Money
and
Banking

Money
and
Banking

CHARLES L. PRATHER, Ph.D., Pd.D.

1969
Ninth Edition

 Richard D. Irwin, Inc., Homewood, Illinois
Irwin-Dorsey Limited, Nobleton, Ontario

Library of Congress Catalog Card No. 69-15547
Printed in the United States of America

Preface

THE current edition of *Money and Banking* presents the elementary principles of money and banking with emphasis on the prevailing problems in the field. In this edition, there was a greater need to update the material than in any preceding revision because the period 1966 through 1968 was one of many changes. In this edition, as in previous ones, the broad concept of monetary policy is used; hence, material is included that embraces the activities of institutions that affect the uses of money and credit as well as those that affect the supply.

In the first three chapters, the author discusses the nature of money, the monetary history of the United States, and the United States monetary system. A description is given of the changes in the monetary role of gold and silver and their replacement with paper money and nonsilver coins. The current international monetary position of gold is discussed in later chapters.

The theory of the value of money was enlarged to include a discussion of the theory of interest in order to clarify the difference in the "value of money" and the "cost of money." Chapters 5 and 6 contain a general description of credit and credit instruments and those traded in the money market. "Liquidity" is discussed in the original sense as "the capacity for being exchanged for money with little or no delay or loss."

The history of commercial and central banking is covered in Chapters 7 and 8 which are followed by six chapters dealing with commercial banks as a source of both money and credit. Now banks are sharing the latter function to a greater extent with noncommercial banking financial intermediaries. Commercial banks are the most important of the financial institutions that deal directly with the general public and they are the largest of the deposit institutions, the main source of short-term credit, and the managers of the check currency or payment system. In their operations, commercial banks come into contact with all segments of the economy—business, household, farm, financial, and the rest of the world—and their activities have a direct effect on the financial decisions of each. Competition has forced banks to offer new financial services formerly offered only by specialists or not at all. In changing from a "wholesale" to a "wholesale-retail" type of business, banks have become more flexible in their operations.

In the chapters on central banking and monetary and fiscal policy, the Federal Reserve banks are discussed both as service institutions and as the means for expanding and stabilizing the supply of money and credit. In these chapters, there is a discussion on how the instruments of monetary policy have been modified to better serve the economy and achieve the goals of monetary policy. It is also recognized that more attention must be given to cost-push inflation and the use of nonmonetary techniques to achieve greater stability in prices.

At one time, discussions of noncommercial banking financial intermediaries in a money and banking book would have been considered out of place but the conviction is growing that an understanding of their functions is essential to a broader appreciation of contemporary economic and financial developments. Government agencies are coordinating their credit policies with those of the Federal Reserve System and their contribution to the liquidity and growth of the economy is greater today than in the past. At the beginning of the current century, most financial assets were held by commercial banks; but, today, they are shared with insurance companies, savings institutions, trusts, pension funds, and investment companies.

In Chapters 21 through 25, the topics covered include capital markets, investment banking, urban and agricultural credit, consumer finance, and trust banking. The last five chapters are devoted to a description of foreign exchange activities of commercial banks and other specialists, international transactions, the international monetary system, development banks, and foreign banking systems. The gold crisis of 1968, the two-gold-price system, and provisions for "special drawing rights" are among the topics discussed and analyzed.

For suggestions made during the preparation of this edition, the author is indebted to Dean H. J. Markle, College of Business and Industry, Memphis State University; Dean Ben B. McNew, School of Business and Government, University of Mississippi; Drs. Jack C. Cashin and Robert D. Mittlen, University of Texas; Dr. Henry J. Frank, Rider College, and Charles M. Prather, Vice President, Republic National Bank of Dallas, Texas. This textbook still reflects the influence of those who made suggestions for earlier editions including Dr. James R. Kay, the University of Texas; Kornelis J. Walraven, Continental Illinois Bank and Trust Company; Herbert W. Hickman, Prudential Insurance Company of America, Newark, New Jersey; T. L. Carlson, Western Michigan University; Irving O. Linger, Texas Agricultural and Mechanical University; D. H. Bellmore, New York University; Charls E. Walker, American Bankers Association; J. H. Stehmen, University of Minnesota; and J. K. Langum, Chicago, Illinois. In the preparation of this manuscript, the author is deeply indebted to his wife, Katherine F. Prather.

February, 1969   CHARLES L. PRATHER

Table of Contents

List of Tables and Charts

CHARTS

ꙅꙅꙅꙅꙅꙅꙅꙅꙅꙅꙅꙅꙅꙅ

CHAPTER 1

The Nature of Money

ꙅꙅꙅꙅꙅꙅꙅꙅꙅꙅꙅꙅꙅꙅꙅꙅꙅꙅꙅꙅꙅꙅꙅꙅꙅꙅꙅꙅꙅ

THE UNITED STATES has a dual monetary system composed of "reserve" and "circulating" money. This system is the product of legislation, some of which was adopted under political pressure that reflected economic developments. For illustration, the speculative demand for gold abroad during 1968 resulted in the adoption of the "two gold price" system. The monetary system of the United States is still related to "monetary" gold having a fixed price of $35 per fine ounce which may differ from the price of gold in the marketplace. Gold is still used as a medium of exchange in international transactions and as international reserve money, but its value as money is no longer the same as its commodity value.

SIGNIFICANCE OF MONEY

In a modern democratic society, all general economic problems tend to cluster around money, and the present complex economic system could not function efficiently without it. The problems of production, distribution, and consumption are simplified because money is paid for goods and services.

The use of money and the market system which it presupposes permits freedom of choice to millions of producers and consumers as to their current and future way of life. Under present-day methods of production, each worker performs only a single process; hence, most of his wants must be satisfied by goods produced by others.

Money and Production. From the viewpoint of economists, production is the creation of economic value; and its correct purpose is to provide man with the necessities, conveniences, and luxuries of life. In modern industrial society, money is used as the device for measuring expenses of and returns from business—a function of money that even the totalitarian governments use. It would be difficult to visualize orderly production without some unit of account in which to keep records. Production is planned and carried out with the objective of making a money profit. Money and the economy it

1

presupposes permit businessmen to concentrate on producing for the marketplace, rather than on meeting production quotas as set by some government control agency. While the profit motive may be criticized, no effective substitute has been found in a free economy. In a world plagued by a conflict of ideologies, the use of money and credit permits individual planning and freedom of action. In addition, money permits a degree of specialization, division of labor, and cooperation not possible in any other type of economy except the most autocratic in which all phases of production are specified by the government.

It is in the marketplace that the decisions of millions of individuals determine the overall efficiency and future growth of the United States. Undirected cooperation is found among those who work upon a good in the different stages of production, from the raw material to the finished product. The need for coordination among these independent producers increases with the increase in quantity and variety of products, the number of specialists, the size of the market, and the number of productive steps between the producer and the ultimate consumer.

The producer, mindful not only of his own plans but also those of his competitors, must estimate the quantity and quality of goods consumers will demand. Thus, while specialization and division of labor increase "the productivity of labor on the technical side," the money economy "tremendously increases the problems of finance and management."[1] The present structure and productive efficiency of American business bear witness to the ability of financiers and entrepreneurs to solve these problems.

Money and Distribution. In economics, the word "distribution" is used in several ways, but here it is used in a technical sense to mean the apportionment of the national income among the four factors of production: wages to labor, interest to capital, rent to land, and profits to the entrepreneur, the recipients being individuals. Money together with the mechanism of the price system permits the heterogeneous mass of goods and services to be distributed among the many individuals who want them. Theoretically, if there is a change in the supply of or demand for goods and services, the resulting change in prices would tend to bring supply and demand into equilibrium. The use of money as a measure of value and the market system

[1] A. H. Hansen, *Business Cycle Theory* (Boston: Ginn & Co., 1927), pp. 120–21.

make it unnecessary for the government to operate elaborate and expensive price control and rationing systems.

In a modern society, the total national income and the shares allotted to the factors of production are computed in terms of money. Wages are the prices paid to laborers for their services; interest is the compensation to capitalists for the use of capital; rent is the price paid to landowners for the use of land; and profit is the money return to the entrepreneur for the assumption of risk. Thus, wages, interest, rent, and profit are all expressed in terms of money. Theoretically, each factor of production shares in the national income according to its contribution, with labor receiving from 65 to 70 percent of the total. Like all value concepts, the contribution of each factor is more easily appraised when expressed in terms of money.

Money and Consumption. In economics, consumption is the use of goods and services to satisfy human wants. The productive energy and economic resources of a nation are limited and, in a free market system, one of the functions of consumers is to determine what is produced. By purchasing more of certain goods, they cast dollar-votes for increased production of these goods. The consumption problem of the individual consumer is to budget his liquid money income in order to care for his immediate and future needs to the best advantage. In making decisions, his choice is determined primarily by the size of his money income and the quantity and quality of goods that can be bought with it. Although the obtaining of money income is the prime motivator of economic effort, the price at which this money can be converted into goods and services is of equal importance. The welfare of a community is dependent upon the size of its "real income" (goods and services that money will buy).

The use of money permits the consumer to shift purchases from one commodity to a second, to buy certain goods today or to postpone purchases, to buy in one community or a second, or to buy from one merchant or another. The consumer's time and place options are important to buyers and sellers. Much of modern advertising is explainable only in terms of this liquid purchasing power, which is always limited in amount and shiftable from goods to goods, from the present to the future, and from market to market.

In modern economics, there is an increasing recognition of the importance of consumption in determining the size of the national income. Since one man's expenditure is another man's income, what is spent in one time period by the community tends to determine the size of the community's income in the period that follows. Of the two types of expenditures—for consumption and for investment—the first is the larger and therefore the more important. On the other hand, the amount of investment is more variable and therefore more troublesome than the amount of consumption. During one phase of the business cycle, the amount of investment rises sharply; during another, it plunges precipitously. A shrinkage in investment means a loss of both current and future income because a decline in investments means less employment and less employment means another decline in national income which would tend to cause a further decline in investments.

FUNCTIONS OF MONEY

Money is a social tool whose origin is buried in antiquity. How it is used reflects the type of society in which one lives, being most important in a free enterprise society wherein production for the marketplace dominates. For such an economy, it is imperative to have a medium of exchange, a store of value, a standard of value, and a standard of deferred payments; because, sooner or later, money is spent for goods and services including the settlement of debts and taxes. The resulting price system is most efficient when there are neither product nor labor monopolies or government intervention with individual markets (as in the case of farm products).

Medium of Exchange.   In a barter transaction, goods and services are exchanged directly for goods and services; but when money is used as a medium of exchange, it is the means by which goods and services are exchanged indirectly for goods and services. Money is the intermediary for which goods are sold and with which purchases are made. This function of money may be shown by the following diagram:

Goods and Services → Money → Goods and Services.

Historically, as communities became more industrialized, family units became less self-sufficient and the number of indirect exchanges increased. The articles that have been used as the exchange medium includes commodities used for display, such as beads, gold, and silver; consumable goods such as knives, nails, pots, and weapons; and tokens such as pieces of leather and fur.

Originally, money was accepted because it had value as an ornament, weapon, or had some other nonmonetary use. It was first used as a third commodity or go-between in barter transactions, serving as

(1) a common denominator in which values of things bartered were expressed, (2) the third article in exchanges when large or "dear" goods were traded for small or inexpensive ones, and (3) the medium when a person with a surplus commodity could not deal with a party that had what he wanted but would accept a third commodity. Now money appears in the form of personal checks, paper currency, and token coins that have little or no value as commodities.

The concept of price is closely related with the general concept of exchange value. By exchange value is meant the ability of one good to command a second in exchange; but, instead of measuring the value of one good in terms of a second, it is customary to compare prices, that is, the exchange value of the two goods expressed in terms of money. If, in a particular market, the price of one good is one dollar and the price of a second is two dollars, the conclusion is that the second is twice as valuable as the first.

The price system refers to the type of economy wherein consumers can obtain goods and services contributed by others at prices acceptable to both buyers and sellers, and one wherein producers can sell goods and services to consumers at prices acceptable to both. The price system presupposes the legal rights of individuals to (1) own property and to dispose of it at their own price and (2) work for themselves or for an employer of their own choosing (not as a serf under the feudal system or a slave under slavery).

Value is the central theme in the treatises on economic principles, but prices are of major interest to businessmen. The use of money as a standard of value permits the substitution of a simple, easily understood price system for an unwieldy, disjointed exchange-value ratio system. It is necessary to remember the price of each item rather then the exchange value of each item in terms of all other items. The standard of value function of money may be illustrated by a price list such as the following:

Oranges, 60 cents per dozen.
Bread, 35 cents per 1½-pound loaf.
Butter, 90 cents per pound.
Potatoes, 89 cents for 10 pounds.
Ham (picnics) 29 cents per pound.

Prices, the functional guide to economic activity, are determined by custom, public authority, and the varying degree of competition in the market. In a free economy the last is the most important because it involves all the problems of demand and supply.

The existence of a common denominator of values makes exchange decisions simpler and more accurate in terms of generally accepted values. Our present pricing system, a convenient marketing device wherein individual prices of goods are set prior to exchange, reflects the dealings of numerous buyers and sellers who transact business only when there is agreement on prices. (The opposite of the free enterprise system is one wherein prices are established by decrees of public officials.) Competition among producers tends to keep prices near their cost of production levels by expanding production when prices are high and contracting production when losses occur.

In a private enterprise economy, most economic planning is done in terms of the monetary unit. The dollar, or a similar unit, is used in weighing the importance of past and current activities and in setting up future goals. In order for the record of achievement and the plans for the future to be more than illusory dollar figures, the monetary unit must be fairly stable in value. A standard of value that is an elastic measuring device is no more satisfactory than would be an elastic standard of weights and measures.

As a standard of value, money is more than a common denominator for expressing exchange ratios as prices. It provides businessmen and others with a standard unit to use in planning future production (budgeting), in measuring current costs and receipts (cost accounting), and in reporting on the income and assets of business enterprises (financial accounting). It would be difficult to visualize orderly production without some unit of account in which to keep records.

Store of Value.   One advantage of the use of money is that the owner may delay spending it until a future time. At any particular moment, a very small percentage of the money supply is being spent or "on the wing"; which means that most of it is being held as a store of value for future spending. The holder of money has options as to time and place, and goods and/or services for which his means of payment are to be spent. These options are among the most valuable privileges accruing from the use of money as a medium of exchange and as a store of value. In effect, the holder of money has a *claim check* on the economy, representing what is called "general purchasing power." The store-of-value function of money may be illustrated by the following diagram:

Goods and services → Money.

Eventually, these spendable balances, money held as a store of value, will be used to buy goods and services or financial assets.

Money serves as an excellent store of value if goods and services are available when required and if money retains its value during the interim; however, during most of the present century, there has been a tendency for the value of money to decrease. Serious disturbances may result from too much or too little spending at a particular time; therefore spending habits are being studied to determine their effects on national income and prices. The instability of money accounts, in part, for the development of monetary management, that is, manipulation of the supply and uses of money by central banks and national governments in such a way as to offset or compensate for what individuals may or may not do with their general purchasing power. While money is not a productive resource, its amount and application may be manipulated so as to influence the use of labor, capital, land, and other resources in order to affect total expenditures and output.

Standard of Deferred Payments. With the growth of debt (now over $1,000 billion or many times the money supply in the United States), the use of money as a standard of deferred payments has become of major importance. Customarily, debts—obligations to pay in the future—are expressed in terms of money. Debts may originate in services rendered today in return for future payment, as in the case of wages and public utility service contracts; in purchases of goods "on time"; in rental or lease contracts for houses, commercial buildings, land, equipment, and other fixed assets; and in loans of money. The written or implied contracts to make money payments in the future may be long term, as in the case of a bond issue maturing in 1995 or the 99-year lease on the land owned by Columbia University on which Rockefeller Center is built; intermediate term, as in the case of many consumer and business contracts calling for payment on the installment plan; or short term, as in the case of obligations due within one year that accompany the current wage system; retailing of goods on time; purchases of goods by wholesalers, jobbers, and manufacturers; and individual, trade, and other borrowings from banks, nonbank financial institutions, and others.

The use of money permits businessmen, consumers, governments, and others to make credit arrangements and future contracts that are repayable in terms of general purchasing power rather than specific items which may or may not be obtainable when the contract is due. A list of prices of United States Treasury issues illustrates the use of money as a standard of deferred payments (see Table 1–1).

Instrument of Economic Policy. If the functions of money were limited to those already discussed, Congress could provide for the addition of a specific amount of money each year and no other

TABLE 1–1

TREASURY NOTES AND BONDS

Coupon (Percent)	Maturity	Offering Price	Yield before Taxes (Percent)
4.0...................2/15/72		95	5.54
4.0...................8/15/73		93–16*	5.47
4⅛...................2/15/74		93–8*	5.54
3¼...................5/15/85		79–8*	5.10
3.0...................2/15/94		79	4.34

* Fractions are quoted in 32nds, so 93–16 = 93.5; 93–8 = 93.25; and 79–8 = 79.25.
Source: Aubrey G. Langston & Co., Inc., *Offering Letter* (July 1, 1968).

monetary legislation would be required. However, changes in the money supply affect employment, prices, output, and other forms of economic activity. Since the discovery that money may be used as an instrument of economic policy, monetary authorities have attempted to use it to achieve the goals of economic policy. With the passage of time, there has been an increase in the number of these goals which, at times, are in conflict with one another. At such times, the problem is that of having the proper "mix," with some being emphasized more than others. The social benefits derived from efficient monetary management are great, as during the 1961–65 period, and the effects of poor monetary management are disastrous, as during the 1930–33 period. Among the most important of the current macroeconomic phenomena that monetary policy may help to correct are unemployment, inflation, balance-of-payments deficits, and lack of sustainable growth.

Customarily, growth is measured in terms of the gross national product (GNP), which is defined as the money value of the total output of goods and services within a country in a given period of time, usually a year, before allowance is made for consumption and depreciation of capital goods. In 1929, GNP reached $100.1 billion and then declined sharply to $55.6 billion in 1933. By 1940, GNP was $99.7 billion and now it is in excess of $800 billion (see Table 1–2).

GNP is the money value of the total output of goods and services and so allowance must be made for price inflation in order to realize how much the real output of things has changed during a period of time. For example, the money value of GNP increased over 8 times from 1929 to 1968 but it increased only 3.3 times in terms of constant dollars (see Table 1–2).

TABLE 1–2

GROSS NATIONAL PRODUCT FOR SELECTED YEARS
(in Billions of Dollars)

Item	1929	1933	1941	1950	1963	1964	1965	1966	1967	1968* Iᵖ
Gross national product	103.1	55.6	124.5	284.8	590.5	632.4	683.9	743.3	785.0	826.7
Final purchases	101.4	57.2	120.1	278.0	584.6	626.6	674.5	729.9	779.8	824.0
Personal consumption expenditures	77.2	45.8	80.6	191.0	375.0	401.2	433.1	465.9	491.7	518.7
Durable goods	9.2	3.5	9.6	30.5	53.9	59.2	66.0	70.3	72.1	78.4
Nondurable goods	37.7	22.3	42.9	98.1	168.6	178.7	191.2	207.5	217.5	228.1
Services	30.3	20.1	28.1	62.4	152.4	163.3	175.9	188.1	202.1	212.1
Gross private domestic investment	16.2	1.4	17.9	54.1	87.1	94.0	107.4	118.0	112.1	118.0
Fixed investment	14.5	3.0	13.4	47.3	81.3	88.2	98.0	104.6	107.0	115.4
Nonresidential	10.6	2.4	9.5	27.9	54.3	61.1	71.1	80.2	82.6	87.2
Structures	5.0	.9	2.9	9.2	19.5	21.2	25.1	27.9	26.8	28.5
Producers' durable equipment	5.6	1.5	6.6	18.7	34.8	39.9	46.0	52.3	55.7	58.7
Residential structures	4.0	.6	3.9	19.4	27.0	27.1	27.0	24.4	24.4	28.2
Nonfarm	3.8	.5	3.7	18.6	26.4	26.6	26.4	23.8	23.9	27.6
Change in business inventories	1.7	−1.6	4.5	6.8	5.9	5.8	9.4	13.4	5.2	2.7
Nonfarm	1.8	−1.4	4.0	6.0	5.1	6.4	8.4	13.7	4.8	1.8
Net exports of goods and services	1.1	.4	1.3	1.8	5.9	8.5	6.9	5.1	4.8	1.7
Exports	7.0	2.4	5.9	13.8	32.3	37.1	39.1	43.0	45.3	47.2
Imports	5.9	2.0	4.6	12.0	26.4	28.6	32.2	37.9	40.6	45.5
Government purchases of goods and services	8.5	8.0	24.8	37.9	122.5	128.7	136.4	154.3	176.3	188.3
Federal	1.3	2.0	16.9	18.4	64.2	65.2	66.8	77.0	89.9	96.2
National defense	....	....	13.8	14.1	50.8	50.0	50.1	60.5	72.5	76.7
Other	....	....	3.1	4.3	13.5	15.2	16.7	16.5	17.4	19.5
State and local	7.2	6.0	7.9	19.5	58.2	63.5	69.6	77.2	86.4	92.1
Gross national product in constant (1958) dollars	203.6	141.5	263.7	355.3	551.0	581.1	616.7	652.6	669.3	689.7

* First quarterly data for 1968 seasonly adjusted preliminary figures.
Source: *Federal Reserve Bulletin*, June, 1968, p. A-66.

CHARACTERISTICS OF MONEY

Although the medium of exchange and the standard of value functions of money are closely related, it is possible for money to serve adequately as a standard of value without having all of the qualities of a good medium of exchange.

Qualities of A Good Medium of Exchange. A good medium of exchange will have the qualities of (1) general acceptability, (2) convenience, (3) durability, (4) recognizability, and (5) uniformity in value.

1. The thing used as money must be generally acceptable, in order to be a satisfactory medium of exchange. Money which has been issued by the government or central bank of a country is usually widely acceptable within the country of origin and to a lesser extent in foreign countries. However, money of private origin, such as personal checks, has limited acceptability. This lack of acceptability may be due to lack of confidence in the drawer of the check or in the bank on which it is drawn, distrust of credit instruments, inconvenience in cashing the check, or the fact that it is not legal tender. The

value of a check depends on the drawer having a sufficient balance in the bank on which it is drawn.

2. Because money is being moved continually from place to place in making sales and purchases, convenience with reference to the physical shape and size of the various units is necessary. Although one may think that the physical forms of checks, paper money, and coins is unimportant, the government, central banks, and commercial banks are giving a great deal of consideration to this problem. By way of illustration, major attention has been given to the development of checks that may be handled by machines (as in the Magnetic Ink Character Recognition System).

Currency (defined to include all coins and paper money) is kept on hand by individuals as a store of ready purchasing power and by banks and business firms as "vault cash" or "till" money and for reserve purposes. Currency should have considerable value in small bulk in order to reduce the burden of moving and storing it; and modern coins, being circular disks of uniform size for each denomination, are easy to handle, stack, and store.

Physical size of currency may affect its acceptability; for illustration, the silver dollar, sometimes called a "cartwheel," was so large that many persons hesitated to accept it; and, while in circulation, the gold dollar and the $2.50 gold coins proved too small for convenience in handling. (All are valuable collectors' items.) Congress demonetized all U.S. gold coins in the Gold Reserve Act of 1934, but for reasons other than physical inconvenience. The need for convenience in size is recognized for paper money and checks as well as for coins. U.S. paper currency issued since 1929 measures $6\frac{5}{16}$ by $2\frac{11}{16}$ inches, which is the same size as the standard bank check. It fits into a business envelope without folding and is easier and more convenient to handle than the larger size it replaced.

3. Money should possess the quality of indestructibility in order to serve as a medium of exchange and a store of value. In the tropics, where paper money tends to deteriorate because of climatic conditions, coins are preferred. Originally, coins were made of pure metals, but, because gold and silver are soft, coins made therefrom were subject to a large amount of abrasion. This problem was solved by adding an alloy to give the coin hardness. The early coins bore a design on only one side, which made it possible to clip or file off a part of the metal. This weakness was corrected by stamping a design on both sides. To prevent clipping (cutting the edges), coins were milled, that is, the edges were furrowed. All U.S. coins except the

1-cent and 5-cent pieces have these edges. A slight rim raised around the edge of all coins facilitates stacking and prevents the weight from resting on the whole surface of the coin. This rim reduces abrasion and protects the design, thereby adding not only to the life of the coin but also to its cognoscibility.

The government's main problem in respect to paper money is increasing its durability. ($1 bills have an average life of about 15 months.) The paper used for checks need not be of the same high quality as that used for paper currency, because checks are not expected to remain in circulation. When a merchant accepts a check in payment or cashes one for a customer, he usually deposits it in his bank promptly; then the check is sent to the bank on which it is drawn, where the drawer's account is debited for the amount and the check is canceled.

4. Money will be more acceptable, and therefore a better medium of exchange, if it is easily recognized. A great deal of thought has been given to designing coins that will be difficult to imitate but easy to recognize. The technique in the manufacture of coins now has reached such a high standard that the problem of cognoscibility largely has been replaced by that of making paper money which cannot be imitated by counterfeiters. Fraudulent currency must be kept at a minimum in order to prevent loss to the public. The existence of even a small percentage of counterfeit bills may lead to a decrease in confidence in all paper money and a loss in its acceptability.

In the United States money is protected by laws covering the conditions under which coins, paper currency, government checks, and other obligations may be reproduced (sec. 474 of Title 18 of the United States Code). Advertisers recognize the fact that pictures of money are sure to attract the attention of the public—everyone seems to be interested in money. In 1951 the law covering the reproduction of currency was changed to permit photographing and printing pictures of coins (Public Law 79, 82d Congress, approved July 16, 1951). By special regulation, the Secretary of the Treasury sometimes allows pictures of savings bonds and stamps to be used to increase their sales, but such pictures are required to be off-size. Although it is permissible to photograph paper money so that it will not be "in the likeness" of genuine money, it is safer to refrain from photographing paper money, checks, or governmental obligations (violators may be subject to a maximum penality of 15 years in prison and/or a fine of $5,000).

All U.S. paper money is printed by the Bureau of Engraving and Printing in Washington, and it is protected from counterfeiting by secret processes in the manufacture of the paper, by secret designs, and by special texture of paper. In spite of these safeguards, imitations of the official currency appear frequently. As a result, Secret Service men are kept busy apprehending counterfeiters, and bank clerks constantly are on the alert for the appearance of the counterfeit bills. In order to obtain greater uniformity and thereby minimize counterfeiting, the Treasury Department placed new designs on all U.S. paper currency on July 10, 1929. The portraits assigned to different denominations and other ways of identification are shown in Table 1–3. Even greater cognoscibility would be achieved if paper money

TABLE 1–3

PAPER CURRENCY: DENOMINATIONS AND IDENTIFICATION

PORTRAITS

$ 1 .... Washington	$ 100 .... Franklin
2 .... Jefferson	500 .... McKinley
5 .... Lincoln	1,000 .... Cleveland
10 .... Hamilton	5,000 .... Madison
20 .... Jackson	10,000 .... Chase
50 .... Grant	

SEALS AND BACKS

The backs of the new currency are printed uniformly in green; the faces in black; and the Treasury seals and the serial numbers in the following colors:
United States notes .... Red
Federal Reserve notes .... Green

varied in size of the denomination (as is true of English and French currency) and if the denominations varied in color, as has been proposed by two Treasurers of the United States (both women). Although it is a good idea, it has not been adopted by the government at this writing.

In 1871 George La Monte invented a "national safety paper" to help prevent widespread check raising and forgeries, which made businessmen and others wary of accepting checks. During subsequent years improvements have been made;[2] and now, national safety paper is in demand not only for checks and drafts but also for railroad, bus, and airplane tickets, gift certificates, cash slips, notes, and other special

[2] The paper currently used has dyes that are applied with a protective coating and by designs, both on the front and back of the check, which make it impossible to alter checks by either mechanical or chemical means without leaving a white spot.

documents. It has been suggested that La Monte's invention of national safety paper should rank with such developments as the telephone and telegraph; without it, the current extensive use of check currency would not exist.

5. The need for different denominations and different kinds of money will be met only by a monetary system in which all forms of money have relatively equivalent value. One hundred pennies, ten dimes, one paper dollar, and one gold dollar all must have the same purchasing power. If two kinds of money have equal nominal value but unequal value in terms of demand, the inferior type tends to drive the preferred type out of circulation. When money has uses that are more attractive than as a domestic medium of exchange (including uses in foreign exchange, hoarding, or as a commodity), it will tend to be used where its value is greatest. The generalization explaining the tendency for the less-valuable money to drive the more valuable out of circulation is called "Gresham's law," so named for Sir Thomas Gresham, who explained this monetary principle to Queen Elizabeth in 1558.[3] It seems a strange contradiction that the best articles capture the market in most lines, whereas with money the poor is used more than the good as a medium of exchange. The reasons for this situation are obvious after one reviews his own experience and considers what is meant by the demand for money. Assume that a person has a new $1 bill and an old one. Most people will spend the old one and keep the new one. The same tendency is noticed in spending coins; the worn ones are spent first, and the new ones are held back from active circulation. If this situation exists when there is no difference in value, it is evident that it would be far more pronounced when two moneys differ in value.

As noted above, money is used not only as a medium of exchange but also as a store of value. At any particular time, most of the money outside of the issuing agencies, "in circulation," will be held as cash balances. It is this store-of-value or "cash balance" market that is captured by the more valuable of two kinds of money. In domestic trade the buyer usually decides which form of legal-tender money he will use, and self-interest results in the use of the cheaper form; but in international trade, not covered by the domestic legal-tender law, a buyer may find it advantageous to use the dearer kind of money (in fact, he may have no option because sellers naturally prefer the more

---

[3] H. D. Macleod first named this principle "Gresham's law." See *The Elements of Economics* (New York: D. Appleton & Co., 1881), Vol. I, pp. 270–72.

valuable type of money). If the cheaper money exists in sufficient quantity, it will replace the more valuable money in domestic trade, and the more valuable money will be exported or hoarded.

Quality of a Good Standard of Value.   The essential characteristic of a good standard of value is stability in value over a period of time. The purchasing power of a monetary unit, such as the dollar, should be fairly constant over a period of time. When prices in general increase, the value of money decreases; and when prices

CHART 1-1

WHOLESALE PRICES, 1801–1967
(Annual Averages, 1957–59 = 100)

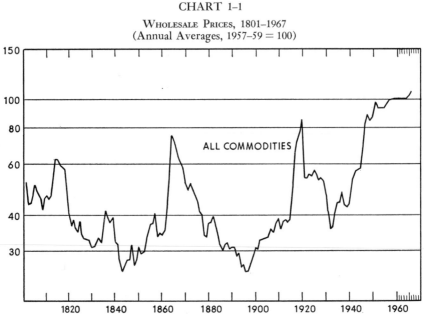

Source: Board of Governors of the Federal Reserve System, *Historical Chart Book, 1967*
(Washington D.C., 1968), p. 101.

decrease, the value of money increases. Therefore, stability in the value of money is synonymous with stability in the general price level.

The major criticism of modern money is that it lacks stability in value. Although the record of the U.S. dollar has been better than that of most foreign monetary units, it has had this same fault as indicated by Chart 1–1, which shows that there has been a sharp increase in prices during war periods (suggesting that the twin evils of war and inflation go together). During much of the time since 1800 there have been periods of falling prices which have been most pronounced following war years, with the exception of the period since 1946.

Historically, the current upward swing in prices has been unusual, and it may be that the political and economic forces at work will cause even higher prices in the future. Among the reasons given for the rise in prices since the close of World War II have been the increase in the supply of money, postwar scarcity of goods, growth in size and monetization of the public debt, increase in money income, and the increase in labor costs passed on to the public in the form of higher prices. Irrespective of the cause, the fact remains that the U.S. dollar lacks the desirable quality of stability in value. The United States always seems to have a money problem of some type, and the predominant one since World War II has been a decline in the value of the dollar. The dollar is now being used as the unit for measuring past, present, and estimated future business performance, the unit of account for credit transactions, and the liquid asset wherein purchasing power is stored. In order to perform these functions adequately, it must be reasonably stable in value.

Legal Qualities of Money. Throughout history, the state has had considerable influence on money. At an early date, it assumed the right to mint coins and to retain the profits therefrom (called seigniorage). Insofar as the state determined the content of coins, the profit (the difference between the cost of the material and their monetary value) could be large or small. Later, banks as well as the state issued paper money, with the latter assuming the right to control the conditions under which such currency was issued and withdrawn from circulation. With the growth in demand deposit in commercial banks and their increased use as money, the state—through its agent, the central bank—regulated the volume of demand deposits. In addition, the state has influenced the acceptability of money by giving it certain legal qualities. The three legal qualities of money, which tend to overlap, are those of "legal tender," "lawful money," and money receivable for a particular thing, such as in payment of customs or import duties (government tender).[4]

1. Legal-tender money is that money which the law requires debtors to offer and creditors to accept when tendered in payment of money obligations. In disputed cases over money values, some method must be provided to fix conclusively when a debt is paid. The mere offering of legal-tender money, without acceptance by the creditor, does not discharge the debtor's obligation, because refusal to accept payment may not be related to the kind of money offered. However,

---

[4] Arthur Kemp, *The Legal Qualities of Money* (New York: Pageant Press, Inc., 1956), p. 5.

if legal-tender money is offered in the correct amount and refused, interest on the obligation ceases; and if the debtor's obligation is not settled, it will eventually be extinguished by the operation of the statutes of limitations.[5] The list of U.S. money given the legal-tender quality by Congress has been extended to include all kinds of U.S. circulating coins and paper money.[6] Usually, the legal-tender quality is not important, and most payments are made with bank checks that represent an optional type of money.

Sometimes governments have given the legal-tender quality to certain types of money as a means of exploiting creditors and of raising revenues for the government (for illustration, the continental currency of the Revolutionary War and the U.S. notes or greenbacks of the Civil War).[7] Although giving legal-tender qualities to money may create some demand for it, no one would expect the legal-tender quality to be sufficient to maintain its value as measured by price index numbers.

2. The term "lawful money" is used here in the technical sense to mean those types of money that are lawful for specific purposes such as gold certificates which are lawful money for reserve purposes for the 12 Federal Reserve banks (it is not used in the popular sense to mean money that has been issued lawfully). Both the federal and state governments use the term "lawful money" to specify things that may be used as legal reserves of banks. Until recently only available deposits at the Federal Reserve banks could be counted as legal reserves for member banks (banks that are members of the Federal Reserve System), but in 1959 Congress authorized the Board of Governors of the Federal Reserve System to permit member banks to count "vault cash" as part of their legal reserves (used for the first time in December, 1959). The legal reserve requirements of state-chartered non-member banks vary considerably, but most of these banks are permitted to use vault cash and deposits in other banks (generally, the latter must be approved as reserve depositories by the appropriate state banking authority—a banking board or state commissioner of banking).

Gold certificates and gold credits are the only types of money

[5] *Ibid.*, pp. 143–44.

[6] Prior to 1933, 1- and 5-cent pieces were legal tender in one payment in amounts up to 25 cents; subsidiary silver coins were legal tender in amounts up to $10. Making all coins legal tender has been criticized because it permits disgruntled debtors to offer small coins as "spite" money in making payments.

[7] Greenbacks were not legal tender for payment of customs duties or for payment of interest on the national debt.

that may be used by the Federal Reserve banks for legal reserve purposes; but under existing laws these gold certificates may not be lawfully held in the United States by individuals, firms, or corporations other than the Federal Reserve banks. In case of need, the gold certificates may be used to obtain gold from the United States Treasury to meet requests for monetary gold from foreign central banks and foreign governments. The Federal Reserve banks must meet the domestic currency needs with their own Federal Reserve notes and United States Treasury currency. Their gold reserves cannot be used to meet their domestic obligations (which violates the concept of something kept in store for special or future use). Federal Reserve notes, the most important type of domestic currency, are "legal tender for all debts, public and private, and are redeemable in lawful money at the United States Treasury, or at any Federal Reserve Bank"; but Congress has not answered the question of what is "lawful money" for this purpose. In practice, it may be the same type of currency or U.S. notes which entitle the bearer to receive money on demand without specifying the type of money.

The concept of lawful money is more inclusive than that of legal-tender money because the former may include bank deposits as well as circulating coins and paper money and gold certificates that do not circulate. Later, it will be shown that reserve requirements are being emphasized as a device to control the supply of money and not as something held back in order to protect a bank's creditors (depositors or noteholders).

3. Governments may specify the kinds of money that may be used to meet obligations due the government, such as for taxes, fees, fines, and so on (called "government tender"). Although provisions for government tender are usually of little importance, they may be significant under certain circumstances. For illustration, they have been used to protect government officials from irate citizens who wanted to use small coins as nuisance money in payment of fines and taxes. In addition, the government may specify (*a*) the kind of money it will use in meeting its obligations to private persons and (*b*) the types of money that debtors may use in meeting obligations to quasi-public corporations, such as banks.

SUMMARY

Money is a medium of exchange, standard of value, store of value, standard of deferred payment, loan medium, and finally, a tool of monetary management. In order to perform these functions efficiently, money must be generally acceptable; should exist in suitable denominations; should be physically convenient, durable, and easy to recognize; and should have stability in value. The complexities of modern economies have made it necessary to develop different kinds of money, and governments have taken steps to keep the value of all kinds of money equivalent in order to prevent the operation of Gresham's law from driving one or more kinds out of circulation.

In making provisions for the creation of money, governments decide which types must be accepted by creditors in payment of debts (legal tender), the type which may be used by administrative authorities such as the United States Treasury as redemption funds or by banks to meet legal reserve requirements (lawful money), and money made receivable for specific purposes. The circulating media of the United States include two current kinds of paper money and coins, all of which have full legal-tender qualities. However, the most important medium of exchange, deposit currency or checkbook money, is classified as optional money.

QUESTIONS AND PROBLEMS

1. Identify: (*a*) barter, (*b*) money, (*c*) price, and (*d*) price system.
2. Why is money important?
3. What are the functions of money?
4. Explain the significance of the following: "The earliest coins were probably made by merchants, but the function of coinage was soon taken over by governments. . . ." (E. Victor Morgan, *A History of Money* [Baltimore, Maryland, Penguin Books, Inc., 1965], p. 13.)
5. What physical qualities should money have in order to be a good medium of exchange? Are the same qualities necessary to have a good standard of value? Explain your answer.
6. Explain how a government may make money more acceptable by the addition of legal qualities.
7. Would it be easier for a country to manage without a medium of exchange than without a standard of value or unit of account? Explain your answer.
8. Discuss: "The most important and most gratifying economic development in 1967 was the maintenance of high employment. The most disturbing economic news was the continuation of creeping inflation that began in 1965." (*Economic Report of the President Transmitted to the Congress February 1968 together with the Annual Report of the Council of Economic Advisers* [Washington, D.C.: U.S. Government Printing Office, 1968], p. 96.)
9. Explain: "Although prices were advancing at a fast pace, consumer purchases in real terms, as well as current dollars, apparently showed

the largest quarterly rise since 1965." (*Federal Reserve Bulletin*, March, 1968, p. 245.)

10. Analyze: "A group of Russian scientists recently visited Copenhagen. They observed to a foreigner: 'Why are the Danish people so poor? Stores are filled with things to buy. But there are no crowds of customers. In our country people have so much money that they queue up to purchase everything in sight.'" (*New York Times*, December 24, 1955, p. 12.)

ꙄꙄꙄꙄꙄꙄꙄꙄꙄꙄꙄꙄꙄ

CHAPTER 2

Monetary History of the United States

ꙄꙄꙄꙄꙄꙄꙄꙄꙄꙄꙄꙄꙄꙄꙄꙄꙄꙄꙄꙄꙄꙄꙄꙄꙄꙄꙄ

THE DOLLAR has been the monetary unit of the United States through-out its history, but there have been changes in the kinds of money in use. The latter have included commodity money, standard coins, token coins, convertible and nonconvertible paper money, and check-book money (demand deposits). Gradually, the emphasis shifted away from the use of valuable money commodities (gold and silver) to token coins, paper money, and checks and bank drafts which have functional rather than commodity value.

INTRODUCTION TO THE HISTORY OF MONEY IN THE UNITED STATES

The U.S. monetary system, as established in 1792, was based on the best monetary principles of that time. Those responsible for its establishment showed a preference for full-bodied money (full-weight gold and silver coins that had a commodity value equal to their exchange value). This preference for hard money was a natural reaction to experiences with inflation caused by overissues of paper money by the colonies, states, and the Continental Congress. To the founding fathers, it seemed improbable that there would ever be too much money if money were made of gold and silver.

Colonial Currency. During the colonial period under liberal policy rules formulated by the British government in London, each colony engaged in promoting and regulating economic activities inde-pendently. A scarcity of coins was a recurring problem; hence com-modities such as beads, corn, tobacco, pelts, and gunpowder were used at various times as money. For short periods when these com-modities were given government tender, their usefulness as money was enhanced. Most of the English coins which the colonists brought with them had been exported to pay for goods imported from Eng-land. The English colonies had a favorable balance of trade with the

20

Spanish colonies, so many coins were imported from them, including the Spanish piaster (or milled dollar), which circulated widely in the colonies.

The colonists thought of banks primarily as a source of paper money, and many were formed to supply needed bank notes.[1] The conditions under which paper money was issued varied, but three types of notes or bills were authorized by the same or different colonial governments at different times and at different places: (1) government bills of exchange, which were to be redeemed out of public revenue after a year or more; (2) paper money issued by government banks and lent at interest (notes were to be redeemed when the loans were paid, usually on an annual installment plan); and (3) bills issued by chartered private banks, which were backed by deeds to land and commodities.[2] Although all these types of paper money provided for ultimate redemption, no provisions were made for current convertibility.

Some of the colonial banking ventures were successful, and their note issues had a beneficial effect on the economies of the areas wherein the notes circulated. However, too often overissuance of notes was followed by depreciation, postponement of redemption and sometimes repudiation. Because of losses incurred, merchants and others protested to the English government and, as a result, parliament prohibited the issuance of paper money in all English colonies.

Continental Currency.   One of the first tasks of the Second Continental Congress was to provide means for financing the Revolutionary War. Because the new government's credit was too poor to permit borrowing and the colonists were opposed to heavy taxes, paper money was issued. In May, 1775, Congress authorized the issuance of notes equivalent to 2,000,000 Spanish milled dollars. The process was repeated many times during the next few years, and more than $240,000,000 were issued. The notes purported to be credit money—a promise of the Continental Congress to pay coins—but, since there were no coins for this purpose, the notes were irredeemable paper money. Because the volume of money in circulation was in

[1] In 1652 Massachusetts established a mint (closed in 1688 by the English government) that coined 3-penny, 6-penny, and the famous "pine tree" shillings. Although some of the other colonies authorized the establishment of mints, they never became operative.

[2] Technically, a bill of exchange is an order to pay, while a note is a promise to pay. Although paper money issues are usually promises to pay, individual items are sometimes referred to as "bills." The first issue of government paper money in the Western world occurred in 1690, when the Massachusetts Bay Colony paid its soldiers with an issue of paper money.

excess of the needs of the predominantly agricultural economy of the period, the value of the government paper money depreciated rapidly, and those who accepted and held it suffered heavy losses.

In 1780 there was an unsuccessful attempt to redeem "old tenor" currency in "new tenor" currency; and, by the next year, the old tenor notes ceased to circulate as money and were bought up by speculators at rates of from 400 to 1 to 1,000 to 1.[3] During this period and later, things that were considered valueless were referred to derisively as "not worth a continental." (Incidentally, Paul Revere made the plates used to print the first continental currency, dated May 10, 1775, and circulated the next year.)

State Issues.   After the outbreak of the Revolutionary War in 1775, without waiting for any Declaration of Independence, the states authorized the issuance of paper money for war financing and other purposes. Every one of the 13 states issued bills of credit (noninterest bearing promises to pay) during 1775, and for several years new issues appeared in most states. In 1778, the Continental Congress appealed successfully to the states to cease issuing paper money in order that the value of the continental currency might be maintained. But in 1780, following the announcement by Congress that it would replace the old continental currency with a "new tenor" issue and would authorize no new paper currency issues, new state issues appeared. Within two years the country was flooded with new state issues.[4]

Specie.   Most of the $4,000,000 in coins which had been in the country at the outbreak of the Revolutionary War was hoarded as a result of the depreciation of paper money. But new coined money came from three sources: (1) Great Britain, which paid for supplies and services (including troop pay) in coins; (2) France, which sent gold and silver directly to the United States and also followed the practice of paying for goods and services in specie; and (3) Spain and the Spanish colonies, which had an unfavorable balance of trade with the United States. By 1780 the supply of specie was sufficient to permit our national government to make its payments in "hard money."

[3] Ten years later, about $6 million was turned in to be redeemed at a rate of 100 to 1 (it is inferred that the rest was destroyed). Secretary of the Treasury Alexander Hamilton insisted that the federal government assume responsibility for the debts created by the Continental Congress and by the states in order to establish the credit of the United States on a sound basis. Hamilton, the first U.S. economic planner, submitted reports to Congress which dealt with such matters as chartering a new national bank, coinage, assumption and funding of the public debt, taxation, and manufacturing.

[4] Ralph V. Barlow, "Aspects of Revolutionary Finance, 1775–1783," *American Historical Review*, Vol. XXXV, p. 68.

Because the shortage of fractional currency continued, some states gave approval to private coinage projects. Many specimens of brass, copper, and tin coins appeared; and some states issued paper money in fractional denominations. Merchants in Boston and New York imported small coins of various descriptions (more than 40 tons of one design reached New York). This situation was bound to cause trouble, and in 1782 several states prohibited the circulation of private coins. While competition among business firms providing goods and services tends to accrue to the advantage of the general public, a similar result would not follow if private firms were to provide currency at their own risk and for profit. Competition in the latter case would lead to debasement and overissuance of coins and, as a result, the cheaper money would capture the market (Gresham's law). Self-interest would cause individuals to hoard the more valuable coins and to use the less valuable in exchange. A similar situation would tend to result if all of the states were permitted to issue coins.

This background helps to explain the provision in the United States Constitution giving Congress the power "to coin money, regulate the value thereof, and of foreign coin . . . ."[5] and forbidding any state "to coin money; emit bills of credit; make anything but gold and silver coin a tender in payment of debts . . . ."[6] While the Constitution established the sovereignty of the federal government over coinage and legal tender, it did not specifically limit the issuance of paper money nor did it mention banks.

BIMETALLISM

Coinage Act of 1792. The first step taken by Congress to meet the pressing need for a safe, uniform, and adequate currency system was the passage of the Coinage Act of 1792. This act provided for a United States Mint, standard gold and silver coins, token copper coins, a mint ratio of 15 to 1 for gold and silver for monetary purposes, free coinage of gold and silver, and legal tender for all U.S. gold and silver coins.

The weight of the silver dollar was fixed at 371.25 grains of fine silver and that of the gold dollar was fixed at 24.75 grains of fine gold. In effect, Congress provided for two competing standards—a gold-coin standard and a silver-coin standard—with silver having been dominant until 1834 and gold thereafter until the Civil War, when the paper dollar became the standard.

During the formative period, Congress also provided for a na-

[5] *The Constitution of the United States*, Art. I, sec. 8.
[6] *Ibid.*, Art. I, sec. 10.

tional bank which was a semipublic institution with one fifth of the capital owned by the federal government. This bank issued paper money, gave fiscal services to the government, dealt in bullion and foreign exchange, made loans to business firms, invested in government securities, and provided central banking services to the state-chartered banks (see Chapter 7).

Gold Underrated. The free coinage of both gold and silver provided "pegs" below which their market prices would not fall (minor allowances must be made for the cost of moving metals, mintage, and other charges). In 1792, for illustration, if one could not sell silver in the market for $1.29 + or gold for $19.39 + per fine ounce, one could take them to the mint and have them minted into silver and gold coins.

The 15 to 1 ratio of the Coinage Act of 1792 overrated the value of silver and underrated the value of gold, which meant that when the mint was opened in Philadelphia in 1794 practically no gold was brought in for coinage. Spain had a 16 to 1 ratio and France, after 1800, had a 15½ to 1 ratio; consequently, silver tended to flow to the more favorable monetary market in the United States where only 15 ounces of silver were equivalent to 1 ounce of gold (as compared to 15½ and 16 elsewhere), and gold was sold abroad or used in the United States for purposes other than money. This left the United States on a *de facto* silver standard, even though the law provided for both gold and silver standard coins.[7]

Theory of Bimetallism. Those who favored the bimetallic system assumed that the mechanism of the bimetallic standard would keep the market ratio of gold and silver in line with mint ratio, thus maintaining the double standard. The principle of bimetallism assumes that the shift of the monetary stock of the underrated metal into the commercial market will decrease its market price because of the increase in supply. At the same time, the increase in monetary work thrown on the metal overrated at the mint and the withdrawal of bullion from the commercial market will increase its value. These two movements, one working so as to decrease the value of the metal underrated at the mint and the other working so as to increase the

[7] Originally, the U.S. silver dollar circulated freely both at home and abroad. In the West Indies, it was at par with the heavier Spanish dollar; consequently, Yankee traders used U.S. dollars to obtain the heavier coins, which they melted down and had reminted into U.S. dollars at a profit of about 2 percent. President Jefferson objected to this practice of using the United States Mint as a source of private profit and closed the Mint to the coinage of silver dollars. From 1805 to 1835 inclusive, there were no issues of U.S. silver dollars, and the silver 50-cent piece was the favorite coin during much of the period prior to the Civil War.

value of the metal overrated at the mint, are expected to keep the mint and market ratios in balance.

Shifting the monetary demand in part from one metal to the other was expected to give the economy a more stable price level than would result from having a single commodity as the standard. The commodity base for the monetary system was expected to be broader, and fluctuations in the volume of money were expected to be smaller. The need for both large- and small-denomination coins was also recognized, and it was assumed that this would be cared for more readily by using both metals.

If all countries had established the same mint ratio, the system might have worked as expected; but this need for a common mint ratio and international cooperation was recognized too late. During the third quarter of the last century the problem of a common mint ratio was discussed at a number of international monetary conferences. In 1865 the Latin Monetary Union was formed by Belgium, France, Italy, and Switzerland (later Greece joined the Union). This was an international bimetallic system which had the same mint ratio and interchangeable coins, but it was in operation for only a few years. After the Franco-Prussian War, Germany received an indemnity of five billion gold francs, and this gold furnished the basis for the shift of Germany from a silver to a gold standard. Fearing a flood of silver released from Germany, France and other members of the Latin Monetary Union discontinued the free coinage of silver. Gradually, all countries recognized the fact that bimetallism could not operate successfully on a national basis, and it was abandoned.

Gold Bill of 1834. In the act of June 28, 1834, sometimes called the "Gold Bill," Congress, in an effort to correct the error of 1792, reduced the gold content of the dollar from 24.75 grains of pure gold to 23.2 grains, without altering the silver content of silver coins. This changed the coinage ratio from 15 to 1 to about 16 to 1. In 1837 gold and silver coins were made $9/10$ fine (previously $11/12$ fine), and the gold content of the dollar was increased slightly to 23.22 grains, thus creating a ratio of slightly less than 16 to 1 (15.988 to 1). The new mint price of gold was $20.67 and that of silver remained at $1.29 + per fine ounce. The weight of the silver dollar in terms of fine silver remained at 371.25 grains as it has been to date.

The acts of 1834 and 1837 were expected to attract gold to the mint, and this expectation was fulfilled particularly after gold was discovered in California. However, Congress did not anticipate the gradual disappearance of full-weight silver coins, and merchants and others were largely dependent on fractional paper money and foreign and token coins. In 1853, Congress made provisions to supply an adequate volume of coins by creating silver coins under the same conditions as the copper 1-cent and ½-cent pieces authorized in 1792.

Silver Subsidiary Coinage Act of 1853.   In the act of February 21, 1853, Congress departed further from the "full-bodied" or "hard money" principle and made all fractional silver coin token money by reducing their silver content by approximately 7 percent and by providing for their "limited" coinage (principles adopted and still adhered to by the rest of the world). The free-coinage system, as applied to silver, had failed to provide the economy with a satisfactory coinage system, but soon after the passage of the silver "limited" coinage act, the country had an adequate supply of coins. In 1857 all acts making foreign coins legal tender in the United States were repealed.

THE GREENBACK PERIOD

Pre-Civil War Bank Paper Money.   From the beginning of its national history, the U.S. currency system included paper money. To be sure, the Fathers of the Constitution assumed that there would be no issues of government paper money under the Constitution,[8] but the federal government as well as state governments chartered commercial banks which issued bank paper money. By 1800 there was at least one chartered state bank in each state which competed with the branch offices of the nationally chartered Bank of the United States, whose main office was located in Philadelphia. The bank paper money issued by the chartered banks soon became an important form of currency.[9] This development of commercial banking under state control represents a departure from the principle that the federal government was to maintain sovereignty over the money supply.

When the second Bank of the United States lost its charter in 1836, the bank notes issued by state-chartered banks became the only kind of paper money. Generally, the note issues of Eastern banks

---

[8] The assumption that the federal and state governments did not have the right to issue paper money was based on the constitutional provision limiting the powers of the states and the principle that the powers of Congress were delegated ones.

[9] In 1819 and 1824 the right of Congress to charter banks was upheld by the Supreme Count under a group of powers including the powers to levy and collect taxes, to borrow money, to regulate commerce, to declare and conduct wars, and to raise and support armies. Although many critics of state banks contended that states were bound by the Constitution not to coin money or issue "bills of credit," in 1837 the Supreme Court affirmed the constitutionality of the chartering of state banks.

were satisfactory, but many of those of Western banks were of questionable value. Often notes were issued by institutions in areas where there were more wildcats than people (called "wildcat" currency).[10] Since bank notes circulated widely, distinguishing between good and bad notes presented a serious problem (augmented by the fact that the existence of so many different kinds of bank notes made counterfeiting easy). Most of the state banking legislation of the pre-Civil War period was directed at making paper-money issues safe; but, when considered from a national viewpoint, the results were unsatisfactory.

Irredeemable Government Paper Money. At the beginning of the Civil War, the requirement of the United States Treasury that banks use cash to pay for government bonds caused a loss of reserves which led to the suspension of specie payments.[11] So, fairly early in the war (February, 1862), Congress authorized the issuance of irredeemable paper money. Soon thereafter, the Bureau of Engraving and Printing was established in Washington, D.C., and the first U.S. notes (greenbacks) were printed for use in meeting war and other governmental expenses. These irredeemable legal-tender notes provided the United States with currency to fill the void caused by the hoarding of gold and silver coins. By 1865, war spending and inflationary financing caused prices to rise more than double their 1861 level. Gold and silver coins circulated only in California and, from 1862 to 1879, the standard money for the remainder of the country was the U.S. note. It was the form in which reserves were kept, debts were repaid, and prices were quoted.

Following the Civil War, prices dropped sharply and continued downward for several years. The volume of national bank notes (provided for in the National Bank Act of 1863 as amended in 1864) was carefully limited, state bank notes had been taxed out of existence, and Confederate currency had disappeared. The currency situation was simpler and, in some respects, sounder than it had been prior

[10] The term "wildcat" first appeared in Michigan, where a bank issued notes that bore the vignette of a panther. Later, when banks failed, they were called "wildcat" banks.

[11] Before as well as since the Civil War, banks' lack of cash reserves often caused a worsening of financial difficulties. For illustration, the panic of 1837 followed the issuance of the President's Specie Circular, which stated that public land would be sold only for specie or bank notes redeemable in coin. (Until that time, receipts from the sale of public land had been the second most important source of government revenue.) The resulting public demand for gold and silver coins was so great that banks' reserves were soon exhausted, and the banks were forced to suspend redemption of their notes.

to the Civil War. Greenbacks, fractional paper money, and national bank notes had replaced specie and the hundreds of different kinds of state bank notes of the prewar years.

The United States was in a postwar depression for several years following the Civil War. The West had borrowed large sums in order to develop its agricultural resources, and the South had borrowed heavily in order to reconstruct its war-devastated communities. Because greenbacks were only slightly below par and could be used to meet debt contracts, certain political leaders considered them to be the solution to the country's monetary problems and wanted more of them in order to stimulate business and to raise prices. Consequently, plans to eliminate the U.S. notes were modified and the amount to be retained was set in terms of the notes then outstanding. By December, 1878, greenbacks were at par in terms of gold, and on January 1, 1879, the shift to a convertible basis was made (required by the act of January 14, 1875) with no internal or external drain on the gold reserves of the Treasury. Thus, the paper money standard policy was officially brought to a close.

National Bank Notes.   Secretary of the Treasury Salmon F. Chase was a proponent of a federally chartered banking system, and he recommended legislation to this end in his report of December, 1861. Although no action was taken on his proposal during the next year, popular support for it increased because bank responsibility was at a low ebb.[12] In December, 1862, Secretary Chase repeated his recommendation for passage of a national banking bill, and one was introduced on January 8, 1863. This bill passed both houses and was signed by President Abraham Lincoln on February 25 (bankers celebrated the 100th anniversary in 1963). Defects discovered in this law were corrected, in part, by the law of June, 1864. These two acts provided for the currency and banking system which remained dominant until the passage of the Federal Reserve Act in 1913.

From the viewpoint of the general public, the most significant change in the currency system during the late 1860's was the replacement of hundreds of state bank note issues of varying quality and degrees of discount by national bank notes, which were safe and

[12] Following the panic of 1861, despite ample gold reserves, banks made no move toward resumption of specie payments. Generally, the banks were profiting from the sale of gold at a premium and were not very helpful in marketing government war bonds and notes. Where state laws permitted them to do so, many of the state-chartered banks expanded their note issues. The situation was most serious in the West, where bank failures were common and losses sustained by noteholders were heavy.

uniform in value throughout the United States. National bank notes were obligations of the issuing bank, and their payment was guaranteed by the U.S. government. In case a bank failed or closed for other reasons, the government paid its notes and reimbursed itself by selling the government bonds which had been pledged as security for the notes.

The National Bank Act required every national bank to accept at par "any and all notes" issued by national banks organized under the provisions of the law, thus preventing these notes from circulating at a discount when far from the place of origin. During the years that followed, the importance of the monopoly of bank note issue given to national banks was largely offset by the increase in the use of deposit currency. However, the "death sentence" tax on note issues of state banks did establish the complete sovereignty of the federal government over the issuance of currency (coin and paper money) in the United States.[13]

Other Currency Legislation. In addition to the provision for redemption of greenbacks in gold, Congress made plans to replace the silver and other coins that had been melted during the Civil War. A bill providing for a revision and codification of scattered coinage laws was passed by Congress and became law in 1873. By omitting the standard silver dollar from the list of U.S. coins, this law eliminated the last remnant of the original free-coinage privilege as it applied to silver.[14] Thus ended legal bimetallism in the United States as provided for in 1792. Since the country was on a paper standard, this change meant nothing at the time, but a few years later it became very important. The act also indicated the intent of Congress to make gold the only standard by declaring that the gold dollar containing 25.8 grains of standard gold nine tenths fine or 23.22 grains of pure gold should be the "unit of value." Gold coinage was to be unlimited, and gold coins were to be legal tender.

---

[13] The Act of March 3, 1865, implemented the National Bank Act by placing a tax of 10 percent on the amount of notes of any state bank or banking association paid out by every national bank, state bank, or state banking association after July 1, 1866. If this had been made applicable to both promises and orders-to-pay money (checks, drafts, etc.), the national bank monopoly of supplying bank money would have been complete.

[14] The Act of 1873 made no provisions for the 2-cent copper coin, half dime, or 3-cent piece; but a new 20-cent silver coin was minted from 1874 to 1878 and a dollar for trade with China was struck from 1874 to 1884. A 3-cent copper coin was minted from 1865 to 1889, and a 5-cent piece since 1866, a 10-cent coin since 1796, and the quarter and half dollar since 1793. See *Annual Report of the Director of the Mint for the Fiscal Year Ended June 30, 1966* (Washington, D.C.: U.S. Government Printing Office, 1967), pp. 80 ff.

Two developments that began in 1874 made the act of 1873 of political significance. One was the discovery of rich silver mines in Nevada, and the other was the fall in the market price of silver below the old mint price. The new silver interests soon discovered that if the free coinage of the silver dollar were permitted they could take their silver bullion to the mint and dispose of it at the mint price of $1.29 + per fine ounce. The drive for the restoration of the bimetallic standard and the return of the standard silver dollar began. Although the silverites have secured many concessions from Congress, including the return of the standard silver dollar, they have not secured a law permitting the free coinage of silver and the return of the bimetallic standard.

The act of February 28, 1878 ("Bland-Allison Act") required the Secretary of the Treasury to purchase from $2,000,000 to $4,000,000 worth of silver each month at the market price and to coin it into standard silver dollars having full legal tender. This was limited coinage, not free coinage, and the silver dollars were but token coins. (This act discontinued the free coinage of the "trade" dollar provided for in 1873.) The amount of silver purchased was expected to equal the output of domestic mines, and the owners of silver dollars could exchange them for silver certificates, which could only be issued when secured by silver dollars.

Gold certificates were first authorized in the act of March 3, 1863, during the greenback or paper money period. Although gold was being mined in large quantities in California, it was flowing either out of the country or into gold hoards, except in California, where the people refused to use U.S. notes as money.[15] In the remainder of the country the only compulsory uses for gold were in payment of customs duties and interest on the federal debt (greenbacks were not government tender for these purposes). The government's receipts of gold were in excess of Treasury needs for interest payments, and this led to the policy of selling gold in the market at the market price, which fluctuated from day to day. This gave rise to speculation in gold and on "Black Friday" (September 24, 1869) Jay Gould and his associates cornered the market. The provision for gold certificates was for the convenience of the users of gold, and this reflected the preference for paper money over "hard" money.

---

[15] Congress not only permitted this situation to exist but also authorized the formation of "gold banks," which were no different from others except that their national bank notes were redeemable in gold instead of greenbacks. This distinction became unimportant in 1879, when the greenbacks were made convertible into gold. The act of February 14, 1880, authorized the conversion of "national gold banks" into ordinary national banks.

As a result of the Civil War and the Reconstruction era which followed, provisions were made for four new types of paper money —the U.S. notes, national bank notes, gold certificates, and silver certificates. From 1879 to 1900 there were heated political debates over the monetary standard and between the "soft" and "hard" money advocates, with some favoring gold, some gold and silver, and others the U.S. note. Unfortunately, a more urgently needed reform, that of the banking system, was delayed until 1913.

GOLD-COIN STANDARD ERA

After the Civil War, the United States was among the countries that joined the United Kingdom in shifting from a bimetallic standard to a gold-coin standard.

Characteristics of the Gold-Coin Standard. The chief characteristics of a gold-coin standard as illustrated by that of the United States were:

(1) The gold value of the dollar was defined as 25.8 grains of standard gold (standard gold means $\frac{9}{10}$ fine—the fine-gold content was 23.22 grains). This meant that the official price of gold was $20.67 per fine ounce.

(2) Unlimited coinage of gold was permitted with only minor charges having been made for refining the metal and for the alloy added to make it "standard" gold. Gold could be bought from or sold to the mint at the official price plus or minus minor handling charges. The effects of free coinage and the purchase of gold at a fixed price were to place a "peg" under the price of gold.

(3) Melting of gold coins was permitted, but penalties were provided for defacing gold coins. The melting-down privilege was used freely when the market value of coins exceeded their monetary value. This tended to increase the value of the remaining supply of gold money and to reduce the value of gold bullion. This contributed to keeping the value of gold coins constant in terms of gold.

(4) All gold coins were full legal tender at face value if not below the "least current weight," otherwise only at their weight value. This assured the holders of gold coins a monetary use for them.

(5) All types of money were convertible, directly or indirectly, into gold coins. This had the effect of keeping the value of all money equal to gold.

(6) Import and export of gold were unrestricted. If import had been restricted, there would have been a tendency for the domestic value of gold to rise above the world value; and if export had been

restricted, there would have been a tendency for the domestic value of gold to fall below the world value. If both import and export had been prohibited, the value relationship at home and abroad would have been determined by whether the United States was mining gold above or below its domestic needs. Technically, such limitations are in violation of the free-coinage principle which makes no distinction between domestic and foreign owners of gold.

(7) Individuals and others could possess gold coins, gold bars, or gold in any form in "unlimited" quantities.

When the United States began redeeming the U.S. notes (greenbacks) in 1879, it was moving into a 21-year era during which bank paper money and subsidiary coins were redeemable in lawful money, U.S. notes and gold certificates were redeemable in gold coins, and silver certificates were redeemable in "standard silver dollars." But what was the status of the standard silver dollar? For all practical purposes the country was on a gold standard, but the uncertainty of the status of the silver dollar caused this period to be known as that of the "limping" gold standard, or the gold standard with a "peg-leg" made of silver.

Purchase of Silver. The act of July 14, 1890, added to the complexity of the monetary system in two ways: (1) it required the monthly purchase of silver to be increased to 4,500,000 ounces per month at the prevailing market price, which doubled the quantity of silver bullion purchased, and (2) it required that the silver purchased be paid for with Treasury or "Sherman" notes (eliminating the delay in obtaining payment by sellers who previously had to wait until the silver bullion was coined). Now the Treasury went through the procedure of buying silver bullion, paying for it with paper money called "Treasury notes," coining silver into silver dollars, issuing silver certificates to retire the Treasury notes, and retaining the silver dollars as a reserve against the silver certificates.

The effect of increasing the amount of silver in the monetary stock was to lessen confidence in the ability of the United States to remain on the gold standard. Several domestic and foreign factors account for the panic of 1893, but the silver issue played an important part. On November 1, 1893, Congress repealed the silver purchase clause of the Sherman Act. From 1893 to 1897 the government had great difficulty in keeping the United States on the gold standard. It was not until the end of the presidential campaign of 1896 that general confidence in the monetary system returned, and with it the pressure upon the country's gold reserves was decreased. Although the candidate of the party favoring the free coinage of silver was defeated in the campaign of 1896, the legal position of the silver dollar was not settled until the passage of the Gold Standard Act of 1900, which provided that "all forms of money issued or coined by the United States shall be maintained at a parity with this standard" and made it the duty of the Secretary of the Treasury "to maintain such parity." Relief from the deflationary effects of the gold standard followed primarily through expansion in (1) deposits in state-chartered banks which were organized and operated under liberal laws and (2) gold supplies flowing from new mines in Alaska.

Despite the economic boom of the first decade of the 20th century, the United States suffered severely from the money panics of 1903 and 1907. Little had been done to lessen the inherent instability in the monetary and banking system. Although fiscal policy had been improved by the willingness of the United States Treasury to deposit cash with banks when they needed reserves, there was a demand for additional money that could be used for reserves and circulation during each crisis.

In 1908, the Aldrich-Vreeland Act provided for (1) appointment of the National Monetary Commission to study the country's monetary and banking system and to make recommendations for needed legislation and (2) issuance of additional national bank notes under conditions that would permit the volume to expand as needed. Banks, individually or in groups, were permitted to issue new national bank notes backed by pledges of commercial paper. Because this paper increases and decreases with trade, it was assumed that the cyclical needs for additional currency would be cared for by banks using their new note-issue privilege.

In its summary report of January, 1912, the National Monetary Commission indicated the money and banking system on numerous counts and the discussions that followed led to the passage of the Federal Reserve Act on December 23, 1913. After the outbreak of World War I, pending the opening of the Federal Reserve banks in November, 1914, some use was made of the power to issue additional national bank notes.[16]

---

[16] The national bank note was given a new lease on life in 1932 when Congress permitted national banks to use any type of government obligation as collateral for new issues for a three-year period. When the three-year period expired, the Secretary of the Treasury called all the outstanding bonds that had the permanent circulation privilege. As a result, all the legalized collateral for national bank notes was canceled and plans had to be made to retire the national bank notes in circulation. The issuing banks deposited cash with the United States Treasury which assumed all responsibility for redeeming the bank notes.

Federal Reserve Currency. Each Federal Reserve bank was empowered to issue (1) Federal Reserve bank notes to replace national bank notes and (2) Federal Reserve notes, a new type of "elastic" currency.

1. Federal Reserve bank notes required no gold reserves and were secured by U.S. government banks in the same way as the national bank notes. Although few such notes were issued in exchange for national bank notes, Federal Reserve bank notes were used under provisions of the Pittman Act of 1918 to retire $350 million in silver certificates. The silver dollars which the latter represented were melted down and most of the bullion was sold to Great Britain (which used it to pay for its purchases from India during World War I). After the war emergency, silver was purchased in the domestic market, and silver money replaced Federal Reserve bank notes.

In 1933, when the nation was in the midst of the Great Depression, Congress again authorized the issuance of Federal Reserve bank notes (called national currency) in an act that broadened the collateral base to include commercial paper and any direct obligations of the U.S. government. Although a large quantity of these notes was printed, the need for additional currency was less than expected, and only a relatively small amount was issued. However in December, 1942, these unissued notes were placed in circulation as an economy measure. In June, 1945, Congress withdrew the power of the Federal Reserve banks to issue Federal Reserve bank notes and made the Treasury responsible for retiring those in circulation with assets provided by the Federal Reserve banks.

2. The Federal Reserve Act provided that Federal Reserve notes were to be obtained in exchange for commercial paper; hence, it was assumed that the need for an elastic currency would be cared for because the amount in circulation would fluctuate with changes in the needs of trade. The framers of this provision reasoned that when trade increases businessmen borrow from banks and the latter rediscount this loan paper with their Federal Reserve banks which, in turn, use the paper as collateral for new Federal Reserve notes. On the other hand, with a decline in trade, businessmen repay loans at banks, the latter repay the Federal Reserve banks, and when the commercial paper pledged is returned an equal amount of Federal Reserve notes is returned to the Federal Reserve agents. However, other factors were involved. For illustration, when the Federal Reserve banks used gold and gold certificates to recover the matured commercial paper held by their Federal Reserve agents, the Federal Reserve notes remained in

circulation and the amount was not directly related to the volume of commercial paper held by the Federal Reserve banks (see Chapter 3).

The assumption that the amount of commercial paper in the banking system during a financial crisis would be adequate to provide a base for additional money was based on the fact that earlier panics had occurred at the height of business booms when business borrowing was at its peak and banks' vaults were "bursting" with promissory notes of merchants and others. However, in 1933, a banking panic came at the bottom of a depression when banks were without adequate supplies of commerical paper eligible as collateral for loans at Federal Reserve banks. Although banks were permitted to use government securities as collateral for borrowing at their Federal Reserve banks, these securities were in short supply (the era of big government debt held by banks was still in the future). During the late 1920's, bank failures and business losses caused many to question the concept that sound money depended on the redemption of currency in gold, and there was a growing conviction that the most urgent monetary need was to protect the nation's most important type of money, demand deposits in commercial banks.

BANKING AND MONETARY CHANGES SINCE 1932

On March 4, 1933, when Franklin D. Roosevelt became President of the United States, one of his first official acts was to declare a national banking holiday (in effect, a moratorium) to replace the moratoria already in effect in most states. In addition to suspending all banking activities except those authorized by the Treasury, the national banking holiday proclamation contained provisions forbidding the hoarding of gold and gold certificates and the exportation of gold. When Congress met on March 9, it confirmed the emergency steps taken by the President and made provisions for reopening the banks as soon as possible. All banks were to be examined, and only the solvent banks were to be permitted to operate without restrictions. Confidence in banks had to be restored. Within 10 days the task was completed, and, when the holiday was over, 13,500 banks had licenses from the Secretary of the Treasury permitting them to operate and the remainder were closed or permitted to do only a "new banking business," which required them to segregate new deposits and assets from the old. Many of the unlicensed banks were hopelessly insolvent and had to be liquidated, and others were reorganized with the financial assistance of the government-owned Reconstruction Finance Corporation.

Usually, when a nation is experiencing a national crisis, the event is reflected in the price being paid for its money in foreign exchange markets; however, during this period the price of the dollar remained at or near par. This confidence seemed justified when the Secretary of the Treasury adopted a fairly liberal policy in regard to granting requests for gold-export licenses. There was no gold scarcity in the United States, and the flow of currency back to the banks and of gold coins and gold certificates to the Federal Reserve banks increased the liquidity of the banking system and improved the reserve position of the Federal Reserve banks.

Devaluation. In April, 1933, the gold policy of the Treasury became more restrictive as became evident with the announcement that gold-export licenses for all ordinary purposes would be suspended and that gold was to be sequestered in the Treasury. In May, devaluation of the gold dollar was indicated when the President in a radio address to the American people stated: "The Administration has the definite objective of raising commodity prices to such an extent that those who have borrowed money will, on the average, be able to repay that money in the same kind of dollar which they borrowed. . . . We do not seek to let them get such a cheap dollar that, in effect, they will be able to pay back a great deal less than they borrowed." Emphasis was to be on raising commodity prices by monetary action as provided for in the Thomas Inflation Bill passed by Congress a few days later. This act empowered the President to reduce the weight of the gold dollar by as much as 50 percent; reestablish bimetallism; accept silver from foreign governments in payment of their debts in an amount of $200 million at a price of 50 cents per ounce; authorize the Secretary of the Treasury to issue $3 billion in U.S. notes; and approve requests of the Federal Reserve Board to make emergency changes in the minimum reserve requirements of member banks.

On October 22, 1933, in another radio address, the President restated his price program and announced his new plan to secure it—governmental purchases of gold at higher prices. The assumption was that, since each increase in the price of gold would increase the number of gold dollars represented by the gold stock, general prices would rise correspondingly. Three days later the Reconstruction Finance Corporation announced that it would purchase all domestic gold at $31.36 per ounce (as compared to the previous government price of $20.67), and the following day governmental purchases were extended to foreign markets by the Federal Reserve Bank of New York. Subsequently, gold-buying prices were increased.

The gold-buying plan aroused a storm of protest from the first. It was not understood by businessmen; and the resulting uncertainty was enough to prevent its successful operation, assuming that it had been scientifically correct in its concept. The fact that the mint price of gold is increased and more paper money (gold certificates) is printed and deposited in Federal Reserve banks is no guarantee that the supply of money will increase. Even if the supply of money does increase, the price level or volume of transactions or both will not increase if businessmen and others hold more funds and spend relatively less. A decrease in the rate of spending or velocity of money may even cause a decline in general prices. The main result of the gold-buying policy was to prepare the country for the devaluation of the gold dollar, which became effective on January 31, 1934.

Gold Reserve Act of 1934. The Gold Reserve Act of 1934 made permanent many of the emergency changes that had taken place since March 4, 1933 and greatly expanded governmental control over the monetary systems. The Act provided for the permanent transfer of the nation's gold stock from the Federal Reserve System to the government; placed responsibility for domestic and foreign gold transactions in the Treasury Department; created a $2 billion stabilization fund to be used by the Treasury to stabilize foreign exchange rates; prohibited coinage of gold into U.S. coins and demonetized those outstanding; changed minimum reserve requirements of the Federal Reserve banks so as to allow gold certificates to be substituted for gold;[17] and specified that the new gold dollar could not be more than 60 percent of its former weight.

After the close of business on January 30, 1934, the President issued a proclamation fixing the weight of the gold dollar at $15\frac{5}{21}$ grains of gold $\frac{9}{10}$ fine, making the mint price $35 per fine ounce troy weight. The new weight was 59.06 percent of the former weight, and this is the basis for reference to the "59-cent dollar."

Immediately following the devaluation proclamation, the Treasury issued regulations that provided for a gold-buying policy at $35 per fine ounce, minus a handling charge of one fourth of 1 percent and a selling policy (1) for artistic, industrial, and professional uses;

---

[17] Section 6 of the Gold Reserve Act reads in part: "Except to the extent permitted in regulations which may be issued hereunder by the Secretary of the Treasury with the approval of the President, no currency of the United States shall be redeemed in gold: *Provided, however,* that gold certificates owned by the Federal Reserve banks shall be redeemed at such times and such amounts as, in the judgment of the Secretary of the Treasury, are necessary to maintain the equal purchasing power of every kind of currency of the United States. . . ."

(2) to Federal Reserve banks for the purposes of settling international balances; and (3) for other purposes not inconsistent with the purposes of the Act.[18] Although the Treasury has followed a policy of selling gold to selected foreign central banks and governments, an element of uncertainty exists because would-be purchasers must be given permission to buy gold by the Treasury. Domestic sales of gold have been regulated carefully, with the negative purpose of preventing the general public from using gold as a store of value or for the positive purpose of keeping gold in the hands of the government to be held as reserves for gold certificates and for international exchange purposes.

The basic function of the Stabilization Fund, administered by the Secretary of the Treasury, is to stabilize the international value of the dollar. Until the past few years, the dollar did not need support because of the strong economic position of the United States; but the deficits in the U.S. balance of payments have changed this situation (see Chapter 27). Only 10 percent of the $2 billion allocated to the Stabilization Fund was placed on deposit with the Federal Reserve Bank of New York; the remainder was carried as "inactive gold" in the Treasury statement of cash holdings until 1945, when Congress authorized that it be used as part payment of the U.S. quota of $2.75 billion due the International Monetary Fund. Until 1945, the use of the Stabilization Fund prevented most of the profits from devaluation from being "monetized"; but the new price of gold made the United States a favorable market in which to buy goods. The increased foreign purchases of American goods caused a disturbing inflationary influx of gold.

During World War II the expansion of the volume of currency and in the volume of Federal Reserve banks' deposits, which serve as reserves of member banks, brought pressure on the Federal Reserve banks' reserve positions; therefore, Congress in the Act of June 12, 1945, changed the minimum Federal Reserve banks' reserve requirements to 25 percent in gold certificates for Federal Reserve notes and eliminated the provision in the Thomas Inflation Act permitting issuance of $3 billion in U.S. notes. On March 4, 1965, Congress eliminated all gold-reserve requirements for deposits in Federal Reserve banks and, in 1968, removed the remaining minimum gold-reserve requirements for Federal Reserve notes in order to make the entire monetary gold stock of the United States available as international

[18] See *Provisional Regulation Issued under the Gold Reserve Act of 1934 as Amended to April 15, 1942* (Washington, D.C.: United States Treasury, 1942).

money. This change did not mean that the United States had abandoned the gold-exchange standard.

Gold Standard Changes.   Under the original gold-coin standard, gold was coined and used as circulating as well as reserve money and to meet deficits in international balances of payments. Years before the full gold standard was legally replaced by the gold-bullion standard, bank reserves were being held in the form of gold bars and the latter were used in international transactions. When national governments wished to economize on the use of gold, they made provisions for the demonetization of gold coins, abolition of gold coinage, and substitution of gold bars for gold coins in meeting reserve requirements. But even before the shift to the gold-bullion standard was complete, many nations had shifted to the use of gold exchange in meeting their international reserve needs.

A country is considered to be operating on a gold-exchange standard when its money is redeemable in drafts drawn on a bank in a country which is operating on the gold-coin or gold-bullion standard. The basic requirement of a gold-exchange standard is the right to buy and sell gold exchange freely in unlimited quantities at established prices. In countries (such as the United States and the United Kingdom) having well-developed money markets, bankers could invest their reserves to secure income and still convert them into cash in case of need without loss or delay. Thus, banks retained the advantage of having the liquid assets required for international payments while obtaining an income therefrom. Hence, the gold-exchange standard was superior to other forms of the gold standard for as long as the "parent" country maintained convertibility of its money into gold.

In 1944, participants of the international monetary conference held at Bretton Woods, New Hampshire, made provisions for the organization of the International Monetary Fund (also the "World Bank," whose official title is International Bank for Reconstruction and Development) wherein the member nations were committed to the gold-exchange standard. The provisions required those nations to define their monetary units in term of gold or the U.S. gold dollar of July 1, 1944 and to maintain parity of their currencies in foreign exchange markets. (See also Chapter 28.)

Early in 1968, the United States and certain other countries took another step toward separating their moneys from gold. As a result of speculators' demands on central banks for gold (much of which came from the United States), the central banks of Belgium, Germany, Italy, the Netherlands, United Kingdom, and the United States agreed: (1) to buy and sell gold at $35 per ounce to one another and to other cooperating central banks and (2) to refrain from providing gold to the London gold market or any other market.[19] This agreement resulted in the two-price or "two-tier" system for gold wherein the market price or commodity value of gold bears little relation to the monetary value of gold. Hence the question may be asked: Is gold, like silver, being "phased out" as a monetary metal?

Silver Changes. From 1933 to 1939, under different Presidential proclamations under authority of the Thomas Inflation Act, the United States Mint accepted all newly mined domestic silver tendered for coinage into silver dollars; but a seigniorage charge of 50 percent reduced the price the miners received to 64.64 + cents per fine ounce. This was not "unlimited" coinage because it was restricted to "newly mined" domestic silver. In 1939, Congress passed a law that embodied this procedure but reducing the seigniorage charge to 45 percent or paying miners 71.11 cents per fine ounce (in 1946 the charge was changed to 30 percent and miners received 90.5 cents per fine ounce).

Until the outbreak of World War II, foreign silver was purchased at the world price under the Silver Purchase Act of 1934. The purpose of this act was to purchase silver until one fourth of the money value of the country's gold and silver stock was in silver. This objective was never achieved; instead, the high price of silver led to the abandonment of silver purchase policies at home and abroad. In the United States this was followed by replacing silver certificates with $1 denomination Federal Reserve notes and "phasing out" silver as a monetary metal for all coins except the half dollar. Gradually the United States has shifted from the use of gold and silver as money to the use of credit money having little or no commodity value.

SUMMARY

The first coinage act passed by the United States Congress under the new Constitution provided for a bimetallic standard including both gold and silver "full-bodied" or standard coins. In addition, provisions were made for a small quantity of token coins, bank credit money (bank notes issued by the Bank of the United States), and deposit currency. Although their constitutionality was challenged, many banks were chartered by state governments. These banks were

---

[19] "Meeting of the Governors of Central Banks Contributing to Gold Pool: Communiqué," *Federal Reserve Bulletin*, March, 1968, p. 254.

given the right to issue paper money and to accept demand deposits. Thus, from the beginning of the history of the United States full-bodied money had to compete with less expensive forms of money.

Because of the failure to make an accurate appraisal of the market ratio prevailing between gold and silver, the bimetallic standard operated unsatisfactorily. In 1853, all silver coins except the standard silver dollar were made token coins. In 1873 free coinage of standard silver dollars was discontinued, but five years later Congress authorized their coinage as token money. At the same time, provisions were made for the replacement of silver dollars in circulation with silver certificates because of the public preference for paper money.

During the Civil War era United States notes were issued, and they became the standard money from 1862 to 1879. State bank notes were eliminated and replaced by new national bank notes that provided the nation with a uniform and safe bank paper money system for the first time in its history. The convertibility of U.S. notes into gold ended the paper standard era in 1879. Although the silver dollar was being coined under a limited coinage law, the situation was confused because no provisions were made to keep these coins at par with gold, and there was no specific declaration by Congress that the gold dollar was the standard coin. This situation was clarified in 1900, when the gold dollar was made the "standard unit of value" and the Secretary of the Treasury was required to maintain the value of all coins at par with the gold dollar.

The Federal Reserve Act led to fundamental changes in the currency and banking situation of the United States. The Federal Reserve note became the most important kind of currency in circulation, replacing gold coins, gold and silver certificates, national bank notes, and Federal Reserve bank notes. By the provisions of the Gold Reserve Act of 1934, together with administrative policies subsequently adopted, the United States Treasury and the Federal Reserve banks were given the task of managing the money supply so as to maintain domestic stability and to keep the international value of the U.S. dollar equal to gold.

The International Monetary Fund agreements of 1944 provided for a new international monetary system which embodied the principles of the gold-exchange standard. In 1968, the link between the monetary and market or commodity value of gold was severed when the United States and other countries established a policy of not buying or selling gold in the market.

QUESTIONS AND PROBLEMS

1. Identify (*a*) colonial currency, (*b*) continental currency, (*c*) state issues of paper money, and (*d*) "private" coins.

2. What are the chief provisions of the Coinage Act of 1792? Was too much expected of "free enterprise"? Explain.

3. What mistake, made in the Coinage Act of 1792, was overcorrected in 1834? How was the mistake made in 1834 corrected in part in 1853?

4. Summarize the changes made in the currency system of the United States from 1861 to 1870 (standard, coins, and paper money). What steps were taken to reconstruct the monetary system from 1873 to 1879?

5. Explain what is meant by the "limping" gold-coin standard. What act brought to an end this period in U.S. monetary history? To what extent may the gold-coin standard (1900–33) be considered a gold-bullion standard in international transactions and a gold-certificate standard in domestic transactions?

6. What is meant by the statement that the different silver-buying acts (1878, 1890, and 1934) did not provide for a bimetallic standard?

7. "Presently, there are seven different types of currency in circulation: gold certificates, silver certificates, United States notes, Federal Reserve bank notes, National bank notes, Treasury notes of 1890, and Federal Reserve notes." (Federal Reserve Bank of Dallas, *Business Review*, July, 1963, p. 3.) Which are classified as bank paper money? As Treasury currency? Why?

8. Justify the following: "Since June, 1967, the Treasury has been withdrawing the old silver coins from circulation. Melting was recommended by the Joint Commission on Coinage as of March 1. The silver will be sold to industrial users." (*The Coin World*, April 17, 1968, p. 1.)

9. Outline the main provisions of the Gold Reserve Act of 1934. As it is being operated today, what is the gold-standard situation in the United States?

10. "Gold has been valued by all peoples. Men have sought for it and fought for it over the ages. But as a medium of exchange between modern nations, gold leaves much to be desired." (*The Austin American*, April 15, 1968, p. 5.) Why?

CHAPTER 3

United States Money

THE MONETARY SYSTEM of the United States consists of gold and money provided by the United States Treasury, Federal Reserve banks, and commercial banks, and the rules and regulations applicable thereto. The monetary agencies control both the creation of money and the machinery for formulating and executing policies in accordance with laws passed by Congress. The United States Treasury is responsible for administering policies pertaining to gold and silver, issuance of coins and United States notes, retirement of obsolete currency and management of Treasury cash balances. The Federal Reserve System is responsible for issuance and retirement of Federal Reserve notes, distribution of currency among commercial banks, creation of reserves for commercial banks, and formulation and execution of general monetary and credit policies of the nation.

The concept of money includes gold, demand deposits in commercial banks, and currency created by the Treasury and the Federal Reserve System. Demand deposits appear as "accounts payable" on commercial banks' statements, and the owners of these deposits create their own private instruments of transfer, usually in the form of checks. Although deposit currency, "checkbook" money, lacks the legal-tender quality, it is the most important means of payment in the United States.

BANKS AND THE MONETARY SYSTEM

Condition Statement for Banks and the Monetary System. The gradual shift from "full-bodied" money is reflected in the Consolidated Condition Statement for Banks and the Monetary System (see Table 3–1). It indicates that the money used by the general public consists of debts of commercial banks (demand deposits adjusted) and currency issued by the goverment and the Federal Reserve banks. The security for the promises to pay that make up the money supply appears as assets in this statement. The largest of the

43

TABLE 3–1

CONSOLIDATED CONDITION STATEMENT FOR BANKS AND THE MONETARY SYSTEM
(May 29, 1968*; in Millions of Dollars)

ASSETS		LIABILITIES AND CAPITAL	
Gold stock	$ 10,400	Money supply:	
Treasury currency		Demand deposits adjusted	$139,900
outstanding	6,800	Currency outside banks	41,100
Loans (net)	282,400	Total money supply	181,000
U.S. Government		Nonmonetary:	
securities	116,000	Foreign deposits	2,100
Other securities	72,800	Time deposits	250,000
		Treasury cash and deposits	7,300
		Capital and miscellaneous (net)	48,000
Total†	$488,400	Total*	$488,400

* Preliminary.
† Amounts may not total because of rounding and interagency adjustments.
Source of statistics: *Federal Reserve Bulletin*, June, 1968, p. A-18.

asset items—loans and U.S. government securities—indicate the extent to which debts dominate the asset side of the statement.

On the liabilities side of the consolidated condition statement, "demand deposits adjusted" are equal to total deposits minus U.S. government deposits, cash items in process of collection, and interbank deposits. These items are deducted because (1) government deposits in commercial banks are ordinarily not subject to check, (2) checks and other items in process of collection still appear on the drawers' banks' statements, and (3) deposits of one bank that are redeposited in another bank have already been counted.

The Consolidated Statement of Condition for Banks and the Monetary System is constructed by combining the balance sheets of commercial and savings banks, Federal Reserve banks, and the United States Treasury, and then deducting interagency transactions and duplicating items (such as gold certificates, interbank deposits, and currency held by banks). In addition to the money supply items, the statement includes nonmonetary items. Of the latter, the most important are time deposits, called "near money," that include savings accounts and other deposits that are payable after the lapse of 30 days or more (see Chapter 11).

GOLD

The present gold policy of the United States commits the United States (1) to buying and selling gold at the official price to cooperating central banks and governments and (2) to regulating the domestic gold market in order to prevent gold from being hoarded. Since the "official" and "commodity" markets for gold are separated, the value of money is no longer linked to gold. Like token coins, an ounce of gold money has value that is not related to its commodity value. For illustration, a foreign central bank may acquire U.S. monetary gold for $35 per fine ounce, but a like purchase in the marketplace by a bullion dealer would be approximately $40. Hence, the value of the dollar in terms of gold is greater in the "official" than in the "commodity" market.

Gold Money.   Over 100 countries now define the par values of their currencies in terms of gold or the U.S. dollar of the weight and fineness in effect on July 1, 1944, in accordance with the provisions of the International Monetary Fund. The *Schedule of Par Value* published by the Fund contains the par value of each member country in grams of gold and its equivalent in U.S. dollars of the "weight and fineness in effect on July 1, 1944."[1] The International Monetary Fund defines the dollar for nations using the metric system as 0.888671 grams of fine gold; but Congress defines it in terms of the troy weight system as $15\frac{5}{21}$ grains of standard gold nine-tenths fine or as $\frac{1}{35}$ of an ounce of fine gold.

The par of exchange between two countries may be found by comparing the amount of gold in their currency units. For illustration, the German mark, the monetary unit of West Germany, contains 0.222168 grams of fine gold, which is one fourth the gold content of the U.S. dollar; hence the par value of the mark is 25 cents.

Gold Policy.   Prior to March, 1968, the United States Treasury redeemed its money abroad (but not at home) in gold at a fixed price of $35 per fine ounce. Due to speculation in and hoarding of gold, the United States and cooperating central banks adopted a new gold policy that led to a two-price system for gold. Under this arrangement, the official price of gold ($35 per ounce) applies only to official transactions among the cooperating central banks and the United States Treasury. Other buyers and sellers are permitted to trade in nonmonetary gold in the marketplace. The Treasury's gold regulations permit (1) domestic producers to sell nonmonetary gold in the domestic and foreign markets, and (2) domestic users to buy gold at home or abroad in amounts and under conditions specified in their licenses. In administering the gold policies of the United States, the

---

[1] International Monetary Fund, *Schedule of Par Values, Forty-fifth Issue* (Washington, D.C.), December 22, 1967, pp. 2–5.

Treasury uses the Federal Reserve Bank of New York as its agent in trading with foreign central banks and governments (see Chapter 18).

Customarily foreign central banks sell gold to obtain dollar exchange, which is left in commercial banks until used to pay for goods, services, and securities. In a transaction of this sort, the United States Treasury pays for the gold with a check drawn on its account with the Federal Reserve Bank of New York, and the foreign central bank deposits its Treasury check with a commercial bank. The latter receives reserve credit when the check is collected. Then, the Treasury replenishes its account with a deposit of gold certificates and earmarks gold as security for the certificates. As a result of these transactions, there will be an increase in the monetary gold stock of the United States, in the gold-certificate reserve account, in member banks' assets and liabilities, and in dollar-exchange holdings of a foreign central bank. When the bookkeeping is completed, an import of $1 million in gold would ordinarily increase the following items by $1 million: the money supply, member-bank reserves, Federal Reserve gold-certificate reserves, and the Treasury's monetary gold stock This may be shown as follows:

Commercial Bank		*Federal Reserve Bank*	
ASSETS	LIABILITIES	ASSETS	LIABILITIES
Reserves, + $1 million	Deposits, + $1 million	Gold certificates, + $1 million	Member-bank reserves, + $1 million

U.S. Treasury	
ASSETS	LIABILITIES
Gold, + $1 million	Gold certificates, + $1 million

When a foreign central bank purchases gold from the United States Treasury, the latter releases the gold from the assay office and cancels an equal amount of gold certificates held by the Federal Reserve Bank of New York, which debits the Treasury's account to offset the loss in gold-certificate reserves. The Treasury's checking account will be replenished when the Federal Reserve bank credits its account for the check given in payment by the foreign gold buyer. At the same time, the foreign buyer's bank account will be debited. As a result of these transactions, there will be a reduction in the monetary gold stock of the United States, in gold-certificate or gold-credit assets of the Federal Reserve System, in deposit liabilities of the Federal Reserve bank, in commercial banks' assets and liabilities, and in dollar-exchange assets of the foreign gold buyer. After all the bookkeeping entailed in an export of $1 million in gold is complete, the changes in the statements of member banks, the Federal Reserve bank, and the United States Treasury will be as follows:

Member Banks		*Federal Reserve Bank*	
ASSETS	LIABILITIES	ASSETS	LIABILITIES
Reserves, — $1 million	Deposits, — $1 million	Gold certificates, — $1million	Deposits, — $1 million

U.S. Treasury	
ASSETS	LIABILITIES
Gold, — $1 million	Gold certificates, — $1 million

Because many countries of the free world keep their monetary gold in the Federal Reserve Bank of New York, an export of gold may consist of a change of title and a shift in location from the United States Assay Office in New York to the Federal Reserve Bank of New York. This foreign-owned gold is earmarked or tagged to indicate the owner. Such gold does not belong to the U.S. government, and the amount is not included in the statistics of the U.S. gold stock.

KINDS OF CURRENCY OUTSTANDING

In the United States, the two monetary authorities and currency-issuing agencies are the United States Treasury and the Federal Reserve System. The Treasury is responsible for gold money and Treasury currency. The latter includes all types of silver money (standard silver dollars, silver bullion, silver certificates, and subsidiary silver coins), minor coins, U.S. notes, and paper money issues in process of retirement.[2] The Federal Reserve System issues only one type of currency, the Federal Reserve note.

The term "currency" is defined to include all circulating coins and paper money. The concept of "currency in circulation" includes all such money outside the United States Treasury and the Federal Reserve banks, and the concept of "kinds of currency outstanding" includes all coins and currency in the Treasury and Federal Reserve banks as well as all currency in circulation (see Table 3–2). Congress permits the Treasury to adjust for coins and currency "lost from circulation," that is, in hoards, lost, and destroyed. If the item is a Federal Reserve note, the credit for the "lost" note is accounted for

---

[2] As shown by the Treasury statements, U.S. currency outstanding includes various types of paper money being retired for which the Treasury is responsible. These types of obsolete but not extinct currency include national bank notes, Federal Reserve bank notes, Treasury notes of 1890, silver certificates, and gold certificates issued before 1934. They are redeemed with cash from the general fund when presented to the Treasury.

TABLE 3–2

UNITED STATES CURRENCY—
KINDS OUTSTANDING AND IN CIRCULATION
(In Millions of Dollars)

| Kind of Currency | Total Outstanding April 30, 1968 | Held in the Treasury | | | Held by Federal Reserve Banks and Agents | Currency in Circulation* April 30, 1968 |
		As Security against Gold and Silver Certificates	Treasury Cash	For Federal Reserve Banks and Agents		
Gold.......................... 10,484		(10,128)	356†	......	.....	......
Gold certificates................(10,128)		....	.....	10,127‡	1	......
Federal Reserve notes........... 43,846		....	152	......	2,876	40,818
Treasury currency—Total....... 6,790		(288)	562	......	425	5,803
Standard silver dollars........... 485		3	......	......	......	482
Silver bullion................... 339		285	54	......	......	......
Silver certificates............... (288)		....	.....	......	5	284
Fractional coin................. 5,559		....	492	......	412	4,656
U.S. notes..................... 323		....	17	......	9	297
In process of retirement§........ 85		....	......	......	......	85
Total—April 30, 1968...... 61,120‖		(10,416)	1,070	10,127	3,302	46,621
March 31, 1968..... 60,643‖		(10,433)	1,084	10,130	3,131	......
April 30, 1967...... 60,527‖		(13,160)	1,365	12,603	2,828	......

* Outside Treasury and Federal Reserve Banks. Includes any paper currency held outside the United States and currency and coin held by banks.

† Includes $245 million gold deposited by and held for the International Monetary Fund.

‡ Consists of credits payable in gold certificates: (1) the Gold Certificate Fund—Board of Governors, Federal Reserve System; and (2) the Redemption Fund for Federal Reserve notes.

§ Redeemable from the general fund of the Treasury.

‖ Does not include all items shown, as some items represent the security for other items; gold certificates are secured by gold, and silver certificates by standard silver dollars and monetized silver bullion. Duplications are shown in parentheses.

Source: *Federal Reserve Bulletin,* June, 1968, p. A–16.

according to instructions given by the Board of Governors of the Federal Reserve System and the remaining forms of paper money are credited to the Treasury's "general fund."

Coins and Coinage. Metals were first used as money in commodity or bullion form, and each transaction entailed weighing and testing for quality. Later merchants, who had more at stake than others, started to stamp pieces of metals of known weight and fineness. This practice of stamping was the first step toward modern coinage.

A coin is a specific weight of metal of a specific fineness that is created to circulate as money (allowances must be made for the striking of a relatively small number of proof sets and commemorative coins not designed for circulation). Coins may be classified in a number of ways, such as according to their composition (copper, nickel, silver, gold, and alloys) and according to their value relationship as token or subsidiary and standard or "full-bodied." On the day of issuance, a token coin has more value as money than as metal, but a "full-bodied" coin has a commodity value equal to its money value.

The colonists began coinage as early as 1652 in Boston, where the famous "pine tree" shilling was struck. The Articles of Confederation, the first U.S. Constitution, gave Congress the power to regulate coinage but did not deny the same right to the states. Between 1778 and 1789, a few states made arrangement for coinage, and the mint established by Massachusetts was an important source of copper coins. Although Congress made plans for the decimal system with silver as the standard metal, no federal coins were struck until 1787 (the Fugio or Franklin cent was privately minted under a federal contract).

The Coinage Act of April 2, 1792, provided for a United States Mint and authorized the free coinage of gold and silver, which meant that owners had the privilege of taking the metals in unlimited amounts to be minted into coins. The term "free coinage" does not mean gratuitous coinage; there was usually a charge for assay and minting costs, and sometimes a seigniorage fee was added. Free coinage existed for gold from 1792 to 1934 and for silver from 1792 to 1873.

Now, all circulating coins in the United States are token coins. They are supplied by the United States Mint, which buys the raw materials in the market, mints the coins according to the needs of the country for small change, distributes them through the Federal Reserve banks, and transfers the profits from coinage (called seigniorage) to the United States Treasury. On request, the mint or a specified government agency redeems or repurchases worn or mutilated coins and any surplus amounts due to changes in buying habits. Most token coins are composed of copper, nickel, and tin, with silver being used only in some "prestige" coins such as the U.S. 50-cent piece. The existing silver dollars and 50-cent pieces struck before 1965 are owned chiefly by collectors, coin dealers, and speculators.

In the Coinage Act of 1965, Congress made provisions for: (1) a half dollar composed of 800 parts silver and 200 parts copper per 1,000 parts by weight clad on a silver-copper alloy so that the composition of each coin is 40 percent silver and 60 percent copper; and (2) 25-cent and 10-cent pieces composed of an alloy of 75 percent copper and 25 percent nickel clad on a core of pure copper. No changes were made in the 5-cent piece (75 percent copper and 25 percent nickel) or the 1-cent piece (95 percent copper and 5 percent tin and zinc).[3]

Gold and Silver Certificates. United States currency includes two types of government credit money and several forms of obsolete

[3] Director of the Mint, *Annual Report for the Fiscal Year Ended June 30, 1966* (Washington, D.C.: U.S. Government Printing Office, 1967), p. 148.

but not extinct paper money. In 1863, Congress authorized the Secretary of the Treasury to receive deposits of gold coin and gold bullion in exchange for gold certificates in denominations of $20 and over (the minimum was changed to $10 in 1907). This policy was one of convenience, but it reduced the loss that normally results from the circulation of coins. Although gold coins and gold certificates were called in 1934, occasionally these certificates are presented to the Treasury for redemption.

Gold certificates issued since 1934 are in denominations of $100,000, and they are secured by an equal amount of gold in bar form held by the United States Treasury.[4] (These certificates never appear in circulation.) For a number of years, Congress has permitted the Treasury to forgo the cost and inconvenience of using gold certificates and to use gold credits instead. The use of gold credits issued to Federal Reserve banks in exchange for Federal Reserve credit means, for example, that a single bookkeeping entry may replace the use of 10,000 pieces of paper representing gold reserves of $10 billion.

In 1878, Congress authorized the Secretary of the Treasury to exchange silver dollars (and later silver bullion) for silver certificates. Originally, the silver certificates were secured by an equal dollar amount of silver dollars, which necessitated useless coinage because silver certificates were seldom redeemed; therefore Congress provided for the use of silver bullion as security. During recent years the demand for silver for use in the arts and industry has been so great as to cause Congress to make provisions for releasing the silver hoard held as security for silver certificates. The role of the silver certificate was one that could be assumed by any kind of paper money, and it is being replaced by the Federal Reserve note.

U.S. Notes.   The U.S. note or "greenback" is unique in being the only type of credit money issued by the U.S. government. Originally, the notes were irredeemable or "fiat" money. These promises to pay of the U.S. government were first issued during the Civil War. Congress added to their acceptability by making them legal tender for all obligations except payment of custom duties and interest on the federal government debt. Although the government took steps to reduce the amount outstanding after the War, the project was

---

[4] The "gold brick" weighing 27 pounds and worth $14,000 is the most popular size of gold bar. The United States Assay Office indicates the weight of each gold bar, but it is rechecked by the receiving central bank or its fiscal agent (such as the Federal Reserve Bank of New York) when ownership changes.

never completed. Late in 1874, Congress set January 1, 1879, as the date for resumption of specie payments and empowered the Secretary of the Treasury to use surplus revenues and to borrow for this purpose. Without waiting for the redemption date, the Treasury retired and canceled almost 10 percent of the legal-tender notes outstanding. Because of the objection of many congresssmen, Congress, in the act of May, 1877, made it illegal for the Secretary of the Treasury to reduce the number outstanding (thereby fixing the amount at $346, 681,000). The Secretary was also required to reissue not only notes received in payment of taxes and other obligations but also those returned as "unfit for circulation."

In 1900, Congress directed the Secretary of the Treasury "to set apart in the Treasury a reserve fund of $150,000,000 in gold coin and gold bullion." As provided in the Federal Reserve Act of 1913, the Secretary of the Treasury may use funds paid to the Treasury from earnings of the Federal Reserve banks to supplement the gold reserves held against outstanding U.S. notes. In March, 1968, the gold reserve requirement for U.S. notes was eliminated in the same act that repealed similar requirements for Federal Reserve notes and Treasury notes of 1890 (Public Law 90–269). Now, United States notes which the Treasury estimates have been destroyed or lost (under provisions of the "Old Currency Act") may be canceled. This explains why the amount outstanding is reported to be less than $325 million.

Obsolete Paper Money.   Obsolete U.S. paper money includes (1) gold certificates, (2) Treasury notes of 1890, (3) Federal Reserve bank notes, (4) national bank notes, and (5) silver certificates. Now, all of these forms of paper money are classified as "Treasury currency" and are redeemable at the Treasury from general funds.

(1) In 1934, provisions were made to retire all gold certificates in circulation and to issue new ones in large denominations to be used only as Federal Reserve bank reserves. (2) Treasury notes of 1890 were issued for a short time in payment for silver bullion left by miners at the mint. Later, when Congress premitted the mint to issue silver certificates against silver bullion as collateral, the issuance of Treasury notes of 1890 was discontinued. (3) Federal Reserve bank notes were first used to replace national bank notes; later, to replace silver certificates when the silver backing for them was sold to the United Kingdom for shipment to India during World War I; and, finally to serve as emergency currency in 1933 and at the beginning of World War II. In 1945, Congress provided for the withdrawal of all Federal Reserve bank notes outstanding. (4) National bank notes

were issued under provisions of the National Bank Act of 1863. They were based on the credit of the issuing banks and collateral, in the form of U.S. government bonds, deposited with the Comptroller of the Currency. Except for the period 1933–36, national banks could use only certain specified bond issues as security; and when these issues were called in 1936, all national bank notes outstanding were made redeemable by the United States Treasury with cash provided by the issuing banks. (5) In 1878, issuance of silver certificates was authorized to replace the less convenient silver dollars. The latter were to be used by the United States Treasury as backing for the silver certificates. These certificates were redeemable in silver dollars or silver bullion at redemption centers until June 25, 1968. Now the remaining silver certificates outstanding are redeemable at the Treasury from general funds.

The European policy of setting a date for redemption of paper money issues and then refusing to honor any notes presented after that date has never been adopted by the United States. Instead, provisions have been made for the redemption of obsolete but not extinct paper money issues any time they are presented to the Treasury. The procedure is for the issuing institution to deposit sufficient funds to cover all their outstanding currency obligations and then for the Treasury to redeem any notes presented in the future.

Federal Reserve Notes. In the United States, paper money issues have included those of state and nationally chartered commercial banks, but currently additional paper money is issued exclusively by the 12 Federal Reserve banks under supervision of the Board of Governors of the Federal Reserve System. Although the United States Treasury replaces torn and worn-out U.S. notes, it does not add to the volume of paper money outstanding.

Provisions for Federal Reserve currency resulted from the agitation for an elastic currency—one which would increase and decrease automatically with the need for more or less currency. Unlike gold and silver certificates (the amounts of which were tied to the supply of gold and silver) and national bank notes (whose quantity was linked to the volume of eligible government bonds which tended to be perversely elastic), the volume of Federal Reserve notes may be changed to meet the needs of the economy. Since 1914, the volume of Federal Reserve notes has increased to more than $40 billion, due in part to the fact that they have filled the gap left by the withdrawal of other types of paper money. The movement toward simplification of the currency system would be completed by retiring outstanding U.S. notes.

In addition to being prior liens on the assets of the issuing Federal Reserve banks, Federal Reserve notes are obligations of the U.S. government. In order to obtain Federal Reserve notes, a Federal Reserve bank makes application to its Federal Reserve agent and accompanies the application with an equal amount of collateral in the form of obligations of the U.S. government: notes, drafts, and bills of exchange that have been acquired under different sections of the Federal Reserve Act and/or gold certificates (see Table 3–3). The Federal Reserve agent must make daily reports to the Board of Governors showing all issues and withdrawals of Federal Reserve notes

TABLE 3–3

FEDERAL RESERVE NOTES—FEDERAL RESERVE AGENTS' ACCOUNTS
(In Millions of Dollars)

	July, 1967	July, 1968
Federal Reserve notes issued to Federal Reserve banks	42,092	44,848
Collateral held by Federal Reserve agents:		
Gold certificates	6,720	4,658
Eligible paper	...	...
U.S. government securities	36,671	41,791
Total collateral	43,391	46,449

Source of statistics: *Federal Reserve Bulletin*, August, 1968, p. A–12.

by his Federal Reserve bank. The Board may at any time request additional collateral from any Federal Reserve bank to protect its outstanding Federal Reserve notes.

Movement of Currency. The amount of money outside of banks is determined by the needs of individuals, business firms, and others for spending—the transaction motive rather than either the precautionary or speculative motive, although there may be an element of all three. Currency is needed in retail trades and personal service industries to meet payrolls and "petty cash" needs. Changes in the needs of a community for paper money reflect changes in the general price level, income, availability of other forms of cash balances, and the use of credit cards, revolving credit plans, and other forms of retail credit.

The general public has little if any contact with the Bureau of Printing and Engraving, which manufactures paper money; the United States Mint, which strikes coins; or the Federal Reserve banks, which issue Federal Reserve notes; hence, the public depends on middlemen, commercial banks, to meet their needs for currency. Commercial banks learn from experience to appraise their own and their communities' needs for coins and paper money and they keep enough currency to meet these needs. Banks are now permitted to count vault cash in computing their legal reserve requirements, and as a result, they tend to hold more currency than in the past.

Commercial banks are confronted with fluctuating weekly, monthly, and seasonal demands for currency and then a return flow of currency after the peaks in needs have passed. Shoppers and tourists obtain pocket money and merchants build up their till cash in preparation for weekend shopping periods. At the end of one month and the beginning of the next, banks prepare for the demand for currency resulting from payment of trade bills and payrolls. Similar preparations are made for seasonal demands for currency associated with Christmas shopping, payrolls, and holiday travel.

During any business day, there is a continuous flow of currency to and from banks, with new deposits tending to offset withdrawals.[5] However, the inflow is never exactly equal to the outflow for any particular bank; therefore all banks hold a little extra money in case it is needed. If the outflow is mounting relative to the inflow, as happens during periods such as the Christmas shopping season, more currency may be obtained from the Federal Reserve banks. When requesting currency, banks generally specify certain denominations but otherwise show no preference for one kind of currency over others. In making deliveries, the Federal Reserve banks may use registered mail, railway express, or armored cars, and the receiving banks' reserve accounts are debited for the amounts. The Federal Reserve banks replenish their stocks of currency by applying to the Board of Governors, which makes the proper arrangements with the United States Treasury for new currency.

Paper money is produced by the Bureau of Printing and Engraving and coins by the United States Mint—both are divisions of the United States Treasury Department. The Federal Reserve System keeps the Mint informed regarding the need for coins; and, after coins are struck, the Federal Reserve banks purchase them at face value. The Board of Governors obtains Federal Reserve notes from the Comptroller of the Currency—the bureau of the Treasury Depart-

---

[5] Currency coming into commercial banks is sorted and the pieces that are worn or mutilated are sent to the Federal Reserve banks along with those types of currency which are being retired.

ment responsible for "execution of all laws passed by Congress relating to the issue and redemption . . . of all Federal Reserve notes, except for the cancellation and destruction, and accounting with respect to such cancellation and destruction, of Federal Reserve notes unfit for circulation. . . ."[6] Some of the unissued notes are kept in Washington, but most of them are sent to the 12 Federal Reserve agents to be held pending requests for them by their Federal Reserve banks.

DEMAND DEPOSITS

Demand deposits are obligations of commercial banks that are used by their owners as a means of payment, that is, as money. In accepting a deposit subject to withdrawal on demand, a bank creates a liability. Later, the depositor creates his own instrument of transfer when he writes a check on the deposit. Although a check has no legal-tender quality, it is the instrument used in most business and a large percentage of household transactions. A check is a negotiable instrument drawn on a bank and payable on demand.[7] However, banks are seldom asked to pay currency because most bearers or holders prefer to keep their cash balances in checking accounts. If a check is deposited in the drawer's bank, only the books are changed; but, if the check is deposited in a second bank, funds must be transferred from the drawer's to the drawee's bank (see Chapter 9).

Deposit Creation. Banks most commonly create deposits by exchanging their promises to pay on demand for the assets of the depositor (currency, checks, and other credit instruments). When banks make loans, they give deposit credit in exchange for their loan customers' interest-bearing promises to pay; thus banks create new money for as long as checks drawn on deposit accounts by their owners are accepted. The general practice of making payments by check rather than with cash permits banks to do business with a relatively small amount of assets held as a reserve to meet deposit withdrawals. Because most banks' earnings are derived from lending and investing, they usually keep cash (a nonearning asset) at a minimum.

Since 1837, legislative bodies have passed laws requiring banks to keep reserves to protect depositors. These required reserves are but a fractional part of deposits; therefore banks may still expand the volume of deposits or deposit currency. If total reserve requirements

[6] *Federal Reserve Act as Amended through November 5, 1966,* Compiled under the Direction of the Board of Governors of the Federal Reserve System in its Legal Division (Washington, D.C., 1967), p. 32.

[7] *Uniform Commercial Code,* Sec. 3–104(2)(b).

were 20 percent, a bank receiving new deposits of $100 will hold $20 in cash and lend or invest the remainder. If other banks follow the same policy, the expansion in the banking system will tend to progress as follows:

Bank A

ASSETS		LIABILITIES	
Required reserves...........$20		Deposits..................$100	
Excess reserves............ 80		Borrower's deposit.......... 80	
Loan..................... 80			

Bank B

ASSETS		LIABILITIES	
Required reserves..........$16		Deposits..................$80	
Excess reserves............ 64		Borrower's deposit.......... 64	
Loan..................... 64			

Bank C

ASSETS		LIABILITIES	
Required reserves........$12.80		Deposits................$64	
Excess reserves.......... 51.20		Borrower's deposit........ 51.20	
Loan.................... 51.20		*To Bank D*	
To Bank D			

At the fourth stage of the expansion based on new reserves of $100, the total volume of deposits will be $295.20 (Bank A, $100; Bank B, $80; Bank C, $64; and Bank D, $51.20). Bank D has excess reserves, so the deposit expansion may continue among all other banks until the balance sheet of the banking system includes an increase in deposits and assets of $500 made up of loans for $400 and reserves of $100.

The probability of expanding bank credit and deposits to the point outlined above is remote. It could happen only if (1) no deposits were withdrawn as currency; (2) the loan demand was sufficient to use all the potential bank credit; and (3) all bankers acted instantaneously in meeting loan requests. Normally, an increase in deposits is accompanied by an increase in demand for currency which reduces available reserves. In addition, loan demand varies from bank to bank and bankers differ as to their policies in regard to keeping legal and working reserves.

Commercial banks destroy as well as create money. When a bank customer pays off his loan, there is a reduction in the amount of deposits if other things remain the same. Customarily, on the due date of a loan, the bank debits the borrower's account for the amount of the loan, stamps the note paid, and mails it to the loan customer. But the bank customer must have the amount of the loan on deposit, and so he sells an asset which is paid for with a check drawn on Bank B. The latter remits for the check but finds that it has a reserve deficiency. If the required reserve is 20 percent and the check is $100, the reserve deficiency is $80. Bank B corrects this situation by selling Treasury bills worth $80 by which the buyer pays for a check drawn on Bank C. When the latter remits cash, it has a reserve deficiency of $64 which must be corrected, and so the process of reserve and deposit contraction continues.

In case of repayment of a loan in currency, the effect would be to reduce the amount of money in the hands of the general public and to increase the amount of reserve money in banks. Assuming that other things remain the same, other depositors will withdraw currency from their banks to fill the void in the currency supply. This would create a reserve deficiency. This reserve deficiency may be corrected by liquidating assets, borrowing, or withdrawing deposits from correspondent banks. If the last method is used, the correspondent banks will have reserve deficiencies which in turn must be corrected by liquidating assets, borrowing, or withdrawing deposits from correspondent banks.

During periods of deposit contraction, the commercial banking system needs a source of new reserves. In most countries, this source is the central bank; and, in the United States, this role is played by the Federal Reserve banks. When a member bank borrows from its Federal Reserve bank, its reserve account at the "Fed" is increased, and this new reserve money makes additional contraction of the money supply unnecessary as illustrated below:

Federal Reserve Bank		*Member Bank*	
ASSETS	LIABILITIES	ASSETS	LIABILITIES
Discounts and advances, + $80	Deposits or member-bank reserves, + $80	Reserves or deposits at Federal Reserve bank, + $80	Note payable, + $80

When in need of reserves, many banks are adverse to borrowing from their Federal Reserve banks because they fear that their customers may interpret such borrowing as a sign of weakness. But when there is a general need for more reserves, the Federal Reserve System may bring about an expansion in reserves by purchasing government securities in the open market. If the sale of securities is made by a member bank, changes on the books of the Federal Reserve bank and the member bank may be as follows:

Federal Reserve Bank		*Member Bank*	
ASSETS	LIABILITIES	ASSETS	LIABILITIES
Government securities, + $80	Deposits or member-bank reserves, + $80	Reserves or deposits at Federal Reserve bank, + $80 Government securities, − $80	

The amount of deposit currency or checkbook money will be determined to a large extent by banks' lending and investing activities. On the other hand, commercial banks may destroy money by curtailing their lending and investing activities.

SUMMARY

The money supply of the United States is increased or decreased by different types of monetary transactions. For illustration, the federal government creates money when it purchases "monetary gold" from abroad and destroys it when it sells gold aboard. Federal Reserve banks create money by lending and investing their credit in the form of deposits and by issuing Federal Reserve notes. Federal Reserve banks also create deposits when they accept liquid assets as deposits and pay for services, salaries, and dividends with Federal Reserve credit. Federal Reserve banks destroy money when they reduce their earning assets and contract the amount of Federal Reserve credit.

Federal Reserve notes are issued by Federal Reserve banks under supervision of the Board of Governors of the Federal Reserve System. The notes are kept in government vaults until they are shipped to the Federal Reserve agents of the Federal Reserve banks for which they were printed. The agents release the notes to their banks' banking departments when the request is accompanied by at least 100 percent collateral in the form of gold certificates or gold credits, eligible paper, and/or United States government securities. These notes are then shipped to member banks upon request and they go into circulation when withdrawn by businessmen and others.

QUESTIONS AND PROBLEMS

1. (*a*) What is the Consolidated Condition Statement for Banks and the Monetary System? (*b*) Is gold an important asset? (*c*) What are the money supply items? (*d*) What are the nonmonetary liabilities in the statement? (*e*) Are there reasons for assuming that U.S. money is based on credit? Give reasons for your answers.
2. What is the present gold policy of the United States? Is the United States on a gold standard? Give reasons for your answers.

3. Explain the relationship between changes in the monetary gold stock and changes in the money supply.

4. Identify: (*a*) demand deposits adjusted, (*b*) obsolete paper money, (*c*) Federal Reserve note, and (*d*) Federal Reserve Agents Account.

5. What is meant by the multiple expansion of bank credit based on new reserves? Illustrate.

6. Analyze: "Among all assets, money is considered unique because of the services it renders and because of the control which monetary authorities can exercise over it." (Federal Reserve Bank of St. Louis, *Review*, December, 1967, p. 5.)

7. Discuss: Before the removal of gold reserve requirements in 1968, the United States "had enough gold in excess of required gold so that the reserve requirements imposed no limitation on monetary expansion. And when reserve requirements threatened to become a limiting factor . . . the law was changed. Thus, the growth of the domestic money has, in reality, been determined by the Federal Reserve. . . ." (Federal Reserve Bank of Richmond, *Monthly Review*, July, 1968, p. 10.)

8. Discuss: In mid-March, 1968 "seven [London] gold-pool nations, led by the U.S., set up a two-tier gold system that would separate monetary demand from the open market. Central banks discontinued selling on the open market to maintain the gold price around $35 an ounce." (*Wall Street Journal*, April 2, 1968, p. 2.)

9. Explain: "The rate of expansion in the daily average money supply—privately held demand deposits plus currency outside of banks—continued to moderate in the first quarter, when the annual rate of growth fell to 4.2 percent from 5.1 percent in the final quarter of 1967." (Federal Reserve Bank of New York, *Monthly Review*, May, 1968, p. 102.)

10. Discuss: "Most of the long-term increase in currency . . . is accounted for by growth in population and in the dollar volume of economic transactions. But the rates of expansion have seldom been parallel over consecutive long periods. . . . [Beginning in 1961] the demand for currency began to accelerate, suggesting that some special factors were at work." Federal Reserve Bank of New York, *Essays in Monetary Credit* [New York, 1964], pp. 16–17.)

2525252525252525252525

CHAPTER 4

The Value of Money and Interest Rates

25252525252525252525252525252525252525252525252

MONEY HAS properties that render it useful and desirable; therefore, it has value. The most important of these properties is purchasing power, the utility that enables its use to satisfy human wants. Obviously, there are many reasons why money is desirable and why it is in demand. For anything to have value, it must be limited in supply—otherwise it would be a "free good"—but, in the case of money, the need for having the supply limited is not always obvious. While any individual may feel that he could not have too much money, nevertheless, if everyone had an unlimited amount of money, money would be worthless.

Monetary theory that explains the value of money is but a statement of tendencies. An individual's desire for an unlimited amount of things—usually associated with general purchasing power (money), on the one hand, and the ease with which modern banks and governments create or destroy money, on the other hand—makes it important for all citizens to understand the theory of the value of money.

VALUE OF MONEY

Because money is used to buy things, its value is commonly referred to as its purchasing power, that is, the amount of things that each monetary unit (dollar in the United States) will buy. If money were used to buy but one thing (gold, for instance), its value would be determined by the value of this one commodity. The fact that money is used as a medium of exchange means that its value must be considered in terms of things for which it is commonly exchanged, and they number in the thousands or millions. Thus, the value of money is its purchasing power over goods and services in general, and not over any particular good. The "value of money" is not synonymous with the "price of money." The former refers to what money

60

will buy and the latter to the price paid for the use of money, that is, the rate of interest. It may be that when the price of money (interest rate) is falling, the value of money is increasing (general prices are falling); and conversely, when the value of money is declining, the price of money is increasing.

In a modern economy the exchange value of things is expressed in terms of money (as prices), and at any particular time a dollar is worth a dollar. Statements to the contrary have no meaning unless reference is made to some preceding period when the purchasing power of the dollar was more or less in terms of things in general (or in terms of gold). As every housewife knows, the volume of things that a dollar will buy has declined during the past 10 years, and those with longer memories may say that the current dollar will buy no more than 25 cents did in 1900 or than 50 cents did before World War II. It is apparent to all that when prices in general are increasing, the value of money is decreasing, and, when prices in general are decreasing, the value of money is increasing. But, at any one time, some prices may be increasing, others may be decreasing, and others may be unchanged. In order to take the guesswork out of whether the value of money is increasing or decreasing, price index numbers are constructed.

Price index numbers are statistical devices for measuring the relative changes in averages of prices of a number of selected goods over a period of time. In the United States, the two most widely used price index numbers are "Consumers' Price Index for Moderate Income Families in Large Cities" and "Wholesale Prices, by Groups of Commodities." Both are constructed and published by the United States Bureau of Labor Statistics.

Although more specialized index numbers are available, either of the above is satisfactory for measuring changes in the value of money. The one used depends on the special problem involved. As an illustration, the consumers' price index number (popularly known as the "cost-of-living" index) is widely used as a basis for adjusting money wages, and the wholesale commodity price index number is used as a basis for adjusting rents and other nonwage money contracts.[1]

Because price index numbers are used for comparative purposes, they usually have a base year (or base period) to which a figure of 1.00 or 100 is assigned. Since the current situation is emphasized, an index number with a fairly recent base is usually more accurate. Now,

---

[1] Since methods used in constructing index numbers are covered in textbooks on statistics, they are omitted here.

items that were nonexistent 10 years ago may represent an important percentage of current family expenditures. In addition, there are changes in tastes and fashions and in the quality of goods that make comparison of the standard of living of two periods difficult.

The United States Bureau of Labor Statistics periodically revises its wholesale commodity and cost-of-living index numbers by adding some and dropping other prices of certain commodities and/or services and changing the "weights" assigned individual items in order to make the current index numbers representative of the wholesale and consumer price structures as a whole. In addition, index numbers are constructed for different groups of goods and services, such as apparel, food, housing, medical care, personal care, reading and recreation, transportation, and other goods and services. Even more price index numbers are constructed for wholesale prices of different commodities, which give businessmen and others information as to price trends in their particular fields of interest.[2]

Most of the emphasis in modern economic writing is on prices; therefore it is important to remember that, as general prices increase or decrease, the value of money decreases or increases by the reciprocal of the price change. (In mathematics, the reciprocal of a fraction is the fraction inverted.) If the index number for a particular year is 125 and the base period is 1947–49, it means that the price level has increased 25 percent above the average during the base period and that the value of money has declined 20 percent (100/125 = 80 as compared to 100 for the base period). The value of one's salary may be computed from time to time simply by dividing the year's current income by the current price index number, which would give one the current value in terms of the base period ($10,000 ÷ 1.25 = $8,000). Similar computations may be made for rent, interest, total national income, the gross national product, and wealth.

QUANTITY THEORY AND THE FLOW OF EXPENDITURES

Quantity Theory.   The quantity theory in its earliest and simplest form stated that the value of money varies in direct proportion to changes in the quantity of money. Aristotle recognized that the value of money fluctuated from time to time and several medieval writers noted a relationship between an increase in the supply of money and an increase in prices. However, it was not until after the discovery of America and the subsequent influx of gold and silver

[2] See current issue of the *Federal Reserve Bulletin*.

from Spanish America that Europeans generally associated rising prices with the increase in the quantity of money.

World War I was accompanied and followed by extreme price changes which many attributed to an expansion in the money supply. Following the war, some writers refined and restated the quantity theory of money. For illustration, Irving Fisher broadened the concept of the velocity of circulation of money, the influence of the volume of production, and the difference between bank deposits and coin and paper money.

One of the chief criticisms of the quantity theory is its emphasis on the stock of money rather than the flow of expenditures or the flow of income. In a price economy there are two continuing flows of things in opposite directions: the flow of goods and services and the flow of money payments for these goods and services. The size of the money stream depends upon the number of dollars and the number of times each dollar is spent over a period of days, weeks, months, or years. In an explanation of the value of money, attention is given first to how changes in the supply (quantity) of money tend to influence its value (the simplest approach to the study of any problem of value determination).

The value of money, like that of any commodity, is influenced by its supply. The supply of money affecting the price level is properly thought of as hand-to-hand money and deposit currency used by the general public for spending. An increase in the money supply would encourage spending, and increased spending would tend to increase general prices or to decrease the value of each monetary unit (each unit would buy less). Obviously, a decrease in the money supply would discourage spending, and decreased spending would tend to decrease general prices or to increase the value of each monetary unit (each unit would buy more).

Although the amount of emphasis varies among monetary economists, all recognize the supply of money as a factor in determining the general price level. John Stuart Mill wrote emphatically: "That an increase in the quantity of money raises prices, and a diminution lowers them, is the most elementary proposition in the theory of currency. . . ."[3] As stated by the late Dr. E. W. Kemmerer: "The difference between the supporters of the quantity theory and its opponents" amounts to "differences in the relative importance attrib-

[3] J. S. Mill, *Principles of Political Economy* (5th ed.; New York: D. Appleton & Co., 1895), Vol. II, p. 33.

uted to certain factors entering into the determination of the general price level."[4] While Dr. Kemmerer emphasized the supply of money, modern economists are inclined to stress the demand for money. Modern money is easily created and destroyed as more or less is demanded by businessmen, homeowners, consumers, and governments. At any particular time, very little of the supply of circulating money is "on the wing." Instead, it is held as till money by business firms, as pocket money by individuals, and in checking accounts as cash balances.

While the mere existence of money may have certain psychological effects, money must be spent in order to be effective. Money is a tool and the use man makes of it is important to the economy. In this respect money is no different from other things used by man. For instance, it may be argued that the existence of 50 million automobiles in the United States has no effect upon the number of "car-miles" driven on the national highways during a year. This is true in the same way that the existence of $150 billion has no effect on the prices of things for which money may be spent. Either automobiles or money must be used in order to be effective, but this does not mean that the number of automobiles and the number of dollars is unimportant, for they are necessary for driving and for spending. In performing their functions, monetary authorities are interested in the amount of money available for spending, so control over the amount of money has a place in monetary management.

Since modern money has little or no intrinsic value, a logical assumption is that most of it will be spent some day. However, if the money supply is increased, the amount by which it is increased may be held temporarily as idle cash balances, or it may be matched by an increase in the supply of things. Thus, an increase in the supply will not necessarily cause an increase in general prices. The least that may be claimed for the relationship between changes in the quantity of money and changes in the general price level is that the former is a factor that conditions spending and therefore the general price level. The quantity theory merely recognizes the importance of having money and the willingness to spend it as factors that affect prices. As stated by Dr. Milton Friedman, "perhaps no other empirical relation in economics that has been observed to recur so uniformly under so wide a variety of circumstances as the relation between substantial

[4] E. W. Kemmerer, *Money and Credit Instruments in Their Relations to General Prices* (New York: Henry Holt & Co., 1909), p. 2.

changes over short periods in the stock of money and in prices; the one is invariably linked with the other and is in the same direction. . . ."[5]

Velocity. An increase in the quantity of money (*M*) does not always cause an increase in prices because the new money may not be spent but held as an idle cash balance. In order to explain this situation, economists developed the idea that it is the flow of money rather than the quantity that determines prices. This flow may be found by multiplying the quantity of money by the velocity of circulation (*V*). The product of *M* and *V* is the total of the sum of all expenditures during a year.

The velocity of money (*V*) is the rate at which a unit of money passes from hand to hand as a medium of exchange during a period of time, usually a year. The rate is found by dividing the total number of dollar transactions by the average number of dollars owned by the general public (currency outside of banks plus demand deposits adjusted). For statistical reasons, this concept is usually limited to the rate of turnover of deposits alone, computed by dividing the recorded debits against demand deposits by the average amount of such deposits existing during a given period.

If the monetary units that make up the money supply were spent regularly, an increase or decrease in the money supply would be reflected immediately in the volume of money payments. In practice, this is not true; therefore, the economy is subject to changes both in the amount of money and in the rate of spending. Statistics are available, in the form of debits to deposit accounts, which indicate changes in the rate of spending. Although such statistics are not all-inclusive, because pocket money leaves no record of the number of times it is spent, they are significant because deposit currency is used in about 90 percent of all money transfers.

In its *Federal Reserve Bulletin,* the Federal Reserve System publishes the annual rate of turnover of demand deposits, exclusive of interbank and United States government demand deposits, for banks located in (1) 233 standard metropolitan statistical areas including New York, (2) 232 standard metropolitan statistical areas excluding New York, (3) 226 other standard metropolitan statistical areas, (4) 6 leading standard metropolitan statistical areas other than New

---

[5] Milton Friedman (ed.), *Studies in the Quantity Theory of Money* (Chicago: University of Chicago Press, 1956), pp. 20–21.

York,[6] and (5) New York standard metropolitan statistical area. The principle behind the omission of New York in some groups is to exclude the effect of major financial transactions on the velocity of money. For example, in February, 1959, dealers in government securities kept an average balance of $34 million in the 14 member banks of the New York Clearinghouse Association, and during this month debits to their accounts amounted to $18,773 million. This is a turnover rate of 556.9 monthly or 6,682.8 yearly. While dealers deposit millions of dollars in their checking accounts each day, they withdraw them about as rapidly. Similarly, other investment dealers and brokers in New York have an abnormally high turnover of demand deposits. Their average balances were $372 million and their monthly debits $9,272 million.[7]

Many corporations keep deposit balances in New York banks and this is another factor in the high yearly turnover of deposits (other than interbank and government) in New York. Currently, corporations are investing in money-market instruments—Treasury bills, negotiable certificates of deposit, commercial paper, and bankers' acceptances—and are making call loans to government securities dealers. The resulting reduction in their demand-deposit accounts has necessitated using the funds remaining more efficiently, and this greater efficiency has contributed to the increase in turnover or velocity of demand deposits.

Obviously, a $1 bill moving rapidly from hand to hand in payment for things will do as much exchanging as a $20 bill moving with only one twentieth the rapidity. This fact is illustrated by the old English axiom: "A nimble sixpence will do the work of a lazy crown." Thus a change in velocity tends to have the same effect on general prices (or the value of money) as a change in the supply of money—an increase tends to increase general prices (to reduce the value of each monetary unit), and a decrease tends to lower general prices (to increase the value of each monetary unit).

In analyzing the reasons for changes in the velocity of money, it is necessary to examine what individuals do "to retard or advance the rate at which they spend their cash balances." Velocity is the "simple resultant of the decisions which the individuals in charge of the

[6] The six leading standard metropolitan statistical areas other than New York are Boston, Philadelphia, Chicago, Detroit, San Francisco–Oakland, and Los Angeles–Long Beach.

[7] "Member Bank Reserve Requirements," *Hearings before the Committee on Banking and Currency* (U.S. Senate [86th Cong., 1st sess. on S. 860 and S. 1120], March 23 and 24, 1959), p. 172.

administration of cash balances make with respect to the size of the cash balance that they choose to keep relative to outlay."[8] This means that all individuals who have funds to spend are responsible for the rate of spending and therefore the velocity of money. If an individual delays purchases on one occasion or speeds up purchases on another, to that extent he decreases or increases the velocity of money.

Volume of Transactions. An increase in the flow of money may not cause an increase in general prices because the increase in demand may be confronted by an increase in the flow of things (T) that are purchased with money. The volume of transactions includes income-creating financial and other transactions such as gambling, sales of secondhand goods and real estate, nonpersonal donations, and grants. Among the income-producing transactions are those involving the purchases of the total current output of goods and services by consumers, businessmen, governments, and foreigners (gross national product).

If the money supply and the rate of turnover remain the same, an increase in the volume of goods, services, and securities offered in the market will depress prices. An increase in the volume of things offered may be due to an increase in production or may result from "bearish" sentiments (anticipation of falling prices). In order to sell things, price reductions will be in order. Conversely, a decrease in the volume of goods, services, and securities offered in the market will tend to increase prices. Buyers will have to compete more actively with others in order to buy things, with a "bullish" effect on prices. A decrease in the volume of things offered may be due to a decrease in production or to an anticipation of higher prices. So an increase in the number of things offered will tend to lower general prices, and a decrease in the number of units offered will tend to increase prices.

The volume of transactions during a period of time is determined not only by the volume of things sold but also by their velocity of circulation. For instance, title to cotton, wheat, metals, and other commodities is exchanged daily in markets throughout the world, and individual items among them may be sold many times before their "end transaction." Manufactured goods remain in channels of production and trade for varying periods of time, and, each time an item is sold, the sale is reflected in the total volume of transactions. To be sure, personal services and some consumer goods are not sold more

[8] A. W. Marget, *The Theory of Prices* (New York: Prentice-Hall, 1938), Vol. I, p. 419 *passim*.

than once, but most commodities entail several purchases and several sales before they reach the ultimate user or consumer.

Financial transactions include borrowing, lending, and trading in securities, the supply of which may remain relatively unchanged. Nevertheless, the dollar value of all financial transactions is great. The stock market, which receives so much attention, is in reality a second-hand market, wherein ownership of previously issued shares changes from day to day. Similarly, most of the trading in government and other securities involves buying and selling credit instruments that represent old debts. However, trading in these securities increases the total volume of transactions, and this is recognized in formulating monetary policy and using devices of credit control (see Chapter 18).

General Prices. Things purchased with money have a price (P), and so the flow of money payments (MV) is equal to the money value of the flow of things (PT) for which money is spent. In this way, one arrives at the equation $MV = PT$. Both sides may be divided by T to give $MV/T = P$, which places the symbols indicating the causes of general prices on one side of the equation and prices on the other. From the equation one may also show that an increase in money and a corresponding decrease in velocity will have no effect on prices if the volume of transactions remains the same. Furthermore, there may be an increase in T with no change in MV, which would cause prices to decrease.

In the marketplace, prices of individual items sold at retail are fixed by businessmen (called administered prices) before sales are made, other prices are determined by negotiation between buyers and sellers as in the commodity and securities markets, and others by auction as on organized stock exchanges. Except under monopolistic conditions, prices are influenced not only by the flow of money payments but also by the flow of things.

Equation of Exchange. A summary of the relationship among the different factors that affect the value of money (or general prices) may be presented as the equation $MV = PT$ which represents "nothing more or less than shorthand expressions designed to indicate the nature of the variables whose operations can be shown to influence prices."[9] The symbols represent the following:

> M = All kinds of money in the hands of the public (currency outside of banks and demand deposits adjusted for interbank balances, cash items in process of collection, and government deposits).

[9] *Ibid.*, p. 91. Italics in the original are omitted.

V = Velocity or turnover of all kinds of money but, for statistical reasons, it is usually limited to demand deposits adjusted.

P = General price level.

T = Total number of monetary transactions during a given period of time.

MV = Total money expenditures during a period of time, usually a year.

PT = Money value of things for which money is spent.

So, during a given period of time in the market, there is a "man-directed" flow of money payments for a stream of things including goods, financial assets, real estate, secondhand goods, and others. Within a given period of time the money value of the two flows will be equal because the dollar value of money given for things must equal the money value of things given for money ($10 given for a book equals the money value of a $10-book).

The size of the money stream is the product of two factors—the number of monetary units multiplied by the velocity at which they circulate. Money is different from things for which it is spent in that it is designed for continued use in the markets. It is this repeated use of money that explains why so much trade can be carried on with a relatively small supply of money. Therefore, in influencing the size of the money stream, changes in the rate of spending (velocity) may be at least as important as changes in the amount of money.

The physical flow of things varies during a given time period. Services of teachers, doctors, barbers, and others appear once, only to be replaced by new services on the following days; goods are withdrawn from the markets to be consumed by individuals; and new securities are purchased by investors to be held for income or appreciation in value. In addition to the number of units of things, the turnover of things in the market is a factor to be reckoned with in explaining the total volume of transactions. For example, a bushel of wheat that appears 10 times in the market has the same effect as 10 bushels that appear but once. Things are sold for money, and the total money value of things sold will be matched by the total money payments.

QUANTITY THEORY AND THE HOLDING OF MONEY

The quantity theory of money, as just presented, has been criticized because it uses the concept "velocity of circulation" which does not explain why money moves more or less rapidly. As a result, it has been suggested that the term "cash balance" be used as a substitute in order to direct attention to the reasons for changes in the velocity of money. A "cash balance" is the reciprocal of the "velocity of circulation"; so if people hold more or less money, velocity changes in the opposite direction. Futhermore, the use of the cash-balance approach permits a discussion of the value of money in terms of demand and supply.

Demand and Supply. The demand for money is defined as the holding of cash balances. Therefore, an increase in the demand for money would indicate a preference for money over things such as goods, services, and investments; and a decrease in the demand for money would indicate a preference for the things which money can buy. If other things remain the same, the value of money will increase (general prices will fall) when there is an increase in the demand for money; conversely, the value of money will decrease (general prices will rise) when there is a decrease in the demand for money.

The amount of money in circulation may be fixed by the monetary authorities, but nevertheless the average size of one's cash balance may change because the demand for money is relative to one's total expenditures (or some other outlay for which money is held). Hence, if total expenditures for a year are $10,000 and one's average cash balance is $1,000, the demand for money would be larger when compared with a second year when total expenditures are $20,000 and the average cash balance is still $1,000. Another way of saying the same things is that during the first year the velocity of money was 10 and during the second year, it was 20.

Reasons for Holding Money. The reasons given for holding money include the (1) transaction motive, (2) precautionary motive, and (3) speculative motive.[10]

1. Individuals and others hold money in order to meet day-to-day needs for things such as food, clothing, transportation, housing, and payments (for insurance, utilities, savings accounts, etc.). The amount of money held as a cash balance, relative to total money transactions, is dependent on various factors including the nature and size (both actual and anticipated) of an individual's money income, his standard of living, and the time interval between receipts of income (the amount tends to increase with a lengthening of this interval). If one's money income is small and received weekly, it will be spent fairly regularly, and the average size of his cash balance will be small compared to his total expenditures. On the other hand, if one's

[10] John M. Keynes, *The General Theory of Employment, Interest, and Money* (New York: Harcourt, Brace & Co., 1936), pp. 166–74.

money income is large but received at irregular intervals, more budgeting is necessary, and the average size of one's cash balance will be large relative to total expenditures.

2. Many consumers, businessmen, and others hold more money than is needed to care for current needs as a precautionary measure. Normally, those responsible for the well-being of a family, farm, or business hold reserves against unforeseen contingencies such as sickness, repairs, and economic reverses. However, the transaction and precautionary demands for money tend to remain fairly stable; therefore, the short-term changes in the demand for money are due largely to fluctuations in the speculative demand for money.

3. The holding of money in order to profit from anticipated changes in the economy constitutes the speculative demand for money. For illustration, one may keep money idle in expectation of a fall in securities prices. If and when the prices fall, the speculator will be in a position to purchase the securities at bargain prices (sufficient to compensate for the loss of interest involved in having held money idle during the interim).

One of the factors that influence the relative size of cash balances, in addition to variations in income and the business cycle, is the nature of the credit system. The ability to buy on credit, to borrow from financial institutions, and to convert liquid assets (saving bonds and other government securities, savings or time deposits, etc.) into money help to explain why some business firms and individuals tend to keep lower cash balances than do other business firms and individuals.

In an economy dominated by cash sales, large cash balances are held. The need for holding cash balances is greater in commercial and industrial regions than in agricultural sections, wherein more of the needs of the people are cared for without the use of money. Today the greater dependence on the marketplace for goods and services tends to cause people to hold larger amounts of money relative to money income. On the other hand, improvements in the banking and credit systems permit businessmen and others to keep relatively smaller cash balances and to borrow or sell assets when cash is needed as well as to buy on credit (with or without credit cards) and to pay by wire or other forms of transfer.

The level of interest rates in the money and capital markets may have considerable influence on the annual rate of turnover of demand deposits, rising when interest rates are high and falling when they are low. Corporate treasurers have found it profitable to keep cash holdings at a minimum and to invest in money market instruments (see Chapter 6).

Cash Balance Equation. The relationship among the factors that determine the value of money may be presented as an equation. The cash-balance or demand theory of money may be expressed as $M = KPT$, wherein the symbols represent:

$M =$ The supply of money as in the quantity theory.
$K =$ The proportion of total expenditures kept in the form of money.
$P =$ The general price level as in the quantity theory.
$T =$ The volume of transactions as in the quantity theory.

Although the transaction theory emphasizes the supply of money, while the cash-balance theory stresses the demand for money, the two theories are similar. For illustration, if the money supply equals $100 million, the volume of transactions equals one billion, the average price per unit equals $1, and the length of time during which control over transactions is held in the form of money is one year, then the equations would be $M = KPT$ ($100,000,000 = \frac{1}{10} \times$ $1 \times 1,000,000,000$) and $MV = PT$ ($100,000,000 \times 10 = \$1 \times$ 1,000,000,000). The cash-balance equation may also be written as $P = M/KT$, and the transaction equation as $P = MV/T$.

QUANTITY OF MONEY AND NATIONAL INCOME

Both the cash-balance and transaction equations include the concept of total transactions which makes it difficult to measure a change in general prices with the use of price index numbers because they are computed for only segments of the economy (such as retail prices, wholesale prices, agricultural prices, etc.). The problem may be solved by using one or more existing price index numbers, but it would not measure the effect of the total flow of money payments on the total flow of the money value of things sold.

At the present time, the tendency is to emphasize factors that affect changes in national income rather than changes in general prices. However, national income statistics include the concept of general prices, and so an income equation of exchange may include a symbol for general price changes. The income theory holds that monetary expenditures for the current output of goods and services determine gross national income.

National income is equal to the aggregate income of all factors used in the production of current goods and services. It includes compensation of employees, income of proprietors, rental income of individuals, corporate profits, inventory valuation adjustments, and net interest (see Table 4–1). National income is equal to gross national product minus capital consumption allowances, indirect business taxes, and other minor items.

In computing the aggregate of prices for goods and services,

TABLE 4–1

NATIONAL INCOME

(In billions of dollars)

Item	1929	1933	1941	1950	1963	1966	1967	1968* Ip
National income	86.8	40.3	104.2	241.1	481.9	616.7	650.2	686.2
Compensation of employees	51.1	29.5	64.8	154.6	341.0	435.7	469.7	497.6
Wages and salaries	50.4	29.0	62.1	146.8	311.1	394.6	423.8	447.6
Private	45.5	23.9	51.9	124.4	251.6	316.7	337.5	355.9
Military	.3	.3	1.9	5.0	10.8	14.7	16.4	17.6
Government civilian	4.6	4.9	8.3	17.4	48.6	63.2	69.8	74.0
Supplements to wages and salaries	.7	.5	2.7	7.8	29.9	41.1	45.9	50.0
Employer contributions for social insurance	.1	.1	2.0	4.0	15.0	20.3	22.6	24.8
Other labor income	.6	.4	.7	3.8	14.9	20.8	23.2	25.2
Proprietors' income	15.1	5.9	17.5	37.5	51.0	59.3	58.4	95.9
Business and professional	9.0	3.3	11.1	24.0	37.9	43.2	43.6	44.4
Farm	6.2	2.6	6.4	13.5	13.1	16.1	14.8	15.5
Rental income of persons	5.4	2.0	3.5	9.4	17.1	19.4	20.1	20.6
Corporate profits and inventory valuation adjustment	10.5	−1.2	15.2	37.7	58.9	82.2	79.6	84.3
Profits before tax	10.0	1.0	17.7	42.6	59.4	83.8	80.7	88.8
Profits tax liability	1.4	.5	7.6	17.8	26.3	34.5	33.2	36.6
Profits after tax	8.6	.4	10.1	24.9	33.1	49.3	47.5	52.2
Dividends	5.8	2.0	4.4	8.8	16.5	21.5	22.8	23.2
Undistributed profits	2.8	−1.6	5.7	16.0	16.6	27.8	24.7	28.9
Inventory valuation adjustment	.5	−2.1	−2.5	−5.0	−.5	−1.6	−1.2	−4.5
Net interest	4.7	4.1	3.2	2.0	13.8	20.2	22.4	23.9

* First quarterly data seasonally adjusted preliminary figures.
Source: *Federal Reserve Bulletin*, June, 1968, p. A–66.

only the final value of the product is used in order to avoid multiple counting. Hence, retail prices are used for consumer goods, and manufacturers' and other users' costs would be used for capital equipment. Costs of raw materials and semifinished products would not be used because these costs would be included in the price of the final product. If there is objection to this method of arriving at the value of the output of the economy, the "value-added" method may be used at each step in the productive process and then the value of a product would be found by adding these figures. For illustration, the value of a loaf of bread may be found as follows:

Firm	Receipts	Paid Other Firms	Value Added
Retailer.....................$0.26	$0.21	$0.05
Baker...................... 0.21	0.10	0.11
Miller..................... 0.10	0.04	0.06
Farmer..................... 0.04	0.00	0.04
Totals...............$0.61	$0.35	$0.26

The total of value-added figures is the same as the price of the final product (retail price). It is also true that the total expenses, including profits of producers minus payments to other firms, is equal to "added value" ($0.61 — $0.35 = $0.26).

The gross national product is equal to the total of personal consumption expenditures, gross private domestic investment, government purchases of goods and services, and net export of goods and services (see Table 1–2,). Each of these in turn may be divided into two or more subdivisions.

The emphasis on *market value* of goods and services means the exclusion of the products of many individuals, of whom the most important are housewives. By taking jobs and employing domestic servants not previously employed, housewives would increase national income in an amount equal to the combined wages of housewives and servants.

The statistics compiled by the Office of Business Economics include values other than those appearing in the market; for illustration, an estimate is included for the value of rent for owner-occupied nonfarm dwellings whose imputed value is about 40 percent of the total net rental income of persons. Similar estimates are included for rent of owner-occupied farms and numerous personal income and consumption expenditures in kind (such as food and fuel produced and consumed on farms, meals and lodging supplied employees, etc.). Also included is imputed interest that originates in private business and personal consumption expenditures in kind not included in personal income. For studies of real income the use of current dollar data would be misleading; therefore, the Office of Business Economics estimates national income in both current and constant dollars.

In the absence of unemployed resources, an increase in the amount of money will tend to generate too much demand for goods which tends to increase domestic prices and to stimulate the import of goods some of which are normally produced at home. At the same time, higher prices will tend to cause a decline in exports resulting in a less favorable balance of trade or an increase in the trade deficit.

Income Equation. The income equation, $M = KPO$ is similar to the cash-balance equation, and it may be written in the Fisherine form as $MV' = PO$. In the first version, the symbols represent:

M = Supply of money as previously defined.
K = Proportion of national income that people hold as money.
P = Price level of consumer goods (not general price level).
O = Current output of goods and services (not total transactions).

In the second version, the symbols represent:

M = Supply of money as previously defined.
V' = Income velocity of money, or the number of times a unit of money is used in income transactions during a year.
P = Price of consumer goods.
O = Current output of goods and services.

Income velocity, V', is the number of times a unit of money is spent in income transactions (rather than the total number of monetary transactions). Income velocity is usually computed by dividing gross national product for a year by the average amount of money in existence during that year. Because gross national product (GNP) excludes all financial transactions, money payments in the various stages in the manufacturing and distribution processes are ignored, as are gifts and similar outlays. Consequently, the figure for income velocity will be smaller than that for the transaction velocity of money.

Costs and Prices. Excessive demand in an economy results in an increase in general prices; hence many conclude that the increase in prices since World War II has been due to excessive demand. However, there is a second possibility—that is, that the increase in general prices may be due to higher costs. The increase in the price of steel, automobiles, and other industrial products may be due to an attempt by management to recapture higher wage costs following union bargaining. If one producer raises prices to cover higher costs, he tends to lose sales to other producers; but when all within an industry are subject to higher costs, they may pass them along to the consumer in the form of higher prices. The consumer income needed to purchase higher priced products is provided by increases in wages and profits. Therefore the equation of exchange would have to be written to indicate that income and prices change before the quantity of money changes (see Chapter 20). Only by adopting policies as to prices and wages and persuading businessmen and union leaders to abide by them is it possible to stabilize general prices.

INTEREST AND PRICES

Interest, the price paid for the use of money, is the most flexible and, at times, the most influential cost factor in the economy. The classical method of preventing inflation is to raise interest rates and to reduce the availability of loanable funds, and the classical method of preventing deflation is to lower interest rates and to increase the availability of loanable funds. Since World War II, the expansion in

CHART 4–1

SHORT-TERM INTEREST RATES

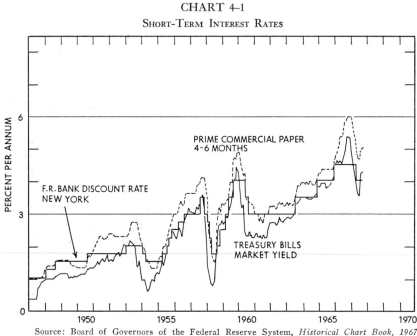

Source: Board of Governors of the Federal Reserve System, *Historical Chart Book, 1967* (Washington, D.C., 1968), p. 27.

demand for loanable funds has been in excess of the rate of increase in the supply of such funds; as a result, there has been a substantial increase in interest rates (see Chart 4–1). The rate of increase has been most rapid during periods of business boom and least rapid during periods of recession.

Many theories have been presented to explain how the rate of interest is determined. With the beginning of the modern commercial and industrial age, many interest-rate theories were formulated to justify the taking of interest which was forbidden by the church. Now, the interest rate is considered to be a price and, like any other price, it is determined by supply and demand.

Classical Theory of Interest. Some economists explain the interest rate in terms of the marginal productivity of real capital and the cost of waiting because goods are produced in a roundabout manner. A businessman would borrow money to produce new capital equipment if and when the expected return from the use of new capital is at least equal to the interest he would pay for borrowed funds. Thus, the interest rate is equal to the marginal cost of production and equal to the reward for postponing consumption for the marginal saver. If the demand for investment capital increases, the interest rate increases and people save more; thus the two are brought into equilibrium at the higher interest rate. This marginal productivity theory may explain why businessmen borrow, but it does not explain why others borrow to finance the purchase of consumer goods.

Time-Preference Theory. The time-preference theory is based on the psychological law that consumption in the present is preferred to that in the future. In other words, most individuals consider present goods to be worth more than future goods. The natural interest rate equates the demand for loanable funds with the supply of loanable funds. Whether considered from the viewpoint of the borrower or the lender, the time preference of present over future goods suggests why interest can and must be paid. The rate of interest will be determined by the time preference of the marginal saver on the supply side.

Liquidity-Preference Theory. The liquidity-preference theory of interest derives its name from Keynes's emphasis on interest as being a reward for parting with liquidity (not the use of money). If an individual holds money, it is because he prefers liquidity to interest from investments or loans. Among the motives for holding cash, only the speculative motive is considered to be sensitive to changes in interest rates. When interest rates are low, the penalty for holding cash is small and the risk of loss on fixed-income investments is great (an increase in interest rates would cause a decline in market value); and, when interest rates are high, the penalty for holding cash is high and the prospects for profit on fixed-income investments are excellent (a decrease in interest rates would cause a rise in market value). When there is an increase in the amount of cash balances (a decrease in investments), there tends to be a decline in production, income, employment, and prices; and, when there is a decrease in cash balances (an increase in investment), there tends to be an increase in output, employment, income, and prices.

In his analysis, Keynes assumes that savings and investments are always equal, but leaves the way open to monetary policy by noting that savings are influenced by the level of income which, in turn, is influenced by investments. Hence, an increase in the supply of money by monetary authorities may be used to reduce interest rates, to encourage investment, to increase income, to increase savings, and so on; and, a decrease in the money supply may be used to increase interest rates, to discourage investment, to reduce income, decrease savings, and so on.

At a given level of income, the height of interest rates is determined by the liquidity preference of the holders of cash balances. Savings may be held as idle cash balances or invested; and, at times, a sharp increase in interest rates may be required to induce investment. Thus, the interest rate will be the price paid for the parting with liquidity for that period, but it may be changed by issuing more or less money. Hence the amount of savings is affected by income, and liquidity preference will determine the amount of savings that will be available for lending.

Loanable-Funds Theory.   The loanable-funds theory is a demand and supply theory of interest that includes most of the ideas contained in the classical, time-preference, and liquidity-preference theories. The sources of supply of loanable funds are: (1) savings of individuals and business corporations, (2) dehoarding, (3) income accounted for as depreciation and similar cost allowances, (4) turnover of working capital, and (5) an increase in the quantity of funds by commercial banks and the monetary authorities.

The bulk of savings that appear in the market originates with individuals who do not spend all of their disposable personal income for consumption. In addition, past savings that have been hoarded may be made available (called dehoarding), thereby increasing the volume of funds offered in the market. Businessmen may add to the supply of loanable funds by dehoarding and lending funds in the market, pending investment in their own firms. The sources of such funds are temporary idle working capital and net income of business units "before deductions for depreciation and other cost items that do not require an expenditure of cash."[11] The monetary authorities and commercial banks may add to or withdraw funds from the market, thereby having the same effect as dehoarding or hoarding funds (that is changes in M and V).

The demand for loanable funds originates with individuals, business firms, governments, and others. It may be for consumption,

[11] Charles L. Prather, *Financing Business Firms* (3rd ed.; Homewood, Ill.: Richard D. Irwin, Inc., 1966), p. 183.

investment, or hoarding purposes. The demand for loanable funds to purchase consumer goods depends on the time-preference schedule of individuals, and the demand for such funds by business firms depends on the anticipated profitability of their investment. However, part of the business demand for loanable funds is for cash balances rather than for capital goods. The chief cause of hoarding funds is a low interest rate and uncertainty regarding the future.

On the supply side of the market, the interest rate will reflect the volume of savings (S), new money (ΔM), and dehoarding (DH). On the demand side of the market, the interest rate will reflect the volume of new investment (In), consumption financed with borrowing (Cb), financial demand (Fb), and hoarding demand (H). Therefore total supply $(S + \Delta M + DH) =$ total demand $(In + Cb + Fb + H)$.

Structure of Interest Rates. The term, structure of interest rates, refers to the relationship among short-term, intermediate-term, and long-term interest rates on credit instruments having similar credit qualities. When these rates are plotted, they give what is called a "yield curve" for the date on which they are drawn. The yield curve changes from day to day, reflecting preferences of the market for different maturities at a particular time. During periods of expanding business and rising interest rates, short-term rates increase faster and rise farther than intermediate rates, and the latter increase faster and rise farther than long-term interest rates.

Although the various sectors of the money and capital markets are connected, differences in interest rates and volatility are due to structural differences in the market. For illustration, commercial banks, because of their secondary reserve and liquidity needs, must concentrate more on shorter maturities than insurance companies, which have long-term contracts (policies). Due to central bank policy, the volume of loanable funds of commercial banks varies countercyclically; but the amount of loanable funds of insurance companies and other savings institutions (including savings departments of commercial banks) tends to vary directly with the business cycle.

Interest-Rate Changes. In our present-day economy when such a large proportion of savings is of a contractual nature (life insurance premiums, social security payments, and others) and debts are repaid on the installment plan, the supply of savings may be relatively inelastic. Many things contribute to the stability of interest rates including custom, corporate financing with net income (accounted for as profits and depreciation and other allowances), relationships of loan customers to banks, and limited competition among lenders.

If the credit markets functioned perfectly, interest-rate changes would be a more accurate indicator of the status of credit conditions, but they would not show the ease or difficulty of obtaining loans, variations in the amount that will be lent to an applicant, collateral, and other requirements for lending, and the time needed to process an application for a loan. Although money and capital markets have different rates and types of lenders, all are interrelated and lending policies therein reflect changes made at the core of the credit system by the Federal Reserve authorities.

As a cost factor, interest payments currently have little effect on business operations of corporations because debtors are permitted, in the current law, to deduct interest payments as a cost in computing their income taxes. However, interest payments may be an important cost to homeowners, municipal governments, and other nonbusiness borrowers. Relative to business firms' expenditures for wages, interest costs are so insignificant that one may question the value of considering interest-rate theories. Nevertheless, interest-rate changes are important and business borrowers, in particular, differ in their sensitivity to changes in them due to (1) the level of income after taxes, (2) different costs of borrowing, (3) the existence or absence of capital and other expenditures that must be made irrespective of credit conditions, (4) the volume of funds from operations that is available for investing, (5) the effects of interest-rate changes on the development of marginal projects, (6) whether a particular firm is in a regulated or nonregulated industry, and (7) the expectation of the permanency of any change in interest rates.

SUMMARY

The various theories of the value of money are but statements of tendencies. At any one time, the value of money is meaningless per se unless compared to its value as of some previous time. Thus it is changes in the value of money that are important, and these changes are measured through the use of price index numbers, statistical devices for comparing groups of prices and measuring their changes. As the value of money changes, prices change reciprocally; that is, as the value of money decreases, prices increase, and as the value of money increases, prices decrease.

The factors that influence the value of money or prices include the supply and velocity of money and the volume and velocity of transactions. The relationship among the factors that determine the value of money is presented as an equation, known as the "equation of exchange." The various equations of exchange, which include the transaction, cash-balance, and income equations, differ as to the factors that are emphasized. The transaction theory stresses spending, the cash-balance theory emphasizes the holding of money, and national income is given special consideration in the income theory. The various theories of interest include the classical, time-preference, liquidity-preference, and loanable-funds theories.

QUESTIONS AND PROBLEMS

1. Identify: (*a*) value of money, (*b*) price index number, (*c*) quantity theory of money, (*d*) demand for money, and (*e*) cost of money.
2. Distinguish between: (*a*) transaction velocity of money and income velocity of money, and (*b*) total expenditures and income expenditures.
3. Explain the significance of the following statement: "It is now widely recognized that money supply has two dimensions: size and velocity. . . . The temporary eclipse of transactions velocity as an element in monetary analysis coincided with a period when monetary policy was relegated to second place. . . . With the re-emergence of a flexible monetary policy, velocity became a more significant, as well as a more meaningful, element in monetary analysis." (George Garvy, *Deposit Velocity and Its Significance* [New York: Federal Reserve Bank of New York, 1959], pp. 86–87.)
4. Variations in the value of money (*P*) may originate in *M*, *V*, or *T*, but most frequently they result from concomitant changes in all three. Discuss, bringing in the fact that it is individuals who are responsible for spending.
5. Analyze: From 1867 to 1960, changes "in the behavior of money stock have been closely associated with changes in economic activity, money income, and prices. . . . The interrelation between monetary and economic change has been highly stable . . . monetary changes have often had an independent origin; they have not been simply a reflection of changes in economic activity." (Milton Friedman and Anna J. Swartz, *Trends and Cycles in the Stock of Money in the United States, 1867–1960* [Princeton, N.J.: Princeton University Press, 1963], p. 676.)
6. Distinguish between the cash-balance equation of exchange and the transaction equation of exchange.
7. Explain the income approach to the theory of the value of money.
8. Explain the loanable-funds theory of interest and note how it differs from (*a*) the classical theory, (*b*) time-preference theory, and (*c*) the liquidity-preference theory.
9. Analyze: Market "expectations of continued inflation tend to put upward pressure on interest rates. Lenders of funds probably demand higher yields to compensate for greater expected future increases in prices. Borrowers . . . are less reluctant to pay higher rates as they

anticipate repaying in dollars depreciated by inflation." (Federal Reserve Bank of St. Louis, *Review*, June, 1968, p. 3.)

10. Explain: "We have to face the fact that our economy is not equipped to deal with the wage-price spiral, a problem that has plagued all free economies of the World." (Senator William Proxmire, "Wage Price Spiral Problem," *Austin American*, July 17, 1968, p. 4.)

CHAPTER 5

Credit Instruments

IN THE CONSTITUTION, Congress was given control over foreign and interstate commerce, including trade with the American Indians[1] (then an important political and military problem); but control over financial transactions was left in the hands of the states. At first, there was little uniformity among state laws in regard to regulation of negotiable instruments, partnerships, investment securities, agency and trust functions, contracts, and other financial and business subjects. When business operations became national in scope, uniform laws were needed. After years of work by lawyers, bankers, businessmen, and others, most states adopted the *Uniform Commercial Code*,[2] which replaces the Uniform Negotiable Instruments Act and the Uniform Stock Transfer Act, as well as others.

CREDIT SYSTEM

The term "credit system" is used to include credit, credit instruments, credit agencies, and laws and customs pertaining to the granting of credit and to the collecting of obligations. The credit system is growing in complexity and size because of the trend in production which is placing more and more emphasis upon indirect rather than direct creation of consumer goods.

The basis for the development of a credit system is a high sense of business morality, which gives creditors who give up present wealth or rights to wealth assurance of repayment in the future. The growth of the credit system has been aided by custom and law. Owners of surplus funds are more willing to lend their funds when they know that they have a legal right of action against debtors if the latter default on their obligations. While credit instruments do repre-

[1] *United States Constitution*, Art. I, sec. 8.

[2] The *Uniform Commercial Code* contains the following sections; (1) general provisions, (2) sales, (3) commercial paper, (4) bank transfers, (7) warehouse receipts, bills of lading, and other documents of title, (8) investment securities, (9) secured transactions: sales of contracts, contract rights, and chattel paper, and (10) effective date and repealer.

sent a legal right of action against debtors, the future of the credit system depends primarily upon the debtors' willingness and ability to repay and upon wise management on the part of those who are responsible for grants of credit. In general, the credit system has had its greatest development in those countries where customs and laws exact the highest moral and business standards, not only from debtors but also from creditors. The shyster lawyer, the fraudulent stock salesman, and the Shylock type of small-loan dealer are as harmful to the credit system as are the deadbeat, the forger, and similar characters. Legitimate dealers in credit fully appreciate this situation, and they have been the leaders in promoting blue-sky, antifraud, and small-loan laws.

The word "credit" has many meanings but in economics it usually refers to the ability to obtain something of value in the present in return for a promise to pay for it at some future time, combining the elements of a promise and of time. (In accounting, entries on the right side of an account refer to "credits" and those on the left side to "debits.") The thing received may be goods, services, securities, or money, and that which is promised to be paid may take the form of goods, services, securities, or money. In any credit transaction there are two parties involved—the creditor, who surrenders the thing borrowed, and the debtor, who assumes the obligation to pay. Ownership, as well as possession, is usually transferred. Otherwise, the renting of houses, where possession alone is transferred, would have to be considered a credit transaction. In banking and allied fields (with the exception of the stock market, where stocks are borrowed daily), a credit transaction usually involves either a promise or an order to pay a definite sum of money. Therefore, the largest and most important of credit transactions are those wherein money is used not only as a medium of lending or investing but also as a medium of repayment.

If the obligations of the debtor and the rights of the creditor are written, the paper is called a "credit instrument." Certain types of credit contracts must be in writing if they are to be enforceable by law, but there are others based on oral agreements alone that are legally binding on both parties. In the latter case there is not credit instrument, although the value of the thing borrowed may be large, as is true when government securities dealers or brokers deal with one another. Credit instruments vary according to purposes, customs, and the statutes of the states in which they originate. In some fields of credit considerable uniformity in credit instruments has resulted from the adoption by states of uniform laws, from the influence of federal legislation, and from the decisions of the courts. The advantages of credit have been extolled by many, among them Daniel Webster, who described it in the following glowing terms: "Credit is the vital air of the system of modern commerce. It has done more, a thousand times more, to enrich nations than all the mines in the world." However, credit is not wealth, nor does it create wealth, since no more goods, no more capital, and no more wealth exist after credit is granted than before. Credit is the agency of transfer. Total wealth, total income, and total well-being are increased by credit only to the degree that land, labor, and other goods may be utilized more efficiently and pleasurably.

Credit enriches consumption by permitting consumers to possess homes, cars, electrical equipment and appliances, and other types of durable consumer goods in the present in return for promises to pay in the future. Credit enables individuals to purchase goods and services to meet the emergency financial needs that accompany births, sickness, and death. Credit is used also in the retail field because it is convenient for both sellers and buyers to charge things purchased. Credit enables businessmen to obtain capital and investors to hold securities without sharing ownership with others.

Credit has contributed to the general increase in size and efficiency of production units. Our modern productive system could not have been developed without credit because few businessmen have adequate funds to purchase land, build plants, buy raw materials and machinery, and pay labor. An honest and capable businessman may obtain these factors of production on a large scale if he has credit. Inactive businessmen, small savers, widows, and orphans lend him funds with which to carry on his business activities. Thus, credit makes it possible to shift capital into the hands of those who are able and willing to use it. Most credit is used for productive purposes, thus making more goods available for exchange. More goods make possible more credit, and the cycle continues unless there is a breakdown in confidence.

Credit is no blessing for those who abuse the privilege of using it because any credit transaction is also a debt transaction. The debtor places a lien on his future income, and, for an individual, the pleasure of having consumer goods in the present may be offset by the burden of forced saving and loss of purchasing power in the future. In the case of a business firm, if profits expected from increased production based on credit do not materialize, the firm is left with less income than expected as well as burdensome fixed debt obligations.

Currently, a considerable portion of the nation's debt is based on the debts of others—those of banks, insurance companies, and other financial institutions—and a serious depression could destroy both the assets and credit worthiness of many debtors. Growth in the size of the debt is related to growth in gross national product (see Chart 5–1). How debt policies may aid in preventing depressions, eliminat-

CHART 5–1

UNITED STATES TOTAL DEBT AND GROSS NATIONAL PRODUCT
(In Billions of Dollars and Ratio Scale)

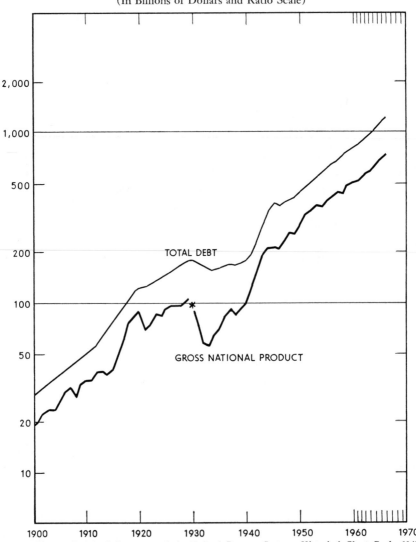

Source: Board of Governors of the Federal Reserve System, *Historical Chart Book, 1967* (Washington, D.C., 1968), p. 66.

ing financial panics, facilitating recovery, and sustaining full employment will be discussed in later chapters.

NEGOTIABLE CREDIT INSTRUMENTS

The wide use of credit instruments has resulted in legal rules covering their purchase and sale and the rights of owners. One of the most important legal features that pertains to them is the quality of negotiability. Ordinary transfers of wealth of property rights pass by assignment, since most types of property possess the legal qualities of salability and transferability. The buyer (assignee) is subject to all the defenses that may exist between original parties. Any defect in the title is passed along from the assignor to the assignee. For example, if a man purchases a stolen car, the original owner may reclaim it by proving that he is the legal owner. The assignee may sue the assignor, if he can find him, but he has no adequate defense against the legal owner.

Most forms of credit instruments have the legal qualities of salability and transferability and many possess the quality of negotiability. The negotiable credit instrument is a special type of contract that appears most commonly in the form of checks, notes, and bills of exchange. It is the quality of negotiability that makes possible the handling of billions of dollars of credit instruments each year by banks and nonmonetary financial institutions. The protection provided by this legal principle is an outgrowth of the struggles of English merchants and bankers since the origin of the bill of exchange in the 15th century to obtain special legal status for "bills."

Negotiability. The normal rule pertaining to property transactions is that a new owner cannot obtain a better title than that possessed by the party from whom it was received. In contrast, when a negotiable credit instrument is acquired under certain conditions, the transferee obtains a title that eliminates the "defenses and equities" of former owners. Otherwise, the buyer would be assuming the risk that the seller has obtained the property improperly (or the party from whom the seller had obtained it had acquired it improperly) and the true owner might claim it if he succeeds in identifying the property and proving his right to it. In such a case, the buyer, with little hope of success, would have to try to recover the purchase price from the seller, who in turn would have to bring suit against the party from whom he acquired it.

Negotiation is the transfer of a credit instrument in a form that makes the transferee become the holder. If an instrument is payable to order, it is negotiated by delivery together with any necessary endorsement; but, if it is payable to bearer, it is negotiable by delivery (*Uniform Commercial Code*, Section 3–202–[1]). The transferee obtains a good title provided he acquires the credit instrument before it is overdue, he is a purchaser for value, and he has no knowledge of any defect or infirmity of the instrument. The intention of the law is to make negotiable instruments transferable from hand to hand, like money, by freeing transferees from defenses that earlier holders may have asserted and therefore from claims of other parties.

Purchasers of credit instruments and stock certificates are not concerned with title search as are buyers of real estate. (Although stock certificates are not credit instruments, they are transferred in much the same way.) The rules governing the transfer of promissory notes, bills of exchange, and investment securities are included in the *Uniform Commercial Code*, which has been adopted by a majority of the states.

In order for a credit instrument to be negotiable, it must have the following characteristics: (1) be in writing and signed by the maker or drawer, (2) contain an unconditional promise or order to pay a certain sum of money, (3) be payable on demand or at a definite time, and (4) be payable to order or bearer. In order to make a credit instrument negotiable, certain procedures, including proper endorsement and presentation, must be followed. If an instrument is drawn payable to bearer, it may be negotiated by delivery without an endorsement but the transferee, who is often a banker, may insist on the transferer's endorsement as a matter of record (*Uniform Commercial Code*, Section 3–104[1]).

Endorsement.   Endorsement is the act of signing one's name, with or without qualifications, to an instrument for the purpose of transfer. Endorsement is necessary whenever a credit instrument is an order or promise to pay to a specified party. If the name of the payee on a credit instrument differs in spelling from his normal signature, he may be required to endorse the instrument in both ways. Endorsement may be special, in blank, restrictive, or qualified. A special endorsement designates to whom or to whose order the instrument is to be paid. For example, a check endorsed as follows: "Pay to John Jones or order," requires the signature of John Jones for further negotiation. An endorsement in blank specifies no endorsee, being signed by the maker (*Uniform Commercial Code*, Section 3–204). If a check is payable to bearer, it may be negotiated by delivery only until it is specifically endorsed.

Restrictive endorsements may be (1) conditional, (2) purport to prohibit further transfer of the credit instrument, (3) include the words "for deposit," "for collection," or a similar one signifying a purpose of deposit or collection, or (4) otherwise state that it is for the benefit of the endorser or another person (*Uniform Commercial Code*, Section 3–205). The most common forms of restriction are found on checks, such as, "for deposit only to the account of," "for collection only," "pay to John Jones only," or "for deposit and collection." The last endorsement requires the bank, as agent for the depositor, to appy funds consistent with the endorsement. Another type of restrictive endorsement is one that conditions the rights of the endorsee on certain happenings. Thus, a father may endorse a check "Payable to my son, John Smith, when he finishes college," signed "Henry Smith" or a businessman may endorse a credit instrument as follows: "Pay to the order of William Brown on the arrival of the *S.S. United States* in New York," signed "Charles Brown."

A qualified endorsement may be made by adding the words "without recourse" to the endorsement. The purpose would be to exempt the endorser from the liability for payment of the credit instrument in the event of it being dishonored at maturity. Such an endorsement not only diminishes the normal liability of the endorser but also places those in financial circles on notice that they must rely solely on the credit of the maker of prior endorsers for payment. The holder who signs an obligation in this way refuses to assume any financial responsibility for the instrument which may impair its acceptability but not its negotiability (*Uniform Commercial Code*, Section 3–417–[3]).

Presentment. Presentment is a demand for acceptance or payment made upon the maker, accepter, drawer, or other payer by or on behalf of the holder (*Uniform Commercial Code*, Section 3–504). The instrument may be presented by mail, through a clearinghouse, or at the place specified in the instrument for acceptance or payment. If no place is specified, it may be presented at the place of business or residence of the payor. If the latter is not present or accessible at his place of business or residence, presentment is excused.

If payment or acceptance is refused, the instrument has been "dishonored," and this action may cause the owner to make a formal protest. The *Uniform Commercial Code* defines "protest" as a "certificate of dishonor under the hand and seal of a United States consul or vice-consul or a notary public or other person authorized to certify dishonor by the law of the place where dishonor occurs."[3] The protest must identify the instrument, certify as to presentment or reason

___

[3] See *Uniform Commercial Code*, Sec. 3–509(1), (2), (3).

why it was excused and that the instrument had been dishonored by nonacceptance or nonpayment. The protest may certify that notice has been given to specified parties or to all parties.

After working for decades to obtain the protection contained in negotiable credit instruments, bankers and others may nullify this protection and increase their liabilities by waiving the requirement for presentment, notice, and protest. For business reasons, a collecting bank may mark a credit instrument "no protest" or "protest waived." In so doing, the bank accepts secondary liability for the instrument without the requirement that the credit instrument be protested if it is dishonored. An endorser or drawer may add words such as "payment guaranteed" to his signature which means that, in case of dishonor, he will pay the instrument without resorting to other names on the instrument; or an endorser may reduce his normal liability by adding the words "without recourse."

Nonnegotiable Instruments. In addition to negotiable credit instruments, there are others that are nonnegotiable because they do not possess the necessary qualifications. These include credit instruments that had been negotiable but which became nonnegotiable because of special endorsements. Briefly, a negotiable instrument is an unconditional promise or order to pay containing the words "to order" or "to bearer" that must be delivered, while a nonnegotiable instrument may be a conditional promise or order to pay which need not be delivered.

Instead of being endorsed, a nonnegotiable credit instrument is assigned and the assignee takes the instrument subject to all the equities of the original party. The endorser of a negotiable credit instrument agrees to pay if the maker or drawer fails to do so; but the assignee does not agree to pay if other parties fail to do so. In addition, there are other instruments of credit that have a degree of negotiability. Of these, the most important are stock certificates that represent ownership of stock in a corporation. Some property certificates, such as bills of lading and warehouse receipts, may be negotiable or nonnegotiable depending on how they are written.

Credit instruments are often ambiguous because of the way they are written; therefore, the *Uniform Commercial Code* provides rules for their construction. For example, (1) if there is doubt whether a credit instrument is a promissory note or a draft, the holder may treat it as either one; (2) when handwritten, typed, and printed terms appear on a credit instrument, the order is: handwritten terms control typewritten and typewritten control printed; (3) if written numerals and figures are not the same (a common mistake on checks), the rule is: words control figures except when the former are ambiguous and then the latter control (*Uniform Commercial Code*, Section 3–118).

MONEY INSTRUMENTS

The term "money instruments" is used to identify negotiable credit instruments having moneylike qualities (see Chapter 6). Those discussed in this section include drafts or bills of exchange, checks, certificates of deposit, and promissory notes.

Draft or Bill of Exchange.   The Uniform Negotiable Instruments Act defines a bill of exchange as "an unconditional order in writing addressed by one person to another, signed by the person giving it, requiring the person to whom it is addressed to pay on demand or at a fixed or determinable future time a sum certain in money to order or to a bearer." The *Uniform Commercial Code* states that a negotiable credit instrument is a draft or a bill of exchange "if it is an order" (see Section 3–104). This order is a direction to pay, and it must identify the one who is to pay with reasonable certainty. It could be addressed to more than one person, jointly or as alternate but not in succession (*Uniform Commercial Code*, Section 3–102).

Originally, bills of exchange appeared as payable on demand, and they were used as a "substitute for money." Demand bills are still widely used in international trade (see Chapter 26). During the Middle Ages, bankers and merchants began the practice of issuing negotiable instruments that were payable at some future date. The assumption was that the payee would wait until the due date of the bill of exchange and then collect it. The payee, rather than the payer or debtor, provided the credit to finance these transactions. Subsequently, the time bill of exchange became salable to bankers and others prior to maturity, which meant that the new owner was financing the transaction. The buyer purchased the bill of exchange at less than its value at maturity, and this discount was large enough to compensate for interest, risks, and the cost of administering the credit transaction.

Bills of exchange are classified as domestic or inland and foreign or international. Under the *Uniform Commercial Code*, only an international bill (one drawn or payable outside the United States and its territories) must be protested, unless waived, to hold all parties liable for loss or damage if the bill is dishonored. A domestic bill (one drawn or payable in the United States or its territories) need not be protested in case of nonacceptance or nonpayment (*Uniform Commercial Code*, Section 3–501–[3]). These provisions differ from those embodied in the Uniform Negotiable Instruments Act which defines an inland bill of exchange as "a bill which is, or on its face purports to be, both drawn and payable within the State. Any other bill is a foreign bill. Unless the contrary appears on the face of the bill, the holder may treat it as an inland bill."

Bills of exchange are classified in terms of the drawee (the one drawn upon or the payer) as trade bills and as bank bills. A trade bill is one drawn on a merchant or purchaser of goods; a bank bill is drawn upon a bank. Trade drafts may be demand or time and secured or unsecured. If the order to pay drawn by the seller of goods on the purchaser of such goods is accepted by the purchaser, it is called a "trade acceptance." The accepting process consists of writing or stamping on the face of the "bill" the word "accepted," followed by the date of the acceptance and the signature of the drawee. This corresponds to the endorsement on a promissory note with this important difference: the accepter is primarily liable for the credit instrument, while the endorser is only secondarily liable. At the end of the credit period (ordinarily 30 or 60 days but it may be longer), the bill of exchange is presented to the drawee a second time—this time for payment. However, the first owner of the trade acceptance may need cash before the end of the credit period, in which case he endorses the trade draft and discounts it at his bank.

Commercial bills or bankers' acceptances are similar to trade acceptances except that the orders to pay are drawn upon banks by the sellers of the goods. (A bank may purchase the rights of the seller of goods and act as the drawer.) The seller usually receives authority to draw upon the bank in a formal letter, called a "commercial letter of credit," which is arranged for by the buyer of the goods (see Chapter 26). Both trade acceptances and commercial bills may be accompanied by a property instrument, such as a bill of lading, that contains title to goods being financed. This document gives the drawer security until his draft is accepted or paid.

The terms of sale covering financing of goods may specify (1) that the bill of exchange is payable on "sight," on "arrival" of the goods, or 30 days, 60 days, or some other number of days after sight or date; (2) that certain documents are to be attached to the "bill"; and (3) that the title document will be released when the "bill" is paid (D/P bill) or when it is accepted (D/A bill). If payment is required, the bill of exchange is canceled; but, if acceptance is required, the credit instrument may be in existence for 30 days, 60 days, etc., from the date of acceptance (30, 60, etc., sight bills) or from the date on which it was drawn (depending on the terms of credit).

A bank draft, an instrument drawn upon one bank by a second bank, is customarily payable on demand, and it differs from a check in that the drawer is a bank instead of a person. Sometimes bank drafts are called "remittance drafts" because of their extensive use in settling for checks and matured instruments. They are sold by banks to their customers who use them to settle obligations in distant places and to nonbank customers that do not have checking accounts.

Check. The *Uniform Commercial Code* specifies that a negotiable instrument is a check "if it is a draft drawn on a bank and payable on demand" (*Uniform Commercial Code*, Section 3–104–[2] [b]). Checks are orders drawn on, and later charged against, drawers' checking accounts in banks. After a check is written and before it is paid, the drawer may stop payment provided the order to do so is received in time and is made in such a manner to give the bank a reasonable opportunity to act. The "stop payment" order may be given orally; but, unless it is confirmed in writing, it is binding on the bank for only 14 days. Written orders are effective for six months, after which they must be renewed in writing to be effective. However, except in the case of a certified check, a bank is under no obligation to pay a "stale" check, that is, one that is not presented until six or more months after the date it was written.

The check of an "incompetent" customer of a bank is treated in the customary way if the bank is not aware of the customer's adjudication of incompetence when the check was issued or accepted for collection. Even death of the bank customer does not revoke the bank's right to accept, collect or pay checks drawn on the deceased's account. Unless a request is made to stop payment by someone claiming an interest in the account, banks may continue to pay checks drawn or certified prior to the date of death of the drawer for 10 days after his death.

Specific forms of checks are cashiers' checks, certified checks, and travelers' checks. A cashier's check is one written by an authorized officer of a bank on his own bank. This type of check is frequently used as a substitute for a bank draft. A certified check is a personal check that has been certified by a bank officer; the amount of the check has been charged against the account of the drawer, which makes the check an obligation of the bank. Certification of a check has the same legal status as acceptance of a bill of exchange. Certification may be requested by a drawer in order to increase the acceptability of his check, or it may be obtained by a holder in order to assure payment. Travelers' checks are sold by banks and the American Express Company (see Chapter 26).

Promissory Notes. As stated in the *Uniform Commercial Code,* a credit instrument is a note if it is a promise to pay; certificates of deposit are exceptions which are treated separately. A note is a written promise to pay a sum of money on demand or on a definite future date to a designated person or bearer. The person making the promise is called the "maker," the one to whom it is made is called the "payee." The maker and the payee may be the same person or firm. Promissory notes may be single name or double name, interest-bearing or noninterest-bearing, secured or unsecured, payable on demand or at the end of a specified period, and payable in one lump sum or in installments that include interest and principal payments at specified times until the note plus interest is paid in full.

The most common types of secured notes are collateral notes, chattel mortgage notes, and real estate mortgage notes. A collateral note is one secured most frequently by intangible personal property in the form of stocks, bonds, insurance policies, leases, savings account passbooks, bills of lading, warehouse receipts, and book accounts. A chattel mortgage note is secured by a chattel mortgage executed by the maker on a specific item of personal property such as an automobile, livestock, or equipment. The basic legal difference between a mortgage and a pledge is that the latter entails a transfer of possession of personal property and a mortgage is a transfer of title to property. To an increasing degree, state laws and courts are regarding a mortgage as merely giving a lien on mortgaged property. A real estate mortgage note is one secured by a mortgage on a specific piece of real property of the maker. Basically, it is the same as a chattel mortgage, except that the property mortgage is on real property. The trust or mortgage deed is given in many states to secure a promissory note, and it is a lien rather than a conveyance of title.

Numerous documents are used in connection with promissory notes, depending in part on the purpose of the transaction and the property pledged as security. When tangible personal property is pledged, the legal document may be a trust receipt (that is, the property is transferred in trust), a conditional-sales contract (which means that certain things are to be done in the future), a warehouse receipt (which serves as a receipt, a contract, and a document of title to the goods it represents), or a bill of lading (which is similar to a warehouse receipt but is issued by a railroad company, steamship company, or some other common carrier). The *Uniform Commercial Code* created a new concept of collateral and security, as a "security interest" in personal property used as security. It may replace the assignment, bailment lease, chattel mortgage, conditional-sale contract, equipment trust, factor's lien, trust receipt, and so on.[4]

Certificate of Deposit. The *Uniform Commercial Code* states that an instrument is a certificate of deposit if it acknowledges a bank's receipt of money with a promise to pay it (*Uniform Commercial Code*, Section 3–104 [2] [a]). Usually such a deposit receipt is treated as a note, but banks are required to hold a percentage of the amount as an asset reserve in the same way as for savings and other time deposits (see Chapter 11). Although a certificate of deposit does not contain the words "order of" or "bearer," usually present in negotiable credit instruments, it states that it is "payable upon the return of this certificate properly indorsed." Like other credit instruments, a certificate of deposit may be negotiable or nonnegotiable, depending on how it is written. During the 1960's, negotiable certificates of deposit became the most important, in dollar amount, among the nongovernment money market instruments (see Chapter 6).

INVESTMENT SECURITIES

Investment securities are issued either in bearer or registered form; and they are a type of security (1) commonly dealt in on securities exchanges or in other securities markets, or (2) commonly recognized in any area in which they are issued or dealt in as a medium for investment. Investment securities may be either one of a class or series of instruments or, by its terms, divisible into a class or series of instruments. Investment securities evidence either (1) a share, a participation or other interest in property or an enterprise or (2) an obligation of the issuer (*Uniform Commercial Code*, Section 8–102 [1] [a]). The two major classes of investment securities are stocks and bonds.

Investment securities and commercial securities are treated separately in the *Uniform Commercial Code*. This move permits continuance of the high standards set for negotiability for commercial paper

---

[4] Following Section 9–102 (3) of the *Uniform Commercial Code* the following note appears: "The adoption of this article should be accompanied by the repeal of existing statutes dealing with conditional sales, trust receipts, factor's liens where the factor is given a non-possessory lien, chattel mortgages, crop mortgages, mortgages on railroad equipment, assignment of accounts and generally statutes regulating security interests in personal property."

(checks, drafts, and notes) without handicapping the securities market. Unlike previous acts, stock as well as bonds are made negotiable instruments (*Uniform Commercial Code*, Section 8–105 [1]).

Bonds. A bond is a written or printed acknowledgment of debt or a contract to pay money issued by a government, public or private corporation, partnership, or individual. Ordinarily, a bond is one of a number of similarly issued instruments; and the individual bonds in the issue may vary as to amount and maturity. Usually a bond is a long-term obligation at the time of issuance and assumes a life expectancy of the borrower to be at least equal to the maturity of the loan. Corporate bonds are classified in many ways, the most common being as debenture bonds, mortgage bonds, collateral trust bonds, and guaranty bonds.

Debenture bonds are unsecured promises to pay, "dignified by a formal indenture, the interposition of a trustee, and marked by the participation of many individual creditors. . . ." The indenture (a written agreement), which is held by a trustee, describes the rights and remedies of holders of bonds for broken promises given by the debtor. In general, limitations are placed upon (1) the issuance of new bonds, (2) dividend payments when working capital is depleted, (3) procedure to be followed by trustees when agreements are violated, and (4) the use of funds raised by the bond sale. As in all types of bond issues, many creditors are participating in advances of funds to but one corporate debtor.

Mortgage bonds differ from debenture bonds in that they are promises to pay secured by special liens or mortgage trust deeds conveying title to all or a specified part of the corporation's assets to the designated trustee as security for the payment of the bonds. The mortgage is held and supervised by a trustee, who acts for the holders of the bonds. When the bonds are paid, title to the mortgaged property reverts to the corporation. The original type of mortgage bonds (with rigid provisions for foreclosure in case of failure to pay interest and taxes, to maintain insurance, and to meet installment-principal payments) has been modified by law and court actions. For these reasons, the indenture agreements now used in this type of financing, as well as for debenture bonds, are of increasing importance.

The collateral trust bond is similar to the mortgage bond, but it is secured by pledges of other securities, which are held by a trustee. As in the case of mortgage bonds, there is a supplementary agreement obliging the debtor to pay if the pledged property is insufficient. Collateral trust bonds most often are issued by holding companies and investment trusts that have chiefly stocks and bonds to offer as security for public borrowing.

From the viewpoint of security, guaranty bonds stand between debenture bonds and those secured by liens on real or personal property. They include bonded debts of one of the other classes of bonds that have been assumed, guaranteed, endorsed, or otherwise protected by the credit of a second corporation, as sometimes happens in case of railroad mergers. Sometimes bonds are the individual and joint obligation of two or more corporations, as illustrated by the bonds of the federal land banks and the federal home loan banks.

Many minor classes of bonds have appeared as corporation finance has become more complex. Bonds may belong to an open-end or to a closed-end issue. If open-end, additional bonds may be issued under certain specified conditions under the indenture agreement, mortgage, and/or collateral trust agreement. If closed-end, no new bonds of the same lien as those already outstanding may be issued. Bonds may be issued with or without convertible features. If convertible, the holder can, under certain conditions, exchange them for shares of stock. The bonds may be callable or noncallable. If callable, the debtor company may call them under certain stipulated conditions. Bonds may be registered both as to principal and as to interest, or they may be registered as to principal only. If bonds are not registered as to principal, they are payable to bearer.

Bonds are also classified according to the provisions made for repayment of the principal. If a certain quantity of the total borrowed is repayable annually or at definite periods, the bonds are called "serials." Serial bond issues are common among public issues, particularly those of local governments. If all bonds are due on a particular date, they are called "term bonds." The term bonds are paid either out of a sinking fund that has been built up over the life of the bond issue for this purpose or with proceeds of a new security sale. If the bonds are put out for a definite period (for example, twenty years) but are callable after a fixed period (say, ten years), they are known as "callable term bonds." This type was common among the federal issues. Perpetual bonds, with no maturity date, are common among government issues in foreign countries.

With one exception, bonds call for interest payments at stated intervals (usually every six months), but the payment of interest on income bonds depends on net profits of the issuing corporation. Such bonds are sometimes called "adjustment bonds" because they are used widely in adjusting fixed-interest debts of bankrupt corporations which has given income bonds a bad name. Since the payment of interest is dependent on earnings, they are similar to preferred stock in this respect. Because of the tax advantage, preference bonds might be used more commonly in place of preferred stock.

In long-term financing, the issuer may delay printing bonds until they have been sold; and, after the sale of an issue, the issuer may give purchasers interim certificates which usually require the debtor or obliger to give the holder a bond at a particular time. Like stock certificates and bonds, interim certificates are negotiable under provisions of the *Uniform Commercial Code* (see Section 8–105).

Stock Certificates.   A stock certificate is a written or printed evidence of ownership of shares of capital of a corporation. A certificate may be issued for any number of shares to indicate a stockholder's total ownership in a corporation, but, if shares are purchased at different times, several stock certificates may be issued to one individual. All shareholders are proprietors or owners rather than creditors of their corporations. A stockholder receives a share in the earnings, which is called a "dividend." In general, dividends are paid only when earned and voted by the board of directors. Most stockholders of large corporations have little to say about the policies of their corporations, and, if they vote at all, it is by proxy. In deciding to buy stock, such investors are guided by investment rather than by managerial motives. This is true particularly of those who buy stocks that are traded actively on organized stock exchanges and in the over-the-counter markets.

There are many ways of classifying shares of stock, but the two most general classes are "preferred" and "common." Preferred stockholders have prior claims to earnings and, in the event of liquidation, usually to assets. In return for this preferred position, preferred stockholders usually accept a limited rate of return and surrender voting rights except when their rights and privileges are involved (such as issuance of new preferred stock with equal or superior rights, cancellation of accrued dividends, voluntary dissolution of the company, and so on). If preferred stock dividends are omitted for a stated period, preferred stockholders may be authorized to vote for all or to elect a specified number of directors.

Preferred stock is called a hybrid security because it has characteristics of both stocks and bonds (see below). Preferred stock may be cumulative or noncumulative, participating or nonparticipating. If it is 6 percent cumulative participating stock, it means that, if dividends are only 3 percent one year because of low earnings, an equal amount becomes an obligation due preferred stockholders that must be paid before dividends are paid to common stockholders. If earnings are above 6 percent, the participating preferred stockholders may share (depending, of course, upon the participation clause) in the excess earnings on the same basis as common stockholders, or on some other basis.

The common stock certificates of a corporation represent the claims of stockholders after creditors and preferred stockholders have received interest and dividends. They may have a definite face or par value, or they may be issued without par value. Owners have a residual claim to earnings and assets. Thus, common stock differs from borrowed capital; it is proprietary, ownership, or equity capital, which means that (1) the business firm using equity capital is not

TABLE 5–1

LEVERAGE OF CAPITAL STRUCTURE

		Earnings			
Type of Security	Capital	3%	4%	5%	6%
Bonds (3%)	$200,000	$6,000	$ 6,000	$ 6,000	$ 6,000
Preferred stock (5%)	100,000	3,300	5,000	5,000	5,000
Common stock	10,000	......	1,400	4,500	7,600
Total	$310,000	$9,300	$12,400	$15,500	$18,600

legally bound to pay any income return to those who provide it, (2) there is no stated time when the funds provided by owners must be returned, and (3) those who own it are responsible, at least in theory, for the control and management of the business enterprise.

In addition to the risk assignable to the nature of the business, there may be an added financial risk assumed by common stockholders owing to the financial structure of the corporation. This risk is determined by the relationship between fixed charges and the income available, after taxes, to meet these fixed charges. If one assumes that a corporation has outstanding $200,000 in 3 percent bonds, 1,000 shares of 5 percent preferred stock with a par value of $100, and 1,000 shares of common stock with a par value of $10, the fixed charges on the bonds will be $6,000 and dividends on the preferred stock will be $5,000.

The effect of changes in earnings assignable to common stock is illustrated in Table 5–1. If one assumes that the preferred stock is noncumulative and nonparticipating, when the corporation has an operating income of 3 percent, after taxes, no income is available for common stock, and dividends on preferred stock are covered only in part. However, an increase in operating income to 6 percent, after taxes, means that $7.60 is available for each share of common stock. This method of financing with senior securities (bonds and preferred stock) is called "trading on equity" (but only in a nontechnical sense, because preferred stock also represents equity in the legal sense). Any increase in earnings is passed through the senior securities and pyramided into a wide fluctuation of earnings assignable to common stock. In financial circles this proportionate change in the return on common stock in excess of operating income is called the "leverage factor."[5]

The danger in the use of borrowed capital is that the corporation will overborrow during good times and will have too large a fixed debt to be serviced when returns on capital are very low. In the past this has been one of the primary reasons for the failure of railroads and other large corporations. Following financial difficulties during the 1930's, corporations began to finance more with funds from operations (accounted for as retained earnings and depreciation allowances), common stock, and short-term and other bonds with callable features. Currently, the pressure to finance with debts is considerable because, in computing the base for payment of federal corporate income taxes as well as many state income taxes, interest on debts is deductible. When corporate taxes are taking almost half the taxable income, the savings that result from financing with debts rather than with common or preferred stock are great. Although financing to a greater extent with stock (equity) is recognized as socially and economically desirable, the use of this method of strengthening our economic system has been retarded by our corporate tax structure. One solution would be to treat dividend payments like interest payments, deducting them as a cost of doing business; another would be to treat interest payments like dividend payments are treated at present. The first, because of its effect on government revenue, would be unacceptable to Congress. However, it is the correct approach because the distinction between the two sources of income is only a technical one from the viewpoint of the average investor.

Subscription Warrant. A subscription warrant may be a short-term, intermediate, or long-term credit instrument. It is a written or

[5] When the financial leverage factor is used, it is called "trading on equity." The term, "financial leverage" should not be confused with the term "operating leverage." The latter refers to the increase in the rate of profit which follows when an increase in production or sales permits a business firm to spread its fixed costs over more units.

printed document that authorizes the owner to subscribe to new stock under the conditions stated therein (price, method of payment, time period, and so on). Sometimes warrants are attached to bonds to enhance their salability, but more often such warrants are issued to represent the preemptive rights of old stockholders to buy new issues of stock or bonds convertible into stock. Stock purchase rights are prorated among existing stockholders according to the number of shares owned; if they are not used within the time specified, the privilege lapses. Arrangements whereby *rights* may be sold to others are usually made by listing the rights on a stock exchange or by arranging for their sale through investment banking houses.

Sometimes corporations give their officers stock-purchase options at or near the market price of the stock when the options are issued. Customarily, such options are for periods of from 10 to 12 years from the date of issue; if the company prospers and the market price of the stock increases, the options may be exercised at the price stated in the option. Usually such stock-purchase options are issued under "executive incentive plans."

SUMMARY

In recognition of the fact that many of the older concepts of common law that originated during the Middle Ages are no longer suitable to the present type of modern business, the framers of the *Uniform Commercial Code* tried to rectify this situation in rewriting the rules applicable to many phases of industry. In this chapter, only the legal rules appropriate to the transfer of commercial paper and investment securities were considered.

Traditionally, bank credit is associated with short-term loans to business firms, the principle being that bank credit should not be used as a substitute for savings. Now, bank credit is invested freely in long-term debts of business firms, homeowners, governments, and others. Some writers feel that this has been a misuse of credit held by commercial banks; however, to the extent that they accept large amounts of savings deposits, banks are justified in financing long-term commitments. Individuals must save money before they can lend or invest it, but commercial banks and the monetary authorities may create bank credit. Expansion in the volume of bank credit has been an important factor in the growth of the credit system.

The extent to which credit instruments are used in the United States is sufficient evidence of their importance. In any one month, practically every adult handles credit instruments of some type. Primary responsibility for the credit system remains in the hands of bankers and the monetary authorities, but every user or granter of credit shares in the responsibility.

QUESTIONS AND PROBLEMS

1. Identify (*a*) credit, (*b*) credit instruments, and (*c*) credit system.
2. What are negotiable credit instruments? Explain the conditions necessary to make a credit instrument negotiable. May a credit instrument be transferable without being negotiable? Illustrate.
3. Assume that you have checks and want to endorse them in order to accomplish the following purposes. Write out your endorsements so as (*a*) to make the check negotiable without further endorsements, (*b*) to limit your financial responsibility, (*c*) to prevent anyone except your bank from collecting, (*d*) to make it necessary for the party to whom you give the check to endorse it, thereby making it easier to trace payments.
4. What is meant by (*a*) presentment? (*b*) money instrument? (*c*) financial leverage? and (*d*) investment securities?
5. Distinguish among the following: (*a*) a draft, (*b*) a check, (*c*) a promissory note, and (*d*) a certificate of deposit.
6. Explain: "Preferred stock is called a hybrid security because it has characteristics of both stocks and bonds. . . ."
7. Explain the legal difference between a stock and a bond.
8. Discuss: "Corporate manufacturers had almost $69 billion of accounts receivable on their books at the end of 1966." Subtracting "accounts payable, these manufacturers were owed about $36 billion by other businesses. In comparison, all commercial banks had outstanding loans to business (only some of which were manufacturers) of $79 billion." (Federal Reserve Bank of Philadelphia, *Business Review*, July, 1967, p. 3.)
9. Explain the terms in the following: "Union Gas Co., of Canada Ltd., offered $20 million of 7¾ percent debentures with a 15-year nonredemption feature. . . . The issue . . . consists of $17 million of 20-year sinking fund depentures and $3 million of three-to-eight year serial debentures." (*Wall Street Journal*, July 19, 1968, p. 13.)
10. Analyze: "In choosing shares you should go for the lowest immediate return you can afford to accept. 'The higher the yield, the greater the risk' is a useful slogan." (Margot Naylor, *Your Money* [Rev. ed.: London, England: Hodder & Stoughton, 1967], p. 63.)

CHAPTER 6

The Money Market

CREDIT INSTRUMENTS are classified as short term, intermediate term, and long term. the first category includes "money instruments," so-called because of their moneylike qualities, which are traded in the money market. In a modern economy these instruments provide all types of banks, business firms, and other institutions that own them with much-needed liquidity. Money market instruments may be sold with practically no loss or delay to obtain cash if needed; hence they are important substitutes for money.

Liquidity is the key in management of financial affairs, and now bankers and businessmen are giving more thought to assets that possess this quality. Although policies as to the degree of liquidity to be maintained vary, no banker would accept the ratio of cash to deposits as a satisfactory test of liquidity. It is true that Congress and the Board of Governors of the Federal Reserve System require member banks to keep a minimum cash-deposit ratio, but the purpose is to restrain the deposit-creating activities of banks (see Chapter 16). Among the assets that meet the bankers' test of liquidity are those which are traded in the money market.

NEW YORK MONEY MARKET

The New York money market is only one of many in the United States, but it is the largest and most important. For about 100 years this market was dominated by call loans made by banks to securities brokers and dealers. Although banks still make short-term loans secured by stock market collateral to brokers and dealers, this business is on a negotiated basis and, with the exception of loans made to government securities dealers, stock market loans are not called when banks need to increase their cash reserves.

The brokers and dealers in the money market are individuals and financial firms who are specialists in trading in the credit instruments bought and sold in this market. As brokers, they act as agents for buyers and sellers and receive commissions for their services. As dealers, they buy and sell money market instruments from and to investors and others and for their own accounts, and are compensated by the spread between their buying and selling prices and the interest earned on securities while they hold them (usually for but a short time).

The money market is one wherein most of the trading is done over the telephone. The network of telephone lines links dealer banks, nonbank dealers and other specialists including the Federal Reserve Bank of New York), and many out-of-town banks; hence it is easy for them to communicate with one another. Unlike the traders and floor brokers on the New York Stock Exchange who deal personally with one another on the floor of the Exchange (see Chapter 21), traders in the money market may never see each other during business hours. Changes in titles of money-market instruments are based on oral agreements made by telephone or wire and later confirmed by letter. These arrangements involving millions of dollars are made by men who do not know each other personally but who trust one another's integrity. The dollar amount of trading in this market exceeds that of any other market.

Large New York banks provide most of the facilities needed for delivery of and payment for money-market instruments and offer messenger and custodian services to those trading in the money market. A large money bank has its own trading department and a money-position officer who watches his bank's "money" or reserve position. The money banks outside of New York are linked by telephone and wire to the New York banks and the broker-dealer specialists.

All of the instruments in the money market are short-term, have impeachable credit quality, and are negotiable. The securities must be short term in order to minimize the effect of changes in money-market interest rates. Obviously, long-term United States Treasury bonds would not qualify even though the Treasury is responsible for them (as it is for United States Treasury bills, the most important among the credit instruments traded in the money market). United States Treasury bonds that were sold at par when issued are now selling at a discount because new issues carry a higher coupon rate. When owners of outstanding bonds wish to sell them in order to buy the higher yielding new bonds, they can only sell the old bonds at a discount, which has the effect of equalizing the new and old market rates.[1] However, prices of credit instruments that are approaching

[1] Aubrey G. Lanston & Co., Inc., Offering Letter, July 22, 1968.

maturity do not reflect changes in market rates to the same degree as do long-term obligations (see Chapter 14).

When banks and other institutional buyers acquire money-market instruments, their first consideration is safety and their second is yield. Money-market assets must have the highest credit rating in order to be acceptable for secondary reserve purposes, otherwise it could be disastrous for banks to depend on them as a source of cash. As might be expected, obligations of the Federal Reserve banks (federal funds), commercial banks (bankers' acceptances), prime business firms and finance companies (commercial paper), government securities dealers (collateral notes secured by U.S. government obligations), and the United States Treasury and government agencies (bills and other obligations approaching maturity) are the preferred forms of liquid assets. Nevertheless, a short-term credit instrument of prime quality would have no place in the money market without the facilities that make it easy to buy and sell such instruments.

The Federal Reserve System uses the facilities of the money market in its "open-market operations"—buying and selling government securities or other assets in order to affect the economy (see Chapter 18). The Federal Reserve Bank of New York acts as money-market agent for both the Federal Reserve banks and the United States Treasury. Commercial banks use the money market as a place to adjust their reserve positions. By lending or investing where funds may be withdrawn quickly in case of need, banks are able to earn an income on assets (called secondary reserves) that otherwise might be held as idle cash balances. If cash reserves are deficient, banks can sell their holdings of money-market paper in the open market at favorable prices.

Although an individual bank may never use the money market as a source of funds or as an outlet for investment, bankers watch the money market because changes therein signal impending changes in the economy. For illustration, a sharp increase in interest rates may suggest the need to tighten up on loans, watch collateral held as security for loans, make certain that loans are paid when due, and advise customers to ease up on purchases and to watch inventories. Just as businessmen are interested in the market for their products and services, bankers are interested in the day-to-day changes in the money market.

The instruments used in the money market include: (1) drafts or checks and transfers drawn or written on member-bank reserve deposits and other deposit accounts in Federal Reserve banks, (2) short-term promises to pay of the U.S. government and its agencies, (3) promissory notes of business firms that borrow in the open market, (4) bills of exchange or orders to pay which have been drawn by commercial firms and endorsed or accepted by commercial banks, (5) negotiable time certificates of deposit that evidence time deposits made by commercial firms, foreign banks, and others in commercial banks, and (6) promissory notes of dealers in U.S. government securities.

MARKET FOR FEDERAL FUNDS

When trading in the money market, dealer banks, nonbank dealers and others use two types of money: (1) clearinghouse money and (2) federal funds. Clearinghouse money consists of checks and drafts on commercial banks that are settled through the clearinghouse the next day. In other words, clearinghouse money is tomorrow's money (see Chapter 9).

Federal funds or Federal Reserve money consists of orders to pay drawn by member banks, the United States Treasury, and others on their deposits with their Federal Reserve banks. The orders may be in the form of checks, drafts, or transfers made by mail, wire, cable, radio, or telephone. When these orders are presented to the Federal Reserve bank, the owners receive immediate Federal Reserve bank credit (today's money). For illustration, if a bank sells government securities from its portfolio, it may specify that the terms be for "immediate" or "cash" delivery "against federal reserve funds." On that day, the government securities will be delivered by messenger to the buyer, and the latter will pay for them with an order on his account at its Federal Reserve bank.

Banks' Need for Reserve Money. A bank, faced with the need for adjusting its reserve position today, is willing to pay a premium (interest) for Federal Reserve money because it gives immediate reserve credit and thereby the bank avoids being penalized for having a deficiency in its reserves. Why then should not a bank with excess reserves earn an income therefrom by allowing another bank with a deficiency in reserves to use its excess reserves? The use of such deposits to adjust member-bank reserve positions emerged when New York banks began to exchange checks, with the lender's check drawn on the Federal Reserve Bank of New York and payable that day and the borrower's check drawn on itself and payable through the clearinghouse the next day. The federal funds market developed out of this situation; and, before the end of the 1920's, it was a common practice among banks to settle interbank obligations in this way.

Beginning with the statement for the week ending September 18, 1968, banks which are members of the Federal Reserve System started to use a new method of computing reserve requirements (see Chapter 16). Now, reserve requirements are based on average weekly deposits for the preceding week rather than on the average deposits for the current week for reserve city banks and two weeks for country banks as was true in the past. Banks know exactly what their reserve requirements will be before they start a week, so there is no longer any need for them to borrow large amounts of federal funds the last day of a reserve period to avoid having a deficiency, as was true previously.[2] The new system has resulted in more efficient utilization of reserves and slightly lower and more stable interest rates for federal funds.

Trading in Reserve Money. Some banks are in the federal funds market more or less continuously as borrowers, while others are in the market more or less continuously as sellers. Sometimes metropolitan banks are both buyers and sellers, using the market not only to adjust their own reserve positions but also to accommodate their correspondent banks and other customers. Since the Comptroller of the Currency has ruled that transactions in federal funds constitute purchases and sales, commercial banks that trade in Federal Reserve money are not subject to lending and borrowing limitations in these transactions. In lending and borrowing transactions, national banks generally may not lend more than 10 percent of their capital and surplus to one borrower, nor may they borrow an amount in excess of their own capital accounts.

The typical transaction in the federal funds market is for one day, and the amount dealt in is large, generally in units of $1 million. Sometimes large banks enter into transactions, as an accommodation to their small correspondent banks, wherein the amounts dealt in are as small as $50,000; but even such accommodation transactions are rarely for less than $200,000. Active trading in the federal funds market is limited to fewer than 300 banks (with the number declining during periods of credit ease), plus 20 government securities dealers who also trade in bankers' acceptances and government obligations. The market is primarily an interbank market, with banks involved in

---

[2] The penalty for a deficiency in reserves is assessed on the deficiency at a rate of 2 percent per annum above the Federal Reserve bank's discount rate applicable on 90-day commercial paper for member banks in effect the first day in which the deficiency occurred. The bank's directors are notified, and failure to correct the deficiency may result in loss of charter by a national bank or loss of membership in the Federal Reserve System by a state-chartered member bank. However, the penalty is usually waived for a bank that did not have a deficiency at the end of the preceding reserve computation period.

about 90 percent of purchases and sales. The New York City banks are the chief buyers and sellers, and the greatest flow of funds is among themselves and with banks in other financial centers.[3]

Dealers in U.S. government securities and agents of foreign central banks also use the federal funds market. Payment for government securities is customarily made in federal funds. Hence when buying or selling these securities, dealers arrange with brokers to find someone to sell or to buy federal funds. For several years the chief middlemen in bringing together buyers and sellers of federal funds have been Garvin, Bartel & Co., (formerly Faber, Garvin & Co.), a member of the New York Stock Exchange, which has acted as broker in trades totaling as much as $100 billion a year. This brokerage house, which has been in the federal funds market for over 40 years, generally makes no charge for its services; instead it is compensated by the brokerage business received from its customers. A few banks prefer to pay the brokerage house a flat fee (usually $\frac{1}{16}$ of 1 percent). Several New York banks now give brokerage services in federal funds to national banks and some give these services to their correspondents on request, acting more often as principal than as broker.

Transactions.   The convenience of the federal funds market attracts buyers and sellers and, if the parties involved in a transaction are New York member banks, the terms are arranged over the telephone. The purchaser receives either a draft or a "transfer" on the Federal Reserve bank for the amount purchased. The transfer is the seller's advice by telephone to the Federal Reserve bank, confirmed by a written statement sent by messenger, to transfer from the seller's reserve account to the buyer's reserve account the amount stated in the contract. The buyer would give the seller a clearinghouse check for the same amount plus interest at the agreed-on rate for one day (two or more days if the transaction is made on Friday or the day before a holiday). This so-called "straight" transaction entails a purchase and sale of federal funds on an overnight unsecured basis. It is the simplest transaction in the money market requiring no note and no collateral and only an exchange of checks or exchange of a transfer order and a check.

If an out-of-town bank is involved, the federal funds transaction is equally simple. After the terms are arranged by telephone, instructions for the transfer of title to deposits at the Federal Reserve bank

---

[3] For statistics on interbank federal funds transactions, see table entitled "Basic Reserve Position and Federal Funds and Related Transactions" in the current issue of the *Federal Reserve Bulletin.*

are made by wire (later confirmed by letter). Customarily, the message is sent free of charge over the wire transfer system of the Federal Reserve System. For illustration, a bank in Buffalo, New York, may telephone a bank in New York City to arrange the terms of a federal funds transaction and then wire the Federal Reserve Bank of New York to transfer the agreed-on amount from the Buffalo bank's reserve deposits to that of the New York bank (followed by a written confirmation). The next banking day, the procedure is reversed. Usually the interest payment is handled separately by remitting a cashier's check or crediting the bank's account, if it is a correspondent bank. When a transaction is between banks in different Federal Reserve districts, the procedure is the same except that the two Federal Reserve banks settle through the Interdistrict Settlement Fund of the Federal Reserve System (see Chapter 9).

Banks sometimes disguise their federal funds transactions by selling government securities to other banks under one-day repurchase contracts or by using two contracts—one to buy and one to sell. Such sales and repayments are in federal funds. The transaction may be handled like a loan with government securities pledged as security for the promissory note.

Interest Rates. Although the interest rate on federal funds varies according to supply and demand, it is usually highest when the Federal Reserve System is following a tight-money policy and not making additional amounts of Federal Reserve credit available by investing in the open market. Because a member bank may borrow from its Federal Reserve bank to adjust its reserve position, it was assumed that the maximum rate on federal funds would be the same as the rediscount rate of the district Federal Reserve bank. However, since 1963, many large commercial banks have been willing to pay a premium rate for federal funds when money is "tight" to avoid questions customarily asked at the "discount window." Trading at interest rates above the discount rate has been common but this may no longer be true after the "Fed" adopts its new discount policy (see Chapter 18).

Although there may be no difference between the interest rate on federal funds and the rate on other open-market paper, borrowing in the federal funds market may be preferred because it entails no loss due to price changes and no costs to be absorbed because of the spread between buying and selling prices (especially if the need for reserves is expected to be temporary). Some banks have a policy of not borrowing at their Federal Reserve banks except in an emergency, preferring the federal funds or other markets as the medium through which to adjust their reserve positions.

SHORT-TERM GOVERNMENT SECURITIES MARKET

The largest among the various divisions of the money market is that wherein short-term promises to pay of the U.S. government are traded. This includes a primary market wherein the securities are first offered for sale by the government and a secondary market wherein these securities are traded until their maturity dates. As the length of time to maturity increases, the money aspect of credit instruments lessens and the credit aspect increases. Therefore, only federal government securities that mature in one year or less are considered to be money market instruments. This limits government securities eligible for trading in the money market to United States Treasury bills and other Treasury securities as they approach maturity.

Treasury Bills.   Although the term "bill" suggests an order to pay, Treasury bills are promises to pay which are issued on a discount basis and are payable at par. Treasury bills with maturities of 91 days (13 weeks) and 182 days (26 weeks) are offered weekly, and bills with maturities of 9 months and one year are offered monthly. Tax anticipation bills (TAB's) have no set maturities; instead each issue runs from the date of issue to the next tax payment date. TAB's generally mature about seven days after a corporate tax date, but they are acceptable at par in payment of taxes. This arrangement gives the taxpayer the equivalent of one week's interest, which is usually reflected in the auction price when the bills are first offered in the market. If TAB's are not used to settle income taxes, they are paid at par on the maturity date. Because they are sold at a discount and repaid at par at maturity, their yield is the difference between the purchase price and the par value. Treasury bills are fully negotiable and are issued in denominations of $1,000 and multiples thereof up to $1 million.

Originally, Treasury bills were regarded as credit instruments to be used by the Treasury to bridge the gap between expenditures and receipts of quarterly income tax payments or to care for interim financing between issues of long-term bonds. Now, new issues of bills are offered to care for repayment of those maturing. Some flexibility in debt management is possible because a new issue of bills may be larger or smaller than the one being retired. In the latter case, the difference would be made up out of Treasury cash obtained in ways other than the sale of new Treasury bills.

Auction for Bills. The Federal Reserve banks, as agents for the Treasury, handle the details of financing and selling issues of bills to the highest bidders. Offers to buy are made in the form of sealed bids submitted to the Federal Reserve banks before the time set for closing (1:30 P.M. in New York, 2 P.M. in Dallas, etc.). Messengers from local banks, government securities dealers, and others arrive at the Federal Reserve bank minutes prior to the closing of the window where tenders to buy are placed. Out-of-town banks and other buyers submit bids by telegraph, letter, or through correspondent banks. Although medium-sized banks, large business corporations, and other investors may enter the bidding, government securities dealers and the large New York banks absorb about two thirds of each weekly issue.

TABLE 6–1

AVERAGE AUCTION RATES FOR UNITED STATES TREASURY BILLS

Auction Dates	3-Month	6-Month	9-Month	12-Month
1968: 6/17............5.578		5.633	. . .	. . .
6/24............5.238		5.485	. . .	. . .
6/25............ . . .		. . .	5.745	5.731
7/1............5.400		5.589	. . .	. . .
7/8............5.368		5.410	. . .	. . .
7/15............5.467		5.554	. . .	. . .

Source: Aubrey G. Langston & Co. Inc., Offering Letter, July 22, 1968.

(On one occasion, a New York bank bid successfully for an entire weekly issue, but it was not allotted the entire amount.)

With the exception of noncompetitive bidders discussed below, all bids are accepted in the order of offering prices, the highest bidder is the first to receive his allotment, and so on down the list until the issue is exhausted. All bids must be accompanied by personal checks or drafts equal to 2 percent of the face amount of the tenders. Noncompetitive bids are allotted in full up to a maximum specified (usually $200,000) from those bills that have been set aside before competitive bids are considered. Noncompetitive bidders are charged the average price paid by the auction investors (see Table 6–1).

The policy of alloting bills to small investors is most helpful to country banks that are not in a position to bid as knowingly as are large investors. Although it may not seem fair for some to pay more for bills than others, the difference between the highest and lowest bids is usually very small. Unlike the English tenderer for British Treasury bills who has the option of taking them any time during the following week, the successful bidder for United States Treasury bills must accept his bills on a specified day.

Auctions are held every Monday, and the following day the United States Treasury releases the detailed results of the auction—total bills applied for, bids accepted, high and low sales prices, and the average price. On the same day (Tuesday), the successful bidders are notified of their allotments and the price they must pay on Thursday when the bills are delivered (payment must be either in federal funds or maturing bills). On Thursday, the Treasury announces the next issue and invites the public to make tenders for it before the next Monday's closing time.

Secondary Market.   Unsuccessful bidders and other investors may acquire Treasury bills from securities dealers who purchase bills for resale to banks and nonbank buyers. After issuance, there is an active market in Treasury bills at prices set by dealers. The Federal Reserve System, through the Federal Reserve Bank of New York as its fiscal agent, is an active participant in the Treasury bill market. Purchases and sales of Treasury bills are made by telephone with negotiations to buy around the dealer's "bid" price and to sell around the dealer's "ask" price. The dealer's profit on bills is the "spread" between his ask price (what he will take to sell) and his bid price (what he will pay). Although the spread is small, profits are substantial because transactions of $5 million and $10 million are common. However, the prices quoted may be in effect only as long as the telephone conversation is in process. United States Treasury bills have been described as "the next thing to money" and, in terms of liquidity, this is true; but in one respect they are superior to money—they are earning assets.

Certificates of Indebtedness.   Prior to December, 1929, when the United States Treasury bill was first used, the Treasury depended on certificates of indebtedness to raise short-term funds. These certificates were interest-bearing obligations on which the principal and interest were paid at maturity. The main advantage claimed for Treasury bills, which to a large extent have replaced certificates of indebtedness, is that they are sold on a discount basis with the market determining the yield. In addition, the Treasury bill is considered to be a more liquid type of instrument and therefore better suited to the needs of banks and other institutional investors. However, the Treasury still uses certificates of indebtedness on occasion, and so they are included among the money-market instruments.

Other Securities. As other government securities approach maturity, they are included in money-market trading. These include Treasury notes (issued with maturities of 1 to 7 years) and government bonds (with original maturities of 7 to 40 years) as they near maturity. Although not government obligations, securities issued by government-sponsored banks and corporations are also traded in the money market. These include maturing issues of the federal home loan banks, federal land banks, federal intermediate credit banks, and the banks for cooperatives.

COMMERCIAL-PAPER MARKET

The oldest among the money-market credit instruments are short-term promissory notes of business firms sold through commercial-paper houses. In recent years, there has been an increase in the number of firms financing in this market due to the appearance of finance companies, many of whom sell their own notes—locating buyers and making sales terms. In open-market financing about 70 finance companies and about 400 business firms, representing most of the different industries in the United States, rely on commercial-paper dealers to sell their promissory notes (see Table 6–2).

TABLE 6–2

OPEN-MARKET COMMERCIAL PAPER AND DOLLAR ACCEPTANCES
(In Millions of Dollars)

| | Commercial and Finance Company Paper | | | Dollar Acceptances (Held by) | | | | |
| | | | | | | Federal Reserve Banks | | |
End of Period	Total	Placed through Dealers*	Placed Directly†	Total	Accepting Banks	Own Account	For Correspondents	Others
1962	6,000	2,088	3,912	2,650	1,153	110	86	1,301
1963	6,747	1,928	4,819	2,890	1,291	162	92	1,345
1964	8,361	2,223	6,138	3,385	1,671	94	122	1,498
1965	9,058	1,903	7,155	3,392	1,223	187	144	1,837
1966	13,279	3,089	10,190	3,603	1,198	193	191	2,022
1967	17,084	4,901	12,183	4,317	1,906	164	156	2,090
1968‡	17,509	5,930	11,579	4,430	1,778	87	118	2,447

* As reported by dealers (includes finance paper).
† As reported by finance companies that place their paper directly with investors.
‡ Data for 1968, for the end of April.
Source: *Federal Reserve Bulletin*, June, 1968, p. A–35.

United States Treasury bills and bankers' acceptances have specific maturity dates; therefore they may not constitute the best type of investment for one who may have to sell them before maturity. Under such circumstances, the investor would have to pay a broker a commission for selling them, and he would also assume the risk of loss due to a decline in price. It might be preferable for the investor to buy promissory notes of business firms and finance companies whose terms may be tailored to fit his needs. Usually, the negotiable promissory notes of business firms offer more flexibility than do Treasury bills or bankers' acceptances, and they carry a higher yield.[4]

Commercial-paper houses usually buy issues outright at a discount and resell the notes at a slightly higher price to investors. The commercial-paper house assumes the risk of loss that may result from a sudden change in money rates in the market, or even worse, of buying an issue that cannot be sold because investors shy away from it. They offer notes to investors with an option of returning them within 10 days or two weeks after purchase (the understanding being that they are to be returned only for adverse credit reasons).

In open-market financing, the relationship between investors and borrowers is impersonal, and notes are not renewed when they come due; therefore, business firms that borrow in the open market must meet high standards of liquidity as well as safety. Most of the firms that borrow in this market have seasonal working capital needs, strong commercial-bank connections, and large lines of credit. Their use of the commercial-paper market is considered as a supplement rather than an alternative to bank borrowing. However, they may finance in the open market to obtain more favorable interest rates and avoid the other costs of borrowing at banks. Traditionally, the prime rate on commercial paper is at least 1 percent below the prime rate charged by commercial banks for loans.

Corporations find it advantageous to finance in the commercial paper market because it advertises their financial strength. In addition, to obtaining lower interest rates, they may borrow larger amounts than they could obtain from commercial banks. Business firms that obtain short-term funds from commercial banks may be required to repay all such loans for part of a year (annual cleanup); and, during this period, they may transfer all financing to the open market rather

---

[4] Promissory notes sold in the commercial-paper market need not be registered with the Securities and Exchange Commission because they are issued for terms not exceeding nine months and cannot be extended, renewed, or automatically rolled over (see Chapter 21).

than to a second bank. After financing in the open market, many firms are able to obtain more favorable terms when they transfer back to banks.

It has been stated that financing in the commercial-paper market would be impossible when the "market gets tight," but a business firm whose financial position is excellent may finance in the market at any time. In recent years, the volume of financing in the open market has increased rapidly (see Table 6–2).

Among the chief investors in open-market commercial paper are small and medium-sized banks, and nonfinancial corporations (such as public utility, oil, steel, chemical, automobile, railroad, airlines, and electrical manufacturing companies). The advantages to banks in holding commercial paper include higher earnings than on other money-market obligations (such as Treasury bills and bankers' acceptances), assured liquidity because notes are paid at maturity (the last loss was in 1936 when the amount involved was 0.0078 percent of the total paper outstanding as of June of that year), greater diversity in assets because promises to pay may be acquired from firms in other areas and in industries outside the community, higher earnings because the bank's loanable funds may be kept more fully employed, and possibility of future expansion in business because of new outside business contacts. In addition, commercial paper is eligible for discount or as security for loans at Federal Reserve banks.

An open-market issue of commercial paper is usually in an even amount (such as $50,000, $100,000, or $1 million), and individual notes that make up an issue usually vary in amounts from $2,500 to $50,000, but they may be smaller or larger. Sometimes an issue of open-market commercial paper is secured by collateral held by a bank or trust company acting as trustee, but such issues are unusual.

Open-market commercial-paper notes are drawn "payable to bearer" or "payable to ourselves" by the maker, who signs and endorses them in blank so that they are negotiable by delivery only. Usually the notes are payable at maturity at a designated bank or banks, are traded at a discount, have maturities varying from 30 to 270 days at the time of issue, and are single-name (if a second name appears, it is usually the endorsement of an officer or of someone closely connected with the business firm or finance company that is borrowing). An issue of negotiable promissory notes is placed in the market by a broker who charges a commission varying from ⅛ of 1 percent computed on an annual basis. In comparing the cost of financing in the open market with the cost of bank borrowing, this fee should be added to the discount on the promissory note when sold. Other costs are minor (fees, cost of printing notes, etc.), and terms of selling may be negotiated over the telephone.

COMMERCIAL-BILL MARKET

One of man's oldest types of credit instruments, the bill of exchange, is traded in the commercial-bill market. Although its origin dates from the Middle Ages, it did not become an important credit instrument in the United States until after national banks were authorized to "accept" drafts from their customers in the Federal Reserve Act (1913). These acceptances are the primary obligations of the accepting bank. During the 1920's bankers' acceptances were the dominant credit instruments in the money market, occupying the same position as that currently held by Treasury bills.

Usually a bankers' acceptance is drawn under a previously issued letter of credit or credit agreement to finance imports, exports, or foreign or domestic storage of goods. Customarily drafts originate with the seller of goods, who draws the draft under provisions of a letter of credit. The draft is then sent to the issuer of the letter of credit and the latter acknowledges his obligation when he stamps or writes "accepted" or "I accept" on the bill followed by the date and appropriate signature on the face of the draft.

After acceptance, the commercial bill will have several weeks or months to run before maturity; and, during this time, it may be sold in the commercial-bill market. In addition to the signature of the drawer of the draft, the instrument carries the name of one of the most highly respected banks in the market. The relatively low discount (they are noninterest bearing like Treasury bills) at which bankers' acceptances are traded indicates that they approach Treasury bills in liquidity and safety.

In making grants of acceptance credit, commercial banks do not lend their funds (which are provided by the buyers of the bills), but they do assume liabilities, and therefore they must use the same care in this type of financing as they use in lending on a straight loan basis. Since no bank funds are committed immediately, there may be a temptation for a bank to resort to this type of financing after it has already committed all its loanable funds. Hence, when a bank's reserves are limited, the loan department may direct customers to its foreign exchange department, which handles requests for both domestic and foreign acceptance credit. However, legal restrictions and regulations of the Board of Governors of the Federal Reserve System under the law not only limit the total amount of acceptance credit that an individual bank may extend at one time but also define the terms of such transactions as to maximum maturity, purpose of financing, and required security (see Chapter 26).

Accepting institutions include state and national banks, a few specialized institutions, private banks, investment houses, and subsidiaries and agencies of foreign banking houses. About two thirds of the volume of acceptances outstanding are the obligations of New York banks and other institutions in New York, with those in San Francisco, Boston, Dallas, and Chicago following in that order. Because of the specialized nature of acceptance credit and the need for foreign banking connections, it is difficult for small banks to enter this field. The Federal Reserve System keeps a list of all banks in the United States that extend acceptance credit and reviews the condition of these banks periodically.

The banks which extend acceptance credit also buy most of the accepted drafts, and their holdings are divided into two classes—"own bills" and "bills bought," with the former representing the bills that were accepted by the bank holding them. A bank's profit on "bills bought" is the discount or the difference between the purchase price and the face amount. Generally commercial banks prefer to hold bills accepted by other banks, often swapping their own for those of other banks. The five active dealers in the bankers' acceptance market also trade in U.S. government securities and other securities.

The dealer's profit on bankers' acceptances is the spread between his buying and selling prices (at present, one eighth of 1 percent). Normally, most dealers sell acceptances immediately after buying them and hold only a small amount overnight. Their chief source of supply is accepting banks that have discounted their own bills at the dealers' buying rate. Usually, these banks expect to buy an equal amount of acceptances of other banks at the dealers' selling rate. Sometimes "swapping" of acceptances is made directly between two banks, thereby saving the spread between the dealers' buying and selling rates. Dealers also acquire bills for inland banks, where no "swapping" is expected.

The most important use of acceptance credit is financing foreign trade wherein the bill is tied to a specific transaction until it is accepted. The most important buyers in the commercial-bill market, which is located in New York, are foreign investors, who prefer bankers' acceptances because of yield, familiarity with this type of credit instrument, tax advantage (foreign holders' incomes from acceptances are not subject to federal income tax), and other features. Foreign banks may request their New York correspondent banks to sell them their own accepted bills or to purchase others for them, adding their own endorsement (thereby making them two-bank bills). (Both the Federal Reserve bank and commercial banks add a fee for the extra risk assumed by endorsement or guarantee.) Although dealers acquire bills for foreign customers, they do not endorse the bills which they handle. In addition to foreign and domestic banks, American business corporations have been attracted to this market by the relatively high yields (showing a preference for the 30-to-60-day maturities), while foreign investors prefer the longer maturities. However, some potential investors are discouraged because of the scarcity of acceptances and the odd denominations in which they appear, while others lack an understanding of the market.

During the formative period of the commercial-bill market, the Federal Reserve banks maintained the liquidity and safety of these instruments by purchasing all bills offered at their posted discount rates, which increased with the time to maturity of the bills offered. They were active buyers from 1915 to 1934 but made only occasional purchases from 1934 to 1955. Since that time, the procedure followed by the Federal Reserve System in buying bankers' acceptances has changed. At the present time, the manager of the Federal Reserve Open Market Account makes sales as well as purchases to parallel Federal Reserve action in the government securities market. Instead of supporting the market by pegging yields, the current policy is to treat buying and selling as an aspect of open-market credit policy (see Chapter 18).

In buying bankers' acceptances, the Federal Reserve System relies on the name of the accepting bank and those of other endorsers, if any. The problem is merely that of verifying the negotiability of the instrument and conformity with regulations of the Board of Governors and established acceptance practice (only rarely will the credit standing of the business firm drawing the acceptance be checked). The change in policy of the Federal Reserve System to selling as well as buying acceptances was initiated to broaden and strengthen the market.

Most businessmen who are eligible for acceptance credit are also eligible for direct bank loans; they may, however, find it advantageous to use acceptance credit if the market rate thereon plus the commission is less than the interest rate on direct loans. Usually, no specific compensatory deposit balance is required as in the case of direct loans, but banks usually give loan customers an interest rebate on prepaid loans, which is seldom done when acceptance credit is used. So some borrowers may regard acceptance credit as being more expensive than financing with direct loans (assuming the interest and other costs are equal).

In financing business transactions, businessmen will use the methods specified by those with whom they deal, and sellers, in turn, will cooperate with their customers in working out acceptable sales terms. These terms may include the use of trade acceptances, which are the same as bankers' acceptances except that the accepter is a name other than a bank (usually the buyer of the goods being financed). If endorsed by an accepting bank, trade acceptances have the same standing in the market as bankers' acceptances.

NEGOTIABLE TIME CERTIFICATES OF DEPOSIT

During the early 1960's, the rapid growth in business activity increased the demand for savings, with the result that the Board of Governors of the Federal Reserve System authorized banks to pay a higher rate of interest on their time and savings deposits.[5] This made it possible for commercial banks to compete with savings and loan associations and other institutions for savings and the surplus funds of corporations (see Chapter 11).

Negotiable time certificates of deposit (called CD's) were developed to attract the surplus funds of business firms, local governments, and other institutions. These credit instruments are promises to pay having variable maturity dates at the time of issue, usually from 30 days to one year. Although they are not payable prior to maturity, they may be sold to others directly or through brokers and/or dealers. Customarily, CD's are issued in denominations of $100,000 and multiples thereof, of which the most common is $1 million. A survey made by the Federal Deposit Insurance Corporation indicated that fewer than 3,700 banks issue negotiable certificates of deposit and fewer than 850 banks issue them in denominations in excess of $100,000. Of the banks that issue CD's in larger denominations, 80 percent hold deposits in excess of $500 million.[6]

[5] In August, 1964, the First National Bank of Boston offered its short-term promises to pay in the money market in order to raise funds. Such short-term notes are not deposits and are therefore not subject to the same reserve requirements as are certificates of deposit. However, few have been issued, since the Board of Governors ruled that all such notes issued by banks would be subject to the same reserve requirements applicable to bank deposits.

[6] K. A. Randall, *Control of Time and Savings Deposits*, an address before the Southwestern Graduate School of Banking, Southern Methodist University, Dallas, Texas, July 27, 1966.

CALL LOANS

A broker's call loan is a promise to pay issued by a "person engaged for all or part of his time in the business of buying and selling securities, who in the transaction concerned acts for or buys a security from or sells a security to a customer," with securities pledged as collateral.[7] The market for call loans developed in New York during the early 1830's and continued to be an important segment of the money market until World War II. At one time, the money market was primarily concerned with call loans made by banks to brokers operating on the New York Stock Exchange. Until 1946, call and demand loans were impersonal, with loan transactions arranged through the money desk of the New York Stock Exchange.

When a commercial bank needed to adjust its reserve position, it would "call" upon brokers to repay their loans. If such calls were widespread, the brokers were forced to sell their securities to raise funds unless they could borrow from other banks. Such forced sales brought down the prices of securities, and the decline in securities prices forced brokers to call upon their "margin" customers for more protection. If they could not supply additional funds or securities, the customers' pledged securities were sold, which resulted in a further decline in the prices of securities.

For many years economists criticized the commercial banking system for its dependence on call loans to brokers and dealers for liquidity, because such loans reflect prices and activities in the stock exchange and other securities which are often dominated by speculators. Now, in appraising the liquidity of the money market, attention should be focused on factors other than fluctuations in the volume of call loans because they are no longer used to adjust bank reserves.

Since 1946, call loans have been negotiated directly with banks. They are now comparable to other customer loans and are seldom called by banks to adjust their reserve positions. The one exception is call loans to U.S. government securities dealers which banks are not hesitant to call and, as agents, to place with other lenders. Nonbank dealers in government securities operate with a small amount of capital and obtain funds primarily from commercial banks, insurance companies, business corporations, and others. Most of their stock-in-trade consists of U.S. government securities, which they pledge as security for loans. The volume of credit needed depends on the

---

[7] *Uniform Commercial Code*, Sec. 8–303.

market for government securities (it may be from $2 billion to $4 billion or more).[8]

SUMMARY

The credit instruments traded in the money market include federal funds, Treasury bills and other short-term promises to pay of the U.S. government and its agencies, promissory notes of business firms, bankers' acceptances, negotiable time certificates of deposit, and promissory notes of dealers in U.S. government securities.

All money-market instruments are highly liquid, but they vary as to their money and credit features, depending on the time element. The drafts and transfers ordering Federal Reserve banks to change title to deposits of member banks (federal funds) are usually on an overnight basis. While the money feature is the dominant characteristic of federal funds, the credit feature appears more prominently in other money-market instruments.

The largest division of the money market is that wherein short-term promises to pay of the federal government are traded. The most important of these is the Treasury bill, but others include obligations maturing in one year or less. Treasury bills are fully negotiable, issued in denominations of $1,000 and multiples thereof, sold at a discount, and repaid at par. The primary market for these securities is an auction market wherein most sales are made on a competitive basis, with details handled by the Federal Reserve banks as fiscal agents for the United States Treasury. In addition to Treasury bills, the government securities traded in the money market include certificates of indebtedness and other securities approaching maturity, as well as short-term and/or maturing issues of government-sponsored banks and corporations.

The instrument traded in the commercial-paper market is commercial paper, the promissory note of a business firm or finance company which is usually unsecured by any pledge of collateral. The commercial-paper market is closely related to the customer loan market, and, from the viewpoint of business firms, these markets supplement each other as sources of funds.

Another segment of the money market is the commercial bill market, wherein the bill of exchange, one of the oldest types of credit instruments, is traded. When these bills of exchange or drafts are "accepted" by a bank, they become bankers' acceptances; when ac-

[8] For current statistics on "dealer transactions," "dealer position," and "dealer financing," see current issue of the *Federal Reserve Bulletin*.

cepted by a name other than a bank, they become trade acceptances. Because acceptances are used to finance specific trade transactions, the volume of acceptances outstanding is closely related to the amount of dollar financing of foreign trade and foreign and domestic storage of goods.

The newest among the money market instruments are the negotiable certificates of deposit which are promises to pay of commercial banks. Although these so-called CD's are not payable prior to maturity, they may be sold to others through brokers and dealers. The brokers' call loan market has been a segment of the money market since the early 1830's. At one time commercial banks relied heavily on call loans to adjust their reserve positions, but they are now generally regarded much as customer loans except those to government security dealers.

QUESTIONS AND PROBLEMS

1. (*a*) What is meant by the New York money market? (*b*) Identify its different divisions.
2. Analyze: "The federal funds market refers to the borrowing and lending of a special kind of money—deposit balances in the Federal Reserve Banks—at a specified rate of interest." (Board of Governors of the Federal Reserve System, *The Federal Funds Market* [Washington, D.C., 1959], p. 1.)
3. Explain: "The money market was continuously firm during April, and Federal funds were generally quoted at a substantial premium over the prevailing discount rate. This premium rose as high as 7/8 percentage point at the start of the month. . . ." (Federal Reserve Bank of New York, *Monthly Review*, May, 1968, p. 97.)
4. "A Treasury bill is simply a promise by the United States to pay a certain sum without interest on a specified future date." (Carl H. Madden, *The Money Side of "The Street"* [New York: Federal Reserve Bank of New York, 1959], p. 48.) Does this mean that investors are not rewarded for holding United States Treasury bills? Explain by describing how new issues are distributed.
5. Explain: Government securities dealer "quotations differ according to the issue under consideration. Treasury bills are quoted on a yield basis. For example, Treasury bills maturing three months from now may be quoted at 4.90 'bid' and 4.80 'asked' !" (Federal Reserve Bank of Cleveland, *Economic Review*, December, 1967, p. 4.)
6. Discuss: "Commercial paper placed directly by a major finance company was as follows: 30 to 119 days, 6⅛%; 120 to 270 days, 6%. Commercial paper sold through dealers, 30 to 270 days, 6¼ to 6½%." (*Wall Street Journal*, July 10, 1968, p. 16.)

7. "During the formative period of the commercial-bill market, the Federal Reserve banks purchased all bills offered at their posted discount rates. . . ." What is the practice in regard to commercial bills at the present time?

8. Analyze: "Being claims against banks, time certificates of deposit are, like the acceptances . . . credit instruments with the lowest degree for risk attainable in the open market for short-term paper." (Lawrence L. Crum, *Time Deposits in Present-Day Commercial Banking*, University of Florida Monographs, Social Science, No. 20 [Gainesville, Florida: University of Florida Press, 1963], p. 43.)

9. Distinguish between (*a*) call loans to brokers on stock exchange collateral and call loans to dealers in federal government securities; (*b*) "today's money" and "tomorrow's money," and (*c*) auction market and negotiated market.

10. In what ways is the New York money market using cash holdings of nonbank firms and eliminating spare cash of banks?

CHAPTER 7

History of Commercial Banking

HISTORICALLY, the creation and development of banks paralleled the growth and development of the United States. Commercial banking is closely linked to money because these banks have always been an important creator of means of payment—first in the form of paper money and later as deposit or checkbook currency. In the United States, emphasis on the money-creating function of banks dates back to colonial times when banks were regarded primarily as a source of currency. However, as indicated by the earning assets which they held, banks were also suppliers of credit. They lend their credit in the form of deposits—exchanging their deposit liabilities for interest-bearing promissory notes of borrowers. This exchange of promises has increased financial assets and financial liabilities by the same amount and, in the process, has added to the liquidity of the economy. Throughout the history of the United States, the dual function of commercial banks—money creation and credit creation—has been the cause of conflict between those who want loanable funds and those who want sound money.

FORMATIVE BANKING, 1782–1862

Chartering Policies. When the Declaration of Independence was signed in 1776, there was not a single incorporated bank in the country. All of the "land banks" of the colonial period had been liquidated after the British parliament made the formation of joint-stock companies illegal without its specific approval (1741). This banking situation was not unusual, because the century of banking was still around the corner. To be sure, the "Old Lady of Threadneedle Street," the Bank of England, had been in existence since 1694, but banking was still in its pioneer stage. Private firms such as merchants, pawnbrokers, and goldsmiths dominated the poorly developed financial machinery of the era. Until the end of the 18th century, commercial banking as well as most other enterprises were carried on by sole or single proprietors or firms consisting of a few partners. A few charters had been granted for the purpose of giving a monopoly or making a concession to certain individuals or groups of individuals.[1]

Prior to 1838, American governments followed the English colonial policy of prohibiting the organization of new banks without the specific approval of Congress or the local state legislature. It was difficult to obtain a charter because of the unfriendly attitude toward banks which were regarded merely as institutions for the issuance of paper money. Those opposed to banks included not only adherents of the "hard money" school but also such famous and influential men as Presidents John Adams, Thomas Jefferson, and Andrew Jackson. The belief that banks were nothing more than institutions for issuing paper money persisted long after the operations of banks had demonstrated otherwise. "As late as 1853 the Secretary of the Treasury expressed the hope that the increase in the supply of the precious metals in this country (following gold discovery in California) would continue a few years longer so that we might yet find it possible to abolish banks and return to a purely metallic currency."[2]

Prior to the Civil War, bank chartering policies varied widely, not only in point of time but also among the various chartering authorities. At different times and in different states, banking was prohibited, practiced as a private monopoly, operated as a public or semipublic monopoly, or free to all under supervision of the government.

Note-Issue Banking. Almost without exception, chartered banks issued paper money in the form of engraved or printed promises to pay in denominations as low as 5 cents and as large as $10,000. Banks used these notes in their day-to-day activities, to pay salaries of employees, to purchase supplies, and to repay depositors. Since the initial cost of forming a bank was that of printing the notes, it was easier to start a bank with the note-issue privilege than without it.[3]

The success of a note-issue bank depended on its ability to lend

[1] For illustration, note the monopoly given to certain colonizing and trade companies famous in American history (London Company, Plymouth Company, Dutch West India Company) and the charters given to individuals (Sir Walter Raleigh, Roger Williams, Lord Baltimore, and William Penn). As a result, the country inherited an animosity toward business monopolies and highly centralized government.

[2] James Guthrie, *Finance Reports* (1853), p. 10; Message of the Governor of Michigan (January 2, 1843), in United States House of Representatives, 29th Cong., 1st sess., Doc. 226, p. 1215 (quoted).

[3] Bagehot justifies the use of the note-issue privilege as follows: "No nation as yet has arrived at a great system of deposit banking without going first through the preliminary stage of note issue. . . ." (Walter Bagehot, *Lombard Street* [14th ed.; London: John Murray, 1915], p. 88.)

and to keep its notes in circulation. Except in larger commercial centers, bank customers made little or no use of checkbook currency, and there was little deposit creation as we know it today. The volume of credit outstanding depended on the use of bank notes as a medium of exchange and as a store of value. From the viewpoint of a bank, the ideal note-issue transaction was one that involved lending bank notes that never came back to the bank for redemption.

The interest of each individual bank in keeping its notes outstanding also explains why a monopoly of note issue was important. While this monopoly might not mean that the total volume of bank paper money would be less, it does mean that the volume issued by a single bank would be more. If there are two or more banks, it is to the interest of each to have fewer of the other banks' notes in circulation. Furthermore, if the existing banks can keep the note-issue field to themselves so much the better; hence, the continuous unsavory political pressure on legislative bodies not to charter new banks and not to renew the charters of existing banks (other than those of the banks exerting the pressure) when old charters expired. However, gradually new banks were formed either through subterfuge[4] or because of changes in chartering policies.

Technically, bank notes and specie were interchangeable but, in practice, this was not the case, because of the inconvenience of remitting notes to the place of issue and the unwillingness or inability of certain individual banks to pay specie on demand. Nonconvertibility by local banks had popular support, especially when requests for conversion came from outside the community. The inconvenience of remitting notes to the place of issue usually meant that these notes were at a discount in terms of local currency. When wildcat banks were located in the wilderness (banking laws required them to have some nominal place of business), this inconvenience of location was exploited in a ruthless way.[5] However, this was not the only trick resorted to by some banks to keep notes from being returned. Inn-

[4] In 1799, the Manhattan Company received a charter containing a provision that permitted it to use its capital not needed in the water business "in the purchase of public or other stocks or any moneyed transactions or operations not inconsistent with the laws and constitution of the state of New York."

[5] The typical wildcat bank of this period has been described as follows: "The speculator comes to Indianapolis with a bundle of bank notes in one hand and the stock in the other; in twenty-four hours he is on his way to some distant point of the union to circulate what he denominates a legal currency. . . ." (A. M. Davis, *The Origin of the National Banking System*, Publications of the National Monetary Commission [Washington, D.C.: U.S. Government Printing Office, 1911], Vol. V, p. 20.)

keepers, who were channels through which notes could be distributed widely, were preferred borrowers of local banks. Borrowers who would accept small-denomination notes were preferred to those who requested large-denomination notes because the former stayed in circulation longer, and borrowers who spent notes outside the community were preferred to those who spent them locally. However, it does not mean that all banks followed these practices.

First Chartered Banks. In January, 1782, the Bank of North America opened for business in Philadelphia (the political and financial capital of the United States at that time), and this event marked the beginning of modern banking in the United States. In chartering the bank, Congress had doubts as to the validity of its act and recommended that the state legislature "pass such laws as might be necessary to give effects to its Act." Subsequently, the bank received charters from other states as well as Pennsylvania, but the Bank of North America operated chiefly under the Pennsylvania charter until 1863, when it became a national bank.[6]

The charter of the Bank of North America provided for share capital equal to $10,000,000, but it began operations with $400,000 in cash, of which $250,000 was provided by the federal government. The bank not only made currency and credit available to merchants and others but also aided in financing the national government and the state of Pennsylvania during the last stages of the Revolutionary War. The government had no voice in management of the bank, and it operated primarily as a private institution throughout its history.

Within a few years after the opening of the Bank of North America, New York, Massachusetts, and other states imitated Pennsylvania in making provisions for state-chartered banks. After 10 years of banking in the United States, there were 14 banks having an average capitalization of $1 million (which was very small compared with the capitalization of today's medium-size and large banks). There were no minimum reserve requirements, but banks' charters limited note circulation in terms of capital (usually equal to but sometimes two or three times a bank's capital). Most of the assets of the banks were in the form of commercial loans, including bills of

[6] In 1863 the Bank of North America entered the National Banking System without changing its name, claiming that it already had a national charter. This position was not seriously challenged by the Comptroller of the Currency. Currently, it is a part of the First Pennsylvania Banking and Trust Company. For additional information on the organization of banks in the United States, see *Federal Banking Laws and Reports, 1780–1912*, (Committee on Banking and Currency, U.S. Senate, 50th Anniversary 1913–1963 [Washington, D.C.: U.S. Government Printing Office, 1963]), pp. 1–6.

exchange arising out of financing foreign and domestic trade. In addition to lending their credit in the form of bank notes, these banks accepted deposits. The early banks were successful, and many of them are still in existence, either under their original names or under new names, changed as a result of mergers, reincorporation under national law, or addition of a trust business. During the first 27 years of American banking, not a single bank failed (the first bank failure occurred in 1809 when the Farmers Exchange Bank of Glocester, Rhode Island, closed).

After 1800, a bank was among the first institutions to be formed in a new community because the need for credit was great. The loans made by such banks differed from the short-term, self-liquidating commercial type loans made by banks in cities on the Atlantic seaboard. Although most of the new banks' loans were short term, they were customarily secured by land, buildings, and other forms of fixed assets. This was not good banking practice, and only a relatively few of these early banks withstood the test of time. Nevertheless, they contributed to bringing land under cultivation, establishing foundries and mills, developing mineral resources, building roads and canals, and settling the continent.

Bank of the United States. Realizing the government's need for a national bank, Alexander Hamilton was influential in obtaining a charter for the first Bank of the United States in 1791 for a 20-year period.[7] This bank, whose main office was in Philadelphia, operated branches in the leading cities of the country. One fifth of the bank's total capital of $10 million was subscribed by the federal government.

The first Bank of the United States issued paper money that was made government tender by Congress for as long as it was convertible into gold or silver coins. The bank's credit, in the form of notes, was used by the state-chartered banks as reserves. As was also the case with the Bank of England at that time, the first Bank of the United States also accepted deposits and made loans to business firms and individuals, combining the activities of a commercial bank with those of a central bank (see Table 7–1). Judging from available reports, the relationship between the bank and the government was very satisfac-

[7] See *Ibid.*, pp. 7–90, and also National Monetary Commission, "Act of February 25, 1791," in *Laws of the United States concerning Money, Banking and Loans, 1778–1909* (Washington, D.C.: U.S. Government Printing Office, 1910), Vol. II, pp. 269–76.

TABLE 7–1

STATEMENT OF THE FIRST BANK OF THE UNITED STATES, JANUARY, 1811

RESOURCES (IN MILLIONS)		LIABILITIES (IN MILLIONS)	
Loans and discounts	$14.6	Capital	$10.0
U.S. 6 percent and other U.S.		Surplus	0.5
stock	2.8	Circulation	5.0
Due from other banks	0.9	Individual deposits	5.9
Real estate	0.5	U.S. government deposits	1.9
Notes of other banks	0.4	Due to other banks	0.6
Specie	5.0	Unpaid drafts outstanding	0.2
Total	$24.2	Total*	$24.2

*Individual items total less than $24,200,000 because of rounding.
Source: *Annual Report of the Comptroller of the Currency, 1916*, Vol. II, p. 912, Table 93.

tory. The bank transacted most of the government's fiscal business and lent money to the Treasury in anticipation of tax revenues. It acted as custodian of public funds and transmitted them from place to place through its branch-banking system.

The three state-chartered banks in existence when the first Bank of the United States began operations were the Bank of North America in Philadelphia, Massachusetts Bank in Boston, and the Bank of New York in New York; but by 1805, there were 75 banks. During this time opposition to rechartering the Bank of the United States increased. State banks objected to competition from the bank's branches and to forced redemption of their note issues. After the rechartering bill was defeated, the assets of the Bank of the United States were sold to private investors. The bank ceased being a federal institution on March 4, 1811; and, when its assets were liquidated, a bonus of $34 was paid on each share of stock.

The liquidation of the Bank of the United States was followed by a trying war period (1812–15), during which (1) the banks suspended specie payments and expanded severalfold the volume of bank paper money; (2) the government issued noninterest-bearing Treasury notes in denominations as low as $3; (3) specie disappeared from circulation, and barbers, bartenders, manufacturers, and others issued fractional paper money; (4) there was more than 100 percent inflation of prices; and (5) the government had all the difficulties in tax collection and borrowing that are associated with a confused currency and banking situation. Most of these difficulties could have been avoided if the Bank of the United States had been rechartered. Following the financial debacle of the War of 1812, one of the reform measures taken by Congress was the chartering of the second Bank of the United States in 1816.[8]

Second Bank of the United States. The second Bank of the United States, chartered in 1816,[9] was capitalized for $35 million. The federal government provided one fifth of its capital and, in return, the bank performed fiscal services such as collecting and holding deposits and transferring them from place to place as requested. The bank provided state banks with reserve money and acted as the regulator of their circulating notes.

Although the charter of the second Bank of the United States was similar to that of the first, there were numerous differences that showed the development of banking principles during the intervening period. All deposits as well as notes were to be redeemed in legal-tender money (reflecting the increased importance of banks' deposit liabilities). Notes were issued in denominations no smaller than $5 and post notes were limited to denominations of $100 or more and to maturities of 60 days or less. Post notes—time promises to pay—were a means of borrowing from the public with or without interest. They were widely used at this time, but often they were issued in such small denominations that the recipients mistook them for demand notes.

The first and second Bank of the United States shared the note-issue privilege with state-chartered banks, but the notes of the former were accepted nationally and were used as reserves by state-chartered banks to redeem their bank notes. Out of the acceptance of government deposits, there developed the central-bank function of regulator of the currency, which is now considered one of the most important functions of a central bank.

When the first and the second Bank of the United States received tax receipts in the form of bank notes of other banks, they became the creditors of these banks (in contrast to Federal Reserve banks, which are debtors to member banks). Possession of these notes gave the "public bank" a simple and effective device for restraining the note-issue practices of other banks. By returning these notes to the

[8] During the interim between the first and second Bank of the United States, Congress chartered the Bank of Washington, Bank of Alexandria, The Mechanics Bank of Alexandria, The Farmers Bank of Alexandria, Bank of the Potomac, and the Union Bank of the District of Columbia. Congress approved of the acts of legislative assemblies in the territories that provided for the organization of banks and continued to charter banks in the District of Columbia after it had passed the Act of April 10, 1816, which provided for the second Bank of the United States. See National Monetary Commission, *op. cit.,* pp. 288–91.

[9] *Ibid.,* pp. 295–310. See also "Act of April 10, 1816," *Federal Banking Law and Reports 1780–1912,* pp. 127–42.

issuing banks for redemption, the Bank of the United States could exert pressure on the issuing banks to keep reserves in the form of bank notes of the Bank of the United States or gold and silver, thereby limiting the volume of other banks' notes (debts) within their ability to pay on demand. The state banks resented the regulation of currency by the Bank of the United States, wanting the right to pay their creditors, including the Bank of the United States, if and when they pleased.[10] The state-chartered banks found support from the agrarian interests, who wanted an abundant supply of cheap credit; from those who felt that the sovereign rights of the states were being violated; and from those who believed in hard money and opposed all banks that issued paper money.[11]

A bill providing for the rechartering of the bank was passed by Congress in 1831 but was vetoed by President Andrew Jackson, and later attempts to recharter the bank failed. (Again there was a general suspension of specie payments during the panic of 1837.) In 1836, the Bank of the United States received a Pennsylvania charter and continued to operate as a state bank until it suspended payments in 1839 and was liquidated in 1841.

Correction of Note-Issue Abuses. One characteristic of American banking is governmental supervision and regulation, which started before the Civil War when it seemed necessary to protect noteholders from losses. Among the earliest steps taken to achieve this objective were laws that (1) limited the paper money issues of banks to a specific proportion of their capital; (2) penalized banks that failed to redeem their notes in specie; and (3) placed a minimum on the size denomination of notes (the homing power of large-denomination notes is greater than that of small-denomination notes).

Although bank notes were convertible at par over the counters of the issuing banks, they often circulated at a discount in distant places because the holders were unwilling to bear the cost of sending them back to the issuing banks for redemption. This meant that

[10] Legal attacks were made on the Bank, and Maryland attempted to tax the Baltimore branch out of existence. The Supreme Court upheld the constitutionality of the chartering act (1819) and also stated that without the consent of Congress a state could not interfere by taxation or otherwise with the operation of a bank chartered by Congress (1824). See *McCulloch* v. *Maryland*, Wheat 316, and *Osborne* v. *United States*, 9 Wheat 738. It was contended that states, as well as the national government, did not have the legal right to charter banks issuing paper money, and it was not until 1837 that the power of states to do so was confirmed by the Supreme Court.

[11] For a reappraisal of the controversy over rechartering of the Bank of the United States see Bray Hammond, "Jackson, Biddle, and the Bank of the United States," *Journal of Economic History*, Vol. VII, No. 1 (May, 1947), pp. 1–23.

businessmen and others were frequently paid in money that was at a discount from face value (as they are today when they accept a check on a nonpar clearing bank). Private bankers, "money brokers" and (later) chartered banks made a profit by buying these notes at a discount with local currency and then collecting them at par for the issuing banks. This business was speculative because there was no assurance that the issuing bank would be able or willing to redeem its notes.

In 1818, the merchants of Boston organized the Suffolk Bank, which announced that it would accept and pay only the notes of the out-of-town banks that maintained redemption deposits with it. Later, the Suffolk Bank presented a plan wherein each country bank was requested to keep a permanent deposit with it and an additional one sufficiently large to redeem at par all the notes received by the Suffolk Bank. In return, the Suffolk Bank received the notes and gave credit for them on the day following their receipts. Notes of country banks were held subject to order of the issuing bank and were sent home for redemption unless the country bank arranged for redemption in Boston. The expenses of operating the plan were cared for (as is true of modern correspondent banking) by fees and by income earned from lending these bankers' balances.

Originally, many interior banks refused to join the Suffolk Banking System, but, after the other seven Boston banks agreed to participate, the interior banks were forced to join. The forcing process used was simple. The notes of interior banks not in the system were promptly sent back for redemption. If the notes were reissued, the process was repeated promptly. By 1825, virtually all New England banks were in the system, and, from then on until the Civil War, the notes of New England banks circulated at par throughout that section and were in considerable demand in other parts of this country and in Canada.

The Suffolk Banking System recognized the importance of convertibility not only at the bank of issue but also in a central redemption center. In a banking system made up of a few banks with a large number of branches, serving a small geographical area, provisions for convertibility at the branch and head offices may be sufficient; but, where there are hundreds of local banks, central redemption is necessary if a discount on notes is to be prevented.[12] This was recognized

---

[12] In May, 1840, the New York State legislature required all banks outside New York, Brooklyn, or Albany to appoint an agent and to open an office in Albany or New York for the purpose of redeeming their notes at no more than one half of 1

by Congress when it required national banks to accept at par the notes of other national banks and to keep a 5 percent redemption fund in Washington where banks could redeem the notes of other banks. Today, the counterpart of bank note issues is personal checks; and, like the Suffolk Bank, the Federal Reserve banks hold deposits of banks to be used in their par clearing and collection operations (see Chapter 9).

A more serious problem than that of preventing discounts on notes was that of preventing losses of noteholders because of bank failures. Before the Civil War, an average of 5 percent of bank notes became worthless each year. One attempt to protect the public from this loss was the creation of the Safety Fund System of New York. Under this system, which was managed by the state government, each bank was subject to a yearly assessment of one half of 1 percent of its capital until 3 percent was paid. If the fund's assets became depleted, additional contributions could be requested at a rate of one half of 1 percent per year. Because the banks were paying dividends in excess of 7 percent, it may be assumed that the burden was not excessive. Although the debates on the bill stressed bank notes, the law was so drawn that both depositors and noteholders were covered.

The Safety-Fund System was tested severely as a result of bank failures (1837–42), and the claims were so great that the fund's assets were depleted. Then the law was changed, limiting the future protected liabilities to notes and freezing future claims until all pending ones were met. By 1866 all banks in the system had secured new charters either under the state "Free" Banking Act of 1838 or under the National Bank Act of 1863, as amended. In the final accounting, all claims presented to the fund were met, and there was a surplus of $13,000 given to the New York treasury. The basis of the contributions (capital) tended to penalize banks that had the largest capital/liability ratio and to favor the more speculative type of bank with the smaller capital/liability ratio. In contrast, Federal Deposit Insurance Corporation assessments are based on total deposit liabilities adjusted.

Reserve Requirements. One characteristic of American banking has been the policy of requiring banks to keep a minimum percentage of deposits and/or notes as a cash reserve, originally to protect

---

percent discount. R. E. Chaddock, "The Safety-Fund Banking System in New York State, 1829–1866," *Banking in the United States before the Civil War* (publication of the National Monetary Commission [Washington, D.C.: U.S. Government Printing Office, 1911]), Vol. IV, p. 307.

holders of banks' promises to pay and later as a credit-control device. In 1837, the state of Virginia made provisions for the first reserve requirement, a cash reserve of 20 percent of banks' note circulation; and, by 1840, Georgia, Mississippi, and Ohio had followed suit.[13] With the passage of the National Bank Act, this principle of reserve requirements was extended to both banks' notes and deposits, and it has since become fairly general throughout the country.[14] However, no modern government has achieved the banking standards embodied in the Louisiana Bank Act of 1842.

Prior to the Civil War, the most restrictive laws pertaining to organization and operation of banks were those of Louisiana. In 1842, its state legislature passed a banking act that made no provisions for new banks, and this was sufficient to check a tendency to create too many banks during business booms. This law forced banks to protect both noteholders and depositors, recognizing that both were fundamentally the same sort of obligation. The unusually high standard set for minimum reserve requirements provided for 100 percent backing for notes and deposits—one third in specie and two thirds in short-term paper. The law also provided for quarterly examinations by state officials, monthly publication of bank statements, and weekly settlement of interbank balances. It also prohibited banks from paying out notes other than their own, and this necessitated sending notes to banks that had issued them, thus testing their ability to redeem them.

One of the most significant provisions of the Louisiana Bank Act of 1842 was that pertaining to reserve requirements (the "Forestall System" named for Edmond J. Forestall, a New Orleans banker who was the author of the bill). Assets to be used as reserves for notes and demand deposits consisted of one third specie and two thirds commercial paper payable in 90 days (renewals were forbidden). Liquidity was emphasized not only by this provision but also by the requirement to segregate the loans and investments made out of a bank's capital funds and to separate so-called "movement" and "deadweight" loans, in modern terminology "liquid" and "nonliquid" loans. The Louisiana Bank Act continued in effect until the Civil War Reconstruction period, but the reserve-requirement system embodied

[13] See Bray Hammond, "Banking Before the Civil War," *Banking and Monetary Studies,* ed. Deane Carson (Homewood, Ill.: Richard D. Irwin, Inc., 1963), pp. 10–11.

[14] Illinois is the only state which does not have a minimum percentage reserve requirement for state-chartered banks. The reserve requirement for banks' notes found in the National Bank Act was later repealed.

therein did not spread widely because of the scarcity of specie and short-term commercial paper. In most sections of the country the need for long-term credit was paramount—not for trade but for exploitation and development of capital resources. Often there was a conflict of interests, with pressure for loans (credit) exceeding the pressure to meet obligations (bank notes and deposits). The Louisiana Bank Act was unique in American banking history in that it linked money and banking in a specific way.

New Chartering Policy. Until 1838 a special act of a state legislature was necessary before a new bank charter could be obtained. The conditions that resulted may be illustrated by the situation in New York State. Prior to 1804, there were only six banks, and they made common cause against all applicants for bank charters. By lavish expenditures of funds, however, bank charters could be secured. The new bank charters invariably went to friends of the political party in power. White summed up the situation as follows: "In short, politics, monopoly, and bribery constitute the key to banking in the early history of the state."[15]

In 1838 New York joined in the nationwide condemnation of banking. An antimonopoly legislature met and passed a general banking law under which charters could be obtained without a special act of the legislature. This law permitted banks to be organized under prescribed standards of organization and operation, which included deposits of collateral with the state comptroller in amounts equal to the volume of notes issued. If a bank failed, the collateral was sold and the proceeds paid to its noteholders.

The democratic nature of the free-banking system and the prospect of abundant paper money and credit appealed to the public, and, within a short time, 14 additional states adopted similar laws.[16] From 1834 to 1861 the number of banks increased from 500 to 1,600, and the states that had enacted free-banking laws, particularly those in the West, accounted for most of the increase in number. (This movement was related to that permitting business firms to incorporate under general laws if they met certain minimum standards.)

The organization of hundreds of banks led to the development

[15] Horace White, *Money and Banking* (5th ed.; Boston: Ginn & Co., 1914), p. 303.

[16] While the free-banking law was being considered by the New York State legislature, Michigan passed a general bank incorporation act. Prior to 1860 the following additional states had passed similar laws: Connecticut, Florida, Illinois, Indiana, Iowa, Louisiana, Ohio, Massachusetts, New Jersey, Pennsylvania, Tennessee, Vermont, Virginia, and Wisconsin.

of correspondent banking out of necessity in a banking system made up of many unit banks. This was an important factor in New York becoming the money market of the nation (New York banks held most of the nation's gold reserves). Growth in the value of check currency led to the organization of the New York Clearinghouse in 1854 (incorporated in 1855), with $1 million contributed by the five largest banks in the area. The Boston Clearinghouse was organized in 1855, and the next year clearinghouses were organized in Philadelphia, Baltimore, and Cleveland (sufficient evidence of the wide use of checks in cities).

Branch Banking.   While unit banking dominated in many states, branch banking developed in others. In some there was only one chartered bank which had offices to serve many communities (Ohio, 1845; Indiana, 1855; and Iowa, 1858). Branch banking had been tried in the Northeast but failed to gain a foothold because local communities had sufficient capital to finance unit banks and local government and civic groups resented any outside interests that might curtail the privileges and benefits that should "rightfully" go to local citizens. However, by 1860 there were 39 banks that operated 222 branches located in Virginia (39), Ohio (36), Missouri (33), Kentucky (31), Indiana (20), North Carolina (19), Tennessee (17), and Iowa (13).[17] Thus, branch banking is an old issue in the United States.

Mixed Ownership.   Many of the early banks were semipublic institutions with state governments owning part of the capital stock of the banks which they chartered. In the East, where banking needed little encouragement, the purpose was to participate in banks' earnings. In the South and West, the chief reason for mixed ownership of banks was the scarcity of private capital.

Private Banking.   During the early history of the country, conditions were favorable to the development of various aspects of private banking. There was a place for the private banker, the broker, the speculator, and the promoter, wherever chartered banking is inadequate or unreliable or handicapped by governmental regulations, currency is in a state of confusion, and business is expanding rapidly.

One group of private bankers was indigenous in origin, and another traces its origin to the financing of international trade and international lending. The first group of private bankers accepted deposits; dealt in domestic exchange; issued paper money in conven-

---

[17] John M. Chapman and Ray B. Westerfield, *Branch Banking* (New York: Harper & Bros., 1942), p. 47.

ient denominations, which circulated as money even though some-times it was disguised as a bill of exchange; bought bank notes of chartered banks at a discount and presented them to the issuing banks for payment; and sold gold and silver at a premium during periods of banks' suspension of specie payments. Many of these private bankers were operators of country stores, carrying on both a mercantile and a banking business. It was natural for the frontier merchant to carry on limited deposit banking, to extend credit, and to participate in the financing of local ventures, such as turnpikes, railroads, and canals. Too often the frontier-chartered banks were formed solely for the purpose of issuing paper money, and the more modern type of bank-ing was left to the merchants and private bankers.

A second group of private bankers developed a banking business as a result of foreign-trade contacts and the need for funds in foreign centers to pay for goods obtained from abroad. Merchant-bankers purchased American securities and sent them abroad to financial cen-ters. When these securities were sold to foreign bankers, the Ameri-can merchant-bankers were given bank credit to use in purchase of goods. Some of the merchant-bankers set up their own branch offices in foreign centers so as to sell securities directly to investors. Later, some of these firms gave up their mercantile businesses to specialize in the purchase and sale of securities, foreign-exchange credit instru-ments, and gold and silver. Others carried on a more general banking business, including, in addition to the above, the acceptance of depos-its, the issuance of paper money disguised as orders to pay and/or as shop notes, and commercial-loan and discount operations.

The private domestic bank and bankers that played a leading role in financing prior to the Civil War included such leading capital-ists as Stephen Girard, Jacob Astor, and David Parish, who helped in financing the War of 1812; E. W. Clarke and Company, which helped to finance the Mexican War; Corcoran and Riggs, of Wash-ington; August Belmont and Company; Jay Cooke (the financier of the Civil War); and Drexel and Company. Among other firms that appeared later were J. and W. Seligman and Company; Kuhn, Loeb and Company; J. P. Morgan and Company, and N. W. Harris and Company. In addition, numerous foreign banks had representatives or agencies in the United States, including Baring Brothers and Com-pany, the Rothschilds, and the French house of Hottinguer.

Independent Treasury System. During 1832 and 1833 the Sec-retary of the Treasury, acting on instructions of the President, shifted government deposits from the Bank of the United States (which had been acting as the fiscal agent for the Treasury) to certain state-chartered banks. President Jackson's purpose in giving this order was to lessen the shock upon the credit and currency systems that was expected to result from the liquidation of the second Bank of the United States with the lapse of its federal charter in 1836. This brought the United States Treasury into direct contact with the problem of the varying values of bank notes. In 1835 the Treasury brought pressure to bear on banks to redeem their notes either in specie or in bank credit of banks that were redeeming their obligations in specie. This was followed by the issuance of the "specie circular" to land agents directing them to accept nothing except specie or notes of specie-paying banks in payment for public land. These measures emphasized the importance of convertibility of bank notes in specie, brought on the Panic of 1837, and demonstrated the importance of fiscal policy when applied to such a routine matter as determining which form of currency is government tender.

During the Panic of 1837 and the depression which followed, the government (along with others) suffered from the inconveniences of inconvertibility, loss of deposits in suspended banks, and loss due to holding paper money of suspended banks. In 1840 and again in 1846 Congress made provisions for the temporary safekeeping of its own funds in its own vaults. It provided for subtreasuries in various cities and for the collection and payment of amounts due to or owed by the government in specie. Thereby the sponsors expected to keep a large supply of coin in the country, to reduce the volume of paper money, to prevent the expansion of bank currency based on government deposits, and to provide for safety of government funds. This so-called Independent Treasury System (independent of banks) had to be modified during the Civil War, but it was adequate while the receipts and expenditures of the Treasury were small.[18] However, it was no substitute for a public bank as a regulator of currency (as some of its sponsors argued that it would be).

NATIONAL BANKING SYSTEM, 1862–1913

Dual Banking.   The provisions for incorporation of private banks under the National Bank Act resulted in a dual banking system. Although the existence of both state-chartered and national banks in the United States has created some problems, the activities of these institutions are more alike than different.

In 1863 Congress, in passing the National Currency Act, or

---

[18] After the Federal Reserve banks took over the subtreasury functions, Congress abolished the Independent Treasury System (1920).

"National Bank Act," adopted the bond-secured system of note issue which had been tested in New York and other "free-banking" states. The objectives of this act were to create (1) a market for United States Treasury bonds, (2) a uniform bank note system, and (3) a better banking system. Two years later, Congress levied a 10 percent tax on any bank that paid out notes of a state-chartered bank (effective July 1, 1866). For all practical purposes, this tax denied the note-issue privilege to state banks and made operating under a national charter more attractive to bankers.

In 1865–66, many state banks were rechartered as national banks and new national banks were organized by private bankers and others. Jay Cooke, the financier of the Civil War, was responsible for organizing three banks, including the First National Bank of Philadelphia, which received Charter No. 1, on July 11, 1863; and the members of his government-bond sales organization were instrumental in organizing many more, particularly in the West, which was more friendly than the East toward the new system.[19] From 1864 to 1866 the number of state banks declined from 1,089 to 297, while national banks increased from 139 to 1,582.

The Comptroller of the Currency. The shift of banks to the National Banking System brought most banks under the supervision of the Office of the Comptroller of the Currency (the first of numerous administrative agencies created by Congress). This bureau, located in the Treasury Department, was made responsible for issuance, redemption, and retirement of national bank notes. Today, it would be more accurate to call the Comptroller the "Superintendent of National Banks," because his chief duties are to supervise the organization, expansion (through amalgamation or establishment of branches), operation, and liquidation of national banks; to perform comparable functions with respect to all banks and certain credit unions in the District of Columbia; to operate an issue and redemption division to handle the engraving and destruction of Federal Reserve notes; to make annual reports to Congress on the condition of national banks; to make legislative recommendations; and to make detailed decisions involving administrative interpretation of the law.

Growth of Deposit Banking. The chief reason for the original shift of banks to incorporation under national law was the desire for the then valuable note-issue privilege. Although deposit banking ri-

---

[19] Older banks were slow in joining the National Banking System, as shown by the fact that the Bank of North America (1781) was given Charter No. 602 and the Bank of Massachusetts (1784), Charter No. 794. The Bank of New York (1784) is still operating under a state charter.

valed or exceeded note-issue banking in importance in metropolitan centers by 1820, banks in pioneer communities, where transportation facilities were poor and daily or weekly contacts with banks were impossible, found a demand for bank notes rather than for deposit currency. The increase in regulation of state banks' note issues, following disastrous bank failures from 1837 to 1841, hastened the movement toward deposit banking, but the shift from note-issue to deposit banking was most rapid after the Civil War.

The shift to deposit banking meant that banks were finding it more profitable to lend their credit in the form of accounts payable (deposit currency) than to lend their credit in the form of bank notes. National banks shared in the growth of this type of lending because their note issues were limited to the amount of their capital and there was no legal limit on the ratio of capital to deposits.

By 1890, the development of deposit currency lessened the importance of the note-issue privilege and eliminated the near-monopoly of commercial banking that national banks enjoyed during the first decade after the Civil War. In the settlement of the West, one of the first business enterprises to be established in a new town was a bank. The minimum capital requirements for state-chartered banks were generally less than for national banks, and they were subject to less restrictive governmental control and enjoyed much broader banking privileges. For illustration, many banks combined banking with farm mortgage, fire insurance and real estate businesses. Later state banks added savings, safe-deposit and trust-banking activities; hence, before the end of the century, state banks exceeded national banks in number.

Correspondent Banking.   Almost from the beginning of banking in the United States, bankers recognized the need for centers for the payment of notes, and later for payment and collection of checks and drafts. Even before the Civil War, banks had made arrangements with other banks outside their communities to act as collection agents and to assist them in other ways. In order to retain the services of these correspondent banks, deposits were kept with them. Out of the original correspondent relationship, two central banking functions developed; namely, holding reserves of the banking system and lending funds to banks when needed. However, the correspondent banks did not have the right to issue paper money or to create new reserve money as needed by the banking system; consequently, the correspondent banking system was not equipped to meet the demands for currency and reserves during financial crises.

Creation of the National Banking System had the unexpected effect of strengthening correspondent banking. National banks were required to keep minimum reserves against deposits (originally, also against bank notes) which varied as to percentages according to the domicile of the bank. Banks in New York and, after 1887, those in Chicago and St. Louis were required to hold all their required reserves of 25 percent against deposits in their own vaults in the form of lawful money (all kinds of currency except national bank notes). Banks located in other designated cities were permitted to carry one half of their legal reserves of 25 percent with other banks as bankers' balances or deposits. The remaining banks were permitted to keep three fifths of their required reserves of 15 percent as bankers' balances. Customarily, interest was paid on interbank balances; consequently, when permissible, bank reserves were kept with other banks and eventually concentrated to a considerable degree in the nine "super" banks in New York City. Until the creation of the Federal Reserve System in 1914, these large banks, having thousands of correspondents, played a major part in determining national credit policy.

National Monetary Commission.   The act which created the National Monetary Commission contained a provision whereby national banks, individually or as a group, could issue national bank notes secured by deposits of commercial paper. This provision for an emergency currency was made pending the establishment of a permanent central banking system. After completing and publishing a number of studies of foreign and domestic banks, the Commission (consisting of eight senators and eight congressmen) made a summary report and recommendations pointing out the need for mobilization of cash reserves for use in time of need, the effects of legal restrictions on the use of bank reserves and on the lending power of banks in the presence of unusual demands, and the absence of an adequate means whereby banks could replenish or increase their reserves to meet unusual or normal demands for bank credit.[20] Although national bank notes were safe and uniform in value, the Commission criticized the inelasticity of national bank note circulation, that is, the failure to expand during a money crisis or in response to seasonal and other demands for more currency and the failure to contract when demands for currency declined.

[20] National Monetary Commission, *Letter from Secretary of the National Monetary Commission Transmitting, Pursuant to Law, the Report of the Commission* (Washington, D.C.: U.S. Government Printing Office, 1912), Vol. XXIV, pp. 6-9.

While recognizing the services of clearinghouse associations, the Commission pointed out the need for "means to insure such effective cooperation on the part of banks as is necessary to protect their own and public interest in times of stress or crisis."[21] The Commission also noted the need for an agency for making the domestic- and foreign-exchange systems more effective. As noted previously, the procedure for handling collection items between banks was slow and inefficient.

The character of the commercial-credit market was criticized because of the lack of commercial paper of an established standard; the flow of bank credit to New York for use of brokers, dealers, and buyers of stocks; the placement of "farmers and others engaged in productive industries at a great disadvantage in securing" credit because national banks could not make loans secured by real estate; and the "lack of equality in credit facilities between different sections of the country." These conditions could be corrected, in part, by an agency that would "aid in securing greater uniformity, steadiness, and reasonableness of rates of discount in all parts of the country" and "provide adequate banking facilities for different regions promptly and on reasonable terms to meet the ordinary or unusual demands for credit or currency necessary for moving crops or for other legitimate purposes."

The provisions for bank supervision and regulation were criticized because there was "no power to enforce the adoption of uniform standards with regard to capital, reserves, examinations, and the character and publicity" of bank reports. The National Monetary Commission also called attention to the need for "American banking institutions in foreign countries" and the inability of national banks to make mortgage loans to farmers and others. The policies of the Independent Treasury System were criticized because they resulted in "irregular withdrawals of money from circulation," and because the attempt to modify the situation, by depositing funds in national banks when needed, resulted in discrimination and favoritism in the treatment of different banks.

Some of the criticisms by the National Monetary Commission in regard to the National Banking System seem to be contradictory. As an illustration, one criticism was based on the need to mobilize

[21] In addition to serving as local clearing and collection centers, clearinghouses sometimes examined members to assure safe banking practices. In addition, during financial panics they issued emergency currency—clearinghouse certificates (in 1860, 1873, 1890, 1893, 1907, and to a minor extent in 1933).

reserves for use in emergencies, while another objected to the centralization of reserves in New York. However, the first referred to the fact that gold money was scattered among thousands of banks; the second referred to the practice of reserve city and country banks of using their option to keep part of their required reserves as bankers' balances in New York, where they were used to make call loans to security dealers and brokers. At that time banks were permitted to pay interest on interbank deposits, and depositing banks took full advantage of this opportunity to derive income from part of their required reserves. Of course, the banks which held interbank balances found it necessary to keep them employed.

Difficulties arose when banks in one area, faced with sizable demands for funds, withdrew their balances with correspondent banks. This pressure was felt by banks all along the line, and it came to a head in New York, where the banks holding large bankers' balances were forced to call their loans to dealers and brokers, and what started as a local financial disturbance ended as a national panic. (There was some justification for calling the National Banking System the "panic breeder.") The correct solution was not elimination of interbank balances but provisions for a source of new bank reserves and currency that could be increased in case of need—in other words, a central bank.

COMMERCIAL BANKING SINCE 1913

Since 1913 the history of commercial banking has been linked to the development and operation of the Federal Reserve System—the machinery designed to provide for the expansion and stabilization of the supply of money and credit. The Federal Reserve Act left unsolved many problems that had faced the people of the United States since before the Civil War. There remained the problem of the weak, poorly managed, small local banks. Bank failures were not eliminated, and banking codes and government regulation were as fruitless in protecting the creditors of banks as they had been before 1914. Branch banking still was restricted or prohibited. Every community thought it necessary to have its own locally owned and locally operated bank; as a result, there were "too many banks and not enough bankers." There was a tendency to lower banking standards, and apparently too much reliance was being placed upon mere membership in the Federal Reserve System. (The popular expression was, "Members of the Federal Reserve System cannot fail.") Even the belief that money panics were impossible under the Federal Reserve

System proved to be false in February and the first three days of March, 1933.

Bank Failures.   The most significant phenomenon of the period between 1921 and 1934 was the large number of bank failures. Before 1930, failures were generally in the agricultural sections of the country where the mortality rate was high among small banks located in communities with populations of less than 1,000 (due largely to the holding of farm mortgage loans made during and after World War I when the price of farms was high). As a result of the Great Depression, bank failures were so widespread that most communities suffered from at least one bank suspension. This led to local, then to state, and finally to a national moratorium. About 11,000 banks failed between 1920 and 1933, and over 4,000 more were suspended during 1933. From a peak of about 29,500 banks in 1921, the number of commercial banks declined to less than 14,000 in 1933.

As a result of the hardships that accompanied the collapse of the banking system, Congress took specific steps to correct abuses inherent therein. The Federal Reserve System's managerial control over money creation and banking activities was strengthened, and the Federal Deposit Insurance Corporation was created to protect small depositors from losses in case of bank failure.

Suppliers of Credit.   As suppliers of credit, commercial banks have always preferred to make short-term commercial loans to business firms to finance seasonal expansion in inventories and goods in transit. In modern times, this type of loan business has declined because of the development of cash payments in the retail trade field and the growth of trade credit in the business area. However, some communities have never had much need for commercial credit; so, from the beginning, some banks had to find other outlets for their loanable funds. Banks in rural areas made loans to farmers to purchase land and buildings, to acquire livestock and farm machinery, and to buy feed, seed, and household goods. Banks in cities supplemented commercial lending with lending to industry and homeowners.

During the 1920's a disproportionate percentage of lending by commercial banks was to business firms, individuals, and brokers to finance trading in corporate stocks and bonds. Following the stock market crash and the severe depression of the early 1930's, banks purchased large quantities of government bonds, continued to make short-term business loans, and developed new types of loans. The new type of loans included term loans to business firms secured by goods stored in warehouses, loans on accounts receivable, real estate loans insured or guaranteed by the Federal Housing Administration, and loans to consumers.

During World War II commercial banks purchased U.S. government securities and made "V-loans" to business firms to finance their production of war goods for the Army and Navy Departments and other divisions of the federal government.[22] Following the war, commercial banks increased their loan activities in all areas except for speculation in securities. Bank financing of consumer installment credit became "big business" (see Chapter 24), and term loans comprised from one third to one half of all business loans (see Chapter 13).

SUMMARY

The development of commercial banking in the United States has reflected the rapidly expanding nature of the economy, the spread of population across the continent, the dual chartering system, the opposition to concentration of financial power in a few institutions, and the wealth of the country. During the formative period, commercial banking was closely allied to note-issue banking, and much of the banking legislation prior to the Civil War had as its primary purpose the protection of bank noteholders. Even the National Bank Act of 1863, as amended in 1864, was regarded by many as primarily a currency-reform measure.

The first and the second Bank of the United States shared the note-issue privilege with state-chartered banks, but the notes of the former were accepted nationally and were used as reserves by state-chartered banks to redeem their bank notes. Both United States banks acted as fiscal agents for the federal government, lent money to the government in anticipation of tax receipts, handled refunding of debts, accepted government deposits, and transferred funds from place to place through their branch-banking systems. Out of the acceptance of government deposits, there developed the central-bank function of regulator of the currency, which is now considered one of the most important functions of a central bank.

[22] Under provisions of the *Defense Production Act of 1950* (Pub. No. 774, 81st Cong., approved September 8, 1950) and subsequent executive orders, different departments and agencies of the federal government are authorized to guarantee any financing institution against loss of interest and principal on any loan or other commitment made "to expedite production and deliveries or services under government contracts for the procurement of materials or performance of services for national defense. . . ." The Federal Reserve System acts as fiscal agent for the guaranteeing agencies. Requests for government-guaranteed loans must follow provisions found in the Board of Governor's Regulation V.

When the first and the second Bank of the United States received tax receipts in the form of bank notes of other banks, they became the creditors of these banks (in contrast to Federal Reserve banks, which are debtors to member banks). Possession of these notes gave the "public bank" a simple and effective device for restraining the note-issue practices of other banks. By returning these notes to the issuing banks for redemption, the Bank of the United States could exert pressure on the issuing banks to keep reserves in the form of bank notes of the Bank of the United States or gold and silver, thereby limiting the volume of other banks' notes (debts) within their ability to pay on demand.

From 1865 to 1914, a dual banking system developed in the United States which had neither the type of central banking system provided for in the Federal Reserve Act of 1913 nor the protection of the banking system's deposit provided for in the Federal Deposit Insurance Act of 1933. The axiom "what is good for business is good for banking" is another way of saying that American banks have influenced and have been influenced by their environment. The number of banks declined by more than one half since the peak in 1921, but the decline in number of banks has been offset by the increase in the number of branch offices and in the size of the average bank. The most significant changes in American banking have been in the quality of bank assets, which have shown a shift in emphasis from short-term commercial-bank lending to investing in government securities and intermediate- and long-term lending to business, homeowners, consumers, and others. At one time, the assets of commercial banks represented 90 percent of the total resources of all financial intermediaries; but the near monopoly they enjoyed was broken by the organization of numerous types of financing institutions which will be the subject matter of later chapters in this book.

QUESTIONS AND PROBLEMS

1. Analyze: "The chartering of new banks represents, in many respects, the most delicate task which confronts the bank regulatory authorities. A new bank represents a new competitor, and a new competitor is rarely welcome in any industry. On the other hand, since bank charters are valuable because they are limited in supply, they are actively sought by competing applicants. The public authorities are thus subjected to intensive pressures both from those who seek charters and those who oppose them." (The Administrator of National Banks, *Studies in Banking Competition and the Banking Situation* [Office of the Comptroller of the Currency, U.S. Treasury Department (Washington, D.C., 1966)], p. 402.)

2. The "best way to diffuse banking in a community is to allow the banker to issue bank notes of small amount that can supersede the metal currency. This amounts to a subsidy to each banker to enable him to keep open a bank till depositors choose to come to it." (Walter Bagehot, *Lombard Street* [14th ed.; London: John Murray, 1915], p. 82.) Was this method used in the United States? Was it successful?

3. The first mistake of a monetary nature was made "when Congress refused to renew the charter of the first Bank of the United States in 1811." (E. C. Jerome, *Governments and Money* [Boston: Little, Brown, & Co., 1935], p. 172.) Was this a serious monetary mistake?

4. Many early bankers issued notes far beyond their ability to redeem. They "hoped that the notes would fly so far that they would never find their way home." Why? Was "home" made as accessible as possible? Why were some of these early banks called "wildcat" banks? What changes were made in the 1840's?

5. The National Bank Act rejected the big-bank idea and enthroned the local-bank system. Explain. What are the duties of the Comptroller of the Currency? What state official may be compared to him?

6. Analyze: "In the 13 years following 1921, the number of commercial banks declined by approximately half. The major part of this reduction took place during the depths of the depression, 1930–1933, when 9,000 banks failed and another 2,300, many of which were in financial difficulties, were absorbed by other banks. Perhaps of greater significance, however, were the more than 5,000 bank suspensions which occurred during the 1921–1929 period while most sectors of the economy were prosperous." (The Administrator of National Banks, *op. cit.*, p. 412.)

7. In 1963, the American Bankers Association celebrated the 100th anniversary of the dual banking system and not the establishment of the National Banking System. Why?

8. Compare the modern concept of a banker to the following: "By custom we call a man a banker who has an open shop, with proper counters, servants, and books, for receiving other people's money, in order to keep it safe and return it upon demand, . . ." (James W. Gilbert, *Principles and Practices of Banking* [new ed.; London: Bell & Daldy, 1871], p. 145.)

9. Discuss: Since the end of World War II, commercial banks have declined in importance relative to other financial institutions, continuing a trend originated around the turn of the century." (Federal Reserve Bank of Cleveland, *Economic Review*, November, 1965, p. 2.)

10. Analyze: One criticism of the National Banking System was "based on the need to mobilize reserves for use in emergencies, while another objected to the centralization of reserves in New York."

CHAPTER 8

Federal Reserve System

CENTRAL BANKS are financial institutions that are distinguished from other banks by their functions. Central banks hold reserves for other banks, act as fiscal agents for their national governments, and issue paper money. In addition, central banks are the instruments for expanding and stabilizing the supply of money and credit. The central bank of a country may not be its largest bank, but it will be the dominant one. Customarily, the central bank has an official or semiofficial status in its government, but the Federal Reserve banks are among the few central banks that are not owned by their national government.

Most of the central banks in the world, now in excess of 100, have been established since World War I; however, the state bank of Sweden (Sveriges-Riksbank) was opened in 1656, the Bank of England in 1794, the Bank of France in 1800, and the German Reichsbank in 1875. The Federal Reserve System was created under provisions of an act signed by President Woodrow Wilson on December 23, 1913. The long title of the Federal Reserve Act is "An Act to provide for the establishment of Federal Reserve banks, to furnish an elastic currency, to afford means of rediscounting commercial paper, to establish a more effective supervision of banking in the United States, and for other purposes."[1]

If "other purposes" were to be given specific legislation today, Congress would doubtless include "to foster orderly economic growth, a high level of employment, a relatively stable general price level, and to achieve a balance in the United States international payments," because these goals have become the objectives of the Federal Reserve System.

During the planning stage ownership of the Federal Reserve banks was an important issue, with some favoring government ownership and others private ownership. The final decision was a compro-

[1] Federal Reserve Act, approved December 23, 1913, 38 Stat. 251, ch. 6.

mise which permitted member banks to own the capital stock but stripped them of most of the traditional rights and privileges of shareholders. After the outbreak of World War I, the organization of the Federal Reserve banks was hastened, and they opened for business in November, 1914.

IMPROVEMENT OF THE BANKING SYSTEM

In 1910, central banks were few in number, the world was still on the gold standard, and nations depended on gold to stabilize their domestic prices, to bring their international balances of payment into equilibrium, and to provide automatic control over the volume of currency. After investigating central banking and currency systems throughout the world, the National Monetary Commission recommended the incorporation of a "National Reserve Association of the United States" with 15 district branches and local associations of participating banks. Because of the change in political control of the federal government, this plan was not adopted, but the new administration provided for banking reform in the Federal Reserve Act which became law on December 23, 1913.

In many respects the Federal Reserve System was similar to the plan proposed by the Commission. The most important differences were the provision for a greater degree of decentralization, which has been largely nullified by subsequent changes in the System, the provision for a more liberal currency and reserve system, and the divorce of the Federal Reserve System from control by banks.

The purpose of the framers of the Federal Reserve System was to strengthen the existing banking structure without making fundamental changes in the existing unit-banking system. Two types of changes were stressed: broadening the banking activities of individual banks and creating a more efficient money and banking system. National banks were authorized to accept savings deposits, to undertake limited mortgage-banking business, to perform trust functions, to grant acceptance credit, and to carry on a foreign finance business. In subsequent legislation, the further liberalization of many of these powers was directed at improving and enlarging the services offered by individual banks. Important as these changes were, the key to improving the money and banking system was the Federal Reserve System with its 12 central banks that have the power to create bank reserves and currency. Congress assumed that it could set up a system wherein there would be automatic expansion and contraction of Federal Reserve credit according to the "needs of trade" and changes in the country's gold supply. The Federal Reserve Act contained no provisions for replacing the existing banking systems but provided a banking structure that was to be superimposed on them.

Mobility of Credit.   One of the requisites of a good banking system is its ability to provide mobility of capital, that is, its ability to move credits from place to place according to the varying requirements of business. The commercial-banking system of the United States is basically local in nature because, for the most part, it is made up of banks that are local in organization, management, and scope of operations. The counterpart of the branch-banking systems of foreign countries is found in the United States in the noncommercial-banking fields, including investment banking, brokerage, sales-finance, and personal-loan fields of finance. (Most of the large bond and investment houses, commission houses, and small-loan and sales-finance companies have branch offices in the leading cities of the country.)

In the United States some mobility of credit is provided by correspondent banks and by facilitating organizations, which take credit instruments of local origin and sell them in the money market. This group includes the acceptance dealers, bill brokers, commercial-paper houses, and mortgage dealers and brokers. It is the local nature of commercial-banking institutions in the United States that makes the facilities of the Federal Reserve System so important. Bank credit is now made available throughout the country at practically uniform rates for bank loans of like size, risk, purpose, and quality. The greatest variation among customer-loan rates in different sections of the country is for small loans, whose rates reflect the presence or lack of competition in local markets. Although the Federal Reserve System has not been the sole contributor to the increased mobility of bank credit (for example, the Federal Housing Administration), it has played the major role by providing for domestic transfers of funds and collection of checks, notes, coupons, and other credit instruments and by creating greater liquidity, which has permitted commercial banks to broaden their lending activities to accommodate various classes of individual, corporate, government, and other borrowers.

Elastic Credit System.   In addition to geographical mobility of credit, the central-banking system should provide an elastic credit system, that is, one capable of expanding and contracting in volume as the credit needs of business expand and contract. With perfect elasticity, two undesirable developments would be avoided—an expansion that outruns the need and causes inflation and a contraction that causes businessmen to liquidate assets and to postpone or curtail production. The index of the efficiency of an elastic credit system is the absence of sharp fluctuations in interest rates in the money market. Where there are compulsory reserve requirements, the need for an emergency source of reserves and currency must be met if periodic breakdowns in the money and banking systems are to be avoided. This need is indicated by the appearance of the word "reserve" in the title "Federal Reserve Act."

A good monetary system embodies a mechanism whereby bank reserves may be transferred among depositors and converted into currency at their request. Although banks had developed a system of correspondent banking for out-of-town clearing and collection of checks and other items, the Federal Reserve System has assumed primary responsibility for the nationwide development of this function so that the nation may have a better monetary system.

In the light of conditions following the panic of 1907 when credit was not available to responsible borrowers, it is not surprising that the objectives of the sponsors of the Federal Reserve System included securing an "elastic" currency system and providing a place to rediscount commercial paper. Both dealt with a temporary or special need; the first stressed an "elastic" rather than the total money supply, and the second emphasized "commercial" credit rather than the total credit needs of the economy. For years, it was not apparent that determination of the total amount of money was the primary function of a central bank. Although statistics of the amount of credit in use have been available for many years, it was not until 1960 that the *Federal Reserve Bulletin* published statistics on the money supply. Even now, information is lacking as to the distribution of the money supply among consumers, business firms, and government institutions.

STRUCTURAL ORGANIZATION

Regional Plan. Due to public suspicion of "big business" and centralized control, the structural plan for the Federal Reserve System contained many compromises; however, with the exception of the creation of the Federal Open Market Committee, the System is much as it was in 1914 (see Chart 8–1). Although many congressmen favored the one-central-bank plan characteristic of foreign central banks, the majority were opposed to such concentration of authority

CHART 8-1.
FEDERAL RESERVE SYSTEM ORGANIZATION CHART

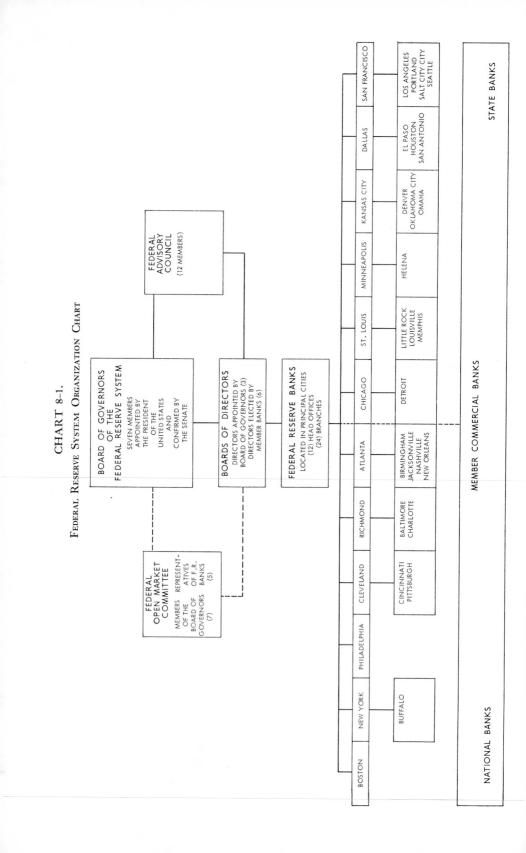

FEDERAL OPEN MARKET COMMITTEE

MEMBERS OF THE BOARD OF GOVERNORS (7)

REPRESENTATIVES OF F.R. BANKS (5)

BOARD OF GOVERNORS OF THE FEDERAL RESERVE SYSTEM

SEVEN MEMBERS APPOINTED BY THE PRESIDENT OF THE UNITED STATES AND CONFIRMED BY THE SENATE

FEDERAL ADVISORY COUNCIL

(12 MEMBERS)

BOARDS OF DIRECTORS

DIRECTORS APPOINTED BY BOARD OF GOVERNORS (3)

DIRECTORS ELECTED BY MEMBER BANKS (6)

FEDERAL RESERVE BANKS

LOCATED IN PRINCIPAL CITIES (12) HEAD OFFICES (24) BRANCHES

| BOSTON | NEW YORK | PHILADELPHIA | CLEVELAND | RICHMOND | ATLANTA | CHICAGO | ST. LOUIS | MINNEAPOLIS | KANSAS CITY | DALLAS | SAN FRANCISCO |

BUFFALO

CINCINNATI PITTSBURGH

BALTIMORE CHARLOTTE

BIRMINGHAM JACKSONVILLE NASHVILLE NEW ORLEANS

DETROIT

LITTLE ROCK LOUISVILLE MEMPHIS

HELENA

DENVER OKLAHOMA CITY OMAHA

EL PASO HOUSTON SAN ANTONIO

LOS ANGELES PORTLAND SALT LAKE CITY SEATTLE

MEMBER COMMERCIAL BANKS

NATIONAL BANKS

STATE BANKS

and voted in favor of a regional plan.[2] Hence the Federal Reserve Act provided that there were to be no more than 12 or less than 8 Federal Reserve banks and districts. The task of dividing the country into districts and selecting sites for Federal Reserve banks was given to an organization committee composed of three men—the Secretary of the Treasury, the Comptroller of the Currency, and the Secretary of Agriculture.

Organization Committee. The Organization Committee held public hearings in 18 cities; gave each national bank an opportunity to state by card ballot its choice of location for the Federal Reserve bank with which it desired to be connected; received petitions from clearinghouse associations, chambers of commerce, or other representatives of 200 cities; and received requests from 37 cities to be designated as the site of a Federal Reserve bank.

After three months of investigation, the Organization Committee announced its decision to create the maximum number of banks and districts, with Federal Reserve banks in the following cities: Boston, New York, Philadelphia, Cleveland, Richmond, Atlanta, Chicago, St. Louis, Minneapolis, Kansas City, Dallas, and San Francisco (see Chart 8–1). The economic factors that guided the Committee in the location of regional banks were existing financial, mercantile, and industrial relations between areas and cities within the proposed districts; normal transportation and communication facilities; prevailing business activities within a region; probable ability of the Federal Reserve bank to serve its district; and equitable distribution of member banks among the districts with particular care taken to see that the future member banks in the district would be able to subscribe the minimum required capital ($4,000,000) for each Reserve bank.

Federal Reserve Board. The members of the Federal Reserve Board, now the Board of Governors of the Federal Reserve System, took office on August 10, 1914. The Board's membership included two members of the Organization Committee (the Secretary of the

[2] In the *Eighth Annual Report* of the Federal Reserve Board the following statements appear: "The Federal Reserve Act did not establish a central bank" but "adopted the regional principle and authorized the establishment of not more than 12 banks to be located in various sections of the country." The Board also stated that "each of these banks is practically independent of the others, in operation as well as in local policies. From a legal standpoint, these banks are private corporations organized under a special act of Congress. . . . Their stockholders are their member banks, each of which is required to subscribe to the capital stock of the Federal Reserve Banks an amount equal to 6 percent of its own capital and surplus, one-half of which amount is required to be paid in." *Eighth Annual Report of the Federal Reserve Board Covering Operations for the Year 1921* (Washington, D.C.: U.S. Government Printing Office, 1922), pp. 88–99.

Treasury and the Comptroller of the Currency) and five others appointed by the President with the consent of the United States Senate. The public nature of the Federal Reserve System is indicated by the presence of the Secretary of the Treasury and the Comptroller of the Currency. Among the original members was the Assistant Secretary of the Treasury, who resigned to accept membership on the Federal Reserve Board. Of the appointive members, one was a college president and three were professional bankers.[3]

Since 1914, the number of members on the Board has been changed twice, with the present makeup being provided for in the Banking Act of 1935. The Board is now composed of seven members appointed by the President of the United States with the consent of the United States Senate. Although it is called the Board of Governors of the Federal Reserve System, it is often referred to as the "Board of Governors" or the "Federal Reserve Board."

Although the Board was authorized to adjust Federal Reserve district boundaries and to change the locations of Federal Reserve banks, no changes were made in the latter, and only minor ones were made in district boundaries, except those resulting from the change in political status of Alaska and Hawaii. When they were admitted to the Union (January 3 and March 18, 1959), both states were added to the Federal Reserve Bank of San Francisco district, and every national bank therein became a member bank within 90 days after their admission to statehood. In 1936 the term of office for members of the Board of Governors was made 14 years, with the terms arranged so as to have one term expiring in January of even-numbered years. However, in case a member resigns another may be appointed for a term of less than 14 years without being disqualified for a second 14-year term. This arrangement assures continuity of policies and a majority of experienced members.

Although the members of the Board of Governors and its staff are often thought of as government employees, they are paid from funds secured from levies on the Federal Reserve banks. Congress fixes the salaries of Board members and of the Board's staff in Washington and passes on those of officers and employees of the Federal Reserve banks. Geographic and economic representation on the Board is assured by the provision requiring the President to have due regard to fair representation of the financial, agricultural, industrial, and

[3] Two of President Woodrow Wilson's original selections for the Board were unable to serve. See also Charles Seymour, *The Intimate Papers of Colonel House* (Boston: Houghton Mifflin Co., 1926), pp. 167–72.

commercial interests and geographic divisions of the country in his appointments. Each member is now called "Governor," and the President appoints one member as chairman and another as vice-chairman, both of whom hold office for four years but may be reappointed until their 14-year terms expire. The chairman is the chief executive officer and spokesman of the Board of Governors but he is subject to the Board's supervision.

The Board of Governors of the Federal Reserve System is the directing agency for the System, and its regulations pertain to the 12 Federal Reserve banks, the member banks, and some other institutions that are not a part of the Federal Reserve System. The Board of Governors has many specific powers over the internal operations of Federal Reserve banks, including the power to permit or require one Reserve bank to rediscount for a second Reserve bank so as to pool the System's resources in case of need. The Board defines the character of paper eligible for rediscount, prescribes the rules as to rediscounting, reviews and fixes the discount rates which are established by each bank every two weeks. The Board is also responsible for fixing margin requirements and setting maximum interest rates payable on time and savings deposits in member banks. In addition, the members of the Board together with the presidents of five of the Federal Reserve banks are in charge of the System's open-market operations, that is, the Federal Reserve System's investments.

In addition to policy matters, the Board of Governors is responsible for routine matters such as examinations of Federal Reserve banks and foreign banking corporations; approval of operating budgets and appointment and salaries of officers; and selection of Federal Reserve agents and Class C directors of the Federal Reserve banks.[4] (Foreign banking corporations may be organized under state laws, in which case they are called "agreement corporations" or under federal law, in which case they are known as "Edge Corporations.")

The Board of Governors supervises and regulates the issue and retirement of Federal Reserve notes, a function that includes the formulation of rules and regulations for safeguarding all securities held as collateral for all Federal Reserve notes in circulation. The Board may withhold issues of Federal Reserve notes and impose

---

[4] The regulations of the Board of Governors that are designated by letters of the alphabet and pertain to the activities of the Federal Reserve banks are *A*, discount for and advances to member banks; *B*, open-market purchases of bills and bankers' acceptances; *E*, purchase of warrants by Federal Reserve banks; *G*, collection of noncash items; *J*, check clearing and collection; *N*, relations with foreign banks and bankers; and *V*, financing of defense pursuant to the Defense Production Act of 1950.

interest charges on those in circulation. The Board acts as a clearing-house for Federal Reserve banks and requires the Federal Reserve banks to act as clearinghouses for member banks. It has the authority to determine charges that may be made for the collection and payment of checks and drafts.

The Board of Governors has many powers pertaining to member banks, including the power to pass on requests for admission of state banks to membership; to expel a bank from membership; to supervise mergers which include member banks; to reduce or suspend a bank's discount privilege; to regulate interlocking directorates; to pass on requests of a state member bank to establish branches and to merge with other banks; and to regulate the granting of acceptance credit and to pass on requests of member banks to accept drafts in excess of 50 percent of their capital and surplus.[5] It may also issue cease-and-desist orders to any member institution, or to an officer or director of such an institution, for illegal operations or for following unsafe or unsound banking practices. The Board's authority permits it to remove officers and directors for participating in illegal or unsound banking practices and to sever banking connections of any person convicted of either any criminal offense or breach of trust, or charged with similar crimes.[6]

In 1933 Congress brought group banking under regulation by requiring any holding company owning or controlling any member bank to obtain a "voting permit" from the Board of Governors. Prior to giving the permit to vote the stock of the member bank, the bank holding company is required to agree to submit to periodic examinations, to file an annual report, and to meet certain standard requirements as to building up "surplus" by retaining earnings. Under provisions of the Bank Holding Company Act of 1956, as amended

[5] The regulations of the Board of Governors that are designated by letters of the alphabet and pertain particularly to the activities of member banks are C, acceptance of drafts and bills of exchange by member banks; D, required member-bank reserves with Federal Reserve banks; H, membership of state banking institutions in the Federal Reserve System; I, changes in capital stock of Reserve banks (owned by member banks) and the issuance of new stock certificates; L, interlocking bank directorates under the Clayton Act; M, foreign branches of national banks and of corporations organized under provisions of Sec. 25 (a) of the Federal Reserve Act; O, loans to executive officers of member banks; Q, maximum rates of interest payable on time and savings deposits by member banks; U, loans for the purpose of carrying stocks registered on national securities exchanges; W, consumer credit; V, financing of defense pursuant to the Defense Production Act of 1950; and X, real estate credit.

[6] The purpose is to give regulatory authorities the power to keep criminals from taking over control of banks and other financial institutions; and, in the Financial Institutions Act of 1966, Congress gave similar powers to other regulatory agencies and the two federal insurance funds (Federal Deposit Insurance Corporation and Federal Savings and Loan Insurance Corporation) until 1972.

by an Act approved July 1, 1966 (Public Law 89–485) the Board of Governors was made responsible for supervising the organization and future expansion of bank holding company systems and the disinvestment of existing holding companies in nonbanking organizations (insurance companies and numerous other business firms).

The greatest breaks with past regulatory policies came when the Board of Governors was authorized to regulate the use of credit by brokers, dealers, and members of national securities exchanges; two temporary provisions were made for regulation of advances of consumer credit by banks and other financial institutions, dealers, retailers, and others; and provision was made for the use of credit in real estate construction (with concurrence of the Administrator of the Housing and Home Finance Agency when the credit is to be used for construction of residential property).[7]

Staff. The chief divisions of the staff of the Board of Governors are: (1) Legal, (2) Research and Statistics, (3) International Finance, (4) Bank Operations, (5) Examinations, (6) Personnel Administration, (7) Administrative Services, and (8) Data Processing. In addition there are the offices of the Secretary, Controller, and Defense Planning. The Board now occupies its own building in Washington and uses the government salary scale in fixing salaries for staff members. The salaries of the members of the Board of Governors are fixed by Congress at $30,000 per year for the chairman and $29,500 for other members.[8]

FEDERAL OPEN MARKET COMMITTEE

Although only minor changes have been made in the framework of the Federal Reserve System, many important changes have taken place within the System. The most significant of these has been the concentration of power in the hands of the Board of Governors, which is responsible for all major decisions with the exception of investing, for which the Federal Open Market Committee is responsible.

The Federal Open Market Committee was authorized by Con-

---

[7] The regulations of the Board of Governors that are designated by letters of the alphabet and pertain, in whole or part, to the activities of institutions other than Federal Reserve banks and member banks are K, banking corporations authorized to do foreign banking business under the terms of Sec. 25 (a) of the Federal Reserve Act; P, holding-company affiliates—voting permits; R, relationship of dealers in securities with Federal Reserve and member banks—generally forbidden to be directors and/or officers; T, credit extended by brokers, dealers, and members of national securities exchanges; W, consumer credit; X, real estate credit (currently W and X are not in effect); and Y, bank holding companies.

[8] See Public Law 90–206, approved December 16, 1967.

gress in 1933, but it had been functioning under policy regulations issued by the Federal Reserve Board as early as 1923. With minor exceptions, its present membership and certain powers date from the passage of the Banking Act of 1935. The Committee now consists of the members of the Board of Governors and five presidents of Federal Reserve banks, four of whom are elected annually. (The fifth is the President of the Federal Reserve Bank of New York, which has continuous representation on the Committee.)[9] Customarily the Chairman of the Board serves as chairman of the Open Market Committee and the President of the Federal Reserve Bank of New York serves as the vice-chairman. Usually the presidents of all Federal Reserve banks attend the committee meetings, and, because membership changes annually, their presence is desirable in order to keep abreast of new developments.

The organization of the Federal Open Market Committee was in recognition of the importance of the Federal Reserve banks' investments in the open market. Prior to 1922, most of the open-market operations of the Federal Reserve banks were in bankers' acceptances in order to support the "bill" market rather than to influence the amount of money and credit. The purpose in purchasing government securities was to obtain income or collateral for issues of Federal Reserve notes.

In May, 1922, the chief executive officers of the Federal Reserve banks appointed a committee for "the centralized execution of purchases and sales of government securities." Little in the way of policy decisions was involved, as the Federal Reserve banks merely wanted to avoid working on both sides of the market at the same time (some banks buying and some selling). Actually, many of the central bankers did not understand how Federal Reserve banks' purchases and sales of government securities could be used to affect the credit situation. Later, the importance of this tool of monetary policy was appreciated, and the Federal Reserve Board required the Open Market Committee to give primary consideration in its open-market operations to the "accommodation of commerce and business" and to the effects of purchases and sales of securities on the general credit situation. The Open Market Committee purchases and holds all of the System's investments and allocates the income among the Federal

[9] The grouping of Federal Reserve banks for selection of the four members on the Open Market Committee is Boston, Philadelphia, and Richmond; Chicago and Cleveland; Atlanta, Dallas, and St. Louis; and Minneapolis, Kansas City, and San Francisco. Presidents of these banks serve in rotation as members of the Federal Open Market Committee.

Reserve banks (except during World War II, when a special policy was followed).

Previous to June, 1955, the Federal Open Market Committee had an executive committee that carried out the decisions of the full Committee. Since improvements in transportation permit members to assemble on less than 24 hours' notice, it was decided to discontinue the executive-committee meetings and to replace them with full membership meetings. Transactions in government securities are executed by the Federal Reserve Bank of New York (as agent), where a staff of economists and specialists is responsible for the daily operations of the System's open-market accounts.

Federal Advisory Council.   The Federal Reserve Act also provided for a Federal Advisory Council, whose function, as the title implies, is purely advisory. Although the Council's advice and recommendations as to Federal Reserve bank operations, Federal Reserve policies, and general economic conditions are not binding on the Board of Governors, they are given consideration by the Board. The Council is composed of 12 commercial bankers, one selected by each of the Federal Reserve banks. This arrangement gave commercial bankers an opportunity to present their views directly to the Federal Reserve Board.

FEDERAL RESERVE BANKS

The twelve Federal Reserve banks are corporations having indeterminate charters issued by the federal government under a special chartering act. All their capital stock is owned by member banks, and since 1916 the maximum 6 percent dividend allowed on stock has been paid every year. While some critics of the Federal Reserve System seem to consider the compulsory investment in Federal Reserve bank stock to be a burden on member banks, the yield on this practically riskless investment has been very attractive, but the amount that may be invested therein is so small relative to a bank's total assets that it has little influence on membership in the Federal Reserve System. The restriction on dividends is a reminder that the Federal Reserve banks are to be operated as public banks, not as private profit-seeking institutions. The income of Federal Reserve banks is used to cover the expenses of the banks, the Board of Governors, and the Open Market Committee and other committees; and the federal government receives all earnings remaining after the banks pay expenses and dividends. If the "surplus" accounts of the Federal Reserve banks were to fall below their paid-in capital, earnings would be retained until the situation could be corrected. Currently, the Federal Reserve banks have their own auditing staffs and use the services of certified public accounting firms of "national repute."

The semipublic nature of the Federal Reserve banks was recognized in the Act by not authorizing them to accept deposits from or lend to the general public. Instead their relations with private institutions were limited to member banks whose legal reserves they were required to hold and whose short-term paper they were authorized to discount without disturbing the business of commercial banks and their customers. They were designated as fiscal agents for the federal government and authorized to accept deposits from the government, governmental agencies, and foreign central banks and governments.

Branches. Branches of Federal Reserve banks are offices of these banks that perform most of the functions of their parent banks. In effect, a branch bank is a miniature Federal Reserve bank, having a seven-man board of directors, of whom three are appointed by the Board of Governors and four by the parent bank. However, these directors serve in an advisory capacity and have no powers corresponding to those of directors of Federal Reserve banks.

The deciding factors in placing branches are geographical and economic. Compact districts within easy reach of the district reserve city, such as districts 1 (Boston) and 3 (Philadelphia), have no branches; others have only one; but in the South and West, where the districts are large, some Federal Reserve banks have three and four branches. Each branch is assigned a territory that includes banks that normally transact business with the city in which the branch is located (currently there are 24 branch offices).

The specific activities of the branches depend upon rules and regulations of the Board and grants of power by the parent bank. Some of the branches carry on independently the same activities as those performed by the parent bank. During World War II the Federal Reserve banks increased the functions and powers of branches in order that they could give better service to member banks and the government. Most of the branches now have fiscal and other central-banking functions comparable to those of the head office.

Board of Directors. Provisions for Management of Reserve banks are similar to those of other large banking institutions. Each of these banks has a board of directors of nine members, each having a term of office of three years. Six of the directors are selected by member banks (stockholders), and three are appointed by the Board of Governors of the Federal Reserve System (Class C directors).

Three of the six directors selected by the member banks must be bankers (Class A directors), and three must represent industry (Class B directors). "Looking at the make-up of Reserve bank board of directors in another way, Class A directors represent lenders of funds, Class B directors represent borrowers, and Class C represent the interest of the general public.[10] Member banks are divided according to size into three groups, and each group elects one Class A and one Class B director from its group (voting is by mail because no annual meeting of stockholders is held), but directors rarely act as representatives of their classes after taking office. Insofar as credit policy is concerned, directors act only on discount rates, which are subject to review and determination by the Board of Governors. Presidents of the Federal Reserve banks, as members of the Federal Open Market Committee, may be influenced by the opinions of their boards of directors, but usually they act independently.

The board of directors of a Federal Reserve bank performs duties comparable to those of directors of any commercial bank, such as adoption of bylaws under which the bank's general business is conducted; selection of officers and their salaries, subject to approval by the Board of Governors; appointment of an auditor in charge of internal auditing of the bank's books; preparation of the annual budget, which is reviewed by the Board; and supervision of the general functioning of the bank.

Directors of Federal Reserve banks also have functions peculiar to these banks, such as appointing a commercial banker to the Federal Advisory Council and four of the seven directors of branch offices. Directors must make recommendations to the Board of Governors on applications for voting permits by holding companies and are required to meet periodically to review credit conditions and pass on discounts and advances, discount rates, and other matters requiring action.

Officers and Staffs. In 1914, the problems encountered in staffing the Federal Reserve banks were similar to those of any new institution wherein there is little knowledge of the amount and nature of the work to be performed. There were misunderstandings over who was to be the chief executive officer, one selected by the bank's board of directors or the chairman of the board, who was selected by the Federal Reserve Board. As a matter of fact, each Federal Reserve bank's board of directors selected a chief executive officer (called governor) and, until 1935, each bank had two executive officers. In

[10] Board of Governors of the Federal Reserve System, *The Federal Reserve System: Its Purposes and Functions* (Washington, D.C., 1947), pp. 53–54.

1935, Congress made provisions for a president for each bank and stripped the chairman of the board of directors of most of his powers.

Now, the president is the chief executive officer of his bank and is responsible for its general functioning. All executive officers except the auditor are directly responsible to him. Although the president is not a member of the board of directors, he attends the meetings and participates in its discussions. His term of office is five years and the salary is sufficient to attract capable men. At one time, commercial bankers were selected as presidents; but now the practice of promoting from within is more common (with economists on the staffs often getting the call).[11]

All Federal Reserve banks have a first vice president, a variable number of other vice presidents, and other officers in charge of departments and branches. There are officers in charge of discounts and advances (loans); collection of notes and other items; collection of checks and transfer of funds; issues of Federal Reserve notes; fiscal agency functions for the government; bank examinations; collection, analysis, and distribution of economic data; and personnel.

One of the Class C directors is, at the same time, the chairman of the board of directors and the Federal Reserve agent of his bank. He presides at all meetings of the board, and in his absence his place is taken by the deputy chairman. The Federal Reserve agent is appointed by and is the official representative of the Board of Governors at his bank (as is the deputy chairman). With the help of assistants, he administers duties in connection with the issuance of Federal Reserve notes and has such other powers as may be specified by the Board of Governors and by the board of directors of his bank.

A state member bank may withdraw from membership after giving six months' notice (a requirement that may be waived by the Board of Governors if the bank's federal deposit insurance has been terminated and/or if its banking practices have been unsound or illegal). Prior to 1952 a state-chartered bank's capital had to be equal to the amount required of a national bank similarly located, but the current rule is that its capital stock and surplus must be adequate in the judgment of the Board of Governors.

By 1920, state-bank membership had increased to over 1,300, but there were still about 20,000 state banks outside the System. Because state member banks, especially large ones, were treated more generously than national banks, the latter found it difficult to compete with

---

[11] One third of the 12 presidents have Ph.D. degrees from outstanding universities, and over half of them have had teaching experience in colleges or universities.

state member banks of similar size for trust, investment, loan, and safe-deposit businesses. Furthermore, the more restrictive rules applicable to branching by national banks stiffled their growth and many reincorporated as state banks. Although many of the larger national banks rechartered as state banks from 1919 to 1926, most of them retained their membership in the Federal Reserve System which indicates that they objected to the discriminatory laws and regulations applicable only to national banks rather than to federal regulation.[12] While these developments reduced the importance of the national banking system, they did not affect the importance of the Federal Reserve System.

MEMBERSHIP

Although the Federal Reserve banks retain the form of private corporations, they posses little of the corporate substance; and, in order to preserve their cooperative aspect, Congress has limited their shareholders to member banks. However there is little danger that any single member bank may acquire a majority interest through stock ownership because the amount of stock that may be owned is fixed at a small percentage of each bank's capital stock and surplus. Stock is not transferable and, when a bank withdraws from membership, its shares are canceled.

Unlike ordinary procedures for voting, each member bank has but one vote regardless of the stock held; and stockholders, as a group, elect six of the nine directors of their Federal Reserve banks. However, each shareholder is assigned to a class of member banks and is permitted to vote for only two of the six directors selected by shareholders. Congress specifies that only one of the two must be from the shareholders' own group and that the other must come from some other occupation. This is the sole role of shareholders in the management of their Federal Reserve banks; because there are no annual meetings to attend, no opportunities to ask questions, and no voice in the amount of dividends is permitted (they are fixed at 6 percent).

The Federal Reserve System was regarded as a cooperative venture; therefore, many argued that membership should be voluntary

---

[12] The large New York banks that gave up their national charters included the Merchants National, Irving National, Bank of New York National Banking Association, Importers and Traders National, and Liberty National. Other banks withdrawing included the Manufacturers and Traders of Buffalo, First National and Union Commerce National of Cleveland, Corn Exchange National of Chicago, Third National of Atlanta, National Bank of Commerce of Kansas City, and Wells Fargo National Bank of San Francisco.

and that each bank should determine for itself whether or not the advantages of membership outweighed the disadvantages. At the other extreme were those who insisted that all banks accepting checking accounts should be compelled to join the System. Most congressmen were aware of the fact that deposit currency was our most important means of payment, which had not been the case in 1866 when the passage of the "death sentence" clause eliminated the circulation of state bank notes.

In the Federal Reserve Act, which was a compromise, Congress again failed to establish sovereignty over our money system when it required only national banks to become members within one year or forfeit their charters and permitted, rather than required, state-chartered banks to become members. National banks have always provided the core of membership, while the majority of state banks have been unfriendly toward membership. The original intent was for all member banks to operate under the same conditions as national banks but so few state banks entered during the first three years that Congress, as a war measure, changed the law so that they could retain their statutory and charter rights as state banks while receiving all the privileges of membership.

Nonmember Banks. Many state-chartered banks obtain central-banking services from correspondent banks and have no desire for membership in the Federal Reserve System because they may carry on more profitable banking outside the System. For example, they often secure considerable revenue from exchange charges on checks forwarded to them for payment, while member banks must remit at par. In addition, nonmember banks have been subject to fewer restrictions on loans and investments and to less rigid examinations, but the most important advantage enjoyed by nonmember banks is that their primary reserves need not be as large as those of member banks. However, the Federal Deposit Insurance Corporation, which has an important financial interest in the well-being of all insured banks, has set standards that have eliminated some of the so-called "advantages" formerly enjoyed by nonmember banks. However, the success of the Federal Deposit Insurance Corporation seems to have made membership even less desirable to nonmember banks.

Some of the privileges associated with membership in the Federal Reserve System have been extended to nonmember banks. These include use of the clearing and collection services of the Federal Reserve System, provided that the clearing nonmember banks keep funds on deposit with the Federal Reserve banks and remit at par for cash items collected, and the privilege of borrowing from the Federal Reserve banks under emergency circumstances.

While the wisdom of including many small banks in the Federal Reserve System has been questioned, the fact remains that, in order to be most effective, national credit policy must apply to all commercial banks. Because membership in the Federal Deposit Insurance Corporation is more attractive than membership in the Federal Reserve System, it has been proposed, as a method of increasing Federal Reserve membership, to make membership in the Federal Reserve System a prerequisite for membership in the Federal Deposit Insurance Corporation (rather than the other way round, as is true today). Ownership of Federal Reserve bank stock is an incentive to membership and, with the recent reductions in member-bank reserve requirements, it may be that membership will be more attractive in the future than it has been in the past; but even more important would be the elimination of more of the archaic laws that restrict the operations of national banks. Although the 1,500 state-chartered and 5,000 national banks that are members of the Federal Reserve System constitute less than 50 percent of the country's commercial banks, these member banks hold 80 percent of the total resources of the commercial banking system.

SUMMARY

The functions of central banks that set them apart from ordinary commercial banks include holding reserves of other banks, acting as fiscal agents for their governments, issuing paper money, and acting as the instruments through which the supply of money and credit is controlled. Although some of the early American banks performed the first three of these functions, they did not have the power or capacity to perform the fourth and could not stave off money panics. The Federal Reserve System was born in bitter controversy, and there was no assurance that it would gain the popular support necessary for its survival. However, the outbreak of war in Europe in 1914 and the series of economic, military, and political events that followed made the Federal Reserve System one of the foremost financial powers among central banks in the world in less than five years.

The main divisions of the Federal Reserve System are the Board of Governors of the Federal Reserve System, the Federal Open Market Committee, the 12 Federal Reserve banks, and the member banks. The central-banking part of the System consists of the Federal Reserve banks and their branches and the central-banking authorities in

Washington—the Board of Governors and the Federal Open Market Committee, which are responsible for all major policy decisions. In effect, the central-banking system of the United States is a group-banking system with major policy authority vested in hands other than the directors and officers of the Federal Reserve banks.

The centralization of policy decisions and control over investment activities of the Federal Reserve banks in Washington reflects the change in emphasis from state and regional affairs to national and international affairs. Today, there is greater awareness of international as well as national problems. The expansion in the size of the economy and the increase in the interdependence of nations has necessitated greater centralization of the Federal Reserve System than was visualized by the framers of the Federal Reserve Act in 1913. Fortunately, the System has sufficient flexibility to make changes as they are needed.

By creating branches, the Federal Reserve authorities have given member banks located in and near branch cities many of the advantages of a Federal Reserve city location. These advantages include faster clearing and collection of checks and other items; reduction in vault cash needed, since new currency can be obtained quickly; and closer personal touch between member banks' officers and Federal Reserve banks' officers.

To fail to make the Federal Reserve System accountable to Congress, as the representative of the general public, would be unthinkable; but, to make the System an agency of the Treasury would be equally deplorable because of difference in the basic philosophies of the two agencies. The Board of Governors may approve unpopular policies but the Secretary of the Treasury must be mindful of the political effects of his decisions on controversial matters. The members of the Board of Governors remain in office for the duration of their terms, while the Secretary of the Treasury may be removed by the President at any time. In order to make monetary and credit policy more effective greater consideration should be given to transferring some of the Treasury's monetary powers to the Board of Governors of the Federal Reserve System.

The most unusual aspect of the Federal Reserve System is the existence of 12 banks that have all the functions of central banks but whose major banking policies are determined for them by the Board of Governors and the Federal Open Market Committee in Washington (instead of by their own boards of directors, as is the case with ordinary banks). Thus, in effect, the Federal Reserve banks are but individual units of a group central-banking system. The minor role currently played by these central banks in making policy decisions was not the original intention, but the United States of today is very different from that of 1913. Equally important developments have taken place in the field of international finance. Following World War I, the United States emerged as one of the most important trade nations in the world, with New York as a leading financial center.

The economic collapse of 1929 ushered in a new philosophy of the role of the government in monetary and other economic affairs. So today we have 12 Federal Reserve banks performing all central-banking functions—issuing notes, holding and creating bank reserves, and acting as fiscal agents for the national government—but carrying out decisions made, for the most part, by the Board of Governors of the Federal Reserve System and the Treasury Department in Washington.

The concentration of power on national credit and monetary policies in Washington has set the stage for a conflict between those in favor of greater government control of the Federal Reserve System and those in favor of "an independent Federal Reserve System." What the Federal Reserve System means by an "independent Federal Reserve System" is one independent of the executive branch of government; but the complete independence from the executive branch is impossible because the latter has fiscal, monetary, and credit powers that could make shambles of any credit policy of the Federal Reserve System. Hence, the two must cooperate.

QUESTIONS AND PROBLEMS

1. Identify (*a*) regional plan of organization of the Federal Reserve System, (*b*) Federal Reserve Board, (*c*) Federal Reserve districts, and (*d*) Federal Reserve banks.

2. What important changes have taken place in the organization of the Federal Reserve System since 1914? In the location of power over credit policies?

3. Explain: "Although the Federal Reserve banks retain the form of private corporations, they possess little of the corporate substance."

4. Identify the Federal Open Market Committee. What changes have been made in its composition and powers since 1922? Why have these changes been made?

5. "To one accustomed to responsibility being centralized in one person, the decentralization of authority and policymaking procedure of the Federal Reserve System may appear confusing and cumbersome." (Federal Reserve Bank of Philadelphia, *Business Review*, August,

1960, p. 9.) Do you agree? Why? What are the advantages and disadvantages?

6. Analyze: For over 20 years, the Secretary of the Treasury was a member of the Board. "The Banking Act of 1935 eliminated [him] as a member because, as Senator Carter Glass admitted, referring to his brief tenure as Secretary of the Treasury, 'I dominated the activities of the Board, and I always directed them in the interest of the Treasury, and so did my predecessor.'" (William B. Widnall, "A Committee Minority Member Views the Patman Hearings," *Banking*, May, 1964, p. 50.)

7. What constitutes membership in the Federal Reserve System? What institutions are compulsory members? Voluntary members? What justification would there be for requiring all United States commercial banks to be members of the Federal Reserve System? What changes have been made recently in the eligibility requirements for membership?

8. Analyze: "Mr. Robertson conceded, in theory at least, that it would be possible for bankers . . . [who elect] five of the 12 members of the [open market] committee, to unduly influence the committee itself." (*New York Times*, January 24, 1964, p. 37.)

9. Discuss: "The Federal Reserve Act . . . moved in a half-blind way toward completion of what had been only partly accomplished 50 years before. The means of . . . regulating the volume (of) . . . deposits in the commercial banks of the country was placed in the hands of an agency of the federal government, the Federal Reserve System." (Allan Sproul, "The Federal Reserve System—Working Partner of the Federal Reserve System for Half a Century," in Dean Carson (ed.), *Banking and Monetary Studies* [Homewood, Illinois: Richard D. Irwin, Inc., 1963], p. 65.)

10. Explain: The "Federal Reserve Organization . . . is far from monolithic, being composed of four main groups—the Board of Governors, the Federal Reserve Banks, the Federal Open Market Committee, and the Federal Advisory Council. . . . Although all parts of the System act in a public capacity, the appearance is one of a mixture of public and private participation." (David P. Eastburn, *The Federal Reserve on Record* [Philadelphia, Pa.: Federal Reserve Bank of Philadelphia, 1965], p. 173.)

CHAPTER 9

Commercial Banks—A Source of Money

IN THE United States and other countries, debts of commercial banks in the form of ledger accounts (called demand deposits) are used by individuals, business firms, governments, and others to settle money obligations whether resulting from long-term contracts or current sales. The most commonly used method of transferring title to a demand deposit from one name to a second is by giving a check written by the debtor (drawer or payer) to the creditor (drawee or payee); but this transfer may be made by an oral, written, or wire request to a bank to debit one account and credit that of a second party.

Banks generally debit deposit accounts of their customers for service charges, rent on safe-deposit boxes, and other amounts due the banks. Many business firms and institutions follow the practice of paying employees by arranging with their banks to credit their employees' accounts with the appropriate monthly salaries and to debit the employers' accounts with the gross amounts transferred. Among financial institutions, the preferred method of payment is by transfers of bank credit on the books of the Federal Reserve banks. The fact that deposit currency and checkless transfers lack the legal-tender quality possessed by coins and paper money is of little or no importance in the United States.

DEVELOPMENT OF DEPOSIT CURRENCY

The existence of deposits is as old as banking, but the practice of transferring title to deposits by orders written by individuals is only of fairly recent development. It resulted logically from the practice of banks in using bank drafts to transfer funds between domestic centers and between foreign countries. Some claim that the Romans invented the check as early as 352 B.C.; but the first organized bank to handle deposit currency was the Bank of Amsterdam.

Bank of Amsterdam.   In 1609, the officials of the city of Amsterdam organized the Bank of Amsterdam to give the community relief from worn and defaced coins. The bank's business was to accept and keep gold and silver coins in perpetuity and to make transfers of credits from one account to another on written orders (an illustration of the 100 percent reserve plan).[1]

When new accounts were opened at the Bank of Amsterdam, the coins deposited were tested and accepted at a 5 percent discount; in addition, the depositor paid a service charge of 10 florins to cover the cost of opening his account. The discount entailed no penalty for the depositor because he had a superior means of payment that could be sold at a premium for coins. Although accounts were not convertible into specie, they could be sold to others (often through brokers). Instead of redeeming its checking accounts, the Bank of Amsterdam employed brokers to repurchase those offered. The Bank also accepted money with the understanding that it would be returned on request, charging a fee for its services (as modern banks do when they rent safe-deposit boxes and accept valuable items for safekeeping). The Bank also accepted special accounts that could be withdrawn at the end of a certain period of time, and a fee was charged the depositor (usually one half of 1 percent for bullion and a smaller amount for coins).

According to the plan, the Bank of Amsterdam was to keep all gold and silver received as a 100 percent reserve against deposits. However, during the Panic of 1672, when the French Army entered the Low Countries, depositors were paid in bullion or coin. In 1790, 180 years after the bank opened for business, it was discovered that a large part of its gold and silver had disappeared 50 years previously. It had been lent illegally to the city government, the provinces of Holland, and the East India Company. As managers of the bank, the city's magistrates had failed in their trust, and the bank failed even though it had been operated under the guaranty of the city.

Goldsmiths.   In England, the development of bank notes and check currency, toward the latter part of the 17th century, was related to the activities of goldsmiths. The goldsmiths accepted gold and silver in exchange for "goldsmith notes," a type of paper money, which was used as a means of payment. In addition, a customer could direct the goldsmith in writing to pay a certain person, or the bearer of the note, a specific sum of money. The orders were similar to

[1] Stephen Coldwell, *The Ways and Means of Payment* (New York: J. B. Lippincott & Co., 1859), pp. 174–81.

modern checks but were not uniform until some years later. About 1722 a private banking firm in London, Messrs. Child and Company, "began to supply their customers with printed cheque forms which they might complete as drafts for any amount and payable to any of their creditors."[2] Goldsmiths lent part of the gold and silver left on deposit with them and kept the rest as a reserve. It was much later, after the check was well established as a means of payment, that banks created deposit by lending and giving the proceeds of the loans as checking accounts rather than in the form of gold and silver.

Checks. Checks may have been used as early as 1680 in Boston, and since that time their use has increased steadily until an average of 80 checks is written per person per year in the United States. At the present time, there are over 50 million checking accounts, and payments made with checks represent between 85 and 90 percent of the dollars spent. If there were but one bank, the process of collecting and paying checks would entail merely charging the accounts of drawers and crediting those of payees for the appropriate amounts. However, there are about 13,800 banks on which millions of people write checks to pay their bills, and there are millions of recipients of these checks who direct these banks to collect them. Obviously, a tremendous amount of bookkeeping, sorting, mailing, and routine handling of check is required.

Over the years, banks have developed an elaborate organization to handle checks, including not only their own transit and bookkeeping departments but also the facilities of local clearinghouses, correspondent banks, and the Federal Reserve System. Now a bank customer is supplied with books of checks imprinted with his name, address, telephone number, zip code, and account number printed in magnetic ink containing iron oxide filings. This ink permits machines to "read" the checks and sort and route them through the clearinghouse or other agency to the banks on which they are drawn. Checks other than those containing the magnetic ink number are treated as "special items" because they cannot be handled by the high-speed electric computers.

Bank tellers are expected to recognize the signatures of their demand-deposit customers so that payments are made only to proper persons. Normally a bank bears the loss if payment is made on a forged signature; therefore, a bank customer should not take it amiss when a bank teller examines his signature and asks for identification.

[2] H. E. Evitt, *Practical Banking* (London: Sir I. Pittman, Ltd., 1935), p. 5.

In addition, bank depositors are expected to examine their statements and to notify their banks of any unauthorized signatures or alterations in any items within a reasonable period of time, not exceeding 14 days.[3]

Unlike legal-tender money, which is generally acceptable, a check's acceptability depends in part on the credit standing of the drawer and on whether or not he is known to the one asked to accept it. Because checks are not expected to circulate widely, there is no official supervision to see that they are drawn correctly. Hence, there is always the possibility that the signature of the drawer may not be genuine, the drawer's account may not be sufficient to cover the amount of the check, the date may be incorrect, the signature may differ from that on the depositor's signature card, the check may have been altered after having been written by the drawer, or the bank on which it is written may be nonexistent.

While losses are incurred by acceptance of counterfeit paper money, the risk is small compared to the risk of accepting fraudulent checks. Although efforts are made constantly by commercial banks and the Federal Reserve System to improve the deposit currency system, there is no way to prevent people from being dishonest; the best that can be done is to minimize the opportunity for misuse of deposit currency and to expose and punish offenders promptly. Individuals should cooperate by presenting checks promptly because the longer checks remain in circulation, the greater is the opportunity for misuse and the greater the risk. However, with the exception of certified checks, banks are under no obligation to pay checks that are more than six months old. Generally, banks must start the procedure for transmitting and presenting checks to payers' banks by the "midnight deadline" (by midnight of the business day after the day of receipt).

COLLECTION OF LOCAL CHECKS

Whether drawn on the bank wherein a check is to be deposited, on another local bank, or on an out-of-town bank, any check deposited with a bank must be collected and returned to the bank on which it is drawn. A check deposited in the bank on which it is drawn is sent to the bookkeeping department to be credited to and debited against individual accounts. If drawn on another local bank, it is sent to the clearinghouse division to be prepared for the local clearinghouse. A check drawn on an out-of-town bank is sent to the transit department

---

[3] See *Uniform Commercial Code*, Sec. 4–406.

to be mailed to a correspondent bank or to the district Federal Reserve bank.

Clearinghouse. A clearinghouse is an association of banks whose primary function is to facilitate the exchange of checks and other items (as agreed upon by members) and to settle any resulting balances so as to avoid needless transfers of funds. Of course, each bank could exchange all items directly with all the other banks in the community, but in a community having 10 banks this would necessitate 45 clearing and settling operations (9 for the first bank, 8 for the second bank, and so on). If the 10 banks participate in a clearinghouse arrangement and regard all their claims as being against the clearinghouse, the number of operations is reduced from 45 to 10.

In preparing for a clearing, each bank sorts and packages all clearinghouse items according to drawee banks, computes the total for each bank, and adds these figures to arrive at the sum due from the clearinghouse. At the appointed time each bank sends a delivery clerk and a settling clerk to the designated building where the clearing is to take place. They carry the bundles of checks previously prepared—one for each of the other clearinghouse members and containing the clearing items and a statement listing the dollar amount of each check in the group, together with the total amount. The settling clerk gives the clearinghouse manager a statement showing the total amount that the clearinghouse owes his bank. After the manager adds the figures presented by the clerks, he will have the total of claims on the clearinghouse (total clearings). When the gong sounds, the delivery clerks will give their bundles of checks to the settling clerks of the other banks. The latter add the total of the figures appearing on the bundles of checks they receive, and the totals are what their banks owe the clearinghouse. Each settling clerk notifies the manager, and the latter adds these figures and then checks the total against the claims on the clearinghouse. The total of the amounts of claims on the clearinghouse must be the same as the total of the amounts owed to the clearinghouse. (In Table 9–1, the same amount is reached by reading down under total credits as by reading across for total debits.)

While the total "claims on" and "amounts owed to" the clearinghouse must be the same, this is not the case with individual banks, and ordinarily the differences must be settled with money. Each settling clerk computes the "credit" and "debit" position of his bank. The clearinghouse manager makes a second check on the accuracy of the clearing process by comparing total "net credits" and "net debits," which must be equal (see Table 9–1). In practice, the clearing opera-

TABLE 9–1

HYPOTHETICAL ILLUSTRATION OF CLEARING

Bank	1	2	3	4	5	Total Credits	Net Credits
1...........	...	$ 400	$ 350	$ 250	$ 200	$1,200	$100
2...........	$ 350	...	200	250	300	1,100	50
3...........	250	100	...	300	400	1,050	...
4...........	300	250	350	...	100	1,000	...
5...........	200	300	200	400	...	1,100	100
Total debits....	$1,100	$1,050	$1,100	$1,200	$1,000	$5,450	....
Net debits...........	...	...	$ 50	$ 200	...	...	$250

tion is very simple, and it usually takes but a few minutes. In smaller communities, where the volume of clearings is small, each bank may be represented by but one clerk, but the same procedures are used in all clearings.

The task of settling is given to the clearinghouse manager, who uses the method previously agreed upon by the members. One of the most popular methods is to use the facilities of the district Federal Reserve bank. Since all banks that are members of the Federal Reserve System must keep reserve deposits with their district Federal Reserve banks, and, since many nonmember banks keep "clearing balances" with these banks, the balances may be credited or debited according to a memorandum, letter, or simply a certified copy of the clearing-house settling sheet sent to the Federal Reserve bank by the clearing-house manager.

If balances are not settled through the Federal Reserve bank, the manager may be authorized to draw checks in favor of the creditor banks upon the debtor banks, which are settled in currency or bank drafts. In some clearinghouse associations, members keep balances in the clearinghouse bank; the manager uses these balances to settle claims by crediting and debiting the accounts of banks according to the day's settlement-sheet record. The recommended practice is to settle the net amount owed or due on the books of the Federal Reserve bank or a correspondent bank on the same day.

As soon as the clearing process is completed (the settling process being left to the clearinghouse manager), the clerks return to their banks with the checks and other items received from other banks. These are taken to the bookkeeping department to be debited against the accounts of the appropriate depositors. If an item has been mis-sent, an account has been overdrawn, or any other mistake has been made, it is adjusted at a second clearing held later the same day. All dishonored checks and missent items are sent back to the banks that presented them at the first clearing.

The clearing principle is hundreds of years old, but the first clearinghouse in the United States was not established until 1853. There may or may not be a clearinghouse building, although the term "clearinghouse" is commonly used to describe the place where the clearing is done. In many communities the place of the clearing is rotated among the members. A centrally located office may be rented when a number of nonclearing functions are to be performed. In Boston all the clearing functions for the clearinghouse are performed by the Federal Reserve Bank of Boston. The New York Clearinghouse owns its building, but most of the remaining 300 clearinghouses have little or no property other than the necessary office equipment, books, and stationery. Fees vary with the size of banks, volume of clearings, and amount of trade association activities, or nonclearing functions.

In addition to clearing and settling functions, clearinghouse associations act on problems common to members. (Some so-called "regional" clearinghouse associations have been organized for purposes exclusive of clearing and settling.) Clearinghouse associations usually take action on many routine problems, such as the establishment of banking hours, clearinghouse meeting hours, holidays, methods of analyzing checking accounts for service charges, amount of service charges and fees, and basis for computing interest payments for time deposits and the rate to be paid.

Clearinghouse associations have adopted policies governing the relationship of local banks to the public. They have adopted rules controlling methods and extent of advertising. In some communities they have eliminated the "buying" of business by offering gifts, donations, and prizes. Mutual resistance has been made against "drive" committees and other pressure salesmen, and maximum donations have been fixed by clearinghouse rules. Educational work done by clearinghouse groups includes sponsoring thrift clubs and distributing home modernization plans, income tax instructions, household budgets, and educational materials to school children and the public.

Frequently clearinghouse associations operate credit bureaus in order to improve credit practices. In the past, clearinghouses frequently examined member institutions, but this practice has become less common because of the costs involved and the superior facilities of other bank-examining agencies. No fewer than 11 times, clearinghouses have assumed leadership in panics when a sudden widespread fright seized depositors, bankers, and other members of the financial community. It was during the Panic of 1857 that the New York Clearinghouse introduced emergency money, the clearinghouse certificate, which was used most recently in 1933. This certificate was a promissory note of the members of the clearinghouse secured by collateral held by an agent.

ILLUSTRATION 9–1

CLEARINGHOUSE CERTIFICATE

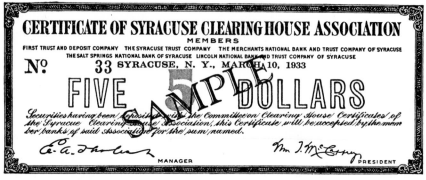

All local banks should participate in local clearings; but, it is not unusual for small banks in some cities to clear through a clearinghouse member. Since over 30 percent of out-of-town checks received by country banks for collection are drawn on banks within a radius of 25 miles, many areas have set up central clearing arrangements (using armored cars) through which checks are presented to the drawees with settlement through a Federal Reserve bank or a correspondent.

Control of the clearinghouse is placed in the hands of an executive committee. Officers—president, vice president, secretary, treasurer, and manager—are elected or appointed. With, perhaps, the exception of the manager, they serve without pay. The president, vice president, and members of the executive committee are usually key men in the banking community where the clearinghouse is located.

CORRESPONDENT BANKING

The oldest method of clearing and collecting out-of-town checks is through the services of so-called correspondent banks. A correspondent bank is one that maintains reciprocal business relations with a bank in another city. Although the two banks participating in a correspondent-banking relationship may be approximately the same size, usually one bank is much larger than the other and located so as to give financial services desired by the smaller bank. This means that services given by the larger bank tend to be dominant in the mutual arrangement and that the smaller bank usually reciprocates by keeping a deposit with the larger bank. These deposits are the means for settling checks handled, and they are usually large enough to compensate the correspondent for handling collection items. When rising interest rates make earning assets more attractive, banks tend to shift some of their idle bank balances into investments. However, the correspondent banks may be able to maintain their services on relatively smaller balances because of technical changes and the increase in earnings on remaining balances.

Today New York banks are acting as correspondents for banks in hundreds of other cities, and some of them hold deposit accounts of hundreds of customer banks. Banks in other large cities are acting as correspondents for banks in smaller cities, and those in small cities are acting as correspondents for banks in towns and villages. In practice, a bank may be keeping bankers' balances, also called "interbank deposits," with several different banks at the same time. As a result, a complex voluntary working relationship among banks blankets the country, and, since certain metropolitan banks (sometimes called "international" banks) have extended these arrangements to include banks in foreign countries, the correspondent-banking system is international in scope of operations.

When a respondent bank sends a check to a correspondent bank for collection, it usually receives immediate credit, even though the check will not be paid by the drawer's bank until later. (This is similar to the immediate credit for checking purposes that most individuals are given when they deposit checks in their banks.) This practice is dangerous, but it simplifies bookkeeping and is justified for that reason. The correspondent bank may present the item to the drawer's bank indirectly through the clearinghouse if drawn on a local bank. If the drawer's bank is located in another city, however, the correspondent may deposit the check with the Federal Reserve bank for collection, mail it to its correspondent in the area where the drawer's bank is located, or send it directly to the bank on which it is drawn for payment.

A bank may keep a deposit with a correspondent bank for the same reasons that any depositor keeps an account with his bank—as a means of payment. A bank in Austin, Texas, may write checks (bank drafts) on its deposit in a New York bank in order to buy bills, notes, government bonds, and other types of assets; or the Austin bank may sell bank drafts on its account with the New York bank to customers so that they can use it as a means of payment. The individual who buys the draft may not have a checking account, or his personal check may or may not be acceptable in payment of some particular obligation. The bank will charge a small fee for its draft, which will vary according to the amount of money involved.

A correspondent bank may provide its respondent bank with services other than those associated with clearing and collecting checks. Among these services are giving advice on investments, loans, collection procedures, insurance protection, advertising, accounting and auditing practices, pension and profit-sharing plans, job analysis, equipment, taxes, and other bank problems; acting as agent in making loans and investments; providing credit information on firms that borrow in the open market; providing foreign-exchange facilities, including commercial and travelers' letters of credit and travelers' checks; sharing large loans; and providing funds or loans in case of need. Thus, the correspondent banking system makes the services and talents of large banks available to small banks.

FEDERAL RESERVE SYSTEM CLEARING AND COLLECTION

The Federal Reserve System, in addition to its responsibility for the flow of money expenditures, helps to improve the quality of money by providing for economical and prompt clearing and collection of checks and noncash items (which include matured notes, drafts, and matured securities except government obligations, which are handled by the Federal Reserve banks as fiscal agents for the government). The Federal Reserve System's procedure for settling balances among banks has greatly reduced the need for shipping currency (see Table 9–2).

Collection of Cash Items.   Now, the Federal Reserve banks ordinarily collect the following as cash items: (1) checks drawn on banks located in any Federal Reserve district if the checks are collectible at par in funds acceptable to the Federal Reserve bank; (2) government checks drawn on the Treasurer of the United States; (3) U.S. postal money orders, and (4) such other items that the Federal Reserve bank is willing to accept as cash items and which must meet the standards set for checks (see Table 9–2).

Member banks and nonmember clearing banks that use the services of the Federal Reserve banks in order to get prompt credit for cash items sort, list and place them in separate "cash" letters according to the Reserve bank's time schedule. For some items, immediate credit

TABLE 9-2

VOLUME OF OPERATIONS IN PRINCIPAL DEPARTMENTS OF FEDERAL RESERVE BANKS, 1964–67
(Number in Thousands; Amounts in Thousands of Dollars)

Operation	1967	1966	1965	1964
Number of Pieces Handled:*				
Discounts and advances....	6	16	11	10
Currency received and counted..............	5,338,781	5,232,806	5,144,345	5,026,311
Coin received and counted..	10,958,606	9,304,120	5,855,884	4,561,704
Checks handled:				
U.S. government checks.	540,065	504,049	491,848	467,288
Postal money orders....	205,343	217,473	223,337	234,094
All other†............	5,419,583	5,021,454	4,606,907‡	4,318,703‡
Collection items handled:				
U.S. government coupons paid...........	14,355	14,305	14,087	15,042
All other.............	25,203	26,712	26,820	27,271
Issues, redemptions, and exchanges of U.S. government securities......	246,289	235,555	222,477	212,267
Transfers of funds........	5,444	4,832	4,389	4,010
Food stamps redeemed....	273,983	166,615	81,885	50,481
Amounts Handled:				
Discounts and advances....	30,968,332	90,667,647	75,684,394	46,551,402
Currency received and counted..............	38,410,969	37,001,390	36,075,114	34,548,507
Coin received and counted..	1,184,616	957,282	496,582	559,588
Checks handled:				
U.S. government checks.	175,068,179	160,014,331	134,806,438	134,585,725
Postal money orders....	4,860,925	4,626,573	4,507,801	4,578,853
All other†............	2,043,772,112	1,893,974,522	1,633,863,858‡	1,462,383,319‡
Collection items handled:				
U.S. government coupons paid...........	6,693,383	5,916,485	5,380,748	5,371,153
All other.............	15,299,519	12,624,804	10,723,571	7,851,274
Issues, redemptions, and exchanges of U.S. government securities......	820,283,379	793,261,958	763,248,392	738,062,697
Transfers of funds........	6,565,594,328	5,555,075,862	4,496,230,723	3,953,186,948
Food stamps redeemed....	368,569	226,508	116,498	73,182

* Packaged items handled as a single item are counted as one piece.
† Exclusive of checks drawn on the F.R. Banks.
‡ Revised.
Source: *Fifty-Fourth Annual Report of the Board of Governors of the Federal Reserve System Covering Operations for the Year 1967*, p. 362.

is given at full face value in the reserve account or clearing account on the day of receipt; and the proceeds are counted as reserves and may be withdrawn or used immediately by the sending bank. For other items, deferred credit is entered on the books at full face value, but the proceeds are not counted as reserves and may not be drawn on or used until the expiration of the time specified in the bank's time schedule.

At the end of that period, credit is transferred to the member bank's reserve account or nonmember bank's clearing account and is available for withdrawal or use by the depositing bank. However, the Federal Reserve bank reserves the right to disapprove withdrawals or use of credit given for any item for which it has not received payment.

Each Federal Reserve bank and branch has its own time schedule, which indicates when checks will be credited to the reserve balances (or clearing accounts of nonmember banks) of the banks that deposit them for collection. Customarily, checks that are drawn on banks in or near the city where the collecting Federal Reserve bank or branch is located are given immediate credit. The time schedule for giving deferred credit was originally as long as two weeks, but with improvements in transportation and changes in Federal Reserve policy the maximum time has been reduced to two days. Thus, the Federal Reserve is moving more closely to the policies followed by correspondent banks in giving immediate credit to customer banks and by local banks in giving immediate credit to old depositors.

Under current conditions it is not possible for the Federal Reserve banks to collect all items within the time limits set on deferred credit. Therefore, on their balance sheets the item "cash items in process of collection" will be larger than the item "deferred availability cash items." The difference between the two is Federal Reserve "float," which represents reserve credit given member banks free of interest. For the Federal Reserve banks, the solution would be to adopt a more realistic time schedule or to give credit only for collected items. The disadvantages of doing so include extra bookkeeping costs and ill will of the commercial banks, who feel that the Federal Reserve banks should be at least as generous with them as they are with their customers.

Check Handling. When the transit department of a Federal Reserve bank receives a package of checks from a member bank, the checks must be sorted and sent in a "cash letter" to the banks on which they are drawn. The receiving bank must remit the amount due on the day of receipt in the form of acceptable and immediately available funds. The cash letter may include checks that must be returned because of insufficient funds or other reasons. The amount of such items is deducted from the remittance (otherwise, it may be deducted from and returned with remittance for the cash letter received the following day).

The Federal Reserve banks handle 90 percent of out-of-town checks and all checks with magnetic ink character symbols are fed into a computer feedbox where the reader-sorter places the checks into the proper pockets; then the lister-printer prints the following on the master list: (1) the amount of each check, (2) the payer bank's electronic address, (3) the dollar amount of checks dropped in each pocket, and (4) the total amount of all checks in all pockets. The bank now has the checks sorted by banks on which they were drawn, the amount owed by each bank, and the total amount that is to be credited to the account of the depository bank. Each computer is able to process 65,000 checks per hour or about 50 times as many as by the older proof-machine method (which is still used to clear the "headache" checks or those that are not "machinable").

The Magnetic Ink Character Recognition program (MICR) has been in operation for about 10 years; but there are still too many checks that require special handling. Among the steps taken by the Federal Reserve banks to discourage use of nonconforming items is to treat those of over $1,000 as noncash items and to charge back and return all others to the sending banks. The latter may be returned to the "Fed" as "noncash items" or as cash items if the sending bank provides the symbol–transit number on the checks.

When a package of checks is received by the Fed for credit, the headache checks must be counted so that the bank has an accurate total of all checks received from each bank. Sending banks will receive credit for cash items within two days or less but will receive credit for noncash items only after they are collected. A check without the MICR symbols that is to be handled as a cash item may be held over for one day. Counter drafts comprise the largest number of nonconforming checks and most business firms are eliminating their use by accepting only personalized checks. As a result their average bad-check losses have been reduced from $1,000 to $100 per month (an unexpected bonus).

Since 1951, a procedure to handle money orders like checks has been used. These orders, not drawn on any particular post office, may be cashed at any post office or bank within one year after the date of issue. After being cashed, the orders are deposited with a Federal Reserve bank or branch, where they are processed and the amounts are charged to the account of the Treasurer of the United States; then they are sent to the regional accounting office of the Post Office Department in the Federal Reserve city of that district. In the collection procedure, punch-proof machines designed and installed for this purpose are used. Orders are printed on "card" checks, prepunched with a serial number and the number of the 12 Post Office regions (which conform generally to Federal Reserve districts). The operator feeds a machine that lists the amount on tape, punches the amount in the order, and sorts the orders by Post Office regions (see Table 9–2).

Collection of Noncash Items. In addition to collecting cash items, the Federal Reserve banks collect noncash items, which are defined to include "items of the following classes payable within the continental United States":[4]

1. Maturing notes, acceptances, bankers' acceptances, certificates of deposit, bills of exchange, and drafts (with or without securities, bills of lading or other documents attached).

2. Drafts and orders on savings deposits with passbooks attached.

3. Checks, drafts, and other cash items which have previously been dishonored or on which special advice of payment or dishonor is required.[5]

4. Maturing bonds and coupons (other than obligations of the United States and agencies which are redeemed by Federal Reserve banks as fiscal agents).

5. State and municipal warrants including both orders to pay addressed to officers of State and political subdivisions thereof and any special or general obligations of States and political subdivisions thereof.

6. All other evidences of indebtedness and orders to pay except checks and bank drafts handled . . . [as cash items] and checks and drafts drawn on or payable by a nonmember bank which can not be collected at par in funds acceptable to the Federal Reserve bank of the district in which such nonmember bank is located.[6]

A Federal Reserve bank acts as agent for the banks for which it collects noncash items and assumes no liability for the transaction "except for its own negligence and its guaranty of prior indorsement of the sending bank." Noncash items that are payable in a second Federal Reserve district are sent to that district's Federal Reserve bank, except when because of the size of the item or for other reasons the item is sent directly to the bank where it is payable. The items may also be sent to another agent for presentment to the person, firm, or corporation on which it is drawn or is payable. Bank drafts or other

---

[4] Board of Governors of the Federal Reserve System, *Regulation G*, p. 1.

[5] Cash items may be handled as noncash items, such as those over $1,000 that lack the proper MICR symbol.

[6] Federal Reserve banks are prohibited from handling noncash items and also cash items drawn on nonpar banks.

forms of remittance used in payment for noncash items are customarily handled as cash items (see Table 9–2).

NONPAR BANKS AND DIRECT ROUTING

Before the creation of the Federal Reserve System banks had developed a reasonably satisfactory system for clearing and collecting checks through correspondent banks, but the system had two main weaknesses—absence of universal par collection and indirect routing of checks to avoid exchange charges.

Par Collection of Checks. A Federal Reserve bank may receive checks for collection from member banks and clearing nonmember banks if such checks are collectible at par in funds acceptable to the Federal Reserve banks. This means that a bank using the collection services of the Federal Reserve System must remit at par for checks in funds acceptable to the System when the checks are presented by mail as well as when presented over the counter. It was a common practice for banks to remit (pay) less than the stated amount for checks presented by mail. If a check for $100 was presented, the drawer's account was debited for that amount, but only $99.90 was remitted to the presenting bank in payment. The drawer's bank kept the 10 cents, calling it an exchange charge. The important thing to note is that merchants and others who accepted checks drawn on nonpar banks were paid in inferior money—money at a discount from face value. It was this situation that caused the Federal Reserve System to refuse to take nonpar checks for collection.

Although the Federal Reserve System has made a great deal of progress in eliminating all money circulating at a discount in the United States, there are still many small banks on the nonpar list published and distributed to member banks by the Board of Governors (see Table 9–3). The adverse effects of nonpar remittance for checks include: increasing the costs of sorting, routing, and handling checks; forcing some banks to forgo, in part, the use of the free collection and clearing services of the Federal Reserve System; and lowering the quality of checkbook money by placing a burden on those receiving nonpar checks. The practice persists because these charges are a major source of income for small banks.

The correct procedure for any commercial bank to follow is to remit at par and then to adopt a system of service and collection charges to compensate for the loss of revenue. The drawee bank should not be permitted to shift the expense incurred in connection

TABLE 9–3

NONPAR BANKING OFFICES
(December, 1967)

State	Banks	Branches and Offices
Alabama	66	12
Alaska	1	...
Arkansas	86	23
Florida	29	...
Georgia	229	16
Louisiana	102	47
Minnesota	389	1
Mississippi	103	73
Missouri	35	...
North Carolina	41	68
South Carolina	29	3
North Dakota	93	36
South Dakota	94	26
Tennessee	56	16
Texas	22	...
Total	1,375	321

Source: *Federal Reserve Bulletin*, February, 1968, p. A–91.

with the collection and remittance for checks drawn on it by its customers to payees or indorsees of the check. The Board of Governors has recommended that all insured banks be required to pay the face amount of all valid checks drawn upon them.[7]

More Direct Routing. The Federal Reserve System has improved the quality of checkbook money not only by working toward the reduction in the number of nonpar banks but also by eliminating a great deal of time-consuming check routing. Member banks, using the Federal Reserve System collection facilities, route their checks so that they usually go directly to the district Federal Reserve bank. Checks received by a Federal Reserve bank that are drawn on banks in its own district are ordinarily forwarded or presented for payment directly to the banks on which they are drawn (intradistrict). Checks drawn on banks in a second Federal Reserve district are ordinarily forwarded for collection to the Federal Reserve bank of the district in which they are payable (interdistrict).

Sometimes arrangements are made whereby the Federal Reserve bank sends interdistrict checks directly to the banks on which they are drawn, with the second Federal Reserve bank being advised of the

[7] *Fifty-Third Annual Report of the Board of Governors of the Federal Reserve System Covering Operations for the Year 1966* (Washington, D.C.: 1966), p. 11.

transaction. This type of direct routing appears most commonly when the drawer's bank is located in adjacent territory (as from the Federal Reserve Bank of New York across the district line to a bank located in eastern Pennsylvania). This direct routing saves both time and handling by a second Federal Reserve bank.

The use of air shipments between Federal Reserve banks and their branches permits most interdistrict checks to be presented to the second Federal Reserve bank (weather permitting) within hours after they have been forwarded by the first Federal Reserve bank. However, there still remains the problem of forwarding or presenting the check to the drawer's bank for payment, as in the case of an intradistrict check. In the future there may be even more direct routing of checks, such as sending them directly to the drawers' banks in adjacent Federal Reserve districts, making direct air shipments of checks to financial centers where there is no Federal Reserve bank or branch, or using the Federal Reserve System to collect all interdistrict items.

INTERDISTRICT SETTLEMENTS

There are two flows in the clearing and collection of checks received by mail—those to be collected flow in one direction and funds for those to be settled for flow in the other. The drawer's bank may either authorize its Federal Reserve bank to deduct the amount of the checks to be collected from its deposit account or remit payment on the date of receipt of the checks. Earlier, the Federal Reserve bank had given credit to the depositing bank; so the settling and collecting processes entail changes in reserve accounts of banks at the district Federal Reserve bank for all intradistict checks.

The settling and collecting processes require an extra procedure when a check drawn on a bank in one Federal Reserve district is deposited in a bank in a second Federal Reserve district. The Federal Reserve bank that first receives the check as a deposit will have no member-bank account to debit because the drawer's bank is in a second district, so it will send the check to the Federal Reserve bank in the drawer's district, where it will be debited against the account of the drawer's bank. This leaves the second Federal Reserve bank owing the first Federal Reserve bank for the check, which will be settled through the Interdistrict Settlement Fund.

In order to facilitate settlement of obligations among the Federal Reserve banks, the Board of Governors of the Federal Reserve System created the so-called Interdistrict Settlement Fund, which consists of funds of the Federal Reserve banks kept in the United States

Treasury in Washington. The fund is managed by the Board of Governors, whose office is linked by private wire to the Federal Reserve banks (see Chart 9–1).

At the close of every business day each Federal Reserve bank and its clearing branches notify the Interdistrict Settlement Fund of the amounts due to the accounts of each of the other Federal Reserve

CHART 9–1

INTERDISTRICT COLLECTION OF CHECKS

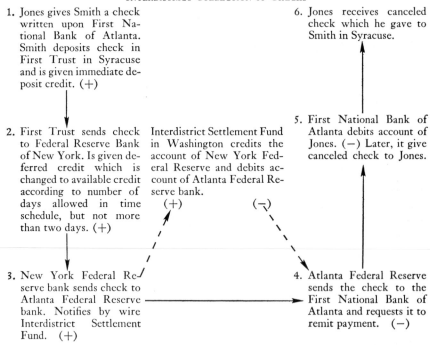

1. Jones gives Smith a check written upon First National Bank of Atlanta. Smith deposits check in First Trust in Syracuse and is given immediate deposit credit. (+)

6. Jones receives canceled check which he gave to Smith in Syracuse.

2. First Trust sends check to Federal Reserve Bank of New York. Is given deferred credit which is changed to available credit according to number of days allowed in time schedule, but not more than two days. (+)

Interdistrict Settlement Fund in Washington credits the account of New York Federal Reserve and debits account of Atlanta Federal Reserve bank. (+)   (−)

5. First National Bank of Atlanta debits account of Jones. (−) Later, it give canceled check to Jones.

3. New York Federal Reserve bank sends check to Atlanta Federal Reserve bank. Notifies by wire Interdistrict Settlement Fund. (+)

4. Atlanta Federal Reserve sends the check to the First National Bank of Atlanta and requests it to remit payment. (−)

banks and their branches as a result of clearings on that day. The accounts of the other banks are credited, and the account of the sending bank is debited. Although all wires are sent at the close of business, they arrive at different hours in Washington because of different time zones. In accordance with the telegrams received, each Federal Reserve bank's share in the total of the Interdistrict Settlement Fund will be changed, and before the start of the next business day each bank will be notified by wire as to the changes. The share of each Reserve bank in the fund is counted as part of its legal reserve maintained against its deposit liabilities and Federal Reserve notes outstanding.

Transfer of Funds. The Interdistrict Settlement Fund is also used to settle interdistrict obligations resulting from wire and mail transfers of United States Treasury funds and commercial banks' collections of such noncash items as maturing notes and acceptances, state and municipal warrants, drafts and orders on savings deposits, and maturing bonds and coupons. The facilities for daily interregional settlements through the fund are used by commercial banks for their own accounts and for their customers'. Banks' reserve accounts are debited and credited when "federal funds" are bought and sold in the money market.

Any member bank or clearing nonmember bank may make arrangements with a Reserve bank to draw drafts against it. These drafts may be used to meet collection charges and other obligations at the Reserve banks. A member bank may also sell "Federal Reserve exchange drafts," which will be accepted by any Federal Reserve bank or branch. When such a draft is used, the issuing bank notifies its Federal Reserve bank on a special form prepared for this purpose, and the Reserve bank immediately debits the account of the bank for the amount sent.

All Federal Reserve banks are linked by the System's telegraph system, whose facilities are made available to member banks for "wiring" money free of charge if the amounts transferred are in round numbers of $100 or multiples thereof. For instance, if Chicago Bank A wants to send $1,000,000 to New York Bank B, it will notify the Federal Reserve Bank of Chicago to debit its account and transfer the sum to the Federal Reserve Bank of New York for the credit of Bank B. The wire transfer that the Chicago bank sends takes but a few minutes, and funds which otherwise would be idle may be put to work immediately. These transfers are made by code in order to lessen the dangers of fraudulent transfers and payment of funds to the wrong party.

Federal Reserve banks also use commercial wires to transfer odd or even amounts for the accounts of banks, individuals, firms, or corporations. They make no charge other than the cost of the necessary telegram. Thus, merely by paying for the commercial wire, a member bank may make specific and immediate transfers of funds for its customers to distant places within the United States. Additional transfers are made over the private wire facilities of commercial banks, some of which are linked by their own wire system, and others are made by commercial wire facilities.

The United States Treasury is one of the chief users of the wire transfer system and settlement services of the Federal Reserve System. Funds from securities sold by the Treasury and taxes that it collects in New York or some other district may be spent in a second Federal Reserve district. In this case, the Federal Reserve Bank of New York will debit the Treasury's checking account and the second Federal Reserve bank will credit the Treasury's account as instructed. The Federal Reserve System also "wires" government securities (which is physically impossible in a literal sense) when they are sold in one place and delivered out of stock, as instructed by wire, in a second place. For illustration, a government-securities dealer in New York may sell United States Treasury bills to a bank in Houston. The Houston bank will be instructed to pick them up at the Houston branch of the Federal Reserve Bank of Dallas, and the Federal Reserve Bank of New York will receive other United States Treasury bills from the New York government-securities dealer. In 1967 over 246 million government securities with a value of over $820 billion were issued or exchanged for the Treasury (see also Table 9–2).

CHECKLESS TRANSFERS

Many steps have been taken to reduce the costs involved in the present deposit currency system, and some bankers visualize a time when transfers of title to deposits will be made without the use of personal checks. Modern electronic devices permit inexpensive transfers of funds between and among accounts without the use of checks. In individual cases, where periodic payments are made, checks may be dispensed with and payment made by transfer of funds from one account to another.

Business corporations and other institutions have made considerable progress in economizing on the use of checks. Some are meeting payrolls by sending letters to their banks authorizing the latter to credit employees' checking accounts for specified amounts and to debit the firm's account for the total amount transferred. (If an employee does not have a bank account, a check is used.) A similar procedure is used in paying dividends; but before this plan can be used by a major company, the problem of having a large number of widely scattered stockholders that change from day to day must be solved. Through the transfer facilities of the Federal Reserve System, the federal government and other governments and institutions are transferring billions of dollar each day.

Consumers share in checkless transactions through the use of credit cards and check-guarantee cards and in other ways (see Chapter 24). Plans have been developed whereby insurance, mortgage, utility, and other payments may be paid automatically by banks.[8] Advocates of the transfer system maintain that all payments now being made by check would be handled faster and more economically by computers. If the payer and payee are depositors in the same bank, almost instantaneous transfer could be made by feeding the information of the authorization into the computer. If they have accounts in different banks, the payer's bank would perform the necessary operations and transmit a copy to the payee's bank.

Among the future checkless transactions envisioned is that of a housewife who (1) pays the family bills by tapping out instructions to the bank's computer over her push-button telephone; (2) pays for daily purchases by inserting a card in the store's special telephone which will permit her to make payment by instructing the bank's computer to transfer the correct amount from her account to that of the store; and (3) uses one bank credit card for all purchases to be paid by her bank with her offsetting obligations charged to her installment account at her bank.[9]

The large number and wide geographical dispersion of American banks makes the adoption of the giro transfer system, used on a national scale in France and Japan, by the U. S. banking system a very remote possibility. In countries where this system is in use it is centered around the post office, central bank, and/or commercial banks that have branches that blanket the country. To start with, each country uses facilities that permit the simplest type of transfers, from the payer to the payee having accounts in the same bank or institution. The transfer agent has offices over a wide area which permits prompt interoffice transfers. The payer's account is charged for the amount of the payment plus a small service fee, and upon receipt of instructions from the paying office the receiving transfer office will credit the account of the payee.

In some countries, there are two or more giro systems, with the post office meeting the need of individuals having small transfer ac-

[8] The Philadelphia Electric Company is among the corporations that have made provisions with banks in their areas "to have monthly service bills deducted automatically from special or regular checking accounts. . . . A customer wishing to pay his bill in this way merely files an authorization for bank deduction with the Company. . . . Each month the customer's bill is sent by the Company to the bank for payment. At the same time, the customer receives a memorandum bill showing the amount of deduction to be made from his account a week later." Philadelphia Electric Company, *Report to Stockholders*, March, 1967.

[9] Federal Reserve Bank of Richmond, "The Giro, the Computer and Checkless Banking," *Monthly Review*, April, 1966, pp. 2–5.

counts and commercial banks handling those of business firms and other large depositors. When banking is highly centralized, there is little need for interbank transfers: but, when highly decentralized, the need for interbank transfers is great.[10]

SUMMARY

In the United States the most important means of payment (in terms of dollars) is deposit currency or checkbook money. This type of money originates in transactions that create bank deposits. Technically, banks create deposits when they give depositors bank credit on their books for hand-to-hand money, checks, and other credit items. Banks cancel deposits when they cash checks for depositors and otherwise settle for checks and other items with currency that is withdrawn from the banking system. In addition, banks not only create bank deposits but also increase the volume of means of payment when they increase their holdings of earning assets. Similarly, banks decrease the volume of means of payment by decreasing their holdings of earning assets.

Clearinghouses were first organized as laborsaving associations, but they soon became the agencies through which banks cooperated on problems of common interest. By the very nature of banking, this covered not only problems among bankers themselves but also most of those associated with their contacts with the general public. In many fields, federal legislation leaves the final decisions to local bankers. This is illustrated by interest-rate regulations, wherein federal legislation has defined deposits eligible for receiving interest and the maximum rates that may be paid—but the actual rate paid is usually decided by local clearinghouse members.

Commercial banks, in cooperation with each other and with the Federal Reserve banks, have contributed to improving the deposit currency system of the nation. Banks clear and collect checks and other items through local clearinghouses, correspondent banks, and the Federal Reserve banks. As a result, the personal check is a means of payment that is cleared at par anywhere in the United States, except for a small number of banks whose checks circulate at a discount in distant places because these banks do not remit at par.

The contribution of the Federal Reserve System in providing the country with better currency and greater mobility of credit includes such services as accepting, handling, and forwarding for collection such cash items as checks, matured drafts, and government coupons,

[10] *Ibid.*, p. 4.

and such noncash items as promissory notes, bankers' acceptances, bonds, and other credit instruments.

By use of the Federal Reserve exchange services, funds may be transferred among banks either in the form of items to be sent by mail or orders sent by wire. Each Federal Reserve bank acts as a regional settlement center for paying credit instruments, and the Board of Governors operates the Interdistrict Settlement Fund, which settles balances resulting between Reserve banks. The use of the Federal Reserve System's wire service permits the transfer of large sums almost simultaneously anywhere in the United States. Creation of new procedures and formation of service corporations should contribute to improvement in our deposit currency system.

QUESTIONS AND PROBLEMS

1. Identify: (*a*) deposit currency, (*b*) checkless transfers of deposits, (*c*) goldsmith notes, and (*d*) Bank of Amsterdam.

2. "Neither paper currency nor deposits have value as a commodity. Intrinsically, a dollar bill is just a piece of paper. Deposits are merely book entries. Coins do have some intrinsic value as metals, but considerably less than their face value. What, then, makes these instruments . . . acceptable at face value in payment of all debts and for other monetary uses?" (Federal Reserve Bank of Chicago, *Modern Money Mechanics* [rev. ed.; Chicago, 1968], p. 2.)

3. Describe the clearing and collection work of a local clearinghouse.

4. Explain: One of the advantages claimed for a strong correspondent banking system is that it gives small banks access to the services and talents of the large banks.

5. Distinguish between (*a*) par collection and nonpar collection, (*b*) cash items and noncash items, (*c*) Federal Reserve district and interdistrict clearing and collection of checks, and (*d*) exchange charges and collection charges.

6. "The establishment of the Interdistrict Settlement Fund of the Federal Reserve System and the provision for daily inter-regional settlements through the Fund have made it possible for commercial banks to effect almost immediate telegraphic transfer of funds across the country for their own accounts or for the accounts of their customers." (Joint Committee on Economic Report, *Monetary Policy and Management of the Public Debt* [Washington, D.C.: U.S. Government Printing Office, 1952], part 1, p. 529.) Explain.

7. Discuss: "Effective September 1, 1967, Federal Reserve Banks will no longer handle checks as checks unless they bear the routing symbol and transit number in magnetic ink." (Federal Reserve Bank of Atlanta, *Monthly Review*, August, 1967, p. 111.)

8. Explain: The giro transfer system "differs chiefly in the manner of effecting these transfers . . . giro transfers are simplest when both the

payor and payee have accounts at the same institution." (Federal Reserve Bank of Richmond, *Monthly Review*, April, 1966, pp. 2–3.

9. Explain: Some "bankers . . . [visualize] the day when customers could receive from their banks one statement a month reflecting—in addition to checking account transactions—savings deposits made, bills paid, personal loans . . . and mortgage payments deducted." ("A Century of Commercial Banking," *Washington Post*, October 6, 1963.)

10. Bob borrowed one of Doug's checks to pay a bill. "But first in the presence of Bob, he carefully inked out Bob's account number and wrote his own above it. The incident was forgotten until Bob received his bank statement, which showed that Doug's $35 check had been debited to his account." (*New York Times*, February 17, 1966, p. 45.) Why?

CHAPTER 10

Banking Structure

THE BANKING SYSTEM of the United States differs in size, complexity, and number of banking units from other banking systems of the free world. The United States banking system developed under laws of states and the federal government and reflects the economic conditions and prejudices of the people served. Although banks are organized under the laws of 50 states, the District of Columbia, and the federal government, their operations show great similarity because of the influence of the Federal Reserve System, Federal Deposit Insurance Corporation, and bankers' own trade associations, such as the American Bankers Association.

In a general way, the banking structure of the United States consists of three types: (1) local or limited branch banking in the East, (2) unit banking (no branch offices) in the central states, and (3) statewide branch banking on the West Coast. Hence a "billion-dollar" bank in New York or Philadelphia will not be the same as one in Chicago or Los Angeles or San Francisco.

CLASSES OF INDIVIDUAL BANKS

Individual banks may be classified in numerous way, the most common classifications are according to (1) source of charter, as national or state banks; (2) type of deposits accepted, as commercial or savings banks; (3) membership in the Federal Reserve System, as member or nonmember banks; (4) insured status, as insured or noninsured by the Federal Deposit Insurance Corporation; (5) form of organization, as unit or branch banks; and (6) method of operation, as unit banks or members of group or chain banking systems (see Table 10–1).

Incorporation. A new commercial bank must incorporate, either under a state charter obtained from the state banking authority or under a national charter obtained from the Comptroller of the Currency.[1] This situation, dual chartering authorities, accounts for the

[1] There are seven nonnational banks in the District of Columbia which are supervised by the Comptroller of the Currency.

TABLE 10-1

NUMBER OF BANKS AND BRANCHES CLASSIFIED BY TYPES, 1967

State and Type of Bank or Office	All Banks			Commercial Banks and Nondeposit Trust Companies						Mutual Savings Banks			Percentage Insured*		
					Insured			Noninsured								
					Members F. R. System		Not Mem-	Banks	Non-deposit Trust				All Banks	Com-mercial	Mutual
	Total	Insured	Non-insured	Total	National	State	bers F. R. System	of De-posit†	Com-panies‡	Total	Insured	Non-insured	of De-posit	Banks of Deposit	Savings Banks
United States—all offices	33,194	32,574	620	31,860	14,974	4,983	11,613	235	55	1,334	1,004	330	98.3	99.3	75.3
Banks	14,244	13,850	394	13,741	4,758	1,312	7,447	177	47	503	333	170	97.6	98.7	66.2
Unit banks	10,412	10,123	289	10,181	3,229	854	5,899	157	42	231	141	90	97.6	98.5	61.0
Banks operating branches	3,832	3,727	105	3,560	1,529	458	1,548	20	5	272	192	80	97.4	99.4	70.6
Branches	18,950	18,724	226	18,119	10,216	3,671	4,166	58	8	831	671	160	98.8	99.7	80.7
50 States and D.C.—all offices	32,983	32,394	589	31,652	14,940	4,983	11,470	205	54	1,331	1,001	330	98.4	99.4	75.2
Banks	14,222	13,840	382	13,721	4,757	1,312	7,440	166	46	501	331	170	97.6	98.8	66.1
Unit banks	10,401	10,121	280	10,171	3,229	854	5,898	149	41	230	140	90	97.7	98.5	60.9
Banks operating branches	3,821	3,719	102	3,550	1,528	458	1,542	17	5	271	191	80	97.5	99.5	70.5
Branches	18,761	18,554	207	17,931	10,183	3,671	4,030	39	8	830	670	160	98.9	99.8	80.7
Other areas—all offices	211	180	31	208	34	...	143	30	1	3	3	...	85.7	85.5	100.0
Banks	22	10	12	20	1	...	7	11	1	2	2	...	47.6	42.1	100.0
Unit banks	11	2	9	10	...	...	1	8	1	1	1	...	20.0	11.1	100.0
Banks operating branches	11	8	3	10	1	...	6	3	...	1	1	...	72.7	70.0	100.0
Branches	189	170	19	188	33	...	136	19	...	1	1	...	89.9	89.9	100.0

* Nondeposit trust companies are excluded in computing these percentages.
† Includes 10 noninsured branches of insured banks (8 in Pacific Islands and 2 in Panama Canal Zone).
‡ Includes one trust company in Massachusetts, member of Federal Reserve System, operating one branch.
Source: *Annual Report of the Federal Deposit Insurance Corporation 1967*, p. 160.

fact that the banking system of the United States is known as a "dual banking system" wherein there are both national- and state-chartered banks in each state. There are about 13,800 commercial banks in the United States, of which over 4,800 operate under national charters and the remainder are classified as state-chartered banks. About 75 of the latter are small unincorporated "private" banks which were organized prior to the required incorporation. State-chartered banks also include savings banks and trust companies. Although most large banks seem to prefer national charters, many of the large New York banks operate under state charters. State banks outnumber national banks almost 2 to 1 (even in states where state chartering got a late start, as in Texas with 598 state banks and 544 national banks)[2] but the average-size state bank is smaller than the average-size national bank.

Banks of Deposit. The chief distinction between a savings bank and a commercial bank is that the latter accepts demand deposits, while the former does not. Thus a commercial bank is a monetary institution (its demand deposits being used freely as a means of payment) which also accepts time and savings deposits. In addition to financing commerce, commercial banks make agricultural, real estate, industrial, and consumer loans. Gradually, commercial banks have become "department stores of finance," providing trust, investment, and other financial services in addition to those related to their monetary and commercial functions. Savings banks are specialized institutions that accept only savings deposits, which they invest almost exclusively in home mortgages. However, a few stock savings banks offer checking accounts, and they are classified as commercial banks.

One of the major sources of confusion in the banking system is the mingling of demand deposits and savings deposits as is done by most commercial banks. When a savings bank makes a loan, it lends existing funds that have been deposited with it (as is the case with individuals and nonmonetary lenders). However, a commercial bank lends its credit. The proceeds of the loan appear as demand deposits, and the lending bank has created a means of payment. When a commercial bank accepts a check written on a customer's demand-deposit account for deposit in his savings account, the effect is to create a surplus reserve because of the difference in minimum required reserves for the two types of deposits.

Membership in the Federal Reserve System. The Federal Reserve Act specified that all nationally chartered banks must be mem-

---

[2] Until 1903, the Texas constitution prohibited the chartering of banks, leaving the market open to nationally chartered banks.

bers of the Federal Reserve System and that qualified state-chartered banks may elect to become members. This arrangement was a compromise between those members of Congress who favored compulsory membership for all commercial banks and those who favored voluntary membership for all banks. Approximately 25 percent of all member banks are state-chartered institutions. Although more then 50 percent of all commercial banks are nonmembers, about 85 percent of the total deposits of the commercial banking system are held by banks which are members of the Federal Reserve System. However the fact that about 15 percent of demand deposits are held in banks beyond the control of the Federal Reserve System weakens the System's control over the money supply to the detriment of the public interest.

Participation in Federal Deposit Insurance. When Congress provided for insurance of deposits in 1933, it took the most important step since 1789 toward bringing all money-creating banks under federal control. Passage of the Banking Act of 1933 paved the way for the development of a "unified national system" of banking. The purpose of the legislation was to restore public confidence in the national banking system, which was at the lowest point since the creation of the system. At the present time, 97 percent of all banks are participating in deposit insurance, and these banks hold 98 percent of all deposits in incorporated banks of deposit. The banks which are not members of the Federal Deposit Insurance Corporation include: (1) unincorporated banks, (2) trust companies that do no regular deposit banking business, (3) a few branches of banks chartered in foreign countries, and (4) the 170 mutual savings banks insured by the Massachusetts Savings Central Fund, Incorporated. Under the Federal Deposit Insurance Corporation system, the $15,000 maximum coverage per depositor means that over 60 percent of deposits in insured banks are covered by FDIC insurance.

Unit and Branch Banks. Foreign commercial banking systems are dominated by a few large banks which operate branches throughout their countries. In the United States, the closest counterpart of this system is found only in California and some other western states where commercial banks have branches scattered throughout the state wherein the main office is located. In the East branching is confined to districts, counties, or cities wherein the main offices are located, and in other areas branch banking is prohibited by state laws.

A unit bank is one having a single place of business, and a branch bank is one having a main office and one or more branch offices.

Almost 80 percent of banks in the United States are unit banks, and about one half of these are in states which prohibit branch banking. The remaining 20 percent of United States banks operate from two to 1,000 branch offices. The largest commercial bank in the world, the Bank of America National Trust Savings Association of California (popularly known as the Bank of America), has assets of over $26 billion. Some of the large United States banks that do not operate domestic branches have either established branches abroad or have formed subsidiaries to establish foreign branches.

In states permitting branch banking, national banks are authorized to operate branches under conditions similar to those applicable to state-chartered banks. Among the proposals made in Congress is one to permit any national bank to operate branches within a 25-mile radius of its main office. Another proposal is to permit any national bank to operate branches within its Federal Reserve district. At the present time, the status of branch banking in the United States does not compare with the nationwide systems of branch banking in Canada and European countries.

The federal government permits national banks to open branch offices in foreign countries but leaves the question of domestic bank branching to the respective state governments. Fourteen states permit branches to be established within the state, 16 permit branch offices to be operated in the area of the main office, and the other 20 disallow all branching (except for branches located on military reservations and other facilities of the federal government). Within the legal limits, there has been a rapid growth in branch banking in the past 25 years but the situation still contrasts sharply with that in foreign countries.

In 1968, the Board of Governors of the Federal Reserve System opened the door to a limited type of multiple-office banking by ruling that opening a loan procurement office does not constitute branching within the meaning of the law. If this ruling is not upset by the federal courts or changed by Congress, it will mean that a member bank may establish and operate such offices anywhere in the United States to solicit loans, assemble credit information, make property inspections and appraisals, secure title information, and prepare applications for loans to be made by the main office or a branch of the bank.

The 13,800 commercial banks in the United States have 17,100 branches, but only one bank out of four has branches. This means that the "unit" or single-office bank is the prevailing type. This reflects the fact that local communities (and even subdivisions of cities) want their own banks whenever possible. Therefore, 50 percent of all banks in the United States have assets of less than $5 million and only 10 percent have resources equal to or in excess of $25 million.

There are many arguments in favor of branch banking, the most important being the claims of superiority as to (1) flexibility in structure, (2) management, (3) diversification of assets, (4) geographical mobility of funds, (5) uniformity in interest rates, (6) economy in reserves, (7) clearing and collection services, and (8) deposit and lending services for retail and other firms that ceased being local in nature. In many cases, a branch bank could operate profitably while a unit bank could not; and, if it became necessary to do so, a branch office could be liquidated more easily and with less unfavorable publicity than would be the case for a unit bank. For illustration, in 1967, 121 branch offices were closed without the unfavorable publicity given to the failure of four relatively small banks located in four states. A branch office of a large bank can offer a small community services comparable to those of its main office which a unit bank similarly located could not match.

If the growth of cities continues to follow the present trend of decentralization (as with community shopping centers, etc.), banks will have to open branch offices or will lose an increasing volume of business to competing institutions (savings banks, savings and loan associations, check-cashing offices, etc.). Most suburbanites are in the middle-income group requiring banking services of all kinds—checking accounts, safekeeping facilities, and real estate, consumer, and small business loans. While the volume of business in each suburb may not justify a new unit bank, it may be more than sufficient to meet the cost of a branch office (called "cubbyhole" banking).

The chief argument against branch banking is that it is monopolistic in nature. This argument against branch banking fails to recognize that there may be competition between branches of different banks in the area, as well as between unit banks, and that often the opening of a branch bank in a town has broken the monopoly formerly enjoyed by the local unit bank. The second argument is that the main office would neglect the needs of small communities. This argument is hard to substantiate in view of the experiences with branch banking in California and other western states. Any good banker desires to make profitable loans, irrespective of the domicile of the borrower, and this desire does not exclude those located in small communities. If one banker fails to make these loans, a rival branch-office manager will make them.

Group and Chain Banking. Recent statistics indicate that the typical commercial bank in the United States is a small bank—72 percent have deposits of less than $10 million, and less than 1 percent have deposits of $500 million or more. Nevertheless these statistics may be misleading because hundreds of small banks are not in reality unit banks, since they belong to "group" or "chain" banking systems.

Group banking exists when two or more banks are controlled by a holding company organized as a corporation or similar type of organization. This type of banking system offers some of the advantages of branch banking and additional ones which are peculiar to this type of organization. In some group-banking systems unit banking and branch banking are combined (for illustration, the Marine Midland group of New York State). A holding company is not a bank and does not come under the general banking laws of states or the federal government. Hence numerous states and the federal government have passed laws providing for regulation of group banking systems.[3]

Congress made the Board of Governors of the Federal Reserve System responsible for the supervision and regulation of bank holding companies (all controlling two or more banks must register with the Board of Governors). At the end of 1967, there were 74 registered companies that included over 560 banks and their 1,800 branches located in 34 states and the District of Columbia, with total deposits of over $41 billion.[4] The size of bank holding company groups ranges from small systems containing two unit banks such as the Commercial Associates, Inc., of Pensacola, Florida, which has deposits of $13 million, to the Western Bank Corporation of Los Angeles, California, which operates in 11 western states and has banks with 559 offices and deposits of $16.7 billion.[5]

The same arguments used to justify branch banking are used to justify the organization of group banking. In the United States it has the advantage of achieving ownership and direction of regional sys-

---

[3] In the Bank Holding Company Act of 1956, Congress defined a bank holding company as one "that directly or indirectly owns, controls, or holds with power to vote 25 per centum or more of the voting shares of two or more banks . . . (or) controls in any manner the election of a majority of the directors of each of two or more banks. . . ." In 1966, an amendment to this act broadened the coverage by repealing certain exceptions from registration, such as when banks were owned by registered investment companies or religious, charitable, and educational institutions. (See Bank Holding Company Act of 1956, as amended effective July 1, 1966 Public Law 84–485).

[4] *Federal Reserve Bulletin*, June, 1968, p. A–91.

[5] Board of Governors of the Federal Reserve System, *Subsidiary Banks of Bank Holding Companies*, December 31, 1966, mimeographed, 25 pages.

tems that cut across state lines. Each bank affiliated with a holding company retains its identity, and its officers have more independence of action than is the case of managers of branch offices. But a system made up of unit banks cannot have the economy in operation or the flexibility in structure (opening and closing of offices) that characterize branch banking. In practice, holding companies that are expanding seem more interested in gaining control of existing successful unit banks than in organizing new banks. Their higher cost of operation may be more than offset by avoiding loss of goodwill that might follow the substitution of a branch office for a local unit bank. Group-bank management has an advantage over branch-bank management in being able to expand over state lines. However, in the past, in states wherein branch-banking laws have been liberalized, many units in group systems have been reorganized as branches.

Chain banking, the second type of multiunit banking, is similar to group banking except that controlling ownership is in the hands of one or more individuals rather than a holding company. Although "chains" are more numerous than "groups," they are smaller both in the number of banks and in the size of the unit banks controlled. The chain type of organization avoids the regulation and requirements applicable to bank holding companies; but, because control is in the hands of individuals or groups of individuals, chains lack the permanency of organization, the stabilizing influence, and the services offered by the head office of a branch-banking institution or of a group-banking holding company.

Although there is no official information as to the chain-banking organizations in existence, it has been estimated that there are 431 chain systems including 1,169 banks, with only 3 of the systems containing more than 10 banks and two thirds controlling only 2 banks. About 73 percent of the banks involved are located in centers where the population is 25,000 or less, and the largest number are found in areas that prohibit or restrict branch banking (in the Kansas City, Dallas, and Chicago Federal Reserve districts).[6]

Mergers. Bank mergers have been a significant factor in the growth in the size of the average bank. The combination of two or more banks is most frequently motivated by the desire to "expand services to customers and to gain representation in certain localities through branches." During 1967, the three federal banking agencies (Comptroller of the Currency, Board of Governors of the Federal

---

[6] Jerome C. Darnell, "Chain Banking," *National Banking Review*, March, 1966, pp. 328–29.

TABLE 10-2

CHANGES IN BANKS AND BRANCHES CLASSIFIED BY TYPE, 1967

Type of Change	All Banks			Commercial Banks and Nondeposit Trust Companies							Mutual Savings Banks		
					Insured				Noninsured				
						Members F. R. System		Not Members F. R. System	Banks of Deposit	Non-deposit Trust Companies*			
	Total	Insured	Non-insured	Total	Total	National	State				Total	Insured	Non-insured
All Banking Offices:													
Number of offices, December 30, 1967†	33,194	32,574	620	31,860	31,570	14,974	4,983	11,613	235	55	1,334	1,004	330
Number of offices, December 31, 1966†	32,136	31,491	645	30,872	30,544	14,436	4,867	11,241	251	77	1,264	947	317
Net change during year	+1,058	+1,083	-25	+988	+1,026	+538	+116	+372	-16	-22	+70	+57	+13
Offices opened	1,335	1,300	35	1,261	1,243	602	224	417	18	...	74	57	17
Banks	109	94	15	109	94	18	3	73	15	...	...	...	...
Branches	1,226	1,206	20	1,152	1,149	584	221	344	3	...	74	57	17
Offices closed	277	240	37	273	238	129	42	67	13	22	4	2	2
Banks	156	140	16	153	139	65	17	57	13	1	3	1	2
Branches	121	100	21	120	99	64	25	10	...	21	1	1	...
Change in classification	...	+23	-23	...	+21	+65	-66	+22	-21	...	...	+2	-2
Among banks	...	+23	-23	...	+21	+6	-24	+39	-21	...	...	+2	-2
Among branches	...	...	...	...	...	+59	-42	-17	...	...	...	...	...
Banks:													
Number of banks, December 30, 1967	14,244	13,850	394	13,741	13,517	4,758	1,312	7,447	177	47	503	333	170
Number of banks, December 31, 1966	14,291	13,873	418	13,785	13,541	4,799	1,350	7,392	196	48	506	332	174
Net change during year	-47	-23	-24	-44	-24	-41	-38	+55	-19	-1	-3	+1	-4
Banks beginning operation	109	94	15	109	94	18	3	73	15	...	...	...	...
New banks	107	94	13	107	94	18	3	73	13	...	...	...	...
Banks added to count	2	...	2	2	...	...	...	...	2	...	...	...	...
Banks ceasing operation	156	140	16	153	139	65	17	57	13	1	3	1	2
Absorptions, consolidations, and mergers	137	132	5	134	131	64	16	51	3	...	3	1	2
Closed-financial difficulties	4	4	...	4	4	1	...	3	...	...	...	...	...
Other liquidations	7	4	3	7	4	...	1	3	3	...	...	...	...
Discontinued deposit operations	4	...	4	4	...	...	...	...	4	...	...	...	...
Banks deleted from count	4	...	4	4	...	...	...	...	3	1	...	...	...
Noninsured banks becoming insured	...	+23	-23	...	+21	...	...	+21	-21	...	...	+2	-2

*Includes one trust company member of the Federal Reserve System.

†Includes facilities established at request of the Treasury or commanding officer of government installations, and also a few seasonal branches that were not in operation as of December 31.

Source: *Annual Report of the Federal Deposit Insurance Corporation 1967*, p. 156.

Reserve System, and the Federal Deposit Insurance Corporation) approved mergers involving 238 banks with assets in excess of $24 billion.[7] The degree of concentration in banking in large cities is high, and the trend is continuing. Outside of California and other western states, the banking system is still dominated by local banks.

In line with the general growth of the economy, banks are under pressure to acquire expensive machinery such as data processing equipment, to pay higher wages, and to meet other rising costs. As a result, the number of small banks is declining while the number of large and medium-sized banks is increasing. Within recent years changes in banking structure have shown a small decrease in the number of banks and a substantial increase in the number of banking offices (see Table 10–2). (In addition to commercial banks, mutual savings banks and savings and loan associations are opening branch offices for the convenience of their customers.)

There are two forms of branching: (1) the formation of new branch offices; and (2) the absorption of existing banks to be operated as branches. The general policy as to branching has been left to state governments, with the result that policies as to branching have been far more restrictive than those applicable to chartering new banks.

BANK CHARTERS

Bank charters are valuable as long as they are limited in number. In any community, a new bank is a competitor rarely welcomed by existing banks; but, because of the monopolistic nature of banking, it is essential to keep the way open for the entry of new banks. This principle is applicable not only to the opening of new banks but also to the establishment of new branches of existing banks that require the approval of public authorities.

If entry control is administered too restrictively, it will stifle change, result in lack of competition, create artificial shortages, and make banking services inadequate and expensive. On the other hand, if entry control is too liberal, bank failures will tend to result in the detriment of bank customers and the communities affected. It is the function of entry control to prevent establishment of inefficient banks rather than to protect existing banks from competition.

The authority to charter new state banks is held by designated state agencies (usually the state superintendent of banking) whose

[7] *Annual Report of the Federal Deposit Insurance Corporation 1967* (Washington, D.C., 1968), pp. 23–24.

standards are determined by their state governments and influenced by the Federal Deposit Insurance Corporation. The presence of the Corporation in state-bank chartering is due to the general practice of arranging for deposit insurance before a bank is opened (organizers realize that a noninsured bank will be unable to compete successfully with insured banks for depositors' funds). During the organizational period, FDIC is desirous of assuring the future safety of the bank and to this end insists on a qualified managerial staff and adequate capital funds. Of all the state and federal bank supervisory agencies, FDIC is the only one having a financial stake in the safety of banks, and this could be a factor in its granting or withholding of deposit insurance.

Any application for a bank charter is carefully screened in terms of local demand for banking services, potential profitability, and anticipated effect on existing institutions. The future prospects of a bank will depend on efficient operation; therefore a proposed bank's managerial staff will be given primary attention. However, even the best managerial staff cannot operate successfully without adequate funds, so chartering authorities must make sure that the minimum capital needs are met and maintained. There is no way to forecast with any degree of certainty what effect a new bank will have on existing banks or whether or not any business venture will succeed or fail; but if an insured bank fails its depositors are protected from loss in whole or part.

The National Bank Act provided that five or more natural persons may apply to the Comptroller of the Currency for a national bank charter. The first formal step is for a member of the group to write to the Comptroller stating the intent of the group and giving the proposed title, location, and capitalization of the bank to be organized. Ordinarily, the proposed title will be reserved for the bank, provided that the word "national" is included and no other bank in the community has the same name.

If the request for title is approved, the organizers will make formal application for a charter on a second form entitled "Application to Organize a National Bank." In the spaces provided there must be given the name and location of the bank; its proposed capital, surplus, and undivided profits; considerable information about the applicants; and other information about the plans for setting up the bank (renting or erecting a banking house; salaries to be paid to various officers and employees; expenditures to be made for furniture, fixtures, stationery, supplies, vaults, etc.). Presumably, the organizers have obtained the services of an attorney, have estimated the cost of equipment, have made a market survey of the area, and have the answers to all questions.

When the Comptroller of the Currency receives the application, his office instructs the chief national bank examiner of the appropriate district to make an investigation. In addition to checking the details contained in the application, the examiner will investigate the character, standing, and business experience of the applicants and others who are to take an active part in managing the bank, and he will appraise the banking needs of the community, the probable earnings of the proposed bank, the adequacy of existing banking facilities, and the expected effects of the bank on existing institutions.

The examiner's report is sent to the Comptroller's office in Washington, where it is checked to see that statutory requirements have been fulfilled and the proposed bank is appraised on its merits. The Comptroller of the Currency obtains reports from the Federal Reserve agent of the district Federal Reserve bank and from the Federal Deposit Insurance Corporation; but, in case of disagreement, the responsibility for any decision is borne by the Comptroller.

When the Comptroller of the Currency approves the application for a charter, the committee will proceed with its plans to organize the bank. The stock of the bank will be offered for sale at a price that will provide the necessary capital and a paid-in surplus (at least 20 percent of the capital and usually more). While minimum capital requirements for new banks are fixed by law, in practice considerably larger amounts of capital funds are needed; therefore, organizers are guided by the needs of the community and the anticipated growth of the bank. The allocation of cash receipts from the sale of capital stock is arranged to give the bank some flexibility in management. The stock is often sold at a price high enough to give the bank an amount of surplus equal to capital as well as a paid-in undivided profit or reserve account. The stockholders meet and elect at least 5 but not more than 25 directors. The directors, in turn, meet and select officers for the bank, including at least a president, vice president, and a cashier. Then two forms, the "Articles of Association" and the "Organization Certificate," are completed and signed, preferably by the same five persons who signed the application for the charter, and copies are sent to the Office of the Comptroller of the Currency.

The articles of association repeat in final form much of the tentative information found in the preliminary papers filed with the Comptroller and also certain specific information with reference to the organization of the bank. The organization certificate is merely an attestation as to the purposes of the organization. It gives the title, location, and capital stock of the bank and the names, net financial worth, and residence of each shareholder, with the number of shares held by each. A bank may not commence business until the Comptroller issues a "Certificate of Authority to Commence Business," which banks commonly refer to as the "charter." The bank must also certify that it has subscribed to stock of the district Federal Reserve bank in an amount equal to 6 percent of its capital stock and surplus and that it has already paid an amount equal to one half of its subscription. A bank must publish its new charter and return an affidavit to the Comptroller signed by the publisher of the newspaper in which the charter has appeared for at least 60 days (as required by law). National bank charters are indeterminate, that is, perpetual unless terminated by legislative action, dissolved by shareholders, forfeited by the bank for violation of the law, or closed voluntarily or by regulatory authorities because of insolvency or illegal action.

Although free banking remains as a statute, it can readily be seen that many proposed charters are rejected by administrative action. The record of successful applicants is high, but this may be due in part to the fact that many would-be organizers are discouraged informally before applications are made. The policies of the Comptroller of the Currency differ at various times, and those in force at the present time are unusually liberal. Organizers of banks are usually substantial businessmen interested in community needs, but they may have personal motives, such as dissatisfaction with present banking facilities, desire for prestige associated with a new bank, hopes for profits from ownership of stock, and prospects of new sources of loans for real estate and other developments. Congress requires all national banks to insure their deposits with the Federal Deposit Insurance Corporation; therefore the Corporation has no "veto power" as to chartering national banks.

BANK MERGERS

Although the number of banking offices and the total volume of bank assets have increased since 1929, the total number of banks has declined, due in part to bank mergers. However, in recent years, increased opposition to bank mergers has led to the passage of the Bank Merger Act of 1960. Under this act, the appropriate federal supervisory agency was directed to consider the effect on competition and any tendency toward monopoly of any merger transaction and then to withhold approval of any transaction not in the public interest.[8] Actions taken on bank mergers are reviewed by the Justice Department, and its opinions and those of the agencies concerned are published in the annual reports of these federal agencies. The list of merger decisions includes all combinations irrespective of whether the transactions were "mergers," "consolidations," or "purchases" (the last term is used to cover the direct or indirect acquisition of the assets and assumption of liabilities of a second bank). In 1967, 238 banks that operated 2,041 branches and held assets in excess of $24 billion were involved in bank mergers.[9]

In the 1966 revision of the Bank Merger Act of 1960, Congress reaffirmed the necessity of obtaining approval of the appropriate federal agency for proposed bank mergers. In giving or withholding approval, the agency must consider the bank's financial history and condition, the adequacy of its capital structure, its future earnings prospects, the character of its management, the need of the community to be served, and "whether or not its corporate powers are consistent with the purposes of this Act."[10]

As has been obvious since the beginning of chartered banks in the United States, one objective of public supervision has been the prevention of destructive competition among banks. The money-creating function of commercial banks is of public interest, and, if we are to have sound money, banks must be sound. While the merger of two or more banks does not insure a sounder bank and an improved banking system, it may be a step in that direction. Furthermore, the competition faced by a bank is not limited to that offered by other banks because the money and capital markets include not only commercial banks but also insurance companies, savings banks, discount or finance companies, savings and loan associations, governmental agencies of many kinds, and other lenders. In order to meet the needs

[8] The responsible federal agency, when "the acquiring, assuming or resulting bank is to be" (1) a national bank or a District [of Columbia] bank, is the Comptroller of the Currency; (2) "a state member bank except a District bank," is the Board of Governors of the Federal Reserve System; and (3) "a nonmember insured bank except a District bank," is the Federal Deposit Insurance Corporation.

[9] *Annual Report of the Federal Deposit Insurance Corporation, 1967* (Washington, D.C., 1968), p. 24.

[10] Public Law 89–357, 89th Cong., S 1698, amended Sec. 18(c) of the Federal Deposit Insurance Act (12 U.S.C. 1828 [c]). The main purpose of the 1966 amendment was to end the conflict among the Courts, the Department of Justice, and the supervisory agencies over standards to use in approving or disapproving mergers. Now, the consummation of a merger cannot take place for 30 days, to give the Department time to contest it in court.

of a growing economy, banking facilities must be expanded because business communities may be handicapped by the existence of too many small banks whose resources are inadequate to care for their needs. Although public officials should make sure that competition is not unduly restricted, it sometimes seems that we are preventing competition in trying to preserve it. A merger may decrease competition in a local market while increasing competition in a regional or national market.

The advantages accruing from large-scale organization may be obtained by banks as well as other forms of business organization. A large bank may use more efficient modern equipment to reduce its per-unit costs and may employ better trained personnel. It is also possible for a large bank (1) to spread the risks of lending over a greater volume of assets drawn from a wider trade area, and (2) to keep lower cash reserves because of its larger flowback of deposits.

In recent years, the increase in the size of banks has been accompanied by improvements in banks' operations and layouts and greater mechanization of operations. In addition, "banking by mail" and "drive-in" banking have facilitated both deposit and withdrawal of funds. However, congestion in downtown areas is testing the ingenuity of bank management, particularly in those states wherein branch banking is prohibited. The growing practice of using expensive land for parking and drive-ins means increased operating costs.

Bank management, while being confronted by increased costs for equipment and salaries and rising interest rates on time deposits, is not free to offset these increases by raising the price of its revenue-producing product—the use of money. In general the level of interest rates is determined by factors beyond the control of an individual bank; hence its continued prosperity will depend primarily on economies in operation and expansion in the volume of business. After expansion, banks are usually able to reduce per-unit costs by spreading overhead, using mechanical and electronic equipment more efficiently, and bidding more successfully for highly qualified personnel. Now banking is a high-volume, low-markup type of business.

The rapid growth in industrial production during and since World War II has led to the formation of business firms having plants and/or distribution outlets throughout the country and the world. Such firms need banking services of all kinds, and their needs are being met by larger banks or by cooperation among banks (despite the opposition of those who associate size with monopoly and those who consider cooperation to be collusion of an antisocial type).[11] Loan demands are coming from business firms in many fields (such as petroleum, metals, chemicals, etc.) and only large banks can afford to employ the specialists needed to handle their accounts (geologists, physicists, chemists, and engineers).

Insofar as commercial banking is a private business motivated by profit, the test of whether or not to merge or to establish branches is the expected increase in net earnings derived therefrom. Although an increase in size is no guarantee of an expansion in earnings, the trend toward expansion in size through mergers and/or branching is expected to continue. Electronic computers have been a factor in the movement of large banks into the areas of high-cost lending, including consumer installment financing, small loans, and the home mortgage market. Now, directly or through subsidiaries, they control the credit card and credit guarantee card business. Computers have also contributed to increased accuracy in computing bank costs so as to fix fees and other charges more realistically.[12]

BANKING, A REGULATED INDUSTRY

Federal supervisory authorities are assuming the major responsibility for administering laws relating to changes in the structure of the commercial banking system as well as taking a leading role in making decisions affecting services offered the general public. Although legislative bodies make provisions for chartering new banks, it may be that the Federal Deposit Insurance Corporation makes the final decision as to opening a new bank or branch (in states permitting branch banking). Without deposit insurance, a new bank charter would be meaningless for all practical purposes.

Uniformity. Many individuals advocate vesting the responsibility for bank supervision in one federal agency so that all banks that

---

[11] International banks have been restricted in their overseas operations because of the balance-of-payments deficit. Because foreign loans earn a higher return than domestic loans, these restrictions tend to reduce bank earnings (see Chapter 27).

[12] Congress has recognized the position of many small banks, unable to compete with large ones without the use of high-priced electronic equipment, by authorizing two or more banks to cooperate in organizing and operating service corporations (Public Law 87–856, 87th Cong., H.R. 8874, October 23, 1962). Any bank examined by a federal agency (all banks except those not participating in the Federal Deposit Insurance plan) may invest not more than 10 percent of its capital and surplus in corporations created to service "check and deposit sorting and posting, computation and posting of interest and other credits and charges, preparation and mailing of checks, statements, notices, and similar items, or any other clerical, bookkeeping, accounting, statistical or similar functions performed for a bank." Before beginning operations, the service corporation and participating banks must give assurances to the appropriate federal examining agency that they will submit to its supervision.

handle demand deposits will operate under the same rules; but those interested in the credit function rather than the money aspect of commercial banking feel that applying the same rules to all banks regardless of size and location would present insurmountable problems.

The approach to the problem of supervision has been from the viewpoint of creditors, but students agree that at least those banks handling checking accounts should be supervised by an agency of the federal government. The power to coin money and to regulate its value is vested in Congress by the Constitution of the United States; therefore, since commercial banks create and destroy deposits, they should be supervised by the federal government. The banking business is national in scope and so lends itself best to federal control and supervision. Finally, banking disturbances are of national importance and can be dealt with most effectively by national action. The courts have never questioned the sovereignty of the federal government over money matters, and today commercial banks are our most important source of money.

National control could be obtained by requiring all commercial banks (1) to secure national charters, which would make them members of the National Banking System, the Federal Reserve System, and the Federal Deposit Insurance System; (2) to insure their deposits with the Federal Deposit Insurance Corporation, or (3) to join the Federal Reserve System, which also would force them to be members of the Federal Deposit Insurance Corporation. The second plan would permit banks to select or reject membership in the Federal Reserve System, and the third plan would permit banks to select either state or national charters, but a modification of this plan would leave all chartering of banks to state governments and require banks that handle checking accounts to be members of the Federal Reserve System (the same principle that applies to railroads and other corporations). The weakest proposal for reform is one that would merely require nonmember commercial banks to keep the same reserves with the Federal Reserve banks that member banks are required to keep with them.

Although the adoption of no one of these plans would clarify all the issues as to supervision and examination, the first plan (that of requiring national charters) would be the simplest procedure. It would have the advantage of making the office of the Comptroller of the Currency responsible for commercial-bank supervision and examination. At present, it is responsible for the examination of more banking assets (in national banks) than the other two federal agencies, which must share their examining and supervisory functions with state authorities. Even under the plan requiring all commercial banks to have national charters, the Federal Deposit Insurance Corporation would be responsible for supervision and examination of mutual savings and other insured noncommercial banks, and the Federal Reserve authorities still would have certain regulatory powers.

In order to avoid raising too many political issues and still place responsibility for examinations in the hands of a single agency, it has been suggested that the Federal Deposit Insurance Corporation be made solely responsible for examining and supervising all insured banks. At the present time, it examines nonmember insured state banks periodically and makes special examinations of other banks. Through its insurance of deposits, the Federal Deposit Insurance Corporation is in contact with over 98 percent of the nation's commercial banks, holding over 99 percent of all commercial banks' deposits, and with almost 50 percent of the mutual savings banks, holding 75 percent of mutual savings banks' deposits.

In its recommendations for the reorganization of the executive branch of the government, the "Hoover Commission" favored placing supervision and examination responsibilities under the control of the Board of Governors of the Federal Reserve System. This recommendation recognized not only the need for eliminating interagency friction but also the importance of avoiding examination policies that might intensify deflation or inflation. It was felt that this might best be avoided by centralizing responsibility for examinations with the Federal Reserve System, whereby credit policies and examining policies would be formulated by the same agency. If examining policy is to be used as a device of credit control, there is considerable justification for this proposal; but, if the primary function of bank supervision is to reassure depositors of the soundness of their banks, the examining and credit-control functions should not be combined.

At present the Federal Deposit Insurance Corporation and the office of the Comptroller of the Currency have regional offices serving districts that are separated along state boundary lines, but Federal Reserve districts cut across state lines, which adds to the difficulty in dealing with state-chartered banks.

Purposes. The chief purpose of bank supervision is to protect the general public by maintaining sound and liquid banks. Supervisory officials stress the financial condition and management of individual banks, which means that monetary aspects of banking may be secondary to them.

1. The first task of the supervisory officials is to see that only qualified individuals are allowed to organize banks, and then only when their banks are capitalized adequately and located where there is an economic need not met by existing banks. In carrying on this activity, regulatory agencies have been handicapped by the American "free-banking" philosophy and by the predominance of the small unit banks in the banking system, but in spite of these handicaps considerable progress has been achieved in keeping down the number of inadequately financed and poorly managed banks.

2. The second task of supervisory officials is to see that banks are operated according to the law and the administrative regulations under the law. The banking code is usually complex and detailed because of the ease with which irresponsible groups may gain control over banks, because of the American "genius for bankruptcy," and because of the American tendency to correct (or try to correct) abuses by legislation. But it does not follow that a bank is being operated wisely just because it is being operated legally. This is demonstrated by the fact that closures of banks for insolvency have been many, while closures for illegal operations have been few.

3. The third task of supervisory officials is to see that banks are sound. These officials receive reports on banks' conditions that are more complete and more informative than those given to the general public. They are required to audit or examine banks periodically and may make such special examinations as may seem necessary. This procedure gives the supervisory authorities firsthand information on the legality of the banks' transactions and an opportunity to verify the existence of assets and to appraise the value of assets that the banks claim to possess. It permits the examiners to review the ability of officers of banks to carry out previous suggestions and to operate their banks successfully.

The chief aim of bank supervision is normally identical with that of good management, but, at a particular time, management may be enmeshed in a local situation wherein potentially harmful practices are being followed. These practices may result from overemphasis on dividends and earnings, from "carrying" some favored customer because of his position on the board of directors, and from other factors. Bank examiners and supervisory agencies raise practical questions as to the gathering of credit information on borrowers, collection practices, accounting reserves, sources of earnings, and adequacy of capital, fidelity insurance, and protective equipment.

Banks must also secure the prior approval of supervisory authorities before changing their capitalization, opening or closing branches, and adding trust-banking functions. Care must be taken to follow the rules in regard to computation and maintenance of required reserves, computation of deposits on which insurance is paid semiannually, and the preparation of cash and noncash items for collection through the Federal Reserve System. Banks must abide by the restrictions in effect on lending and investing. However, not all the restrictions placed on banks are of a character that places the soundness of banks foremost, since some are of a monetary nature. Among these are (or have been) the high primary-reserve requirements and the high margin requirements on loans made for the purpose of purchasing and carrying stocks bought and sold on national exchanges, installment loans to consumers, and those made with real estate pledged as security.

4. Although bank supervisory agencies do not relish the responsibility, the final task that they must perform is to close any bank that continues to violate the law or is insolvent and to reorganize or close others whose capital has been impaired.

Although banks have been supervised in one or more of the states since the 1830's and by the federal government since the Civil War, there is still no uniformity of opinion among members of Congress, regulatory personnel, commercial bankers, businessmen, lawyers, and economists as to solutions to current problems relative to branch banking, mergers, number of new charters, optimum size of banks, and new banking services offered. While all may agree that the basic purpose of regulation is to keep the values of free enterprise while preventing abuse, no two individuals may agree as to how this may be accomplished. The difficulty of answering this question should encourage periodic review of all rules pertaining to bank regulation, because many were conceived and adopted for some narrow purpose that is no longer applicable. Otherwise, bank regulation may stifle progress, encourage the organization of less efficient substitutes, and be more harmful to the industry and the general public than would a system of no supervision or only nominal supervision. For illustration, by forming one-bank holding companies which, through subsidiary companies, perform services for their customers that the bank is not permitted to perform, banks are now taking advantage of the loop-hole in the law that does not bring under regulation holding companies that control but one bank.

BANK MANAGEMENT

Banks are organized along the same lines as other corporations, with stockholders, directors, officers, and employees and management in the hands of officers and directors. Banks are permitted to issue both common and preferred stock, but they have made little use of their power to issue preferred stock. In addition to providing the original capital, stockholders may be assessed to restore their bank's capital if it has become impaired through losses. Under national and most state laws however, stockholders are no longer subject to "double liability" in case of bank failure. This means that they are no longer subject to assessment in amounts up to 100 percent of the par value of each share held in order to provide cash to pay the bank's creditors. As a substitute, banks are generally required by state or federal law to retain earnings until surplus is at least equal to capital.

At the time of organization, a bank's stock may be owned only by natural persons, but, later, stock may be acquired by corporations (which permits holding companies to gain control over banks). Usually a stockholder of record is entitled to one vote for each share held. However, in electing directors, each national bank stockholder has the privilege of cumulative voting. Thus if a stockholder owns 5 shares and there are 20 directors to be elected, he may cast a maximum of 100 votes for 1 candidate, 50 votes for 2 candidates, etc., rather than 5 votes for each of 20 candidates, as would be the case under noncumulative voting rules.

A national bank is required by law to have a board of directors of not less than 5 or more than 25 members. Each director is elected for a term of one year and serves until his successor has legally qualified to serve in his position. All directors must be citizens of the United States, and two thirds must have resided, for at least a year prior to election, within the state wherein the bank is located or within 100 miles of the bank. In addition, each director must own stock in the bank equal to at least $1,000 par value, except where the bank's capital is $25,000, in which case the minimum is $500. These are but modest minimums and are not representative of the typical stockholdings of directors. Directors must take an oath that they will "diligently and honestly administer" the affairs of their bank. Usually, men and women are selected as bank directors because of their professional or business standing in the community.

The president of a bank must be one of the bank's directors, and other members of the official staff may also be directors. However, such "inside" directors are usually in the minority, which tends to assure better representation for outside interests. A bank's board of directors customarily meets monthly, or more often if desired, and is presided over by the president of the bank or the chairman of the board. Between meetings most of the work of the board of directors is done by committees, the most important of which are the executive and the loan or discount committees. The board of directors formulates major policies, selects the bank's officers, enacts bylaws, and otherwise controls the bank's operations.

Directors are subject to common-law penalties, both civil and criminal. They are liable for neglect of duty and lack of ordinary diligence in supervising their banks. When cases come before the court, the test is "the degree of care which ordinarily prudent and diligent men would exercise under similar circumstances" (the "prudent man" theory). In addition to common-law penalties, bank directors, as well as officers and employees, are liable under national law for criminal prosecution. Space does not permit a discussion of all the legal responsibilities of directors, but enough has been presented to show the intent of Congress, which is to protect the general public from losses caused by illegal or careless operations. However, no law or series of laws can insure proper and profitable operations of any bank; this is the function of the bank management.

The chief officers of a bank are known as president, vice president, and cashier, or by similar titles. Their duties may be defined in the bylaws formulated by the board of directors and adopted by the shareholders. The president is selected by the board from among its own members to serve for one year but usually is reelected from year to year. The president may be a trained banker, developed by years of experience in banks, or he may be a lawyer or a businessman who has been active in the bank's affairs. In most banks the president is a trained banker, but exceptions are common in rural communities. The president and cashier must sign certain documents and attest to reports to supervisory officials.

The national and most state banking codes require that each bank have at least one vice president. If there are two or more vice presidents, one is designated as the senior or first vice president in order to fix responsibility for the president's duties when the latter is not present. The specific duties of vice presidents depend primarily on their assignments, and these in turn depend on the size and organization of the bank. Customarily, a vice president is placed in charge of each major department (see Chart 10–1) and in charge of large branch offices, if the bank has branch offices.

The cashier is a trained banker with years of experience. He is usually the executive officer second only in importance to the president in the administration of the internal affairs of the bank. In small banks he assumes all the nonstatutory functions of the president. Unless otherwise delegated, the cashier is responsible for the bank's

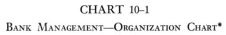

CHART 10–1

BANK MANAGEMENT—ORGANIZATION CHART*

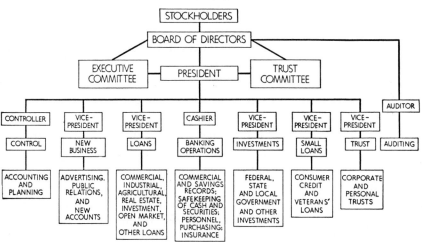

* This chart is based on the organization of a medium-sized commercial bank and is presented to show the channels of administrative responsibilities of the chief officers. The number of departments will vary according to the volume of business of the bank. Foreign-exchange, bond, real estate, savings, branch-management, legal, and other departments may be added as needed. In small banks all the activities of the bank may be in the banking operations department.

funds, the safekeeping of earning assets, the employment of junior members of the staff, the purchase of supplies, and the arrangement for insurance. He signs cashiers' checks, bank drafts, and vouchers, and he has charge of the transactions when his bank sells securities, borrows money, or rediscounts paper. He signs certificates of stock, takes charge of the stock ledger and dividend books, and has charge of the bank's correspondence. He endorses notes and drafts before they are sent to other banks for collection. The cashier is primarily responsible for all the actual transactions after lines of policy have been determined by the president and the board of directors.

Many large banks have an officer known as the "chairman of the board of directors," who may be the chief administrative officer; but usually his activities are less routine than those of the president, being in the nature of "policy forming," "public relations," and "new business." The chairman's banking activities will be determined by his personality, business and social contacts, ability, and "power" within and outside the bank.

The titles and duties of junior officers are not uniform, but next in rank are the assistants to the chairman of the board, the president, the vice president, and the cashier. These titles give no indication as to their functions, but among the junior officers are tellers, chief clerks, and head bookkeepers; among the employees are accountants, stenographers, typists, file clerks, machine operators, junior clerks, and many others.

Since 90 percent of the customers never come in contact with the senior officers of a bank, it is the employees who are responsible for the impression that the general public has of the bank. This is recognized generally by those who select new employees, and consequently, neatness and personality are emphasized. Since most bank jobs are routine or technical in nature, the qualities of accuracy, dependability, and speed are also essential in employees.

Promotion from within the ranks of any organization is a basic requirement in any sound personnel policy, and banking is no exception. Most of the current banking leaders have risen through the ranks, and surveys made of bank officers' training and experience support the conclusion that most of them have had many years of banking experience (but not necessarily with the same bank). At present there are 600,000 bank officers and bank employees, of whom over one half are women. Banking, like teaching, is handicapped in obtaining personnel because of its reputation for paying low salaries and for giving little opportunity for advancement. However there are many advantages to working in a bank, including job security, pleasant surroundings, prestige, and, in spite of the reputation to the contrary, excellent chances for promotion. Banks are growing so rapidly and the officer-to-employee ratio is such as to necessitate eventual promotion of all qualified, experienced permanent employees to officer rank. Salaries paid to bank employees are about the same as those paid other office workers and above those paid in retail stores, but, if relative responsibilities are considered, they may be below those paid in industry. Gradually the salaries of bank officers and employees have been increased to a competitive level, and the fringe benefits provided staff members (educational, hospitalization insurance, pensions, profit sharing, recreational, retirement, sickness, and others) exceed those of any other major industry. Because of the nature of banking, the sharp division between management and labor found in industry is lacking, and this may explain the absence of organized labor in banks, except in some metropolitan areas and part of the West Coast.

SUMMARY

Banks are classified according to the source of charters, principal types of deposits and use made thereof, affiliation with federal agencies, type of structure and size. During the past 15 years, while there has been a decline in the number of banks, the number of branches has increased. Part of the decline in numbers is attributable to mergers, and this has raised the cry of "monopoly" by some while others are more concerned over destructive competition among banks which has been a factor in the rising cost of banking.

The aim in bank supervision is to assure sound banks and to provide the general public with adequate banking services. To this end, applications for bank charters are scrutinized carefully within the framework of the so-called "free banking" system. The only guarantee of sound banks is capable, responsible bank management; however, the responsibility is shared by all bank directors, officers, and employees and to some extent by stockholders and depositors. The soundness and profitability of a bank may be indicated by its published statements of condition and its profit-and-loss or earnings statements.

QUESTIONS AND PROBLEMS

1. Distinguish between or among banks classified as follows: (*a*) state and national, (*b*) commercial and savings, (*c*) member and nonmember, (*d*) insured and uninsured, (*e*) unit and branch, and (*f*) large, middle-size, and small.
2. Explain the difference between multiunit and branch banking. Which do you favor? Why?
3. Discuss: "The only proper basis for the restriction of branching is the suitability of this means of bank expansion in particular banking markets. Under this principle, the regulatory authorities should have the full discretion to authorize the formation of branches wherever they may serve the public interest to best advantage." (The Administrator of National Banks, *Studies in Banking Competition and the Banking Structure*, [Office of the Comptroller of the Currency, U.S. Treasury Department (Washington, D.C., 1966)], pp. 405–6.)
4. Analyze: "The desire to merge is critically affected by the power to branch. Merger applications rarely appear in no-branch States be-

cause a merger under those conditions usually requires the closing of one of the merged banks." (*Ibid.*, p. 406.)

5. Outline the general procedure in chartering a bank. Is there any danger of monopoly as long as there is "free entry"?

6. Discuss the ownership and management of commercial banks.

7. What are the main changes that have taken place in the structure of commercial banks in the United States since World War II?

8. Discuss: "During the year there were net declines of 16 national and 55 State member banks. The decline in the number of national banks reflected 48 conversions to branches incident to mergers and absorptions and 7 conversions to nonmember banks, which was partly offset by the organization of 25 new national banks and the conversion of 10 nonmember banks to national banks." (*Fifty-Third Annual Report of the Board of Governors of the Federal Reserve System Covering Operations for the Year 1966* [Washington, D.C., 1967], p. 301.)

9. Analyze: "A further element of difficulty has been the vast complex of regulation . . . which banks have had to live with. On the regulatory front, we at the Chase had some experience in this regard in our abortive attempts to acquire the Diners Club and to affiliate with a group of Upstate banks in New York." (Chase Manhattan Bank, N.A., *Perspective on Banking* [New York, 1968], p. 2).

10. Explain: "One might expect chain systems with all members located in the same country to be more popular in states that prohibit branching. To a certain extent this expectation is borne out; Illinois and Texas have unit banking and rank first and second in number of chain systems, with 34 and 27, respectively." (Jerome C. Darnell, "Chain Banking," *National Banking Review*, March, 1966, p. 316.)

CHAPTER 11

Source of Bank Assets

STUDENTS are particularly interested in commercial banks because of the monetary nature of their deposit liabilities; but this does not explain why commercial banks are willing to assume debts payable on demand, or at the end of a short-term period, that amount to over $415 billion. Banks are profit-seeking organizations and the most important source of cash assets which they lend or invest is depositors—individuals, corporations, governments, and others—who exchange their cash for bank debts. In addition, banks obtain assets from owners and lenders, and they also retain some of their earnings from operations. Unlike most other business firms, the smallest percentage of a bank's assets comes from the last three sources.

BANK CAPITAL

Banks need capital funds to meet legal requirements and to assure confidence of depositors, loan customers, and the general public. The percentage of bank assets obtained from funds provided by owners, including retained earnings, has been declining steadily for many years. Currently, owners provide about 8 percent of banks' total assets; depositors, 87.5 percent; and other sources (such as borrowing in the money and capital markets and from Federal Reserve and correspondent banks), about 4.5 percent. The total equity of stockholders, or "total capital account," consists of capital stock, surplus, undivided profits, and any other proprietory claim (see Table 11-1). The book value of each share of stock is found by dividing the total capital account figure by the number of shares. Although stockholders' equity represents only about 8 percent of the average bank's total assets, it has a dual function.[1] First, it acts as a shock absorber to

---

[1] Many years ago Walter Bagehot wrote that "the main source of profitableness of established banking is the smallness of the requisite capital. Being only wanted as a 'moral influence,' it needs not be more than is necessary to secure that influence." Walter Bagehot, *Lombard Street* (Homewood, Ill.: Richard D. Irwin, Inc., 1962), reprinted from Scribner, Armstrong & Co. edition printed in New York in 1873 (with minor editorial changes), p. 120.

TABLE 11-1

CAPITAL ACCOUNTS OF COMMERCIAL BANKS,
JUNE 30, 1967

(In Thousands of Dollars)

Capital accounts—total $33,418,529
　Capital notes and debentures 1,988,062
　Preferred stock   65,197
　Common stock 9,259,094
　Surplus 14,548,615
　Undivided profits and reserves 7,557,561

Source: *Annual Report of the Federal Deposit Insurance Corporation, 1967* (Washington, D.C., 1968), p. 173.

protect depositors and shareholders in case of bank losses; and, second, it gives bank management cash to use in obtaining buildings, fixtures, machinery and other fixed assets as well as income-producing securities. Each capital account item has certain features that distinguish it from the others.

Capital Stock.　The capital stock of a bank is the amount of capital as stated in the bank's charter, and it has been described as a trust fund for depositors that must be kept unimpaired at all times. Hence, depositors are assured that stockholders always will have a financial stake in their bank equal to the capital item. If, for any reason, this stake is impaired by losses, regulatory officers are responsible for such action as will protect the community, the depositors, and the bank. In cooperation with other governmental agencies the directors and officers of the bank and others in the community may raise new capital funds to keep the bank functioning or may close it and later either reorganize it or liquidate it. The capital stock of a bank may be increased or decreased by appropriate legal action.

There are two main classes of capital stock, common stock and preferred stock. Holders of common stock are entitled to net earnings after taxes and all other obligations of the bank are met. They are the risk takers, who in theory, at least, are responsible for management. Owners of preferred stock have preference as to dividends and assets in the event of liquidation of their bank. No dividends may be paid on common stock until dividends have been paid on preferred stock, and no cash from liquidation of assets is paid to common stockholders until the claims of preferred stockholders have been satisfied. In return for their priority position, preferred stockholders' dividends are usually limited and they may not have the right to vote for directors and on other matters brought before the stockholders' annual and special meetings.

Surplus. Largest among the various capital account items is "surplus," which is an accounting item representing an amount in excess of the par value of stock paid in at the time of organization and/or the earnings of the bank which have been retained by management and placed in this account. It differs from the capital stock in that it may be impaired without making the bank subject to reorganization.

Undivided Profits. The undivided profits account is an accounting item showing bank earnings that have not been paid out as dividends or placed in the surplus account or in one of the reserve accounts that banks keep to offset losses or some expenses that are certain. In some cases it includes funds paid into a bank in excess of capital and surplus at the time of organization. When retained earnings are accounted for in the undivided profits account, management has much greater freedom of action than when they are accounted for in the surplus account. Therefore, the undivided profits item is becoming more important on bank statements. The funds accounted for in the undivided profits account may be transferred to the surplus account, added to one of the reserve accounts for contingencies, or paid out to stockholders as dividends. Most banks prefer to have a stable dividend policy, which means that the undivided profits account will be built up during good years and paid out during lean years.

Accounting Reserves. Customarily, banks make bookkeeping allowances for payment of taxes, payrolls, interest, and other accrued expenses due in 1, 3, 6, or 12 months, by spreading the expense items proportionately throughout the year (called "accrued taxes and other expense" items). Other deductions from income may be made for anticipated losses on loans and/or investments. The term "reserve" is used here in a technical sense and does not refer to an "asset reserve" or something set aside for future use.

The largest of the reserve accounts is "reserve for contingencies" which functions as a general reserve to absorb charges for nonrecurring expenses and unforeseen losses including those on securities (bad-debt losses are treated separately for tax reasons, as explained below). Management may retain income in amounts in excess of reserve needs, and so the excessive part of all reserve accounts should be considered as part of total capital accounts.

The policy of reserve for anticipated costs and losses of any particular bank depends on its management, its financial position, the outlook for future profits, the attitude of regulatory officials, and sometimes the source of profits. For illustration, a bank having a large trading profit on investments would usually set aside a large "reserve for contingencies" to offset possible future trading losses.

In banking, losses on loans usually occur during depressions; therefore, it would be logical to create accounting reserves during prosperous years to absorb them when they occur. Following the disastrous experiences of banks during the early 1930's, the Internal Revenue Service encouraged this practice by permitting banks to make deductions from income to create reserve accounts for losses on loans before computing federal income taxes. When a loss occurs on a loan both the asset affected and its related reserve are reduced by the amount of the loss, and the bank's reported current income for the accounting period is not affected.

In order to prevent abuse of this tax-free privilege, the Bureau of Internal Revenue Services places limits on the annual deduction from current earnings and on the size of this reserve account. The procedure followed has been changed several times, but the one now in effect permits banks to deduct from income 0.8 percent of the amount of their "risk" loans outstanding at the end of the year and to add the amount deducted to the reserve account for losses on loans.[2] The size of the reserve account is limited to an amount equal to 2.4 percent of the "risk" loans outstanding at the end of the year.

Sales-Leaseback. Banks may increase their "surplus" by selling their bank premises and leasing them back. The sale may be made to a subsidiary corporation created by management to purchase and hold title to the building. If one assumes that the bank is carrying the value of the building on its books at the original cost less depreciation, or $2 million, and the selling price is $20 million, there would be $18 million profit to be added to "surplus" and $20 million in cash to be lent or invested. (A part of the profit would be invested in the stock of the subsidiary corporation which will borrow most of the cash it uses to buy the bank building from an insurance company or other institutional investor.)

Growth. Currently, commercial banks' capital accounts are divided approximately as follows: common stock, 27 percent; surplus, 44 percent; preferred stock, 6 percent; and undivided profits and reserves, 23 percent. However, the percentage composition of these items changes from year to year; for illustration, in 1967, retained

[2] Internal Revenue Service, Ruling 65–92, dated March 15, 1965. The amount of loans guaranteed or insured by an agency of the federal government is subtracted from total loans as "riskless" loans.

earnings accounted for 71 percent of the increase in total capital accounts for member banks as compared with 76 percent the preceding year.[3]

At times, new issues of common stock represent an important source of new capital; but most of the growth in common stock has been due to capitalization of retained earnings and issuance of stock dividends. Some banks capitalize their retained earnings periodically by distributing stock dividends and reducing surplus and/or undivided profit accounts. Retaining a large percentage of earnings necessitates low dividends, which makes bank stock less attractive to some investors. If banks were to reverse this procedure, it would facilitate their financing new capital needs by the sale of capital stock. Preferred stock is not popular, and banks have issued only a small amount. (Many associate preferred stock of banks with the distressed conditions under which it was issued in 1933 and 1934.) Although the growth in banks' capital accounts had been rapid, it has not kept pace with the expansion in total bank assets.

Adequacy. Bankers, supervisory officials, depositors, and others are interested in the adequacy of banks' capital. Although there is no answer as to the amount that would be needed to insure solvency in case of large losses due to a major catastrophe, certain guides as to the "ideal" amount of capital have been formulated. Among these, the earliest was that capital should equal or exceed 10 percent of deposits. Later this formula was abandoned in favor of using a risk assets to capital ratio because the need for capital is best measured by the risk a bank assumes. A bank's assets differ as to the degree of risk, and so a more complete analysis would compute capital needs in terms of different assets. Since "cash and due from banks" are practically risk-free, no capital would be needed to protect them, but "work out assets" contain much risk of loss and so the reasoning might be that the capital needs should equal 50 percent of such assets.

Unquestionably, the "adjusted risk assets" treatment for appraising risks is superior to the general "capital/risk asset" or "capital/deposit" ratios, but this approach fails to recognize the fact that although a bank may have losses, it may be only a matter of time until changes in the economic climate (from depression to prosperity) and improvements in earnings would permit the bank to recover. Certainly, many of the banks that were closed in 1933 would have regained solvency if they had been given the opportunity. Now, more attention is being given to (1) quality of management, (2) liquidity

[3] *Federal Reserve Bulletin*, May, 1968, p. 413.

of assets, (3) history of earnings and retention thereof, (4) quality and character of ownership, (5) burden of meeting occupancy expenses, (6) potential velocity of deposit structure, (7) quality of operating procedures, and (8) capacity to meet present and future financial needs of its trade area in view of its competitors.[4]

Because of the remoteness of the possibility of an economic collapse comparable to that of the 1930–34 period, the lack of general concern with the question of adequacy of banks' capital seems justified.[5] The current distribution of capital among the different capital account items is such as to provide protection to shareholders. The capital account items that may be used before capital is impaired seems to be sufficient to absorb any foreseeable losses (they now comprise about 75 percent of all capital account items).

Debt Financing.   Although long-term notes and bonds have been an important source of long-term funds for corporations other than banks, the latter have made little use of them until recently. As reported by the Federal Deposit Insurance Corporation, "In the two years ended December 31, 1965, capital notes and debentures of banks increased from $168 million to $1,701 million." This increase of $1,533 million represents fewer than 200 issues but "comprises 30 percent of the amount in 'total capital and surplus accounts' of all banks during the period."[6]

The feature that makes long-term debt financing tolerable to depositors is that such debt obligations are made subordinate to deposits and other liabilities (in case of liquidation, depositors and other creditors would be paid in full before any payments could be made on capital notes). Interest paid on capital notes is a cost and is deductible before computing federal and state income taxes. In contrast, dividends paid on bank stock are not a cost and are not deductible as an expense before computing a bank's tax liability. However, financing with debt instruments has one disadvantage not found in equity financing—debts must be repaid. On the other hand, many banks are finding it profitable to borrow at 4.5 or 5 percent when net income after taxes is at the present level (in 1967, member banks earned 9.6 percent on their total capital accounts).[7]

---

[4] Department of the Treasury, Comptroller of the Currency (12 c.F.R., parts 7, 10–14), *Corporate Practices and Procedures of National Banking Associations* mimeographed, no date, p. 11. Although these rules were tentative, they were later adopted with only minor changes.

[5] See Roland I. Robinson and Richard H. Pettway, *Policies for Optimum Bank Capital* (Chicago: Association of Reserve City Bankers, 1967).

[6] *Annual Report of the Federal Deposit Insurance Corporation, 1965* (Washington, D.C.: U.S. Government Printing Office, 1966), p. 106.

[7] *Federal Reserve Bulletin*, May, 1968, p. 413.

BANK DEPOSITS

Although owners and long-term lenders provide banks with capital funds, the chief source of bank assets is depositors, whose funds are classified in various ways such as availability, insurance status, security, ownership, and origin. In the aggregate, banks' total deposits are obtained from thousands of individuals, business firms, and others who keep funds in their banks for various reasons. The characteristics of these deposits vary greatly. For illustration, some depositors seldom withdraw any funds from their savings accounts, building them up to care for retirement needs; while government-securities dealers may have deposit turnovers at a rate in excess of 6,600 times per year.

Availability. When deposits are classified according to availability, the two classes are demand deposits and time deposits. De-

TABLE 11–2

TOTAL DEPOSITS OF COMMERCIAL BANKS, JUNE 30, 1967
(In Thousands of Dollars)

Business and personal deposits—total	$300,467,414
Individuals, partnerships, and corporations—demand	137,942,098
Deposits of savings and loan associations	2,255,300
Other deposits of individuals, partnerships, and corporations	135,686,798
Individuals, partnerships, and corporations—time	154,973,753
Savings deposits	91,769,473
Deposits accumulated for payment of personal loans	1,276,052
Deposits of savings and loan associations	822,227
Other deposits of individuals, partnerships, and corporations	61,106,001
Certified and officers' checks, letters of credit, travelers' checks, etc.	7,551,563
Government deposits—total	36,515,231
United States Government—demand	5,176,614
United States Government—time	290,044
States and subdivisions—demand	15,316,304
States and subdivisions—time	15,732,269
Domestic interbank deposits—total	17,603,332
Commercial banks in the U.S.—demand	15,439,089
Commercial banks in the U.S.—time	708,202
Mutual savings banks in the U.S.—demand	929,361
Mutual savings banks in the U.S.—time	526,680
Foreign government and bank deposits—total	7,899,561
Foreign governments, central banks, etc.—demand	823,278
Foreign governments, central banks, etc.—time	5,114,136
Banks in foreign countries—demand	1,692,231
Banks in foreign countries—time	269,916
Total deposits	362,485,538
Demand	184,870,538
Time	177,615,000

Source: *Annual Report of the Federal Deposit Insurance Corporation, 1967* (Washington, D.C., 1968), p. 173.

mand deposits are so-called because they may be transferred or with-drawn on demand, that is, without prior notice of withdrawal (the "ledger clerk" function of commercial banks). Generally, time deposits are those that may not be withdrawn until after the elapse of a specified time period; but, for regulatory purposes, time deposits are those wherein the original time element is 30 days or more.

The classification of deposits as demand and time deposits is the basis for setting member-bank minimum reserve requirements. Con-

TABLE 11–3

RESERVE REQUIREMENTS OF MEMBER BANKS
(Percent of Deposits, Beginning July 14, 1966)

Effective Date	Net Demand Deposits*				Time Deposits† (All Classes of Banks)		
	Reserve City Banks		Country Banks		Savings Deposits	Other Time Deposits	
	Under $5 Million	Over $5 Million	Under $5 Million	Over $5 Million		Under $5 Million	Over $5 Million
1966—July 14, 21	16½		12		4	4	5
September 8, 15	...		...		...	...	6
1967—March 2	...		...		3½	3½	...
March 16	...		...		3	3	...
1968—January 11, 18	16½	17	12	12½	...	...	...
In effect April 30, 1968	16½	17	12	12½	3	3	6
Present legal requirement:							
Minimum	10		7		3	3	3
Maximum	22		14		10	10	10

* Net demand deposits are gross demand deposits minus cash items in process of collection and demand deposits due from domestic banks.
† For reserve purposes, Christmas and vacation club accounts are subject to the same reserve requirements as savings deposits.
Source: *Federal Reserve Bulletin*, June, 1968, p. A–11.

gress has specified that minimum and maximum for savings and other time deposits and for demand deposits in the two classes of member banks—reserve city and country banks; but the regulatory authorities have broad powers to set actual rates within these limits (see Table 11–3).

The maximum interest rate payable on savings and time deposits in banks is subject to regulation by the Board of Governors of the Federal Reserve System and the Federal Deposit Insurance Corporation. In order to best achieve the objectives of interest-rate payments the Board of Governors now classifies time deposits as "savings deposits" and as "other time deposits." The latter is also divided into "multiple" and "single" maturity deposits (see Table 11–4).

Savings deposits are evidenced by passbooks and only individuals and nonprofit corporations (churches, educational institutions, fraternal organizations, and similar institutions) are permitted to open them with insured banks. They are opened with banks under a statutory provision that permits the latter to require a 30-day written notice of intent to withdraw them before a withdrawal is made, but most banks

TABLE 11–4

MAXIMUM INTEREST RATES PAYABLE ON SAVINGS
AND OTHER TIME DEPOSITS
(Percent per Annum, Rates Beginning July 20, 1966)

Type of Deposit	Effective Date		
	July 20, 1966	September 26, 1966	April 19, 1968
Savings deposits....................	4	4	4
Other time deposits:*			
Multiple maturity:†			
90 days or more............	5	5	5
Less than 90 days (30–89 days)...................	4	4	4
Single maturity:			
Less than $100,000..........	5½	5	5
$100,000 or more:			
30–59 days..............			5½
60–89 days..............			5¾
90–179 days............	5½	5½	6
180 days and over........			6¼

* At this time, time deposits of foreign governments and of monetary and financial organizations of which the United States is a member are exempt from maximum interest-rate regulation.
† Includes deposits that are automatically renewable at maturity without action by the depositor and deposits payable after written notice of withdrawal.
Source: *Federal Reserve Bulletin*, June, 1968, p. A–11.

customarily waive this requirement. If and when they do apply it, the rule must be uniformly applicable to all savings depositors.

Multiple maturity deposits are time deposits that (*a*) are payable at the option of the depositor on more than one date (March 30, June 30, September 30, etc.) or after the elapse of a specific amount of time after the deposit date (30 days, 60 days, etc.); (*b*) is payable after written notice of withdrawal; or (*c*) has an underlying instrument, contract, informal understanding, or agreement that provides for automatic renewal at maturity.

During 1964 and 1965, metropolitan and other city banks were encroaching on the savings bank business by issuing certificates of deposit having more than one optional maturity date. The effect was to give such deposits some of the flexibility contained in ordinary savings deposits. For the purpose of fixing maximum interest rates payable on multiple-maturity deposits, the latter are divided into two maturity classes, those maturing in 90 days or more and those maturing in from 30 to 89 days. (Those with longer maturities usually have higher interest-rate ceilings.)

The multiple-maturity time class of deposits includes one type that is usually considered to be an ordinary savings deposit—"time deposits–open accounts." This type of deposit entails a contract that specifies that neither the whole or any part of a deposit made for 30 days or more may be withdrawn by check or otherwise before the date of maturity or until expiration of 30 days following written notice of intent to withdraw it. Christmas Club, Vacation Club and similar deposit accounts may permit withdrawal even before the end of the period and still qualify as "time deposit–open accounts." If these deposits are not withdrawn at maturity, they usually are continued automatically without action by depositors.

Single-maturity time deposits are usually evidenced by negotiable or nonnegotiable certificates of deposit issued in large denominations and varying in maturity from 1 to 12 months, with shorter maturities being more popular with depositors. The interest rates paid on time and savings deposits vary according to conditions in the money market.

Insurance.   Under laws enacted after the 1933 banking crisis, most bank accounts are protected by insurance provided by the Federal Deposit Insurance Corporation. Although coverage is limited to $15,000 for each deposit account maintained by one depositor in a bank, the Corporation estimates that 99 percent of all accounts are fully protected. Nevertheless, the remaining 1 percent represents many large accounts; hence, it is estimated that only 58 percent of deposits is covered by insurance. Of the banks that do not participate in the FDIC insurance plan, two thirds are mutual savings banks in Massachusetts which are covered by their own insurance program, and the remainder are either unable or unwilling to meet the standards set for federal deposit insurance.

Ownership.   Deposits are customarily classified according to ownership as (1) business and personal, (2) government, (3) domestic interbank, and (4) foreign government and bank deposits (see Table 11–2). Each of these classes of deposits has several subdivisions.

1. Business and personal deposits include (*a*) demand deposits, (*b*) time deposits and (*c*) others earmarked for certified and officers' checks, letters of credit, travelers' checks, and similar liabilities. The most important of the deposits of individuals, partnerships, and corporations with commercial banks are in the form of demand deposits (see Table 11–2).

2. Government deposits include those of the federal government and those of the states and their different political subdivisions. The federal government keeps its checking accounts with Federal Reserve banks and its tax and loan accounts with commercial banks (see Chapter 19). The federal government holds only a small part of its deposits as time deposits. In contrast, state and local government deposits are divided almost equally as time and as demand deposits (see Table 11–2).

3. Domestic interbank balances are assets of one bank which are kept with a second bank for the same reasons that other corporations keep deposits with their banks. Often a bank located in a small community will want the payment and collection, lending, advisory, and other services that a larger bank can give to a smaller one. This practice of maintaining correspondent banking relations with other banks has been strengthened by state laws that permit state-chartered banks to keep all or part of their legal reserves with designated depositories. Interbank balances amount to between 5 and 6 percent of total commercial bank deposits.

4. New York, being the financial center of the "free" world, attracts deposits of many foreign governments and foreign central banks. These banks as well as others in metropolitan areas give the same type of correspondent banking services to foreign depositors as they provide their domestic bank customers (see Chapter 26).

Security. Secured deposits are similar to other secured credits in that something has been pledged specifically to assure their payment. The two most common kinds of secured deposits are "trust" and "public" deposits. This means that public deposits (federal, state, city, county, and other subdivisions of the state) and trust funds left on deposit are secured by a special lien on the bank's assets, earmarked for this purpose. Like preferred creditors of any debtor, these creditors have preferred claims to the pledged assets—which, in case of failure of the bank, places their rights (to what are usually the best assets of the bank) ahead of the Federal Deposit Insurance Corporation and other unsecured creditors.

Unsecured deposits are all deposits that are not secured by something specifically pledged to assure their payment. If and when a bank is liquidated, the unsecured creditors as a group will lose to the extent that the secured creditors gain. While this situation does not present a special problem for those whose deposits are fully insured, it is significant for large depositors and the Federal Deposit Insurance Corporation. The reason for the discrimination in favor of certain types of depositors is that the laws covering the deposit of these funds require this special protection. There are therefore two ways to regard the advertisement "depository for federal [state, city, etc.] funds": (1) the bank is so strong that the government has selected it as a depository, or (2) the bank gives less protection to my deposit than it does to government and trust deposits. Seemingly, if public and trust funds require special protection, it should be provided by means other than increasing the risks assumed by general depositors and the Federal Deposit Insurance Corporation.

Origin. When classified according to origin, the two classes of deposits are primary and derivative. Primary deposits are those resulting from the collection of cash items or deposits of currency. They are traced to deposits of checks, drafts, interest coupons, and currency and to collection of mail and wire transfers, notes, and other obligations that are due. The significant fact to recognize is that primary deposits give an individual bank new funds to invest or to lend. A bank usually gains primary deposits when its competitive position is improving and/or when the banking system as a whole is expanding.

Derivative deposits are those that result from the lending and investing operations of the bank, and such deposits tend to increase when its primary deposits are increasing and, conversely, to decrease when its primary deposits are decreasing. In other words, banks lend and invest more when they have available reserves provided by primary depositors.

CHECKING ACCOUNTS

Customarily, demand deposits are kept as checking accounts with banks. No interest may be paid on them, but these interest-free accounts may be so expensive for a bank to service that there would be a loss in handling them if the bank did not make service charges. Check handling and record keeping occupies the time of most of the employees of banks. Banks are deprived of the use of a fraction of each deposit because of legal and working reserve requirements and items in process of collection.

Although there is a tendency for the general public to assume that opening a deposit account is a right rather than a privilege, banks sometimes refuse to open deposit accounts for individuals, partnerships, and corporations, including governments. Among the reasons for refusal are: the account would fail to meet some technical requirements, such as maintaining a minimum balance; the prospective depositor's reputation may be such as to lead the bank's officers to conclude that having the account would be harmful to the bank; and the nature of the account would make it difficult for the bank to service it properly and/or profitably.

Partnership accounts are opened on the same basis as individual accounts except that filing a copy of the partnership agreement is required. In the case of a corporation's account the bank customarily requires the board of directors of the corporation to authorize the opening of the account by resolution, to specify those authorized to sign checks and other credit instruments, to indicate who may endorse credit instruments and sign promissory notes, and to certify that there is nothing in the corporation's bylaws or charter that would impair or limit the authority conferred in the resolution. Banks have printed forms that cover these requirements, and, when these are properly filled in and signed, the account is opened.

Banks also open checking and other accounts in the names of two or more persons, most commonly husband and wife. The privileges of the participants may be either as "tenants in common" or as "joint tenants." In both legal arrangements, deposits may be made by either party, but, in case of tenants in common, both parties must act jointly when making withdrawals. As joint tenants, either party may write checks for all or any part of the funds on deposit. In the case of death, as tenants in common, the survivor's share in the account (one half) may be withdrawn after furnishing such proof of death of the other party as the bank may require, and the remainder of the account becomes part of the estate of the deceased; as joint tenants, the survivor may withdraw the deposit upon filing a tax waiver with the bank.

Banks accept deposits of cash, properly endorsed checks, sight drafts, and matured interest coupons. Ordinarily, in making such deposits, the depositor fills in a deposit slip according to the directions thereon and presents it over the counter or by mail. Instructions for making out deposit slips should be followed carefully, and, if the depositor has been given an account number, it should be written in the space provided or on the deposit slip. Usually, the bank keeps the original deposit slip and provides the depositor with a machine-printed receipt. In order to reduce the cost of bookkeeping, banks customarily give immediate credit in the deposit accounts for credit items which they collect. But, in order to prevent "kiting"[8] and the use of funds prior to collection, there must be some relationship between the checks written on an account and the funds collected.

A depositor's checking account may be increased by borrowing from his bank and having his deposit account credited with the proceeds of the loan, by depositing currency, or by leaving credit instruments with his bank to be collected and the proceeds credited to his account. These "collection items" include drafts used in domestic and foreign trade, such as acceptances and drafts that have documents attached (surrendered on acceptance or payment of the drafts). In addition, other credit instruments that may be deposited for collection include coupons, matured bonds, notes, installment contracts, and other obligations that require special handling. Local collections are made by messengers of the bank or the clearinghouse from payers at their places of business, homes, or banks; out-of-town collections are made by mail through the nationwide services of the collection department of its Federal Reserve bank or through its correspondent banks. Presumably, all costs are covered by the collection fees charged, but the charges made by Federal Reserve banks do not cover the cost of operating their collection departments.

Depositors use bank buildings most frequently to make deposits and to cash checks. In modernizing buildings, banks have tried to make them more attractive to customers, as reflected in the layouts of bank lobbies, the elimination of the grillwork and high screens around tellers' windows, and the replacement of high counters with low ones. In addition, emphasis has shifted from dark woodwork and furniture, massive columns, and high ceilings to brighter interiors marked by better lighting, more attractive fixtures, and pleasantly colored draperies and walls.

Some of the changes that banks have made in their operations have helped not only their depositors but also the banks. For a number of years banks have used the unit-teller system, whereby the same teller receives and pays deposits. This relieves the customer from the necessity of waiting in line at two different windows. New equipment and operating procedures permit tellers to do their work more rapidly and more efficiently. Coin cashiers have cut the time required to cash checks by an estimated 35 percent. Sorting and packaging machines

[8] "Kiting," as used in banking, refers to the practice of writing checks for amounts in excess of the funds in a checking account. The drawer takes advantage of the time needed to collect the checks. He may set up a kiting arrangement with others wherein two or more banks are involved, and, by keeping a flow of checks in the process of collection, he has the use of bank credit which he does not own. Sometimes the word "kiting" is used when checks are altered by raising the amount.

are also time-saving devices, as are window machines that receipt deposits and provide the depositor with a printed receipt (thus elimi- nating the use of duplicate deposit slips and passbooks). Tellers are using portable teller units, which may be locked when the teller must leave his cage. Extra ones may be rolled to the counter when more teller help is needed and rolled away when the need passes. The purpose of these units is to give tellers control over the currency for which they are responsible and to permit more efficient use of banks' staff members. Some banks use "split windows," whereby the teller receives the check on one side of a vertical panel and delivers the currency and coins on the other side. This keeps the customers mov- ing and permits a teller to serve more customers.

As has been stated previously, one advantage in the use of checks is that they serve as receipts upon cancellation and return to the drawers. Even if a canceled check is lost, a record of payment re- mains, because banks photograph all checks and keep the films on record. This practice also helps banks when they have difficulties with a customer who may disavow having written a specific check or claim that the amount of the check charged against his account is erroneous (questions that may arise after a bank depositor receives his monthly statement).

Ordinarily, a bank prepares a monthly statement for each depos- itor. This statement shows transactions that affect the account—de- posits made, withdrawals, bank charges against the account, and the amount on deposit at the beginning and at the end of the period. The depositor should check this statement for errors; if any are found, they should be reported to the bank immediately. This reconciliation is fairly simple for an individual account but more difficult for a business account. Although errors are seldom made, the depositor's full cooperation is helpful in disclosing unauthorized withdrawals, raised checks, and forgeries. Under some circumstances, failure to report unauthorized signatures and/or alterations may give the bank valid defense against any claim of the customer for payment of the item.[9]

The operational steps entailed in handling checking accounts are burdensome, time-consuming,[10] and expensive; therefore banks are

---

[9] *Uniform Commercial Code*, Sec. 4–406.

[10] The procedure followed by banks in the "process of posting," that is, paying and recording items, includes one or more of the following: "(*a*) verification of any signature; (*b*) ascertaining that sufficient funds are available; (*c*) affixing a 'paid' or other stamp; (*d*) entering a charge or entry to a customer's account; (*e*) correcting or revising an entry or erroneous action with respect to the item." See *Uniform Commercial Code*, Sec. 4–109.

looking for procedures and techniques which will not only lighten this burden but also provide better service for their customers. There are various means by which the number of checks written may be reduced, such as direct payroll processing, loan payments, and additions to savings accounts without the issuance of checks. While the total cost incurred when a company writes a check may be as much as $2.50, a bank can handle the same transfer for a few cents. Banks are experimenting with many new types of deposit transfers such as collecting public utility bills and processing accounts receivable for business firms.

Service charges are explained by the fact that banks operate on the principle that each checking account must pay its own way. An account may be unprofitable because it is too small relative to the number of checks written, the number of deposits made, and the overhead costs involved. Before service charges are made, the accounts of business firms may be analyzed, but those of individuals are treated more simply (to reduce expenses) under a measured or meter system or Simplified Analysis Plan. They are usually charged a flat amount per month as an overhead charge and per-item charges for checks written and items deposited. In addition, special charges are usually made for returned items, stop-payment orders, and other special services such as mailing the monthly statement. These service charges may be offset, in whole or part, by an "earning credit," which may be fixed arbitrarily at 10 or 15 cents for each $100 in the minimum or average balance, or calculated more scientifically in terms of what the bank may earn on the available balance (the amount left after cash reserves and uncollected items are subtracted).

Many banks offer a popular kind of checking account in which no minimum balance is required. This consists of selling a book of checks with the depositor's name on each check. As now used by banks in most large cities, there is no minimum-balance rule, but each depositor pays a service charge each month plus so much per month for each check written or simply so much for each check written without any monthly service charge. This type of personal checking account is economical and therefore an effective device to bring new customers to banks. The social implications resulting from such "thrifty" or pay-as-you-go checking accounts are far-reaching because the chief critics of banks are the nonusers of their services. Many individuals who cannot afford regular checking accounts are now enjoying the benefits of "thrifty" accounts.

Once an individual has become a depositor of a bank, it is but natural for him to use other services of the bank. Among these, the first he may want to use is the loan service to finance an automobile, a home, or business assets (inventories, equipment, machinery, etc.). In order to be eligible for a bank loan, a good credit rating is essential, and one of the best procedures for building up a good credit standing is to have and maintain a good deposit account.

Since depositors leave funds with banks for safekeeping, it is not surprising for them to expect their banks to keep other things of value such as jewelry, silver, securities, and other valuable papers. Most banks are equipped with safe-deposit boxes and vaults, which are rented to customers at an annual fee. This fee varies according to the location of the bank, the size of the box, and other variables. (The smallest and most popular box rents for about $5 per year plus federal tax.) Some banks also keep valuables in their vaults for customers.

SEGREGATION OF SAVINGS DEPOSITS

In recent years, bankers have given more attention to the management of liabilities on the assumption that, when loans are profitable enough, they may pay more for funds and increase their assets. Bankers no longer assume that the level of deposits is beyond their control. By paying higher interest rates on time and savings deposits, funds may be diverted from the money market and from other financial institutions.

When time and savings deposits are accepted by commercial banks, the funds are mingled with other assets of these banks. Since the very nature of commercial banking requires that more risks be assumed than in the case of savings banking, time deposits are subject to more risks when left with commercial banks than with mutual savings banks (part of these risks may be shifted from depositors to the Federal Deposit Insurance Corporation). The savings depositors do not benefit from the risk associated with commercial banking, since they are not commercial borrowers and do not have the privilege of using their deposits as a means of payment.

During the 70 years from 1865 to 1934, 75 percent of the total losses due to bank failures were taken by depositors with accounts of $5,000 or less.[11] Many bankers now regard the Federal Deposit Insurance Corporation as the solution to the problem of the need for protection of the small time and demand deposits, but a more equitable solution is the proposal for the complete segregation of the two

[11] "Losses to Depositors in Suspended Commercial Banks, 1865-1934," *Annual Report of the Federal Deposit Insurance Corporation for the Year Ended December 31, 1934* (Washington, D.C.: U.S. Government Printing Office, 1935), pp. 73-110.

types of banking, even though they may be carried on by the same bank.

Segregation of savings deposits would require the complete legal separation of the savings department from the rest of the bank, allocation of a proportionate share of the bank's capital and surplus to this department, and investment of savings deposits in assets similar to those purchased by mutual savings banks. The two legal entities would be operated as a single firm, using the same personnel and premises, having the same ownership, and serving the same customers; but cash and earning assets which are the basis for money creation (demand deposits) would be separated from assets arising from savings. Thus, savings deposits in commercial banks would be treated as they are in other savings institutions.

FEDERAL DEPOSIT INSURANCE CORPORATION

Among the banking systems of the world that of the United States was unique until 1967 in that banks' deposits were insured by an agency of the federal government (see Chapter 30). The Federal Deposit Insurance Corporation was formed in 1934 to restore the badly shaken confidence of depositors in banks.[12] It is supported by a "tax" on deposits of insured banks and earnings from the government securities in the Corporation's "insurance fund." The statutory annual rate is one twelfth of 1 percent of assessable deposits. However, the Federal Deposit Insurance Act of 1950 provided for an "assessment credit," and the current effective rate is one thirty-second of 1 percent of assessable deposits.[13]

The Federal Deposit Insurance Corporation has no capital stock and is managed by a board of three directors (the Comptroller of the Currency and two others representing different political parties appointed by the President with the consent of the United States Senate). In 1967, the country was divided into 14 districts with new district offices in Philadelphia and Memphis (district boundaries which follow state lines were rearranged).

Congress gave the Federal Deposit Insurance Corporation examining powers over all nonmember insured banks and the right to reject

[12] For a history of guaranty or insurance of bank deposits see *Annual Report of the Federal Deposit Insurance Corporation for the Year Ended December 31, 1950* (Washington, D.C.: U.S. Government Printing Office, 1951), pp. 61–101.

[13] Assessment credit is applied to future assessments which are paid semiannually. It is found by deducting FDIC costs and expenses from total assessments which came due during the year and then taking two thirds of this amount. The remainder of the net assessment income is transferred to the deposit insurance fund, which amounts to $3.5 billion. See *Annual Report of the Federal Deposit Insurance Corporation for the Year Ended December 31, 1967*, p. 36.

any nonmember bank's application for insurance for failure to achieve and maintain a safe and sound bank. In acting on applications, the Corporation considers the following factors: (1) financial history and condition of the bank, (2) adequacy of its capital structure, (3) prospects for future earnings, (4) general character of management, (5) location and banking needs of the area served, (6) whether or not the bank's corporate powers are consistent with the purposes of the Federal Deposit Insurance Act.

The Corporation has been responsible not only for removing most of the fear of bank failure but also for the achievement of better banking standards and practices. Since World War II, insured bank closures have averaged three per year (ranging from none in 1962 to seven in 1966). When the Corporation was established, it fell heir to hundreds of financially weak banks; so, during the first 10 years, the activities of the Corporation were concentrated on paying off depositors of insolvent banks placed in liquidation and absorbing assets of other weak banks so that they could be merged with other banks or become the nucleus for new banks (called Deposit Insurance National banks).[14]

It is not generally understood that deposit insurance is provided by an independent agency that could become insolvent if its losses became excessive. Although the federal government has pledged to lend the Corporation $3 billion in case of need, its legal responsibilities under current law do not go beyond this commitment. Presumably, more funds would be appropriated if they were needed, because there is no question as to the popularity of deposit insurance in the United States.

During the 1934–67 period, the Corporation fully reimbursed 99.3 percent of the 1.6 million depositors in 470 insured banks either by deposit payoff or assumption of liabilities by a second insured bank. By the end of this period, 96.7 percent of all deposits in failed banks had been paid or made available to claimants. The losses of FDIC have amounted to $53.0 million and those of depositors to $26 million (including amounts not yet available because some assets of failed banks have not been liquidated).[15] When compared with total insured deposits, these losses have been surprisingly small.

[14] Deposit Insurance National banks are organized to give limited temporary banking services to communities when a bank fails. The temporary bank must either be transferred to private ownership or be liquidated within two years.

[15] In cases of liquidation, FDIC must be appointed as receiver for all national banks and for all state-insured banks where state legislatures have made it mandatory; and the Corporation may be appointed in other cases. As a receiver, FDIC is more efficient and less expensive than are others acting in similar capacities.

Following the failure of the First National Bank of Marlin, Texas, in 1964, Public Law 88–593, was signed by the President on September 12, 1964. This law requires the president or chief executive of an insured bank to report to its federal supervisory agency (1) any change in ownership of the bank's outstanding voting stock that alters control of the bank, (2) any of their loans secured by 25 percent or more of the stock of any insured bank, and (3) "any changes or replacement of its chief executive officer or any director occuring in the next 12-month period, including . . . a statement of the past and current business and professional affiliations of the new chief executive officer or director." In 1967, four banks were closed, and FDIC disbursed $7.8 million to protect depositors. As has been the case in recent years, the chief cause of failures was managerial weakness and illegal practices (including "fraudulent use of unissued stock certificates, fictitious loans and self-serving financial operations by leading officers of the banks").[16]

SUMMARY

Depositors, the bearers of assets, are sought after by their banks because they supply over 90 percent of the total assets used by commercial banks. Although the costs of handling demand deposits are high, they are the least expensive of the raw materials used by commercial banks. Under these circumstances, it is but natural for banks to compete among themselves for deposits. Neither the growth of savings in financial institutions other than commercial banks nor the expansion in investments can affect adversely the volume of deposits in the commercial-banking system. The key to deposit contraction and expansion is held by the Federal Reserve banks who may withhold or expand Federal Reserve credit that serves as member bank reserves.

Bank deposits are classified in various ways, but the one most important to banks and to the general public is according to availability as demand and time deposits. Although the use of demand deposits as money is purely incidental from the viewpoint of bankers, it is of major significance from the viewpoint of the public. It was the desire on the part of Congress to protect the circulating medium (deposit currency) of the country that justified the creation of the Federal Deposit Insurance Corporation, which has increased depositors' confidence in banks. Although this has meant "better money" for the

---

[16] *Annual Report of the Federal Deposit Insurance Corporation, 1967* (Washington, D.C.: 1968), p. 19.

nation, the supervisory agencies and FDIC alone cannot assure the nation of a safe deposit currency system, because this basic responsibility rests with banks and their depositors.

Some of the claims made for the Federal Deposit Insurance Corporation are reminiscent of those made for the Federal Reserve System, such as that "a member bank cannot fail" and that "the Federal Reserve eliminates all money panics." Thus we hear that FDIC has eliminated the danger of "runs" on banks, with no thought given to the fact that there are a great many depositors whose positions have not changed materially by deposit insurance of only $15,000. The interest of these depositors is to keep funds in strong banks and avoid weak ones; consequently, in the future, as in the past, the most disturbing presuspension withdrawals of bank deposits will be those of large depositors. Assuming most ideal circumstances, the need for deposit insurance could be eliminated by wise management of banks by bankers themselves. While supervisory officials may assist, the burden of preventing deposit insurance from attracting poor bankers and fostering laxity in bank management rests primarily on bankers.

QUESTIONS AND PROBLEMS

1. Identify: (*a*) common stock, (*b*) preferred stock, (*c*) surplus, (*d*) undivided profits, (*e*) reserves for losses, and (*f*) sales-leaseback financing.
2. Analyze: "The greater . . . use of borrowed capital [by banks] has been stimulated generally by tax advantages and the possibility, through greater leverage, of increased earnings." (*Annual Report of the Federal Deposit Insurance Corporation, 1965* [Washington, D.C., 1966], p. 106.)
3. Discuss: "The indebtedness of the Bank evidenced by the Notes . . . is to be subordinate and junior in right of payment to its obligations to its depositors, its obligations under banker's acceptances and letters of credit, [and] its obligations to any Federal Reserve Bank and . . . other creditors" except as to any long-term debt. The notes rank on a parity with the capital notes of 1990. (Chase Manhattan Bank, *4⅞% Convertible Capital Notes Due 1993* [New York, April 19, 1968], p. 13.)
4. Distinguish between (*a*) public and private deposits, (*b*) secured and unsecured deposits, (*c*) primary and derivative deposits, and (*d*) insured and uninsured deposits.
5. What relationship, if any, exists between increases in service charges and increases in the amount of money in circulation? Is it true that service charges "drive people out of banks"?
6. When insured banks are placed in receivership, how does the Federal

Deposit Insurance Corporation protect depositors (*a*) fully covered under the $15,000 maximum rule and (*b*) not fully covered under the maximum rule?

7. Explain: "The reserve for possible loan losses totaled $242 million at year end. . . . This reserve was the maximum permitted with accompanying tax benefits under Internal Revenue Service regulation." (Chase-Manhattan Bank N. A., *Annual Report 1967* [New York, 1968], p. 8.)

8. Discuss: "The growing role of commercial banks in the credit markets is due in large part to the aggressiveness of banks in competing for the liquid balances of the nonbanking sector of the economy." (Federal Reserve Bank of New York, *Monthly Review* [February, 1966], p. 29.)

9. Explain: "Common share book value was $22.68 as compared with $21.54 at the close of 1966. When reserves for possible loan losses are added to per share book values, the figures increase to $30.06 and $28.44." (Marine Midland Corporation, *1967 Annual Report* [Buffalo, New York, 1968], p. 7.)

10. Explain: "Time deposits at commercial banks increased by 16 percent in 1967, almost double the rise in the preceding year." (Federal Reserve Bank of New York, *Annual Report, 1967* [New York, 1968], p. 30.)

CHAPTER 12

Management of Bank Funds

BANK MANAGEMENT has the primary responsibility for the safety of banks. The nature of a bank's liabilities together with the thin layer of equity on which it operates makes the problem of management of a bank's funds a challenging one. Management must balance the use of funds in order to assure liquidity on one hand and safety on the other. The first may be achieved by keeping all assets in the form of cash, the second by investing all assets in long-term government bonds. However, vault cash does not generate earnings, and long-term bonds do not provide adequate liquidity. Hence balancing the two is a major problem of senior bank management.

The managerial problems of large and small banks differ widely in areas such as personnel, equipment, services offered, structural organization, and size of loans and investments. However, there are problems that are common to all commercial banks regardless of size; namely, the risks of banking and the use of bank resources to protect depositors while earning an income. Any bank, after making provisions for bank premises and equipment, will use part of its resources to meet legal reserve requirements and depositors' requests for currency (primary reserves), part for protective investments in liquid assets (secondary reserves), and the remainder for income-producing loans and investments.

RISKS OF BANKING

Will a Bank Have Customers? Banks are like other private business firms in that they seek to make a profit for their owners. Commercial banks try to attract creditors (depositors) in order to obtain their assets with or without payment of interest thereon. Some "time" deposits are of the money market type, devoid of any personal relationship between the banker and the depositor; but most time and demand depositors are interested in how efficiently their banks serve them. In unit-banking states, many small banks may operate under a monopolistic situation and give less than adequate banking services but this is not the usual situation.

Since the establishment of federal deposit insurance, many bank depositors (creditors) seem less concerned with their banks' ability to pay on demand and more concerned with their accuracy and efficiency in handling their checking accounts. Today, among banks in cities competition for creditors' assets (deposits) is intense, but this competition takes the form of offering better service rather than offering higher interest rates. Now, bankers more or less take for granted the confidence of their small depositors, but they must convince larger depositors that hold accounts in excess of $15,000 that their bank is able to meet its obligations on demand.[1]

The success of a bank will depend in part on its ability to attract good borrowers and then to serve them so well that they will not transfer their loan business to a second lender. Bank management must be prepared to assume some risk and, as a result, to take small losses. Hence, bankers must so arrange their assets that they can absorb losses without affecting their banks' solvency. In addition, they must maintain a liquid position in order to care for not only their depositors' demands for cash but also borrowers' requests for new loans.

Meaning of Liquidity.   Liquidity is a term used by bankers to indicate the ability of their banks to meet the demands of depositors and borrowers for cash. Since banks may reject loan applications, emphasis may be on their legal obligations to depositors, but good bankers do not ignore the needs of their loan customers. Hence, a bank will hold either cash or other assets that may be converted into cash without loss or delay.

In the bankers' test for liquidity, long-term government bonds would be excluded. They are traded in the government securities market and can be sold without delay; but when there is an increase in the rate of interest, bonds will be sold at a capital loss. In addition to having a ready market and being practically risk free, a liquid credit instrument must be short term and transferable without a capital loss.

Liquidity Theories.   The traditional theory of bank liquidity is that its earning assets must be in the form of short-term credit instruments, which have arisen out of financing the processing of goods and

---

[1] At the end of 1967 about 58.2 percent of total deposits of $448.1 billion in all insured banks were covered within the $15,000 limit, leaving 41.8 percent or $187.3 billion uninsured. See *Annual Report of the Federal Deposit Insurance Corporation, 1967* (Washington, D.C., 1968), p. 22.

their movement through the market from producers into the possession of the ultimate consumers. Bank loans made to finance any step in this movement will be repaid with cash obtained from the completion of the transaction. These so-called "self-liquidating" loans will be repaid if banks continue to lend and invest. If, for any reason, bankers do not extend credit but wait until the maturities of outstanding loans to provide them with cash, they will discover that their loan customers will be unable to sell their inventories, collect their receivables, and repay their bank loans. By refusing to lend and/or invest, bankers have reduced general purchasing power and total expenditures and have changed the quality of their assets from "liquid" to "congealed" or "frozen." Hence a self-liquidating loan loses its preferred quality if the banking system contracts credit.

Commercial banks make loans primarily to local business firms, and these loans tend to be among the least liquid of a bank's assets when there is an emergency need for money (due to drought, tornado, flood, or any other disaster). Fairly early in the history of banking banks placed some of their resources on deposit with correspondent banks and acquired earning assets that originated outside their communities, so that they could obtain financial help from outside sources during local financial crises.

Usually, banks keep correspondent bank balances with more than one bank. When they need funds they may withdraw them from one or more of their correspondents and the latter, in turn, may withdraw funds from their correspondents until the shock of deposit withdrawal from one bank is felt by many others. This situation may be avoided if the first bank in need of funds transfers its demand from its correspondents to its Federal Reserve bank which may create new currency and bank reserves without involving those of other banks (see Chapter 16). Demand deposits kept with other banks are non-earning assets; so banks that make use of the shiftability theory to protect against nonliquidity may prefer to invest in earning assets such as United States Treasury bills and other credit instruments traded in the money market.

At the present time, banks hold a large amount of loans that are repaid on the installment plan out of the debtors' normal income. If the debtors' anticipated income from such loans is estimated accurately, the bank will have a flow of funds that can be used to meet depositors' claims and/or other loan demands. During normal times, bank lending of this type would function in much the same way as lending based on the commercial-loan theory.

Danger of Bank Runs.   A banker takes in stride the day-to-day demands for cash due to unfavorable balances resulting from clearing of checks and ordinary currency withdrawals, but he is not prepared for "lobby" or "clearinghouse" runs due to a loss of confidence in the bank. When this occurs, depositors either come "on the run" to convert their deposits into currency at the bank or write checks on their accounts and deposit them in other banks. If the transfer of deposits takes place over a period of time, the bank loses funds because of "seepage" of cash rather than because of runs.

The clearinghouse type of run is most serious to a bank because it involves larger accounts. While it would take a teller a long time to count and pay out currency totaling $1 million, it would take the treasurer of a corporation less than one minute to write a check transferring this amount to a second bank. In addition to raising cash by selling money-market instruments, member banks may borrow from their Federal Reserve banks, and both member and nonmember banks may borrow from their correspondent banks. For as long as the Federal Reserve banks are capable of issuing Federal Reserve notes and creating reserves, banks that hold sound assets will be able to care for "lobby" or clearinghouse runs. Balances in Federal Reserve banks serve member banks not only as reserves but also as "payment funds" at distant places. Balances in correspondent banks are used similarly by nonmember banks and by member banks as additional "payment and reserve funds."

Risk of Insolvency.   In their lending and investing operations, banks must take the usual lenders' risk—the possibility of nonpayment of funds lent or invested. Like any business firm, a bank is insolvent when its liabilities exceed its assets; hence, nonrepayment of its loans and investments or a decline in their value may result in the insolvency of a bank. Even small losses may embarrass a bank because the capital margin on which it operates is smaller than that of any other major business enterprise. Furthermore, there is a legal requirement that a bank's capital must not be impaired. While corporations other than banks may operate while insolvent, a bank not only must be solvent but also must be able to show assets equal to liabilities plus capital stock. While a bank's liquidity is important, the danger of nonliquidity is minor compared to the danger of insolvency. Following examinations that reveal insolvency, a bank is usually closed (for example, the thousands of banks closed during the national bank holiday of March, 1933). A few bad loans, one unsound investment, or one dishonest employee may cause a bank to become insolvent.

In the course of their work, bank examiners find it necessary to "write down" or "write off" questionable assets; and, what may have been a solvent bank without impairment of its capital is reported to the state or national headquarters as one whose capital structure needs correction. This may be illustrated as follows:

CASE 1

SOLVENT BANK (CAPITAL UNIMPAIRED)
(In Millions of Dollars)

Before loss:

ASSETS		LIABILITIES AND CAPITAL	
Cash	16.1	Deposits	89.6
Loans and discounts	58.2	Other liabilities	0.4
Investments	23.1	Capital stock	6.1
Other assets	2.6	Other capital items	3.9
	100.0		100.0

CASE 2

SOLVENT BANK (CAPITAL IMPAIRED)

After loss:

ASSETS		LIABILITIES AND CAPITAL	
Cash	16.1	Deposits	89.6
Loans and discounts	50.2	Other liabilities	0.4
Investments	22.0	Capital stock	6.1
Other assets	2.6	Deficit	−5.2
	90.9		90.9

Although the directors of the bank assessed shareholders an amount equal to the par value of their stock, deterioration of assets continued. A special examination was made before the assessments were paid, with results as follows:

CASE 3

INSOLVENT BANK (AFTER EXAMINATION)

ASSETS		LIABILITIES AND CAPITAL	
Cash	14.1	Deposits	89.6
Loans and discounts	44.0	Other liabilities	0.4
Investments	22.0	Deficit	−7.3
Other assets	2.6		
	82.7		82.7

Although the noncapital items in Case 2 were sufficient to protect depositors against loss, they were not sufficient to protect shareholders. The "double liability" provision for assessing shareholders of suspended banks has been repealed by the federal government and most state governments; however, the directors were within their rights when they assessed shareholders of a solvent bank. In Case 3, when additional losses were written off, the amount of capital was insufficient to cover losses and the bank was closed with insufficient funds to pay off depositors in full.

Risk of Defalcation.   A common excuse given by bankers and their apologists for bank failures is an unfavorable environment that caused banks to hold too many "substandard assets." However, conditions have changed and now most bank failures are due in part to illegal practices and appropriation of funds by officers and employees. Each year there are other less widely publicized bank losses due to theft and embezzlement by staff members and employees of banks. Automation of bank operations has slowed down the growth in the number of bank employees but losses from crimes against banks by bank employees are increasing. In 1947, one writer listed 210 methods used to defraud banks and apparently many of them are still in use.[2]

Bankers are concerned about defalcations and embezzlements not only because of the sums involved but also because the rate at which thefts occur has been increasing. Large losses traced to officers and employees are the most damaging of all types of bank exposures, and the publicity given them does much to destroy the goodwill sought through millions of dollars worth of advertising. Many of the basic safeguards consist of fraud- and error-prevention devices built into a bank's organizational and operational procedures and into its accounting, internal auditing, and control systems.[3]

A bank may protect itself from loss resulting from defalcation by purchasing a bankers' blanket bond insurance policy; and, by paying a small fee, it may secure an added feature that will protect stockholders and depositors from extreme fidelity losses. The Insurance and Protective Committee of the American Bankers Association periodically recommends how much fidelity insurance banks should carry (it is relatively more for small banks than for large banks). Although banks are not obliged to follow the Committee's suggestions, supervisory officials usually insist that banks purchase at least the suggested minimum amount of coverage.

In July, 1968, Congress passed a law requiring the appropriate federal supervisory agency to establish the minimum safety standards

[2] L. A. Pratt, *Bank Frauds, Their Detection and Prevention* (New York: Ronald Press Co., 1947), pp. 221–32, appendix.

[3] Ben B. McNew and Charles L. Prather, *Fraud Control for Commercial Banks* (Homewood, Ill.: Richard D. Irwin, Inc., 1962), 186 pages.

that each bank and savings and loan association must install, maintain, and operate "to discourage robberies, burglaries, and larcenies and to assist in the identification and apprehension of persons who commit such acts." The installation and maintenance of proper safety devices and procedures should reduce the risk of loss and be accompanied by a lower premium rate for bond insurance. Therefore, Congress authorized the federal supervisory agencies to consult with such insurers "to determine the feasibility and desirability of premium rate differentials" based on the use of the proposed safety devices.[4] A bank or savings and loan association that violates the safety rules is subject to a civil penalty not to exceed $100 per day for each day of violation.

Banks could avoid many of their difficulties by improving bank administration, such as by clarifying duties of officers and employees and improving auditing systems. The last includes continuous checking (preauditing), staff cooperation, and frequent postaudits. However, no system can prevent an individual from being dishonest if he is so inclined. The best that can be done is to screen prospective bank personnel carefully, control the opportunities for theft, and shorten the time between commitment of an offense and exposure. When losses not covered by insurance occur they may be "written off" without causing insolvency when the bank's reserve, undivided profits, and surplus accounts are large enough to cover the loss.

Losses on loans and investments constitute another important cause of bank failure. Management may take certain precautions to prevent them such as limiting investment to federal government securities, diversifying loans and investments, setting up valuation reserves, and strengthening the bank's capital structure so as to provide a larger cushion between capital stock and deposit liabilities.

War and Emergency Risks. Since World War II, American banks have been subject to the potential risks inherent in warfare. The massive destruction due to nuclear weapons has added to the potential risk of loss due to use of conventional instruments of war. Experiences of European banks during World War II indicate the necessity for keeping duplicate records in safe places. If ever needed, such duplicates would permit banks to resume operations. Without them it would be impossible for banks to ascertain their obligations to depositors. In addition to the risks due to bombing, the rampages of nature present a potential risk—hurricanes, floods, and other so-called "Acts of God."

[4] See *Bank Protection Act of 1968* (Public Law 90–389), approved July 7, 1968.

In addition to placing duplicates of banks' records in safe places, such as bomb- and fireproof shelters, certain other changes could be made. For illustration, if bearer bonds were replaced with registered bonds and notes, it would provide a record of ownership at places of their origin. In addition, the federal government could sell bonds by giving buyers credit on its books (similar to giving Federal Reserve banks "gold credits" for gold certificates) and dispense with issuance of securities.

FIXED ASSETS AND CAPITAL STOCK

Unlike funds provided by depositors, those supplied by stockholders are not subject to withdrawal; therefore, they may be invested in buildings, equipment, machinery, and other fixed assets. In addition, funds obtained from the sale of capital stock may be used to acquire the corporate stock of institutions related to, or which form a part of, the operations of the bank. A bank may or must hold stock issued by (1) its Federal Reserve bank, (2) a corporation from which the bank leases its bank building, (3) "Edge" or "agreement" foreign banking corporations, (4) small business investment corporations, (5) the Federal National Mortgage Association, (6) bank service corporations, and (7) shares of any corporation established to perform at its place or places of business any function the bank is authorized to perform directly. In addition, stock that has come into a bank's possession as a result of default on loans may be held for a limited period of time.

1. As noted in Chapter 8, one of the requirements for membership in the Federal Reserve System is ownership of stock of the district Federal Reserve bank in an amount equal to 3 percent of the bank's unimpaired capital and surplus. (On admission, the bank actually subscribes to 6 percent, so the other 3 percent may be called by the Board of Governors of the Federal Reserve System at any time; however such a call appears unlikely.) This stock is not transferable and, if a member bank is liquidated or withdraws from membership, the stock held by the bank is redeemed at par and canceled. Additional stock must be purchased when a bank increases its capital and surplus, or canceled if it reduces its capital and surplus in order to maintain its holding at 3 percent of its capital and surplus.

2. Banks are usually permitted to own stock in a corporation organized to own the building in which the bank is located, but without the prior approval of the Comptroller of the Currency a national bank may not invest in the stock or obligations of such a

corporation or make loans thereto in amount in excess of the bank's capital stock. The creation of a subsidiary corporation to hold title to a bank's building limits the liability of the parent bank to its investment (which means that creditors may not seize the general assets of the bank in case of default on the obligations of the subsidiary corporation). Sometimes a bank will be permitted to buy stock in a corporation that operates a parking lot or garage near the bank so that the bank may give free parking privileges to its customers.

3. If a national bank has a capital and surplus of $1,000,000, it may receive permission from the Board of Governors of the Federal Reserve System to invest no more than 10 percent of its capital stock in a corporation or corporations formed under state, national, or foreign laws to engage in foreign banking or other financial transactions including agreement and Edge corporations (see Chapter 26).

4. National, member, and other banks (when authorized by state law) may invest in the stock of small business investment companies organized under the Small Business Investment Act of 1958 as amended, in an amount not to exceed 5 percent of their capital and surplus.[5]

5. Commercial banks that sell Federal Housing Administration (FHA) insured mortgages and Veterans Administration (VA) guaranteed mortgages to the Federal National Mortgage Association are required to buy stock in the Association in amounts equal to no more than 2 percent or less than 1 percent of the unpaid principal amount of the mortgages sold (see Chapter 22).

6. As noted in Chapter 9, banks are permitted to invest in "bank service corporations," formed to enable them "to make use of modern automated equipment." The service corporations are forbidden to perform activities other than rendering bank services "such as check and deposit sorting and posting computation and posting of interest and other credits and charges, preparation and mailing of checks, statements, notices and similar items, or any other clerical, bookkeeping, accounting, statistical, or similar functions performed for a bank."[6] The amount invested in the stock of a bank service company may not exceed 10 percent of the unimpaired capital and surplus of two or more banks.

7. In August, 1968, the Board of Governors of the Federal

---

[5] Public Law 90–104, October 11, 1967, limits investments of a bank in the stock of any one small business investment company to 50 percent of its stock having actual or potential voting rights.

[6] See Public Law 87–856, October 23, 1962; 12 United States Code, 1816–20.

Reserve System ruled that any member banks, insofar as federal law is concerned, may purchase stock for its own account in any corporation organized to perform at its place or places of business any function that the bank may perform directly. Unless this ruling is set aside by the courts or changed by Congress, it means that a bank may establish and hold stock in innumerable subsidiary corporations.[7] In addition, all banks may, for a "reasonable" time, hold corporate stock that has come into their possession as the result of default on loans. Without this privilege banks would be unable to protect themselves when stock has been pledged as collateral for bank loans that are in default.

Some state laws permit state-chartered banks to own special types of corporate stock (such as savings and loan association shares in Texas) or limited amounts of preferred stock of some companies.

PRIMARY RESERVES

Primary reserves are the assets that make up a bank's first line of defense against technical insolvency that would follow if it failed to meet its obligations on demand. The terms "primary reserves" and "secondary reserves" stress the functional nature of various assets and they are not found in published statements of condition of balance sheets of banks. However, asset items appearing in a traditional balance sheet may be rearranged to form a functional balance sheet (see Table 12–1).

In the overall management of banks' assets, the first objective is meet minimum percentage reserve requirements and the cash needs for "working balances." Because lending is an important bank function, banks must have cash available to finance the needs of their loan customers. Thus, the liquidity of a bank must be adequate to satisfy reserve requirements, loan demands, and cash withdrawals of depositors without management being forced to sell long-term investments at a possible loss.

Liquidity Needs. The peak liquidity needs of an individual bank depend on local factors that cause changes in deposits and loan demands and these can best be estimated by management from past experience. However, there are certain general changes that tend to affect the liquidity position of the banking system as a whole. (1) There are seasonal fluctuations in both deposits and loans, with both declining the first half of the year and increasing the second half. (2) Four times each year, during the Federal income tax periods, there is

[7] See *Federal Reserve Bulletin* (August, 1968), p. 682.

TABLE 12–1

BANK ASSETS—BALANCE SHEET

Traditional		Functional	
ASSETS:		*ASSETS:*	
Cash and due from banks...	$ 4,198,201	Primary reserves........	$ 4,198,201
U.S. Treasury bills........	977,000	Secondary reserves.......	$ 1,337,600
U.S. government bonds....	2,000,098	U.S. Treasury bills.....	(977,000)
Public Housing Authority		Money-market notes...	(360,600)
bonds................	350,945		
Federal Land Bank bonds...	50,109		
Municipal bonds..........	1,685,989	Customer Loans........	15,013,188
Loans and discounts.......	15,373,788	Investments for Income...	4,097,141
Federal Reserve bank stock.	36,000	U.S. government bonds.	(2,000,098)
Banking house............	369,399	Federal Land Bank	
Furniture and fixtures......	126,616	bonds.............	(50,109)
Other real estate..........	134,178	Municipal bonds.......	(1,695,989)
Other assets.............	124,451	Fixed assets............	790,644
Total assets.........$26,440,534		Banking house.........	(369,399)
		Furniture and fixtures...	(126,616)
		Other real estate.......	(134,178)
		Federal Reserve bank	
		stock..............	(36,000)
		Other assets..........	(124,451)
		Total assets........$26,440,534	

an increase in bank loans, a decrease in deposits owned by the general public, and an increase in deposits in the United States Treasury's "tax and loan" accounts. (3) The long-run or trend increase in deposits and loans is most rapid during relatively poor business years when the Federal Reserve System has an "easy" money policy and the least rapid when the "Fed" has a "tight" money policy. In other words, economic stagnation increases the relative need for liquidity, and growth decreases the need for it.

In anticipating the need for liquidity to care for deposit withdrawal, the following general principles are applicable: (1) abnormally large deposits of individuals are extremely volatile ("hot money") and need special liquidity protection because of the likelihood of sudden withdrawal. To a lesser extent, deposits of the federal, state, and local governments and those of trusts are in the same category. (2) Small savings deposits of individuals are the most stable of the various types of deposits and they need the least liquidity protection.

Customarily, a bank's needs for primary reserves or cash assets are met by its normal operations. In its daily operations, a bank receives new deposits of currency and cash items and collects maturing promissory notes and other earning assets. However, as bankers know, legal reserves are never adequate to meet a large withdrawal of funds because the reserve held against a deposit is a fractional one. For illustration, if a bank were to suffer a 10 percent loss in deposits, the results may be as follows:

Before loss of 10 percent of deposits (in millions of dollars):

ASSETS		LIABILITIES AND CAPITAL	
Legal reserve	10.3	Demand deposits	86.0
Balances in other banks	8.0	Other liabilities	4.1
Secondary reserves	17.2	Capital items	9.9
Loans and discounts	50.2		
Investments	12.2		
Other assets	2.1		
	100.0		100.0

After loss of 10 percent of deposits:

ASSETS		LIABILITIES AND CAPITAL	
Legal reserve	9.3	Demand deposits	77.4
Balances in other banks	4.0	Other liabilities	4.1
Secondary reserves	13.6	Capital items	9.9
Loans and discounts	50.2		
Investments	12.2		
Other assets	2.1		
	91.4		91.4

The withdrawal of $8.6 million in deposits is met by a reduction of $1 million in legal reserves, and the rest of the funds are drawn from balances in other banks ($4 million) and sale of secondary reserves ($3.6 million). As is evident, a bank's protection against nonliquidity is furnished primarily (90 percent) by assets other than those kept as legal reserves.

Cash and Due from Banks.   A bank's primary reserves include (1) coins and paper money, (2) cash items in process of collection, (3) deposits with correspondent banks, and (4) deposits with its Federal Reserve bank. These appear under the "cash and due from banks" item in a bank's statement of condition.

1. Only a small amount of cash is held to meet day-to-day requests for currency because the outflow of currency is usually matched by the inflow. Thus the amount of vault cash will average less than 1½ percent of total deposits, with the banks in Federal Reserve cities holding the smallest percentages and those located in areas least accessible to Federal Reserve banks and branches holding the largest percentages. Because the cost of shipping currency to and from Federal Reserve banks is borne by the latter, there is no need for commercial banks to assume the extra burden or risk of holding excess

currency. On the other hand, preparing currency for shipment involves time and labor and the urgency to return it no longer exists since vault cash as well as deposits in Federal Reserve banks count as legal reserves of member banks. The chief reason for returning currency is to lessen the danger of theft and defalcation and the cost of protecting it (such as larger vaults, added insurance, and more auditing).

2. Cash items in process of collection appear as primary reserves. They represent near-cash for which credit is given by the collecting bank on or before collection. Such items fluctuate from day to day and from season to season, being largest the first part of each month when checks are written to pay monthly bills and at the peak of the Christmas shopping season when they represent more than 10 percent of the assets of banks. Obviously, there is no feasible way to reduce the volume of cash items in process of collection in an emergency; hence, they are not a practical source of liquidity. After collection such items are canceled but similar items take their place. The total volume of these items outstanding at any one time emphasizes the need for reducing this cost of doing business by improving procedures and machinery for clearing and collecting checks and increasing the use of the transfer system of making payments as previously indicated in Chapter 9 (see Table 12–2).

Correspondent bank balances have been a feature of commercial banking in the United States throughout most of its history. As the country grew, the rising tide of commercial and industrial activity

TABLE 12–2

PRIMARY RESERVES OF INSURED COMMERCIAL BANKS
(Amounts in Thousands of Dollars)

Assets	Insured Commercial Banks				
	December 20, 1963	December 31, 1964	December 31, 1965	December 31, 1966	December 30, 1967
Total assets.............................	311,790,848	345,130,205	375,394,111	402,946,336	450,712,578
Cash, balances with other banks, and cash collection items—total...............	50,445,462	60,032,916	60,436,719	68,651,850	77,532,592
Currency and coin......................	4,053,057	4,551,889	4,865,803	5,457,281	5,953,155
Reserve with Federal Reserve Banks (member banks)...........................	17,149,613	17,580,743	17,992,395	19,068,820	20,275,051
Demand balances with banks in the United States (except private banks and American branches of foreign banks)..........	11,644,517	14,090,586	14,354,186	15,136,611	16,520,060
Other balances with banks in the United States.............................	367,817	558,335	484,817	257,066	544,658
Balances with banks in foreign countries...	298,992	300,841	255,865	250,872	280,249
Cash items in process of collection........	16,931,466	22,950,522	22,483,653	28,481,200	33,959,419

Source: *Annual Report of the Federal Deposit Insurance Corporation, 1967* (Washington, D.C.: 1968), p. 176

was paralleled by an expansion in the amount of money moving across the country, first as currency and bank drafts and later as checks and money transfers. Because the country lacked a nationwide branch-banking system, cooperation among banks for collection and payment purposes was imperative. Fairly early, New York, Philadelphia, and Boston became so-called "payment centers"; and, as population moved westward, banks in other cities shared this function and outlying banks kept deposits in metropolitan banks for various reasons (note the element of compulsion in the Suffolk Banking System).

3. Now, state laws permit nonmember banks to hold part of their reserves as balances with other banks, and member banks maintain accounts with other commercial banks as compensation for numerous services supplied by their correspondents. These services make it possible for small banks to give their customers a broader range of services and to improve the efficiency of their banking operations. They should not be discontinued; therefore, they are not considered to be an ordinary source of liquidity. While balances in correspondent banks should be large enough to compensate for services, they should not be unnecessarily large.

4. Member banks' legal reserve requirements vary according to the time classification of deposits, the geographic location of the bank, and the form in which the reserves are kept. The Federal Reserve Act provides for different reserve percentages not only for demand and time deposits but also for banks classified as reserve city banks and country banks.

The geographical classification of banks dates from the passage of the National Bank Act (1863), and it was incorporated in the Federal Reserve Act (1913). Originally, the differential in reserve requirements was based on the liquidity or convertibility concept of bank assets. The attitude was that correspondent banks, holding large interbank deposits, must be prepared to meet deposit withdrawals of other banks, particularly so when these deposits counted as part of the legal reserves of the other banks (national banks before 1913, member banks from 1913 to 1917, and nonmember banks today). The present-day attitude of bankers toward legal-reserve requirements is that reserves are a device for making monetary policy effective and that current high legal reserves are not necessary. Actually, some central banks have carried out their monetary policies without the use of any legal-reserve requirements (illustrated by the old Reichsbank and the first and second Bank of the United States, which obtained the same results by manipulating the currency supply).

During the early 1960's, Congress improved the required reserve situation by permitting member banks to count vault cash in computing their required reserves. The latter seemed desirable for two reasons: (1) currency, which is chiefly in the form of Federal Reserve notes, is basically the same as member-bank reserve accounts in Federal Reserve banks, and (2) normally, banks located a considerable distance from Federal Reserve banks must hold more vault cash than those closer to their source of new currency.

The increased mobility of bank funds and their sudden movement to and from banks having different reserve requirements increases the problem of reserve control. The central bank may expect to have a surplus of reserve money and then have a shortage occur because of a shift of money away from country banks to their city correspondent banks (where the required reserve percentage is higher).

Management of "Money" Position. The amount of primary reserves that any particular bank should keep depends on its legal-reserve requirements, its loan demands, and the pattern of its customers' deposit withdrawals. Bankers can compute their loan demands and legal-reserve requirements with a great deal of accuracy, and they may use their past experience with customers as a basis for estimating deposit withdrawals. Customarily, the one in charge of the bank's money position will keep cash reserves to a minimum and will keep all the remaining funds fully lent and/or invested.

A member bank's required reserves for its net demand deposits,[8] savings deposits, and other time deposits are computed daily upon the amount and types of deposits at the close of business each business day by multiplying it by the applicable reserve percentage. (For nonbusiness days, such as Saturday and Sunday and bank holidays, the deposit figures at the close of the last preceding banking day are used.) For illustration, if a country bank has net demand deposits of $200 million, the one in charge of the bank's cash position will compute the required reserve by multiplying the first $5 million by 12 percent and the remainder by $12\frac{1}{2}$ percent and then add the two to get the required reserves for net demand deposits. If the bank has $10 million in savings deposits, it will arrive at the required reserve by multiplying this figure by 3 percent. Finally, if the bank has $50 million in other time deposits, the required reserve is computed by multiplying the first $5 million by 3 percent and the remainder by 6 percent and then

[8] Net demand deposits equal total demand deposits minus cash items in process of collection and demand balances due from domestic banks.

adding the two. Hence, the required reserves will be the total of the reserves required for (1) net demand deposits, (2) total savings deposits, and (3) total time deposits.

Under the computation system prevailing before September, 1968, member banks were required not only to compute the reserve needs for the reserve period (weekly for reserve city banks and bimonthly for country banks) but also to maintain the necessary reserves for that period. Since banks did not know what their reserve needs would be until the morning of the last day of the reserve period (Wednesday for reserve city banks and the 15th and last of the month for country banks), there was usually a scramble for additional reserves before the close of business on the part of banks faced with a reserve deficiency.[9]

Under the present system for computing reserve requirements there is a week between the end of the base period for reporting deposits and other related information to the Federal Reserve banks and the maintenance of reserves for that period (stated in terms of daily average figures). For example, member banks were required to report their deposits for the week beginning Thursday, August 29, 1968, and begin the maintenance of required reserves against the week beginning September 12, 1968. Hence, member banks and the Federal Reserve banks had a week in which to compute required reserves and compare results before the related reserve period started. Furthermore, bankers knew before a reserve period started how much their required reserves would be.

Separation of the reserve computation or base period from the related reserve period may cause hardships for banks that have fluctuating deposits. For illustration, a bank that receives and holds a relatively large deposit for a few days must hold a reserve against it a week or two later during the reserve maintenance period even though it does not have the cash. Banks will be keeping required reserves but the amount will not be related to current deposits. Furthermore, country banks are now reporting the amount of their deposits and other related data the same day as reserve city banks, which makes the statistical information pertaining to banking more meaningful.

[9] Penalties are assessed monthly at a rate of 2 percent per annum above the Federal Reserve bank discount rate, applicable to 90-day commercial paper. However, this penalty may be waived if a review shows that the deficiency was due to a clerical error, illness, or a delay in mail or currency in transit. In addition, exceptions are made when (1) the deficiency does not exceed 2 percent, (2) there was no deficiency in the preceding period, and (3) the deficiency is made up in the next reserve computation period. This flexibility permits banks to manage their money positions more economically.

PROTECTIVE INVESTMENTS

Secondary Reserves. When a bank keeps its cash assets at a minimum, it must provide for necessary liquidity by investing in money-market instruments that may be converted into cash with practically no loss or delay. This liquidity account is called the bank's "secondary reserve account" or "protective investment account." It is the key part of a bank's functional balance sheet when liquidity needs are stressed.

Secondary reserves are income-producing assets held by banks to provide primary reserves whenever the latter become depleted. Two general situations may be involved—seasonal and emergency. Banks are subject to seasonal losses of primary reserves because of seasonal lending and withdrawal of deposits. Since both these movements tend to come during the last half of the year, secondary reserves must be arranged to meet these needs. In addition, banks must be in a position to meet emergency and other withdrawals of deposits, some of which may not be predictable. Finally, bank management must meet interest payments due time depositors and cash dividends on stock when declared by the board of directors.

Secondary reserves of the seasonal type may be in the form of Treasury bills or short-term government securities, certificates of deposit, bankers' acceptances, and/or commercial paper notes. Now, the abundance of short-term government obligations makes it possible for banks to hold all of the secondary reserves desired in any scientifically planned portfolio in this form.

Secondary reserves of the nonseasonal type may be selected from the promises to pay of the federal, state, and local governments and of public utility and similar types of corporations. All these assets must have two characteristics: prime quality and a maturity of less than four or five years. By careful spacing of the maturities of secondary reserves, a bank may have a continuous return of funds to meet unexpected demands for primary reserves. If a bank regards its secondary-reserve account as a revolving fund to be reinvested in similar securities as they mature, it will be able to maintain the liquidity of its portfolio and still show satisfactory earnings on these assets.

The policies as to a particular bank's secondary reserves will be influenced by factors such as the character of deposit liabilities, capital structure, the nature and soundness of other assets, and the business cycle. Fewer secondary reserves will be required when a bank's deposit have great stability, and this stability depends upon the type and size of the deposits and their location. Time deposits are more stable than demand deposits; small deposits are more stable than large ones; deposits in city banks are more stable than those in country banks and other time deposits are more volatile than savings deposits.

A bank's capital deposit or capital asset ratio is an important factor in planning its secondary-reserve program because a bank having a relatively small amount of equity, assume 1 to 20 ratio of capital to deposits, may have its capital impaired and made insolvent by a loss in assets equal to no more than 5 percent of its deposits. For a second bank having a relatively large amount of equity, assume a 1 to 10 ratio of capital to deposits, similar losses would be serious, but the danger of impairment of capital and of insolvency would be greatly reduced. A general rule is that the lower the percentage of capital accounts relative to deposits, the higher the secondary-reserve position of the bank must be.

The nature of a bank's loans and investments is also important in determining a bank's secondary-reserve position. A bank whose loan and investment account is dominated by real estate loans and long-term bonds must of necessity keep a higher secondary-reserve position than a second bank whose loan and investment portfolio is dominated by short-term commercial loans and highly marketable investments. The first bank must be in a position to avoid losses on security sales when security prices decline and be able to acquire new cash when real estate and other loans become frozen.

Because of the Federal Reserve System's policy of stabilizing the amount of money, preparing for cyclical change in a bank's total deposits is no longer a major problem, but management may give some thought to the subject. By using data covering deposits over a five-year period and plotting this data on a 12-month basis, bank management will have a picture not only of deposit growth but also of seasonal and unusual changes that could be used as a basis for establishing a plan of using the bank's funds. A trend line below the actual deposit figures will give management a clue as to the volume of (1) stable deposits (below the trend line) to be used as cash, customer loans, and investments for income, and (2) unstable deposits (above the line) to be invested in secondary reserves or liquidity assets. A similar chart for customer loans would help to indicate liquidity needs. The trend line for loans would appear above the actual data figures to show the customer loan ceiling. The difference between the two at any one point would suggest the need for liquidity.

LOANS AND INVESTMENTS

The lending and investing of a bank's funds should not be thought of as a water faucet that is shut off when no new cash is coming into the bank and turned on only when new deposits or cash from repaid loans and investments are available. What actually happens is that the faucets are always open, with the rate of flow regulated so as to keep stable the level of funds in the cash reservoir (see Chart 12–1). It must be emphasized, however, that in the use of bank assets bankers may use their discretion only within the limits provided by law and rules of supervisory officials, and then only insofar as local and general economic conditions permit. In some communities, banks

CHART 12–1

FLOW OF BANK FUNDS

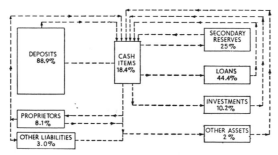

may be highly selective in making loans because of the loan demand; in other communities, banks must go outside their communities to find investment or loan outlets for their loanable funds.

Customer Loans. Of the five divisions of the functional balance sheet of a commercial bank, customer loans usually constitute the largest item. The lending policies of banks greatly affect the allocation of local resources among business firms, consumers, and others in their communities. Lending is the most profitable activity of a bank, but the costs entailed are greater than in investing. Lending is more profitable than investing not only because the rate of return is greater but also because borrowers keep deposit balances in their banks and use other services offered by them. The loan policies of any individual bank involve questions as to the percentage of assets to be placed in loans and discounts after its primary- and secondary-reserve requirements have been met. If the demand for loans from acceptable prospective borrowers is adequate, there is no reason for not lending the remaining available funds (see Chapter 13).

Investments. The final division of the functional balance sheet is "investments." If the capital, primary reserves, secondary reserves, and customer loans divisions do not absorb all of a bank's funds, the remaining funds should be invested for income. This category of assets includes long-term loans that are purchased in the capital market and have no direct local customer connection (such as the guaranteed or insured mortgage loans purchased from mortgage dealers). To illustrate the justification of classifying such loans as investments, assume that the president of a large bank calls the head of the bank's mortgage loan department and asks him to increase its holding of nonconventional mortgages by $25 million. The latter would contact a mortgage banker and ask him to supply that volume of Federal Housing Administration and/or Veterans' Administration insured or guaranteed mortgages before the end of the next business day. The procedure would be the same if the bank's president asked the head of the bond or investment department to purchase a similar amount of United States Treasury bonds.

Commercial banks prefer to invest in federal government bonds, including guaranteed bonds, because there is little or no credit risk, bank examiners permit their value to be carried on the books at cost or par (that is, normal value), they may be used to secure public deposits, and they are more marketable than most other types of bonds. However, state- and local-government securities are also popular investments because of their high ratings and their tax-exemption feature. The fact that they appear in serial form gives banks an opportunity to select the maturities that fit into their investment programs. When a bank or investor is in the 48 percent income tax bracket for marginal income, tax exemption on a 4 percent bond means that its interest equivalent on a taxable bond is over 7.69 percent:

$$4.00 \div [1 - 0.48] = 7.69+.$$

Other securities held by banks include securities of federal government agencies and corporations (not guaranteed), corporate obligations, and other long-term promises to pay (such as issues of foreign governments, the International Bank for Reconstruction and Development, schools, and other nonprofit institutions). Most corporations whose credit standings are high enough to warrant bank purchases of their securities raise their long-term capital by selling bonds with callable features. Because credit risks may be great, this group of securities presents a more difficult portfolio management problem than do other types of investments, and the volume of such bonds held by commercial banks is relatively small. (Today, the corporate-bond market is dominated by other institutional investors, chiefly life insurance companies.) The way in which the funds of commercial banks are administered is reflected by the distribution of their assets, on a percentage of total assets basis, for different years.

The distribution of banks' assets among the different nonfunctional classes over a period of years is affected by the regulations of supervisory agencies and general economic conditions as well as by

TABLE 12–3

PERCENTAGE DISTRIBUTION OF ASSETS OF INSURED COMMERCIAL BANKS

Asset Items	December 10, 1963	December 31, 1964	December 31, 1965	December 31, 1966	December 30, 1967
To total assets:					
Cash and balances with other banks	16.2%	17.4%	16.1%	17.0%	17.2%
U.S. government obligations, direct and guaranteed	20.1	18.2	15.8	13.9	13.8
Other securities	11.1	11.1	11.8	12.0	13.5
Loans and discounts	50.0	50.7	53.6	54.2	52.5
Other assets	2.6	2.6	2.7	2.9	2.9
Total capital accounts	8.1	8.0	8.0	7.9	7.5
To total assets other than cash and U.S. government obligations:					
Total capital accounts	12.8	12.4	11.7	11.4	10.9

Source: *Annual Report of the Federal Deposit Insurance Corporation, 1967* (Washington, D.C.: 1968), p. 177.

the policies of bank management. For illustration, the decline in primary reserves of banks (cash and due from banks) since 1950 has been due to (1) lowering of reserve requirements, (2) permitting banks to count their vault cash as required reserves, and (3) the relative decline in demand deposits and the increase in time and savings deposits.

In recent years, banks have reduced their proportional investments in federal government securities in order to have additional funds to care for the increased needs of their loan customers (see Table 12–4). However, they have increased their proportional investments in other securities, chiefly, municipal securities because of their tax-exempt status which has become increasingly important due to the rising costs of loanable funds stemming from rising interest payments on time and savings deposits.

TABLE 12–4

REPUBLIC NATIONAL BANK OF DALLAS, STATEMENT OF CONDITION,
DECEMBER 31, 1966 AND 1967

	1967	1966
Resources:		
Cash and due from banks.....................$	443,645,721.90	$ 408,189,343.91
U.S. government obligations, direct and fully		
guaranteed............................	121,811,970.66	106,767,304.82
Public Housing Authority obligations.........	19,625,166.85	21,743,462.52
State and municipal obligations...............	167,896,101.76	160,871,076.31
Other securities..........................	15,060,267.59	6,524,695.02
Federal funds sold........................	28,500,000.00	8,750,000.00
Loans and discounts.......................	880,051,635.12	843,789,576.55
Bank premises and equipment................	16,395,621.46	16,539,687.56
Customers' acceptance liability...............	24,813,052.78	28,467,984.80
Other assets.............................	14,891,816.79	15,637,176.42
Total.............................$	1,732,691,354.91	$1,617,280,307.91
Liabilities:		
Capital..................................$	51,234,972.00	$ 51,234,972.00
Surplus..................................	64,765,028.00	64,765,028.00
Undivided profits.........................	10,707,402.12	8,682,423.20
Total capital funds....................$	126,707,402.12	$ 124,682,423.20
Reserve for possible loan losses...............	20,848,762.62	19,314,849.43
Bond valuation reserve.....................	4,976,431.29	3,919,793.14
Federal funds purchased....................	69,855,000.00	73,040,000.00
Other funds borrowed......................	96,779,977.36	57,321,325.74
Acceptances outstanding....................	24,813,052.78	28,541,984.80
Other liabilities..........................	24,509,017.50	17,406,580.28
Demand deposits:		
Individuals and business...................	578,688,982.25	539,420,773.51
Banks.................................	256,979,057.73	252,222,998.90
U.S. government and other public funds......	46,995,421.10	52,128,199.61
Total demand deposits...................$	882,663,461.08	$ 843,771,972.02
Time deposits...........................	481,538,250.16	449,281,379.30
Total deposits.........................$	1,364,201,711.24	$1,293,053,351.32
Total.............................$	1,732,691,354.91	$1,617,280,307.91

Source: Republic National Bank of Dallas, *Annual Report, 1967* (Dallas, Texas, 1968). Courtesy, Dr. Keith Baker, senior vice president.

BANKS' FINANCIAL STATEMENTS

For years, there had been dissatisfaction with banks' reports to shareholders which almost uniformly consisted of a condensed statement of condition and no profit and loss or earnings statement. Complete reports are given to supervisory agencies, but they are considered confidential. Reports are published in the aggregate, but this is of little help to shareholders or potential investors in any particular bank.

Disclosure Requirements. Since 1964, any bank having assets of $1 million or more and a minimum of 750 shareholders is required to (1) file an original registration statement with its federal supervisory agency containing financial, legal, administrative, and historical information regarding its business; (2) keep the registration statement up to date by filing supplemental and amendatory documents as well as annual and periodic reports; and (3) submit proxy information prior to using it. The law (Public Law 88–467) of August 20, 1964 also requires certain shareholders, directors, and officers to file monthly reports listing changes in their holdings of stock of their banks. Small banks are exempt from these requirements because they have fewer stockholders, and public interest in them is limited. Although some bankers have opposed more complete reporting because of fear of unfavorable legislation, disturbance of public confidence, and misuse of information by competitors, speculators, and others, large banks are now issuing more complete information about their affairs.

TABLE 12–5

REPUBLIC NATIONAL BANK OF DALLAS, INCOME AND EXPENSES

	December 31, 1967	December 31, 1966
Operating Income:		
Interest and fees on loans	$53,128,958.85	$53,144,454.78
Interest and dividends on:		
U.S. government obligations	4,467,710.85	3,570,618.03
State and municipal bonds	6,699,163.91	5,789,845.72
Other securities	611,285.20	227,805.06
Service charges on deposit accounts	1,034,777.75	804,073.76
Trust fees	3,291,826.61	2,819,776.75
Other	3,295,356.84	2,873,518.32
Total	$72,529,080.01	$69,230,092.42
Operating expenses:		
Salaries	$ 9,989,441.35	$ 9,306,979.49
Employee benefits	2,404,164.27	2,074,140.84
Interest on deposits	19,505,939.83	21,582,311.89
Interest on other funds	7,948,089.02	7,351,451.45
Net occupancy—Bank premises	3,783,108.53	3,650,027.52
Equipment rentals, depreciation, maintenance	1,617,392.26	1,303,300.01
Other	7,827,821.60	7,299,259.07
Total	$53,075,956.86	$52,567,470.27
Operating Earnings Before Income Tax	$19,453,123.15	$16,662,622.15
Income taxes applicable to operating earnings	6,190,000.48	5,187,996.33
Net Operating Earnings	$13,263,122.67	$11,474,625.82
The Howard Corporation, *et al.*, payment	1,200,000.00	1,200.000.00
Net Income	$14,463,122.67	$12,674,625.82
	Per Share	
Net operating earnings	$ 1.55	$ 1.34
Net income	1.69	1.48

Source: Republic National Bank of Dallas, *Annual Report, 1967* (Dallas, Texas, 1968). Courtesy Dr. Keith Baker, senior vice president.

Bank Statement. A bank statement is a report setting forth the financial condition of a bank at a particular time. It is submitted to the proper federal and/or state banking authorities, to depositors, and to the general public (see Table 12–4). However, bank statements sent to stockholders and published in newspapers do not present all of the detailed information submitted to supervisory authorities as required under Public Law 88–467.

Sources and Uses of Income. Over a period of years a sound bank must earn enough to pay all its expenses, to cover losses, and to provide a reasonable return on its capital accounts. Otherwise, it is only a question of time until losses eliminate all capital account items that provide the cushion between claims of depositors and other creditors and the capital of the bank (see Table 12–5).

A commercial bank's chief source of income is interest derived from loans and investments in federal government and other securities. Other sources of income include service charges and fees on bank loans, service charges on deposit accounts, other service charges, commissions and fees, exchange and collection charges, earnings of trust departments, and other current operating earnings.

The sources of nonoperating income of banks include profits from the sale and/or redemption of securities and profits resulting from accounting changes—such as transfers from reserve accounts—and recoveries on loans and investments that previously had been "written down" or "charged off" as losses. (Conversely, there are nonoperating expenses of the same sort.) A statistical review of small

TABLE 12–6

PERCENTAGE DISTRIBUTION, SOURCES AND DISPOSITION OF INCOME, INSURED COMMERCIAL BANKS, 1959–67

	1959	1960	1961	1962	1963	1964	1965	1966	1967
Total income	100.0%	100.0%	100.0%	100.0%	100.0%	100.0%	100.0%	100.0%	100.0%
Sources:									
Loans	59.7	60.2	59.5	60.8	62.0	63.8	65.1	66.9	66.0
U.S. government obligations	17.3	15.9	16.2	16.5	15.6	14.6	12.9	11.7	11.7
Other securities	5.5	5.1	5.3	6.0	6.6	7.1	7.5	7.7	8.6
Service charges on deposits	5.3	5.2	5.4	5.4	5.2	5.1	4.9	4.6	4.4
Other current income	8.9	8.5	7.6	7.6	7.2	7.3	7.3	7.4	7.4
Recoveries, etc	3.3	5.1	6.0	3.7	3.4	2.1	2.3	1.7	1.9
Disposition:									
Salaries and wages	26.3	25.3	28.3	28.0	27.2	26.6	25.4	24.0	23.9
Interest on deposits	15.8	15.8	17.9	22.4	24.8	26.6	29.5	31.5	33.2
Other current expenses	20.6	20.3	17.0	17.2	17.5	17.8	17.7	17.7	17.5
Charge-offs, etc.	13.6	8.6	7.9	6.6	6.3	6.6	6.8	8.0	6.0
Income taxes	8.8	12.2	11.9	10.0	8.8	7.5	6.0	5.2	5.3
Dividends and interest on capital	7.8	7.4	7.6	7.4	7.1	7.1	7.0	6.6	6.4
Additions to capital accounts	7.1	10.4	9.4	8.4	8.3	7.8	7.6	7.0	7.7

Source: *Annual Report of the Federal Deposit Insurance Corporation, 1967* (Washington, D.C., 1968), p. 191.

but significant changes in the sources of a bank's income and its disposition for a number of selected years is most revealing when items are presented as percentages of total income (see Table 12–6).

SUMMARY

As substantiated by the history of business and bank failures, the risks involved in banking are greater than are those of other businesses. This greater risk is due to a number of factors, including the nature of banks' liabilities, the thin layer of equity capital on which banks operate, and the high standards of safety set by law and supervisory agencies. Since commercial banks create and destroy money, banking is regulated in greater detail than is any other business.

In managing their affairs, commercial bankers must protect their depositors while earning enough to meet the costs of operating their banks. As a result, banks hold more idle cash funds (primary reserves) than do all other business firms combined. In addition, a large percentage of their earning assets are invested in securities having a low rate of return (secondary reserves). Banks, like other lenders, must assume risks. Their greatest risks, as well as their most profitable sources of earnings, are represented by loans to local businessmen, consumers, and others. However, banks also assume risks in buying long-term government securities—the risk of capital loss if interest rates increase.

QUESTIONS AND PROBLEMS

1. Distinguish among the "traditional," "shiftability," and "anticipated-income" theories of the liquidity of banks' assets. During serious financial disturbances, upon what does the liquidity of banks' assets depend?
2. Explain "risks of banking." How do they differ from those assumed by other business enterprises? What is meant by a "run" on a bank? "Clearinghouse run"? Is there a need for "fidelity insurance"? Explain.
3. During depressions, which is more troublesome to banks, remaining liquid or remaining solvent? Distinguish between the two problems that are involved.
4. What is meant by the statement: "A bank's capital must not be impaired"?
5. Identify (*a*) primary reserve and the bank items that are included and (*b*) secondary reserves and the bank items that are included. What are the functions of primary and secondary reserves?
6. Are businessmen who borrow from commercial banks better-than-average credit risks? How does their credit standing compare with the credit standing of those who borrow in the money and capital markets?

7. What is meant by the "flow of bank funds"? Which of the different items in the chart showing the flow of bank funds (Chart 12–1) are relatively "active" and which are relatively "passive"? Explain.

8. Explain: "Banking, along with certain of the other regulated industries, represents the one major segment of the economy in which this basic principle of freedom of trade has not been fully applied. As a result, many banks have been barred from the complete realization of production economies, and many communities have been deprived of the broader range of banking services which could have been provided to them." (Administrator of National Banks, *Studies in Banking Competition and the Banking Structure*, [Office of the Comptroller of the Currency, U.S. Treasury Department (Washington, D.C., 1966), p. 419.])

9. Analyze: "It is probably a classic admonition to a bank director not to brag to your associates about the cashier of your bank who hasn't taken a vacation for 20 years. It may turn out that he has been too busy protecting defalcations to take any time off." (Guy W. Betts, "Legal Responsibilities of Bank Directors," in *Responsibilities of Bank Directors* [Gainesville, Florida: College of Business Administration, University of Florida and Division of General Extension, 1963], p. 11.)

10. Discuss: Growth and "early adoption to trends in the money market enabled us to increase net income . . . by 14% in 1966 . . . [and] 20% in 1965." This made it possible for us to . . . "declare a 10% stock dividend . . . increase regular quarterly cash dividends . . . increase capital funds [and] loan reserve . . . absorb costs of expanding management training . . . of expanding activities of service departments to include Trust, Correspondent Banking, etc., [and provide] additional fringe benefits and increase profit sharing" for employees. (The First National Bank of Montgomery, *Annual Report, 1966* [Montgomery, Alabama, 1967], p. 7.)

CHAPTER 13

Credit-Granting Services of Commercial Banks

THE CHIEF SOURCE of income for American commercial banks is derived from their lending operations. However, the components of banks' loan portfolios differ widely because of lack of uniformity in size, geographical locations, and policies. On the average, the largest percentage of bank loans are made to business firms.

CREDIT DEPARTMENT

Banks must assume risks when they lend or invest. If they are too exacting in their requirements, they may lose income by refusing to make certain loans or investments; if they are too careless in selecting borrowers or investments, they may suffer large losses. When a bank receives an application for a loan, pertinent information about the applicant is essential; if it is not available, the information must be gathered and analyzed by the bank's credit department. Every commercial bank has a credit department, a division or an officer who is responsible for assembling, recording, and analyzing credit information. While a small bank is not in a position to have many specialists on its staff, someone must be responsible for these activities.

Most of the work of a bank's credit department consists of gathering information about actual and potential borrowers in order to assist the lending officers and to answer inquiries from correspondent banks and others. In addition, the credit department may be asked to check on customers who are not borrowers, to analyze checking accounts, and to compute service charges. Analyzing a checking account is not as far out of line with the primary function of the credit department as it may seem, because such an analysis is an excellent source of credit information. Analyzing an individual's account reveals a great deal about the depositor's sources of income and his spending and saving habits, and analyzing a business account may be equally illuminating. When a borrower draws a check in excess of his deposit, the bank should investigate his credit position immediately.

Sources of credit information include borrowers themselves, credit-reporting agencies, and others. Current information about borrowers is essential in making bank loans and must come from the borrowers directly or indirectly. This necessitates a close relationship between the borrower and his bank, with the former (in case of a business loan) providing the bank with signed financial and operating statements, submitting to specific and general questioning (orally or by correspondence) as to accounting and other items, and permitting the bank to investigate the plant or business firm. The bank not only makes trade checks, but also checks with other banks having had experience with the borrower.

Investigation within the borrower's trade area usually reveals how he meets his obligations. Failure to take cash discounts usually is a danger signal that calls for immediate investigation. It may reflect ignorance or lack of cash—both unfavorable credit factors. When used to supplement other sources of information including borrowers themselves, reports of credit-reporting and mercantile agencies are of value in giving the history and background of the borrower. Mercantile agencies or attorneys may make special investigations for banks, and other information may be found in public records (transfer of property, judgments rendered, and suits pending) and in newspapers, magazines, circulars, government bulletins, and trade-association and other directories.

An analysis of the credit standing of a large business firm usually includes the construction of comparative balance sheets for five years or more and the computation of important credit ratios. Among the ratios used are current assets to current debts (current ratio), annual net profits to annual net sales, tangible net worth to annual new sales, net receivables to annual net credit sales (average collection period), current debt to tangible net worth, and total debt to tangible net worth. A separate folder or file is kept on each borrower, and subsequent information on each name is assembled, recorded, and analyzed methodically, so that the credit file on each active borrower is kept up to date. A credit file consists of a large number of small items that, to the expert, give a picture of the credit-worthiness of the borrower or potential borrower. The credit officer may or may not participate in the lending transactions, but, because someday he will be a loan officer, the average bank will want him to have the experience associated with sitting in on the loan committee's review of applications, interviews with borrowers, conferences with business firms' accountants, and preparations of specific recommendations.

The responsibility for making bank loans rests with the senior officers, the loan committee, and the board of directors. While the overall lending practices of banks are considered to be satisfactory, criticisms made of the loan administration of some banks are: failure to require definite repayment plans; emphasis on collateral instead of borrowers' ability to repay out of earnings; failure to use information available; use of inefficient, lenient, and tardy collection procedures; making too many loans on the basis of "good neighbor," "character," and outdated information; giving extensions and permitting pyramiding of loans by marginal loan customers; and making loans which do not contain adequate legal provisions to protect the bank in case of collection difficulties.

BANK LENDING

Those who borrow from commercial banks are confronted with variations in the attitude of bank management toward their loan applications. At times, bankers may welcome certain classes of loans that they are hesitant to approve at other times. For illustration, during the first six months of 1967 many banks showed special interest in consumer installment loans, mortgage loans on family dwellings and nonresidential properties, and term loans to business firms; but, during the rest of the year, the interest of banks in these three major types of loans declined, and they became more interested in making short-term loans to business firms.[1]

Negotiating Terms. In negotiating terms of a loan with an applicant, a banker is influenced by both his bank's policy and the general business outlook. In an individual case, the banker will be guided by the bank's experience with the borrower both as a creditor and a depositor and by the estimate of the credit department as to his credit worthiness. In deciding on terms, the lender must remember that banking is a competitive business and that the borrower may go elsewhere if terms are too restrictive. In addition, tradition and government regulation affect the terms found in any loan contract.

Generally, short-term loans are made on a discount basis and medium- and long-term loans are usually on a loan basis. Technically, a loan transaction is one where interest is paid at the end of the loan period along with repayment of principal, or periodically throughout

[1] *Federal Reserve Bulletin*, April, 1968, pp. 363 ff.

the period. In a discount transaction, interest is deducted from the principal amount at the time the credit is arranged; but it would be impractical to make long-term business loans on this basis (nevertheless the federal government does sell discount bonds).

Endorsement.   Many consumer loans carry the names of two or more parties, but promissory notes of business firms are usually single name, and if a second name appears it is usually that of someone closely connected with the firm. For illustration, the president who is also the chief stockholder of a small family corporation may add his name to that of the firm in order to secure better credit terms. Sometimes a second party may add his endorsement as an accommodation to the maker. Although popular at one time, "accommodation" loans proved unsatisfactory; and, as a substitute, borrowers began to pledge assets as security for loans. Later, improved accounting practices and credit analysis procedures permitted banks to lend on an unsecured basis. Now, accommodation endorsements are more or less limited to consumer lending (making the endorser a surety for the party at whose request he signed the credit instrument).

Security.   Many bank loans are made without requiring the borrower to pledge specific assets for the loan; however, most of them are secured. The range of collateral accepted by banks includes most types of tangible and intangible property (staple commodities, inventories, equipment, oil runs, real property, mortgages, stocks, bonds, life insurance policies, accounts receivable, royalties, assignments of claims, and others). The *Uniform Commercial Code* has made secured lending on personal property easier by substituting a "security interest" for the pledge, chattel mortgage, conditional-sales contract, warehouse receipt, assignment of accounts, factors' liens, and trust receipts.[2]

A security interest may be created by either of two methods (1) making an oral agreement and delivering possession to the creditor, or (2) executing a written agreement (called security agreement) "which contains a description of the collateral and in addition, when the security interest covers crops or oil, gas or minerals to be extracted or timber to be cut, a description of the land concerned."[3] In order to obtain an effective security interest in documents of title or instruments, a bank must acquire possession of them, which would eliminate the necessity of an additional written agreement.

[2] *Uniform Commercial Code*, Art. 9, "Secured Transactions; Sales of Accounts, Contract Rights, and Chattel Paper."
[3] *Ibid.*, Sec. 9–203 (1) (b).

A bank usually wants collateral for the protection given to loans, but sometimes security may be requested because it may be used as a means of disciplining the borrower. Threats of seizure and sale of mortgaged or assigned property may cause the debtor to make an extra effort to meet his obligation. In comparison, legal proceedings to collect for nonpayment of an unsecured note may be less effective. In other cases, a bank may request collateral so that it may lend an amount in excess of the limit fixed by the 10 percent rule, an amount fixed at 10 percent of a bank's capital and surplus (a bill in Congress would increase the percentage to 20 percent). Under the 10 percent rule, a bank having unimpaired capital and surplus of $1,000,000 could not legally lend more than $100,000 to one name on an unsecured basis. Often banks with capital and surplus of $1,000,000 have total assets of $20,000,000 or more; for them, individual loans of $200,000 to $500,000 would not be excessive.[4]

Although secured loans are more numerous in the business field, unsecured loans are more important in the aggregate because the average unsecured loan is larger than the average secured loan. This is due in part to the fact that large borrowers keep better financial records of their firms' business affairs than do small ones, and one maxim of bank lending is that all loans above a specified figure (determined by the board of directors) must be made against adequate financial statements or pledges of assets.

Maturity. The terms of a loan may stipulate that the principal is repayable on demand, at the end of a specified number or days, months, or years, or that principal and interest are to be repaid in installments over a specified period of time. A call or demand loan is one repayable at the option of either the lender or the borrower at any time during a business day. Such loans have been associated with financing the securities markets, but they may be used in business and other loan transactions. Many brokers and dealers in securities and commodities borrow on call, and many buyers of securities finance their purchases on margin with funds obtained with loan contracts containing no specific maturity. Although borrowers may prize the convenience of obtaining loans with no maturity dates, from the viewpoint of the lender, the weakness of this type of loan contract is

[4] There are 13 exceptions to the so-called "10 percent rule," including drafts, bills of exchange, commercial paper, credit instruments secured by goods and commodities in process of shipment, bankers' acceptances, obligations secured by government securities, and several others. For a discussion of these exemptions, see National Bank Division, American Bankers Association, *Manual of Laws Relating to Loans and Investments by National Banks*, Part 1, pp. 1–60.

that the borrower's credit position may not be reviewed periodically. Failure to have a firm understanding as to repayment of loans in whole or part has been one of the chief causes of bank losses on loans.

Banks most commonly make seasonal loans to department stores, fuel dealers, clothing manufacturers, and others having a peak demand for their goods. A typical conversion cycle of such a loan may be illustrated as follows: a department store obtains a loan to buy inventories to care for Christmas shopping demands; sales are made for cash and to charge account customers; accounts receivable are collected; and the bank loan is repaid. In the process, it is not imperative for the store to make a profit to repay the loan; the important thing is the cash flow, which includes depreciation charges. So, the seasonal loan is one that increases the current assets of a business and is repaid later in the same fiscal year by reducing these assets. Customarily, seasonal loans are made under lines of credit (see below).

Short-term loans may be made under "revolving credit" arrangements which contain certain clauses that indicate the maximum amount of loans that may be made at one time and the final maturity of the contract, and other clauses to protect the lender, such as restrictions on borrowing from other lenders, the minimum level of net current assets, sales of fixed assets, and others found in term loan agreements (see below). As long as the borrower meets the terms of the agreement, he may renew any short-term not up to the full amount of the credit arranged for during the credit period. For illustration, if a loan customer arranges for a $50,000 revolving credit agreement for three years, then borrows $10,000 for three months and repays the note at maturity, the $50,000 revolving credit will be reestablished for the remainder of the period. The borrower usually pays interest on the actual amount borrowed plus a small amount on the "standby credit."

A second type of nonseasonal working capital loan is informal in character, being evidenced by a short-term promissory note which is renewable at maturity or paid off with funds borrowed from a second bank. One advantage resulting from this alternative is that the borrower is forced to submit to credit analysis by a second bank. The disadvantages inherent in the practice of renewing notes led to the wider use of "term" loans.

A so-called term loan is defined as a loan to a business firm that is repayable after the lapse of a year or more. Such a loan usually runs from one to five years (but it may be longer), and it is usually repayable periodically during the life of the loan. Loans of this type are well adapted to financing the credit needs of a business whose ability to repay is related to its anticipated earning power. Most of the funds obtained from term loans are used to increase working capital, purchase equipment and machinery, and expand or purchase facilities.

Since the risks assumed by the lender increase as the length of time increases, a number of things that the creditor must do, or may not do, are embodied in the term-loan agreement. A clause in the agreement makes the loan due and payable if any one of these provisions is violated (the acceleration clause). By specifying these provisions in detail in the loan agreement, the bank is seeking to protect both the lender and the borrower.

In addition to provisions covering interest and repayment of principal, other provisions commonly found are those prohibiting the pledging or mortgaging of any of the assets of the company to anyone else, merging with another company, guaranteeing or assuming obligations of another company, paying excessive dividends and salaries, borrowing from other sources, discounting receivables, and using funds borrowed for purposes other than those prescribed in the agreement. The borrower usually agrees to maintain certain minimum current ratios, keep plant and equipment in good repair, include property hereinafter acquired in the covenant (the after-acquired property clause), and provide the lender with complete financial information. Similar provisions are found in the indenture agreements that are used in open-market financing when bonds are sold to investors. Term loans may be secured by any form of property, including real estate, transportation equipment (aircraft, trailers, tractors, and other motors), inventories, machinery, and other forms of durable producer goods.

Customarily term loans are repaid on the installment plan, with payments geared to depreciation allowances on the goods being financed. The use of term loans has made it possible for commercial banks to assume the major role in financing the medium-term credit needs of business firms such as those in retailing, manufacture, transportation, public utilities, extractive industries, and others.

LENDING POLICIES

When a bank's board of directors establishes a loan policy (a stated course of action), it means that some decisions have been made in advance for loan officers. For illustration, a bank's policy may be (1) to limit the maturity of term loans to five years without specific approval of the board of directors; (2) to require that 75 to 80 percent of the bank's real estate loans on urban property be of the unconventional type; and (3) to refrain from lending to a business firm of which a director of the bank is an officer or large stockholder without the prior approval of each member of the board of directors.

Background. The lending policies of a bank depend primarily on the economic environment of the area it serves, whether national, regional or local. For illustration, only banks located in farming areas maintain agricultural departments, employ farm specialists and have special policies covering loans to farmers and ranchers. The economic environment of its area will also affect a bank's lending policies when making loans to local business firms, real estate companies, and consumers. In general, what is good (or bad) for a community is also good (or bad) for banking within the community.

The major part of any bank's earning assets, including risk assets, is found in its loan portfolio. In formulating lending policies, bank management should balance the desire for maximum profits with the greater necessity of maintaining safety for depositors' funds. Officers may be directed to avoid high-risk loans such as those to business firms with poor charge-off records or without established earning records. They may be instructed to reject nonmarketable securities as collateral for loans and to refuse to grant loans to new firms on an unsecured basis when the proceeds of such a loan would represent most of a new firm's capital. The use of a bank's loan policy as a marketing device may result in attracting and keeping new accounts. For illustration, a bank may inform a business firm that it has opened an unsolicited line of credit under certain conditions for the firm.

Although a banker generally prefers to make only local loans, it may be necessary to make or participate in loans to firms outside the business area in order to employ all of the bank's resources and/or to diversify its assets. The term "diversification" refers to spreading loan risks over different companies, industries, names, geographical areas, and maturities (however, diversification is no substitute for quality, because a thousand times zero is still zero).

During the past 15 years, while the assets of banks have increased, the percentage of demand deposits has declined and the percentage of savings and other time deposits has increased. This, along with higher interest rates on the latter, helps to explain the decline in banks' holdings of short-term loans and the increase in their less liquid higher yielding loans such as mortgage, consumer, and farm loans. Apparently, commercial bankers regard most of the increase in time and savings deposits as long-term savings rather than as re-classified demand deposits.

Loan/Deposit Ratio. The loan/deposit ratio is an index of a bank's liquidity. The higher the ratio of loans to deposits, the less liquid is the bank; and, conversely the lower the ratio, the more liquid is the bank. If a bank's loans equal 65 percent of its deposits, only 35 percent of its deposits plus funds obtained from capital accounts would be available for primary and secondary reserves and fixed capital investments. Within recent years, the loan deposit ratio of New York City and other banks has been near or above 60 percent. Twenty years ago, such a high ratio could have brought bank examiners on the run; but a number of changes in the banking situation have made such high loan-deposit ratios more bearable.

The need for liquidity is now less than in the past because banks' liabilities have become progressively less volatile due to the increase in savings and other time deposits. Another factor has been the increase in the amount of funds that may be lent due to the reduction in minimum reserve requirements. (For illustration, a bank lending savings and other time deposits may use $95 of each $100 as compared to $88 of each $100 when using demand deposits, assuming minimum percentage reserve requirements are 5 and 12 percent.) Furthermore, a larger percentage of bank loans are made under arrangements calling for repayment over the life of the loan. Therefore a bank may improve its liquidity position by refraining from making new loans and collecting installment payments of principal and interest on consumer, business, and mortgage loans.

Today commercial bankers must live with business changes, referred to as the "business cycle," and the Federal Reserve authorities' policy to flatten cyclical changes without stifling economic growth. Commercial bankers must expect changes in interest rates, the price paid for the use of bank credit, which is a bank's most important product. Monetary measures affect the economy as a whole, including the ability of borrowers to repay their debts, the demand for new loans, and the market value of investments. In a matter of days, a banker's loan-management policies may shift from rationing existing loan customers, turning away new applicants for loans, increasing collateral requirements, and insisting on maintenance of compensatory balances to policies conditioned by an easy-money situation wherein loanable funds are abundant and new loan customers are courted. As a result, a bank's loan policies must be reviewed and revised regularly; otherwise a loan policy may be harmful rather than helpful. For illustration, for many years bankers opposed consumer lending, because they considered such loans to be "unproductive." Hence, instead of the commercial banks developing procedures for financing consumers, other financial institutions were created to finance them (see Chapter 24).

Interest-Rate Policy. In setting up its interest-rate policy a bank should provide for the same interest rate for all loans of the same type in order to avoid loss of goodwill among customers. In constructing a schedule of interest rates for the guidance of loan officers, management may set the prime or lowest rate for customers having the highest credit rating who borrow on an unsecured basis for no more than 90 days, a slightly higher rate for those borrowing on a secured basis for the same period, and so on, with the rate rising as the maturity of loans increases and/or credit worthiness decreases.

In creating an interest-rate structure, consideration must be given to the range of expenses involved in making and servicing loans, from a minimum for large short-term unsecured loans entailing the least risk to a maximum for small high-risk consumer loans. Aside from the risk element, the cost of administering loans per dollar of bank funds is much less for a large loan than for a small one, so interest rates tend to vary inversely with the size of loans. Large borrowers, who are able to shop around and/or borrow money in the money or capital market, obtain lower interest rates on bank loans for a number of reasons. (1) Most large firms are incorporated and many small ones are not, and bankers as well as other lenders prefer to make business loans to firms organized as corporations because of their greater permanence. (2) Large firms keep better financial records than the average small firm, which permits the credit worthiness of the former to be appraised more accurately. (3) Large firms tend to have higher credit ratings with credit agencies, such as Dun and Bradstreet, that gives them an advantage in negotiating terms of loans. (4) Finally, large firms have more stable earnings due to diversification, which is especially advantageous in intermediate- and long-term borrowing.

The interest rates charged as well as the types of loans made by banks are affected by legal restrictions. For illustration, when interest rates are high many banks shift from originating nonconventional real estate loans to conventional mortgage loans or to limiting their real estate loans to purchases in the secondary market (see Chapter 22). Although the interest-rate policy of many small banks consists of avoiding illegal rates, the interest-rate policy of most banks is flexible enough to reflect the level of interest rates in the money and capital markets. Even though business firm A and firm B may pay the same interest rates on their bank loans, the burden of credit may vary considerably because of differences in provisions as to compensatory balances, prepayment, collateral requirements, and restrictions on business operations and activities.

LENDING PRACTICES

When a bank makes loans to consumers and homeowners, it uses techniques that are similar to those used and developed by competing specialized institutions (see Chapters 22 and 24). To avoid repetition, the discussion in this section is limited to lending practices in regard to business loans of banks.

Lines of Credit. In order to avoid costly delays when faced with the need for funds, many large borrowers with adequate credit standing secure lines of credit from their banks at the beginning of their fiscal years. A line of credit is an informal understanding between the borrower and his bank as to the maximum amount of credit that the bank will provide at any time, but it is not a guarantee that the amount of credit arranged for will be available when requested. A bank usually honors a line of credit, but the amount may be reduced sharply or the line canceled if the financial position of the firm or industry deteriorates. Before a line of credit is granted, the credit position of the borrower is analyzed, and the amount of the line of credit is fixed by the bank's loan committee and/or the board of directors.

Usually, a line of credit is opened at the request of the borrower; but, in some cases, lines of credit are established by a bank for nonbank customers as a new-business promotion device. A bank in search of new business may notify a prospective business-firm customer that it is ready to open a line of credit of $250,000 for the firm on favorable terms. Such lending usually requires the firm to maintain a minimum compensatory balance computed as a percentage of the line of credit or as a specific percentage of actual loans. Banks' minimum-balance rules are usually enforced more rigidly during periods of "tight" money than during periods of "easy" money. Although some banks have no minimum-balance rules, they expect customers to keep satisfactory deposit balances. Usually minimum-balance rules are applicable only to seasonal borrowers who tend to pay the lowest interest rates on their bank loans.

When a borrower wishes to use the entire proceeds of a bank loan but is prevented from doing so because of the required compensating balance, he may arrange with a third party to deposit the amount needed to care for this balance. There are many varieties of this type of so-called "link financing" because of variations in terms and parties; but a common type may be illustrated as follows: A businessman arranges for a $5 million loan at his bank and is required to keep a compensating balance of 10 percent (this percentage varies with the business cycle and type of borrower). He arranges with his insurance company to make the $500,000 deposit which may be in the form of a negotiable certificate of deposit, in which case it may be sold in the money market. The borrower obtains the full $5 million loan, the bank its $500,000 balance, and the insurance company receives interest on its certificate of deposit (if not sold), plus any fee received from the businessman.

From the viewpoint of the lending bank, the compensatory balance is an indirect compensation for making credit available in case of need; from the viewpoint of the customer, it is an asset reserve that strengthens his financial position. Business firms customarily keep a part of their working capital (cash) in the form of deposits in banks, and the minimum-balance requirement merely encourages them to keep such funds in the banks wherein they have established lines of credit. If the minimum balance is in excess of the amount the borrower would normally need, it would have the same effect as a higher interest rate.

Term Loans. Some banks prefer to use the short-term loan contract despite the fact that the borrower may negotiate for a renewal when the note matures. On the other hand, many borrowers prefer to finance with loans having maturities of one year or longer, and the lending policies of most banks are flexible enough to meet such requests. A term loan, one having a maturity of one year or longer, is negotiated between the borrower and the lender, and about one half of these loans are secured. If the funds requested are usually large, two or more banks and sometimes life insurance companies may participate in the loan.

When a loan is syndicated, that is, divided among several lenders, one of the lenders administers the loan—handles repayments, collects interest, sees that clauses in the loan agreement are followed, and prorates receipts among the lenders. This syndicate manager is usually compensated by a service fee paid by the borrower. In the credit analysis work that precedes term lending, more emphasis is placed on investment factors pertinent to anticipated earnings than is the case in credit analysis preceding short-term lending, wherein liquidity or marketability of inventories and other assets is more important. Interest rates on term loans are usually higher than on short-term loans, and many term-loan contracts contain the escalator clause (interest rates increase as the Federal Reserve bank or some other specified interest rates increase). Term borrowing is least popular with business firms having relatively few fixed assets (such as sales-finance companies, commodity dealers, and firms in the wholesale trade) and most popular with firms having large amounts of fixed assets (such as public utility, transportation, and communication companies, and producers or manufacturers of petroleum, chemical, coal, and rubber products). Larger companies are the chief users of term credit, but the relative importance of term borrowing by small companies is increasing.

Some business firms' loan needs are so uncertain and irregular as to make line-of-credit arrangements impractical, and such firms usually apply for loans when the need arises. A business firm of this type whose financial affairs are sound, as shown by financial statements, usually keeps a deposit balance with its bank in about the same proportion to its loans as would a line-of-credit customer.

Sometimes businessmen arrange for loan commitments or revolving credit arrangements from their banks in order to avoid the uncertainties associated with lines of credit. Generally, loan commitments are binding legal agreements between the customers and their banks, the terms of which are so drawn as to meet varying needs and circumstances. (For example, during World War II loan commitments were made in anticipation of government war contracts.) Loan commitments involve the payment of fees based on the size of the anticipated loans and payment of interest if and when loans are made. A loan commitment may be obtained from a bank in anticipation of purchasing new equipment, remodeling buildings, improving facilities, or meeting many other anticipated needs. When the terms of a loan agreement permit a borrower, after repayment of prior loans, to make new ones, it is known as a revolving credit arrangement.

During years of expansion in industrial production and commerce, there is a corresponding increase in the demand for bank loans to finance the enlarged volume of inventories and receivables as well as increased expenses for wages and other items associated with expansion in output (including higher taxes, additional depreciation costs, and enlargement of facilities). The growth in inventories and receivables has encouraged banks to adopt or create procedures whereby these business assets may be used as security for working capital loans. When financing inventories, banks now use field warehousing and when financing receivables they use techniques developed by finance companies (see Chapter 24).

Lease Financing. A lease is a contract whereby one party (lessor) conveys real or personal property to another party (lessee) during the lease period. When a bank finances property needed by a business firm in its operations by a lease arrangement rather than a loan, the bank (lessor) assumes the responsibility for providing the needed property (such as a machine or equipment) to the lessee and for disposing of it at the end of the lease period. The bank usually pays the income tax on the rental payments but the business firm usually pays the property tax and maintenance charges. In financial leasing, rental payments are large enough in the aggregate to repay the amount paid for the property plus interest.

Currently, many business firms lease items such as office equipment, automobiles, road-building machinery, and factory equipment and machines. Banks assist in lease financing by (1) making loans to leasing companies, (2) purchasing lease contracts, and/or (3) purchasing property and leasing it to business firms. In the last case, the bank is the lessor and the user is the lessee who contracts to pay rent on the property and to keep it in good condition. The lease period is related to the useful life of the property which varies from 3 to 20 years (automobiles as compared with freight cars or diesel locomotives).

Although there are other types of leases in use, it is the "finance" type that is most frequently used by banks to finance fleets of automobiles, general office machinery, and equipment and other needs of factories and public utility companies. Lease financing by banks has expanded rapidly during the last 10 years, and there is every indication that the trend will continue as an ever-increasing number of businessmen seem to find its use to their advantage. Among the advantages claimed for lease arrangement as compared with loan contracts are (1) rental terms may be arranged to meet the needs of the lessee, (2) loss due to obsolescence of property is avoided, (3) sometimes there are tax savings, (4) appearance of debt items on balance sheets is avoided, and (5) costs are less.[5]

Three "P's" of Loan Administration. While the three "C's of credit" are important in credit analysis, the three "P's," which are purpose, protection, and payment, are important to loan administra-

---

[5] See Charles L. Prather, *Financing Business Firms* (3rd ed.; Homewood, Ill.: Richard D. Irwin, Inc., 1966), pp. 366–74.

tion. The oft-repeated story of the person who borrowed a sum of money from his bank, placed it in his safe deposit box, and repaid the bank promptly when the note was due in order to establish his credit, is a reflection on the loan officer of the bank. Such a transaction would be impossible in a well-administered bank because the loan officer's first question would be to determine the purpose for which the money borrowed is to be used. Some bank customers may resent this question, but it is simply good bank policy to ascertain the purpose for which a loan is made. Businessmen look to their banks for sound financial advice and it cannot be given without all the facts.

In addition to their responsibility to individuals and businessmen, banks also have a social responsibility in granting credit. When credit is tight, a bank must prorate the amount available wisely among its applicants for loans. Obviously, some loan requests must be rejected and others must be reduced in size. Some discrimination will be made between large and small borrowers, home buyers and securities speculators, old and new customers, and so on. However, banks must cooperate with the policies of the central banks and government monetary and fiscal authorities, even though it means loss of earnings.

When the purpose of a loan is sound, there may be no need for added protection. However, business and other affairs rarely develop as planned; therefore, bankers are justified in seeking extra protection in the form of a pledge of property and/or guarantee or endorsement of a second party (nonconventional mortgage loans have both pledge of property and the guarantee of a federal agency). Financial institutions pledge property when they borrow because of their small capital protection—the ratio of capital to liabilities—which is similar to that of commercial banks. Many loans contracts limit dividend payments, withdrawal of principal, uses of borrowed funds, and borrowing from other lenders, and they contain other provisions such as subordination clauses. Bankers are using money which belongs to other people, and they are responsible for protecting them.

Since World War II, bank loans secured by commodities (inventory financing) have increased, due in part to the development of field warehousing. For illustration, a dealer in construction materials may avoid the expense of moving his supplies to a bonded warehouse by creating one on his own premises, by enclosing a section of his property wherein the materials are stored.

Bank examiners criticize bankers' management of loans for failure to follow well-established collection procedures. For illustration, sometimes banks (1) make loans on the installment plan and then fail to follow up to see that the installment payments are paid when due,

(2) renew single-payment notes without reappraisal of debtors, and (3) allow demand notes (without provisions for repayment except on call) to "sleep" in their portfolios without review or partial payment. The collection problems of banks may be due to improper analysis of the loan application and failure to check on the purpose of the loan and the credit worthiness of the applicant. In other cases, good loans are permitted to go "sour" because of inadequate follow-up by the loan officer and credit department.

CLASSIFICATION OF BANK LOANS

Statistics of commercial banks' loans are presented according to the type of borrower, type of security, or the purpose for which funds are used. Statistics are based on "call" figures supplied by banks as of the date fixed by the supervisory agencies (see Table 13–1).

Commercial and Industrial Loans. Of the total loans made by commercial banks, a little over one third are classified as commercial and industrial, or business loans, which include seasonal loans, working-capital loans, term loans, and open-market paper. Such loans are usually much more important both relatively and absolutely for metropolitan banks than for middle-size and small banks. Approximately two thirds of the loans in this category are held by banks with deposits of $250 million or more. All secured and unsecured loans, except those secured by real estate, are included if the proceeds are used for commercial or industrial purposes.

Agricultural Loans. Loans made to farmers for short-term, intermediate-term, and long-term needs, other than for the purchase of real estate, are classified as agricultural loans. Financing farmers is a repeat type of business entailing "steady customers that need credit from crop to crop" which may be secured under a crop lien. To a large extent, lending to farmers is limited to banks located in agricultural areas; and such loans tend to increase in importance with the decrease in size of banks, with two thirds of them being held by banks with deposits of less than $10 million. Part of the agricultural paper held by larger banks consists of certificates of interest in pooled agricultural paper, which is sold by the Commodity Credit Corporation. The volume of such paper fluctuates widely because of variations in the amount of farm crops in storage under provisions of the federal government's farm price-support program. Although farm loans secured by real estate are excluded, those made to finance farmers' household and personal expenditures are included.

Agricultural loans made by commercial banks are obtained to

TABLE 13-1

LOANS OF INSURED BANKS FOR SELECTED YEARS
(In Millions of Dollars)

End of Year	Federal Funds*	Commercial and Industrial	Agricultural†	For Purchasing and Carrying Securities		To Financial Institutions		Real Estate	Others to Individuals	All Others†	Total except Federal Funds‡
				Brokers and Dealers	Others	Banks	Others				
1941	n.a.	$ 9,214	$1,450	$ 614	$ 662	$ 40	$ n.a.	$ 4,773	4,505		$ 21,259
1945	n.a.	9,461	1,314	3,164	3,606	49	n.a.	4,677	$ 2,361	$1,132	25,765
1947	n.a.	18,012	1,610	823	1,190	114	n.a.	9,266	5,654	914	37,583
1965	$2,064	70,887	8,191	5,088	3,172	2,093	13,148	49,026	45,290	5,155	198,045
1966	2,461	80,060	8,536	5,643	3,148	2,131	13,148	53,686	47,770	5,127	214,918
1967	3,919	87,870	9,250	6,017	3,719	1,848	12,394	58,209	51,395	5,606	231,583

* Includes securities purchased under resale agreements prior to June 30, 1967. Most of them were in loans to banks.
† Beginning with June 30, 1966, loans to farmers guaranteed by Commodity Credit Corporation were reclassified as "other securities" and Export-Import Bank portfolio fund participation was reclassified from loans to other securities. This increased "other securities" by almost $1 billion.
‡ Breakdown of loans, investments, and deposit classification not available prior to 1947.
Source: *Federal Reserve Bulletin*, July, 1968, p. A-24.

finance necessities such as seed, fertilizer, feed, fuel, and living expenses, as well as less pressing wants such as farm improvements, new machinery, modernization of dwellings, and new livestock. To handle this business more efficiently, many banks have set up agricultural departments and are using specialists to operate them.

Loans for Purchasing and Carrying Securities. Loans made by banks for the purpose of purchasing and carrying securities are divided into two classes, those to brokers and dealers in securities and those to others, including those made to individuals and others who are speculating in securities. Banks customarily make such loans, which usually carry a low interest rate, on a secured basis because brokers, dealers, and investment bankers, like merchants, use their inventories as security for loans. The volume of loans secured by stocks and bonds is small compared with the amount of trading in securities on the New York and other stock exchanges and in the over-the-counter market. The amount of loans in this category tends to fall when margin requirements are raised and to increase when they are lowered. These loans are of little or no importance to the smallest banks but increase in importance with the size of banks, with the majority of such loans being made by the large metropolitan banks located in financial centers.

Financial Institutions. Loans made by banks to financial institutions are divided into two classes, those made to domestic commercial banks and foreign banks and those made to others including sales finance, personal finance, insurance, and mortgage companies; factors; mutual savings banks; savings and loan institutions; federal lending agencies, and other business and personal credit agencies. Although these institutions are competitors of commercial banks for short-term, intermediate-term, and long-term loans, they are like other business firms in being deposit and loan customers of banks (see Chapters 22–24).

Real Estate Loans. The classification "real estate loans" includes all loans secured by real estate irrespective of purpose. The categories of mortgage loans include (1) loans on residential urban property insured or guaranteed by Federal Housing Administration or Veterans Administration (called nonconventional mortgage loans); (2) loans on residential urban property not insured or guaranteed by FHA or VA (called conventional loans), (3) loans secured by nonfarm nonresidential property, such as business, industrial, hotel, and office buildings and churches); and (4) loans on farm land and improvements thereon (see Chapter 23).

The category of real estate loans, which is second to business loans in importance, has shown steady growth since World War II. Their high yield makes them popular with banks but they are less liquid than other types of bank loans. In addition to being secured by real property, some loans on residential property are insured or guaranteed by the Federal Housing Administration and the Veterans Administration. The larger commercial banks have favored these nonconventional loans, while the conventional types of loans are more popular with banks having deposits of less than $50 million. The Federal National Mortgage Association, a federal government agency, buys nonconventional mortgages from commercial banks and others, thereby giving these loans a limited liquidity. Real estate loans are widely dispersed among banks of different sizes, but those secured by farm property are proportionately the largest among the banks having deposits of less than $10 million. Commercial banks help to finance real estate purchases by making loans not only to individual purchasers but also to mortgage companies, insurance companies, and other mortgage lenders who hold mortgages pending their resale or placement with permanent investors (see Chapters 22 and 23). Since all real estate loans are included in this classification, it is less revealing than the "purpose" or "borrower" classification.

Other Loans to Individuals. The classification "other loans to individuals" includes retail automobile installment paper, other retail installment paper, repair and modernization loans, and single-payment loans made to individuals for household, family, and other personal expenditures (see Chapter 24). These consumer loans are popular because of their high yield, but they are relatively most important to middle-size banks. In the aggregate they rank third in volume among the different categories of banks' loans. Among the most rapidly growing among service loans made by banks are those to pay hospital, doctors', and dentists' bills, to finance vacations and travel, and to meet home and automobile maintenance costs, and funeral expenses.

Travel has become big business, and credit plans developed by travel agencies, airlines, and transportation companies are financed in part with bank loans. Sometimes, banks make direct loans to finance their customers and others who have been recommended by resort and hotel operators and/or travel agents. A few banks finance the credit card business either directly or through subsidiary corporations.

Although banks have aided in financing college educations for their customers' children for many years, this loan business has expanded greatly in recent years. Originally, such loans were arranged so as to be repaid at the end of the school year; but the current practice is to arrange for funds for a four-year period providing for periodic disbursements of cash and no repayment until three or four months after the student's graduation. Such educational loans are usually made to students' parents or guardians but others are made by banks directly if they are guaranteed by a state, federal, or responsible private agency.

All Other Loans. The last category of commercial bank loans, "all other loans," is the catchall category including overdrafts and loans to charitable and educational institutions, churches, clubs, and all others not included in any of the other classes of loans.

REGULATIONS

The lending policies of commercial banks reflect the restrictions found in laws regarding bank loans. As already noted, the 10 percent rule means that a bank may not lend an amount in excess of 10 percent of its capital and surplus to one name unless the loan falls into one of 13 exceptions, most of which are not applicable to ordinary business loans. At first, this rule limited loans of national banks to 10 percent of the lending bank's capital, the reason being to permit more borrowers to participate in the limited amount of bank credit available. Now, the reason given most commonly for its existence in its present modified form is to protect banks by forcing them to diversify their loans. However, diversification is no substitute for sound loans and so this rule should either be eliminated or changed to permit banks to lend to one name an amount equal to a larger percentage of their capital stock and surplus.

Loans to Bank Officers. In the Banking Act of 1933, Congress eliminated one banking malpractice by prohibiting any executive officer of a member bank from being indebted to his own bank in an amount in excess of $2,500. Furthermore, if any officer became indebted to a second bank, he was obliged to make a complete report of his indebtedness to his own bank's board of directors. In 1967 and 1968, Congress and the Board of Governors of the Federal Reserve System liberalized these restrictions by excluding many junior officers and exempting executive officers' loans to finance (1) purchase of a home up to $30,000, (2) education of children up to $10,000 outstanding at any one time, and (3) other purposes not specified up to $5,000 outstanding at any one time. However, any extension of credit to an executive officer must (1) be reported promptly to his bank's board of directors, (2) be of a type a bank is authorized to make to borrowers other than bank officers, (3) carry terms similar to those of other borrowers with like credit standing, (4) be preceded by a complete detailed financial report, and (5) be made subject to call if the officer is ever indebted to other banks at any time in an amount greater than his own banks could have extended to him in that category of loans (for example, if a bank officer obtains a $40,000 real estate loan from a savings and loan association, his bank may or may not call his $30,000 home mortgage loan).

Loans to Examiners. The Criminal Code forbids a bank to make a loan to a bank examiner authorized to examine the bank, for obvious reasons. Nevertheless, the Board of Governors favors modification of this rule under proper safeguards so that an insured bank may make a mortgage loan to a bank examiner in an amount not in excess of $30,000. (The mere fact that an examiner is authorized to examine an insured bank does not mean that he will ever examine that particular bank.)

Real Estate Loans. Until the passage of the Federal Reserve Act in 1913, national banks were not permitted to make loans secured by real estate. At first, Congress made only limited provisions for real estate loans, but gradually restrictions were relaxed. Currently, a national bank's real estate loans may not exceed its unimpaired capital and surplus or 70 percent of its savings and other time deposits, whichever is greater. No restrictions are placed on the amount of individual nonconventional loans (those insured or guaranteed by a state or federal agency).

In the past, real estate financing was the primary responsibility of institutions other than commercial banks (see Chapter 22); but, in recent years, commercial banks have expanded lending in this field. Commercial banks do not segregate their savings bank business, and so their funds may be withdrawn from the mortgage market at any time and used for commercial and industrial lending.

Limitations on conventional real estate loans are stated in terms of the appraised value of the mortgaged property, and they vary according to the amortization plan and the terms of the loan. A conventional real estate loan must be a first lien (not a second mortgage) and may be up to (1) 80 percent of the appraised value of the property offered as security if the terms do not exceed 25 years and the principal is fully amortized during the life of the loan; (2) 66.66

percent of the appraised value, if 40 percent of the loan is amortized in 10 years; and (3) 50 percent of the appraised value, if the maturity of the loan does not exceed 5 years.

Banks may make nonconventional loans secured by real property on terms specified by the Federal Housing Administration (FHA) and/or Veterans Administration (VA). These loans are not subject to the limitations applicable to conventional loans because they are insured or guaranteed by a federal agency (see Chapter 23).

Other Real Estate Loans. National banks are permitted to make single-payment real estate loans secured by first liens on forest tracts for no more than 60 percent of the appraised fair market value of growing timber, land, and improvements offered as security for a term of no longer than 3 years, and to make amortized loans up to 15 years with no less than 6.66 percent of the principal retired each year. A bank's total forest tract loans may not exceed 50 percent of its capital stock plus 50 percent of its surplus.

Loans may be made to finance construction of commercial and industrial buildings for terms not exceeding 24 months if a responsible lender—such as an insurance company, savings and loan association, or mutual savings bank—contracts to advance the full amount of the bank's loan upon completion of the building. A national bank's total volume of construction loans may not exceed 100 percent of its unimpaired capital and surplus. Construction loans to finance residential or farm buildings with maturities of 24 months or less are classified as ordinary commercial loans; and, when such loans have maturities of 9 months or less, they may be rediscounted at a Federal Reserve bank.

Among the other loans secured by real property but not classified as real estate loans are industrial and commercial loans participated in on an immediate or deferred basis by Small Business Administration; and manufacturing and industrial loans wherein the bank depends on repayment out of the borrower's business operations. In such cases the mortgage is obtained merely as a precautionary measure against contingencies.

SUMMARY

Loans and investments are the chief sources of a bank's income. Bank loans are classified as secured and unsecured loans, short-term and long-term loans, call and time loans, single-payment and installment-payment loans, and over-the-counter and open-market loans. Banks are required to report their loans according to the purposes for which funds are used: commercial and industrial, agricultural, real estate, for carrying securities, other loans to individuals, and all others.

Lending practices of banks involving business loans include the use of lines of credit, loan commitments, loans made in participation with others, loans guaranteed in whole or part, and loans made by different departments of a bank to one name. A bank's lending is influenced by information made available by its credit department and is limited by governmental regulations. The primary purpose of each is to safeguard the quality of bank assets. A secondary purpose of government regulation stresses interest rates that may be charged by banks.

QUESTIONS AND PROBLEMS

1. What are the chief sources of credit information available to a commercial bank? How are they used?

2. Distinguish between (*a*) secured and unsecured loans, (*b*) short-term and long-term loans, (*c*) call and time loans, (*d*) single-payment and installment loans, (*e*) over-the-counter and open-market loans, and (*f*) reporting classes of loans.

3. Analyze: "Loan demand, if substantial and sustained, contributes to credit tightening. As corporations borrow, these proceeds usually are credited to their checking accounts which increases the banks' deposits. The banks, in turn, have to set aside greater reserves to offset these increased deposits." (*Wall Street Journal,* May 4, 1968, p. 3.)

4. Discuss: In term lending, the business firm's "ability to pay is related to its anticipated earning power."

5. Identify (*a*) lines of credit, (*b*) proportionate balances, (*c*) credit department of a bank, (*d*) guaranteed loans, (*e*) loan commitments, (*f*) participation loans, (*g*) 10 percent rule, (*h*) acceleration clause, (*i*) escalator clause, and (*j*) "link" financing.

6. Explain: "One of the principles of bank lending is to know the purpose for which a proposed loan is intended, and to consult with the applicant regarding it." (Bank Management Commission, American Bankers Association, "Statement of Principles of Commercial Banking," *Banking,* November, 1936, p. 37.)

7. Explain: "One of the outstanding features of lending to business by New York City banks is its strong orientation toward medium-term lending. Term lending has developed unevenly over the past three decades, . . . The latest rise in term lending—an increase of about 70 per cent from mid-1964 to late 1966—established term loans as the largest single category of assets in the portfolios of New York City banks." (Federal Reserve Bank of New York, *Monthly Review,* October, 1967, p. 199.)

8. Analyze: "Throughout the post-war years the over-all loan-deposit ratio of the banking system has moved upward . . . at slightly more than 63 per cent, this ratio currently is around the highest level since

the 1920's . . . . As a measure of liquidity, the loan ratio of banks has traditionally been employed to assess their ability to withstand deposit withdrawals and to judge their willingness to meet loan demand by reducing their cash assets and their investment in securities." (Federal Reserve Bank of New York, *Monthly Review*, March, 1966, p. 65.)

9. (*a*) How may change in regulations affect banks' lending to their own officers? (*b*) Is the proposed change in policy in regard to bank lending to bank examiners dangerous? Why?

10. Analyze: "The Comptroller of the Currency has in recent months issued certain rulings allowing national banks broader scope for their financial activities. National banks now are allowed to do direct leasing. There is . . . very little economic difference between direct leasing and making loans secured by equipment." (Paul M. Horvitz," Stimulating Bank Competition," *The Journal of Finance*, March, 1965, p. 11.)

CHAPTER 14

Investments of Commercial Banks

FOR MANY YEARS commercial bankers gave little attention to investments because their theory of sound banking was that bank funds
must be lent. Everywhere, bankers were seeking assets that would
give their banks the proper combination of profit and liquidity. Economic stagnation of the 1930's reduced the opportunities for lending
along traditional lines, and so bankers had to find other outlets for
their funds.

Somtimes bank policies are determined by events over which
bankers have little or no control, and an extreme example would be
the financing of World War II. The banks were used to finance the
war needs of the government and, when the war closed, banks' assets
consisted primarily of federal government securities. Not until recent
years has the loan deposit ratio of banks been near the level that was
considered normal before the 1930's. However, this ratio conceals the
fact that bank loans are now largely intermediate- and long-term
(mortgage loans, term loans to business, and others maturing in more
than one year).

The growth of "mixed banking" has led banks to invest in the
obligations of the federal, state, and local governments, federal
agencies, and nongovernment institutions in search of both liquidity
and income. Now, investments are considered to be a permanent part
of a commercial bank's assets, and increasing attention is being given
to their proper management.

INVESTMENT DEPARTMENT

The investment policy of a bank is formulated by its board of
directors, which designates an officer as head of the bank's investment
department and to administer its policies.

Meaning of Investment. Traditionally, the concept of investing
carries with it the idea of committing or laying out funds for the
purpose of obtaining income or profit over a period of time. Accordingly, a bank's investment will include its holdings of home mortgages, bonds, and other long-term credit instruments (in fact, all

earnings assets except short-term loans). Basically, the time distinction between savings or capital and bank credit has disappeared, and commercial banks' investments and loans must be distinguished on the basis of purpose and source of loanable funds.

Insofar as bankers are concerned, lending includes those transactions in which borrowers come to the bank for funds (customer-loan transactions), while investing generally includes those transactions in which bankers take the initiative (open-market transactions). In a loan transaction the bank is usually the only creditor, but in an investment transaction the bank is usually one of many creditors. Although open-market commercial-paper notes held by banks are reported as loans, this rule generally holds. Finally, banks' lending transactions are usually evidenced by promises or orders to pay, while investments may be evidenced by both credit instruments and stock certificates.

The Banking Act of 1935 permitted national banks to purchase for their own accounts "investment securities under such limitations and restrictions as the Comptroller of the Currency may prescribe." The law defined the term "investment securities" to mean "marketable obligations evidencing indebtedness of any person, copartnership, association, or corporation in the form of bonds, notes and/or debentures . . ." Unless permitted or provided by law or by ruling of the Board of Governors of the Federal Reserve System, national banks may not purchase for their "own account of any stock of any corporation."[1]

Subsequently, the Comptroller of the Currency defined "investment security" to mean any "marketable obligation" and specifically excluded those "which are predominantly speculative in nature."[2] Congress exempts from regulation public securities, including those issued by the federal government, general obligations of states and their political subdivisions, and those issued under authority of three international and numerous domestic governmental agencies.[3]

Investment Risks. When a bank invests, it assumes two kinds of risk: credit risk (the risk that the creditor will default on the

[1] United States, Revised Statutes, sec. 5136, para. 7.

[2] See Comptroller's Investment Securities Regulation of September 13, 1963.

[3] Generally the obligations of the following are exempt from the restriction placed by Congress on banks' investments in and underwriting of securities: federal land banks, banks for cooperatives, and federal intermediate credit banks (see Chapter 23); federal home loan banks, Federal Housing Administrator, Federal National Housing Association, Housing and Home Finance Administrator, and public dwelling, university, and dormitory revenue bonds (see Chapter 22); International Bank for Reconstruction and Development, Inter-American Development Bank, and Asian Development Bank (see Chapter 29); and Tennessee Valley Authority.

obligation) and money risk (the risk that interest rates will change, causing the market prices of investments to change). So the price of any bond is determined by the credit standing of the obligor and the level of money rates in the market. Where there is practically no question of the credit standing of the debtor, bond price fluctuations are dominated by money-market risks—the higher the money rates of interest, the lower will be the prices of bonds, and, conversely, the lower the interest rates, the higher will be the price of bonds. When a 20-year $100 government bond has a rate of 4.5 percent and the market rate is similar, the bond will be selling at par ($100), but, if the market rate increases to 4.6 percent, the market price will be $98.70. If the market rate were to decline to 4.4 percent, the market price of the bond would rise to $101.32. The influence of money-market rate changes on investment values is greater on long-term than on short-term obligations. (Where the credit risk is large, the market price of a bond will be influenced more by changes in economic conditions— credit position of the debtor, the industry, and the country—than by changes in interest rates.)

Banks may limit the "money risk" by restricting their investments to short-term obligations, on which the yield is usually lower than on longer maturities. Since the risks on long-term investments appear excessive and the yields on short-term obligations are sometimes inadequate, banks have been diversifying by "spacing maturities." In order to be able to provide depositors or new borrowers with funds, without disturbing their bond portfolios, banks may arrange the maturities of their loans and investments so that a percentage of these assets mature each year with allowances for renewals.

Investment Activities.   The investment activities of most banks consist of (1) supervising the investment portfolio, (2) managing the common trust fund and assisting the trust department in investing individual trust accounts, (3) providing advisory and brokerage services to corporate and individual customers of the bank's commercial department and to local governments, and (4) making investment services available to correspondent banks.

1. The most obvious activities of a bank's investment department are those pertaining to the selection and supervision of the bank's own investments in securities. These holdings must be supervised to assure their liquidity and legality (compliance with legal requirements) as well as their meeting the bank's objectives and policies.

In general, national banks may purchase for their own account any type of marketable fixed-income security that is not speculative in nature. They may buy bonds which are convertible into stock at the option of the holder, if the book value of the security is written down to a level that reflects only its value independent of its conversion feature. In selecting securities for purchase, bankers must act like prudent men and base their judgment on reliable evidence that the (1) obligor will be able to meet his interest and principal payments and (2) the security "may be sold with reasonable promptness" at a fair price. A bank may not purchase for its own account obligations of one issuer in an amount exceeding 10 percent of its unimpaired capital and surplus, except for public securities and others exempt from regulation (as noted above).

2. In smaller banks, those in charge of their banks' investment portfolios handle the problems connected with the common trust funds and the banks' trust accounts; but, in large banks, the investment work of the trust department may be entirely separated from the bank's investment department. Although the latter arrangement may result in needless duplication of personnel, investments of the trust department are not subject to the same rules as those applicable to the investments of a bank for its own account (see Chapter 25).

3. Many corporate as well as individual customers of commercial banks regard their bankers as the proper source of all kinds of advice, including recommendations as to investments. This is due in part to banks advertising slogans, "consult your banker before you invest" and "one-stop banking." Although bankers normally offer advice, they seldom make specific recommendations; however, some large banks offer advisory services and establish investment management divisions. City and other government officials expect their bankers to act as fiscal agents, depositories, and advisers on financial matters. Furthermore, local banks are not only local governments' chief source of short-term funds but also supporters of their long-term bond issues (sometimes being the successful bidder for an entire issue).

4. Finally, banks offer investment services and advice to their correspondent banks. Customarily, these services pertain to areas of investment in which the larger bank is interested, and so very little extra work is required. This service is often of great importance to smaller country banks whose officers, although well versed in bank lending, ordinarily have limited knowledge of investments. By taking advantage of its correspondent's day-to-day investment services, a country bank will be able to profit from new investment opportunities without neglecting its loan customers.

Brokerage Business.   A commercial bank may act as broker or agent for customers in buying and/or selling stocks and bonds. This is a common practice particularly in small communities without the services of brokerage firms. Upon execution of a transaction, the bank will charge a brokerage fee or commission which may be a flat amount or a percentage of the amount handled; but, according to the rules of the Comptroller of the Currency, it should not "substantially exceed" the cost of such services.

Acting as Dealers.   At the present time, the investment departments of a few large banks operate underwriting sections to handle new issues permitted under federal law. During the late 1920's, the bond departments and investment affiliates of banks retailed over one half of all new securities distributed, and they seemed to be destined to dominate the securities business in the same way that foreign-exchange departments of commercial banks had come to dominate the foreign-exchange markets. During the 1930–33 depression the dangers of the commercial–investment banking tie became apparent. The loss of prestige of investment bankers in general not only hurt the investment affiliate companies but also threatened the lives of the parent commercial banks. The failure of one large bank in 1931 was traced directly to its investment affiliate situation. The possibility of losses stemming from a conflict of interest in bank underwriting (sales of bonds to both banks and their customers) led Congress to the conclusion that commercial banking should be separated from the securities business. (See Chapter 21.)

The Banking Act of 1933 gave member banks one year in which to dispose of their investment affiliates.[4] Since restrictions were to be placed on the investment banking activities of commercial banks, their spokesmen asked Congress to place restrictions upon the deposit banking business of investment banking houses, which seemed reasonable enough. So the Banking Act of 1933 contains provisions that forced the investment houses either to qualify as commercial banks and give up underwriting of securities or to give up their deposit banking business.

When J. P. Morgan and Company gave up its investment banking business in order to keep its deposit banking business, the world's

---

[4] Section 20 of the Banking Act of June 16, 1933 (48 Stat. 188), as amended, reads in part as follows: "After one year from the date of the enactment of this Act, no member bank shall be affiliated in any manner . . . with any corporation, association, business, trust, or similar organization engaged principally in the issue, flotation, underwriting, public sale, or distribution at wholesale or retail or through syndicate participation of stocks, bonds, debentures, notes, or other securities. . . ."

foremost investment banker withdrew from the investment field (now Morgan Guaranty Trust Company). Morgan, Stanley and Company was formed in 1935 by some of the former partners of J. P. Morgan and Company and the grandson of J. P. Morgan. The firm was incorporated, and it assumed most of the investment business formerly held by the elder Morgan's firm. Upon the liquidation of the National City Company, an affiliate of the National City Bank of New York, the world's leading distributor disappeared.

The Banking Act of 1933 forced commercial banks to withdraw from the business of buying and selling securities ("one who as a merchant buys securities and sells them to customers with a view to the gains and profits that may be derived therefrom") but, from the beginning, exceptions were made to this restriction. Now, a member bank may underwrite and distribute the following types of securities: (1) obligations of the U.S. government, (2) general obligations of any state or any of its political subdivisions, (3) obligations issued by federal land banks and banks for cooperatives and others issued under provisions of the National Housing Act, as amended (see Chapter 22), (4) obligations of federal home loan banks (see Chapter 23), (5) obligations of the Tennessee Valley Authority, and (6) obligations of the Inter-American and Asian development banks and the International Bank for Reconstruction and Development (see Chapter 29).

Most of the underwriting by national banks pertains to general obligations of states, cities, and other local governments. A ruling by the Comptroller of the Currency that "general obligations" and "local governments" included issues of political authorities created to finance superhighways, toll bridges, electric light and power companies, and other public utilities was declared illegal by a Federal District Court. A bill in Congress that would do the same thing as the Comptroller's ruling faces heavy opposition by the Investment Bankers Association.[5] Nevertheless, Congress authorized national and state member banks to underwrite revenue bonds issued to finance public housing and university and dormitory projects (effective August 1, 1968).[6] Of the 6,000 member banks, 130 are underwriters and dealers, but most of the underwriting is done by a few large banks.

INVESTMENT POLICY

General Principles.   Most of the investment work of a commercial bank consists of investing the bank's own funds in securities.

---

[5] Paul M. Horvitz, "Stimulating Bank Competition," *Journal of Finance*, March, 1965, pp. 11–12.

[6] *Wall Street Journal*, August 4, 1968, p. 27.

The bank may make investments without any particular plan, or its investment officer may be required to follow a written investment policy. In order to keep such a policy from becoming outdated, the bank's board of directors, by resolution, may authorize a departure from it at any time, and usually the board of directors reviews the bank's investments in their entirety at least annually. Many banks make no distinction between securities that meet secondary reserve standards and others in the investment portfolio; but larger banks usually divide investment into two parts, one classified as a secondary-reserve investment account and the other as an investment account.

The size of a bank's investment account for income may depend on the amount of funds available after providing for primary and secondary reserves and "loans and discounts," or it may be a definite percentage of its resources remaining after primary and secondary reserve needs are met. Because most banks give the last priority in the use of bank funds to investment for income, the size of this account will fluctuate with a bank's loan demand, being large when loan demand is slack and small when approaching a position where the bank is "fully loaned up."

The first principle of portfolio management is to maximize earnings within the framework of rulings of regulatory agencies and the "prudent-man" theory. The legal requirements of bank investment practices are in general terms, and the standards set are not high. As in the case of bank loans, the 10 percent rule also applies to investments; that is, the securities held of one debtor may not exceed 10 percent of a bank's capital and surplus. However, obligations of the U.S. government, state and local governments, and federal agencies are exempt.

The second principle is to give consideration to marketability of securities as well as the income derived therefrom. Usually, the marketability of nonmonetary securities (those containing a risk element) will be impaired during a financial crisis. With the current practice of placing more bank funds in real estate loans, term loans, and other nonseasonal loans, bank management may find it wise to purchase only highly liquid securities. However, this conclusion may be modified if the bank's nonliquid assets are being financed with funds provided by owners and savings depositors. In brief, the investment policy of a bank must fit into the bank's overall position relative to (1) liquidity and soundness of other assets, (2) characteristics of the bank's loans, (3) composition of deposit liabilities, and (4) the bank's capital structure.

By using ratios, a bank may ascertain its liquidity position, the nature of its deposits, and the adequacy of its capital account. It may then compare its position with that of similar size state and national banks. However, any conclusion based on such comparisons may be misleading because the requirements of individual banks vary according to local conditions. On the other hand, if the bank's ratios are out of line it is management's responsibility to find out why.

Certain principles are applicable to all situations: Assuming other things are the same, a bank that is strongly capitalized can better afford to hold long-term securities than one which is thinly capitalized. A bank with a large loan/deposit ratio must be more conservative in its investment than one with a smaller loan/deposit ratio. A bank with a high ratio of total capital accounts to total assets minus cash and U.S. government obligations need not be as conservative in its investments as one having a smaller ratio.

Diversification. Most banks try to spread the risk by diversifying their investment portfolios by acquiring securities from different debtors located in different sections of the country, representing different industries, and/or having different maturities. For illustration, a bank's policy statement may specify that (1) the maximum maturity of any obligation is to be 15 years, (2) the investment account is to be divided almost equally among the different maturities, (3) the total amount of securities must be divided so that (*a*) no less than 50 percent of the account is in U.S. government direct and indirect obligations, and (*b*) no more than 15 percent is in state and municipal obligations, and (4) any remainder shall be invested in nonlocal corporate obligations of public utility, industrial, and/or commercial companies.

Usually a bank is financially committed to the needs of local business firms in its loan portfolio; in which case, a bank's board of directors would be justified in ruling against the purchase of local corporate securities in order to obtain overall geographical diversification. In a few cases, this policy is extended to exclude obligations of local governments (but this procedure is not general for political reasons).

Maturities of federal government obligations may be arranged so that the amount of longer term obligations will be greater at the top of the business cycle than at the bottom. On the other hand, bank management may plan maturity diversification by arranging for equal amounts to mature in successive years, the "ladder of maturities" approach. This method has the advantage of being simple and producing reliable results; but it may mean loss of profits because of failure to take profits and losses (see below).

Quality. When banks lend they assume risks, so the policy of most banks is to limit their investments to securities that are practically riskless. These include direct and indirect obligations of the national, state, and local governments, promises to pay of government agencies, and obligations of others that possess the quality of marketability and give evidence of the obligor's ability to meet all debt service obligations. In order to broaden the scope of banks' investments, the Comptroller of the Currency permits banks to invest an amount equal to 5 percent of their capital and surplus in securities of companies whose records are not satisfactory but have prospects for improved performance. When in doubt about a security's eligibility for a bank's investment and/or underwriting for its own account, bankers may request the Comptroller of Currency to rule on its eligibility.

No government agency can assume responsibility for the future value of securities because today's soundest assets may be tomorrow's risk assets. So, the final responsibility for wise investment rests with a bank's board of directors. Banks may continue to hold securities that no longer qualify if they had investment qualities at the time of acquisition. They may also hold substandard bonds and stocks acquired in good faith—through foreclosure on collateral, by way of compromise of a doubtful claim, and/or to avoid an apprehended loss on a debt previously contracted.

In 1938, the three federal and the various state supervisory agencies agreed to appraise "investment securities" in banks as follows: Group I contains only securities in which the chief characteristic is predominantly investment. It includes general market obligations in the four highest grades and "unrated securities" of equivalent value. The latter includes the direct and indirect obligations of the federal, state, and local governments and those of a number of specialized banks having federal charters, such as federal land banks, federal intermediate credit banks, banks for cooperatives, and federal home loan banks (no one would expect a sovereign state or the federal government to permit a regulatory agency to rule on its credit worthiness or that of an institution for which it is responsible). In bank examiners' reports, all securities in Group I are valued at cost, and no allowance is made for appreciation or depreciation, except that any premium paid above par must be amortized.

Group II contains securities whose chief characteristic is speculative, and it includes general market obligations rated below the four highest grades and others of similar value that are not rated. For examiners' reports, they are appraised at "normal" value, that is, the average market price of the security for 18 months immediately preceding the examination. In determining a bank's solvency, at least 50 percent of their net depreciation (if any) must be deducted from some capital account item.

The two remaining groups include securities in default and stocks and similar holdings. The value of Group III securities, those in default, must be written down to market price and the loss charged against the appropriate accounting reserve account. The value of Group IV securities, stocks and similar holdings, must be valued like those in Group III, and any depreciation must be charged off immediately.

Other Policy Matters. In its policy statement, a bank's board of directors may require investments to be valued on the basis of cost, with provisions for amortization of premiums and discounts over the life of the asset. As a result the total valuation of investments appearing in the bank's published statement of condition may be more or less than the amount found in the examiner's report. The policy statement may also provide that all profits resulting from the sale of securities be placed in a special reserve account against which losses on the sale of securities may be charged. A bank's policy may or may not prohibit "trading" or "switching" into or out of securities for tax reasons or to take advantage of price changes. An annual review of investment policy is usually provided for and investment officers are permitted to confer with the investment committee or board of directors at any time on policy matters. Normally, the correct procedure is for the bank's investment officer to go directly to the president in regard to changes in policy.

TRADING IN GOVERNMENT SECURITIES

A bank's investment program may be based on the assumption that interest rates will increase (bond price will fall) during periods of business expansion and that interest rates will decline (bond prices will rise) during periods of recession. Accordingly, banks will find it profitable to buy and sell government securities with changes in yield or interest rates; that is, they would shorten maturities when the yield curve is upsweeping during business recessions and lengthen maturities when the yield curve is flat or downsweeping (see Chart 14–1). This would result in banks taking capital gains during recessions and capital losses during booms. Normally, operating profits are lowest when there are capital gains and highest when there are capital losses. The effect would be to reduce banks' income subject to tax (banks are permitted to deduct net losses from operating income for tax purposes).

"*Tax Swapping.*" Banks take advantage of changes in interest rates during the business cycle to improve their earning positions after taxes by taking capital losses when their current operating earnings are greatest (when business is booming and loan demand is large). Since net capital losses may be charged against ordinary income, capital gains are avoided (bankers refer to certain years as "loss"

CHART 14-1

YIELD CURVE FOR U. S. GOVERNMENT SECURITIES

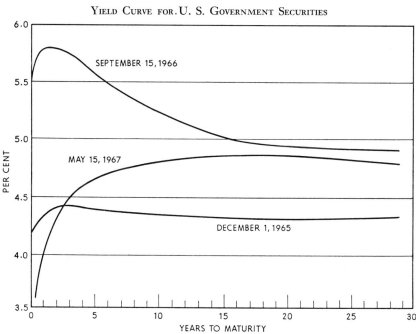

Source: *Savings and Loan News,* June, 1967, p. 11.

years). During booms, bankers sell government securities when their market prices are well below the average price and buy longer maturities in anticipation of higher prices which are sure to come during the next recession. When that time comes, banks will switch again to short-term securities in anticipation of higher yields and lower prices.

Although capital losses taken by commercial banks during boom years reduce their income taxes, this alone is no justification for taking losses. Bank management plans to be in a position to make capital gains sufficiently large during the next recession to offset all capital losses and to make a profit after taxes. Banks have the tax advantage of being able to charge losses against ordinary income and having their profits from sales taxed at the 25 percent rate for capital gains (if securities are held for six months).[7] One of the paradoxes that results from tax swapping is that banks, in the aggregate, show larger earnings during recession years (1954, 1957–58, 1960–62, and 1967) than during boom years (1955–56, 1959, and 1962–65).

Interest-Rate Movements. If interest-rate movements are studied during a business cycle, it will be noted that all interest rates fluctuate with general business, increasing when business activity increases and decreasing when business slumps; but the range of short-term interest rates is greater than for longer maturities. There are several reasons for this situation. First, banks hold their secondary reserves primarily in short-term government securities and, when their loan demand increases because of better business, they permit securities to mature without replacing them and sell others in the money market (pulling down their prices and pushing up yields). At the same time, the Federal Reserve System will be selling securities from its portfolio, also contributing to lowering prices (raising yields) for short-term government securities because most of the System's operations are still in short-term and intermediate-term government securities markets.

During depressions and periods of declining business activity, business loans are repaid and banks have funds to invest, preferably in short-term obligations. At the same time, the Federal Reserve System, as an antidepression policy, will buy government securities, chiefly short-term United States government issues. The purchases by commercial banks and the Federal Reserve System will increase prices (reduce yields) of government securities, particularly short-term rates.

Government Securities Prices. Yield curves may be constructed to show the influence of market conditions on different maturities of government obligations as of a particular time. This market, containing fairly homogeneous groups of credit-risk-free securities, is not only the largest but also the most sensitive to economic change. At one extreme are U.S. Treasury obligations maturing in a week or less and at the other is a $3.4 billion bond issue maturing on November 15, 1998.

---

[7] "Losses on nonoperating transactions dropped sharply during the year [1967], and this decline was a major factor in the increase in member bank net income. . . . Losses and charge-offs on securities dropped from the record level of $416 million in 1966 to $33 million in 1967." *Federal Reserve Bulletin*, May, 1968, p. 408.

As a result of its huge size and the variety of issues, the U.S. government securities market has credit instruments for every type of investor ranging from commercial banks and businessmen who seek a temporary outlet for funds to managers of pension funds, life insurance companies, and other long-term investors who seek yield plus safety. Commercial banks' demands for short-term obligations will be greatest during months of slack business when there is relatively little demand for loans, and smallest during months when business is expanding and loan demand is large. In fact, during the latter periods some banks not only refrain from buying Treasury bills but also liquidate those they have in order to care for their customers' loan demands.

As a result of purchases and sales by investors, prices of U.S. Treasury bills and, to a lesser extent, other federal government securities have a contracyclical movement. In other words, when business is expanding, the yield on government securities is increasing (prices are falling); and when business is contracting, the yield on government securities is decreasing (prices are rising). While all prices of government securities change with changes in business activity, prices of bills and other short-term obligations change most. For illustration, on September 15, 1966, the yield on government securities was high (prices were low) as compared with December 1, 1965, but the greatest change in yield was for those maturing in from 1 to 5 years (see Chart 14–1). However, the situation in the short-term and intermediate-term markets on September 15, 1966, was somewhat artificial because Congress does not permit the Treasury to issue bonds bearing a coupon rate in excess of $4\frac{1}{4}$ percent. Hence, the Treasury was forced to borrow in markets other than the bond market where the maximum maturity for new issues was 5 years (later changed to 7 years). If all buyers were equally interested in the different maturities, the yield on all maturities would be practically the same as on December 1, 1967 (see Chart 14–1).

Types of Yield Curves. The foregoing discussion suggests that there may be yield curves of different types, with many variations between periods of high and low interest rates. The three major types of yield curves are upsweeping, linear or flat, and downsweeping. An upsweeping yield curve is associated with low interest rates, relatively low or contracting business outlays, declines in business loans, increases in banks' sales of long-term investments and their replacement with shorter term obligations, capital gains, and low operating income of banks. On the other hand, a downsweeping or inverted yield curve is associated with high interest rates, an overextended or inflated business situation, a high loan-deposit ratio, sales of long-term bonds and their replacement with longer term bonds, capital losses, and high operating income of banks.

The manager of a commercial bank's investment portfolio may use his knowledge of yield curves to increase his bank's earnings by changing the maturity structure of investments. The basic assumption is that interest rates will increase when business is expanding and fall when business is contracting. Unless provisions are made for a permanent bond portfolio, the investment officer may find that funds will be available for investing only when interest rates are low. When interest rates are low, banks that keep part of their assets invested in government securities may find it advantageous to sell long-term bonds to take capital gains and to purchase shorter term government obligations. When interest rates are high, it may be advantageous to sell long-term obligations to take capital losses and to reinvest in longer term obligations.

When interest rates are low and earnings from operations are relatively low, taking a capital gain may be profitable because capital gains are taxed at 25 percent and operating income at 48 percent. Thereby a bank could reduce that part of its income subject to the 48 percent rate and increase that part subject to the 25 percent rate. When interest rates are high and earnings from operations are large, taking capital losses may be profitable because the federal tax law permits a bank to deduct capital losses before computing its corporate income tax.

COMMERCIAL BANK INVESTMENTS

During the 1960's, the relative importance of banks' investments declined as compared with the growth in total assets and in bank loans. However, while total investments declined, banks' holdings of obligations of states and local governments increased.

U.S. Government Obligations. Banks' investment are primarily in U.S. government securities, which are attractive to commercial banks because they possess the qualities of safety, there being no danger of any modern national government's defaulting on obligations payable in its own currency; relative stability in price, particularly as long as the Federal Reserve System guarantees an "orderly" market; preferred treatment by supervisory officials and bank examiners, who permit banks to carry them at cost (less reserves for amortization of premium if purchased above par) irrespective of market value; acceptability as collateral for loans at Federal Reserve banks; usability as security for public deposits; and availability in almost any desired maturity. In other words, U.S. government securities possess all the desired characteristics of bank investments except a high yield when compared with other marketable securities.

Marketable federal government securities include: (1) Treasury bills, (2) certificates of indebtedness, (3) Treasury notes, and (4) Treasury bonds. Usually obligations of government agencies and banks are considered to be in approximately the same investment category as those of the federal government.

1. United States Treasury bills bear no interest; instead, they are traded on a discount basis.[8] They are bought and sold in the money market and have moneylike qualities that make them ideal short-term investments for commercial banks. Each week, the Treasury offers 91-day and 182-day bills; each month, 6-month and one-year bills; and at irregular intervals, tax anticipation bills (TABs). The maturity dates of tax anticipation bills are usually set for one week after a tax date. They are accepted at par in payment of taxes, giving the investor the equivalent of a week's interest. This bonus feature is reflected in their original auction price when offered in the market.

2. Certificates of indebtedness are promises to pay customarily issued at par by the United States Treasury. Their maturity is usually one year or less, and the entire interest is payable at maturity. The interest rate on certificates of indebtedness reflects the market rate at the time of issuance, but later the certificates may sell above or below par because of money-market interest-rate fluctuations. At the present time, instead of using certificates of indebtedness, the Treasury is relying on one-year Treasury bills to smooth the maturity cycle and to reduce the number of securities falling due each quarter.

3. United States Treasury notes are promises to pay having maturities of from one to seven years at the time of issue. Customarily they are issued at par, with provisions to pay interest semiannually (except when the last interest-payment date is close to the maturity date, in which case it is payable at maturity, as in the case of certificates of indebtedness). The use of Treasury notes permits financing in the market wherein intermediate-term obligations are preferred.

4. United States Treasury bonds are similar to Treasury notes

[8] Treasury bills are traded on a yield basis and in order to find the discount price, the following formula is used $\$100 - a \times b/360$, where $a =$ Income per \$100 and $b =$ Number of days to maturity. Thus, a 90-day bill yielding 5 percent sells at a discount of \$1.25, the equivalent value or price is \$98.75 ($\$5 \times 90/360 = \$1.25$ and $\$100 - \$1.25 = \$98.75$).

except that their maturities are in excess of seven years at the time of issue. The longest term bond issued in recent years was one having a maturity of 40 years. Treasury bonds were issued with a first optional call date (usually five years before final maturity), which means that the Treasury may elect to pay off the issue at par on any interest-payment date thereafter until the final maturity date. The Treasury usually exercises the call privilege if it is advantageous to do so; therefore, the best rule to follow in estimating the maturity date is to use the first optional call date if the bond is selling at or above 100 (par) and the maturity date if it is selling below 100.

In recent years, Treasury bonds have been issued without the optional call date; instead, the Treasury has used the "advanced re-funding" technique which involves exchanging new securities for outstanding bonds that have several years to run before maturity. The privilege of exchanging bonds remains with owners; and, to induce them to do so, the yield and other features of the new issue must be made attractive. When most government bonds are selling at a discount, the "optional call date" is of no value to the Treasury and advanced refunding is an aid to debt management in that it gives greater flexibility in financing the government debt. (The Secretary of the Treasury may allow holders of the refunded securities to postpone, for tax purposes, any gain or loss on such transactions.)

Obligations of federal government agencies are also purchased by commercial banks. These obligations include those issued by the federal land banks, federal intermediate credit banks, banks for cooperatives, federal home loan banks, Federal National Mortgage Association, and the Export-Import Bank of Washington. Some of the securities issued by these agencies are the joint and several obligations of the group of central banks in their fields (such as the 12 federal land banks and the 12 home loan banks).

Obligations of States and Their Subdivisions.   Second in importance to U.S. government securities among the investments of commercial banks are obligations of states and their political subdivisions. Owing to the increase in banks' operating expenses and in the interest rate paid on time and savings deposits, there has been an increase in holdings of "municipals" (see Table 14–1). Commercial banks' investments in such issues reflect not only the increase in debt financing by these governments but also the attractiveness of their tax-exempt quality. For illustration, the taxable equivalent yield of a 3 percent municipal bond is 5.77+ percent when the applicable tax rate is 48 percent ($3.00 \div [100–48] = 5.77+$).

Securities issued by school and improvement districts, towns, cities, and counties are often purchased by local banks motivated by the desire to support their communities. This may mean that the local

TABLE 14–1

INVESTMENTS OF INSURED BANKS FOR SELECTED YEARS
(In Millions of Dollars)

| End of period | Total | U.S. Government Securities* | | | State and Local Gov- ernments | Other Securities† |
		Bills and Certificates	Notes	Bonds		
1941	$21,046	$ 988	$ 3,159	$16,899	$ 3,651	$ 3,333
1945	88,912	21,526	16,045	51,342	3,873	3,258
1947	67,941	9,676	5,918	52,347	5,129	3,621
1965	59,120	13,134	13,233	33,858	38,419	5,945
1966	55,788	12,080	13,439	31,536	40,761	7,545
1967	62,094	n.a.	n.a.	n.a.	49,737	11,204

* Beginning with December 31, 1965, figures for the components are shown at par rather than at book value. They do not add to the total of U.S. government securities, as this item is shown at book value figures.
† Beginning with June 30, 1966, direct guaranteed loans of Commodity Credit Corporation to farmers and Export-Import Bank portfolio fund participation certificates were reclassified as "other securities."
Source: *Federal Reserve Bulletin*, July, 1968, p. A–24.

bank is duplicating its loan portfolio in its investment account and thereby depriving itself of geographical diversification in its earning assets.

During the last 10 years, the after-tax yield on state and local issues has been 1 percent higher than on United States Treasury bonds. However, the current popularity of such issues is due not only to their higher after-tax yields but also to (1) the adequacy of supply due to the growth in debt; (2) the availability of short-term, intermediate- and long-term obligations because of the use of serial issues; and (3) the fact that they possess the qualities of safety and marketability (but to a lesser degree than federal government issues).[9] Although bankers realize that they lose some liquidity when they buy municipals, they contend that there is less need for liquidity than previously because of (1) the increase in their time and savings deposits which are more stable than demand deposits; (2) the additional liquidity provided by the money market; and (3) the stabilization of the overall economy by the Federal Reserve System and the United States Treasury.

[9] Small municipal bond issues such as those of school districts, towns, and townships appeal to local investors but tend to be more difficult to sell in the secondary market.

Other Bonds, Notes, and Debentures.   Other bonds, notes, and debentures are promises to pay other than those of the federal, state, and local governments. These obligations include those of railroads, public utility companies, business corporations, foreign governments, schools, churches, hospitals, and other nonprofit organizations. In general, all such obligations are eligible for bank investment, provided that they are marketable and have investment qualities. Since there is "credit" as well as "money-market" risk attached to these obligations, bankers must decide whether the difference in yield between them and "governments" is sufficiently large to justify the extra risks and the costs of their investment analysis. Some banks purchase small quantities of corporate bonds, but many banks purchase none. (Today, most of the bank financing of the corporate needs for credit of more than one year is with term loans.)

Corporate Stock.   The general rule is that a national bank may not purchase or acquire corporate stock except to protect itself against losses on debts owed the bank or as permitted by law in special cases.

SUMMARY

The concept of investing carries with it the idea of committing or laying out money for the purpose of obtaining an income or profit. Insofar as banks are concerned, investments represent earning assets, which must be safe to insure the bank's solvency and marketable to insure its liquidity. Federal government obligations represent a source of investments that is both safe and liquid, because among these issues may be found securities of any desired maturity, and their liquidity has been assured by liberalization of Federal Reserve policy.

The size of a bank's investment department will depend, for the most part, on the size of the bank, but in all cases the bank's board of directors is responsible for formulating and administering the bank's investment program. In addition to fulfilling the bank's needs for earning assets, which will depend on its size, the nature of its deposit liabilities, and its capital structure, a bank's investments must meet the standards set by regulatory agencies.

The classes of government obligations that may be owned by commercial banks include Treasury bills, certificates of indebtedness, Treasury notes, and Treasury bonds. Commercial banks may also invest in municipal securities—those issued by states and their political subdivisions—but, because of their tax exemption quality, such securities are in great demand, and this is reflected in their price. The category "other securities" is of minor importance as an outlet for commercial banks' funds.

QUESTIONS AND PROBLEMS

1. From a banker's viewpoint, what is the difference between a loan and an investment?

2. Why is the credit department of a commercial bank usually much larger than the investment department? What services does the investment department of a commercial bank give to individuals, to correspondent banks, and to the trust department?

3. What important factors must be considered in formulating a commercial bank's investment policy? What should be the objectives of any bank's investment program? What specific items should be included in the written investment program?

4. How are banks' investments allocated among U.S. government obligations, state and municipal securities, and other securities? Account for changes since 1947.

5. Explain why banks hold corporate stock. Illustrate.

6. Explain: "Over the five years ended December 1966, commercial banks liquidated $10.4 billion of United States Government securities, whereas in 1967 they increased their holdings of these securities by over $6 billion." (Federal Reserve Bank of New York, *Annual Report, 1967*, New York, 1968, pp. 27–28.)

7. Analyze: The Treasury's new six-year note was heavily oversubscribed, with the allotment ratio being a relatively small 18%. Subscriptions from the public totaled almost $24 billion—a huge amount by any standard. It even surpassed the subscriptions for the five year note offered in the February 1967 refunding, and in that instance the commercial banks' prime loan rate was dropped after the announcement but before the subscription books opened." (Aubrey G. Lanston Co., Inc., Offering Letter, August 12, 1968.

8. Analyze: The "expanded business demand for external funds was met only in part by new securities flotations: . . . [Corporate borrowing] from banks was probably due to the relatively favorable terms on which bank credit could be obtained. . . . [The prime rate] was maintained at 4½ per cent, only very slightly above offering rates on prime new corporate bond issues." (Federal Reserve Bank of New York, *Monthly Review*, October, 1967, p. 201.)

9. Explain how banks' investment portfolios were affected by the following changes: "Two decades ago, states and local governments owed about 57¢ out of every $10 of public debt outstanding. The Federal Government owed the remaining $9.43. Now the proportions are $2.40 and $7.60, respectively. At the same time, ownership of the debt has been changing; a much smaller proportion of the Federal debt and a larger proportion of state and local government now are

held by private investors." (Federal Reserve Bank of Philadelphia, *Business Review*, September, 1967, p. 10.)

10. Explain: When "an investor's income touches the 40% [tax] bracket a yield of 3% from a municipal bond is equivalent to 5% from a taxable investment . . . and at the 60% bracket 7½%." (Bache and Co., *Tax Free Income.*)

CHAPTER 15

The Role of Federal Reserve Banks

THE TWELVE Federal Reserve banks are the institutions that carry out the policies of the Board of Governors of the Federal Reserve System, the Federal Open Market Committee, and the banks' own boards of directors and officers (which are referred to in the aggregate as the Federal Reserve authorities). In addition, these banks, in the capacity of fiscal agents, perform many services for the federal government, foreign governments, central banks, and others. The growth in size of the Federal Reserve banks has more than kept pace with the growth in the gross national product. This is important during an era of big government, big business, big labor unions, and big commercial banks because of the key position that the Federal Reserve banks hold in the economy.

Although the Federal Reserve banks have been very profitable, the main reason for their existence is to support national policies (such as achieving full employment, stable prices, economic growth, and balance-of-payments equilibrium). The Federal Reserve banks have little to do with determining policy, which is the responsibility of the Board of Governors and the Federal Open Market Committee. This means that the staffs of the Federal Reserve banks are free to carry out policies and to fulfill other duties. It is relatively easy for the Board of Governors or a committee to decide what should be done, but the real burden falls on those who are to carry out or administer these decisions or policies. The fact that the presidents of the Federal Reserve banks are paid higher salaries than the members of the Board of Governors suggests that the work of the presidents is more difficult (see Table 15–1). While the Federal Reserve banks have become less important as decision-making institutions, they have become more important as service institutions.

A majority of the staff members of Federal Reserve banks carry on the routine work entailed in services rendered member banks, the United States Treasury, and the Board of Governors of the Federal Reserve System. Some of these activities have been discussed in pre-

TABLE 15–1

NUMBER AND SALARIES OF OFFICERS AND EMPLOYEES OF
FEDERAL RESERVE BANKS, DECEMBER 31, 1967

Federal Reserve Bank (including Branches)	President Annual Salary	Other Officers		Employees*		Total	
		Num-ber	Annual Salaries	Num-ber	Annual Salaries	Num-ber	Annual Salaries
Boston..............	$ 40,000	25	$ 453,000	1,191	$ 7,027,919	1,217	$ 7,520,919
New York...........	75,000	76	1,708,000	3,935	26,971,807	4,012	28,754,807
Philadelphia.........	45,000	31	578,500	855	5,056,102	887	5,679,602
Cleveland...........	45,000	31	566,000	1,296	7,826,559	1,328	8,437,559
Richmond...........	45,000	41	745,500	1,386	7,624,715	1,428	8,415,215
Atlanta.............	35,000	37	614,500	1,402	7,365,344	1,440	8,014,844
Chicago............	60,000	49	891,500	2,801	15,787,867	2,851	16,739,367
St. Louis...........	35,000	39	697,000	1,131	6,229,916	1,171	6,961,916
Minneapolis.........	42,500	26	441,000	627	3,656,707	654	4,140,207
Kansas City........	42,500	38	619,850	1,135	5,901,932	1,174	6,564,282
Dallas..............	45,000	37	579,600	950	4,995,257	988	5,619,857
San Francisco.......	46,000	43	693,800	1,802	10,261,742	18,996	11,001,542
Total.........	$556,000	473	$8,588,250	18,511	$108,705,867	18,996	$117,850,117

* Includes 1,012 part-time employees.

Source: *Fifty-Fourth Annual Report of the Board of Governors of the Federal Reserve System Covering Operations for the Year 1967* (Washington, D.C., 1968), p. 262.

ceding chapters and others are treated below or in later chapters. They include (1) collecting checks, drafts, and other transfers and handling transfers of federal funds, and maturing bills, coupons, and notes; (2) providing paper money and handling coins and paper money for banks; (3) supervising and examining state member banks; (4) creating reserves for member banks by lending or investing; and (5) acting as fiscal agents, depositories, and custodians for the federal government and government agencies.

STATEMENT OF CONDITION

After a study of the preceding chapters, there should be no difficulty in identifying each of the items in the Consolidated Statement of Condition of All Federal Reserve Banks (see Table 15–2) that appears each Friday in major newspapers and once a month in the *Federal Reserve Bulletin.* The financial and other information contained in this statement and others provides a statistical picture of the operation of the Federal Reserve banks. It shows the decline that has taken place in the Federal Reserve System's gold-certificate reserves, while the liabilities of the Federal Reserve banks have increased.

Earning assets are distributed among discounts and advances, bankers' acceptances, and U.S. government securities, with the last being the chief source of income (see Table 15–2). These assets plus the "float" (the difference between "cash items in process of collection" and "deferred availability cash items") indicate the amount of

TABLE 15–2

Consolidated Statement of Condition of All Federal Reserve Banks
(In Billions of Dollars)

Item	End of month 1968 June 30	1968 May 31	1967 June 30
Assets			
Gold certificate account..	$10,025	$10,026	$12,610
Cash..	432	424	322
Discounts and advances:			
Member bank borrowings................................	292	1,013	53
Other..	13	13	15
Acceptances:			
Bought outright...	59	56	91
Held under repurchase agreements.........................	75	...	45
Federal agency obligations—Held under repurchase agreements......	...	...	1
U.S. government securities:			
Bought outright:			
Bills...	18,380	16,976	14,006
Certificates—Special..................................	...	...	...
Other..	...	...	4,353
Notes...	27,746	27,626	21,737
Bonds...	6,104	6,023	6,538
Total bought outright..................................	$52,230	$50,625	$46,634
Held under repurchase agreements.........................	...	...	84
Total U.S. government securities............................	$52,230	$50,625	$46,718
Total loans and securities..................................	52,669	51,707	46,923
Cash items in process of collection...........................	7,612	6,944	6,532
Bank premises..	113	113	109
Other assets:			
Denominated in foreign currencies.........................	1,009	1,926	578
IMF gold deposited*.....................................	230	247	233
All other..	441	321	321
Total assets..	$72,531	$71,708	$67,628
Liabilities			
F.R. notes...	$41,862	$41,466	$39,396
Deposits:			
Member-bank reserves....................................	21,462	21,334	19,505
U.S. Treasurer—General account...........................	1,074	956	1,311
Foreign...	153	422	147
Other:			
IMF gold deposit*.....................................	230	247	233
All other..	277	258	278
Total deposits...	$23,196	$23,217	$21,474
Deferred availability cash items..............................	5,671	5,215	5,187
Other liabilities and accrued dividends.........................	366	378	250
Total liabilities...	$71,095	$70,276	$66,307
Capital accounts			
Capital paid in...	617	615	585
Surplus..	598	598	570
Other capital accounts......................................	221	219	166
Total liabilities and capital accounts.........................	$72,531	$71,708	$67,628
Contingent liability on acceptances purchased for foreign correspondents..	$ 112	$ 132	$ 379
U.S. government securities held in custody for foreign account.......	7,676	8,328	7,667

* Includes gold deposited by the International Monetary Fund to mitigate the impact on U.S. gold of foreign purchases for the purpose of making gold subscriptions to the IMF under quota increases.
Source: *Federal Reserve Bulletin*, July, 1968, p. A–12.

Federal Reserve credit in use. During the 1960's, the volume of earning assets expanded rapidly due to the increased demand for money and credit by the economy, together with the fact that Federal Reserve credit has replaced other forms of money.

Most of the liabilities of the Federal Reserve banks are in the form of Federal Reserve notes (over 41 billion) and member-bank reserve deposits (over $21 billion). Most of the notes are owned by the general public (except a small amount held as reserves by commercial banks). When member-banks' earning assets increase, there tends to be a corresponding increase in the amount of Federal Reserve notes and commercial-bank reserve money. Because of the nature of their business and laws requiring them to hold minimum percentage cash reserves, commercial banks are very sensitive about any change in their reserve or money positions, and hence want to be in a position to tap the only important source of new money when needed. It is true Congress has the power to create and regulate the value of money, but it has delegated its responsibility to the Federal Reserve System and has made it what is known as the "lender of the last resort." Without the right to create money, the Federal Reserve System would not be the powerful control agency that it is. The general public is not permitted to hold Federal Reserve bank deposits, and so any increase in Federal Reserve banks' liabilities must affect their holdings of money through the operations of commercial banks.

The mere existence of a source of additional money has a marked effect on the daily operations of commercial banks. When a bank knows it may "tap" an outside source of new money, it is less concerned about holding a large amount of cash for an emergency. Therefore, it keeps a larger percentage of its resources in the form of earning assets. The simplest way that member banks acquire additional money is to apply to their Federal Reserve banks for loans (technically called "advances"). A member bank may remove from its loan portfolio a credit instrument which it endorses and then sells to its Federal Reserve bank (known as a "discount"). The volume of discounts and advances, shown among the assets of the Federal Reserve banks, indicates that borrowing is not an important method used by banks to obtain new money (less than $0.5 billion) when compared to the System's investment in U.S. government securities (over $52 billion).

When the Federal Reserve System buys U.S. government securities, it increases not only the assets of the Federal Reserve banks but also their liabilities. When a purchase is made from a government securities dealer, the latter receives a Federal Reserve check, which he deposits in his commercial bank. His bank will deposit the check in its Federal Reserve bank for member-bank reserve credit. When needed this reserve deposit may be exchanged for Federal Reserve notes.

Hence the investment in U.S. government securities may result in an increase in either member-bank reserves or hand-to-hand money.

Among the other liabilities of the Federal Reserve banks are deposits of the United States Treasury, foreign central banks, international financial organizations, and various government agencies.[1] Deposits of the Treasury and other agencies are kept with Federal Reserve banks in order to obtain the Federal Reserve banks' depository, fiscal, agency, and custodianship services.

The "deferred availability cash items" has reference to the cash items in process of collection (which have been supplied by member banks). The offsetting item among the Federal Reserve banks' assets is "cash items in process of collection." The two items are not equal because of the Federal Reserve System's policy of giving member-bank reserve credit for some items before they are collected. This difference is the "float" that represents noninterest-bearing credit the Federal Reserve banks give banks that are using their clearing and collection services.

Fluctuations in "cash items in process of collection" are due to changes in the volume of business and financial transactions and the billing and paying customs of business firms and individuals. For illustration, most wholesalers "bill" credit customers at the end of the month (EOM) and allow a cash discount if payment is made within a 10-day period after the billing date. As a result, the volume of cash items in process of collection is largest during the second week of each month.

Relative to total assets, investment in banks' premises is small and subject to little change from year to year. The item "other assets" includes a new component, assets "denominated in foreign currencies," which refers to deposits and other assets of Federal Reserve banks in or held by foreign central banks. Other assets consists of miscellaneous items such as the International Monetary Fund's deposit of gold in the Federal Reserve Bank of New York.

LOANS AND DISCOUNTS

At this writing, the principles used by the Federal Reserve banks in judging applications for loans are set forth in Regulation A of the

---

[1] Wholly-owned and mixed government corporations and independent government corporations and agencies that may keep accounts with the Federal Reserve banks include, among others, the Federal Deposit Insurance Corporation, Commodity Credit Corporation, Post Office Department, Federal Crop Insurance Corporation, and Federal National Mortgage Association.

Board of Governors of the Federal Reserve System, which reads in part as follows:

Federal Reserve credit is generally extended on a short-term basis to a member bank in order to enable it to adjust its asset position when necessary because of developments such as a sudden withdrawal of deposits or seasonal requirements for credit beyond those which can reasonably be met by use of the bank's own resources. . . . Under ordinary conditions, the continuous use of Federal Reserve credit by a member bank over a considerable period of time is not regarded as appropriate.

In considering a request for credit accommodation, each Federal Reserve Bank gives due regard to the purpose of the credit and to its probable effects upon the maintenance of sound credit conditions, both as to the individual institution and the economy generally. It keeps informed of and takes into account the general character and amount of the loans and investments of the member banks. It considers whether the bank is borrowing principally for the purpose of obtaining a tax advantage or profiting from rate differentials and whether the bank is extending an undue amount of credit for the speculative carrying of or trading in securities, real estate, or commodities, or otherwise.[2]

New Proposals. The Federal Reserve Act states that the Federal Reserve banks *may* make loans (the technical term is "advances") and *may* rediscount eligible paper, which means that any application for a loan or rediscount may be granted or rejected. Following a reappraisal of the Federal Reserve System's discount mechanism, the following policies were recommended:[3]

1. Each soundly operated member bank be given a "basic borrowing privilege" that would permit it "to borrow limited amounts of funds from its Federal Reserve Bank upon request in as many as half of its weekly reserve periods."[4] The loans would be made without any administrative interference from Federal Reserve bank officials except to see that the borrowing bank is not in an unsatisfactory condition and not selling funds in the federal funds market. The Federal Reserve would not look kindly on borrowing from the Fed to lend to other banks in the money market (in effect, retailing Federal Reserve credit and profiting from the difference in rates and the fact that interest is a cost that may be subtracted before computing federal

---

[2] Board of Governors of the Federal Reserve System, Regulation A.

[3] See *Federal Reserve Bulletin*, August, 1968, pp. 545–51 and *Reappraisal of the Federal Reserve Discount Mechanism: Report of a System Committee* (Washington, D.C.: Board of Governors of the Federal Reserve System, 1968), 23 pages.

[4] The amount borrowed would be a percentage of the bank's capital stock and surplus and the percentage would decrease with an increase in the amount of the loans (such as 20–40 percent for the first million of a bank's capital and surplus, 10–20 percent of the next 9 million, and 10 percent of the remainder. Thus a bank with $20 million capital stock and surplus could borrow $3.2 million from the Fed under its "basic borrowing privilege").

corporate income taxes). If this proposal is accepted, member banks will be less reluctant to borrow from the Federal Reserve because they would not be subject to the normal interrogation preceding lending by Federal Reserve banks.

2. Second among the proposals pertaining to borrowing from Federal Reserve banks is one that would give member banks supplemental discount accommodations subject to administrative review by the Federal Reserve bank. The purpose would be to help a member bank meet temporary needs that are too large or needed for too long a period to be handled under the basic borrowing privilege. No loan would be made under this "other adjustment credit" procedure until the situation was carefully appraised.

3. Member banks located where there is an industry having a definite seasonal pattern, in or near a tourist center, or an agricultural area may need larger and longer seasonal loans than can be arranged under present procedures. So, the third suggested change in the discount policy is to permit Federal Reserve banks to make seasonal loans in such amounts and for such time as necessary to lessen the seasonal pressures on member banks. Prearrangements for seasonal loans may be made by management of the member bank and the discount officer of the Federal Reserve bank. The estimate of a seasonal need would be based on the bank's pattern of loans and discounts during past years. Borrowing under the "seasonal borrowing privilege" would not reduce the bank's ability to borrow under the "basic borrowing privilege."

4. The next proposal for a change in discount policy pertains to making emergency loans by Federal Reserve banks to member banks. At any time the position of a member bank may be jeopardized by a loss of assets or of deposits due to a natural or social disaster such as a flood, fire, drought, or racial violence. The credit needs of the bank may be for an indefinite period and under conditions that will call for "continuous and thoroughgoing surveillance" by the Fed. In cooperation with the bank, a workable program would be developed and followed until the difficulties of the bank and the community are reduced.

Adoption of the foregoing proposals by the Federal Reserve System and their addition to the policy statement (Regulation A) would stimulate borrowing by member banks. It might necessitate frequent changes in the rediscount rate and possibly the use of a multiple rediscount rate structure.

5. The last proposal for a change in the discount policy of the Federal Reserve System pertains to its power to make loans to individ-

uals, corporations, and institutions other than member banks. Loans to individuals and institutions other than banks has been an important part of the activities of certain foreign central banks, but in the United States lending of this type has been unusual and of minor importance.

During the 1931–34 period, the collapse of banking in many sections of the country made it difficult for borrowers to obtain funds for business purposes, and so the Federal Reserve Act was amended to permit the Federal Reserve banks to make loans to individuals, partnerships, and corporations, including nonmember banks. This permissive provision was strictly limited to "unusual and exigent circumstances," to paper that is eligible for discount by member banks, and to situations wherein the applicant "is unable to secure adequate accommodations from other banking institutions."[5] A year later the Federal Reserve banks were permitted to make loans to nonmember banks when the promissory note offered was secured by direct obligations of the U.S. government.[6]

Under the new proposal, when lending to nonmember institutions the Federal Reserve banks would act in cooperation with the appropriate supervisory agency such as the Federal Home Loan Bank Board when lending to a federal savings and loan association. The "advance" would be extended through a "conduit arrangement" with a member bank under emergency conditions and at a higher interest rate than charged on loans to member banks.

The loans would be subject to the same "continuous and thoroughgoing surveillance" as applicable to emergency loans to member banks. The borrower would be required to use all other "practicable" sources of credit before making a request for a loan from a Federal Reserve bank. In lending to other than member banks, the Federal Reserve banks are merely performing their economic function as the "lender of last resort."[7]

CURRENT DISCOUNT PROCEDURES

A member bank may borrow under more than one section of the Federal Reserve Act. Its choice will depend on how long the funds

[5] Act of July 21, 1932 (47 Stat. 715); and amended in the Act of August 23, 1935 (49 Stat. 714).

[6] Act of March 9, 1933 (48 Stat. 7).

[7] In June, 1966, the Federal Reserve System made arrangements for the possible extension of its credit to mutual savings banks, savings and loan associations, and other savings institutions, but none were required. J. L. Robertson, "Statement to Congress," *Federal Reserve Bulletin*, April, 1968, pp. 370–71.

are needed, the type of collateral that must be pledged, and the ease of borrowing. Loan requests must be accompanied by a statement of the bank's financial condition and a certification that paper being offered with the application has not been acquired from a nonmember bank (except as permitted in Regulation A).

Direct obligations of the United States Treasury and those of federal agencies are among the investments of most member banks; hence they have found it most convenient to offer them as security when borrowing from Federal Reserve banks. Customarily, member banks keep their government securities and those of federal agencies with their Federal Reserve banks for safekeeping; and so an application for an advance is processed by removing such securities from the safekeeping category to the pledged category. The borrowing bank sends a note stating the amount of funds required, the government obligations to be pledged, and a letter authorizing the Federal Reserve bank to transfer the securities from safekeeping. When borrowing is anticipated, a member bank may leave a signed note with its Federal Reserve bank, and when funds are needed, the terms may be arranged by telephone. The application is dated, the promissory note is completed, the bank's securities are transferred, and the principal amount of the note minus the discount is credited to the borrower's reserve account. The effect on the statements of the two banks are as follows:

Federal Reserve Bank		*Member Bank*	
ASSETS	LIABILITIES	ASSETS	LIABILITIES
Discounts and advances......+	Member-bank reserves.......+	Member-bank reserves......+	Notes payable.......+

When the note matures, the borrower's reserve account is debited for the principal amount of the note, the note is canceled and returned to the borrower, and the pledged securities are reclassified as "safekeeping" items. The time period for this type of Federal Reserve bank advance may range from one night to 15 days with renewal privileges, but for no longer than 90 days.

When a member bank offers "eligible" paper as collateral for an advance from its Federal Reserve bank, the paper must consist of promissory notes of business firms or individuals operating in commercial, industrial, or agricultural industries and possessing certain characteristics, including maturities not in excess of 90 days (except agricultural paper that may have maturities up to nine months) from the date of the advance to the member bank. The same rate is applicable to advances secured by direct obligations of the United States Treasury and federal agencies as to those secured by eligible paper, but the latter require the borrower to supply more information.[8]

When only collateral requirements are considered, the most generous provision for borrowing from Federal Reserve banks is found in Section 10(b) of the Federal Reserve Act, which permits Federal Reserve banks, under conditions specified by the Board of Governors, to make advances to member banks on their time or demand notes having maturities of no more than four months if secured to the satisfaction of the Federal Reserve bank in question. The rate applicable to such a loan must be at least one half of 1 percent above the Federal Reserve discount rate on the date of the note.

The provisions for borrowing by member banks are unnecessarily burdensome. Although Congress has authorized the Federal Reserve banks to accept any type of collateral as security for advances under exceptional conditions, this authorization is seldom used. Most member banks have an adequate supply of government securities, but the trend is downward because many banks are replacing them with municipal bonds, securities of government agencies, and corporate paper. Hence, it may be preferable for Congress to eliminate all the current requirements as to collateral and to permit Federal Reserve banks to make advances when they consider the applications for credit to be adequately secured.

Rediscounts for Member Banks.   Originally, it was assumed that member banks would obtain Federal Reserve bank credit by discounting or rediscounting eligible paper rather than by borrowing on their own promissory notes. (If a member bank offers paper which it has discounted, the second transaction is called a "rediscount.") A discount transaction entails giving the same type of information as that required when eligible paper is offered as collateral for a member-bank's own note. When paper is discounted, it is sold to the

---

[8] For illustration (1) the application must list each individual note, draft, or bill of exchange offered as collateral; (2) the loan list must bear the unrestricted endorsement of the member bank; and (3) the application package must contain current financial statements of the bank's customers whose credit instruments are pledged (except those instruments secured by direct obligations of the United States). In addition, information must be filed with the Federal Reserve banks as to the collateral pledged for each credit instrument on the loan list (such as warehouse receipts, insurance policies, or commodity pledged). Finally, the officer who has been authorized to borrow by resolution of the member bank's board of directors must endorse the application form, promissory note, collateral, and other papers.

Federal Reserve bank and carries the unrestricted endorsement of the Federal Reserve bank. In addition to the disadvantages already cited, the use of eligible paper is objectionable for other reasons. First, many businessmen and other borrowers are adverse to having their promises to pay rediscounted. Second, member banks are frequently unable to provide the financial statements and other information required by the Federal Reserve banks about the names on the paper submitted for rediscount. Third, member banks often want to borrow for only a few days (in order to build up their reserves or for other reasons), and eligible paper of the correct maturity (1, 2, 5, 10 or 15 days) and the exact amount may not be available. Finally, the Federal Reserve banks must collect the discounted paper when due and recapture all the collection costs from the member bank.

Loans to Foreign Central Banks. The statutory powers of the Federal Reserve banks permit them to operate in the field of international finance, and they have frequently made loans secured by gold to foreign central banks. When credit needs are temporary, foreign central banks obtain loans by pledging gold as security instead of selling gold. Thereby they avoid the handling charges of the United States Treasury on sales and purchases of gold and the uncertainty in regard to obtaining a permit from the Treasury to buy gold.

OPEN-MARKET OPERATIONS

In addition to making advances and rediscounting for member banks and other institutions, the Federal Reserve banks are authorized to buy and sell certain types of securities in the open market under rules and regulations prescribed by the Board of Governors of the Federal Reserve System. Now all open-market operations are centralized under the Federal Open Market Committee. The latter determines policies, and the Federal Reserve Bank of New York administers them. In order to keep the assets of the Federal Reserve banks in liquid and safe form, open-market operations are limited by law to the following four classes of securities:

a) Cable transfers, bankers' acceptances, and bills of exchange of the kind and maturities eligible for rediscount "with or without an indorsement of a member bank."

b) Direct and indirect obligations of the U.S. government and government agencies.

c) Bills, notes, revenue bonds, and warrants with maturity of six months or less, issued in anticipation of taxes or assured revenues by the state, county, municipality, or other political subdivisions within the United States.

d) Acceptances or debentures of federal intermediate credit banks, national agricultural credit corporations, and other agricultural institutions.

When the Federal Reserve System invests in government securities, member-bank reserves are created. The effects of a purchase of $100 on the statements of the Federal Reserve bank and the member bank are as follows:

Federal Reserve Bank		*Member Bank*	
ASSETS	**LIABILITIES**	**ASSETS**	**LIABILITIES**
U.S. government securities..+$100	Member-bank deposits..+$100	Required reserves.....+$20 Excess reserves..$80	Deposits ...+$100

The procedure involved may be shown as follows:

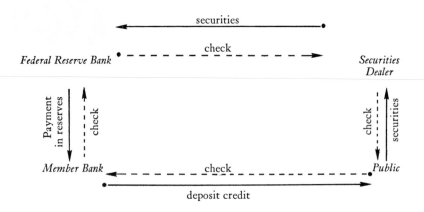

When the Federal Reserve System sells $100 in securities, it destroys an equal amount of member-bank reserves. The effects on the bank statements of the Federal Reserve and member bank and the procedure involved are summarized as shown at the top of page 323.

Bills and Acceptances. The Federal Reserve Bank of New York, as agent for the System, purchases bills and acceptances that are eligible for rediscount with or without the endorsement of a member bank provided they (1) have "been accepted by the drawee prior to purchase"; or (2) "bear a satisfactory bank indorsement"; or (3) are "accompanied or secured by shipping documents" or by terminal,

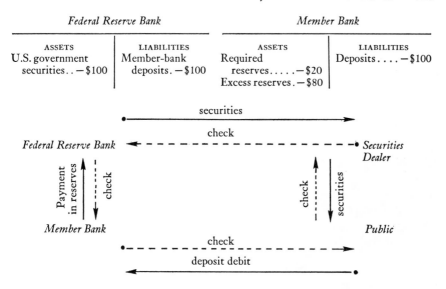

warehouse, "or similar receipts conveying security title." However, a bankers' acceptance resulting from import or export of goods must have a maturity not in excess of six months, and those resulting from storage of goods in the United States (which have been contracted for but not delivered or paid for) must protect the acceptor by a pledge of the goods.

Lacking endorsement by a member bank, a bill of exchange is eligible for purchase by the Federal Reserve System if it is accompanied by a satisfactory financial statement of one or more of the parties; and a bankers' acceptance that has not been endorsed by a member bank may be purchased if the acceptor provides a satisfactory statement of its financial condition and agrees in writing to furnish the Federal Reserve System upon request with information pertaining to the business transaction underlying the acceptance.[9]

For many years it was the policy of the Federal Reserve System to encourage the development of the bill market by buying all bills offered at the Federal Reserve banks' posted buying rates. These rates were usually less favorable than those of other buyers, hence the Federal Reserve banks were usually out of the market. In case a panic situation developed, dealers could sell bills to the Federal Reserve banks and thereby limit their losses to the difference in their purchase

---

[9] Board of Governors of the Federal Reserve System, *Open Market Purchases of Bills of Exchange, Trade Acceptances, and Bankers' Acceptances under Section 14 (Regulation B)*, May 1, 1960, pp. 3–4.

prices and the posted rates for the types of bills involved. Although this support was important during the 1920's, it was of no consequence during the long period of easy money that followed the 1929 stock market break. Since 1955, the System has purchased "acceptances" to stimulate greater activity in this market and to carry out its policy objectives. Buying rates are no longer posted by the Federal Reserve banks; instead, the Federal Reserve Bank of New York, as agent for the Open Market Committee, negotiates at the market price for acceptances acquired under directions issued by the Committee.

Foreign Exchange Transactions. Transactions in foreign currency are handled by the Federal Reserve Bank of New York under directives issued by the Federal Open Market Committee, and these operations may be linked to the purchases and sales of foreign currency by the United States Treasury which uses the Federal Reserve Bank of New York as fiscal agent. Dealings in foreign exchange are more complicated than trading in government securities or bankers' acceptances in that they necessitate correspondent relationships with foreign central banks. (See Chapter 26.) Hence, the Open Market Committee gives the special manager of this account additional instructions in a detailed statement of guidelines (considered more fully in the section dealing with current problems of international finance).

Purchases of foreign money should be recognized as an unusual type of open-market operation in that they are not made with the purpose of influencing the money supply. The basic purposes of the Federal Reserve System's operations in foreign currency are (1) to help safeguard the value of the dollar in foreign exchange markets, (2) to aid in preventing disorderly conditions in the exchange market, (3) to cooperate with central banks and international agencies in monetary matters, (4) to help in moderating temporary imbalances in international payments, and (5) to make possible long-run growth in liquid assets. In order to prevent such purchases from affecting the money supply, the Federal Reserve System may match its purchases of foreign currency with sales of government securities.

Currently, the Federal Reserve banks are holding foreign currency to meet the demands for foreign money. Instead of shipping gold, they write checks or drafts on deposits kept in foreign central banks. Such deposits may be created by buying foreign drafts in the New York market or by "swap" or exchange agreements with foreign central banks. These exchange agreements are made for short periods, such as three months, but they may be renewed. In a swap, the counterpart of an increase in the System's holdings of foreign currency is usually an increase in the volume of short-term American securities held by foreign central banks. During 1966, reciprocal currency arrangements with 11 foreign central banks and the Bank for International Settlements were increased from $2.8 billion to $14.5 billion. In meeting heavy withdrawals owing to the United States deficit in balance of payments and the English pound crisis, the Federal Reserve System used swap drawings totaling $570 million.

Government Securities. The Federal Reserve Bank of New York carries out the operations of the Federal Open Market Committee in government securities and holds this account which is in excess of $45 billion consisting of United States Treasury bills, notes, certificates, and bonds. The chief reason for buying and selling government securities is to influence the money supply by increasing or decreasing the total volume of Federal Reserve credit; but there may be situations which call for the System's having a policy within a policy. For illustration, the System may have a general policy of encouraging business recovery and a secondary one of making the money market more attractive to foreign banks. The first objective will call for increasing total investments to augment the money supply, and the second may be achieved by selling Treasury bills and notes approaching maturity (which lowers their price and makes them more attractive to institutional investors). If the policy of the System is to make the capital market more attractive to domestic borrowers, it may do so by limiting its investments in the long-term Treasury bonds.

When the Federal Open Market Committee is not in session, the Federal Reserve Bank of New York functions under guidelines in a "continuing directive" that may limit increases or decreases in the amount of securities to a stated amount, such as $1 billion, between meetings of the Committee. By introducing a "proviso" clause in the directive, the Committee has permitted the Federal Reserve Bank to deal more effectively with changes in market conditions. For illustration, the directive may state that a less restrictive policy is to be followed unless "bank credit appears to be resuming a rapid rate of expansion." In this case, the manager is expected to reverse the policy without waiting for the next meeting of the Open Market Committee.

The Federal Reserve Bank of New York deals through a limited number of government securities dealers in order to conceal its day-to-day operations, minimize the number of transactions, and make its policies more effective. By making purchases through some dealers and sales through others, traders cannot be sure of which side of the market the System is on. If they knew, they would buy (or sell) in anticipation of the System's purchases (or sales), to the detriment of the market and Federal Reserve policy. The System obtains most of its earnings from investments in government securities; for illustration, in 1966, the average daily holdings of earning assets was in excess of $42.6 billion, of which over 98 percent was in government securities.

BANKERS OF THE FEDERAL GOVERNMENT

Historically, one of the principal functions of a central bank is to act as the fiscal agent for its central government; and, as would be expected, the U.S. government has been by far the largest and most important single customer of the Federal Reserve banks. They act as depositories and custodians as well as fiscal agents for the United States Treasury and various government agencies.

Depository Functions.   The Federal Reserve banks hold the checking accounts of the United States Treasury through which most of the disbursements of the federal government are made. On the other hand, most of the Treasury's receipts are checks drawn on commercial banks by taxpayers, buyers of government securities, and users of various governmental services. If the Treasury were to transfer all of these funds directly to the Federal Reserve banks, it would have a disturbing effect on commercial banks' reserve positions and would hamper their ability to finance business firms.

When the government makes disbursements, the flow of funds is in the opposite direction. Because the two flows of funds are not synchronized, special procedures have been developed to prevent disturbances to the economy. First, receipts are deposited in Treasury "tax and loan accounts" in about 11,600 special depository banks in order to avoid immediate reserve losses. However, the tax and loan accounts are not subject to check; so the second step is to transfer funds from commercial banks to Federal Reserve banks. As funds are needed, the Treasury shifts small amounts, such as 5 to 10 percent of tax and loan accounts, to the Treasury's "general account" at the Federal Reserve bank.

While the aggregate amount in the general fund is kept fairly stable, funds in tax and loan accounts in special depositories will vary greatly. These accounts absorb the fluctuations in Treasury funds caused by differences in timing of government receipts and expenditures. However, during periods of largest receipts, the banks' increases in Treasury deposits tend to be offset by losses in deposits of individuals and business firms; and, during periods of heavy governmental disbursements, banks' losses in government deposits tend to be offset by increases in individual and business firms' deposits.

To facilitate administration of tax and loan accounts, banks are classified periodically according to the average amount of their tax and loan accounts, with banks being designated as Class A, B, and C for call purposes. Class A banks have the smallest average holdings of tax and loan accounts; Class C banks have the largest average holdings; and Class B banks have holdings between the two. Regular calls are made on Class B and Class C banks on Monday for payment the following Friday and Monday; then additional calls may be announced on Thursday for the next Tuesday, Wednesday, and Thursday. Calls on Class A (smaller) banks are made less often, and transfers may take place only once or twice per month.

Services Relative to the Public Debt.   As agents for the United States Treasury, the fiscal agency departments of the Federal Reserve banks are responsible for the issuance, redemption, and exchange of direct obligations of the U.S. government. These obligations include both marketable and nonmarketable debt instruments. Government bonds, which constitute the largest number of issues, include both registered and nonregistered, or coupon, bonds. Savings bonds, issued and redeemed by local banks, are among the nonmarketable issues. Although there are no periodic interest payments on them, there are special problems pertaining to them (such as reissue because of marriage, death, or divorce) that are handled by the Federal Reserve banks.

Most United States Treasury bonds are of the nonregistered type that have interest coupons attached. The latter are clipped on or after the date indicated thereon and mailed to the Federal Reserve banks for payment. The Federal Reserve banks are also responsible for mailing interest checks to owners of registered bonds, some of which are special nonmarketable issues held by governmental agencies, trust funds, and others. On request, holders may exchange registered for nonregistered bonds (and vice versa) and also exchange denominations (for example, five $1,000 bonds for one $5,000 bond, etc.). The Reserve banks will make "wire transfer" deliveries of securities, which means that locally held bonds sold in New York will be delivered to the local Federal Reserve bank and canceled and that a wire will be sent to the Federal Reserve Bank of New York to deliver similar securities out of stock. Since sales of government securities made by individual banks and other institutions may involve millions of dollars, the savings in time and expense of delivery are important.

In addition to processing obligations of the U.S. government, the Federal Reserve banks act in a similar capacity for different government banks and agencies such as the Commodity Credit Corporation, Export-Import Bank of Washington, Federal Farm Credit Administration, and the Housing and Home Financing Agency, which are considered in later chapters. The location of the Federal Reserve banks and branches has facilitated the work of the United States Treasury and other departments and government agencies. It has been estimated that one fourth of the total personnel of the Federal Reserve banks is engaged in performing services that before 1914 would have been rendered by the subtreasuries of the government.

Other Operations. The routine activities of the Federal Reserve banks include receiving, counting, and sorting coins and paper money. The number of such items, over 14.5 billion, is in excess of all other items handled by the bank; however, the dollar value of U.S. government checks, postal money orders, and checks from banks and other is far in excess of the dollar value of currency handled. The largest dollar amount item handled, transfer of funds, represents the device used to move money from place to place by the government, central banks, and other financial institutions. The expansion in this item indicates the rapid increase in the transaction velocity of money and in financial transactions.

The Federal Reserve banks, as fiscal agents for various departments, divisions, and agencies of the federal government, handle guaranteed loans made under the Defense Production Act of 1950 to finance the production of goods, machinery, and equipment ordered by procurement agencies.[10] The Board of Governors prescribes the maximum interest rate, guarantee fee, and commitment applicable to these so-called "V-loans" (made under Regulation V of the Board of Governors, which outlines the objectives, procedures, rates, and fees that may be charged).

International Banking Services. The decentralization of our central banking system was due in large part to public mistrust of big business; however, decentralization could not prevent one or more of the Federal Reserve banks from becoming more important than others. The Federal Reserve Bank of New York is located in the world's wealthiest city, wherein the clearinghouse banks alone own

---

[10] The procurement agencies are the Army, Navy, Air Force, Defense Supply Agency of the Department of Defense, General Services Administration, National Aeronautics and Space Administration, Atomic Energy Commission, and the Departments of Commerce, Interior, and Agriculture.

more banking resources than do all the banks in the United Kingdom. So it is not surprising that this bank's size and activities reflect the fact that it is located in the most important money, capital, foreign-exchange, and commodities market of the United States. Its activities are more truly those of a central bank than are those of the other Federal Reserve banks. In addition, many of the fiscal operations of the U.S. government and the international transactions of the United States Treasury are centered in New York. Consequently, the Federal Reserve Bank of New York has become the most important central bank in the world (even though policy decisions are made elsewhere).

The Federal Reserve Bank of New York is the depository through which foreign central banks and governments transact most of their banking business in the United States; and, in this capacity, the bank acts as their fiscal agent in the purchase and sale of U.S. government obligations and other liquid assets such as bankers' acceptances, which it may endorse if requested to do so.

An interesting part of the Federal Reserve Bank of New York is its foreign-exchange department, which is actually a "bank within a bank." It acts in its own behalf and also as agent for the United States Treasury and the Federal Reserve System. In addition, it holds the accounts of foreign central banks and governments, international institutions (such as the Bank for International Settlements, "World" Bank, International Monetary Fund, and Inter-American Development Bank), and groups of foreign banks.[11] The total number of foreign accounts is small, but the assets therein amount to over $30 billion.[12] The Federal Reserve Bank of New York frequently makes loans to foreign banks on the security of earmarked gold held by the Bank.

The foreign-exchange department certifies to the Treasury the rate of exchange (used in administering customs duties); handles the in-and-out flow of dollar balances in wholesale lots, but has no retail letter-of-credit business; and arranges for gold exports for the Treasury. In addition, the Federal Reserve Bank of New York operates the Stabilization Fund for the United States Treasury and administers

[11] In 1966, new accounts were opened in the names of the Asian Development Bank and the Central banks of Ethiopia, Guyana, and Tanzania.

[12] "Total holdings of gold, dollar balances, and other assets for foreign and international accounts rose to a record $30.6 billion. . . . Holdings for international organizations were slightly lower at $9.4 billion, but holdings for foreign accounts . . . at $21.2 billion were higher by about $2.4 billion . . . ." Federal Reserve Bank of New York, *Fifty-Third Annual Report for the Year Ended on December 31, 1967*, p. 51.

Treasury regulations pertaining to assets and financial transactions with the governments and nationals of Communist China and North Korea.

EARNINGS AND EXPENSES

Federal Reserve banks' total earnings for the year 1967 amounted to $2.19 billion, of which over 98 percent ($2.15 billion) was derived from the System's investments in government securities. In comparison, the expenses of the Federal Reserve banks were small ($0.212 billion). The Federal Reserve banks assume all the expenses connected with issuance of Federal Reserve notes, and they are assessed for the expenses of the Board of Governors. The Federal Reserve banks are reimbursed by the United States Treasury, federal agencies, international organizations, and others for expenditures in connection with performance of fiscal agency and other services for them.

After all current expense items are subtracted from the current earnings of the Federal Reserve banks, their net earnings were over $1.97 billion, or more than their paid-in capital and surplus ($1.2 billion for the same date. The policy pertaining to the distribution of Federal Reserve banks' earnings has changed several times during the history of the Federal Reserve System.

Prior to January 1, 1934, each Federal Reserve bank was permitted to carry net earnings, after dividends, to the "surplus account" until it equaled the bank's capitalization (which is twice the paid-in capital); thereafter, 10 percent was to be retained by each Federal Reserve bank and 90 percent was to be paid to the government. This franchise-tax provision was repealed when the Federal Reserve banks were required to buy stock of the Federal Deposit Insurance Corporation in amounts equal to one half of their surplus as of January 1, 1933 (over $139 million). Subsequently, the surplus accounts of the Federal Reserve banks were rebuilt until they were equal to twice their paid-in capital. Then, the Board of Governors of the Federal Reserve System reinstated the policy in effect prior to 1934, by charging each bank interest on its Federal Reserve notes.[13]

The next change in policy occurred in 1965 when each Federal Reserve bank was required (1) to remit an amount equal to the

---

[13] Federal Reserve Act, Sec. 16, para. 6, permits the Board of Governors of the Federal Reserve System to accept or reject in whole or part applications of any Federal Reserve bank for Federal Reserve notes "and such bank shall be charged with the amount of notes issued to it and shall pay such rate of interest as may be established by the Board of Governors of the Federal Reserve System."

difference between its surplus account and its paid-in capital to the United States Treasury; and (2) in the future, to pay to the Treasury all earnings in excess of "statutory dividends" and the amount necessary to keep surplus accounts equal to paid-in capital. For the period 1914 to 1967, the Federal Reserve banks paid over $14 billion to the United States Treasury, $691 billion as dividends, and transferred $728 million to surplus (see Table 15–3).

TABLE 15–3

Earnings and Expenses of Federal Reserve Banks
(In Millions of Dollars)

	1960	*1966*	*1967*	*Total 1914–67*
Current earnings..........................	$1,103	$1,908	$2,190	$19,424
Current expenses.........................	154	207	220	3,790
Net earnings before payments to United States Treasury*......................	963	1,702	1,972	15,698
Dividends paid...........................	24	34	35	691
Payment to United States Treasury:				
Franchise tax...........................	...	...	...	149
Under Section 13b.....................	...	...	...	2
Interest on U.S. notes..................	897	1,649	1,907	14,127
Transferred to surplus (Section 13b).........	...	...	...	†
Transferred to surplus (Section 7)..........	43	19	30	728‡

* Current earnings less current expenses, plus or minus adjustment for profit and loss items.
† Minus $3,657.
‡ Transfer to surplus was reduced by $500,000 chargeoff on bank premises (1927), $139,299,557 for contribution to capital of Federal Deposit Insurance Corporation (1934) and $3,657 net upon elimination of Section B surplus (1958), and was increased by $11,131,013 transferred from reserves for contingencies (1945), leaving a balance of $599,741,000 on December 31, 1967.
Details may not add to totals because of rounding.
Source: *Fifty-Fourth Annual Report of the Board of Governors of the Federal Reserve System Covering Operations for the Year 1967* (Washington, D.C.: U.S. Government Printing Office, 1968), p. 361.

SUMMARY

Federal Reserve credit is made available to the economy primarily through the lending by Federal Reserve banks and the open-market transactions of the Federal Reserve banks and the Federal Open Market Committee.

The ways in which member-bank reserve accounts are affected by the investing and lending of the Federal Reserve System are reflected in the statement of condition of the Federal Reserve banks and the statement of the Federal Reserve banks' earnings and expenses. Of minor importance are the other ways in which Federal Reserve credit is made available to the economy—industrial and emergency loans to borrowers (other than member banks), discounting for acceptance dealers, and the Federal Reserve "float."

In addition to credit functions the Federal Reserve banks act as fiscal (that is, financial) agents for the United States Treasury. The Federal Reserve banks hold the most important of the checking accounts of the government and also supervise the "tax and loan" accounts in other banks (chiefly commercial banks). The Federal Reserve banks also help the United States Treasury in handling its government debt and act as fiscal agents for U.S. government agencies, foreign governments, and central banks. Because of its location, the Federal Reserve Bank of New York has been given the responsibility for administering matters of policy that have been decided by the United States Treasury, the Board of Governors of the Federal Reserve System, and the Federal Open Market Committee. In addition to the services provided the United States Treasury, the Federal Reserve banks also provide the banks of the nation with currency and assist them in the clearing and collection of cash and noncash items. The public nature of the Federal Reserve banks is suggested by the allocation of their net earnings, with the bulk going to the United States Treasury.

QUESTIONS AND PROBLEMS

1. How important is lending by Federal Reserve banks? Who are the chief borrowers? Why do foreign central banks sometimes pledge gold as security for loans? Are other loans made by Federal Reserve banks well secured? Explain.
2. Explain: A "System committee . . . has completed . . . [a] 3-year restudy of Federal Reserve lending policies [and] proposes several significant changes in lending policies and procedures aimed at providing more liberal and clear-cut access for member banks to Federal Reserve lending facilities." (*Federal Reserve Bulletin*, July, 1968, p. 545.)
3. Discuss: Purchases of government securities by the Federal Open Market Committee (the Federal Reserve Bank of New York acts as fiscal agent) will increase the volume of reserves available to member banks. Conversely, sales of government securities by the Federal Open Market Committee will decrease the volume of reserves available to member banks.
4. What services do Federal Reserve banks perform for the United States Treasury? Other governmental agencies?
5. Explain the greater importance of the Federal Reserve Bank of New York. Compare its functions with those of other Federal Reserve banks.
6. Explain: "It now appears that the regional structure of the [Federal Reserve] System, while satisfying a legitimate need at an earlier time,

has much less rationale at the moment." (Eli Shapiro, *The Structure of the Federal Reserve System* [Manufacturers Hanover Trust, February, 1966].

7. Identify the problems that result from most of the disbursements of the Treasury being made by checks drawn on Federal Reserve banks and most of the Treasury's receipts being in the form of checks drawn on commercial banks.

8. Explain: "Payments to the Treasury as interest on Federal Reserve notes totaled $1,907 million for the year, compared with $1,649 million in 1966. This amount consists of all net earnings after dividends and the amount necessary to bring surplus to the level of paid-in capital." (*Fifty-Fourth Annual Report of Board of Governors of the Federal Reserve System Covering Operations for the Year 1967* [Washington, D.C.: U.S. Government Printing Office, 1968], p. 336.)

9. Discuss: "On August 17, 1967, the Federal Reserve Bank of New York informed the Treasury that reports in the securities market gave reason to believe that terms of the Treasury offering that day had 'leaked' before the official release time. Investigation by the Treasury revealed [that the rumor was true]." Later, "new procedures were developed by the Treasury and Federal Reserve to prevent the possibility of a recurrence." (*Ibid.*, p. 338.)

10. The following questions are based on the Statement of Condition of Federal Reserve Banks (Table 15–2).

    (*a*) What is the ratio of capital and surplus to deposits and notes? Is it too low? How does it compare with a similar ratio for member banks?

    (*b*) What item or items show the amount of Federal Reserve credit in use?

    (*c*) Identify "bills discounted."

    (*d*) Are the types of government securities held significant? Why?

    (*e*) Identify "uncollected items" and "deferred availability items." Why are they not equal in amounts?

CHAPTER 16

Creation of Reserves

THE INFLUENCE of the Federal Reserve System on the economy is due to the ability of the Federal Reserve banks to increase or decrease the volume of bank reserves and thereby increase or decrease the ability of commercial banks to expand or contract credit. Any change in the cost and/or availability of bank credit will tend to affect spending by consumers, business firms, and others. The immediate impact of a change in the volume of member-bank reserves is on the lending power of banks and therefore the quantity of money and interest rates; but the ultimate objectives of monetary policy are to achieve and maintain full employment, growth in the economy, stable general prices, and equilibrium in the balance of international payments.

SOURCES AND USES OF RESERVES

Member-bank reserves are the key to money policy, and Federal Reserve authorities give careful attention to reserve changes as an integral part of the daily operations of the Federal Reserve System. Hence an excellent starting point for the study of Federal Reserve policy is a description of the major factors affecting the sources and uses of member-bank reserves.

Among the factors that affect the volume of member-bank reserves, the most important are changes in (1) monetary gold, (2) Treasury currency outstanding, (3) Federal Reserve bank credit, (4) Treasury cash holdings, (5) currency in circulation, (6) deposits of the Treasury, foreign banks, and foreign agencies in the Federal Reserve banks, and (7) other Federal Reserve accounts except member-bank reserves.

Sources of Reserves. The monetary gold stock, Treasury currency outstanding and Federal Reserve credit are all sources of member-bank reserves (see Table 16–1). Any increase in these sources will tend to increase member-bank reserves, and any decrease in them will tend to decrease member-bank reserves. At the present time, Federal Reserve credit is the primary source of member-bank reserves, and

TABLE 16–1

Sources and Uses of Federal Reserve Funds, June, 1968
(In Millions of Dollars)

Sources		Uses	
(1) Gold stock..............	$10,369	(4) Currency in circulation.......	$47,466
(2) Treasury currency outstanding...........	6,744	(5) U.S. Treasury cash holdings.................	973
(3) Federal Reserve credit:....		(6) Federal Reserve deposits except member bank:	
U.S. government securities..	51,306	U.S. Treasury..............	960
Discounts and advances	705	Foreign...................	181
Float..................	1,712	Other.....................	471
Acceptances............	91	(7) Other Federal Reserve accounts.................	−474
		Member-bank reserves with Federal Reserve banks......	21,350
Total sources......$70,927		Total uses...........$70,927	

Source of statistics: *Federal Reserve Bulletin*, July, 1968, p. A–4.
Note: Member banks held $4,355 million of currency and coins, and so total member-bank reserves were $25,705 million.

the total amount is determined largely by the Federal Reserve authorities.

Monetary Gold and Treasury Currency. The amount of Treasury currency outstanding and of monetary gold stock is determined by factors outside the control of the Federal Reserve System. However, if there are fluctuations in these two items that do not conform to the objectives of monetary policy, the Federal Reserve authorities may compensate for them through the System's open-market operations. For illustration, since 1960 the depression effects of losses of monetary gold have been compensated for by increasing the volume of member-bank credit (see Chart 16–1). Since the adoption of the two gold price system in March, 1968, monetary gold movements have had little or no effect on member-bank reserves, and the only way that the stock of Treasury currency is increased is by minting new coins.

Customarily, new coins are delivered by the Mint to a Federal Reserve bank, which credits the Treasury's general account for them. Member bank's reserves will increase when the Treasury activates these new deposits by writing checks for goods and services that will be deposited in commercial banks, and the deposits will flow back to the Federal Reserve banks as member-bank reserves. Although the United States Treasury normally replaces withdrawals from its checking account by transfers from its tax-and-loan accounts, the

CHART 16-1

MEMBER-BANK RESERVES AND RELATED ITEMS

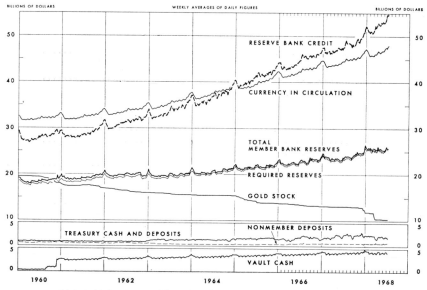

Source: Board of Governors of the Federal Reserve System, *Federal Reserve Chart Book,* July, 1968, p. 2

deposit of coins has the effect of leaving reserves of member banks undisturbed for a longer period of time.

Federal Reserve Credit. The primary way whereby member-bank reserves are increased or decreased is by increasing or decreasing the earning assets of the Federal Reserve banks. The only other imporant source of Federal Reserve credit is an increase or decrease in that part of the Federal Reserve "float" that counts as member-bank reserves. The earning assets of Federal Reserve banks are: (1) U.S. government securities, (2) Federal Reserve banks' discounts and advances, (3) bankers' acceptances, and (4) foreign currency. Of the total amount of Federal Reserve credit, usually 95 percent or more is due to the System's investments in U.S. government securities.

The Federal Reserve System takes the initiative in trading in government securities, bankers' acceptances, and foreign currency; but member banks take the initiative in applying for discounts and advances. The System's transactions in government securities are executed by the Federal Reserve Bank of New York, under instructions of the Federal Open Market Committee. Each Federal Reserve bank participates in the earnings from total investments according to the percentage of its assets of the total assets of the Federal Reserve System.

Repurchase agreements are arrangements between the Federal Reserve System and nonbank securities dealers whereby the System purchases securities from the dealer in order to meet the latter's need for credit. The dealer contracts to repurchase the securities within a stipulated period of time, usually less than 15 days. Since dealer banks may borrow at the Federal Reserve banks and nonbank dealers may not, repurchase agreements are limited to the latter.

Federal Reserve banks' discounts and advances are loans to member banks. At present, the amount of Federal Reserve bank lending represents a relatively small part of Federal Reserve bank credit; but, if the proposals made for changing discount policy considered in the last chapter are adopted, the relative unimportance of discount policy may change.

Bankers' acceptances and foreign currency are purchased by the Federal Reserve Bank of New York for the Federal Reserve System under instructions of the Federal Open Market Committee. Until 1955, Federal Reserve banks purchased acceptances at their posted buying rates in order to prevent fluctuations in the market. Rates were increased or decreased to encourage or discourage sales to the System. Since 1955, the Federal Reserve Bank of New York has been buying acceptances at the market rate as authorized by the Federal Open Market Committee. Sometimes dealers arrange with the Federal Reserve System to sell bankers' acceptances under repurchase agreements which are similar to those made with nonbank government securities dealers. Now, bankers' acceptances are a relatively unimportant source of Federal Reserve credit, as are transactions in foreign currency.

When the Federal Reserve System buys securities in the open market, the Federal Reserve Bank of New York, as agent for the System's open-market account, pays the government security dealer with a Federal Reserve check. When the latter deposits it in his bank, the bank in turn sends it to the Federal Reserve bank for collection. The effects on the balance sheets of the Federal Reserve bank and the member bank (using $100 as a convenient figure) are as follows:

Federal Reserve Bank		*Member Bank*	
ASSETS	LIABILITIES	ASSETS	LIABILITIES
Government securities...+$100	Member-bank reserves...+$100	Member-bank reserves...+$100	Deposits.....+$100

When the Federal Reserve System sells securities in the open market, the Federal Reserve Bank of New York, as agent for the System's open-market account, receives a check in payment which it presents to the bank on which it is drawn and debits the account of that bank at the Federal Reserve bank. The effects on the balance sheets of the Federal Reserve bank and the member bank will be as follows:

Federal Reserve Bank		*Member Bank*	
ASSETS	LIABILITIES	ASSETS	LIABILITIES
Government securities.. −$100	Member-bank reserves... −$100	Member-bank reserves... −$100	Deposits..... −$100

Uses of Reserve Money.   Among those competing with member banks for reserve money are (1) the general public, (2) the United States Treasury, and (3) others who have accounts with the Federal Reserve banks.

1. The general public uses the largest amount of reserves in the form of coins and paper money. Any change in the amount of money in circulation outside of member banks will tend to have the opposite dollar-for-dollar effect on member-bank reserves. Member banks obtain currency from the Federal Reserve banks which may be in the form of Treasury currency or Federal Reserve notes. If the Federal Reserve bank ships only Treasury currency, its assets and liabilities are decreased; but, if it ships only Federal Reserve notes, only the form of the liabilities of the Reserve bank is changed (member-bank deposit liabilities are decreased, and Federal Reserve bank note liabilities are increased).

Federal Reserve notes comprise about 90 percent of the total money in circulation, hence one may expect shipments of currency to and from Federal Reserve banks to contain about 10 percent Treasury currency and 90 percent Federal Reserve notes. An increase in the amount of money in circulation which, in turn, is accompanied by an increase in money outside of member banks will have the following effects on the balance sheets of the Federal Reserve bank and the member bank.

Federal Reserve Bank		*Member Bank*	
ASSETS	LIABILITIES	ASSETS	LIABILITIES
Treasury currency.. −$10	Member-bank reserves... −$100 Federal Reserve notes...... +$90	Member-bank reserves... −$100	Deposits..... −$100

Although the amount of currency in the hands of the public changes from day to day, week to week, month to month, and year to year, there is an upward trend due to the increase in population, growth in business, and increase in general prices.

Unusual developments in the economy, such as those which occurred during the 1931–34 period and during World War II, may cause a sharp increase in the amount of money in circulation. During the Great Depression, the fear of bank failures led to the withdrawal of large amounts of currency. During World War II, there was a sharp increase in the demand for currency due to the increase in the number of men and women in the Armed Forces and the growth in number of transient workers. Other new demand factors were the hoarding demand to evade federal income taxes and to conceal black market profits and, in addition, more currency was needed to purchase the same amount of goods due to the increase in prices.

During the early 1960's, there was another sizable increase in the amount of money in circulation due in part to the increased demand for coins for use in coin-operated selling devices (vending machines, parking meters, highway tolls, Laundromats, etc.), changes in the law that permitted member banks to count vault cash in computing required reserves, the increase in number and income of workers not having checking accounts, the increase in domestic and foreign travel, and higher bank service charges for checking accounts. Superimposed on the trend and unusual changes in the demand for currency are those due to business cycle movements, seasonal fluctuations in business, and changes in buying and paying habits of consumers and business firms.

2. Although most of the cash assets of the United States Treasury are kept as deposits with the Federal Reserve banks and in special depositories, the Secretary of the Treasury may keep part of the government's cash assets in the Treasury's own vaults (as under the Independent Treasury System). The cash holdings include United States coins, paper money, "free" gold, and silver bullion. Any change in these items will have the opposite effect on member-bank reserves.

3. The United States Treasury, foreign banks and governments, international institutions, nonmember banks, and others keep deposit accounts at the Federal Reserve banks, and any change in their amounts means a change in the opposite direction in member-bank reserves. When foreign governments and central banks and/or certain U.S. government banks and agencies collect checks drawn on member banks, settlement usually entails crediting their accounts at the Fed-

eral Reserve banks and debiting the accounts of member banks; for illustration, the effects on Federal Reserve and member banks may be shown as follows:

Federal Reserve Bank		Member Bank	
ASSETS	LIABILITIES	ASSETS	LIABILITIES
	Federal Reserve deposits... +$100 Member-bank reserves... −$100	Member-bank reserves... −$100	Deposits.... −$100

When the account of a clearing nonmember bank at its Federal Reserve bank is being credited with a cash item, the account of a member bank is being debited unless the cash item is drawn on a second nonmember bank (in this case there would be no change in total nonmember banks' reserves); however, our interest is in changes that affect the location of reserves among different groups as a unit.

"Other accounts" includes other liabilities plus capital account items; and any change in these will tend to have the opposite effect on member-bank reserves. For illustration, if a member bank transfers $100,000 from its undivided profits account to its surplus account, it must invest 3 percent of that amount in additional Federal Reserve bank stock. This would be done by drawing a check on its account at the Federal Reserve bank payable to the bank. When collected, the amount of member-bank reserves would be reduced and the amount of Federal Reserve bank stock would be increased. Conversely, if a member bank were to reduce its holding of Federal Reserve bank stock, member-bank reserves would be increased by the amount of the reduction.

In conclusion, the sum of the factors which supply reserve money must equal the sum of the factors that use reserve money. The total of gold stock, U.S. currency outstanding, and Federal Reserve credit equals the total of currency in circulation, United States Treasury cash holdings, and Federal Reserve bank deposits and accounts. The volume of member-bank reserves may be found by using the following formula:

$$(1 + 2 + 3) - (4 + 5 + 6 + 7) = \text{Member-bank reserves}$$

wherein the numbers represent (1) gold stock, (2) Treasury currency outstanding, (3) Federal Reserve bank credit outstanding, (4) currency in circulation, (5) United States Treasury cash holdings, (6) Federal Reserve bank deposits other than member banks' deposits, and (7) other Federal Reserve accounts (see Table 16–1).

REQUIRED, EXCESS, AND FREE RESERVES

The correlation between the total amount of member-bank reserves and the volume of bank credit and money is never perfect, because there are variations in the way banks manage their reserve positions. While some banks customarily carry an excess reserve position from one computation period to the next, others rarely do so.

Required Reserves.   Member banks are required to keep a minimum percentage reserve against their deposits in the form of balances with their Federal Reserve banks and in the form of currency and coins held as vault cash "or such part thereof as the Board by regulation prescribes." The Board of Governors is authorized to set the minimum required reserve ratio within limits designated by Congress.[1] At the present time these limits are as follows: (1) for savings and other time deposits in all member banks, a minimum of 3 percent and a maximum of 10 percent, and (2) for net demand deposits in "country" banks, a minimum of 7 percent and a maximum of 14 percent, and for "reserve city" banks, a minimum of 10 percent and a maximum of 22 percent. The actual reserve requirements in effect are set by the Board of Governors of the Federal Reserve System within these limits (see Table 16–2).

Excess Reserves.   Reserves are nonearning assets, and so most banks try to keep them as low as possible without jeopardizing their legal minimum-reserve requirements.[2] If a bank is to avoid having excess reserves, time must be given to management of its "cash" or "money" position. Some banks keep larger reserves than needed in order to avoid the expense of making daily calculations of their reserve positions.

The current system of computing average reserve needs over a weekly period, together with the operations of the federal funds market, have made it easier for banks to employ all available funds. However, miscalculations do occur, and bank management prefers to err on the side of safety. Furthermore, many banks may fail to find suitable loan or investment outlets as soon as extra funds are received. Because of these factors, an excess reserve situation is nor-

---

[1] Public Law 89–597, Sec. 2(c), 89th Cong., H.R. 1402G, September 21, 1966.

[2] According to current regulations, an individual bank may, with the approval of the Board of Governors, have a reserve deficiency of no more than 2 percent during a given reserve period if there was no deficiency during the preceding period and if its reserves during the following period are large enough to bring the average for the two periods to a satisfactory level. Use of this privilege is not condoned as a policy but rather as an emergency when deficiencies are due to errors in forecasting reserve needs.

TABLE 16-2

RESERVE REQUIREMENTS OF MEMBER BANKS
(Percent of Deposits, Beginning July 14, 1966)

| Effective Date* | Net Demand Deposits† | | | | Time Deposits§ (All Classes of Banks) | | |
| | Reserve City Banks‡ | | Country Banks | | | Other Time Deposits | |
	Under $5 Million	Over $5 Million	Under $5 Million	Over $5 Million	Savings Deposits	Under $5 Million	Over $5 Million
1966—July 14, 21.	16½‖		12‖		4‖	4	5
September 8, 15.	...		...		...	...	6
1967—March 2....	...		...		3½	3½	...
March 16....	...		...		3	3	...
1968—January 11, 18...	16½	17	12	12½	...	...	...
In effect June 30, 1968...	16½	17	12	12½	3	3	6
Present legal requirement:							
Minimum.........	10		7		3	3	3
Maximum.........	22		14		10	10	10

* When two dates are shown, the first applies to the change at reserve city banks and the second to the change at country banks. For changes prior to 1950 see Board's Annual Reports.

† Demand deposits subject to reserve requirements are gross demand deposits minus cash items in process of collection and demand balances due from domestic banks.

‡ Authority of the Board of Governors to classify or reclassify cities as central reserve cities was terminated effective July 28, 1962.

§ Effective Jan. 5, 1967, time deposits such as Christmas and vacation club accounts became subject to same requirements as savings deposits.

‖ See preceding columns for earliest effective date of this rate.

Note: All required reserves were held on deposit with Federal Reserve Banks June 21, 1917, until December, 1959. From December, 1959 to November, 1960, member banks were allowed to count part of their currency and coin as reserves; effective Nov. 24, 1960, they were allowed to count all as reserves. For further details, see Board's Annual Reports.

Source: *Federal Reserve Bulletin*, July, 1968, p. A–10.

mal. So two policy conclusions may be drawn: (1) during periods when the Federal Reserve System is creating new reserves to stimulate spending, the total must be large enough not only to have the desired effect but also to meet the demands of the banking system for unused reserves; and (2) when the System is absorbing reserves to discourage spending, the amount withdrawn must be large enough not only to have the desired effect but also to absorb excess reserves.

Reducing Excess Reserves. Reserve management is becoming more efficient, and there has been a reduction in excess reserves for all classes of banks. This tendency has been accelerated by higher interest rates which increase the penalty (loss of income) for keeping funds idle. At the same time, the increase in size of the average bank means that more bank funds are being traded in the federal funds market. Large correspondent banks are permitting their customer banks to participate in their loans, hence there is less justification for keeping surplus funds idle.

During a year the amount of excess reserves shows a wide range depending chiefly on changes in the amount of money in circulation and the Federal Reserve bank "float." The after-Christmas return flow of currency usually creates an excess reserve situation and this may be amplified when collection time for cash items runs longer than normal. Almost every bank transaction affects banks' reserve positions; but normally those changes due to weekly or monthly factors are short-lived, and banks may adjust their policies to correct excess reserve positions in a relatively short time.

The Federal Reserve authorities may determine the upper limits of the money supply and bank credit by reserve creation; but they cannot expect perfect correlation between changes in total member-bank reserves and changes in total member-bank deposits. Usually an increase in reserves indicates an increase in the supply of funds available for lending, but the effect of any change will depend on the banks that own them. If most of the excess reserves are held by small banks, they may have little effect on the volume of lending; but, if excess reserves are held by large city banks, they may have an immediate effect on the volume of credit. Hence, in planning credit policy the Federal Reserve authorities must consider not only the level of excess reserves but also their location.

Free Reserves. Free reserves are defined as excess reserves minus borrowed reserves, and they may be negative as well as positive. They are positive when the excess reserves held by banks exceed the amount of reserves borrowed by other banks; and conversely, they are negative when the excess reserves held by banks are less than the amount of reserves borrowed by other banks. The figure showing the net position of member banks is found by subtracting the average volume of borrowing from the Federal Reserve banks for a period from the average excess reserves for the same period. (See Chart 16–2.)

Free reserves, like excess reserves, may be misleading when used as a guide to credit policy because they may increase as a result of a shift in location of deposits from city to country banks and decrease as a result of a shift of deposits from country to city banks. Although the Federal Reserve System is able to "mop up" excess reserves, its problem of controlling credit is made more difficult by the lack of uniformity in reserve requirements for all commercial banks.

Free reserves may indicate different things at different times. For illustration, when the demand for bank credit is high, free reserves may indicate unused bank credit expansion or a temporary situation

CHART 16–2

RESERVE POSITION OF MEMBER BANKS

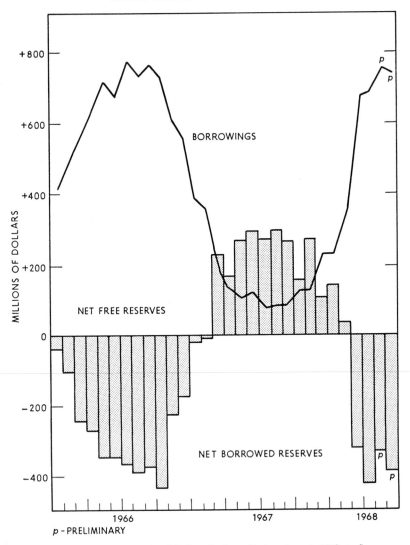

Source: Federal Reserve Bank of Dallas, *Business Review,* August, 1968, p. 7.

caused by an increase in Federal Reserve float. In considering the loan capacity of a bank, its secondary-reserve position is more significant than its holding of excess reserves.

The Federal Reserve System keeps fairly close control over total member-bank reserves by creating or absorbing reserves to offset the effect of other users and suppliers on the total amount available to member banks. Although movements in total reserves correspond to changes in bank credit, their significance is reduced when there is a shift by the general public between checking accounts and savings or time accounts in banks. Because of the higher reserve requirements for demand deposits, growth in the volume of total reserves may be inhibited or even stopped by a shift of deposits from checking accounts to savings or time deposit accounts.

In conclusion, neither excess reserves nor free reserves are satisfactory as measures of the credit position of banks; and now the Fed uses changes in member-bank deposits subject to reserve requirements as its guide to policy (see Chapter 18).

CHANGES IN LEGAL-RESERVE REQUIREMENTS

The Board of Governors of the Federal Reserve System is authorized to change required reserve percentages of member banks within limits specified by law (now for time and savings deposits, from 3 to 10 percent, and for net demand deposits, from 7 to 14 percent for country banks and from 10 to 22 percent for reserve city banks). A change in reserve requirements may apply to different classes of time and savings deposits and/or demand deposits, but there must be no discrimination among individual member banks.[3]

Reserve Classification of Banks. The classification of banks for reserve purposes originated in the National Bank Act of 1863 when nine cities were designated as redemption centers. They were permitted to receive and hold three fifths of the required reserves of national banks. The next year 17 cities were designated as redemption centers, and New York was recognized as the financial center when its banks were permitted to receive half of the required reserves of the national banks in the 17 redemption centers. However, some cities felt that they were discriminated against, and as a result, in 1887, Congress authorized the Comptroller of the Currency to name additional cities as redemption centers. (In this Act, the terms "central reserve cities" and "reserve cities" were first used.) In 1913, Congress shifted this power from the Comptroller of the Currency to the Federal Reserve Board.

There were 49 reserve cities and two central reserve cities (New York and Chicago) until the representatives of the latter argued successfully that there was no longer any justification for the central

[3] In the summer of 1948, Congress authorized the Board of Governors to increase minimum percentage reserve requirements beyond their statutory limits until June 30, 1949.

reserve city classification. In 1960, Congress abolished this classification but still permits the Board of Governors to add to the number of cities classified as reserve cities or to terminate their designation as such. Under present policy, the Board reviews the reserve situation and every three years reclassifies cities as reserve cities as conditions seem to justify.

The reasons for elimination of the central reserve city classification for reserve requirements seem to justify the removal of the remaining distinction between "reserve city" and "country" banks. Often banks in the latter category are larger and performing more correspondent banking functions than some banks in reserve cities. Furthermore, the arbitrary division of member banks into two classes for requiring reserves against demand deposits is an obstacle in the way of creating a more equitable reserve system.

Vault Cash Reserves.   Member banks are permitted to count their vault cash as part of their required reserves. When Congress authorized this change, two inequities were eliminated:

1. All member banks do not have the same convenient access to Federal Reserve banks because of their location, and those less favorably situated keep a larger percentage of assets as vault cash than do the more conveniently located banks. Banks located near Federal Reserve banks or their branches may replace till money or vault cash in minutes, hence it is not necessary for them to keep a large percentage of cash relative to deposits. Banks less conveniently located must keep more vault cash, but since they may count it as part of their required reserves, they are no longer penalized. Reserve balances and vault cash are interchangeable, and changes in either have the same effect on the volume of bank credit.

Additional advantages resulting from permitting vault cash to be counted as required reserves are (*a*) it has facilitated distributing stocks of currency over a wide area for use in a national emergency, and (*b*) it has reduced the expense entailed in transporting currency to and from the Federal Reserve banks.

2. Reserve requirements established by state governments for nonmember banks permits these banks to count their vault cash in computing their reserve requirements. So, when member banks were given the same privilege, the state-chartered banks lost part of their competitive advantage. But there are still inequities between member and nonmember banks that could best be eliminated by requiring all insured banks handling demand deposits to meet identical reserve

requirements. Demand deposits in nonmember banks are part of the nation's money supply, and their exemption from the Federal Reserve System's reserve requirements is not in the interest of the general public.

Objectives in Changing Reserve Requirements. The most common reason for changing reserve requirements in the past was to absorb excess member-bank reserves that result from the import of gold; but, since the early 1950's, the loss of gold and contraction in member-bank reserves has required a general downward movement in percentage reserve requirements. However, in September, 1966, Congress made provisions in the law to permit the Board of Governors of the Federal Reserve System to raise the maximum required reserves for time and savings deposits to 10 percent (see Table 11–2).

In 1966, the Board of Governors increased reserve requirements for large time deposits ($5 million and over) in order to reduce the competition for savings between commercial banks and savings institutions. Savings and loan associations and savings banks invest most of their loanable funds in home mortgages, so the diversion of funds to commercial banks was handicapping the home mortgage market. This use of changes in reserve requirements as a "sector" tool of credit control has been criticized as being discriminatory. However, any monetary tool used to restrict bank credit tends to raise interest rates, and so has an adverse effect on the home mortgage industry. Hence the use of higher percentage reserve requirements for savings and other time deposits in commercial banks in order to make them less attractive to bankers tends to offset the discriminatory effects of a restrictive monetary policy (see Chapter 22).

Using changes in percentage reserve requirements to offset seasonal and cyclical changes in bank credit has been criticized as being an awkward and blunt instrument to affect the availability of member-bank reserves (changes do not affect the amount of reserves but do affect their availability). What actually follows a change in the required legal-reserve percentage depends on the reserve position of individual member banks. If reserve requirements are increased, the lending and investing practices of banks having ample reserves may not be affected, but other banks may have reserve deficiencies that may be corrected by borrowing at their Federal Reserve banks, selling assets, and/or not renewing loans of customers when they come due. Usually, when member-bank reserve requirements are increased, there is some increase in Federal Reserve credit, which is due either to borrowing from Federal Reserve banks by member banks or purchasing of government securities by the System to relieve some of the pressure on member banks.

It is difficult to predict the effects of changes in reserve requirements, but adjusting to such changes is usually more difficult for country banks than for large city banks that have developed the management of their money positions to a point where they make daily adjustments in their money-market holdings in keeping with their money positions. A secondary effect of changes in reserve requirements is that an increase tends to reduce earnings of member banks and to increase those of Federal Reserve banks; and, conversely, a decrease tends to increase earnings of member banks and to reduce those of Federal Reserve banks.

PROPOSALS FOR CHANGES IN RESERVES

The system of requiring reserves has been a part of American banking since 1837. It was lack of prudence on the part of some bankers that led to the system of requiring reserves, first to protect note holders and later owners of both bank notes and deposits. In recent years, various proposals have been made to change reserve requirements including those calling for uniform reserves, basing reserves required on the velocity of deposits, basing reserves on total or on earning assets instead of deposits, requiring secondary reserves, and requiring reserves of 100 percent on demand deposits (as in the 100 percent reserve plan).

The reduction in legal reserve ratios has increased the potential expansion of money and bank credit by commercial banks and has made the problem of control by the Federal Reserve System more difficult. This may be illustrated as follows:

Reserve Ratio	Reserve	Potential Expansion
100 percent	$1	$ 1
50 percent	1	2
25 percent	1	4
10 percent	1	10
5 percent	1	20

Uniform Reserves. If the Federal Reserve authorities are to regulate the supply of money and credit effectively, a more uniform and equitable legal-reserve structure is needed. The Board of Governors favors fixing reserve requirements on a graduated basis according to the amount of deposits in individual banks and then extending these reserve requirements to all banks whose deposits are insured by the Federal Deposit Insurance Corporation. For illustration, a bank could be required to hold a 7 percent reserve against the first $25 million in deposits, 7.5 percent against the second $25 million, and so on until the specified maximum is reached. It would not eliminate reserve changes that follow when funds are shifted from a country bank to a larger reserve city bank. Although a graduated reserve requirement would tend to penalize the largest and often the most efficient banks, it would be superior to the current classification according to location (as country and reserve city banks).

Probably the only way to achieve a fair and equitable reserve system would be for the Board of Governors of the Federal Reserve System, within limits set by Congress, to require commercial banks (1) to meet the same reserve requirement ratio irrespective of the amount of demand deposits held or the location of the bank, (2) to hold the same reserves for time deposits evidenced by negotiable certificates of deposit, and (3) to segregate the savings-deposit business from the commercial banking business.

It seems incongruous that Congress should require a bank to adhere to an increase in reserve requirements merely because it is a member of the Federal Reserve System while its chief competitor, a nonmember bank on the next corner, is not required to do so. This arrangement does not meet the American concept of fair play. (It is not surprising that many small banks are not members of the Federal Reserve System.)

Relating Reserves to Velocity of Deposits. In 1931, a Committee on Bank Reserves of the Federal Reserve System suggested a new approach to the problem of bank reserves and recommended that all deposits be treated alike for reserve purposes and that the activity of deposits as well as the volume of deposits of individual banks be the base for required reserves. The Committee adopted the principle that the "volume of bank credit needed to meet the legitimate needs of trade and industry depends on the rate at which credit is being used as well as on its aggregate amount. . . ." Therefore, it is necessary "that legal requirements differentiate in operation between highly active deposits and deposits of a less active character" (similar to the distinction between time and demand deposits).[4]

According to this proposal, banks located in the vicinity of

---

[4] *Member Bank Reserves: A Report of the Committee on Bank Reserves of the Federal Reserve System* (Washington, D.C.: U.S. Government Printing Office, 1931), p. 5.

Federal Reserve banks and their branches would keep four fifths of their required reserves in their Federal Reserve banks and the remainder as vault cash or on deposit with their Federal Reserve banks. Other banks would be required to keep two fifths of their required reserves in Federal Reserve banks and the remainder as vault cash or on deposit with Federal Reserve banks. The most novel aspect of this proposal is that member banks would keep not only required reserves equal to 5 percent of total net deposits, both demand and time, but also additional reserves equal to one half of the daily debits to deposit accounts. Thus, an inactive account would carry a reserve requirement of only 5 percent; and an active account, wherein withdrawals are current as shown by debit entries on the bank's books, would carry a reserve requirement for the period equal to one half of the withdrawals. In order to prevent this formula from imposing too great a burden on special types of deposits, it was further proposed that in no case would the required reserve be more than 15 percent of gross deposits. The most active accounts are those of government securities dealers, "money banks" in New York and Chicago, and other brokers and dealers in the money market.[5] The advocates of the plan expected that adoption of its provisions would be effective in checking unsound credit situations resulting from increased spending and would provide an automatic brake during crucial years, such as 1928 and 1929, when there was an unprecedented increase in the activity or turnover of bank deposits.

For member banks to report debits weekly or monthly would entail considerable time and effort which might necessitate a change to quarterly or semiannual reporting and computing of required reserve percentages.[6] Under the current system, the Federal Reserve System controls the volume of reserves held and the amount of reserves required; but adoption of a system based in part on deposit turnover would add another feature to the reserve control system.

---

[5] Neil Jacoby, "The Structure and Use of Variable Reserve Requirements," *Banking and Monetary Studies*, Deane Carson (ed.) (Homewood, Ill.: Richard D. Irwin, Inc., 1963), pp. 228–30.

[6] The most extreme fluctuations in single deposits are those of government-securities dealers whose deposit accounts are depleted and built up several times each business day, with the total checks written exceeding the total deposits at the beginning of the day. In New York the rate of turnover of accounts of dealers in U.S. government securities was estimated to be 938.7 times monthly, or 11,264.4 times per year. *Member Bank Reserve Requirements*, (Hearings before the Committee on Banking and Currency, U.S. Senate, 86th Cong., 1st sess. on S. 860 and S. 1120, March 23, and 24, 1959), p. 89.

Using Assets as a Base. Since minimum-reserve requirements are being used as a device of credit control, it has been suggested that assets, rather than deposits, be used to compute required reserve percentages. The adoption of this proposal would penalize those banks that lend the most freely, thereby adding to the supply of money and credit. Since most banking difficulties are traced to unwise or careless lending, the asset-reserve plan would tend to penalize such operations. If lower reserves were required of banks that have most of their funds invested in riskless assets, such as federal government securities, there would be a tendency for banks to favor this type of investment, but, if higher reserves were required when banks use funds to make loans wherein risks are great, the higher reserve required would tend to check such lending.

It was argued that, if reserve requirements were made high enough, banks would be forced to increase interest rates on loans to offset the higher costs of keeping reserves and that this would result in a loss of banks' loan customers to other lenders—insurance companies, savings institutions, and others not subject to this reserve requirement. As a consequence, banks would shift from lending to investing to avoid being required to keep other than conventional reserves, and the total money supply would not be affected.

Earning Assets as Reserves. Primary-reserve requirements necessitate keeping bank resources uninvested without providing much protection to depositors in case of bank failure. At various times, the U.S. banking system has had experience with reserve requirements that necessitated keeping earning assets in some designated form to protect creditors of banks (such as the collateral requirement for state bank-note circulation prior to the Civil War and national bank notes in circulation from 1862 to 1936). The Louisiana Banking Act of 1842 provided for 100 percent backing for notes and deposits, one third in specie and two thirds in short-term paper, thus combining the cash-reserve and earning-asset types of reserve requirements.

In recent years, some state laws have permitted state-chartered banks to use earning assets (generally, U.S. government and state and municipal obligations) as part of their reserves for both time and demand deposits (Colorado, Connecticut, Florida, Idaho, Massachusetts, Nebraska, Pennsylvania, South Dakota, Vermont, and Wisconsin); and other states have permitted the use of earnings assets only for time deposits (California, Georgia, Maryland, Michigan, and Ohio). It is now argued that deposit insurance protects small depositors and that large ones can take care of themselves; therefore, adoption of secondary-reserve requirements would be considered an instrument of monetary policy, not a protective measure for depositors.

Among the arguments in favor of a secondary-reserve requirement in the form of Treasury bills and other short-term government obligations are that it would save interest on the public debt, reduce fluctuations in the market price of government securities, and increase the Federal Reserve System's control over commercial banks' lending powers. From the viewpoint of monetary control, the last of these arguments is most significant because, if heavy reliance is to be placed on monetary control, the conditions under which it may be applied should permit control to be as effective as possible.

At the present time, it is common practice for commercial banks to reduce their holdings of government securities during periods of tight money so as to increase their loans to business and other borrowers. If the volume of such switching were to be reduced by a secondary-reserve requirement, banks would have to scrutinize applications for loans more carefully and reject or curtail those of marginal applicants. Although the money supply would not be changed, the rate at which it is spent would be affected.

The use of assets as reserves in place of money would improve banks' earnings and would give equal protection to depositors if the assets eligible to be held as reserves were limited to United States Treasury bills. Treasury bills are not only safe as money but are also earnings assets; and, under current money market conditions, they are almost as liquid as money.

Individual banks have the dual problem of remaining in a position to meet customers' deposit withdrawals and of keeping most of their funds invested in earning assets so that they may earn a profit for their owners. The answer to both parts of this problem lies in economizing on the holding of cash and depending on holdings of short-term credit instruments, the money market, and the Federal Reserve System for liquidity as well as earnings. So commercial banks are relying primarily on working reserves and short-term assets for liquidity and only to a minor degree, if at all, on cash reserves. Furthermore, in the past, central banks have been able to control the amount of money and credit, in the absence of legal-reserve requirements, by changing the amount of central bank money and credit. In today's highly sensitive money and credit economy, central banks would be able to control bank credit if legal-reserve requirements were eliminated.

The 100 Percent Reserve Proposal. The last proposal to be
considered in regard to changing the reserve requirement system is a
return to the original type of deposit banking wherein 100 percent
reserves were required. Under this system all banks would be required
to keep vault cash or deposits with Federal Reserve banks equal to 100
percent of their demand deposits.

The 100 percent reserve plan would provide a simple means of
bringing the supply of money under control of the monetary authorities. If deemed desirable by Congress, the plan could be extended one
step further by directing the Federal Reserve authorities to expand the
money supply by a given percentage each year, thereby eliminating
discretionary monetary management. While central bankers quote
freely, "Money will not manage itself," they never add, "neither will
it mismanage itself." It is dissatisfaction with the record of discretionary monetary management that accounts for the interest in the 100
percent reserve plan.[7]

If the 100 percent reserve plan were adopted, the transition from
fractional-reserve banking to 100 percent reserve banking could be
made by requiring banks holding checking accounts to shift additional assets to the Federal Reserve banks for deposit credit or
currency until reserves of commercial banks equaled their demand
deposits (reserve requirements for time and savings deposits would not
be affected).

Changes in the money supply would be brought about by open-
market operations of the Federal Reserve System. When government
securities are purchased by the System, the seller is given a Federal
Reserve bank check which is deposited in his bank—thereby increasing the seller's money supply and the bank's reserves by the same
amount when the check is paid. In case of a sale by the Federal
Reserve System, when the investor's check for the securities is collected, the drawer's account and that of his bank at the Federal
Reserve bank are debited—thereby decreasing both bank reserves and
the money supply.

Under the 100 percent reserve plan, if a check were cashed,
there would be a reduction in both the amount of checkbook money
and the amount of reserves, but the total amount of money in the
hands of the public would remain the same. Interchangeability of
money and deposit currency would be assured, and the solvency of

[7] Edward S. Shaw, "Money Supply and Stable Economic Growth," *United
States Monetary Policy* (New York: The American Assembly, Columbia University,
1958), pp. 49–71.

banks would be related to their lending of savings deposits and the honesty of bank officers and employees. The rules in regard to savings and time-deposit withdrawals would have to be made more stringent so that they could not be used as money. Banking habits of individual depositors would remain the same, but they would probably be subject to higher service charges.

The 100 percent reserve plan is primarily a monetary one, and the credit aspects thereof are essentially by-products. Grass-root changes in the money supply now depend on the reactions of thousands of banks' loan officers to the requests of customers for business, consumer, homeowner, and other loans and on the investments of these banks' officers in federal government, municipal, and other securities. Similarly, the quality of the money supply depends on how well these lenders and investors perform their economic functions.

The 100 percent reserve plan would enable the monetary authorities to separate the money needs from the credit needs of the nation. On one hand, the monetary authorities are subjected to the clamor for lower interest rates, easier credit terms, and a more abundant supply of loanable funds; and, on the other hand they are subjected to the demand for higher interest rates, a more restrictive credit policy, and a less abundant money supply to check inflation. This is a current problem, but it is also as old as fractional reserve banking.

For those who argue that shifting the problem of money creation to the Federal Reserve System would be no improvement, the advocates of the 100 percent reserve plan have an answer—to eliminate all discretionary control of money and to make the Federal Reserve banks responsible for carrying out a nondiscretionary policy as determined by Congress. For those who ask where loan funds are to come from, the answer is that they would come from the same place as today except that loans would be made with existing money and there would be no confusion between "credit" and "money" problems.

Commercial banks would obtain loanable funds by (1) selling stock, capital notes, and negotiable time certificates of deposit; (2) acquiring time and savings deposits; and (3) retaining earnings. In other words, they would acquire loanable funds in the same ways as do savings and loan associations, mutual savings banks, credit unions, pension funds, and other thrift institutions. Because bank lending would be reduced, commercial banks would experience a loss in income unless the Federal Reserve banks agreed to pay interest on their deposit or the federal government subsidized them in some way.

Either would be feasible because all excess earnings of the Federal Reserve banks, except dividends paid stockholders, are paid to the United States Treasury.

SUMMARY

In the United States, the monetary authorities use required reserves as an instrument for influencing the volume, availability, and cost of money and credit. The sources of bank reserves are Treasury currency outstanding, gold, and Federal Reserve credit. Member banks must compete with the general public, the United States Treasury, foreign central banks, and others for these reserve funds.

The Board of Governors of the Federal Reserve System has used its power to change member-bank reserve requirements to offset the inflationary and deflationary effects of changes in the gold stock; but, the Board's most important credit control device is controlling the volume of member-bank reserves through its open-market operations. The Federal Reserve System's credit control policies could be made more effective if all commercial banks were subject to the same reserve requirements. Among the various suggestions made for improving control of the reserve situations are (1) relating changes in reserve requirements to changes in the velocity of deposits, (2) using assets as a reserve basis, (3) using earnings assets as reserves, and (4) establishing the 100 percent reserve plan.

QUESTIONS AND PROBLEMS

1. Identify the factors supplying reserve funds. Which is the most important? Why? Which is the least predictable? Explain.
2. Identify the factors absorbing reserve funds. Which is the most important? Explain.
3. Distinguish between (*a*) "currency outstanding" and "currency in circulation," (*b*) "Excess reserves" and "free reserves," and (*c*) "primary" and "secondary" reserve requirements.
4. Explain: "While many banks find it advantageous to try to maintain reserves at the required level on a daily basis, daily reserve balancing is not required." (Federal Reserve Bank of Richmond, *Monthly Review*, September, 1966, p. 2.)
5. Discuss: "Such deposits in nonmember banks are part of the country's money supply just as are those in member banks, their exemption from Federally imposed reserve requirements cannot be justified." (*Fifty-Fourth Annual Report of the Board of Governors of the Federal Reserve System Covering Operations for the Year 1967* [Washington, D.C.: U. S. Government Printing Office, 1968], pp. 330–31.)
6. Analyze: "In the days of the National Bank Act and in the early

period covered by the Federal Reserve Act, it was believed that higher legal reserve requirements were necessary to assure that ample liquidity was maintained in banks which had volatile deposits, such as bank balances. In recent years no recognized monetary authority has contended that the provision of liquidity was the main function of required reserves." (*Member Bank Reserve Requirements*, [Hearings before the Committee on Banking and Currency U.S. Senate, 86th Cong., 1st sess. on S. 860 and S. 1120, March, 1959], p. 61.)

7. "Each banker must consider the cost of carrying . . . excess reserves. What is this cost? It is the revenues foregone by not holding earning assets." However, "there is the cost of carrying an insufficient amount of non-earning liquid assets." What is this cost? Discuss. (Federal Reserve Bank of Philadelphia, *Business Review*, April, 1967, p. 11.)

8. What would be the net change in member-bank reserves if the following changes took place? Federal Reserve banks' loans and advances increased $100 million; money in circulation increased $350 million; United States Treasury deposits with Federal Reserve banks increased $500 million; deposits with Federal Reserve banks other than those of the United States treasury and member banks increased $50 million; gold stock decreased $100 million; Federal Reserve "float" increased $200 million; vault cash increased $50 million; and investments of the Federal Reserve System increased $600 million.

9. Analyze: "Ideally, a legal reserve system should make legal reserve ratios proportional to the rate of deposit use." (Frank E. Norton and Neil H. Jacoby, *Bank Deposits and Legal Reserve Requirements* [Los Angeles: University of California Press, 1959], p. 116.)

10. Discuss: "We can scarcely hope for any great improvement of the American monetary system until it comes to be realized that chequing deposits are money, that their creation and destruction are matters of public concern, and that to avoid major monetary disturbances these deposits must be watched and regulated." Albert G. Hart, "The 'Chicago Plan' of Banking Reform," *Readings in Monetary Theory* [New York, the Blakiston Co., 1951], p. 456.)

CHAPTER 17

Evolution of Monetary Policy

FROM A narrow point of view, monetary policy consists of regulating the supply of money (currency and bank credit in the hands of the general public) by discretionary action of the Federal Reserve System and the United States Treasury to achieve the objectives of monetary policy. Emphasis is on the monetary standard, types of currency, commercial-bank deposits, international monetary relationships, and the tools and procedures used to regulate the supply of money and credit by the central banking system, the Federal Reserve System. From the viewpoint of presentation, this approach has much to recommend it, but it has the disadvantage of disregarding other governmental measures that affect private and public expenditures and prices by their effects on the velocity of money.

When considered from a broad point of view, monetary policy includes all measures taken by the government, the Federal Reserve System, and the Treasury to affect the amount, availability, and use of money and credit. In addition to the problems and procedures covered in the narrower concept of monetary policy, those involved in the broader concept include activities of financial intermediaries and the fiscal policies of the United States Treasury.

MONETARY POLICY AND THE GOLD STANDARD

During the early history of the United States, it was generally agreed that no monetary policy other than adherence to the principles of a commodity standard was needed. It was believed that an automatic regulator of the currency would result from maintaining convertibility of all currency into the standard unit. As long as money is composed of or is backed by one or more commodities, it retains some of the features of full-bodied or commodity currency. But, from the beginning, the American people undermined the use of gold and silver as money by using token coins, paper currency, and demand deposits as money.

In the United States, gold became the *de facto* standard in 1834, following the accidental overvaluation of gold at the Mint, and the legal standard in 1873 when Congress discontinued the free coinage of silver. However, Congress did not take any positive action to make gold the single standard until passage of the Gold Standard Act of 1900.

Insofar as possible, the gold standard was made self-regulatory. The federal government depended on private initiative to provide the gold used for standard coins (free coinage). Thus, the quantity of money depended largely on the flow of gold into and out of the monetary system. When token and credit money appeared, the issuers were forced to give them "gold-coin" qualities by keeping their value equal to gold. One of the first monetary management functions of the federal government was to limit the amount of token coins so as to insure their value; this was done by providing for their convertibility (in reasonable quantities) into standard money. The development of the commercial banking system, which added two types of means of payment, bank paper money and deposit currency, further complicated the problem of maintaining parity between gold and other forms of money.

The most direct way to assure the public that all types of money are "as good as gold" is to maintain convertibility, that is, to allow all types of money to be exchanged for gold on request. This necessitated holding large gold reserves; and, the larger these reserves, relative to other means of payment, the more goldlike was the currency. Thus the ratio of gold reserves to the total means of payment was used as the criterion for judging the soundness of the monetary system.

During the history of the gold-coin standard, the ratio between the gold stock and other means of payment decreased progressively, which meant that any decrease or increase in the gold stock tended to be magnified manyfold in the decrease or increase in the volume of circulating media. If the ratio was 1 to 2 ($1 billion in gold to $2 billion in other means of payment), a loss of gold would mean twice that amount of decrease in the volume of circulating media; but, when the ratio was 1 to 20, a loss of gold tended to cause 20 times the shrinkage in the circulating media. Although these hypothetical changes in the money supply did not follow automatically in exact proportion, they illustrate the growing instability of the theoretical automatic gold standard and the inevitability of replacing "automation" with monetary management. With increased management of note issue and later of deposit currency, the gold-coin standard became something very different from the automatic "regulator of the currency" which it had been considered to be when first adopted. However, monetary policy still required that all types of money be redeemable in gold, which was not possible when a mass demand for conversion occurred.

MONETARY THEORY AND THE BUSINESS CYCLE

During the formative period of the Federal Reserve System, economic theory left little room for monetary policy. In their long-run analysis of the economy, theorists concluded that the rate of interest is determined by the demand for and supply of real capital; therefore, interest-rate changes are largely independent of changes in the quantity of money. In the time-preference theory of interest, emphasis was on the preference for current goods over future goods, leaving no place for consideration of the effects of changes in the quantity of money on interest rates. This meant that the attention of monetary authorities was more or less confined to problems pertaining to the value of money.

As a result of the inflation that accompanied and followed World War I, some theorists recognized that changes in the quantity of money affected the interest rate, thereby opening the door to additional objectives of monetary policy. For illustration, Irving Fisher noted that changes in the quantity of money affect prices and therefore the market rate of interest. If the market rate is below the natural rate of interest (the rate which equates demand and supply of capital without price changes), businessmen will borrow; and, if the market rate is above the natural rate of interest, businessmen will refrain from borrowing. Hence, the Federal Reserve authorities, by increasing the supply of money, may depress the market rate below the natural rate to encourage businessmen to borrow.

During the upswing in the business cycle, the market rate of interest increases less rapidly than the natural rate. If the increase in the market rate is insufficient to compensate for the loss in the value of money due to higher prices, the natural and the market rates of interest will remain in disequilibrium. For illustration, if a borrower promises to pay 4 percent for a loan of $100, a year later he should repay $105.25 if the price level has increased by 1 percent. The natural rate of interest would be 5.25 percent (1 percent for loss of real value of the loan plus .25 percent for loss on the $4 interest payment).

If inflation is expected to continue, lenders are justified in expecting an increase in the market rate until the gap between the market and natural rates is closed. By following a "tight" money policy, central bankers may hasten the closure; and, by following an "easy" money policy, they may continue or even widen the gap between the natural and market rates of interest.

Fairly early in the history of commercial banking, some economists linked their operations with changes in business conditions known as the business cycle. Business cycles are cyclical fluctuations in business activity that occur at fairly regular intervals such as once in every 8 to 10 years. During the upswing in business there is an expansion in income, prices, costs, wages, profits, employment, and production that continues for four or five years. Then the expansion ceases and the downswing begins with a fall in income, prices, costs, wages, profits, employment, and production. This period is followed by one of leveling off, and then the upward movement begins again. Although these cycles seem to be inevitable, no two of them are exactly alike in duration or intensity.

From the Civil War to 1893, the business cycles were superimposed on a falling price trend during which each successive price peak was lower than the preceding one and each trough deeper than the last one. From 1893 to 1930, business cycles were superimposed on a rising price trend, and each price peak was higher than the preceding one and each trough was less deep than the preceding one.

The tendency was to treat the recession phase of the cycle as an interruption in the normal growth of business and an inevitable reaction to the previous excess in the use of bank credit. Therefore, the proper way to forestall a crisis is to prevent excessive expansion in credit.

Bankers, however, consider their role to be passive in the excessive expansion of credit because they are governed by the demands of businessmen and others for loans. Although an individual banker may feel that he should not make a loan, he knows that if he does not some other banker on the street will do so; and, if he is "out of step" with others, his bank will have an increase in reserve funds. If funds are kept idle, he may be "fired" by his bank's board of directors for not making more "sound" loans. In brief, the task of maintaining cyclical stability belongs to the central bank and the government rather than to the individual commercial banker.

When credit conditions are inflated, any new bank loan becomes a causal factor in the continued expansion of the economy. Unless checked by some outside force, the cycle continues until people become alarmed, make runs on banks demanding coins and currency in place of bank credit and thereby force banks to call loans. This leads to the liquidation of assets in a falling market and the situation becomes progressively worse until this phase of the business cycle has run its course. Most current theories of the business cycle recognize the importance of variations in the money supply as a factor in business fluctuations, but few consider it to be the only factor. If it were, the central bank's control of the business cycle would be complete and it would be in a position to eliminate all booms and recessions.

There is general agreement among orthodox economists that the recovery phase begins with an increase in investments, and this may be due to a number of factors including lower costs, lower interest rates, an abundant supply of loanable funds, improved outlook for profits, and increased spending for consumption. Increased spending for investment creates an increase in income which, in turn, results in increased spending for goods and services. The expanded demand for raw materials, equipment, factories, shops, and transportation facilities means growth in employment and spending and rising prices. However, before full employment is reached, the heavy industries may find that their capital resources have been overexpanded. Consequently, they curtail investment which will be followed by a decline in employment, production, income, and consumption and the beginning of the downswing in the business cycle.

The explanation for the fact that swings in business investment are greater than fluctuations in consumption is based on the acceleration principle, which states that a small change in the output of consumer goods industries may lead to accelerated changes in the capital goods industries. Thus a small increase (or decrease) in output of the former will tend to lead to a much larger increase (or decrease) in the latter.

BEGINNINGS OF CENTRAL-BANKING POLICY

When the Federal Reserve Act was passed in 1913, the members of Congress were still thinking in terms of the past and accepted the concepts of the gold standard and the commercial-banking theory. According to this theory (called the "real-bills doctrine" in England) the right amount of money would be supplied if banks would lend only to finance short-term needs of commerce and industry. In terms of the equation of exchange, there would be a temporary increase in M due to a short-term business loan which would be offset by an increase in T without any change in P. At the end of the conversion period (the time needed to convert cash into inventory, accounts receivable, and back to cash), the decrease in T would be offset by the decrease in M when the loan is repaid with no change in P.[1]

In passing the Federal Reserve Act, the monetary goals of Congress were to provide an elastic note-issue system by rediscounting commercial paper and to create a pool of member-bank reserves for use in emergencies. (It was not until later that the possibility of reserve creation by the Federal Reserve banks was recognized.) The outflow and inflow of gold was accepted as part of the workings of the international gold standard.

During the World War I period, the System's efforts were directed toward assisting the Treasury in financing the war. The Federal Reserve banks were operated by commercial bankers who, although not trained in central banking, were well equipped to head bond-selling drives.

Originally, the staffs of most of the Federal Reserve banks were small, but they were enlarged rapidly as the banks assumed more and more of the work of the Treasury. Under war conditions, it is not surprising that monetary policy was subordinated to fiscal policy. During World War I, commercial banks were discouraged from buying bonds as bank investments but were encouraged to make loans to their customers so that they could buy them. The Federal Reserve banks provided federal reserve credit to support the expansion in member-bank credit and to meet the demands for Federal Reserve notes. (In contrast, during World War II, government securities were sold to commercial banks, where they remained for some time as a basis for postwar bank credit.)

Following the close of World War I, there was almost continuous inflation which carried general prices 30 percent above the 1918 level. In exercising monetary policy, the Federal Reserve banks used the traditional device of raising rediscount rates. When gold losses occurred in 1919, discount rates were increased; but the Reserve banks continued to rediscount freely at the higher rates. Prices reached their peak in May, 1919 and then fell sharply (about 45 percent). As a result, economists and others stressed the importance of

---

[1] The main defect in the commercial-loan theory is that money value rather than fixed physical units serve as the basis of credit. When M is expanding, the money value of collateral is expanding and this means that the quantity of M can be increased in excess of the changes in *real* value of the collateral. Thus each round of bank credit expansion provides the basis for a second round of lending and money expansion. In addition, after being created money may enter into many transactions before being retired. So changes in M and T are not matched again until the loan is retired.

the stabilization of general prices, and many favored a congressional price stabilization directive to the Federal Reserve Board.[2]

The Federal Reserve banks kept the rediscount rate high for a year after the onset of the recession, which did not help businessmen, farmers, and others who were suffering from lower prices. The policy was designed to attract capital from abroad and to reverse the gold outflow; but the postwar environment was ill-adapted to free movements of gold in international trade.[3]

Although industry recovered quickly from the recession, the collapse in commodity and farm prices had a permanent effect on the farm sector of the economy. Production had expanded greatly to meet the worldwide food shortages brought on by the war; but, because it is difficult to curtail crop production, output exceeded the postwar demand. Consequently, agricultural prices fell more rapidly and farther than nonfarm prices and recovered more slowly or not at all.

Banks in agricultural sections held farm mortgages and other promises to pay that could not be collected; and as a result, many rural banks were closed because of insolvency. However, insolvency was not the only factor in the decline in the number of banks from 30,456 in 1921 to 23,679 in 1930. During this decade, improvements in transportation made it possible for the general public to be served by fewer banks, and a decline in the number of banks, especially in small communities, was inevitable.

An influx of gold following World War I permitted the System to shift its emphasis to economic goals rather than follow the traditional financial guides to central-banking policy, including the reserve ratio, the import or export of gold, and the differentials in interest rates among international markets. At least temporarily, the rules of the international gold standard were abandoned to the extent that little of the new gold was permitted to be used as a basis for credit

[2] The Strong Bill (named for Congressman James G. Strong of Kansas) would have added to paragraph (d), Section 14 of the Federal Reserve Act "and promoting a stable price level for commodities in general. All of the powers of the Federal Reserve System shall be used for promoting stability in the price level." *Stabilization* (Hearings before the Committee on Banking and Currency, House of Representatives, 69th Cong., 1st sess., on H.R. 7895 (Washington, D.C.: U.S. Government Printing Office, 1927), p. 1. See also *Stabilization*, Hearings on H.R. 7895, 70th Cong., 1st sess. (Washington, D.C.: U.S. Government Printing Office, 1929), p. 1.

[3] In November, 1919, the Federal Reserve Board authorized the Federal Reserve Bank of New York to suspend reserve requirements, and this privilege was used several times in 1920. Part of the New York bank's deficiencies were due to loans that it made to other Federal Reserve banks. The New York bank paid over $20,000 in penalties on its reserve deficiencies.

expansion. Emphasis was on stability at home—stable prices, business activity, and employment—and on assisting foreign central banks to achieve monetary reconstruction in order to bring about stability abroad.

In its annual report for 1923, the Federal Reserve Board recognized the use of open-market operations for the first time. It stated that, in "carrying out . . . policy the system has not relied upon changes in discount rates as the only means of influencing the general credit situation. The open-market transactions of the Federal reserve banks during 1923 . . . as well as their discount policy, have reflected Federal reserve credit policy. Furthermore, the experience of several of the reserve banks is demonstrating that change in discount rates need not be in all circumstances the main reliance or in any situation the exclusive reliance in making credit policy of reserve banks."[4]

The original objective of the Federal Reserve System's use of open-market operations was to make its discount-rate policy more effective. The use of open-market operations may have accounted for the fact that fewer changes were made in discount rates in 1923 than in any other year in the previous history of the System.

The comments of the Board of Governors on "guides to credit policy" were equally indicative of a new era in central banking. It noted, "It is to the reserve ratio that the public in most countries looks to get an indication of changes in the banking position and in the credit situation. This habit of looking at the reserve ratio as an indicator is particularly prevalent in the United States, because the United States is more than any other the country of legally regulated reserves."[5] The Board then discussed the reasons why the reserve ratio had lost its significance, which the Board traced to the abandonment of the gold standard in foreign countries, and recognized the need "to develop or devise other working bases." It rejected a policy of stabilizing general prices because no "credit system could undertake to perform the function of regulating credit by reference to prices without failing in the endeavor . . . [for] the interrelationship of prices and credit is too complex to admit of any simple statement, still less of a formula of invariable application."

The Board recognized that no "statistical mechanism alone, however carefully contrived, can furnish an adequate guide to credit administration." The Board then turned to the Federal Reserve Act

---

[4] *Tenth Annual Report of the Federal Reserve Board Covering Operations for the Year 1923* (Washington, D.C.: U.S. Government Printing Office, 1924), p. 3.

[5] *Ibid.*, pp. 29 ff.

and noted the congressional directives that the Reserve banks and the Board should use in the administration of the credit facilities of the Federal Reserve Banks. They were (1) "accommodating commerce and business," (2) providing credit for "agricultural, industrial or commercial purposes," and (3) denying credit for purposes of "carrying or trading in stocks, bonds, or other investment securities, except bonds and notes of the United States. . . ."

The Board also recognized the need for quantitative as well as qualitative guides and looked for guidance in "information concerning the state of industry and trade and . . . credit. . . . A proper and effective credit policy, considered in its broader aspects, must therefore, be based on that wide variety of economic facts which, when brought together, throw light on the changes taking place in the business situation and their relation to current banking and credit trends." In its treatment of guides to policy, the Board closed with the following prophetic statement: "It is the belief of the Board that out of the experience of the United States and other countries that are now endeavoring to adapt their banking systems to the changing conditions and needs of industry during this period of unprecedented disturbance, there may result a larger concept of the function of these banking systems and the development of a new and more competent basis of credit administration."

Although the Federal Reserve officials were not opposed to the idea of price stabilization, they took the position that stabilization should apply to all aspects of the economy. The Federal Reserve Board was not desirous of having any directive from Congress that would possibly set an unattainable goal, preferring to follow its own discretionary policy.

Although commodity prices declined during most of the 1920's, inflation developed in urban real estate markets and the stock market. During 1928 and 1929, when speculation in the stock market called for a tight-money policy, the international situation and other conditions called for easier money. Because the Federal Reserve System lacked the authority to establish margin requirements for loans on securities, it could only reduce the amount of credit used for speculation by limiting the total amount of bank credit.

The Federal Reserve Board used its open-market and discount "tools" to check speculation in securities; but, because it feared that business would be harmed by a too restrictive policy, it was ineffective in restraining credit expansion. The Board issued several warnings as to the effects of inflation but failed to obtain the general support of commercial bankers, including some who were directors of Federal Reserve banks.

The events that followed the stock market crash in the fall of 1929, after an uninterrupted rise over an eight-year period, provided the greatest peacetime test of the Federal Reserve System. From 1930 to 1933, the general policy of the System was one of credit ease, with the exception of September, 1931. During the 1920's, the Federal Reserve System had worked consistently for the return of European and other countries to the gold standard which had been largely achieved by the end of 1929. Unfortunately, the Bank of England was forced to suspend specie payments in September, 1931.

The international crisis originated in the failure of the Credit Anstalt in Austria and the departure of Germany and other countries from the gold standard. As a consequence, the United States lost $725 million in gold following the middle of September, 1931. It was during this period that the Federal Reserve banks increased their discount rates to protect gold reserves; and, although the gold drain stopped, the tightening of credit made a bad situation worse. Although the outflow of gold was resumed in 1932, credit policy continued to be one of ease expressed through the purchase of United States government securities in the open market and through the reduction of rates charged for discounts and for acceptances.

THE GREAT DEPRESSION

During the decade 1919 to 1929, the United States experienced one of the most rapid expansions in history, with investments almost doubling between 1919 and 1927. As is characteristic of trade cycles, investments flattened out in 1928 and declined in 1929. But past experience provided no precedent for the severity of the depression that followed. Among the most obvious reasons for its intensity was the general loss of confidence of the business community following the stock market crash and the collapse of the banking system. Less obvious was the fact that the decline in investments led to a much greater decline in consumption and in national income (adding to the existing surplus productive capacity and causing a further decline in investments). Beween 1929 and 1932, national income declined by one third and investments by three fourths.

The Federal Reserve banks were criticized for not providing more help to banks which were being suspended at a record rate because of insolvency or nonliquidity; but the restrictions on lending by the Federal Reserve banks handicapped their operations. First, the Reserve banks were required to meet the 100 percent collateral requirement in gold or eligible paper and the 40 percent gold reserve requirement for Federal Reserve notes. Second, member banks were required to use government securities or eligible paper as security for their promissory notes; and third, nonmember banks were not permitted to borrow from the Federal Reserve banks. In view of the fact that the panic of 1907 occurred at the peak of the business cycle when banks' loan portfolios were bulging with commercial paper, it seemed unthinkable that the next financial crisis would take place at the bottom of a depression when financially distressed banks were devoid of commercial paper.

In the Glass-Steagall Act of February 27, 1932, Congress belatedly permitted the Federal Reserve banks to use federal government obligations as collateral for Federal Reserve notes. Later, this provision, as well as the more liberal collateral requirements for member-bank loans, became a permanent part of the Federal Reserve Act. During the 1931–34 period, Congress aided business recovery by creation of many new financing institutions, including Federal Home Loan Banks, Federal Deposit Insurance Corporations, Commodity Credit Corporation, Home Owners' Loan Corporation, Federal Housing Administration, Federal National Mortgage Association, Federal Savings and Loan Insurance Corporation, and banks for cooperatives.

The popular explanation for the large number of bank failures was "excessive speculation." Therefore, Congress took steps to prevent its recurrence by passing the Securities Exchange Act of June, 1934, which gave the Federal Reserve Board the power to fix margin requirements (loan values) of securities bought and sold on national securities exchanges. In addition, laws were passed that provided for punishment of those who abuse their position of trust (such as bankers who borrow money from their banks to speculate in the bank's stock and "insiders" who take advantage of their positions to buy or sell stock of their own companies).

During the Great Depression, the use of discount policy as an instrument of monetary policy was discredited. Low interest rates did not stimulate business recovery; therefore attention was turned toward fiscal policy. The New Deal reversed many of the policies of preceding administrations and introduced polices such as compensatory spending and deficit financing which involved (1) spending large sums for public buildings, roads, and other forms of public works in order to increase employment, (2) operating with a deficit in the national budget, and (3) financing the federal government deficit by issuing short-term securities.

During the late 1930's, governmental policies reflected the influence of Keynes's book, *The General Theory of Employment, Interest, and Money*, which appeared in 1936.[6] Emphasis was on effective demand (spending), which originates in spending for consumption and investment. Although Keynes oversimplified the problem by omission of expenditures by governments and foreign investors, his treatment focused attention on the two main sources of current income.

An individual's consumption is determined primarily by his income; but, for different reasons, the average household saves part of its income. The amount saved may be large if the family income is large or small or nonexistent if family income is small. Furthermore, in the short run the proportion of one's income spent for consumption tends to decrease as one's income increases; and, the proportion of income spent on consumption tends to increase as one's income decreases. Hence the conclusion may be drawn that as a society becomes richer a smaller percentage of income will be spent for consumption and a larger percentage will be saved. Although this conclusion is valid for the short run, it may not be true for the long run due to many factors (such as changes in standard of living, reduction in the inequality of income between rich and poor, modern advertising, and new selling gimmicks). Consumption spending is a stabilizing feature of the business cycle because people will spend a smaller percentage of their income during the upswing in the business cycle and a larger percentage during the downswing.

According to Keynes, the amount of money spent on investment depends on the anticipated yield and the cost of borrowing the money needed to finance the investment (that is, the investment yield as compared to the rate of interest). If the monetary authorities increase the supply of money in order to reduce interest rates, it will tend to encourage investment. An increase in investment will stimulate expenditures, production, and national income. With an increase in national income, there will be an increase in savings and expenditures for capital goods and so recovery continues.

If the level of effective demand (expenditures) is not large enough to use all the resources of the economy, there will be idle labor and machines. In this case, it is the responsibility of central bankers to issue more money in order to lower interest rates and thereby stimulate investment by businessmen. At the same time, the government may contribute to raising the level of output and income by spending more for goods and services and/or taxing less. Jointly,

[6] John Maynard Keynes, *The General Theory of Employment, Interest, and Money* (New York: Harcourt, Brace, & Co., 1936).

central bankers and the government may achieve and maintain full employment. If there is an increase in effective demand when available economic resources are in use, the result will be higher prices; therefore, central bankers and the government will be required to modify their policies.

RECOVERY PERIOD

The Federal Reserve Board was reorganized in 1936 and, from then until 1941, its main contribution to recovery was providing member banks with reserves by open-market operations and keeping rediscount rates at record low figures. The "gold avalanche" from abroad that followed the devaluation of the gold dollar contributed to excess reserves of member banks and easy money conditions. The main change in Federal Reserve policy was the use of its new powers to change member-bank minimum reserve requirement. In three stages from August, 1936 to May, 1937, reserve requirements were doubled for demand and time deposits in all classes of banks. Unfortunately, a short but serious recession followed and the Board lowered reserve requirements by a small percentage in April, 1938.

Consumer and Real Estate Credit. In August, 1941, the president of the United States, under powers given to him in the Trading with the Enemy Act of October, 1917 (40 Stat. 415), authorized the Board of Governors of the Federal Reserve System, in an Executive order, to regulate consumer credit so as to maximize the use of national resources for war purposes. The Board required the grantors of consumer credit to obtain licenses which were not issued until the applicants agreed to conform to provisions in its Regulation W. In brief, Regulation W required large minimum down payments for purchases on credit and relatively short periods for maturities of promises to pay.

In 1946, Congress withdrew the authority of the Federal Reserve System to exercise control over consumer credit but reestablished it for one year at the height of the 1948 inflation and again in 1950 during the Korean War period. On the last occasion, the Board of Governors with the consent of the Housing and Home Finance Administration (see Chapter 22) was authorized to regulate real estate credit.

WARS AND MONETARY POLICY

Even before the sneak attack on Pearl Harbor in December, 1941, the United States was feeling the effects of defense spending.

Again, as during World War I, the full assistance of the Federal Reserve System was used in war financing. In order to raise funds, the Treasury resorted to both taxation and borrowing; and the Federal Reserve banks handled the distribution of savings bonds, special issues, and marketable securities. However the major contribution of the System was the creation of an environment wherein government securities could be sold at low interest rates throughout the war period. Although the proportion of expenditures covered by borrowing was less than during World War I, the federal debt increased from $40.3 billion in 1940 to $259 billion in 1946. About one third of this new federal debt was financed by commercial-bank credit, either by purchases of securities by banks for their own accounts or by loans extended to banks' customers to finance their purchases.[7] The Federal Reserve System provided the new reserves needed to support this expansion in commercial-bank credit and also the additional currency demanded by the general public.

During wars there is a tendency on the part of investors to postpone buying government securities because they expect higher interest rates on new issues and a decline in the prices of outstanding ones. This resistance to purchasing government securities which characterized financing during World War I was avoided during World War II by the Treasury's issuance of nonmarketable convertible savings bonds to be sold to individuals and by the Federal Reserve System's stabilization of prices of outstanding marketable government securities.

Among the measures taken by the Federal Reserve System to stabilize the government securities market were: (1) establishment of a preferential discount rate of one half of 1 percent on 15-day advances to member banks secured by short-term government securities, and (2) maintenance of a structure of interest rates at about the same levels that existed at the beginning of the war by purchasing government securities. In handling its own purchases of Treasury obligations, the Federal Reserve System adopted the policy of permitting member and nonmember banks to sell Treasury bills to the Federal Reserve banks at a discount rate of three eighths of 1 percent, and certificates of indebtedness at a discount rate of seven eighths of 1

[7] The deficits of the United States Treasury financed by banks were 30 percent during World War I, of which 18 percent was on their own accounts and 12 percent by loans to customers; during World War II, the deficits financed were 34 percent, of which 31 percent was on their own accounts and 3 percent by loans to customers. Marshall A. Robinson, "Federal Debt Management: Civil War, World War I, and World War II," *American Economic Review,* Vol. XLV, No. 2 (May, 1955), p. 398.

percent. Other securities were purchased in the open market in order to maintain the "pegged" rates. The pattern of interest rates agreed on by the Treasury and the Federal Reserve System ranged from three eighths of 1 percent on 90-day Treasury bills to 2.5 percent on bonds of longest maturities.

When the liquidity of government securities is guaranteed by the Federal Reserve System, there would seem to be little reason for investors to hesitate to buy long-term government bonds. However, many investors expected the stabilization policy to fail and others followed old habits of buying short-term securities. If this had not been the case, from the beginning, the entire burden of making a market for short-term obligations would have fallen on the System. As a matter of fact, before the end of the war, most of the United States Treasury bills had been acquired by the Federal Reserve System.

When the mechanics are considered, the purchase of all bills offered by the Federal Reserve banks had the advantage of placing credit in the hands of individual banks in need of reserves. While the traditional type of open-market operation increases the supply of Federal Reserve credit in use, it does not follow that the new bank reserves will be acquired by the banks that need them most for reserve purposes. The principles involved were the same as those entailed in purchasing bankers' acceptances, namely, establishment by Federal Reserve banks of uniform discount or buying rates with the initiative for selling left to commercial banks. The revolutionary nature of the war-financing measure was due to the volume of Federal Reserve credit that could be created (while bankers' acceptances outstanding amounted to millions of dollars, Treasury bills amounted to billions of dollars) and to the relatively high price paid for Treasury bills.

In financing the war, the United States Treasury tried to limit the amount of bank credit expansion by borrowing from nonbank investors. For illustration, after the first two Treasury issues, commercial banks were not permitted to subscribe for new issues and could not own them until the lapse of a specified period of time. However, insurance companies raised funds to purchase the Treasury issues by selling their old government bonds to banks. Consequently, the banking system acquired a considerable portion of the federal government debt. During the war, the effect of excess demand on prices was held in check by price control, rationing, and other measures that froze prices, wages, and other costs.

POST–WORLD WAR II MONETARY POLICIES

The Federal Reserve policy of stabilizing the price of government securities during World War II was a success (the average rate of interest on government securities actually declined as the war continued because of an increase in the relative importance of inter-mediate- and short-term obligations); however, serious postwar problems were created.

After the end of World War II the shift from war to peacetime financing was slow. With the removal of direct price control in 1946, the sharp increase in commodity prices disproved the assumption that deflation would be a problem after the war. The amount of the national debt had increased from $40 billion to over $280 billion, and most of the obligations representing this debt had been purchased at the low interest rates prevailing during the war. Since a sharp rise in interest rates would have meant a sharp fall in the market price of outstanding marketable issues, thereby threatening the solvency of commercial banks, it may not seem surprising that the Federal Reserve System continued the policy of maintaining relatively stable prices for government securities for some time. In effect, monetary policy was blocked by the practice of stabilizing prices of government securities. Stable prices are desirable in any market, provided that they are not due to monopolistic practices, but the price paid for stability in the government-securities market was more inflation.

The Federal Reserve System moved slowly in abandoning the special measures adopted to help in war financing, which it felt were no longer needed. In 1946, the System discontinued the one half of 1 percent discount rate on 15-day advances to member banks, raised margin requirements to 100 percent, and increased the rediscount on bankers' acceptances. The following year, the System dropped the three eighths of 1 percent buying rate on United States Treasury bills which had been in effect since 1942.

During the recession of 1949, banks and other lenders used cash from repaid loans to purchase government securities, and the Federal Reserve System took this occasion to make the announcement that it would acquire government securities "to meet the needs of commerce, business, and agriculture," with "primary regard to the general business and credit situation," and would continue "the policy of maintaining orderly conditions in the Government security market" so as to maintain "the confidence of investors in Government bonds."

Economic Policy and Inflation. One of the weaknesses of the declaration of economic policy found in the Employment Act of

1946[8] is that it contains no specific mention of a policy to prevent inflation. As a result, an interpretation of this statement as a directive might lead to the erroneous conclusion that the Federal Reserve System is to promote expansion of employment and production regardless of the means employed. When this directive was being formulated, it was predicted that there would be a decline in government expenditures with the end of the war, which would reduce the national income by some $50 billion and lead to the unemployment of from 10 to 15 million. The Federal Reserve Bank of Philadelphia was among the few that predicted that inflation would follow the war (which was like a voice crying in the wilderness).

Although the Employment Act of 1946 stresses expansionary policies, this does not mean that credit policies that lead to inflation, with its injurious effects on real income and on redistribution of wealth and income, are to be tolerated. If the long-run interpretation of the economic directive is accepted, the employment theory is in keeping with the traditional policy of central banking, that is, to provide stable prices at a high level of employment.

The Federal Reserve System and other agencies are jointly responsible for initiating and following policies that interpret the phrase "to foster and promote free competitive enterprise" and the "general welfare" to mean to foster and promote a free economy wherein the real income in the hands of the public is increased. The concept of a free economy is antithetical to that of a communistic, socialistic, or any other type of regimented state. When there is maximum employment (for "those able, willing, and seeking to work") and maximum production, then additional supplies of money income created by spending new bank credit would merely cause inflation and would not increase real income.

Conditions of maladjustment or distortion occur among and within different segments of the economy during inflationary periods. Industries selling goods and services that are fairly stable in price (railroads and utilities) are adversely affected. The relationships between costs and receipts and between income and expenditures are variously affected—some favorably and others unfavorably. Statements of net profits, after taxes, give a distorted picture of the situation because replacement costs of capital are greater as a result of higher prices. "General welfare" is not served by the redistribution of wealth and income that takes place among classes and individuals during rising prices. Commendable as direct price control, rationing, wage control, and allocations of scarce materials may seem, they are

[8] U.S.C. 1021, 60 Stat. 23.

hardly compatible with the directive "to foster and promote free competitive enterprise."

At work in the economy at any one time are a number of inflationary and deflationary factors that tend to increase or decrease the national income. Since any type of spending is inflationary and any type of nonspending is deflationary, and since there are millions of spending and/or nonspending units, how accurately can the future of business conditions be forecast? Behind each spending or non-spending decision of businessmen is the expectation of profits, and behind each individual consumer's decision are such factors as current and expected future needs, size of income, need for cash balances, and profitable outlets for savings.

Late in the summer of 1948 the President called Congress into special session to take action on bills proposed to check inflation. Authority was granted to raise member-bank reserve requirements and to reestablish the regulation of consumer credit. Between the summer of 1948 and the spring of 1949, while the temporary powers were being put into effect, the picture changed rapidly, and, with business and prices turning downward, the business situation warranted adoption of a policy of easy credit. So on June 30, 1949, emergency anti-inflationary measures were allowed to elapse and reserve requirements were reduced.

In 1950 inflationary pressures reappeared and the Korean War raised the possibility of new large-scale federal financing, but the United States Treasury made it clear that it would not agree to flexible interest rates on government bonds. So the Federal Reserve System agreed to support them at par temporarily, but not for long. The United States Treasury and the Federal Reserve System finally met on matters of policy and issued the so-called "Accord" of March 4, 1951. The agreement resulted in a long-term commitment by the Federal Reserve System to keep the long-term government-bond market orderly but to permit bond prices to seek their own levels and a number of short-term commitments by the System to support the market during refunding operations for the remainder of 1951. Thus, the Federal Reserve System regained its freedom to use all of its credit-control tools to stabilize general business conditions.

FLEXIBLE MONETARY POLICY

Rediscount policy was revived in 1951 after the United States Treasury and the Federal Reserve System agreed on policies pertaining to the support of the bond market for Treasury obligations. Since

1951, the discount rate has varied from a low of 2.5 percent to a recent high of 5.5 percent.

During the 1950's, the U.S. economy was characterized by two business cycles. The first reached a peak in July, 1953, and the downswing that followed continued until August, 1954. The next peak occurred in July, 1957, and the downswing that followed lasted until April, 1958. During the recession phases, the Federal Reserve System increased the volume of available member-bank reserves primarily by open-market operations and reductions in reserve requirements; and, during the "booms," the System decreased the volume of available member-bank reserves primarily by reducing its investments in Treasury bills. In other words, when the Federal Reserve authorities recognized a turning point in general business conditions, they reversed the direction of the System's policy so as to moderate the pace of advance during expansion and to stimulate it during contractions. Between the peak and the trough of a business cycle, the Federal Reserve System's policy is shifted from one direction to the other. For illustration, during the upswing the policy shifts to credit restraint and during the downswing to create ease, largely through the sale or purchase of Treasury bills.

The effects of Federal Reserve credit policy are felt first in the money market, next in the intermediate- and long-term securities markets, and eventually in the customer-loan markets. Although commercial banks depend on qualitative control or "loan screening" during tight money periods,[9] they are sensitive to the level of interest rates in the money market and regard any change therein as being indicative of present and anticipated business conditions. Changes in interest rates in the customer-loan market usually start with one of the leading New York banks, then spread to other large banks and eventually to all commercial banks. In addition to increasing the cost of borrowing, higher interest rates reduce the liquidity of the economy. The decrease in market value of fixed-income securities and the need to conserve cash tend to have a depressing effect on expenditures.[10]

Because financial institutions' assets are predominately in the form of credit instruments, higher interest rates would mean capital losses if they were sold in order to make new loans and investments; therefore, banks are in a "locked-in" position. This "locking-in" or

[9] See "Quarterly Survey of Changes in Bank Lending Practices," *Federal Reserve Bulletin*, April, 1968, pp. 362–67.

[10] A 4-percent, 15-year obligation will sell for $94.07 when the market rate is 4.5 percent and will drop to $89.53 if the market rate increases to 5 percent (see your bond tables).

freezing of investment portfolios tends to limit new bank lending and investing, but if institutional managers anticipate another increase in interest rates, they may switch their capital investments immediately in order to avoid a greater capital loss. Furthermore, commercial banks may find it advantageous to take capital losses for tax reasons as previously noted in Chapter 14.

Business borrowers are usually less concerned about increased interest costs than about the scarcity of loanable funds (although both usually occur at the same time); but high interest rates tend to be an effective deterrent to borrowing by homeowners and state and local governments. Being primarily lending institutions, commercial banks prefer to liquidate their investments rather than turn away applicants for loans. Hence, it is not surprising that the business cycle is accompanied by wide swings in interest rates, particularly on money-market instruments. During most of the 1960–65 period, the Federal Reserve System followed a general policy of credit ease to facilitate business growth; but, by the end of 1965, inflationary pressures brought about a policy of credit restraint (see Chapter 18).

SUMMARY

Monetary policy in its broadest sense includes all measures taken by the government, the Federal Reserve authorities, and the Treasury to affect the amount, availability, and use of money and credit. The Federal Reserve System, which has been delegated to manage and administer monetary policy, is expected to provide member-bank reserves and currency in amounts sufficient to promote long-run economic growth, to make adjustments to care for seasonal needs of the economy, and to iron out the fluctuations in the business cycle. In the last assignment, the Federal Reserve authorities must take actions that will offset those taken by the general public and the commercial banks that tend to have the effect of intensifying the boom and recession phases of the business cycle.

Prior to the 1920's, the Federal Reserve policy was one of promoting economic well-being by maintaining parity between gold and nongold dollars through raising or lowering the discount rate. In the 1920's, the System added open-market operations as a credit-control device and it became the most important instrument of credit policy. During the major depression of the 1930's, Congress provided for a flexible reserve system when it authorized the Board of Governors to change reserve requirements within certain statutory limits and introduced the qualitative type of control when it authorized the Board to set minimum collateral requirements for loans secured by securities.

During wars the long-run objectives of monetary policy must be put aside and other policies must be substituted to attain the immediate objectives desired. To attain these objectives, the Federal Reserve System becomes the servant of the United States Treasury in the expansion of credit and the sale of government obligations. As an aftermath of World War II, the economy was faced with the problems arising from the fact that a large amount of resources had been diverted to the war effort, one third of the new government debt was in the hands of the commercial-banking system, interest rates were abnormally low, and the volume of bank credit was at an inflationary level. It was the task of the Federal Reserve System to aid in correcting the situation with the least harm and loss to those involved, so that it could return to its normal function of administering monetary policy.

QUESTIONS AND PROBLEMS

1. Explain what is meant by "monetary policy." What was the monetary policy of the United States when it was on the gold standard?
2. Discuss: The preamble or long title of the Federal Reserve Act is "To provide for the establishment of Federal reserve banks, to furnish an elastic currency, to afford means of rediscounting commercial paper, to establish a more effective supervision of banking in the United States and for other purposes."
3. Analyze: On November 19, 1967 the Federal Reserve gave as the purpose of its current policy: "To assure the continuing orderly functioning of U.S. financial markets following the devaluation of the British pound, and to maintain the availability of reserves to the banking system on terms and conditions that would foster sustainable economic growth at home and a sound international position for the dollar." (*Fifty-Fourth Annual Report of the Board of Governors of the Federal Reserve System Covering Operations for the Year 1967* [Washington, D.C.: U.S. Government Printing Office, 1968], p. 23.)
4. Identify: (*a*) business cycle, (*b*) role of investments in the business cycle, (*c*) commercial-bank theory, (*d*) effective demand, (*e*) locked-in theory, and (*f*) flexible monetary policy.
5. Explain: "During the twenties, belief in the efficiency of monetary policy was high. In the thirties it dropped almost to zero. After the 'accord' in 1951 it was revived. More recently, it has declined again." (David P. Eastburn, "Where is the Fed Heading?" (Federal Reserve Bank of Philadelphia, *Business Review*, January, 1964, p. 4.)
6. Analyze: "In common with other nations whose energies were devoted primarily to winning the victory, the United States had no choice, under the exigencies of a global war, except to use monetary powers in furtherance of essential war financing and not as an 'anti-inflationary weapon.'" (*Thirty-Second Annual Report of the Board of*

*Governors of the Federal Reserve System Covering Operations for
the Year 1945* [Washington, D.C.: U.S. Government Printing Office,
1946], p. 1.)

7. Analyze: "During the early part of the year . . . inflationary pressures in the private sector of the economy continued and the extension of bank credit . . . proceeded at an unusually rapid rate." It
   became clear that "inflationary credit and monetary measures could
   not be made effective—in fact, that credit and monetary developments would tend to be inflationary—as long as Government securities
   were given 'money quality' by support of their prices." (*Thirty-
   Eighth Annual Report of the Board of Governors of the Federal
   Reserve System Covering Operations for the Year 1951* [Washington,
   D.C.: U.S. Government Printing Office, 1952], pp. 3–4.)

8. Distinguish between (*a*) "market" and "natural" rate of interest and
   (*b*) "monetary" and "credit" policy.

9. Discuss how a general tightening of credit and an increase in interest
   rates is expected to counteract inflation.

10. Discuss: "The desire to help build up a soundly based banking system
    and develop an active and independent monetary policy has continued
    to encourage the establishment of central banks. . . . During the last
    three years alone, fifteen such institutions have opened their doors."
    (Federal Reserve Bank of New York, *Monthly Review*, January,
    1967, p. 15.)

CHAPTER 18

Instruments of Monetary Control

THE FEDERAL RESERVE SYSTEM has at its disposal several instruments that may be used to influence the amount of member-bank reserves and how they are used. In addition to the traditional one, that of changing the discount rate, other devices of credit control include open-market operations, changing minimum percentage reserve requirements, placing ceilings on interest payments on savings and other time deposits, and moral suasion.

DISCOUNT POLICY

The oldest among the devices of credit control is that of increasing or decreasing the discount rate so as to make borrowing from the Federal Reserve banks more or less expensive. Discount-rate policy refers to changes in the rate of interest charged by the Federal Reserve banks on their short-term loans to member banks in order to influence conditions in the money market.

Discount Rate. The Federal Reserve banks' discount rates as posted cover discounts and advances to member banks and other borrowers. Customarily one rate is charged member banks on advances (loans) secured by government obligations and eligible paper and discounts of eligible paper, and a higher rate is charged on other secured advances. The rate known as *the* discount rate is the one applicable to discounts and advances to member banks secured by government obligations and/or eligible paper. Usually the highest rate posted is on advances (loans) to individuals, partnerships, and corporations other than member banks secured by direct obligations of the federal government. Each Federal Reserve bank usually changes its various rates at the same time, and some type of action is expected by them every 14 days. Any action taken is subject to "review and determination" by the Board of Governors, which makes the final decision. Obviously, varying the discount rate would be a much more "timely" tool if the power to use it were held solely by the Board of Governors.

379

Theory.   The theory of the discount rate as an instrument of monetary policy is that changes in the rate will make borrowing more or less expensive. When the discount rate is low and money is "cheap," an increase in borrowing is anticipated, an expansion in spending for goods and services is expected, and a rise in national income is foreseen. When the discount rate is raised and money becomes "dear," a decrease in borrowing, a contraction in spending, and a lowering of national income are expected to follow. However, if business is expanding and the outlook for profits is favorable, high interest rates may not deter businessmen from borrowing; and, when business is depressed and the outlook for profits is bleak, low interest rates may fail to induce businessmen to borrow. The psychological effect of changing discount rates may be more significant than the change in interest costs. When the discount rate is increased, businessmen usually expect a scarcity of loanable funds, a decline in sales, and a worsening of general business conditions. Conversely, when there is a decrease in discount rates, they expect an abundance of loanable funds, an increase in sales, and improvement in general business conditions.

The Federal Reserve System is committed to a policy of maintaining an "orderly" market for government securities; therefore, they may delay changing discount rates when doing so would have an adverse effect on the market. Because discount-rates changes are used in conjunction with other devices of credit control, the same policy of postponement may be followed in regard to these other devices until government financing has been accomplished. However, such delays are minor and represent no serious modification of the System's basic credit policy. As a matter of fact, the Federal Reserve System may fulfill its commitment to maintain an orderly market for government obligations through its open-market operations by changing its emphasis as to the type of securities traded. For illustration, it may add support to the marketing of a new 20-year bond issue by selling short-term securities from the System's portfolio and buying outstanding long-term bonds.

Flexibility.   The discount mechanism is well suited to supplying individual member banks with new reserves when there is a temporary or seasonal need for them. In contrast, open-market purchases of government securities by the Federal Reserve System increase the total Federal Reserve credit outstanding, and banks not in need of new federal funds may participate in the reserve expansion more fully than may those in need of them. During periods of financial stress, reserves can be supplied directly and efficiently to banks in difficulty, and, when they come to the Federal Reserve banks for loans, negotiations may be such as to promote the broader aspects of credit policy. In addition, the discount mechanism provides a device for "disciplining" member-bank borrowers (the same type of disciplinary action that other prospective borrowers must face). Borrowing at the Federal Reserve banks is a privilege, *not* a right, and it may be refused at any time if abused.

The discount mechanism is more flexible than are other methods of credit control because there may be differences in the rediscount or discount rates to member banks among the Federal Reserve banks. However, the mobility of funds may make maintenance of different discount rates among the Reserve banks impractical when there is an active demand for funds; banks in low-interest-rate districts may borrow through the federal funds market in order to lend in the high-interest-rate districts.

Simplicity. Changing discount rates is a simple and easily understood technique of making known the monetary authorities' views on the economic and credit situation. The danger in reducing discount rates is that it may have serious repercussions in business as well as financial circles. The expectation of a business depression will cause businessmen to adopt the policy of using up inventories to meet sales, making downward revisions on plans for capital spending, and reducing output. Even spending plans of consumers for automobiles and other durable goods and investments in homes will be modified or postponed. Thus, anticipated as well as actual effects of discount rate changes have considerable effect on market psychology. Sometimes a change in rates is discounted in advance, being viewed merely as bringing the discount rate in line with market rates (confirming past events); at other times the money market is caught by surprise, with considerable psychological effect (either bearish or bullish, depending on circumstances). Often commercial banks wait until a change in the discount rate is announced before changing their interest rates on customers' loans. In some cases, the escalator clause in term-loan agreements provides for an automatic change in the interest rate on term loans with changes in the Federal Reserve banks' discount rate on loans to member banks.

Tradition. While following a restrictive credit policy, the Federal Reserve authorities are aided by the tradition against member-bank borrowing. Before the existence of the Federal Reserve System, most commercial bankers considered it to be a sign of weakness to have the item "rediscounts and bills payable" appear on their bank statements. Such loans are secured and take precedence over claims of depositors and may be criticized by large depositors. So member banks are more willing to lend and invest when their indebtedness to the Reserve banks is small and less likely to do so when their indebtedness is large. Inasmuch as member banks are reluctant to remain in debt, reserves borrowed from their Federal Reserve banks are usually extinguished promptly when the need for them passes.

The tradition against borrowing has continued, but it is complicated by the fact that sensitiveness to indebtedness is not the same among different banks and is not the same among all banks during different phases of the business cycle. The aversion toward borrowing is greatest among New York banks that, because of their contacts with the money market, are in the best position to avoid all except very short-term indebtedness at their Reserve bank. Other city banks are second in their avoidance of borrowing, while country banks are least reluctant to borrow. Customarily, the interest rate charged by commercial banks is higher than the rediscount rate; this increases the temptation to rediscount or borrow.

Alternate Sources of Reserves.   Most banks are able to adjust their reserve positions by using the federal funds market, borrowing from other banks, or selling assets in the money and/or capital market; however, during periods of rising and strong loan demand, these sources of funds are unattractive because of higher interest rates and other increased costs. Although the correct solution would be for banks to reduce their loans because this would have the desired effect of reducing bank credit, most banks find this policy both difficult and distasteful when the demand for loans is great.

In 1965–66, many commercial banks were able to continue lending by attracting funds from savings depositors and reducing their investments in securities; however, in 1966, both of these sources became more expensive, the first because of increases in interest rates and in reserve requirements and the second because sales involved capital losses. Therefore, it was not surprising that banks increased their borrowings from the Federal Reserve banks. Even though member banks are less dependent on the discount window for reserves, the discount mechanism is still a useful tool of credit control that affects member banks' lending rates and pace of lending.

Proposed Changes.   The discount policy being only one item in the "package of instruments" that monetary authorities may use, it has been suggested that the central banking discount mechanism be used more frequently so that member banks may service the credit needs of their communities more completely. As noted in Chapter 15, banks would be given "basic borrowing privileges," "other adjustment credit," "seasonal borrowing privileges," and "emergency credit" for "unusual or exigent circumstances" to avoid financial disruption.

The significance and use made of discount policy as an instrument of monetary management varies from Australia, where there is no official or public discount rate (all loans are negotiated as to rates and terms)[1] to the United Kingdom, where the discount-rate-change mechanism is used to reduce or increase pressure on the market and to correct deficits or surpluses in the balance of international payments. A central bank is recognized universally as the "lender of last resort," and one of the proposed changes in Federal Reserve discount policy would permit Federal Reserve credit to be channeled through member banks to nonmember financial institutions having financial difficulties.

OPEN-MARKET OPERATIONS

The term open-market operations refers to the purchase and sale of securities in the open market by the central bank to influence the volume of member-bank reserves. If other things remain the same, the volume of member-bank reserves is increased by purchases of securities by the Federal Reserve System and decreased by sales of securities by the System.

Theory. In its open-market operations, the Federal Open Market Committee limits its trading to a relatively short list of securities, including federal government direct obligations and issues of government agencies, commercial bills or bankers' acceptances, and foreign drafts and bills of exchange. All money-market operations are initiated and executed by the Securities Department of the Federal Reserve Bank of New York (popularly known as the Trading Desk), which is responsible for managing the System's Open Market Account under instructions of the Federal Open Market Committee. Trading is with government securities dealers and other specialists in the market.

---

[1] Note: "The term 'discount rate' came to be used for the rate of interest charged by the central bank on its short-term loans to the trading [commercial] banks. But this rate was never published and it had none of the monetary policy functions of the Bank of England bank rate." H. W. Arndt and C. P. Harris, *The Australian Trading Banks* (3rd ed.; Melbourne, Australia: F. W. Cheshire, 1965), p. 195.

When purchases are made for the System, dealers are paid with Federal Reserve checks, which the recipients deposit in their commercial banks from where they are sent to the Federal Reserve bank. When the checks are collected, the dealers' deposit accounts are increased and the volume of Federal Reserve bank credit is expanded. In addition, the commercial banks will have gained reserves which they may use to retire outstanding debt, to lend to customers, and/or to invest in the money or capital market (thereby increasing the volume of money). When this new money is spent, there will be an increase in investments, output, and national income.

When sales are made by the Federal Reserve Bank of New York, the dealers remit checks drawn on commercial banks; and, when the checks are collected, there will be a decrease in the buyers' checking accounts and commercial banks' reserve balances. The banks will have to care for their reserve deficiencies by means such as borrowing from their Federal Reserve banks, calling loans, and reducing deposits. Therefore, there will be less money to spend; and, if other things remain the same, there will be a decline in investments, production, and national income.

Directives.   At each of its meetings, the Federal Open Market Committee takes any action deemed necessary to modify its directives to the Federal Reserve Bank of New York pertaining to open-market transactions in government securities and a second one covering operations in foreign currency operations. For illustration, on January 9, 1968, the directive affecting the System's account was in part:

In this situation, it is the policy of the Federal Open Market Committee to foster financial conditions conducive to resistance of inflationary pressures and progress toward reasonable equilibrium in the country's balance of payments.

To implement this policy, System open market operations until the next meeting of the Committee shall be conducted with a view to maintaining the somewhat firmer conditions that have developed in the money market in recent weeks, partly as a result of the increase in reserve requirements announced to become effective in mid-January,[2] provided, however, that operations shall be modified as needed to moderate any apparently significant deviations of bank credit from current expectations.[3]

---

[2] On January 11, 1968, reserve requirements against demand deposits in excess of $5 million were raised for (*a*) country banks from 12 percent to 12½ percent and (*b*) reserve city banks from 16½ percent to 17 percent.

[3] *Federal Reserve Bulletin*, April, 1968, p. 380.

"Bank Credit Proxy." The rate of growth of bank credit has always been of major concern to the Federal Reserve authorities. When business expansion seems too rapid, they strive to slow the rate of growth in commercial bank lending and investing; when business expansion seems too sluggish, they take steps to increase the rate of growth in bank lending and investing. Unfortunately, the System has been forced to base its day-to-day policy on information as to bank lending and investing which has not been sufficiently inclusive and timely. In their search for a better guide, the Federal Reserve authorities selected member-bank deposits subject to reserve requirements, including those of the government as well as those of private depositors.

The reasons for selecting member-bank deposits subject to reserve requirements, the so-called "bank credit proxy," include: (1) the close relationship between changes in the volume of deposits and in bank credit (earning assets), the conclusion being that what is happening to one is also happening to the other; and (2) current data as to member-bank deposits is available (large banks report deposit figures daily and other banks report their deposit figures weekly). The Federal Reserve officials, in using the bank credit proxy, find it desirable to make adjustments for seasonal variations caused by United States Treasury financing and other developments that affect member banks' balance sheets. These include: (1) shifts in the share of deposits held by member banks to or from nonmember banks, (2) changes in the ratio between deposits and nonearning assets (cash and fixed assets), and (3) the use of more capital funds (including debenture notes) to finance lending and investing.

Proviso Clause. In May, 1966, the Committee increased the effectiveness of open-market policy by giving the manager of the open-market account some discretion by inserting a "proviso" clause which permits open-market operations to be modified when correctives are needed. As a result, the timing of changes in open-market operations improved (much can happen during the three or four weeks between meetings of the Open Market Committee). For illustration, the May 10, 1966 directive stated the objectives of monetary policy as follows:

to resist inflationary pressures and to strengthen efforts to restore reasonable equilibrium in the country's balance of payments, by restricting the growth in the reserve base, bank credit, and the money supply.

To implement this policy, while taking into account the current

Treasury financing, System open market operations until the next meeting of the Committee shall be conducted with a view to attaining some further gradual reduction in net reserve availability, and *a greater reduction if growth in required reserves does not moderate substantially*.[4]

Orderly Market for Foreign Exchange. Foreign money, in the form of bank deposits, is traded in the foreign exchange markets of New York, Chicago, and other financial centers. Because of the fact that foreign exchange prices may fluctuate violently, the Federal Reserve Bank of New York (as agent for the United States Treasury) assists foreign central banks and treasuries to create a "first line of defense against disorderly speculation in foreign exchange markets." Since 1962, the Federal Open Market Committee in conjunction with the Treasury has had a program of open-market operations in foreign exchange administered by the Federal Reserve Bank of New York. Trading is usually in cable and sight exchange in both the domestic and foreign "spot" and "forward" markets in the major currencies of the free world (see Chapter 26).

The Federal Reserve System's currency directive for January 1, 1967 stated:

1. The Federal Open Market Committee authorizes and directs the Federal Reserve Bank of New York, for System Open Market Account, to the extent necessary to carry out the Committee's foreign currency directive.

A. To purchase and sell the following foreign currencies in the form of cable transfers through spot or forward transactions on open market at home and abroad, including transactions with the U.S. Stabilization Fund . . . , with foreign monetary authorities, and with the Bank for International Settlements Austrian schillings, Belgian francs, Canadian dollars, Pounds sterling, French francs, German marks, Italian lire, Japanese yen, Netherlands guilders, Swedish kronor, [and] Swiss francs.[5]

In other parts of the directive, the Open Market Committee authorized the Federal Reserve Bank of New York as its agent to hold the foreign currencies listed above in limited amounts to fulfill outstanding forward commitments, to exert an influence on the market and to meet special arrangements. The Open Market Committee directs the Federal Reserve Bank of New York to maintain reciprocal lines of credit (swap arrangements) with different foreign banks and

---

[4] *Fifty-Third Annual Report of the Board of Governors of the Federal Reserve System Covering Operations for the Year 1966* (Washington, D.C.: U.S. Government Printing Office, 1967), pp. 147–48. Italics added.

[5] *Fifty-Fourth Annual Report of the Board of Governors of the Federal Reserve System Covering Operations for the Year 1967* (Washington, D.C.: U.S. Government Printing Office, 1968), pp. 88–89.

the Bank for International Settlements, so that the System may borrow from them in case of need (by telephoning a "partner" country, the Fed may have foreign currency balances at its disposal in a foreign central bank within a few hours).

Daily transactions in foreign exchange may result from interest arbitrage that takes place because of differences in interest rates in domestic and foreign markets. For illustration, if the interest rate for a 60-day Treasury bill is 6 percent in London and 4 percent in New York, it may be profitable to invest in London. If a New York bank buys £100,000 cable at an exchange rate of $2.40 and purchases 6 percent Treasury bills, the bank will earn £1,000, or $2,400, on the transaction ($800 more than on a similar transaction at home under the conditions assumed).

Customarily, banks bring their funds home after they invest in foreign money markets. Therefore, when they transfer funds abroad they not only buy cable in the spot market but also sell sterling cable in the forward or futures market. If the rate is $2.395, the bank would receive $241,850 for a 60-day forward cable for $242,400 (principal plus interest). Hence the return on the transaction would be $1,850 as compared to $1,600 from the domestic investment. After deducting costs, interest abritrage under the above circumstances would be profitable, and funds would flow abroad.

The Open Market Committee may change the circumstances outlined above by selling cable exchange in the forward market or by buying cable in the spot market or both at the same time. This would result in increasing the spread between the cable rate of exchange for sterling in the spot and futures markets. For illustration, purchases and sales may have increased the spot rate to $240.05 and decreased the futures rate to $2.39. Now, the bank would have to invest $500 more in the transaction and would receive $3.33 more from the domestic investment (a total of $1,603.33). The sale would yield $512 less, reducing the gross return from the foreign transaction from $1,850 to $1,338. Without deducting costs, the international short-term investment would be unprofitable. Sometimes, the discount or premium on forward exchange favors London, and this must be measured against the interest rate differential (see Table 18–1).

The Open Market Committee may authorize the special manager in charge of foreign currency operations to acquire foreign currency up to a specified amount (such as the equivalent of $300 million for the pound sterling) and to make forward commitments to deliver foreign currency up to a specified amount (such as the equivalent of

TABLE 18–1

ARBITRAGE ON 91-DAY TREASURY BILLS

(Selected Dates)

Date	Treasury Bill Rates*		Spread in Favor of London	Premium (+) or Discount (−) on Forward Pound†	Net Incentive (Favor of London)
	U.K.	U.S.			
1967					
September 1........5.14		4.33	.81	− .80	+ .01
October 6..........5.33		4.47	.86	− .69	+ .17
November 3........5.73		4.56	1.17	−1.11	+ .06
December 1........7.33		4.93	2.40	−1.17	+1.23
1968					
January 3..........7.26		4.95	2.31	−2.50	− .19
February..........7.38		4.81	2.57	−2.59	− .02
March 1...........7.24		5.00	2.24	−3.09	− .85
March 14..........7.15		5.33	1.82	−8.75	−6.93
April 5............6.90		5.23	1.67	−4.83	−3.16
May 3.............6.94		5.44	1.50	−4.06	−2.56
June 7.............7.03		5.62	1.41	−6.10	−4.69
July 5.............7.03		5.35	1.68	−5.56	−3.88

* U.K. interest rates are Friday morning opening market-offer rates in London, and U.S. rates are for the latest 91-day issues of bills.

† The exchange rates per annum are computed on the basis of the midpoint quotations (between bid and offer) at 11 A.M. Friday in New York for both spot and forward pound sterling.

Source: *Federal Reserve Bulletin*, July, 1968, p. A–89.

$500 million Italian lire and other currencies up to $275 million each). In addition, the Federal Open Market Committee has made numerous "swaps" of dollars for foreign currencies under reciprocal credit arrangements (see Chapter 28).

Orderly Market for Government Securities. Within the debt limit set by Congress, the United States Treasury has the authority to sell United States securities. At the present time, the Treasury is offering new obligations once or twice each week and it is important that participants be assured that the market will not fluctuate widely from day-to-day and hour-to-hour (a responsibility assumed by the Federal Reserve System). Government securities dealers, the middlemen in the federal government securities market, absorb new issues each week and facilitate trading in outstanding issues. The major risk in their operations is a change in value of their inventories which are pledged as security for call loans (see Table 18–2). The dealers may obtain funds from Federal Reserve banks under repurchase agreements, so they are not forced to sell their securities in order to repay their call loans. Furthermore, the Open Market Committee may increase or decrease its purchases to prevent extreme price changes. In addition to open-market purchases, the Federal Reserve System may

TABLE 18–2

DEALERS' INVENTORIES AND SOURCE OF FUNDS
(In Millions of Dollars)

	Inventories		Source of Funds				
Period	U.S. Govern-ment*	U.S. Govern-ment Agencies	Commercial Banks		Corpora-tions†	All Others	Total
			N.Y. City	Others			
1967							
February.....$4,442		$467	$1,391	$1,331	$1,069	$740	$4,530
May......... 3,375		371	935	1,156	764	757	3,612
August....... 2,903		265	835	734	868	280	2,717
November.... 3,109		312	650	640	1,176	397	2,863
1968							
February..... 3,762		369	1,072	1,008	1,071	648	3,799
March........ 2,438		361	678	643	829	501	2,631
April........ 2,981		403	794	832	937	510	3,073
May......... 3,204		382	699	923	844	696	3,162

* Par value of securities, based on average daily figures for number of trading days in period. Includes all securities sold by dealers under repurchase contracts unless the contract is matched by a repurchase agreement or delayed delivery sale with the same maturity and involving the same amount of securities.
† All business corporations except banks and insurance companies.
Source: *Federal Reserve Bulletin*, April, 1968, p. A–38 and July, 1968, p. A–42.

also buy securities directly from the United States Treasury in an amount up to the maximum fixed by Congress (now, 1.5 billion).

Under different circumstances, the Federal Reserve System may want to "mop up" a sudden increase in member-bank reserves resulting from a temporary change, such as an unexpected increase in the float. This may be followed by a matched sale-purchase which is made through a technique known as a "go-around."[6] In a typical transaction, the Desk will contact government securities dealers by telephone and inform them that during the next 10 or 15 minutes it is selling a specific Treasury security (assume a 23-day Treasury bill) at a discount rate of 4.5 percent, which is the money-market rate at that time, under a matched sale-purchase contract. The dealers are requested (1) to bid for the bills at a rate of 4.5 percent and (2) to offer the same bills for delivery the next day at a discount rate to be selected by them in competition with other dealers. From this list, the Desk selects the successful bidder, whose rate may be 4.5 percent. The purchase price for each 1 million for 23-day bills will be $997,125, and the next day they are sold back to the Desk for $997,250 (giving a return of $125 for one day for each $1 million invested). The return

[6] Federal Reserve Bank of Cleveland, "Federal Reserve Operations: Matched Sale-Purchases," *Economic Review*, May, 1968, pp. 2 ff.

of $125 on a $997,125 investment is equivalent to an interest rate of 4.58 percent (125 ÷ 997,125 × 365 days = .0458).

Operation Twist. During the early 1960's the monetary authorities' two objectives were to keep the interest rate high so as to attract funds from abroad, thereby reducing the gold outflow, and to maintain low interest rates to encourage business investment, thereby increasing production and national income. These two conflicting objectives were realized by the so-called "operation twist."

In order to secure and maintain high short-term interest rates, the Federal Reserve System directed its open-market purchases away from the short-term market to the intermediate- and long-term markets for government securities. At the same time, the United States Treasury financed more heavily in the short-term market and less in the intermediate- and long-term markets. This increase in supply and decrease in demand had the desired effect—the price of 91-day Treasury bills fell from about 99.25 to 99, and increase in the annual discount rate from 3 percent to 4 percent. At the same time, the decrease in supply and increase in demand for intermediate- and long-term obligations increased their prices and reduced their yields.

Operation twist was continued until the new demand for funds in the United States and abroad raised interest rates to new postwar heights. Hence, the objectives of the Federal Reserve System's purchases of government securities may be threefold: to influence general or specific economic conditions, to stabilize prices of federal government securities, and to improve the U.S. international reserve position by increasing its short-term liabilities in order to reduce the outflow of gold.

OTHER INSTRUMENTS OF CREDIT POLICY

Being a flexible instrument of credit control, open-market operations would probably be adequate to care for any situation if accompanied by sufficiently vigorous fiscal policy (see Chapter 19). Other instruments of credit control include changes in (1) member-bank reserve requirements, (2) margin requirements, (3) interest-rate ceilings on savings and other time deposits, and (4) moral suasion.

Changes in Minimum Reserve Requirements. In theory, any change in member-banks' minimum reserve requirements will have the opposite effect on the volume of available member-bank reserves. Thus, if reserve requirements are increased, the banking system will have a reserve deficiency, which will necessitate calling loans and reducing deposits. (Individual banks may escape the reserve "squeeze" by maintaining excess reserves or by borrowing from their Federal Reserve banks.) When minimum percentage reserve requirements are increased, if other things remain the same, there will be a decline in the quantity of money, investments, production, and national income. On the other hand, a reduction in minimum percentage reserve requirements will tend to cause an increase in the volume of loanable funds, money, investment, production, and national income.

By 1966 conditions in the money market were becoming reminiscent of the 1927–29 period. Big corporations and other large depositors were shifting funds from checking accounts into negotiable time certificates of deposit to take advantage of the high interest rates paid thereon. Furthermore, savings institutions other than commercial banks which normally finance home buyers were experiencing difficulties in obtaining and keeping savings funds because of the high interest rates being paid by commercial banks, which were trying to meet the rapidly expanding loan demands of consumers and business firms.

The Federal Reserve System made the savings and other time deposit business less attractive to all except small banks by raising the minimum percentage reserve requirement from 4 to 5 percent and later to 6 percent for all savings and other time deposits in member banks in excess of $5 million. The Federal Reserve authorities were successful in directing a larger percentage of the savings into the home mortgage market and in curbing the inflationary expansion in commercial bank loans. Since the Fed uses several devices of credit control (the "package" approach), the inflationary movement of 1966 was brought under temporary control by use of all methods of credit control; but it was the first time that the device of differential minimum percentage reserve requirement was used to help one segment of the economy, the home building industry.[7]

In 1968, the differential minimum reserve requirement principle was applied to demand deposits in excess of $5 million when reserve requirements for these deposits were raised from 16.5 to 17 percent

[7] Sec. 19(j) Federal Reserve Act as amended states in part "The Board may prescribe different rate limitations for different classes of deposits, for deposits of different amounts or with different maturities or subject to different conditions regarding withdrawal or repayment, according to the nature or location of member banks or their depositors, or according to such other reasonable bases as the Board may deem desirable in the public interest." Exempt from these regulations are (1) deposits of American banks in foreign countries and (2) time deposits in the United States of foreign governments, foreign central banks, foreign monetary financial agencies, and international financial institutions of which the United States is a member. See Board of Governors of the Federal Reserve System, *Federal Reserve Act as Amended through November 5, 1966* (Washington, D.C., 1967), p. 69.

for reserve city banks and from 12 percent to 12.5 percent for other member banks. The old reserve requirements were still in effect for the first $5 million in demand deposits. These changes were applicable in varying degrees to all banks with demand deposits in excess of $5 million, of which there are over 2,000 banks that conduct 75 percent of the banking business of the United States.

In recent years, some banks have raised funds by the sale of promissory notes to investors. This method is more economical than selling negotiable certificates of deposit if interest rates are the same on the two credit instruments. In order to bring these promissory notes under control, the Board of Governors of the Federal Reserve System ruled that the funds involved were deposits. When the maturity dates were less than two years, they were made subject to the same reserve and interest ceiling regulations as other deposits.

Margin Requirements. In the United States securities are often purchased in part on credit provided by brokers and banks, which permits buyers to purchase more securities than they could with their own available funds. The minimum ownership interest that buyers must have at the time of purchase is called "margin." There are two types of margin requirements, the "initial" one and the "maintenance" requirement. When the price of the security purchased on margin falls, the purchaser may receive a "margin call" or notice to increase his equity. If he does not do so with cash or acceptable additional securities, the lender may sell enough of the borrower's securities to build up the owner's equity to the required percentage.

In order to prevent the excessive use of credit for speculation in securities, the Board of Governors of the Federal Reserve System was authorized in the Securities Exchange Act of 1934 "to prescribe the rules and regulations with respect to the amount of credit that could be initially extended and subsequently maintained" on equity securities registered on national securities exchanges and bonds convertible into listed stocks. The regulations of the Board cover credit transactions financed by dealers and brokers in both "purchase" and "short" sales transactions and by banks and others in purchase transactions.[8] (*Regulation T* applies to brokers and dealers, *Regulation U* to banks, and *Regulation G* to others—see Table 18–3.) The minimum down payment or margin is usually the same for each group and

---

[8] Congress is considering extending margin requirements to stock actively traded in the over-the-counter market so as to permit the Board to treat all lenders (brokers, banks, and others) more equitably in its regulation of credit used for speculation in securities.

TABLE 18-3

MARGIN REQUIREMENTS

(Percent of Market Value)

Regulation	Effective date								
	April 23, 1955	January 16, 1958	August 5, 1958	October 16, 1958	July 28, 1960	July 10, 1962	November 6, 1963	March 11, 1968	June 8, 1968
Regulation T:									
For credit extended by brokers and dealers on:									
Listed stocks	70	50	70	90	70	50	70	70	80
Listed bonds convertible into stocks	..	..	..	..	..	..	..	50	60
For short sales	70	50	70	90	70	50	70	70	80
Regulation U:									
For credit extended by banks on:									
Stocks	70	50	70	90	70	50	70	70	80
Bonds convertible into listed stocks	..	..	..	..	..	..	..	50	60
Regulation G:									
For credit extended by others than brokers and dealers and banks on:									
Listed stocks	..	..	..	..	..	..	..	70	80
Bonds convertible into listed stocks	..	..	..	..	..	..	..	50	60

Source: *Federal Reserve Bulletin,* July, 1968, p. A-10.

is now 80 percent for stock and 60 percent for bonds convertible into stock. The Board of Governors has no "maintenance" margin requirement but the different stock exchanges do. The stock exchanges and brokerage houses usually supplement initial margin requirements on low-priced stocks; and, under certain conditions, they prohibit members from advancing credit on other securities.

The regulation of credit used in speculating in securities is to prevent excessive use of credit for trading purposes, which many feel is tying up funds in nonproductive activities. In addition, it may have the secondary effect of reducing fluctuations in stock market prices. Speculative interest in equities is usually greatest when business is booming, and raising margin requirements is but one of the instruments of credit control at the disposal of the Board of Governors to use to check inflationary developments in that sector of the economy.

Interest-Rate Ceiling. In 1933, Congress prohibited the payment of interest on demand deposits and made the Board of Governors of the Federal Reserve System responsible for establishing maximum interest rates which member banks may pay on time and savings deposits. This legislation followed the banking disturbances of the early 1930's, which many in Congress blamed on excessive competition for deposits during the 1920's. Banks operate under the principle of decreasing per-unit costs; therefore, a loss of deposits reduces a bank's loan volume and also increases its unit costs. Whenever there is an expanding loan demand, banks compete actively in order to increase assets. This type of "cutthroat" competition increased expenses and necessitated making high-risk loans and investments in order to cover costs. It was this situation that Congress wanted to eliminate when it provided for regulation of interest payments on savings and other time deposits.

From 1936 through 1956, the maximum interest rates payable on banks' savings and other time deposits under Regulation Q remained unchanged. In January, 1957, the upward trend in interest rates set in and continued, with only cyclical downward movements to the present time. Ceilings on interest rates were increased so that commercial banks could compete with other financial institutions for funds (insurance companies, mutual investment companies, and others), but it was not anticipated that commercial banks would attract savings from savings banks and savings and loan associations and destroy the home mortgage market. Now, the Board faces the problem of reducing commercial banks' competitive advantage over other deposit-type financial institutions.

Following passage of enabling legislation in September, 1966, which permitted a more flexible policy in regard to fixing ceilings on interest rates (Regulation Q), the Board of Governors reduced the ceiling rate on time deposits of less than $100,000 from 5.5 percent to 5 percent, on deposits maturing in 90 days or more from 5.5 to 5 percent, and those having less than 90 days maturing from 5.5 to 4 percent (the same as the rate on savings deposits). But the rate on time deposits of $100,000 or more remained at 5.5 percent until 1968, when it was increased to 6.25 percent. Similar action was taken by the Federal Deposit Insurance Corporation and the Federal Home Loan Bank Board. This meant that the FDIC ceiling rate was applicable to all insured nonmember banks, including insured mutual savings banks, and the Federal Home Loan Bank Board rate was applicable to all savings and loan associations and savings banks that were members of the system, except the insured mutual savings banks.

Moral Suasion. The Federal Reserve authorities are in a position to influence credit conditions by appealing to commercial bankers to conform voluntarily to specific objectives. For illustration, in 1966, in letters sent by the Presidents of the Federal Reserve banks to member banks, a "qualitative" rather than "quantitative" credit policy was suggested. Loans to industry were to be restricted, but banks were to retain their investments with the help of the Federal Reserve banks if necessary. The Presidents' letter reads in part:

Further substantial adjustments through bank liquidation of municipal securities or other investments would add to pressures on financial markets. Hence, the System believes that a greater share of member bank adjustments should take the form of moderation in the rate of expansion of loans, and particularly business loans.

Accordingly, this objective will be kept in mind by the Federal Reserve Banks in their extensions of credit to member banks through the discount window. Member banks will be expected to cooperate in the System's efforts to hold down the rate of business loan expansion—apart from normal seasonal needs—and to use the discount facilities of the Reserve banks in a manner consistent with these efforts.[10]

The most significant part of the Presidents' letter was the offer of financial help to member banks in financing their securities holdings through the discount window. In effect, member banks were told to borrow from their Federal Reserve banks rather than to liquidate

---

[9] Public Law 89-597, Section 2(c), 89th Cong., H.R. 14026, September 21, 1966.

[10] *Fifty-Third Annual Report of the Board of Governors of the Federal Reserve System Covering Operations for the Year 1966* (Washington, D.C.: U.S. Government Printing Office, 1967), p. 103.

securities when in need of cash. This is in keeping with the "lender of last resort" theory of central banking. The market for municipal securities was having the same difficulties as the home mortgage market because banks had been "dumping" their municipals to make business loans. By December 27, 1966, the inflationary expansion in the economy had relaxed and the System shifted to an easier credit policy and rescinded the directives in the Presidents' letter because they were no longer applicable.

In the Financial Institutions Supervisory Act of 1966 (due to expire on June 30, 1972 unless renewed), the Board of Governors of the Federal Reserve System and other supervisory agencies were authorized to issue "cease and desist" orders not only in the case of illegal, unsafe, or unsound banking practices but also in cases wherein the agencies have "reasonable cause to believe that the bank is about to" engage in such practices.[11] A cease-and-desist order may be issued to a bank and/or its officers or directors.

The public relations activities of the members of the Board of Governors of the Federal Reserve System and the presidents and other officers of the Federal Reserve banks play a vital part in the functioning of the Federal Reserve System. Unlike the situation in the United Kingdom and other foreign countries where contact with a score of men is sufficient to place the views of central bankers before the banking industry, in the United States thousands of bankers must be contacted.

COORDINATION OF CREDIT-CONTROL INSTRUMENTS

Successful regulation of credit necessitates the use of a "package deal" policy, that is, the use of several devices of credit control at the same time. Within the framework of the Federal Reserve System, policy formation is centralized in the Federal Open Market Committee. It would be difficult to imagine intelligent men approving a more decentralized system of statutory control than that in effect at the present time: (1) The 12 Federal Reserve banks, with the approval of

[11] Section 8 of the Federal Deposit Insurance Act (12 U.S.C. 1818) was amended and subsections (b) through (n) were added. The first sentence of (b)(1) states that "If in the opinion of the appropriate Federal banking agency, any insured bank or bank which has insured deposits is engaging or has engaged, or the agency has reasonable cause to believe that the bank is about to violate a law, rule, or regulation, or any condition imposed in writing by the agency in connection with the granting of any application or other request by the bank, or any written agreement entered into with the agency, the agency may issue and serve upon the bank a notice of charges in respect thereof." This order may "require the bank and its directors, officers, employees, and agents to cease and desist from the same, and, further, to take affirmative action to correct the conditions resulting from any such violation or practice." Title II, Public Law 89–695, 89th Cong., S. 3158, October 16, 1966.

the Board of Governors, set discount rates; (2) the Open Market Committee is responsible for the investments of the System in open market paper; and (3) the Board of Governors determines (*a*) margin requirements, (*b*) member-bank reserve requirements, and (*c*) ceilings on interest payments on savings and other time deposits in member banks.

Coordination of policies does take place at the meetings of the Federal Open Market Committee. Perhaps better timing in decision making and improved administration of policies would follow if exclusive control of all instruments were given to one group such as the Federal Open Market Committee or the Board of Governors of the Federal Reserve System. Currently, the main obstacle to better coordination of monetary policy involves the United States Treasury. The absence of timely and adequate support by the Treasury may cause the Federal Reserve System to apply credit "brakes" so heavily as to barely avert a financial panic (as in 1966).

Although increased reliance is being placed on monetary tools to achieve economic stability, the results during 1966 (when monetary policy was one of record stringency) would seem to justify increased use of fiscal policy along with selective instruments of credit control. The tight-money policy had little effect on investments of large business firms as compared with the "shock" effect it had on the mortgage market.[12] Nonfinancial factors, such as sales outlook and net earnings, have greater influence on business corporations' investment outlays than do interest rates or the availability of bank loans.

In the spring of 1967 when the pace of business expansion slackened, the Federal Reserve System shifted to an easy-money policy. It lowered reserve requirements for savings deposits and the first $5 million of time deposits from 4.5 percent to 3 percent, and reduced the rediscount rate from 4.5 percent to 4 percent. However, this policy was reversed before the end of the year because costs and prices were rising, labor resources were under strain, and there were numerous indications that the economy was expanding at an inflationary pace.

In November, 1967 the rediscount rate was increased to 4.5 percent and in March and April, 1968, in two steps to 5.5 percent. The interest-rate ceiling on deposits of $100,000 or more was increased from 5.5 to 6.25 percent. Reserve requirements on net demand deposits in excess of $5 million were raised from 16.5 to 17 percent for

---

[12] Jean Crockett, Irwin Friend, and Henry Shavell, "The Impact of Monetary Stringency on Business Investment," *Survey of Current Business*, August, 1967, pp. 10 ff.

reserve city banks and from 12 to 12.5 percent for other banks. Member banks were required to hold a 3 percent reserve against savings deposits, time deposits open accounts, and other time deposits up to $5 million and a 6 percent reserve for such deposits in excess of $5 million. The international gold crisis had shaken confidence in the dollar, and Congress had delayed in taking positive action on the proposed surtax. Apparently, the Federal Reserve System was determined to defend the dollar at home and abroad with or without the help of fiscal policy.

SUMMARY

The instruments at the disposal of the Federal Reserve System for use in regulating member-bank reserves include changing (1) the discount rate to make Federal Reserve credit more or less expensive, (2) open-market operations, or the buying and selling of securities in the open market, to influence the volume of member-bank reserves, (3) percentage minimum reserve requirements to make the volume of member-bank reserves more or less available, (4) margin requirements to make speculation in securities more or less expensive, (5) ceilings on interest rates payable on savings and other time deposits so as to limit competition for deposits, and (6) moral suasion, or appeals to commercial bankers to accept practices designed to facilitate achievement of the goals of monetary policy.

Discount policy is effective when member banks must use the discount window and may be most effective when the Federal Reserve banks use their right to refuse banks' requests. Merely increasing the rate of interest will probably exert little influence on member banks. Open-market operations have been used to influence not only the general credit situation but also the market for foreign currencies and federal government securities. The administration of open-market policy has been improved by the inclusion of a "proviso clause" in instructions to the manager of the open-market account and by giving him a short-term guide to policy, called the "bank credit proxy." Other devices are being used more frequently as instruments of credit control, but the greatest need is for more cooperation between those responsible for fiscal policy and those responsible for monetary policy (see Chapter 19).

QUESTIONS AND PROBLEMS

1. How do central banks influence the money supply?
2. What effects may be expected from a change in the Federal Reserve banks' discount rate?

3. Explain: "The Federal Reserve System's most flexible tool for influencing monetary and credit expansion or contraction is its ability to alter member bank reserves by purchasing or selling Government securities." (Federal Reserve Bank of St. Louis, *Review*, May, 1967, p. 8).

4. Analyze: "Average borrowings from Reserve Banks fell substantially, reflecting both improved availability of reserves and a marked decline in the average level of excess reserves carried by the 'country' banks. Average net borrowed reserves of all member banks were $199 million . . . in July compared with $398 million in June." (Federal Reserve Bank of New York, *Monthly Review*, August, 1968, p. 159).

5. What are the mechanics involved in open-market operations? How do they differ from "repurchase agreement" transactions?

6. Identify: (*a*) margin requirements, (*b*) Regulations G, T, and U, and (*c*) moral suasion.

7. Illustrate how moral suasion "sometimes referred to less elegantly as 'jawbone' or 'open-mouth' policy . . . has played a role from time to time throughout Federal Reserve history." (David P. Eastburn, *The Federal Reserve on Record* [Philadelphia: Federal Reserve Bank of Philadelphia, 1965], p. 150.) Why is it more effective in the United Kingdom or Canada?

8. What were the effects of the following situation and how was it changed? The "Federal Reserve System raised the certificate of deposit rate to 5½ precent without anticipating that . . . many banks would adopt the certificate of deposit as a means of attracting 'ordinary' savings. The Federal Reserve was thinking in terms of million-dollar certificates of deposit issued to giant corporations and investors, but the banks responded by developing certificates in amounts as small as $20, . . ." (*Regulation of Maximum Rates of Interest Paid on Savings*, Hearings Before the Committee on Banking and Currency, U.S. Senate, 89th Cong., 2nd sess. on S 3687 and H.R. 14026, 1966, p. 54.)

9. How may credit policy be strengthened by changing the present system of required minimum reserves? Explain.

10. Discuss: "The policy of monetary restraint pursued by the Federal Reserve during most of 1966 was carried out through a wide variety of instruments—including open market operations, discount window administration, reserve requirements, and policy regarding maximum interest rates on time deposits." (*Fifty-Third Annual Report of the Board of Governors of the Federal Reserve System Covering Operations for the Year 1966* [Washington, D.C.: U.S. Government Printing Office, 1967], p. 25.)

CHAPTER 19

Fiscal Policy and Debt Management

FISCAL POLICY is a commonsense recognition of the fact that financial activities of the government have inflationary and deflationary effects on the economy and that such activities may be planned to facilitate economic stabilization. Most of the principles applicable to monetary and credit policy are also applicable to fiscal policy and debt management. The elements of fiscal policy include expenditures for investment and consumption and taxation both as to amount and incidence. The Secretary of the United States Treasury may influence the quantity of money, and therefore the economy, by the way he manages the existing debt. By changing the form of instruments in which the national debt appears, he may influence the amount held by commercial banks and therefore the amount of money.

BACKGROUND FOR FISCAL POLICY

Prior to the 1930's, it was generally assumed that the forces of depression were self-correcting, but the 1929–33 recession was so severe as to demand government action. However, the steps taken by the government were in the nature of expediencies or actions suitable to the ends in view; there was certainly no policy in the sense of a settled course of action. "Pump priming," as the term suggests, was no more than a temporary government expenditure that it was hoped would set in motion the normal forces of recovery; relief expenditures were to aid the unemployed; and loans to local governments, business firms, banks, and other financial institutions were also stopgap measures. It was out of this situation that the modern concept of fiscal policy developed—the need for action by the government to end unemployment and then to stabilize the economy at a high level of employment.

Compensatory Principle. Fiscal policy may be thought of as being similar in principle to central-bank policy—as an instrument to check booms or depressions by decreasing or increasing expenditures. During the downswing in the business cycle and during depressions, government spending will be increased, taxes will be lowered, debt retirement will be retarded or stopped, and new funds will be borrowed from commercial banks. During the boom phase of the business cycle, government spending will be decreased, taxes will be raised, debt retirement will be accelerated, and borrowing will be curtailed or stopped.

From a budgetary viewpoint, compensatory action is reflected in the size of the government's deficit or surplus. During the downswing in business, corrective measures will be reflected in an increase in the size of the deficit (or at least a reduction in the size of the surplus); during the upswing, corrective measures will be reflected in an increase in the size of the surplus (or at least a reduction in the size of the deficit). Unless a surplus is assumed, compensatory spending would be an expediency rather than a policy. The only exception would be in the case of a mature economy wherein a secular deficiency exists. If according to this stagnation theory, expenditures in the private sector are not adequate to assure full employment, the government must borrow and spend so that all of the potential capacity of the economy may be used.

A budgetary deficit may result from a decline in tax income or a rise in government expenditures or both; conversely, a budgetary surplus may result from a rise in tax income or a decline in government expenditures or both. A compensatory budgetary policy may stress either fluctuating tax income, which would reduce the danger of misspending, or fluctuating government spending, which would incease the danger of misspending. While the first would be easier to administer, the second would be more adaptable to financing certain basic social needs. In practice, both are involved in fiscal policy.

In brief, fiscal policy commits the government to compensate the economy for action which may or may not be taken by the private sector of the economy. During recessions, when business fails to provide labor with income, the government will provide income either by payments of unemployment insurance or creation of new jobs. Thus, when business spending declines, government spending increases; and when individuals do not borrow, the government does. By reducing taxes, the government leaves more income in the hands of the private sector; and by borrowing at commercial banks to finance more of its needs, the government adds to the money supply while the private sector is reducing the money supply by repaying loans at commercial banks. During boom periods, the government follows the opposite of these policies in order to counteract excessive private spending and borrowing.

When a deficit is being financed, the method of financing may be selected so as to maximize the expansionary effects on the money supply and to minimize the deflationary effects on consumer spending and production. Theorists urge that, during recessions, borrowing should be from commercial banks where new funds may be created. When the Treasury obtains new funds by borrowing from commercial banks (the Federal Reserve banks must provide new reserves), new money is forthcoming without reducing the volume of funds in the hands of consumers and producers. This would not only give the Treasury cash but also increase the money supply. Purchases of government securities by the Federal Reserve banks would have the same primary results and, in addition, would have secondary ones because of the expansion in the supply of member-bank reserves. Since funds would not be obtained from consumers and producers, spending by these groups would not be discouraged.

If the economy is in a business boom, new financing may be planned so as to appeal to consumers and institutional investors other than commercial banks, thereby absorbing savings in the hands of these groups. The interest rate, maturity, provisions for redemption, and the call feature would have to be planned to make the issue attractive. The problem is one of channeling purchasing power away from the private sector of the economy to the government without resulting in monetization of the debt.

If there is a governmental surplus, a net reduction in the federal debt is possible. In order to get the maximum monetary benefit when reducing the federal debt, the Treasury should concentrate on the short-end of the market when times are good; but, if a surplus should occur when times are bad, it should shift to the long-end.

Employment Act of 1946. The passage of the Employment Act of 1946 represents the culmination of the development of the philosophy concerning the role of the government in economic affairs. The statement of economic policy contained in this act, which is applicable to all agencies of the federal government, including the Federal Reserve authorities and Federal Reserve banks, is as follows:

> The Congress hereby declares that it is the continuing policy and responsibility of the Federal Government to use all practicable means consistent with its needs and obligations and other essential considerations of national policy, with the assistance and cooperation of industry, agriculture, labor, and State and local governments, to coordinate and utilize all its plans, functions, and resources for the purpose of creating and maintaining, in a manner calculated to foster and promote free competitve enterprise and the general welfare, conditions under which there will be afforded useful employment opportunities, including self-employment,

for those able, willing, and seeking to work, and to promote maximum employment, production, and purchasing power.[1]

FEDERAL BUDGETS

Prior to 1968, three separate budgets were used by the federal government: (1) the administrative budget, which constituted the basic planning document, (2) the consolidated cash budget, which measured the cash flow between the government and the rest of the economy, and (3) the national income budget, which included the federal government's receipts and expenditures in national income accounts to show how federal fiscal transactions affect the flow of income. Collectively, the three were referred to as the "budget document."

Administrative Budget. As the basic planning document of the federal government, the administrative document contained the proposed expenditures and taxes requiring congressional action. It was through this budget that the President submitted his program for the approaching fiscal year. It was developed by the Bureau of the Budget to coordinate the spending requests of various departments of the government and to unify the tax and other proposals for financing them. This was the budget submitted to Congress and the one most frequently referred to in tax hearings and the press. Receipts were accounted for on a collection basis and expenditures were considered to date from the time checks were issued (except for interest payments, which were on an accrual basis). Cash expenditures, not included in the budget, arose because (1) goods ordered the preceding year were not paid for, (2) "obligatory authority" appropriations of previous years had not expired, and (3) trust fund expenditures were excluded.

The administrative budget, presented to Congress for the first time in 1921, was approved as being superior to the previous uncoordinated system whereby Congress, rather than the President, initiated plans for expenditures and taxes. In the 1930's, Congress expanded the regular departments of the government, created new and independent agencies, and set up trust funds to finance different social security programs that were not under the administrative budget (such as unemployment benefits, social security, medicare, veterans' insurance, and many others). Trusts accept receipts from special taxes and make expenditures that must be considered in fiscal policy, because such

[1] U.S.C. S. 1021, 60 Stat. 23.

expenditures may constitute either stabilizing or destabilizing factors. When receipts and expenditures of the trust accounts and independent spending agencies were combined with those of the administrative budget, the result was the "cash consolidated budget" or simply, the "cash budget."

Cash Budget. The cash budget was an attempt to cover all expenditures and receipts from the public from all sources, including trust funds and independent lending agencies. It was helpful to the government in estimating its borrowing needs and therefore, the impact of federal government financing on the money and capital markets. In the cash budget, receipts were recorded as of the date of collection, and expenditures were accounted for as of the date checks were paid.

National Income Accounts Budget. The Department of Commerce prepared the national income accounts budget as part of national income accounting in order to relate the federal government sector to the consumer, business, state and local governments, and international sectors of national income and product accounts. The purpose was to measure the impact on the flow of current income of changes in the government's provisions for expenditures and in tax rates, as well as other expenditures continued under existing laws (including accounts of government-owned agencies as well as those of all government departments and trust funds). Transactions were recorded as additions to or subtractions from national income (see Chart 19–1).

New Unified Budget. In 1967, the President's Commission on Budget Concepts recommended that the administrative budget, consolidated cash budget, and national income accounts budget be replaced by a new unified budget called the "Budget of the United States."[2] These recommendations were used for the first time in the President's budget document sent to Congress for the fiscal year starting July 1, 1968 and ending June 30, 1969. The most important change made in the new administrative budget was to include expenditures and receipts of the trust funds, thereby increasing each by more than $30 billion.

The "Budget Summary" has four major subdivisions that start logically with appropriations, then continue through receipts, expenditures, and lending to the resulting deficit, the means of financing it

[2] *Report of the President's Commission on Budget Concepts* (Washington, D.C.: U.S. Government Printing Office, 1967).

CHART 19-1

RECEIPTS AND EXPENDITURES OF THE FEDERAL GOVERNMENT
(National Income Accounts)

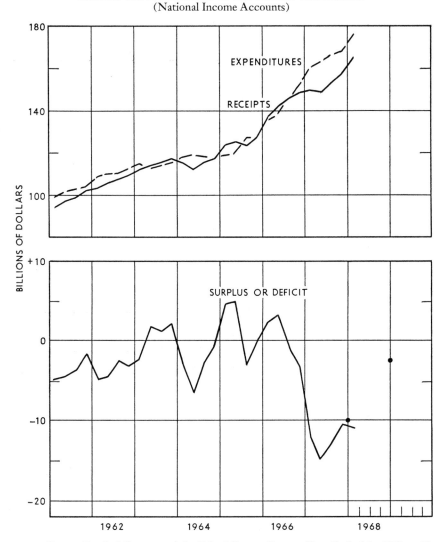

Source: Board of Governors of the Federal Reserve System, *Chart Book,* July, 1968, p. 36.

and how this financing affects the outstanding federal government debt. Quite properly, the new budget summary gives attention to both current requests for appropriations and those remaining from previous budgets, with comparisons for current and "latest actual years" (see Table 19-1).

TABLE 19–1

BUDGET SUMMARY

(In Billions of Dollars)

Description	1967 Actual	1968 Estimate	1969 Estimate
I. Budget authority:			
Requiring current action by Congress:			
Previously enacted..........................	$135.4	$125.1	$.....
Proposed in this budget......................	.....	3.3	$141.5
Becoming available without current action by			
Congress................................	58.7	69.9	73.1
Deductions for interfund and intragovernmental			
transactions and applicable receipts..........	−11.5	−11.8	−12.9
Total, budget authority................	$182.6	$186.5	$201.7
II. Receipts, expenditures, and net lending:			
Expenditure account:			
Receipts...................................	$149.6	$155.8	$178.1
Expenditures (excludes net lending)............	153.2	169.9	182.8
Expenditure deficit (−).....................	−3.6	−14.0	−4.7
Loan account:			
Loan disbursements........................	17.8	20.9	20.4
Loan repayments...........................	12.6	15.1	17.1
Net lending..........................	$ 5.2	$ 5.8	$ 3.3
Total budget:			
Receipts...................................	$149.6	$155.8	$178.1
Expenditures and net lending.................	158.4	175.6	186.1
Budget deficit (−)...................	$ −8.8	$ −19.8	$ −8.0
III. Budget financing:			
Borrowing from the public.....................	$ 3.6	$ 20.8	$ 8.0
Reduction of cash balances, etc.................	5.3	−1.0	*
Total, budget financing................	$ 8.8	$ 19.8	$ 8.0
IV. Outstanding debt, end of year:			
Gross amount outstanding.....................	$341.3	$370.0	$387.2
Held by the public...........................	269.2	290.0	298.0

* Less than $50 million.
Source: *The Budget of the United States Government, 1969* (Washington, D.C.: U.S. Government Printing Office, 1968), p. 51.

The budgets of the United Kingdom and many other foreign countries are usually accepted without legislative change, but this is not the case in the United States, where Congress may accept, modify, or reject any proposal in the President's budget that requires action by Congress. Actual spending has its origin in the appropriation process, and it is here that selections between alternate programs are made. In order to have a better understanding of the impact of actual spending on the economy, it is suggested that all federal government accounting be shifted entirely from a cash to an accrual basis[3] and that frequent reports be published showing cumulative totals of appropriations by fiscal years as they are approved by Congress, with the estimated effects of congressional action on national expenditures and resources. The size of the federal budget was increased by the inclusion of trust funds, but it was reduced by the exclusion of privately owned institutions (especially federal home loan banks and federal land banks described in Chapters 22 and 23). The budget of the District of Columbia is excluded—but not the federal subsidy— because it is something apart from the federal government.

The federal government acts as a banker in various capacities, the most important being a source of loans. Loans of the nonrecourse type, made by the Commodity Credit Corporation to farmers under the price support program, are not loans in the market sense; therefore, they are treated as expenditures. However, loans to foreign governments that could be made in the market are shown as "net lending," and the totals of lending and repayments are given separately.

Some independent government agencies, such as the Federal National Mortgage Association ("Fannie Mae") and the Export-Import Bank of Washington, have been using "participation certificates" to raise funds in the capital market. The new budget treats such sales as borrowing and the amount outstanding as part of the federal debt held by the public. The budget also distinguishes between the debt held by the public and that held by government agencies (the Federal Reserve System is treated as a part of the private sector of the economy).

Budget estimates are prepared months or years in advance; hence mistakes in expenditures and receipts may be sizable. Congress may add or subtract from estimates of receipts and expenditures and add new taxes and new expenditure items that do not appear in the President's budget.

---

[3] Accrual accounting—the system of allocating revenue and expense items on the basis of when the revenue is earned or the expense incurred—will give a more timely estimate of the effects on the economy of spending than the cash budget, because the economic impact is felt before cash is paid. For illustration, it takes years to meet the government's contract for airplanes that must meet Defense Department specifications; and, during the interim, resources are being used that affect national income, and accural accounting recognizes this impact (but not cash accounting). The use of accural accounting reduces the danger of confusing "cash flow" with "income."

GENERAL FUND

The General Fund includes the Treasury's operating balance, balances in other depositories, amounts in Federal Reserve banks in process of collection, unclassified collections, and silver, coins, and currency (see Table 19–2).

Treasury Operating Balance. Treasury cash recepits are customarily received in the form of checks drawn by taxpayers, investors in government securities, and others on personal checking accounts in commercial banks; and Treasury cash disbursements are customarily made with Treasury checks drawn on "the available funds in Federal Reserve banks." Checks drawn by disbursing officers on the Federal

TABLE 19–2

GENERAL FUND, MAY, 1968

(In Millions of Dollars)

Type of Assets	Amounts
Treasury operating balance:	
Available funds in Federal Reserve banks	$ 956
Tax-and-loan accounts in special depositories	4,225
Gold in Treasury fund	112
Total in operating balance	$(5,293)
Balances in other depositories	$ 101
Amounts in Federal Reserve banks in process of collection	214
Unclassified collections, etc	65
Silver, coin, and currency	833
Total assets	$ 6,506

Source: *Treasury Bulletin*, June, 1968, p. 14.

Reserve banks in payment for purchases of goods and services are deposited in commercial banks by the recipients, and the commercial banks, in turn, deposit them in their Federal Reserve banks to be credited to their reserve accounts.[4] As a result of the governmental expenditures, there will be an increase in member banks' deposits and reserve accounts and a decrease in the amount of cash in the Treasury's operating balance. After cancellation, the government checks are sent to the Treasury Department; where they are compared with the monthly record of the disbursing officers showing all checks written (the Bureau of Accounts in Washington records appropriations, cash balances, expenditures, liabilities, and receipts). Before the

[4] See Ernest Block, "The Treasury's Deposit Balances and the Banking System," *Essays in Money and Credit* (New York: Federal Reserve Bank of New York, 1964), pp. 19–24.

balance in the General Fund is depleted it is restored by transfers of funds from tax-and-loan accounts in thousands of commercial
banks.

The tax-and-loan accounts in commercial banks are essentially a
device whereby local banks are permitted to collect federal government taxes and receipts from sales of government securities and deposit them in these special accounts. Since payments for securities and
taxes are usually made by the customers of the collecting banks, the
payment procedure followed is to debit the payee's account for the
check and credit the tax-and-loan account of the government. No
funds leave the community immediately, and the bank's position is not
affected because both the payer's and payee's accounts are demand
accounts requiring the same percentage reserves. Title to billions of
dollars is shifted periodically from taxpayers to the government with
little or no effect on the money market where banking disturbances
are first indicated by changes in interest rates.

When deposits are transferred from member banks to the Federal Reserve banks, there is a loss of member-bank reserves, therefore
transfers are made gradually. For this purpose, banks are classified
into three groups according to the volume of their deposits or the
average amount of tax-and-loan accounts held. The Class A (small)
banks' tax-and-loan accounts are subject to having calls made on them
once or twice a month after prior notice of one week. The accounts in
Class B (medium-size) banks and in Class C (large) banks are subject
to the same call dates, with withdrawals made daily from Monday
through Friday after prior announcement of four to seven days by the
Treasury. In addition, large banks which are able to adjust their
reserve positions most easily in the money market are subject to
subsequent adjustments as to amounts on a particular date. For illustration, if the Monday call is for 10 percent of tax-and-loan accounts
in Class C banks with the withdrawal on Friday or Monday, the
Treasury may announce an increase or decrease on that day.[5]

About 85 percent of United States commercial banks hold
Treasury tax-and-loan accounts, of which over 10,000 are Class A,
about 1,500 Class B, and about 50 Class C banks. Tax-and-loan deposits are classified as demand deposits, on which no interest is paid; but
they must be secured by collateral kept with Federal Reserve banks

[5] If the Treasury has announced an increase or decrease and discovers later
that it does not need the extra amount or needs more, it has the right to change the
amount after the transfer has been made.

for this purpose (adjusted downward for the amount insured by FDIC).[6]

Gold in Treasury fund, the third item of the Treasury's *operating balance,* is gold held during the interim between purchase of gold bullion and issuance of gold certificates by the Treasury. Following devaluation of the gold dollar in 1934, "free gold" amounted to $2.8 billion, but since that time, this gold has been "monetized" by issuance of gold certificates to the Federal Reserve banks. Any increase in free gold tends to decrease Federal Reserve bank reserves and any decrease tends to increase them. When free gold increases, usually the next step is to increase the amount of funds transferred from the tax-and-loan accounts of member banks to the available-fund account in Federal Reserve banks. As a result, there is a decline in both gold certificates and member-bank reserves at the Reserve banks. When this policy is reversed, there is an increase in gold certificates and in the amount of member-bank reserves.

Other Assets in General Fund. In addition to the banks which hold tax-and-loan accounts, there are other "general depositories" that accept funds that must be transferred on the day received to Federal Reserve banks or branches. These depositories are compensated by earnings from time deposits kept with them by the Treasury in amounts commensurate with the services rendered by them. Similar time deposits are kept with other banks which provide government services, such as maintaining banking facilities on or near 400 military posts, handling state unemployment benefit payments, cashing government payroll checks, and furnishing cash requirements of government officials.

Other assets in the General Fund include cash items in process of collection held by Federal Reserve banks and other unclassified items.[7] In addition to other assets, which are credited to deposit accounts when collected, the Treasury's General Fund contains paper money and coins held pending release to Federal Reserve banks for distribution to the public through the banking system. When delivered, Treasury deposit accounts at the Federal Reserve banks are increased, and the size of this account is decreased.

Policy. The United States Treasury follows the policy of keep-

[6] The Subcommittee on Domestic Finance of the Committee on Banking and Currency is considering a bill that would require banks to pay interest on government deposits and to receive fees in payment for their services.

[7] Funds "in process of collection" are received by the Cash Division of the Treasury Department, while "unclassified" collections are deposited in the Treasury's accounts at Federal Reserve banks.

ing the account of the Treasurer (General Fund) low relative to total expenditures. However, the location of cash balances may be used as an instrument of fiscal policy, which is done by increasing the rate at which cash balances are shifted away from commercial banks during periods of business boom. This would tend to decrease the reserves of the banks and to have a dampening effect on inflationary lending. Conversely, keeping cash balances with commercial banks for a longer period during recessions would tend to increase their reserves and to have an expansionary effect on their lending and investing operations. Similarly, during inflationary periods, the Treasury may shift cash balances away from the Federal Reserve banks or refrain from depositing them, that is, keep them as Treasury cash holdings. During recessions, the Treasury may follow the opposite policies.

In effect, the United States Treasury, as well as the Federal Reserve System, has a mechanism whereby it may have its own open-market policy. Normally, the Treasury leaves the problem of adjusting member-bank reserves to the Federal Reserve System, but there have been times when the Treasury has come to the assistance of the System—as in December, 1936, when it put a plan into effect to sterilize gold imports (because of a recession, the policy was reversed the next year). The Treasury may not only affect the reserves of member banks by the location of its cash balance but may also affect the gold certificate reserves of the Federal Reserve banks by either using its gold as security for gold certificates or keeping it as "free" gold.

The United States gold stock that is inactive or "free" may be used in the future as a base for more gold certificates or for export purposes. Hence, the Treasury may influence the amount of reserve money by its gold policy. An interesting experience pertains to its windfall profits that resulted from the devaluation of the gold dollar in January, 1934. When the price of gold was increased from $20.67 per fine ounce to $35, it meant that the United States had a surplus of gold dollars over its gold-certificate and other reserve commitments. Part of this gold was made available to the Stabilization Fund, but most of it was kept as United States Treasury cash holdings. Subsequently, a small amount was monetized, and the money was used to finance lending under provisions of the Industrial Loan Act of 1934, and a part was used to retire United States bonds supporting national bank notes. However, most of the gold remained dormant in the Treasury until after World War II, when Congress directed the Secretary of the Treasury to use it to meet part of the United States government commitments to the International Monetary Fund and the International Bank for Reconstruction and Development (World Bank).

With the exception of the 1930's, little use has been made of the power of the United States Treasury to influence the gold-certificate reserves of the Federal Reserve banks. However, in 1953, the Treasury monetized free gold in its vaults in an amount of $500 million, and this was used to retire that amount of Treasury obligations held by the Federal Reserve banks in order to keep the national debt below the statutory debt limit.

TAX POLICY

Federal Government Cash Receipts. The chief sources of cash receipts of the government are income tax payments of individuals and corporations and payments for unemployment, social security, and excise taxes. In addition, there are minor sources including customs duties, estate and gift taxes, and receipts from numerous government enterprises such as the United States Post Office, Commodity Credit Corporation, Federal National Mortgage Association, Export-Import Bank of Washington, and Tennessee Valley Authority. Funds obtained from the sale of securities are not counted as receipts (see Table 19–3).

Most income taxes of individuals are withheld from wages and salaries and paid to the government monthly or weekly; and the remainder are paid under an estimated-tax payment plan with payments made quarterly (January, April, June, and September) and any tax liability, not previously withheld or met by estimated payments, is due April 15.

Countercyclical Tax Policy. A countercyclical tax policy provides for an increase in government receipts during business booms and a decline during recessions. The combined taxes levied by all governments in the United States, currently about $140 billion, may be either a valuable stabilizing factor or a disastrously destablizing one.

Of the current taxes levied by governments, assuming no change in tax rates, the one most countercyclical in its effects is the progressive personal income tax. With an increase in taxable personal income during business recovery, there is an increase in tax payments not only because the amount of taxable income is larger but also because a higher tax rate is applicable to the upper level of income. Conversely, with each decrease in taxable personal income during business reces-

TABLE 19–3

FEDERAL GOVERNMENT CASH RECEIPTS AND PAYMENTS, 1967

(In million of dollars)

Cash Receipts from the Public		Cash Payments to the Public	
Corporate income tax	$ 34,918	National Defense	$ 70,092
Individual income tax:		International affairs	4,650
Withheld	50,521	Space and research	5,423
Not withheld	18,850	Agriculture	4,377
Social insurance taxes	33,616	National resources	2,132
Estate and gift taxes	3,014	Commerce and transportation	7,446
Excise taxes	14,114	Housing and coml. development	2,285
Customs	1,972	Health, labor, and welfare	40,084
Interest and Repayments	1,805	Education	4,047
Refunds	9,581	Veterans	6,898
Others	362	Interest	10,280
Total	$149,591	General government	2,454
Deficit	$ 8,823	Total	$158,414
	$158,414		

Source of statistics: *Federal Reserve Bulletin,* July, 1968, p. A–39.

sions, there is a decrease in tax payments because of a decrease in both the amount of taxable income and the tax rate applicable. Generally, corporate income and other business, property, and other taxes are proportional taxes, and the receipts therefrom will rise with business recovery and decline with business recessions.

The tax system of the federal government acts as an automatic stabilizer because it depends so heavily on personal and corporate income taxes. Any decline in economic activity reduces income and therefore tax receipts, even if tax rates are not changed. Reductions in taxes cause more tax-free dollars to be left with individuals and corporations to cushion the effects of a recession. On the other hand, an increase in economic activity increases incomes and therefore taxes. With an increase in taxes, fewer tax-free dollars are left with individuals and corporations to "overheat" the business boom.

In seeking an effective and flexible economic stabilization policy, the proposal to give the President limited discretionary powers to adjust tax rates is the most significant. If the President could have increased tax rates in 1966, the record of the economy would have been less inflationary. When any suggestion is made for Congress to surrender any of its powers over taxation, the claim is that "it would not be constitutional." However, Congress has already set a precedent for transferring tax power to the President in the Reciprocal Trade Agreements Act of 1934 (subsequently tested and upheld as constitutional by the Supreme Court). In this act, Congress gave the President wide discretionary powers over custom duties, one of the oldest taxes in our national history.

The Revenue and Expenditure Control Act of 1968 provides for (1) a 10 percent surcharge on corporate and individual incomes, (2) a reduction in proposed federal expenditures for the fiscal year 1969, (3) an extension of excise taxes on telephone service and automobiles, and (4) an acceleration in the payment of corporate income taxes. Congress placed a ceiling of $180 billion on federal government expenditures ($6 billion below the amount projected in the budget). However, expenditures are expected to exceed $180 billion because four categories are exempt, including expenditures for the war in Vietnam, interest on the national debt, veterans' benefits, and benefits paid from social security trust funds.

Stable Budget Plan.   In administration of a tax program, just as in compensatory spending by the government, faulty practices may lead to destabilizing rather than stabilizing results. As an illustration, Congress may change the tax rate in the wrong direction—a reduction during a boom, when the government has a surplus, or an increase during a recession, when the government has a deficit. In order to prevent changes of this kind, it has been proposed that both individual and corporate taxes be fixed at rates that will balance the federal government budget when labor is just short of full employment, will provide a surplus when labor is fully employed, and will cause a deficit when there is a certain percentage of unemployment. But regardless of how the tax rate schedules are determined, the important features of this proposal are that tax rates would not be changed throughout the business cycle and that tax rates would be fixed high enough to balance the federal budget over the business cycle, with budgetary surpluses during good years to offset budgetary deficits during bad years.

Stimulating Private Investment.   Congress has not adopted the stable budget plan, but during the 1960's several steps were taken to stimulate production and consumption. In 1962, two changes were made to expand private investment—depreciation allowances were liberalized and a tax credit of 7 percent was given to buyers of new machinery and equipment (both measures were reversed in 1966).[8]

When any method of rapid depreciation is used, the cost of doing business is increased, and taxable income is decreased during

---

[8] Congress continued the tax credit for the first $15,000 outlay for machinery and equipment and retained one form of accelerated depreciation–150 percent of the declining-balance method.

the early years of the life of the depreciable assets. For illustration, under the straight-line method of depreciation, a machine which costs $10,000 with a useful life of five years and no salvage value, will be depreciated by $2,000 each year. On the other hand, if the sum-of-the-years-digits method is used $(5/15 + 4/15 + 3/15 + 2/15 + 1/15 = 1)$, the depreciation charge would be five fifteenths of $10,000 or $3,333.33 the first year, $2,666.67 the second year, $2,000 the third year, $1,333.33 the fourth year, and $666.67 the last year. Hence, the use of the sum-of-the-years-digits method as compared with the straight-line method of depreciation means expenses have increased and taxes have been less during the first and second years, but expenses were less and taxes more during the fourth and fifth years. The theory is that rapid depreciation will encourage early abandonment of old machines and equipment and their replacement with new and more efficient ones. As a result, investment and national income will increase, thereby increasing receipts from income taxes.

Stimulating Consumption. The Kennedy Administration was interested in stimulating both investment and consumption by reducing income taxes. With the nation struggling for years to attain full employment, more drastic measures were deemed necessary. President Kennedy's proposed reduction in personal and corporate income taxes was opposed by congressmen, with the support of a majority of voters. The general reaction to a tax cut was that it would stimulate price inflation and increase the federal government's budget deficit. Few realized that the chief causes of price inflation were cost-push factors rather than excessive governmental spending. Actually, the United States has had only four balanced administrative budgets since 1946 and less price inflation than most of the countries of the "free" world. After the assassination of President Kennedy and changes in the attitude of the public toward his policies, President Johnson succeeded in obtaining a reduction in income taxes in 1964 and in certain indirect taxes in 1965.

The Revenue Act of 1964 reduced personal income liabilities by one fifth in two stages and corporate income liabilities by one tenth (when added to the tax reduction of 1962, it amounted to about one fifth of their tax liabilities). As a result of these changes, total tax liabilities were reduced about $15 billion. According to the President's Council of Economic Advisers, the "effects of the tax reduction on private demand were clear and drastic. An upsurge in consumer spending indicated that most of the extra take-home pay resulting from tax reduction was being spent in the Nation's shops and markets. . . . The gains in income produced a huge rebound in Federal receipts, bringing the Federal sector into surplus in the first half of 1965."[9]

Theory of a Tax Rate Cut.   In 1963 and 1964 there was considerable discussion in and out of Congress on the theories behind the Revenue Act of 1964 that provided for reductions in individual and corporate income tax rates. Those who opposed the proposed cuts pointed to the large deficits already in the federal government budget at the time; while its proponents advanced the argument that tax reduction would stimulate production and consumption, increase national income, and would yield more tax income than before because of the increased base.

The theory behind the tax cut in the Revenue Act of 1964 is based on the "multiplier" and "acceleration" principles. The first relates to consumption and the second to investment. In earlier recessions, a reduction in taxes increased the amount of disposable personal income in the hands of taxpayers, and this is the objective of the 1964 tax rate reduction. Usually consumers spend from 92 to 94 percent of their disposable personal income, and therefore an increase in consumption is anticipated from a reduction in personal income taxes. The expectation is that business firms will use the additional receipts from increased consumer spending to pay wages, salaries, interest, and dividends to a second group of consumers which, in turn, will flow through expanding business channels to third, fourth, and other groups of consumers.

The expansion could go on indefinitely if, in each round, there were no "leakages" caused by repayment of debts and increases in personal savings, corporations' retained earnings, imports, and federal, state, and local taxes. The amount of leakage depends, in part, on the marginal propensity to consume. If one half of each new dollar of disposable personal income is spent during each round of expansion, expenditures will increase by 50, 25, 12.5, and 6.25 cents at successive rounds of expansion and will continue downward progressively, with total expansion totaling $2 for each new dollar of disposable personal income. The formula for computing this multiplier is

$$M = \frac{1}{1 - \dfrac{\Delta C}{\Delta Y}}$$

[9] *Economic Report of the President Transmitted to the Congress February, 1968, together with the Annual Report of the Council of Economic Advisers* (Washington, D.C.: U.S. Government Printing Office, 1968), p. 67.

in which M represents the multiplier, $\triangle C$ marginal propensity to consume, and $\triangle Y$ marginal income. Thus, if a 20 percent leakage is assumed, the multiplier would be 5 or the reciprocal of the leakage $(1.00/[1.00 - .80] = 1.00/.20 = 5)$. However, if 50 percent is a more reasonable assumption, the expected decrease of $9 or $10 billion in personal income taxes will increase national income by twice that amount. However, time is required for the multiplier to work itself out; so the full impact of a tax cut would not be felt in the current year.

At the same time that the multiplier is affecting consumption, the increase in spending may be having an even greater proportional effect on investment, because of the operation of the "acceleration" principle. Theoretically, capital expansion is based on the business practice of maintaining a fixed relationship between capital equipment

TABLE 19–4

ACCELERATION PRINCIPLE

Period	Desired Units of Production	Total Machines Needed	Replace-ment Demand	Machines Added	Total Demand for Machines
1	1,000,000	1,000	100	0	100
2	1,100,000	1,100	100	100	200
3	1,200,000	1,200	100	100	200
4	1,100,000	1,100	(100)	−100	0

and normal demand for products. Assuming that no industrial facilities are idle, managers of business firms will increase investments to maintain their capital to sales, or capital to output, ratio; provided they are convinced that the increase in demand is permanent (otherwise, there may be only a replacement demand). Of course, the expansion in investments by business firms results in an increase in consumption and additional rounds of expansion because of acceleration, which again pushes upward the total effect on consumption.

The acceleration principle may be illustrated by the hypothetical statistics presented as Table 19–4. If it is assumed that one machine is needed for each 10,000 units produced during each of five periods and that they are depreciated over 10 years, the total number of machines needed will increase by 100 for each 100,000 units of increased production, increasing the replacement demand by 100 in the second and third periods and thus accelerating by doubling the investment demand while consumption is increasing 10 percent. The same type of acceleration takes place in reverse with the decrease in the desired amount of output, decreasing during the fourth period when there is no need to replace obsolete machines or to buy new ones. The tax cut applies also to corporations, giving them additional funds to invest; therefore the effect of the multiplier principle on corporate expenditures as well as the effect of the acceleration principle must be considered in computing the total effect of the tax cut on the economy. In the practical world of business, it is difficult to anticipate the total combined effects of the multiplier and acceleration principles on national income, but it may be three or four times the original increase in disposable personal income, because of the tax cut.

Employment Taxes.   Some of the funds that flow into the Treasury are earmarked for special purposes, such as those collected to protect individuals and their families against income losses or disability. Separate trust accounts or insurance trust funds, created for these and other purposes, are administered under the new budget. Old-age and survivors' benefits are financed by taxes withheld from wages and salaries, excises imposed on employers, and tax levied on self-employed persons. Similarly, railroad retirement benefits are financed by levies on wages and salaries of those in the railroad industry plus an excise tax on employers. Unemployment insurance is a state program with standards set by the federal government and financed through a federal excise tax on employers. In addition, there is a federal program for railroad employees financed by levies on employers (linked to wages that are paid).

Trust Funds.   The largest of the trust funds is that created to provide old-age and survivors' benefits. The increase in the size of this fund has been due to the broadening of social security coverage, increased tax rates, raising the maximum earnings subject to tax (from $6,600 to $7,800 as of January 1, 1968), and expanded payrolls.[10] On the other hand, the increase in benefit payments has placed a drain on the fund and slowed down its growth. Among the other trust funds, that resulting from the federal-state unemployment system is second in size. This fund has increased at an average annual rate of about 4 percent, declining during recessions when drawn upon and increasing during periods of business expansion. Other trust and insurance funds include the two veterans' life insurance programs, the railroad and civil service retirement fund, medicare funds, the Indian tribal trust fund, the federal disability insurance fund, and the highway trust fund.

[10] As of January 1, 1969, the combined employee-employer contribution is to increase from 8.8 percent to 9.6 percent, one fourth of which is for hospital insurance.

Currently, government pension funds are not fully funded (that is, if contributions were discontinued, reserves would not cover all accrued benefit liabilities), and they are not on a pay-as-you-go basis (that is, benefits are not wholly paid out of current income). Being a mixture of both, the future size of these trust funds will depend on how future benefits are to be financed. If there were a shift toward "funding," it would mean increasing them, but if the shift were toward a pay-as-you-go basis, the size of the trust funds would increase less rapidly. Disbursements of some trust funds are counter-cyclical, such as unemployment payments, because they increase during recessions and decrease during periods of business expansion. Other trust fund payments may be managed so as to increase the amount during recessions and decrease it during periods of expansion. For illustration, dividend payments on veterans' life insurance policies have been distributed at times when it was most stimulating to business; and payments from the highway trust fund have been withheld during boom years (such as 1966).

GOVERNMENT SPENDING

In a modern economy government expenditures for goods and services account for a considerable percentage of the national income, currently about 20 percent. In addition to expenditures for goods and services, there are interest payments on public debt and transfer payments, which are important because they affect the size of disposable personal income. Government spending tends to stabilize national income when the amount that governments spend is increased during business recessions and decreased during booms. Generally, it is easy to initiate new government-spending projects during recessions, but it is difficult, if not impossible, to reduce or eliminate them during booms; therefore, experiences with curtailing government expenditures during a boom, as an element of fiscal policy, have been disappointing (as illustrated by events from 1966 to 1968).

Defense Spending. The chief factor in the increase in governmental expenditures has been spending for defense, and these outlays are of such a nature as to leave little room for cyclical flexibility. To reduce them during business booms, with the expectation of increasing them during the next recession, may be ineffective and dangerous; to increase them during recessions, with the expectation of reducing them during business booms, may be unsatisfactory if not impossible. For illustration, from mid-1965 to the end of 1967 defense purchases of goods and services increased by $22.5 billion, because of the war in Vietnam.

State and Local Governments.   Second in magnitude to defense spending are the expenditures of state and local governments for goods and services, including outlays for education, highways, streets, and a variety of other purposes (health, public safety, buildings, and capital for public utility companies). Some of these are financed with borrowed funds; therefore, they may be affected by monetary policy that encourages borrowing by creating easy-money conditions and discourages it by creating tight-money conditions. Although there is more cyclical flexibility in public expenditures of this type than in defense spending, the extent to which the construction of new school buildings, highways, streets, public housing, and other projects should be delayed because of a business boom and then constructed during a recession is debatable. If the need for them is urgent, postponing their construction would be unwise.

Transfer Payments.   The third major outlay of governments is for transfer payments, which are significant because they affect disposable personal income. Over the past 20 years, transfer payments have increased rapidly because of the expansion in various social security programs and the increase in the interest on the public debt. The social security programs include those for old-age and survivors' insurance (both government and private), unemployment insurance, and military personnel pensions. The expenditures are partly offset by receipts, such as contributions for social security, but the net amount of payments is still large. Among these transfer payments, the one which is countercyclical in nature is the unemployment insurance benefit. The amount spent by the government automatically increases during recessions and automatically decreases during business recoveries; hence, such items are known as "automatic" or "built-in" stabilizers. However, some of the transfer payments do not lend themselves to countercyclical adjustments, and, for those that do, there is no guarantee that they will be spent by the recipients. In the 18 months prior to January 1, 1968, old-age, survivors', disability, hospital and related insurance, and grants, interest, and subsidy payments increased by $7 billion. The inflationary effects of these changes were partly offset by an increase in old-age, survivors', disability, and hospital and related insurance payroll deductions and taxes of $5.5 billion.[11]

Other Policies.   In two areas of government expenditures that lend themselves to greater cyclical flexibility, namely, outlays for support of agricultural prices and foreign aid, political and other

[11] *Ibid.,* p. 67.

factors make countercyclical adjustments difficult or impossible. The rate of private spending for residential housing is sensitive to interest-rate changes; so, as a countercyclical adjustment, federal insurance of mortgage credit could be reduced or eliminated during boom periods. However, when the fixed interest rates on nonconventional home mortgages (those insured or guaranteed by a government agency) worked in that direction in recent years, Congress increased the maximum permissible rates that could be charged.

Those who favor government policies designed to promote private long-term capital investment argue for more liberal depreciation allowances and lower corporate income taxes to increase the amount of corporate earnings retained for investment. During recessions these concessions may be augmented by government contributions and tax credits to subsidize business firms that are expanding their investments in plants and equipment.

Timing. The effectiveness of any stabilization measure depends upon its timing. If action is taken soon enough, inflationary or deflationary developments will be checked before they set off the chain reaction known as the "spirals of inflation and deflation." Since there is more fear of deflation than of inflation (traced to the depression of the early 1930's and the slow recovery that followed), antideflationary rather than anti-inflationary measures have been stressed. Members of Congress and government officials are always subjected to group and individual pressure to spend from both outside and within the government. So it is easier to "go along" with an antideflationary policy than an anti-inflationary one. In short, it is "good politics." When major emphasis is on countercyclical spending policies by the government, the danger of misspending is great.

Spending for Investment. In approaching the problem of countercyclical spending, there seems to be a preference for spending for investment rather than for consumption. Perhaps this is short-sighted, because the elimination of idleness, disease, and squalor may be much more desirable than new roads, dams, buildings, and so on. The problem of timing most public expenditures to coincide with the need of promoting economic stability is difficult because the nature and purposes of most of such expenditures make them ill-adapted to prompt change. Some emergency expenditures may not be postponed until a recession develops (for instance, those for war and defense). On the other hand, certain public works plans may be kept "on the shelf" until a recession occurs, but, if public works are justifiable economically, even the wisdom of these postponements may be questioned. (For illustration, how much justification was there for post-poning construction of public schools and some veterans' emergency housing projects following World War II?)

Since the United States is a democracy, to what extent may the blueprints for the next depression be permitted to stand in the way of the construction of new roads, public buildings, harbors, and dams? Floods do not wait for depressions, and neither do democracies. If additional public works are to be planned as a countercyclical measure, there is danger that the spending aspects will be stressed, with little regard to the economic needs for such expenditures. Many public projects are of such a nature that months and years are required for completion, and the outlays for them may continue or even increase after the need for countercyclical spending has passed.

The use of public works as a device for stabilizing the economy, which seems attractive on paper, would be less flexible and would tend to be more wasteful than other devices. If the sphere of government enterprise were enlarged to include public ownership of railroads and public utilities (which would be socialism), the fields for public outlays would be broadened, and the stabilizing influence of overall government spending would be greater. If compensatory government spending were extended to include payments to all those who lose income during recessions (so that they would have a guaranteed annual income), greater stability in national income would result.

The main weakness in the use of fiscal policy stems from the difficulty in determining the correct changes to be made in expenditures and tax rates and the timing of such changes. For example, Congress delayed action on the proposed 10 percent surcharge on individual income taxes for over two years because the administration did not agree to reduce expenditures by $6 billion. This tax was needed as early as 1966 to reduce inflationary developments which were serious due to the increase in governmental demand on an economy whose resources were practically fully employed.

With the exception of the built-in or automatic budgetary stabilizers, increasing government expenditures to counter a recession is objected to because of the difficulty of increasing such expenditures wisely, timing them correctly, and administering them efficiently. Federal government budgets are based on 18-month economic forecasts (the fiscal year starts July 1, but the budget is submitted to Congress in January). If the forecast is inaccurate for any part of the period (and it usually is), the estimated income will be incorrect, and the tax and spending policies based thereon will be inadequate to foster economic growth and stabilization. Although tax and spending policies may be changed, it is difficult to time such changes promptly enough to prevent the government program from having a destabilizing impact on the economy.

Because the federal budget is prepared, presented, and processed in a political atmosphere, it is doubtful that a policy of compensatory spending, in amounts sufficient to eliminate cyclical loss of income, could be followed. More may be expected in the way of a successful anticyclical policy from taxes and debt management.

In using fiscal policy, it should be remembered that only one type of governmental expenditure increases national income, that is, expenditures for goods and services currently produced; however, others are important in that they increase the amount of disposable personal income and, like monetary policy, may have great influence on spending. Likewise, fiscal tax policies affect the amount of personal disposable income rather than the amount of national income. This principle should be kept in mind because it dominates current fiscal policy; but, irrespective of the immediate effects on national income, the budgetary consequences of a countercyclical policy are a deficit during business recessions and a surplus during business booms.

DEBT MANAGEMENT

For almost 150 years, the generally accepted debt management policy of the United States was to retire the national debt as rapidly as government revenues permitted. Alexander Hamilton persuaded Congress to assume not only the debt obligations issued by the previous national government but also those issued by state governments (many of which were incurred during the Revolutionary War). The new federal government bonds were issued for a definite period of time, thereby establishing the principle that only dated securities were to be offered to investors.

Thomas Jefferson believed in the "living generation" thesis of responsibility for retiring debts created by that generation, hence that all public debts should be retired in 20 years. Andrew Jackson considered public debt to be an evil, representing extravagant spending that was tolerable only in case of war. Debt in any form was a sign of weakness, and government debt was considered to be an economic burden that handicapped the economy. The assumption was that capital borrowed by the government was unproductive and interest thereon was paid to the wealthy out of the income of labor; therefore, repayment of the debt would return capital to productive uses and the burden on wage earners would be removed. Economic theorists supported the no public debt policy and there were relatively few dissenters until the theories of J. M. Keynes brought about a revolution in regard to the attitude toward national debt management. Now, the federal government debt is regarded as a permanent and indispensable part of the financial structure of the United States (see Table 19–5).

Debt-Burden Argument. The chief argument against the national debt is that it places a burden on the next generation which must pay more taxes because of the interest charges on the debt. This is true, but those who present this argument fail to note that this burden is offset by the interest received on the debt. These interest payments are transfers of cash from those who pay taxes to those who receive interest, and so long as all of the debt is domestically held, there is no loss to the nation. However, if any part of the debt is held in foreign countries, resources would be transferred abroad to meet interest obligations.

The statement that interest payments (to domestic holders) on the federal government debt do not represent loss of resources to the country does not mean that such payments may not be harmful. For illustration, the existence of debt may prevent the federal government from embarking on some beneficial projects. Furthermore, it is possible that one's tax bill may be so large as to discourage business ventures (there is little evidence that this is the case) and to destroy the incentive to save. Those who inherit government securities may, on the assumption that they are rich, make no contribution to the economy. However, if there is a decline in savings and in productive activity, the economy becomes more vulnerable to inflationary pressures.

The argument that national debt diverts capital (savings) from productive to nonproductive uses is challenged on two counts. First, an increase in public debt is often matched by an increase in fixed assets—highways, bridges, dams, buildings, machines, and equipment. Second, an increase in the national debt may be justified because of its effects on output, employment, and national income, and therefore on savings. However the argument that the national debt diverts savings from productive to nonproductive use is directed at the creation of debt rather than at its existence.

Form of the Debt. Without any change in the total national debt, the United States Treasury may influence the economy by

TABLE 19-5

NATIONAL DEBT BY TYPES OF SECURITIES FOR SELECTED YEARS
(In Billions of Dollars)

End of Year	Total (Gross)*	Public Issues†										Special Issues‖
		Total	Marketable*						Nonmarketable			
			Total	Bills	Certificates	Notes	Bonds‡	Convertible Bonds§	Total	Savings Bonds and Notes		
1941	$ 64.3	$ 50.5	$ 41.6	$ 2.0	...	$ 6.0	$ 33.6	...	$ 8.9	$ 6.1		$ 7.0
1945	278.7	255.7	198.8	17.0	$38.2	23.0	120.6	...	56.9	48.2		20.0
1960	290.4	242.5	189.0	39.4	18.4	51.3	79.8	$5.7	47.8	47.2		44.3
1965	321.4	270.3	214.6	60.2	...	50.2	104.2	2.8	52.9	50.3		46.3
1967	345.2	284.0	226.5	69.9	...	61.4	95.3	2.6	54.9	51.7		57.2

* Includes noninterest-bearing debts and guaranteed securities not shown elsewhere.
† Includes amounts held by U.S. government agencies and trust funds.
‡ Includes Treasury bonds and minor amounts of Panama Canal and postal savings bonds.
§ Includes depository bonds, retirement-plan bonds, foreign currency series, foreign issues and Armed forces leave bonds issued before 1954, tax and savings bonds issued before 1956, and Series A investment bonds issued before October, 1965.
‖ Held only by U.S. agencies and trust funds.
Source: *Federal Reserve Bulletin*, July, 1968, p. A-40.

changing the maturities of the securities in the debt structure. Opportunities to do so arise when existing securities reach maturity and when new ones are to be issued. Each week the federal government has millions of dollars in Treasury bills coming due, and these are normally refinanced with similar short-term obligations. If the monetary authorities fear price inflation, the Treasury may refinance these bills with Treasury notes maturing in seven years. Commercial banks are less interested in longer term securities and may therefore accept cash for their maturing bills; but insurance companies and other institutional investors buy the longer term securities. When the latter write checks in payment for them, the new cash holdings of commercial banks are transferred to the government. Both the assets and demand deposit liabilities of commercial banks (that is the money supply) have been decreased, leaving the economy in a less liquid position. Hence the offering of securities more (or less) attractive to commercial banks may increase (or decrease) the liquidity of the economy.

It must be remembered that a decrease in deposit liabilities will leave commercial banks with surplus reserves which may be reinvested in short-term assets. Therefore, unless the Federal Reserve System takes steps to absorb the surplus reserves before they are invested, the effects of Treasury refinancing may be temporary. But if the policy of substituting longer term obligations for Treasury bills is continued, it will handicap bank management in its search for liquid assets. This shrinkage in the volume of liquid assets will also affect the policies of business corporations and others that hold Treasury bills to meet their liquidity needs.

Under different circumstances, the Treasury may flood the economy with liquid assets by financing more with Treasury bills. By selling more securities to the Federal Reserve System and the commercial banks the treasury will increase bank reserves and money as counter entries (deposits).

Market for the National Debt. Borrowing $1 million by the United States Treasury to repay an equal amount of similar debt will rarely have any noticeable effect on the economy, but if different maturities are chosen for the new obligations a useful purpose may be served, such as decreasing or increasing liquidity. When making such a change, the Treasury must work closely with the market to prevent making the wrong choice.

At one end of the market are commercial banks, foreign central banks, large business corporations, and others who prefer Treasury bills and other short-term obligations; at the other end are insurance companies, savings institutions, and others who are interested in long-term obligations. Although primarily interested in liquidity, the first group may enter the intermediate- and long-term markets; and, the second group interested primarily in yield may enter the short-term market.

The government securities market is in competition with other markets for funds, and investors shift from one to the other when they find it profitable to do so. For illustration, in order to meet the increased demands of business firms for loanable funds during the expansionary phase of the business cycle, banks sell part of their Treasury bills and other short-term obligations. As a result, prices of short-term securities decline, and their yields increase. Although intermediate-term and long-term securities are more firmly held, their market prices are adversely affected but not to the degree sustained by short-term securities. Holders of long-term securities tend to hold them rather than take a loss (the locked-in theory).

The United States Treasury may finance and refinance relatively more in the long-term market and less in the short-term market in order to attract funds of insurance companies and savings institutions and to avoid creation of more bank credit based on investments in Treasury bills. Under recession conditions, the economy would need more liquidity and emphasis would shift to financing in the short-term market. Hence, a major responsibility of the Treasury in management of the national debt is to have a debt structure which meets the economy's need for more or less liquidity.

In managing the debt, the Treasury is aided by the fact that federal agencies and trust funds hold over 22 percent of the debt, the Federal Reserve banks hold 14 percent, and in addition there are an unknown number of other investors who are not likely to disturb the market. The last group includes individuals who own nonmarketable securities in the form of savings bonds and notes in an amount equal to about 14 percent of the total debt (see Table 19–6).

Debt Management Policy. In managing the debt, the United States Treasury must contend with those in the market who are interested in liquidity and profit as well as the general taxpayer who wants the debt financed as cheaply as possible. Although the Treasury has the authority to specify the terms of new and/or replacement issues, it must keep the total debt below the statutory limit (now $358 billion) and the interest rate on bonds at a rate not to exceed the statutory ceiling of 4.25 percent.

TABLE 19-6

OWNERSHIP OF NATIONAL DEBT: DIRECT AND FULLY GUARANTEED
(In Billions of Dollars)

Holders	Dec. 31, 1941	Dec. 31, 1945	Dec. 31, 1960	Dec. 31, 1967	May 31, 1968
U.S. government agencies and trust funds	$ 9.5	$ 27.0	$ 55.1	$ 76.0	$ 78.3
Federal Reserve banks	2.3	24.3	27.4	49.1	50.6
Commercial banks	21.4	90.8	62.1	63.9	60.9
Mutual savings banks	3.7	10.7	6.3	4.2	4.1
Insurance companies	8.2	24.0	11.9	8.7	8.5
Other corporations	4.0	22.2	18.7	12.5	15.8
State and local governments	0.7	6.5	18.7	25.1	26.7
Individuals:					
Savings bonds	5.4	42.9	45.6	51.1	51.2
Other securities	8.2	21.2	20.5	22.7	23.9
Foreign and international*	0.4	2.4	13.0	15.8	14.4
Miscellaneous†	0.5	6.6	11.2	16.2	18.6
Total (gross)	$64.3	$278.7	$290.4	$345.2	$352.9

* Includes investment of foreign balances and international accounts in United States.
† Includes holdings of savings and loan associations, dealers and brokers, nonprofit institutions, and corporate pension funds.
Source: *Federal Reserve Bulletin*, July, 1968, p. A-40.

The policy of the Treasury in managing the debt may be, at one extreme, to finance the debt as cheaply as possible or, at the other extreme, to ignore interest costs and follow a countercyclical policy, or it may follow a policy between these extremes. If a countercyclical policy is followed, the Treasury will shift from short-term issues to longer term issues during periods of business booms, credit restraint, and high interest rates; and, conversely, will shift from longer term issues to short-term issues during periods of recession, credit ease, and low interest rates. This policy supplements monetary management but increases the level of interest rates on the government debt and adds to the cost of debt financing.

The critics of countercyclical debt policy favor refinancing with short-term securities during boom periods, when it would be uneconomical to issue long-term bonds, and with long-term bonds during recessions, when credit conditions are easy. However, short-term issues may be acquired by commercial banks which would add inflationary pressure on the money supply at the wrong time; similarly, the sale of bonds during recessions may attract savings that might otherwise be invested.

While the United States Treasury must consider the cost of servicing the federal government debt, it cannot ignore the economic effects of new security issues. Decisions must be made as to whether a new issue is to be attractive to savers or commercial banks, whether liquidity is to be increased by issuing 91-day bills or reduced by issuing 20-year bonds, whether or not an issue of Treasury bills will disrupt Federal Reserve credit policy, and the kind of issue which would ease the current imbalance in international payments. The Treasury must also consider how a proposed issue will fit into the debt structure which includes marketable and nonmarketable issues, "discount" and "coupon" issues, callable and noncallable bonds, special and regular issues, securities which may or may not be used at par for tax purposes (such as certain Treasury bills for income taxes and bonds for estate or inheritance taxes), and existing maturity schedules of the securities composing the total federal debt. Owing to the use of "advanced refunding," the Treasury is able to choose and set the terms of new issues within limits set by Congress and the overall debt limit.

Advanced Refunding. Funding consists of conversion of short-term obligations into longer term obligations, and "advanced refunding" refers to making this conversion prior to the maturity dates of the securities being converted. Of course, the option to convert may or may not be used by the owners of the securities. The Treasury first used the advanced refunding technique in June, 1960, and, since that time, it has been used to obtain a better balanced and more satisfactory debt structure.[12] Advanced refunding has permitted the Treasury to take the initiative in readjusting maturities by offering holders of debt instruments an option to exchange their securities for new ones of a different maturity.

Usually, the average maturity of the government debt tends to be short because of a number of factors, including the passage of time (long-term bonds becoming short-term with the approach of maturity), an increase in short-term financing due to the balance-of-payments deficit of recent years, and the 4.25 percent interest-rate limit on Treasury bonds. Because of the development of advanced refunding, the Treasury is no longer required to wait until securities mature or become callable; instead, the Treasury may decide on the issue to be replaced, determine the coupon rate and maturity of the new issue, and choose the time for making the offer. This flexibility of scheduling the time for refinancing and maturities of issues permits the Treas-

---

[12] See Joseph Scherer, "Advance Refunding: A Technique of Debt Management," *Essays in Money and Credit* (New York: Federal Reserve Bank of New York, 1964), pp. 125–31.

ury to coordinate its policies with those of the Federal Reserve System so as to (1) reduce the burden of maintaining an orderly market for government securities; and (2) support the System's policy as to regulation of the liquidity of the economy.

SUMMARY

Fiscal policy refers to the use of the federal government's taxing, borrowing, spending, and other powers to maintain a high level of employment while carrying on its activities. The techniques of fiscal policy include deficit financing, preferably with new money during depressions, and debt retirement, with surplus funds during boom periods after making allowance for the growth factor in the economy. Compensatory financing works both ways, except in the case of a mature economy, when there would be a need for offsetting a secular deficiency in private spending.

In adoption of taxation policies, there are problems relative to the amount and incidence of taxes as well as their timing. As a result, there is general approval of the reliance on progressive personal income taxes and proportional income taxes on business firms at rates fixed so as to create a deficit during depressions and a surplus during business booms.

In adoption of expenditure policies, the normal needs of the government are recognized, but, in addition, there are built-in stabilizers that will increase the government's disbursements to the unemployed, farmers, and others during business recessions and will decrease these disbursements during business booms.

Until 1966, fiscal and monetary policies were geared to solve the problem of unemployment; since that time, the fiscal and monetary authorities have been faced with the problem of slowing down the rapid increase in price inflation which has taken place along with near full employment. At best, it seems that the basic principles of fiscal policy are being followed most reluctantly, with serious consequences to the economy.

Debt management involves such problems as from whom to borrow, in what form, and on what terms. The objective is to change the amount and to manipulate the ownership of the federal debt so as to influence the money supply and the propensity to consume and/or to invest. In management of United States Treasury balances, the objective is to help in stabilizing money-market conditions by influencing member-bank reserve balances. The purpose behind fiscal policy is to stabilize the flow of money payments so as to maintain a high level of employment. Perhaps the main criticism that can be made of the administration of fiscal policy and debt management as instruments of economic stabilization is that they have not been used more extensively.

QUESTIONS AND PROBLEMS

1. Identify fiscal policy. Distinguish between the principles used in monetary policy and fiscal policy.
2. What is meant by the General Fund? Identify its chief parts. Why does the Treasury keep part of its operating balance with commercial banks?
3. Identify: (*a*) Employment Act of 1946, (*b*) unified federal budget, (*c*) "built-in" stabilizers, (*d*) stable budget plan, and (*e*) advanced refunding.
4. Explain: "From a budgetary viewpoint, compensatory action by the government is reflected in the size of the government's deficit or surplus."
5. What is meant by countercyclical government spending? What are the chief weaknesses of such a policy? Are all types of government spending income-creating? How important are transfer payments? How flexible are current government expenditures?
6. Analyze: "Moreover, attempts to vary tax rates and spending to help smooth the business cycle may well have perverse effects. Changes in tax rates and spending may sometimes take so long to plan, legislate, and put into effect that many months may elapse from the time the need for action becomes clear until the change in budget position affects total spending." (Robert B. Anderson, "Fiscal Policies for Sustainable Growth," *Journal of Finance*, May, 1960, p. 132.)
7. Discuss: "Under present circumstances . . . with rapidly expanding demands and essentially full employment, the main restraining impact of the tax increase will be on prices, and only secondarily on output. Under current circumstances, the tax increase will add to Federal revenues." (*Economic Report of the President Transmitted to Congress, February, 1968 together with the Annual Report of the Council of Economic Advisers* [Washington, D.C.: U.S. Government Printing Office, 1968], p. 86.)
8. Explain: "The exceptional gain in personal transfers marks the third straight year that increases in this category have amounted to $5 billion or better. The estimated rise from fiscal 1966 to fiscal 1969 is over $16 billion, an amount close to the entire increase in transfers in the previous 10 years." (Office of Business Economics, United States Department of Commerce, *Survey of Current Business*, February, 1968, p. 16.)
9. Explain: "The shorter the [federal government] debt, the more it resembles—and serves the liquidity purposes of—money. A Federal debt that does not grow . . . can gradually become more and more

like money. The effects can be at least a little like the inflation-creating tendencies of the additions to the money supply." (C. L. Harris, *The Federal Debt* [Manufacturers Hanover Trust, October, 1967].)

10. Analyze: "It is clear that the key to monetary policy is the budget. We cannot expect monetary policy to move along ignoring the Treasury when a debt of problem size must be financed. If the budget strays far off course, monetary policy will be pulled off course also. And where these policies go, the economy will tend to follow." (Paul W. McCracken, "Federal Expenditure Policy," *Proceedings of a Symposium on the Federal Budget in a Dynamic Economy* [New York: American Bankers Association, 1968], p. 115.)

CHAPTER 20

Price Stabilization and Growth

FISCAL POLICY as well as monetary policy is being directed toward stabilizing monetary expenditures so as to keep them in balance with the growing needs of the economy at a high level of employment without inflating or deflating general prices and adversely affecting the balance-of-payments situation. When the term stabilization is used it may refer to stabilization in the general economy, in employment, in productive credit, in wages, in prices, or in any other aspect of the economic system. However, stabilization in all of these special areas is dependent, in large part, on the stabilization of general prices.

INSTABILITY OF GENERAL PRICES

Among the constitutional powers of Congress is the right to regulate the value of money; but the United States (and other free nations) has been unsuccessful in ridding the economy of the evil of fluctuating general prices. From 1961 to 1967, the consumer price stability record of the United States was better than that of other leading industrial countries; but this was only partially true for the 18 months preceding November, 1967 (see Table 20–1).

Since World War II, the United States has followed monetary and fiscal policies that stressed full employment with excellent results, but these policies have not succeeded in solving the international balance-of-payments problem or in stabilizing the general price level. Within recent years, the expansion in consumer prices has been more rapid than in wholesale prices because services are included in the former. Since the United States has become an "affluent" society, the service industries (retail and wholesale trades, communications, transportation, public utilities, real estate, insurance, banking, entertainment, and government and personal services such as medical, beautification, nonpublic education, and many others) have generated more national income than the primary and manufacturing industries. The main reason for the greater increase in the consumer price index number, as compared to the wholesale price index number, is the

TABLE 20-1

CONSUMER PRICE INCREASES, 1961-65

	Percentage Increase per Year	
Country	January, 1961 to November, 1967	June, 1965 to November, 1967
United States	1.9	2.8
Belgium	3.0	3.3
Canada	2.3	3.5
France	3.5	2.4
Germany	2.6	1.7
Italy	4.4	2.8
Japan	5.7	4.3
Netherlands	3.8	2.7
Sweden	4.1	5.1
Switzerland	3.8	4.3
United Kingdom	3.4	2.8

Source: *Economic Report of the President Transmitted to Congress February, 1968 together with the Annual Report of the Council of Economic Advisers* (Washington, D.C.: U.S. Government Printing Office, 1968), p. 97.

out-of-line increases in the price of personal services, as illustrated by prices charged by barbers, beauticians, doctors, and hospitals (see Table 20-2).

Money Illusion. As long as the level of output is high, many individuals make the serious mistake of dismissing price inflation as being unimportant. They fail to realize first, that there may be prosperity without inflation, and, second, that price inflation may ruin prosperity. Inflation redistributes wealth and income unfairly, reduces economic efficiency, and lowers the country's ability to compete in world markets. Prosperity may exist during years of stable or declining prices, such as 1925 to 1929.

Linking rising prices with prosperity is due in part to the money illusion—general prices may change but the value of money is always the same. Living in a monetary atmosphere, people blame rising general prices on farmers, chain stores, big business, labor unions, and/or the government without recognizing the fact that the value of the dollar has declined. Price stability is compatible with expansion in wages and other forms of real income. When there is a decline in the per-unit cost of goods due to the use of new inventions, the socially ideal policy would be to divide the fruits from the improvement with labor in the form of higher wages, with owners in the form of higher dividends, and with the general public in the form of lower prices.

TABLE 20-2
CONSUMER PRICES
(1957–59 = 100)

Period	All Items	Food	Housing Total	Rent	Home-Ownership	Fuel Oil and Coal	Gas and Electricity	Furnishings and Operation	Apparel and Upkeep	Transportation	Health and Recreation Total	Medical Care	Personal Care	Reading and Recreation	Other Goods and Services
1929	59.7	55.6	...	85.4	...	...	...	...	...	...	...	...	...	...	...
1933	45.1	35.3	...	60.8	...	...	88.3	...	...	...	...	...	...	...	...
1941	51.3	44.2	61.4	64.3	...	45.2	86.4	...	...	51.2	...	50.6	47.6	57.3	58.2
1945	62.7	58.4	67.5	66.1	...	53.6	...	...	...	55.4	...	57.5	63.6	75.0	67.3
1958	100.7	101.9	100.2	100.1	100.4	99.0	100.3	99.9	99.8	99.7	100.3	100.1	100.4	100.8	99.8
1959	101.5	100.3	101.3	101.6	101.4	100.2	102.8	100.7	100.6	103.8	102.8	104.4	102.4	102.4	101.8
1960	103.1	101.4	103.1	103.1	103.7	99.5	107.0	101.5	102.2	103.8	105.4	108.1	104.1	104.9	103.8
1961	104.2	102.6	103.9	104.4	104.4	101.6	107.9	101.4	103.0	105.0	107.3	111.3	104.6	107.2	104.6
1962	105.4	103.6	104.8	105.7	105.6	102.1	107.9	101.5	103.6	107.2	109.4	114.2	106.5	109.6	105.3
1963	106.7	105.1	106.0	106.8	107.0	104.0	107.8	102.4	104.8	107.8	111.4	117.0	107.9	111.5	107.1
1964	108.1	106.4	107.2	107.8	107.8	103.5	107.9	102.8	105.7	109.3	113.6	119.4	109.2	114.1	108.8
1965	109.9	108.8	108.5	108.9	109.1	105.6	107.8	103.1	106.8	111.1	115.6	122.3	109.9	115.2	111.4
1966	113.1	114.2	111.1	110.4	111.4	108.3	108.1	105.0	109.6	112.7	119.0	127.7	112.2	117.1	114.9
1967	116.3	115.2	114.3	112.4	115.7	111.6	108.5	108.2	114.0	115.9	123.8	136.7	115.5	120.1	118.2
1968 May	120.3	118.8	117.8	114.6	120.2	115.3	109.5	112.5	119.5	119.1	129.2	144.0	119.6	125.3	122.6

Source: *Federal Reserve Bulletin*, July, 1968, p. A-64.

BURDEN OF INFLATION

By "general prices" is meant the average of selected individual prices, and changes therein are measured by index numbers such as those published by the Bureau of Labor Statistics. The use of the wholesale price index number is favored as a guide to monetary policy because it changes first, and proper timing is important in achieving stability. If prices of commodities included in the wholesale price index are sensitive to changes in economic conditions, this index is superior from the point of view of timing monetary action. In addition, wholesale prices are reflected in nonservice retail prices, and this would tend to have a stabilizing effect on them. Nevertheless, an increase or decrease in the consumer price index number is of greater interest to the general public.

By stable prices is meant general prices that remain fairly stable over a period of time; therefore, stabilizing the general price level does not refer to stabilizing individual commodity prices which fluctuate due to changes in demand and supply. The objective of price stability does not entail holding any individual price constant.

Types of Price Changes. Inflation and deflation are the two types of general price changes, but there are changes in sector prices such as those for farm and food products, industrial goods, and different kinds of services. Inflation is most commonly defined as an economic situation wherein prices are rising, and deflation as one wherein prices are falling. Usually, inflation occurs when there is an increase in total expenditures (MV), and deflation when there is a decline in total expenditures. In general, the public is more concerned over deflation than inflation because values are computed in terms of monetary units. (Inflation tends to increase one's money income, making it more acceptable than deflation, which has the opposite effect.)

The amount of gains and losses and the total effect of general price changes on the economy depend on the rapidity and amplitude of changes. Thus, a 10 percent decline in prices in a three-month period would have a tremendous effect on the economy, while a 10 percent decline over a 10-year period would have relatively minor effects.

Rising prices affect the economy most seriously during periods of hyperinflation, that is, when the rapidity and amplitude of changes is inconceivably large. During such times normal business comes to a virtual stop, values of fixed income disappear, and claims of creditors become worthless. The ownership of the real wealth of the economy is shifted to speculators, shareholders, and some businessmen. For illustration, assume that a corporation is financed for $2 million, with equal amounts of debt and equity. After a hundredfold increase in general prices, the dollar value of the debt will remain at $1 million, but the dollar value of stockholders' equity will have increased to $199 million. Although this example of rampant price increase may seem exaggerated, it is an understatement compared with price disturbances that occurred in many foreign countries during and following the two 20th-century World Wars.

Fortunately, the inflationary periods in the United States since the end of the Revolutionary War have not been of the hyperinflation types; however, there is no assurance that the current inflationary trend will be checked soon enough to avert this type of economic disaster. It is inconceivable that general prices would ever fall to zero, but there is no theoretical limit to the height that general prices could rise.

As a class, creditors tend to lose from rising prices, and debtors tend to gain. For example, a farmer having a 5 percent, $25,000 mortgage on his farm will be able to meet his $1,250 interest payment by selling 1,250 bushels of wheat when the price is $1 per bushel, but if the price of wheat rises to $2 per bushel he will be able to discharge his interest obligation by selling only 625 bushels. In addition, his equity interest in his farm will have been increased proportionately. The total public and private debt of the United States is now in excess of $1,400 billion, and when the general price level rises 1 percent, the holders of debt obligations lose $14 billion in purchasing power. Debtors, who gain from inflation, are no longer the impoverished individuals, but the federal, state, and local governments, corporations, nonincorporated business firms, and individuals who have home mortgage and consumer financing debts are.

The search for financial security has led to an unprecedented expansion in life insurance policies and private pension funds. Americans now own $1,000 billion of life insurance issued by legal-reserve life insurance companies; but the holders of such policies should realize that the value of their contracts is eroding with each increase in general prices.

Among those able to adjust their incomes to keep pace with price increases, the most favored group is organized labor, which holds contracts containing the escalator clause which means that wage rates change with fluctuations in the cost-of-living index. The escalator clause sometimes appears in other long-term contracts such as debt instruments, leases, and service policies, wherein money payments are adjusted according to price indexes. The favored few who are covered by such agreements may be spared serious loss of real income during periods of inflation.

Redistribution of Wealth and Income. Deflation has not been a problem in the United States since the early 1930's; therefore inflation is emphasized in the following pages. (The effects of deflation on different economic groups tend to be the opposite of those of inflation.) The effects of inflation on the economy are neither uniform nor equitable, with some groups harmed more than others (also true in the case of deflation).

Inflation tends to cause a shift of income from the inactive to the active. For illustration, a retired farmer who is receiving $3,000 annually from the mortgage on his farm may find it inadequate for his needs. Consumer prices have increased almost one third in the past 20 years. Today, almost 10 percent of the population is over 65 years of age. Along with disabled individuals, widows, orphans, and other inactive members of society, they are dependent largely on fixed incomes from social security, military and other pensions, and income from investments of past savings in insurance, bonds, and savings accounts.

Effect on International Balance of Payments. In its fiscal and monetary policies, the United States has given major attention to its internal problems—growth, unemployment, and inflation—and relatively little to its balance of international payments deficits. Higher domestic prices tend to reduce foreign spending in the United States and thereby reduce exports. In addition, Americans find it more economical to buy abroad; hence there is an increase in imports and a reduction in domestic sales. These two factors tend to cause an imbalance in trade. Steps taken by the government to reduce the export of capital and curtail foreign travel by Americans and to encourage foreigners to travel and to buy more goods in the United States have failed to bring the balance of payments into equilibrium (see Chapter 27).

If costs and prices in the United States are kept below world prices, American businessmen will be able to sell more abroad, and traders in world markets will be seeking bargains in the United States. As a result, there would be an increase in American exports and a decrease in imports which would provide a large trade surplus to offset deficits due to foreign travel, foreign investment, and foreign commitments. Unless there is a slowing down in the present upward movement of wages, profits, and prices, the balance-of-payments deficit may grow even larger before it declines.

Reduction in Efficiency. If prices changed uniformly, the inequities of inflation would be reduced but not eliminated. Prices in some industries respond immediately to changes in economic conditions, but in others the response is slow or virtually nonexistent. In the latter category are railroads, public utilities, and communications companies that are subject to governmental rate regulation. The loss in purchasing power of such companies due to price inflation may be offset by an increase in volume of sales and reduction in debts (as illustrated by electric light and power companies). Insurance companies, banks, and many other financial institutions are in a "hedge" position, because the decline in the value of their assets is matched by the decline in the value of their liabilities.

Inflation may play havoc with managerial practices because of "phony" profits that tend to result from inflation. For illustration, following World War II corporate management was subject to higher income taxes, wage increases, and pressure from stockholders for higher dividends. At the same time, the replacement costs for machinery, equipment, and plants had increased substantially and depreciation allowances, based on original costs, were inadequate. In reality, many corporations paid taxes, wages, and dividends in part at least out of capital.

The purchasing power lost by some groups is not destroyed but is transferred to others. Thus, governments, railroads, business corporations, and financial intermediaries tend to gain from a shift in purchasing power from creditors to debtors. Consequently, there is a tendency for the financially strong to become stronger at the expense of the financially weak (such as the 100 million or more small savers and beneficiaries of social security, insurance, and pension plans). Since World War II, the value of the dollar as measured by the consumer price index has fallen 50 percent. Under such conditions, special concessions have been obtained from Congress "through the ballot box" by pressure groups, such as agriculture, labor, business, and veterans, to mention the most successful.

One of the reasons given to justify "a little inflation" is that it seems to stimulate production and, at times, it is accompanied by economic progress. In the latter case, the national output might have been much larger without the practices and procedures that usually accompany rising prices. For instance, during such periods there is an increase in the number and severity of strikes and other forms of labor warfare which hamper output. Various forms of speculation develop —in inventories, plant capacity, real estate, and corporate stock. Because business is booming, and workers and stockholders are prospering, extravagance and inefficiency are tolerated. In anticipation of future needs, all types of hoarding, including that of both materials and trained personnel (accountants, chemists, and engineers), take place.

COSTS AND PRICES

The definition of inflation either as (1) a "disproportionate and relatively sharp increase in the quantity of money or credit or both, relative to the amount of exchange business . . . always produces a rise in the price level" or as (2) a situation wherein "money income is increasing faster than the flow of goods and services on which it is spent" is not satisfactory when referring to the so-called "new types of inflation." A starting point in discussing these types is to recognize that there has been an increase in the general price level that is not explainable in terms of an increase in the "quantity of money and credit or both" or an increase in "money income" (that is, pressure on the price level from the demand side). Instead, rising costs are stressed, particularly wage costs, administered prices, and lack of competition or monopolies, as causing higher or rising prices. Thus, as opposed to a "demand-pull" type of inflation, there is a "cost-push" type.

Cost Theory. There is nothing new in recognizing cost as a price-determining factor, but what may be new is the assumption that price increases are due solely to pressure from the cost side. The cost price theory was generally accepted during the last century, but it was modified when attention was called to the things that had great value without much cost being involved (such as diamonds, antiques, and paintings). Although the cost price theory is not applicable in all cases, the prices of the items to which the theory is not applicable have little or no weight in determining the general price level.

In estimating the effect of cost on prices, emphasis is on the per-unit cost of output, which entails depreciation, interest, raw material, labor, and other charges. The part of the total per-unit cost of a product assigned to each of these cost items varies with the industry, plant, time, and product, and the best estimate of accountants and engineers are but approximations.[1] In most industries, labor costs are the most important item in the production cost of goods and services, and anything that affects labor costs has a corresponding effect on total costs. If wages remain the same, the wage factor in cost becomes proportionately smaller when the productivity of labor increases; and when the labor cost rises by the same amount as the productivity of labor, the wage cost per unit remains the same.[2] After arriving at the cost figure the next step, in order to arrive at the cost price, is to add the profit margin.

In modern society the profit margin depends on the degree of competition and the volume of sales. If there is active competition, an increase in productivity will be passed along to the general public in the form of lower prices and better services; but if there is a lack of competition because of formal or informal price agreements, prices remain about the same.[3] Hence, when there are falling costs and falling prices, profit margins will remain the same; but, when there are falling costs and rigid prices, profit margins increase.

In most industries an increase in sales has been more important in explaining higher profits than a decrease in costs (usually the two are present at the same time). If total demand is small profits are small, and when sales increase profits also increase. Profits will increase more rapidly than sales not only because of the increase in volume but also the increase in profit margin. The cost price theory has the advantage of explaining why there may be an increase in demand.

When prices increase, the normal conclusion is that there will be a decrease in sales, and this would be true if money income remained the same. However, higher costs, higher prices, and higher profits

[1] Pricing practices of business corporations are so varied that it is impossible to make accurate general statements about them. This is true for different business firms and also for the pricing procedures for different products of the same company. See also A. D. H. Kaplan, J. B. Dirlan, and R. F. Lanzillotti, *Pricing in Big Business* (Washington, D.C.: Brookings Institution, 1958).

[2] For illustration, if a worker's output per man-hour is 10 units, he will produce 400 units during a 40-hour week. If he is paid $160 per week, the unit labor cost is 40 cents. If his output is increased by 3 percent (12 units) and his wages increased by the same amount ($160 × .03 = $4.80), the unit labor cost will remain the same ($164.80 ÷ 412 = $.40). If labor costs constitute 60 percent of the total cost, the amount available to pay other factors of production will increase when the 12 additional units are sold (presumably at the old price).

[3] Under oligopoly a few sellers act to some extent as a group because each seller would be influenced by and would influence the action of others. When one raises or lowers prices, similar price changes are usually made by others in the industry. Oligopoly price is largely established by custom and by open or tacit agreement, and the change in output may not respond rapidly to shifts in marginal cost curves.

mean that some individuals' money incomes are higher. This higher income brings one back to the demand theory of prices and the concept that higher prices must be supported by an increase in demand.

Fixed Costs.   There are three types of costs: fixed, semifixed, and variable. Irrespective of the level of output, any business firm will be subject to certain costs which are fixed, others that change with the volume of business, and some that have characteristics of both. Fixed costs include those for salaries of executives, property taxes, insurance of fixed assets, depreciation, and interest charges on debt. Today, these costs are large and increasing due in part to emphasis on research and development requiring more expensive plants and equipment; these in turn account for increasing property taxes, insurance payments, depreciation charges, and maintenance costs.[4] When fixed charges are large, there must be a greater volume of sales before the break-even point is reached (costs and income are equal); but thereafter profits will increase much more rapidly than sales because fixed costs are distributed over a larger volume of sales (principle of operating leverage).

If prices were fixed according to costs, they would be lowest during business booms when the per-unit costs are lowest, because of the high volume of sales; and conversely, they should be highest during business recessions when per-unit costs are highest due to the relatively small volume of sales. If prices of industrial products were based entirely on costs, they would follow a countercyclical pattern, rising during recessions and falling during booms.

Postwar Inflation.   Since World War II, general prices have been increasing and one might conclude that monetary and fiscal authorities are responsible, through creating too much demand. This conclusion would be justified if demand were the only factor in determining prices. In other words, an important factor in rising prices may be costs pushing up prices, rather than demand pulling them higher.

---

[4] Dr. Schultze wrote that between 1955 and 1957 the "largest part of the rise in total costs was accounted for not by the increase in wage costs but by the increase in salary and overhead costs. . . . Business firms purchased large amounts of new equipment, hired expensive professional, technical, sales and clerical staffs, and speeded up research and development projects." See Charles L. Schultze, *Recent Inflation in the United States*, Study Paper No. 1 of material prepared in connection with the Study of Employment, Growth and Price Levels for Joint Economic Committee, U.S. Congress (Washington, D.C.: U.S. Government Printing Office, 1959), p. 2.

It is difficult to distinguish between a situation wherein prices are being pushed up by costs from below and one wherein demand is pulling them up from above, but the principles involved are simple. In demand-pull inflation, the demand for goods exceeds the supply at current prices, and so prices increase until demand and supply are in equilibrium at a higher price level. In cost-push inflation, the increase in the cost of producing goods causes producers to raise prices to recover costs even though there has been no change in demand. Except in a monopolistic situation, normally an individual producer cannot raise prices without losing sales to competitors; but when all producers are raising prices, this is not true. For most business firms, the chief cost of production is labor; hence collective bargaining may be an important monopolistic element causing costs to increase ahead of prices. Management may be willing to meet the demands of labor if the increased costs can be recaptured by raising prices.

GUIDEPOSTS

Monetary authorities recognize the fact that if restrictive measures applicable to the demand-pull type of inflation are used to check the cost-push type of inflation, it would normally cause unemployment of labor and equipment. Now most modern governments are committed to a policy of full employment; as a result, many laborers feel that they have a better collective bargaining position irrespective of the size of wage increase the union is seeking. Employers no longer fear loss of profits if they can increase prices sufficiently to cover the higher wage costs and to maintain or even increase their profits. As a result, wages and profits in the postwar period increased faster than output and general prices. While competition is the chief determinant of market prices in a free economy, in some industries labor unions and management have found that they have considerable discretion in setting wages and prices.

In January, 1962, the Council of Economic Advisers first presented the wage and price "guideposts" to guide labor union and industrial leaders in their wage and price policies and to give the informed public standards by which to measure their performance. In 1968, former President Lyndon B. Johnson announced his establishment of a "Cabinet Committee on Price Stability" (consisting of the Secretaries of the Treasury, Commerce, and Labor, the Director of the Budget, and the Chairman of the Council of Economic Advisers) and stated that "Through this machinery, we seek to achieve a new and more effective cooperation among business, labor, and government in the pursuit of price stability in a free market economy."[5] This committee will supplement and lend prestige to the Council's recommendations on prices by preparing and publishing studies on industries which are the chief sources of inflationary developments and on government policies that affect prices, and it will consult and work with representatives of business, labor, and the general public in order to achieve price stability in a free-market economy. The guideposts appeal for general restraint and offer "guidance to individual unions and firms as to the specific behavior of wages and prices which would be consistent with general price stability as well as efficient allocation of resources."[6]

Productivity.   The basic principle used in formulating the guidelines for wages is that hourly compensation must stay within limits set by the trend rate of productivity growth for the economy as a whole. In setting wage policies, the general assumption is that wages would be the same, that is "like pay for like work," irrespective of the industry or company. In order to meet the increase in labor costs, management is permitted to increase prices if and when necessary; but, if the increase in productivity is just sufficient to meet the higher costs, prices should be stable; and, if the increase in productivity is in excess of the increase in costs, prices should be lowered. Thus, the guidepost calls for a price increase when the industry's productivity is below the average national trend, price stability when productivity is about equal to the average national trend, and price reduction when productivity is above the average national trend.

In industries wherein wages are not decided at the bargaining table by labor and management, and wherein prices are not set by discretionary powers of large firms (as in agriculture), the "workings of competitive markets may be expected to yield results similar to those prescribed by the guideposts so long as the general movement of wages and prices is consistent with the guideposts" in an "environment of general price stability."[7]

Changes in productivity may not be the best guide to wage and price increases, because demand is ignored. According to the productivity directive, a firm swamped with orders due to greater

---

[5] *Economic Report of the President Transmitted to the Congress February, 1968 together with the Annual Report of the Council of Economic Advisers* (Washington, D.C.: U.S. Government Printing Office, 1968), p. 21.

[6] *Ibid.*, p. 120.

[7] *Ibid.*, p. 121.

efficiency would be expected to lower prices when the classical solution would be to raise them in order to allocate its products properly as dictated by the price system. (Consumers normally bid up prices in the marketplace when demand exceeds supply.) According to the guideposts, less efficient firms would raise prices to meet higher per-unit labor costs when national productivity is increasing, but the operation of the free enterprise system would cause prices to fall in order to increase the demand for the firms' products.

The guideposts were followed reasonably well until the middle of 1966, but during the latter part of that year a number of wage and price increases were in excess of the amount recommended by the guideposts. Labor unions did not cooperate because of the increase in living costs due to higher prices of foods and services (agricultural products and personal services are not covered by the guideposts). In addition, labor wanted an increased share in corporate profits which, in the aggregate, had increased more rapidly than wages.

Product price fixing by management is a convenient mechanism of modern marketing. However, this does not mean that all competition is absent, even though prices do not move freely up and down as they do on the commodity and securities exchanges. Monopolistic and oligopolistic prices are always administered prices, and that is the connotation given by some to all administered prices. Although prices of things are fixed before they are sold, it does not follow that they may not be changed by negotiation. To support higher administered prices, there must be buying power. The discussion of the cost theory of inflation calls attention to the needs for "big business" and larger unions to support the guidelines.

Although the wage and price guideposts are not dead, experience with them has raised questions such as: Would adherence to them by all those in the areas where they apply be sufficient to stop inflation? This question poses a second: Would labor and management be willing to accept the government's guideposts in the face of an increase in the cost of living due to higher prices for foods and services? A third question may be raised: Are the only alternatives to the guideposts rationing, price control, licensing of raw materials, exchange control, tariffs, and import quotas? Finally: Are decisions as to business spending to be removed from the hands of private management and placed in the hands of government agencies? This would mean direct control over wages, capital formation, allocation of resources, import and export restrictions, and so on. If carried to the degree prevalent in war years, there would be no serious problem of unemployment and, if combined with government price fixing, there would be no general price fluctuations. It would mean the end of the free enterprise system.

CREEPING INFLATION

Present indications are that the current century will go down in history as one of creeping inflation. There are several reasons for the assumption that general prices will continue to follow the present trend.

1. No modern government will permit the development of a serious depression. To this end, governments will not hesitate to operate with large and continuing deficits to support economic expansion.

2. Certain cost factors will continue to push up prices, such as wage contracts containing escalator clauses and farm price-support programs which are tied to the concept of parity prices. With every increase in general prices, one may expect a renewed demand for purchasing-power savings bonds, more generous depreciation allowances in the computation of business income for tax purposes, retirement incomes computed in terms of purchasing power, and wage-rate and salary adjustments linked to changes in the general price level.

3. The easy-money policy will be continued because of the size of the national debt, and currently there is emphasis on the need for easy money to promote rapid economic growth. While there may be some increases in money rates, when the real pinch comes central banks will not be permitted to interfere seriously with financing deficits through the use of commercial-bank credit.

4. International tensions will continue for a long time, and this means continuing large expenditures for past and future wars and more expenditures for an increasing number of veterans. Foreign investments and foreign economic and military aid by the United States also are expected to continue. Such expenditures are inflationary because they create money income in the United States that is not offset by a flow of goods and services.

5. Life expectancy will probably continue to increase, and this means more old-age pension payments. Pension payments that are in excess of cash receipts tend to be inflationary.

6. Finally, the mere fact that inflation is expected leads people to do things that cause inflation. People spend more freely, and, in order to do so, they borrow more freely. They are looking for hedges against inflation—such as owning stock and real estate. This increase

in spending tends to increase prices. Other hedges against inflation are inflationary in that they tend to place more money income in the hands of consumers and/or producers when prices are increasing.

Adjusting to Inflation.   One approach to the problem of inflation is to "relax and enjoy it after taking as many steps as possible to offset the injustices of inflation."

1. For years, labor unions have been able to obtain wage contracts from management that provide for automatic increases in money wages to offset the loss in purchasing power as measured by cost-of-living index number.

2. Although life insurance companies are important institutional investors whose avowed function is to provide protection from loss of income due to death or old age, they have done little to protect their policy holders from loss of purchasing power due to inflation. Customarily life insurance benefits are paid in one lump sum or as retirement income of a predetermined amount for a given number of payments or for life. Unfortunately, inflation has reduced much of the value of these benefits. For illustration, by 1965 a $10,000 policy purchased in 1940 would have lost more than 50 percent of its purchasing power. Now, an increasing number of insurance companies are offering variable-annuity policies which provide income that is linked to some previously selected index, such as the value of the fund supporting these annuities. Normally, all or part of these funds are invested in common stock, which tends to change in price as general prices change.

3. In the United States, 30 million persons are covered by private pension plans, and over 95 million participate in social security (old-age, survivors' and disability insurance). Most states now permit life insurance companies to manage pension funds with a separate investment account kept for each. They operate under laws covering their investments that are liberal enough to permit them to compete with banks and other institutions for this type of business. Some private pension plans contain a cost-of-living clause that protects pensioners from loss in purchasing power due to inflation. Although bills have been introduced in Congress to insert a similar clause in social security policies, no approval has been given to date. However, Congress has increased social security benefits to offset some of the effects of inflation.

4. Holders of credit instruments could be protected from the loss in value of their investments due to inflation if their contracts called for repayment in a sum of money having the same purchasing

power as the amount lent, and if interest payments were similarly adjusted so that the rate would change with changes in purchasing power. For illustration, a $1,000, 5 percent, 20-year stabilized debenture bond issued January 1, 1969, would bear interest on July 1 and January 1 in an amount equal to the purchasing power of $2.50 on January 1, 1969, as measured by previously selected index numbers. When the bond matures on December 31, 1989, the sum repaid would equal the purchasing power of the $1,000 on January 1, 1969. If general prices had increased 50 percent during the 20-year period, the creditor would receive $1,500 for each bond held.

During the 1940's, millions of individuals became bondholders by purchasing United States savings bonds, including those on which interest is paid periodically and discount bonds. (In the latter case, a $100, 10-year bond would be sold for $75, and $100 would be paid at maturity.) Because of the rapid inflation following World War II, these bonds were retired with sums of money which had purchasing power that was considerably less than the purchasing power of the sums invested.

The chief debtor in the United States is the federal government. Its creditors include purchasers of over $50 million in savings bonds. Numerous bills have been introduced in Congress to issue savings bonds containing the cost-of-living clause in order to protect these small investors; but to date no action has been taken, largely because of the opposition of the Treasury. Hence, the most loyal and most defenseless small investors are still being sold savings bonds that contain no protection against inflation. The more knowledgeable investor is now placing a considerable part of his funds in common stock and real property as a hedge against inflation.

5. The growing awareness of the declining value of the dollar is the most significant aspect of the problem of protection of one's income and/or investments from loss of value. As this awareness becomes more widespread, it will tend to result in increases in consumption (together with a decline in savings), in capital formation, and in the growth rate of the economy. If funds normally saved and invested in plants, equipment, and inventories are used for consumption, invested in speculative enterprises, or used as a hedge against inflation, the lack of capital funds may cause growth of business firms to level off or decline. The Federal Reserve System might encourage commercial banks to fill the gap by creation of new bank credit, but this would tend to cause additional inflation.

It should be obvious that any policy that accepts inflation is undesirable and dangerous, because too much is at stake. The adoption of escalator clauses in an increasing number of contracts is not the answer, because it would accelerate inflation by increasing the amount of income available for spending when prices are rising. Moreover, higher prices would handicap American businessmen who must compete at home and abroad with foreign producers. Finally, rising prices tend to cause greater imbalance in the international payments position of the United States.

Greater Stability. Fortunately, there are factors in the economy that tend to stabilize prices.

1. The most encouraging one has been the unusual stability in general prices during the 1961–66 expansion period. Adherence of labor and management to wage-price guideposts, although not complete, resulted in a fair degree of stability in the average unit labor cost, the most important requisite for price stability. If too much reliance is placed on monetary and fiscal policies to halt inflation, there is danger that a choice will have to be made between price stability and full employment.

2. Another alternative is to lessen the role of the government in determining prices, create a better bargaining balance between labor and management, and eliminate monopoly and other restrictions on pricing in the marketplace. Application of the antitrust laws to large labor unions is but one of the proposals for solving the cost-push type of inflation. Then improved technology, automation, and better management would reduce per-unit costs of goods and services and permit lowering of prices for the benefit of the general public. A return to a more competitive and more efficient economy would necessitate elimination of "featherbedding" in both management and labor circles and withdrawal of business and farm subsidies. Modifying the farm program, in order to make better use of land and other resources, would mean a more rapid shift to a higher productive economy.

3. Foreign output is increasing, which means not only less dependence on the United States for economic and military aid but also more imports of foreign goods for American markets, both of which will tend to keep prices down. A more efficient U.S. economy will permit American business firms to compete more successfully in foreign markets, because exports are needed to meet international balance-of-payments problems.

4. Higher prices tend to check inflationary expenditures when potential buyers are "priced out of the market." Of course, these potential buyers may be replaced by new buyers who have gained

from inflation. More stable prices will eliminate or at least reduce the popularity of escalator clauses, which have been a factor in the increased cost of production.

GROWTH

Since the 1950's, the United States has placed more emphasis on the growth rate in order to (1) meet the economic challenge from the Soviet Union and other communist countries, (2) raise the standard of living in the United States, (3) increase production and export of goods, (4) help underdeveloped countries, and (5) assure the ability of the United States to meet adequately its economic, military, and political committments to foreign countries. For years, the monetary and fiscal authorities have given most of their attention to conquering unemployment, preventing inflation, and reducing the balance-of-payments deficit, without realizing that a satisfactory rate of growth might be the answer to all three problems (assuming a solution of cost price inflation).

Productivity. The concept of normal growth contains allowances for increases in productivity and in population. The increase in productivity is an index of the efficiency with which the nation's resources are used to produce goods and services measured in terms of output per machine, per unit of capital, or a combination of both. The most comprehensive measure of productivity available is output per unit of labor and capital, because it is an indicator of the productive efficiency of all resources.

During the past 75 years, the increased efficiency of capital and of labor have contributed about equally to the expansion in output; however, since the close of World War II, the rate of increase in output per unit of labor (man-hours of work) has been less than the rate of increase in output per unit of labor and capital. The shortening of the number of work hours has been more than offset by the increase in efficiency, which suggests an improvement in the standard of living. The key to further betterment in the standard of living is a continuing rise in productive efficiency through the use of more efficient plants and equipment and improvements in workers' skills.

Gross National Product. As noted previously, the gross national product (GNP) is the market value of goods and services produced by a nation's economy before depreciation and other allowances for institutional and business consumption in the accounting period are deducted. The gross national product includes an amount equal to (1) personal consumption expenditures, (2) gross private

TABLE 20-3

GROSS NATIONAL PRODUCT, 1964–67

	Millions of Dollars			
	1964	*1965*	*1966*	*1967*
Gross national product..............	$632,410	$684,884	$747,568	$789,663
Personal consumption expenditures....	401,221	432,839	465,487	492,232
Durable goods.................	59,237	66,308	70,459	72,647
Nondurable goods............	178,683	191,059	206,692	215,754
Services.....................	163,301	175,472	188,336	203,831
Gross private domestic investment....	94,032	108,139	120,830	114,269
Fixed investment.................	88,197	98,519	106,095	108,199
Nonresidential..............	61,071	71,291	81,295	83,640
Structures................	21,178	25,530	28,473	27,899
Producers' durable equipment..............	39,893	45,761	52,822	55,741
Residential structures.........	27,126	27,228	24,800	24,559
Nonfarm.................	26,588	26,707	24,254	23,978
Farm....................	538	521	546	581
Change in business inventories...	5,835	9,620	14,735	6,070
Nonfarm..................	6,429	8,647	14,919	5,589
Farm.....................	−594	973	−184	481
Net exports of goods and services....	8,462	6,901	5,080	4,768
Exports......................	37,099	39,196	43,142	45,756
Imports.....................	28,637	32,295	38,063	40,989
Government purchases of goods and services........................	128,695	137,005	156,171	178,394
Federal......................	65,166	66,897	77,390	90,562
National defense.............	49,992	50,134	60,583	72,390
Other....................	15,174	16,763	16,807	18,172
State and local................	63,529	70,108	78,781	87,832

Note: Totals may not add because of rounding.

Source: U.S. Department of Commerce, Office of Business Economics, *Survey of Current Business*, July, 1968, p. 19.

domestic investment including changes in business inventories for the period, (3) net foreign investment, and (4) government purchases of goods and services (see Table 20–3).

Personal Consumption Expenditures. Spending by individuals is for durable consumer goods, nondurable consumer goods, and services. Although the first is subject to cyclical fluctuations, the other two are fairly stable. When there is an increase in income, consumers adopt new habits of consumption which they retain during periods of declining incomes. Goods and services may be purchased with income formerly saved or with borrowed funds, both being stabilizing factors.

Conversely, instability in consumption expenditures is due in part to unequal distribution of income among classes. For illustration, labor union demands for higher wages and fringe benefits for union members are usually triggered by policies of management. Prices which are too high often result from maintenance of inflexible profit margins (which means the absorption of declines in costs due to an increase in productivity), and labor may seek to share in these profits. Union demands for paid vacations, guaranteed annual wages, profit-sharing privileges, and other benefits are to give laborers some of the advantages that companies give to management. An unfair distribution of goods and services is a constant threat to the economic stability of the economy, provoking labor disturbances and wage and price increases.

Some individuals are opposed to full employment because they hold to the false assumption that a "reserve of labor" (that is, unemployed) is necessary to prevent price inflation. Their reasoning—when union members fear a loss of their jobs to the unemployed they will not demand higher wages—assumes (1) that one laborer may replace a second irrespective of the type of job, (2) the nonexistence of union shops, and (3) the immobility of labor. However, "economic managers" may be forced to compromise between objectives and to depend on management and labor leaders to remove obstacles to maximum growth without price inflation and the more equitable distribution of goods and services.

Gross Private Domestic Investment. The two types of domestic investment are for business inventories and fixed capital goods. Changes in investments in inventories have a marked cyclical pattern, but the shift from a goods economy to a service economy is reducing the impact of their fluctuations on national income. Investments in fixed capital goods include those for (*a*) nonresidential buildings and producer durable equipment, and (*b*) urban and nonurban houses and other buildings. During periods of financial reverses, business investment may be postponed until revenues are more normal. As a result, investments in plants and equipment tend to follow a cyclical pattern. When fixed investments are financed with credit, they are discouraged by high interest rates. Consequently, investments in urban and rural housing and other buildings follows a countercyclical pattern. Because of the increasing importance of the service sector of the American economy, more funds are being "invested" in men—doctors, lawyers, teachers, and so on—and relatively less in machines.

Net Exports of Goods and Services. The excess of exports over imports is the amount of goods and services produced in the United States and consumed abroad that is not matched by the consumption of foreign goods and services imported from abroad. During periods of prosperity, imports of goods tend to increase more rapidly than exports, but this situation could be reversed by keeping costs and prices at a level which would permit successful competition with foreign producers.

Government Purchases of Goods and Services. Growth in the economy brings pressure on governmental bodies to increase expenditures. An increase in the standard of living will mean (*a*) more cars on the highways and more spending for roads, bridges, and traffic control; (*b*) more children going to school for a longer period and more spending for school buildings, equipment, and teachers; (*c*) more and better public housing; and (*d*) a greater demand for public parks, beaches, civic centers, and public entertainment.

Theoretically, changes in public spending are to offset changes in private spending, but state and local officials are not inclined to follow countercyclical policies and federal officials seem reluctant to assume the role of economic statesmen. When total expenditures exceed the national productive capacity at the current price level, the market allocates the limited amount of products to the highest bidders, and so general prices increase.

COORDINATION OF MONETARY AND FISCAL POLICY

For convenience, monetary and fiscal policies have been treated separately; in practice, they are interdependent and function as one policy. For illustration, if the Treasury's cash receipts are in excess of its cash expenditures, a reduction in the amount of funds at the disposal of the public will result. Conversely, if the Treasury's cash expenditures exceed its cash receipts, an increase in the amount of funds at the disposal of the public will result. If the governmental surplus is used to reduce the federal debt, the effect on the economy may be offset by the Federal Reserve System's open-market policy of buying government securities. Conversely, the effect of a governmental deficit financed by borrowing from commercial banks may be offset by the open-market sale of government securities by the Federal Reserve System. Hence the effectiveness of "deficit financing" as a countercyclical measure during a recession depends on the support of the Federal Reserve System and commercial banks.

Transfer payments and cyclical tax policies affect the amount of disposable income available for private spending in the same way that monetary policy affects the amount of money and credit available for private and government spending. The purpose of monetary policy is to regulate the amount of credit used to supplement income in day-to-day spending. In times of depression, there is no increase in demand unless the money is spent. Similarly, there is no increase in total demand unless disposable personal income, increased by lower taxes or larger transfer payments, is spent.

Government purchases of currently produced goods and services are income producing and therefore differ from other aspects of fiscal and monetary policy. At present, the government is the chief purchaser of goods and services in the American economy, and its needs are so great that over one fourth (26 out of 100 persons) of those employed work directly or indirectly for the federal, state, or local governments.

Monetary policy seems to be preferred to fiscal policy because it is easier to administer, is subject to less political interference, and can be timed more judiciously. Flexibility is a major advantage of monetary policy, and the lack of flexibility is a serious weakness of fiscal policy because it takes months for laws to be prepared, passed, and put into effect through the federal budget. Although automatic or built-in stabilizers tend to adjust to changes in employment and production, they are only a partial solution to the need for better timing of fiscal policy. A proposal to give the President standby authority to change the tax rate by 5 percent across the board under specified business conditions has received little support from Congress. Similarly, Congress has displayed no enthusiasm for a standby tax law that could be put into effect by a joint resolution of both houses. The same difficulty is present when countercyclical adjustments are being considered in expenditures for goods and services, such as for defense and administrative departments.

Although one may argue that it is unnecessary to use fiscal policy, not to do so would be unwise and also impossible. The state of the federal budget, as well as the size and composition of the national debt, has an influence on the economy at all times. The Federal Reserve authorities are forced to adjust the day-to-day use of open-market operations to changes in the location of United States Treasury cash balances and the debt management procedures of the United States Treasury. The problem is not which is better, but how the two may be coordinated to achieve the objectives of monetary and fiscal policies—a high level of employment without inflation.

The need for coordination of monetary and fiscal policies is evident when consideration is given to the fact that the more restrictive fiscal policy is, the more permissive credit and monetary policies may be. Conversely, as fiscal policies become more permissive, credit and monetary policies may become more restrictive.

One plan for coordination of monetary and fiscal policies would entail removal of the discretionary managerial aspects of these policies.[8] This plan would require the adoption of the 100 percent reserve system and would link the supply of new money to a government budgetary deficit or surplus, with a deficit calling for an increase and a surplus calling for a decrease in the supply of new money. The volume of government expenditures for goods and services, defined to exclude all transfer payments, would be determined without any attempt to change them in response to cyclical fluctuations in business activity. It is presumed that this policy would lead to a fairly stable volume of expenditures for goods and services because, except during war times, the basic things for which governments spend change slowly.

A predetermined program of transfer payments would change the volume of government expenditures automatically with changes in the business cycle. A progressive tax system at fixed rates, with emphasis on personal income taxes, would provide flexibility in revenue yields over the business cycle. The hypothetical yield should balance government expenditures over the business cycle with a small allowance for a deficit, whose financing with new money would provide for a secular or long-run increase in the supply of money (4 or 5 percent each year). No changes would be made in the tax rates except to finance a change in the level of government purchases of goods and services.

These proposals illustrate different aspects of monetary and fiscal policies that have been considered, and the novel aspect of this plan is its automatic features. The money supply and transfer payments would increase during recessions and decrease during business recoveries. Government expenditures would be financed either by tax revenues or by the creation of money. The Federal Reserve System would not operate in the open market, and no interest-bearing securities would be issued to the general public. There are many objections to this plan, and there is no certainty that it would function as presumed, but the ideas are thought provoking and point up the need for coordination of monetary and fiscal policies. This need is widely recognized and was the basis for two proposals to create a money and

---

[8] Milton Friedman, "A Monetary and Fiscal Framework for Economic Stability," *Readings in Monetary Theory* (New York: Blakiston Co., 1951), pp. 369-93.

credit council to coordinate the different monetary, fiscal, and credit activities of the Federal Reserve System, the United States Treasury, and other federal credit agencies.

The "Hoover Commission" (officially, the Commission on Organization of the Executive Branch of the Government)[9] recommended that Congress create a "National Monetary and Credit Council" similar to the National Advisory Council on International Monetary and Fiscal Problems, which is concerned with foreign lending. The council would be composed of the Secretary of the Treasury as chairman, the chairman of the Board of Governors of the Federal Reserve System, the director of the Bureau of the Budget, and a representative of the Federal Farm Credit Administration and/or Housing and Home Financing Agency.

In 1950 the subcommittee of the Joint Committee on the Economic Report recognized the need for coordination of monetary and fiscal policies, as indicated by the following:

> We recommend the creation of a National Monetary Council which would include the Secretary of the Treasury, the Chairman of the Board of Governors of the Federal Reserve System, the Comptroller of the Currency, the Chairman of the Federal Deposit Insurance Corporation, and the heads of the other principal Federal agencies that lend and guarantee loans. This Council should be established by legislative action, should be required to make periodic reports to Congress, and should be headed by the Chairman of the Council of Economic Advisers. Its purpose should be purely consultative and advisory, and it should not have directive power over its members.[10]

In both these semiofficial recommendations, the importance of coordinating monetary, fiscal, and credit policies is recognized. Within the past 30 years, the economic system of the United States has undergone revolutionary changes, and our present complex financial system has developed out of these changes. The chief reason for the existence of so many financial institutions is to make the most effective use of credit, but, unless the activities of these institutions are coordinated with monetary and fiscal policies, their lending operations may weaken monetary and credit policies. The proposals for coordinating the work of the different federal agencies were made

[9] The Commission on Organization of the Executive Branch of the Government, *Treasury Department: A Report to Congress* (Washington, D.C.: U.S. Government Printing Office, March, 1949), p. 9.

[10] Subcommittee of the Joint Committee on the Economic Report, *Monetary, Credit, and Fiscal Policies* (Washington, D.C.: U.S. Government Printing Office, 1950), p. 4.

more than a decade ago, and, although no positive action has been taken, some cooperation is being obtained by informal action.

SUMMARY

One of the most important objectives of monetary policy is stable general prices; however, Congress has not succeeded in regulating the value of money nor has it instructed the Federal Reserve System to do so. Although the Employment Act of 1946 directed the System "to assist in realizing a more stable purchasing power of the dollar," the Act contained no specific directive to prevent inflation. Although the Employment Act of 1946 directed the Federal Reserve System to promote employment, the System is responsible only for that part due to lack of effective demand. Any expansionary program to correct nonmonetary, that is, frictional and chronic, unemployment would not only fail in this respect but would also cause serious dislocations in the price structure and increase unemployment.

The discussion of the new types of inflation calls attention to the need for "big business" and large labor unions to support the fiscal and monetary policies of the government and the Federal Reserve System. The two approaches to the determination of prices, demand and cost, are not new, and they are not mutually exclusive, so there is no reason that both should not be considered in explaining price movements. Generally cost-push inflation can take place only when there are favorable demand conditions, and these conditions may be due to credit and monetary expansion, to an increase in the velocity of money, and/or to fiscal policy.

Growth results from an increase in population and in its efficiency which is due to the energy and skills of management and labor. In the final analysis, the rate of growth depends upon the choice of the people who may prefer more leisure and less work or more work and less leisure. Unfortunately, many persons may be overworked while others are unemployed. To achieve a better balance in the work force, there is need for better education in those areas that will fit a greater number of individuals for skilled jobs in our modern industrial society. The most important factor in growth is men with the ability and educational background to develop ideas, products, and new techniques. Such men have aided and been aided by research and technology, education, the patent system, and an abundance of raw materials, natural resources, and capital.

The President's Council of Economic Advisers has presented wage and price guideposts for use in collective bargaining; and, as

long as the leaders of business and labor adhere to them, the inflationary bias that is a characteristic of a high-employment economy will be
weakened. Although there are many factors in our economy that tend
to lead to creeping inflation, there are others that tend to offset them.
But whether or not the present inflationary trend is kept under control will depend on how well and how courageously the devices of
fiscal and credit control are used by the United States Treasury and
the Federal Reserve System.

QUESTIONS AND PROBLEMS

1. Identify: (*a*) price stability, (*b*) money illusion, and (*c*) hyperinflation.
2. Explain why inflation affects some groups more adversely than others.
3. Explain why (*a*) business firms tend to lose efficiency and (*b*) the
foreign-trade surplus tends to decline during periods of increasing
prices.
4. Note and explain the cost price theory.
5. Identify: (*a*) escalator clause, (*b*) wage-price guideposts, and (*c*) how
(*a*) and (*b*) tend to affect general prices.
6. What is the significance of the following: "Labor costs accelerated
sharply in January (1968). The combination of a sizable increase in
employers' social security tax payments and a modest decline in
output per man-hour resulted in a very large 1.4 per cent increase in
labor costs per unit of output. In January, the index of unit labor costs
in manufacturing stood . . . 3.8 per cent above January 1967 level."
(Federal Reserve Bank of New York, *Monthly Review*, March, 1968,
p. 55.)
7. Discuss: "Once a deceleration (in prices) is achieved, it can become
self-reinforcing. As wage increases slow down, unit labor costs and
prices will move up less rapidly. The successive upward adjustments
of wages to prices and of prices to wages can progressively shrink."
(*Economic Report of the President Transmitted to the Congress
February 1968 together with the Annual Report of the Council of
Economic Advisers* [Washington, D.C.: U.S. Government Printing
Office, 1968], p. 102.)
8. Explain: "Prices of medical care services have been rising faster than
any other component of the CPI [consumer price index]. After
increases of approximately 2½ percent in the quarters immediately
following the initiation of Medicare in mid-1966, the rate of increase
tapered off starting in the spring of 1967 but rose more than 2 percent
from last December to this March. Charges for hospital services and
fees of doctors and dentists continued to climb sharply." (Office of
Business Economics, United States Department of Commerce, *Survey
of Current Business*, May, 1968, p. 2.)

9. Explain: "Fear of pressure from Washington is the principal reason Detroit will hold down the size of its [price] increases. . . . One Auto official, even before the steel industry's price backdown [stated that the auto executives] don't want to get kicked around. . . . General Motors Corp. . . . has reviewed prices with the President's Council of Economic Advisers every year since 1964." (*Wall Street Journal,* August 8, 1968, p. 1.)

10. Analyze: "It is one thing to say 'some degree of inflation' is inevitable but let us try to limit its extent, and it is quite another thing to say 'inflation will happen anyway and we can do nothing about it.'" (Federal Reserve Bank of New York, *Monthly Review,* February, 1967, p. 24.)

CHAPTER 21

Capital Markets and Investment Banking

THE SAVINGS-INVESTMENT process is an important element in the growth of the U.S. economy. A characteristic of the financing of business' corporations is the use of funds obtained from internal sources (retained earnings and depreciation allowances); but there is some dependence on external sources, that is, funds obtained by selling notes, bonds, and stock in the capital market and borrowing from financial intermediaries.

To supplement their operating surplus and federal grants, state and local governments use the capital market to obtain funds to finance the construction of schools, roads, buildings, and other forms of fixed social capital goods. The importance of banks and other financial institutions in the management of capital resources is suggested by Table 21–1.

CAPITAL MARKET

The capital market is the place where long-term securities are bought and sold.[1] Unlike the money market wherein repayment of debts depends on the flow of funds, in the capital market obligations are long-term and repayment is over a period of time from income. Therefore, in analyzing the capital market emphasis is on real and anticipated income rather than on the credit standing of the borrower. This does not mean that all credit instruments traded in the capital market are repaid out of income because borrowers may refinance their debts (bonds and notes) on or before maturity. The

---

[1] The *Commercial Code*, Art. 8–102 (1) (a) defines a "security" as an instrument which (1) "is issued in bearer or registered form," (2) "is a type commonly dealt in upon securities exchanges or markets or commonly recognized in any area in which it is issued or dealt in as a medium for investment," (3) "is either one of a class or series or by its terms is divisible into a class or a series of instruments," and (4) "evidences a share participation or other interest in property or in an enterprise or evidences an obligation of the issuer."

market for capital instruments includes corporate ownership or equity instruments that most commonly appear as common and preferred stock (no equity instruments are traded in the money market).

The capital market is similar to the money market in being made up of the customer-loan market and the open market. A customer loan is usually negotiated between the borrower and one lender; but, if the amount is large, the loan may be participated in by several lenders. Sometimes, after negotiation, customer loans appear in the capital market. For illustration, some mortgage loans are sold by

TABLE 21-1

ASSETS OF INSTITUTIONAL INVESTOR

Institution	Amount (Billions of Dollars)	Percent
Commercial banks	$ 357	34.4
Bank trust departments	250	24.0
Mutual savings banks	61	5.9
Savings and loan associations	134	12.9
Life insurance companies	162	15.6
Other insurance companies	40	3.8
Open-end investment companies	34	3.3
Total	$1,040	100.0

Source: *Commercial Banks and Their Trust Activities; Emerging Influence on the American Economy* (Staff Report for the Subcommittee on Domestic Finance, Committee on Banking and Currency, House of Representatives, 90th Cong., 2d sess., July 8, 1968), Vol. 1, p. 19.

mortgage companies, brokers, or dealers to other permanent investors while others are held by the originating mortgage-financing institution (see Chapter 22). Commercial banks provide some of the loanable funds in the capital market, but the amount of new funds in the form of bank credit from this source is small compared with the amount provided by intermediary financial institutions that receive most of their funds from individual savers.

An individual may invest his savings (the amount of current income which he withdraws for investment) directly in his own business or indirectly in acquiring real estate mortgages and/or securities, or he may invest them indirectly through one or more financial institutions. The fact that many savers have chosen the latter method accounts for one of the most significant characteristics of the capital market, namely, the degree to which it is dominated on the supply side by financial institutions. The chief borrowers in the capital market are homeowners, business corporations, and governments.

Securities Markets. That part of the capital market in which long-term credit instruments and stocks are bought and sold is known as the open market, and it includes not only the primary market for new securities but also the secondary, or "secondhand" market for those outstanding. The middlemen in the securities markets are investment houses, brokerage firms, and securities dealers and brokers. Other financial intermediaries who are interested in the securities markets as permanent investors include life insurance companies, government and private pensions funds, and trust companies. Since a large percentage of the assets of these financial intermediaries is in stocks and corporate bonds, it means that a large segment of the population is indirectly affected by the securities markets.

Investment Houses. The economic function of an investment house is to provide long-term of fixed-capital funds for business and government enterprises. This is done by gathering "other people's money" (savings) through the sale of stocks, bonds, notes, and other instruments of issuers[2] (governments, public utility companies, railroads, industrial companies, and other corporations). It is the task of the investment house or investment banker to service both borrowers and lenders. Basically, the investment banker is a merchandising middleman whose primary function is to bring together users and suppliers of long-term capital funds. He originates new security issues, underwrites them, and distributed them to buyers. An investment house usually participates with others in underwriting millions of dollars of new securities each year (see Table 21–2). For illustration, in 1966, First Boston Corporation participated in underwriting securities of $2.63 billion.

INVESTMENT BANKING

A business corporation that needs to supplement its capital funds by borrowing or selling stock in the open market would ordinarily consult its investment bankers, who investigate the corporation's needs and recommend methods of financing. Often two or more plans are submitted, so that the one that best meets the needs of the issuer and fits the "tone of the market" on the day that the issue is to be offered may be used. The offering may be common stock, preferred stock, a bond or note issue, or some combination or two or more of

[2] The *Commercial Code*, Art. 8–201 1(a) defines an issuer broadly to include one who "places or authorizes the placing of his name on a security (otherwise than as authenticating trustee, registrar, transfer agent or the like) to evidence that it represents a share participation or other interest in his property or in an enterprise or to evidence his duty to perform an obligation evidenced by the security. . . ."

TABLE 21-2
Total New Issues
(In Millions of Dollars)

Period	Total	Noncorporate U.S. Government[2]	Noncorporate U.S. Government Agency[3]	Noncorporate U.S. State and Local	Noncorporate Other[4]	Corporate Total	Corporate Bonds Total	Corporate Bonds Publicly Offered	Corporate Bonds Privately Placed	Corporate Stock Preferred	Corporate Stock Common	Proposed Use Total	New Capital Total	New Capital New Money[6]	New Capital Other Purposes	Retirement of Securities[5]
1960	$27,541	$7,906	$1,672	$7,230	$579	$10,154	$8,081	$4,806	$3,275	$409	$1,664	$9,924	$9,653	$8,758	$895	$271
1961	35,527	12,253	1,448	8,360	303	13,165	9,420	4,700	4,720	450	3,294	12,885	12,017	10,715	1,302	868
1962	29,956	8,590	1,188	8,558	915	10,705	8,969	4,440	4,529	422	1,314	10,501	9,747	8,240	1,507	754
1963	35,199	10,827	1,168	10,107	887	12,211	10,856	4,713	6,143	343	1,011	12,049	10,523	8,898	1,625	1,526
1964	37,122	10,656	1,205	10,544	760	13,957	10,865	3,623	7,243	412	2,679	13,792	13,038	11,233	1,805	754
1965	40,108	9,348	2,731	11,148	889	15,992	13,720	5,570	8,150	725	1,547	15,801	14,805	13,063	1,741	996
1966	45,015	8,231	6,806	11,089	815	18,074	15,561	8,018	7,542	574	1,939	17,841	17,601	15,806	1,795	241
1967	68,514	19,431	8,180	14,288	1,817	24,798	21,954	14,990	6,964	885	1,959	24,409	24,097	22,233	1,867	312
1967—Apr.	4,229	393	650	1,129	41	2,015	1,778	1,368	410	144	94	1,985	1,973	1,891	82	12
May	4,002	438	810	1,209	26	1,518	1,361	965	396	47	111	1,493	1,474	1,418	56	19
June	5,373	410	650	1,461	179	2,674	2,343	1,684	659	17	313	2,631	2,611	2,363	248	20
July	4,375	415	407	925	39	2,589	2,375	1,889	486	85	130	2,546	2,457	2,181	275	89
Aug.	10,625	6,458	250	840	596	2,481	2,231	1,813	418	105	144	2,440	2,406	2,184	222	34
Sept.	4,218	362	599	1,273	220	1,763	1,549	902	647	41	173	1,732	1,723	1,581	142	10
Oct.	4,609	422	708	991	78	2,409	1,940	1,375	566	231	238	2,367	2,289	2,120	168	79
Nov.	8,732	5,054	710	1,320	147	1,500	1,196	645	551	81	222	1,470	1,467	1,305	163	3
Dec.	4,483	371	612	1,093	22	2,385	2,107	1,087	1,020	42	235	2,343	2,336	2,113	223	8
1968—Jan.	4,556	481	999	1,162	144	1,771	1,449	903	546	46	276	1,732	1,705	1,588	117	27
Feb.	8,072	4,719	550	1,134	61	1,608	1,382	796	585	58	169	1,585	1,568	1,447	121	16
Mar.	5,069	418	1,370	1,363	118	1,799	1,359	766	593	145	295	1,765	1,740	1,592	149	24
Apr.	3,448	405	225	1,276	88	1,453	1,184	719	465	49	221	1,422	1,413	1,222	191	9

Column groups: *Gross Proceeds, All Issues*[1] — Noncorporate and Corporate. *Proposed Use of Net Proceeds, All Corporate Issues*[5] — Total, New Capital (Total, New Money, Other Purposes), Retirement of Securities. Stock: Preferred and Common.

[1] Gross proceeds are derived by multiplying principal amounts or number of units by offering price.
[2] Includes guaranteed issues.
[3] Issues not guaranteed.
[4] Foreign governments, International Bank for Reconstruction and Development, and domestic nonprofit organizations.
[5] Estimated gross proceeds less cost of flotation.
[6] For plant and equipment and working capital.
Source: *Federal Reserve Bulletin*, July, 1968, p. A-44.

these basic types of instruments. However, in the case of governments or noncorporate borrowers, the offering would be limited to some form of bond or note issue.

An issue may be sold (1) by competitive bidding to the highest responsible bidder, (2) through private placement with one or more investors, (3) through negotiation to investment bankers, (4) directly by the issuer to investors, and (5) by the issuer to old stockholders. In all cases, the issuer, with the advice of his investment banker, tries to adopt the offering of securities to meet the requirements of the market without ignoring the basic interests of the issuing corporation. As financial advisor, the investment banker recommends the type of security to be issued, the collateral if any is to be used, and terms of the offering, price, and other details.[3]

Competitive Bidding. When credit risk is small and the securities offered are of standard quality requiring little credit investigation, an issue may be sold to the highest responsible bidder. Syndicates, that is, investment houses in association and under formal agreement with each other, submit sealed bids to be opened at the specified time. Customarily syndicates wait until the last minute to place bids so as to have the most recent estimate of the market in which the securities are to be distributed. Buying committees of syndicates study the market prices of similar securities; hence bid prices tend to vary but little (in a few cases when bids were identical, the outcome was decided by the toss of a coin).

Competitive bidding is required by the Interstate Commerce Commission in selling securities of railroad companies under its jurisdiction, except stock issues and a few other special issues. The Securities and Exchange Commission requires registered public utility holding companies and their operating subsidiary companies to sell their new securities and others from their portfolios to the highest responsible bidder.[4] The Federal Power Commission has adopted similar rules for the sale of securities of corporations under its jurisdiction. The United States Treasury sells Treasury bills at its weekly auction, and, in general, the auction method of selling is required by state laws for

[3] Investment houses are represented on the boards of directors and/or finance committees of most of the large corporations, and they participate in plans for new financing from the beginning.

[4] Exceptions to the Securities and Exchange Commission's requirement for competitive sales include those (1) sold under preemptive rights or privileges to old stockholders; (2) debt instruments maturing within 10 years if sold to financial institutions when they are not to be resold and no finder's fee is paid to a third person; (c) issue resulting from mergers and reorganizations; and (4) securities issued to registered holding companies or subsidiaries.

issues of state and local governments and, in some states, for issues of public utility companies.

The practice of selling issues by competitive bidding has disrupted some of the previously established relationships between issuers and their investment bankers, thereby tending to weaken the positions of the older houses (which have had banker-borrower relationships with large corporations for many years) and to strengthen that of the newer ones. Nevertheless, the older "prestige" firms have been able to retain most of their corporate business.[5]

Private Placement.   Private placement refers to the sale of securities by an issuer directly to investors, such as one or more insurance companies. Private placement has the advantages of simplicity, flexibility, and lower cost or financial advantage. The simplicity of private placement refers to the fact that the registration and disclosure requirements of the Securities and Exchange Commission are avoided as well as the registration fee, the 20-day waiting period, and dissemination of detailed information. The investor purchases the securities directly without the services of an investment banker.

In private placement, the terms of the issue result from negotiation between the issuer and the investor; hence there is considerable flexibility as to the size of the particular issue, its maturity, interest rate, and other details. After the original negotiation, terms may be altered if there is a change in market conditions or in the requirements of participants. If the original agreement is satisfactory, it is usually followed by other transactions which may be in the form of firm commitments to the mutual advantage of the parties involved.[6]

The most important reason for direct placement may be the financial advantage to both parties. The two costs involved in issuing fixed-income securities are the flotation costs and the interest charges on the debt. Usually, the costs entailed "in negotiating direct placements are significantly less than the costs of floating a registered public offering."[7] Although the interest rate on privately placed issues

---

[5] Kuhn, Loeb & Co., which has been a partnership since 1867, has been doing business with some railroads for over 100 years. Among the older houses are Kidder, Peabody & Co., Goldman, Sachs & Co., and Lehman Brothers. Some of the newer houses are descendants of old firms, such as Morgan Stanley & Co. and Smith, Barney & Co.

[6] Since 1958, Prudential Life Insurance Company has not purchased a corporate bond in the open market. The company's investments of over $7 billion are divided among loan customers which include such giants as IBM and General Motors Acceptance Corporation, each of whom borrowed in excess of $100 million, and about 400 others, each of whom borrowed $100 thousand to a few million. See Robert Sheehan, "That Mighty Pump, Prudential," *Fortune,* January, 1964, pp. 102 *ff.*

[7] Federal Reserve Bank of Cleveland, *Economic Review,* March, 1965, p. 6.

is usually higher than on issues sold in the market, the differential may be more than offset by the savings on flotation costs. In the case of relatively small bond issues, particularly those of smaller corporations, private placement is usually the most economical method of financing.

Factors in the higher price (lower interest rate) at which publicly offered issues are sold are traced in part to the value of special services of investment bankers, who are more objective in appraising the credit status of the borrower and are able to time and shape offerings so as to command the best market price. Nevertheless, issuers are often willing to forgo a more favorable price for their securities in order to obtain funds sooner by private placement, avoid the costs of registration, and evade the publicity associated with public offerings.

Negotiation. Many corporations negotiate with their investment bankers when planning to offer new issues of securities. The investment banker chosen is usually one with whom the corporation has had previous experience; and he, in cooperation with other investment houses, will agree to give the issuer a check in return for the bonds or stock certificates that constitute the issue. Negotiation will determine the type of bond or stock issue to be offered, the time of offering, provisions for meeting registration requirements, terms of the offering—such as interest rate, maturity, sinking-fund provisions, redemption prices, security for bonds, restrictions on the corporation, and price.[8]

Negotiation is the oldest method of placing securities on the market. At one time, it was about the only method of selling securities through financial intermediaries not only for business corporations but also for federal, state, and local governments.

In order to determine the investment quality of a proposed issue, the investment banker must make a thorough analysis of the credit worthiness of the applicant, with consideration given to both short-term and long-term factors. Because the cost of investigation is considerable, the investment banker usually obtains an option to underwrite the issue before making more than the briefest type of investigation. Then, with the aid of accountants, business analysts, economists, and lawyers, he checks the prospective issuer as to the following: (1) earning and earning prospects, (2) condition and efficiency

---

[8] Restrictions which commonly appear in bond indentures or contracts limit additional financing, dividend payments, contractual obligations such as leases, and possibly mergers.

of equipment and plant, (3) anticipated uses of new funds, (4) capital structure, (5) corporate powers, and (6) financial statements. The investment banker must then estimate the reaction of the market to the proposed issue and determine how the terms can be drawn so as to make the issue command the best price (in case of bonds, the interest rate, maturity, call features, conversion features, timing of offering, price to the investment banker, and price to the public).

Although investment bankers seldom buy securities to hold as investments, they want to make a profit and at the same time establish a reputation for sound merchandising. They realize that the maxim "a commodity which is well bought is half sold" applies to security selling equally as well as to any other type of merchandising. In order to remain in business, they must have satisfied clients who will buy their new offerings. Usually the reputation of the investment banking house is an important sales factor especially when the issuer is relatively unknown. Although most of the underwriting business of investment bankers is for repeat clients, new customers are obtained through promoters, finders, and agents. In some cases, prospective issuers bring their needs directly to the attention of investment houses.

Underwriting. In investment banking, "underwriting" means that the investment bankers are guaranteeing to provide the issuer a definite sum of money on a definite date in return for an issue of bonds or stock. Underwriters buy issues by competitive bidding or negotiation with the hope of selling the securities promptly at a profit. In some cases, an underwriting contract may be made with the owner of a large block of stock rather than the issuing company, as illustrated by a public offering of Ford Motor Company stock by the Ford Foundation (when the securities are sold, it is called a "secondary distribution"). A second more common variation in the standard type of underwriting contract is one in which the underwriter agrees to purchase any part of an issue not otherwise sold (called "standby underwriting").

Issues of bonds or stocks that are underwritten by investment bankers are usually for large dollar amounts; therefore, two or more firms will form an underwriting syndicate to handle each individual issue. The number of participants in such syndicates varies with the size of the issue, the resources of the investment houses, the risk nature of the issue, and conditions of the market. Usually, each syndicate member agrees to buy a fixed amount of the issue, thus assuring a broad market for the securities. Sometimes the size of the public offering is such as to justify the use of hundreds of investment houses in the distribution process. For example, when the common stock of the Ford Motor Company was sold to the public in 1956, 7 syndicate managers and 2,000 other members of the underwriting syndicate shared in selling more than 10,000,000 shares to the public. However, in March, 1964, the American Telephone and Telegraph Company offered an issue of 12,250,000 shares of common stock to its stock-holders at the rate of 1 new share for each 20 held without any underwriting being involved.

A typical originating house will have several issues in different stages of processing, the ideal situation being one in which there will be a steady stream of issues from the issuers through investment banking channels into the hands of investors. The originating house is usually the syndicate manager, who handles the details and signs the purchase contract with the issuer, thus binding the members of the syndicate. The responsibilities, rights, and privileges of each member of the purchasing syndicate are covered in the syndicate agreement.

The risks assumed by investment houses are similar to those assumed by merchants generally, chiefly loss in value of inventories. Being extremely sensitive to adverse news—political, economic, and-/or psychological, the market for securities may change abruptly between the time securities are obtained from the issuer and the time they are offered to investors. Because investment houses depend to a large extent on borrowed funds obtained from commercial banks, they spread the risk among a large number of houses by forming temporary partnerships (called "syndicates") to handle each large issue. (If an issue looks particularly attractive, the investment banking house and individual members of the organization may invest in the securities for themselves.) In addition to the gross profit, the "spread" between the purchase price and the "offering" price, underwriters receive fees and collect other charges from borrowers or issuing companies. (If not represented, underwriters may arrange for the election of one of their officers or partners to the company's board of directors.)

SALE OF SECURITIES IN NEW ISSUES

Issues are purchased by investment houses for resale, and the syndicate agreement may provide that the entire issue is to be pro-rated among the members of the purchasing syndicate, with each participant responsible for selling his share. In other syndicate agreements, the members are individually and jointly responsible for unsold securities. However, the typical agreement, one that limits the liability of participants, is commonly used in handling issues of states and political subdivisions (called "municipal issues") and the highest quality issues in the corporate field (such as equipment trust obligations of railroads and bonds and notes of communications companies and others in the public utility field). In handling some corporate issues, other investment houses in addition to the members of the purchasing syndicate may be invited to participate as brokers in the distribution of the securities in order to get more selling pressure behind the issues.

During the distribution period, the Securities and Exchange Commission permits the underwriting syndicate to buy and sell the securities in the over-the-counter market in order to stabilize their price; but, if confronted with adverse news, it may be impossible to sell securities at the offering price. Therefore, to prevent heavy losses because of forced sales, the investment bankers must be in a position to hold securities until market conditions become more favorable.

For a number of reasons, investment bankers no longer dominate the capital market as they did during the 1920's. Currently, many business firms finance their capital needs by obtaining term loans from commercial banks and insurance companies. In addition, when an issue is sold to the highest bidder, it may be acquired by a life insurance company or other large investor for its own portfolio without investment bankers participating in the distribution. The largest borrower of all, the United States Treasury, with the assistance of the Federal Reserve banks, offers its own securities to investors. While the history of the United States provides many illustrations of the dependence of the Treasury on investment bankers, this dependence no longer exists. After U.S. government securities are distributed through the Federal Reserve banks, the chief reliance for making a market for them is placed on government-securities dealers and dealer banks.

There are two types of corporations that handle their own sales of securities without underwriting services of investment bankers: (1) small companies that are not well known and whose credit rating would make underwriting too expensive; and (2) corporations at the other extreme that can sell their securities without underwriting because of their reputation and credit standing. However, investment bankers may assist the former as agents in selling securities on a "best-effort" basis and the latter by contracting to buy all the securities unsold by the issuer on a "stand-by" underwriting basis, or they may act as advisers deciding on the characteristics and offering price of the issue.

In recent years considerable use has been made of the "best-effort" method of distributing new issues. When this method is used, the investment bankers do not buy the issue but agree to do their best to sell the securities to investors. The investment bankers may sign (1) a group agreement, which may be as detailed as the syndicate agreement signed by members of a purchasing or underwriting syndicate, and (2) a selling agreement between the investment bankers and the issuer. If securities are unsold, the investment bankers are under no obligation to the issuer, and the issuer benefits only to the extent that his selling costs are reduced through the services of investment bankers. In some cases, the "best-effort" basis of handling an issue will be combined with a purchase agreement covering a given number of bonds, notes or shares, with the sale of the remainder of the issue on a best-effort basis.

When an established company offers new shares of stock (or bonds that may be converted into common stock), the current procedure is for the company to make the offering directly to the old stockholders. One reason for this practice is to protect the board of directors from legal action that otherwise might follow if the old stockholders could prove losses as a result of the dilution of their equity in the company and a second reason is to "sweeten the issue." Old stockholders are therefore given "rights" to buy the new stock (or bonds convertible into stock), which they may use, sell, or permit to lapse. The world's largest private business corporation—the American Telephone and Telegraph Company—has financed part of its post–World War II capital needs by selling common stock, or debentures convertible into common stock, to its stockholders.

When small firms are raising funds to start a business or to enlarge an existing one, they often sell securities directly to investors. The issues are usually too small to warrant the assistance of investment houses, which are more interested in handling the issues of large and well-established borrowers. This is true because the costs of investigating and selling are large and the profit margins are small.

During the 1920's some public utility companies experimented with customer ownership plans, which meant that they sold their securities (stocks and bonds) to the users of their services; and other companies experimented with employee ownership plans, wherein their securities were sold to employees. Because of the heavy losses taken by investors from 1929 to 1933, little use was made of either customer ownership or employee ownership plans of raising new capital until after World War II. Many large companies now offer shares of stock to employees under various retirement, pension, or personnel plans, but raising new capital is not the primary motive. At the present time, one of the attractive features associated with working for many large corporations is the fact that their officers and employees are given the opportunity to acquire stock under option, employee ownership, bonus, and other plans.[9]

The justification for the existence of the investment banker, like that of any specialist, is that he can do certain things better than others can do them. By knowing investment conditions better and by having contacts with prospective investors, the investment banker is able to raise capital funds more successfully for governments and business corporations. Without their services, the development of business and urban centers would have been severely handicapped. Although the large investment houses are concentrated in or near Wall Street in New York and La Salle Street in Chicago, the market for securities is nationwide in scope.

LIFE INSURANCE COMPANIES, PRIVATE PENSION FUNDS, AND TRUSTS

Three of the nonmonetary financial intermediaries that have shown rapid growth since the end of World War II are life insurance companies, private pension funds, and personal trust funds.

Life Insurance Companies. Life insurance companies issue many kinds of claims on themselves in the form of policies or contracts in which they agree to make certain cash payments—lump sum or installments—to the beneficiaries in the event of death, on reaching a certain age, in case of disability, or on meeting other specified conditions. Life insurance companies in the United States number over 1,400 and have combined assets equal to approximately one sixth of the assets of all financial institutions.

Insurance seeks to protect the individual by spreading the economic risk, and insurance companies amass large funds which they

---

[9] For illustration, during 1963, officers of the Chrysler Corporation realized profits of $4.2 million on stock option transactions. The corporation's president gained $744,000, and the chairman acquired profits on paper of $2.3 million from increases in the market value of common stock purchased through an option plan. The tax law requires the executive to hold his stock for six months to be eligible to pay taxes based on long-term capital gains. Usually stocks are acquired with borrowed money, which may necessitate their sale at the end of six months. The spread between the option price and the market price when the option is granted may be no more than 5 percent if capital gains taxes are to be avoided.

invest to lower the cost of protection. Customarily, the insured make payments periodically, as prescribed in their contracts, and these payments or premiums are usually arranged so that the same amount is paid annually. While the savings function of insurance companies is secondary, they hold the second largest pool of savings among the private nonmonetary financial intermediaries in the Unitd States. Life insurance companies' assets are growing, and their cash collections are in excess of current payments due to the increase in the volume of insurance, improvement in health, and increased life expectancy. Although the liquidity needs of life insurance companies are small, some of their assets must be in cash and short-term securities to meet legal requirements and short-term demands for funds. Each year the amount of new investments is larger than the net increase in assets due to the reinvestment of cash received from maturing obligations, amortization of mortgage loans, redeemed bonds, prepayment of obligations, and sale of assets. The two factors that affect the investment requirements of life insurance companies are state regulations and the nature of their insurance contracts.

Life insurance companies operate under state charters and are regulated by insurance commissioners of the respective states in which they do business. State regulations vary as to type and purpose but, in general, they restrict these companies' investments to debt obligations—high-grade bonds and real estate mortgages—in order to protect the interests of policyholders. The laws of some states permit the purchase of a limited amount of stock and limited investments in rental housing projects and certain types of commercial and industrial properties. Life insurance companies' investments are mainly in mortgages and bonds of industrial, public utility, railroad, and other companies. Their other assets include obligations of federal, state, local, and foreign governments, policy loans, corporate stock, real estate, cash, and miscellaneous assets.[10]

While insurance companies are buying bonds offered by investment houses at retail prices, they are also competing with them in the wholesale market; and in some cases, they are the successful bidders for issues sold to the highest bidder. In addition insurance companies may also act as members of purchasing syndicates, and in many cases they negotiate successfully with issuers (borrowers). The competitive position of insurance companies for issues has been strengthened by the rapid growth of their assets, the increase in "competitive

---

[10] *Life Insurance Fact Book 1967* (New York: Institute of Life Insurance, 1967), pp. 61–64.

bidding," and the Securities Act of 1933, which has encouraged private placement of securities by exempting such securities from registration.

Private insurance companies are still providing the largest share of external capital used by American industrial and other business corporations. In addition to their investments represented by corporate bonds, notes, and stock, they are extending credit in return for mortgage notes on business property. The last is the chief source of intermediate and working capital for small business firms, especially those which are not incorporated.

The yield advantage of corporate securities over government securities is considerable, but corporate securities are less marketable and entail higher administrative costs and greater risks. However, liquidity is less important to life insurance companies than to commercial banks because the liabilities of insurance companies are predominantly long term. An insurance company sets promises to pay against promises to pay; thus it is in a hedge position, in which any loss in the value of its assets caused by inflation is offset by a decline in the value of its obligations.

Private Pension Funds. The search for individual and family security has been an important factor in the rapid growth not only of life insurance companies but also of private pension funds. These funds, which are financed by employers and employees, should not be confused with social security programs of the federal government.[11] Many of the pension funds call for retirement payments to beneficiaries equal to from one third to one half of the employee's average annual income as measured by the income received during the 5 or 10 years preceding retirement (these payments are usually in addition to social security retirement benefits).[12]

Private pension funds have grown rapidly since the end of World War II, and most of them are managed by trust departments of commercial banks. (In 1955 pension funds were estimated to have been $27.4 billion and, by the end of 1967, in excess of $100 billion.) Generally, the managers of pension funds are interested in yield and appreciation from their investments, and most of the funds under their control are placed in gilt-edged common stock. Since such purchases are long-term investments, they exert a significant stabilizing

---

[11] The present market value of all pension fund exceeds $150 billion, of which more than half is held by private noninsured funds.

[12] Although an adequate retirement income is considered to be between 50 and 60 percent of one's final annual salary, the percentage should be larger for persons in the low-income groups.

influence on the stock market. In addition, they provide a steady stream of new capital for use of industry and governments ($6 to $7 billion per year).

Large amounts of funds flow regularly into pension funds, thus permitting pension fund managers to go into the stock market weekly or monthly and to follow generally accepted investment principles such as dollar averaging.[13] Since managers have a fiduciary relationship to the ultimate beneficiaries, they are interested chiefly in low-risk (blue chip) common stocks, corporate bonds, mortgages, U.S. government securities, and miscellaneous assets of high quality.[14] Liquidity of assets is relatively less important than safety, yield, and appreciation. The new funds received by private pension funds, like those received by life insurance companies, generally represent new savings.

The total assets of private noninsured pension funds have a book value of over $64 billion, and the amount is increasing rapidly, with receipts exceeding expenditures (namely, benefit payments) by over $6 billion. While the investment policies of individual pension funds vary, the general procedure is to build up common stock holdings until they equal 50 percent of the fund's investment portfolio. In addition to the noninsured pension funds, there are insured pension plans (those managed by life insurance companies), Federal Old-Age and Survivors' Insurance, Federal Disability Insurance, state and local governments' plans, Civil Service, Railroad Retirement, and numerous others.[15]

The growth in pension funds and insurance companies illustrates the national preoccupation with personal security and problems of old age. Pension funds are one of the most important areas for negotiation between employees and employers, and they have contributed to greater economic stability and growth because of their effects on disposable personal income and individual and corporate savings and investments.

[13] Dollar averaging is the policy of regularly buying the same dollar amount of a security regardless of the price, which means that the largest number of shares is acquired when prices are low. The average price per share purchased is always less than the average of the market prices at which shares were acquired.

[14] Many corporations have rules preventing their pension funds from being invested in their own stock. However, there are exceptions such as the Sears, Roebuck & Co. fund, which has about 85 percent of its funds invested in Sears stock. *Wall Street Journal*, January 29, 1964, pp. 1 *passim*.

[15] The Keogh Act permits self-employed persons to place 10 percent of their net earnings or $2,500, whichever is smaller, into pension funds and since 1967 to deduct the full amount from taxable income. Now, the American Institute of Certified Public Accountants, the American Bar Association, and the American Medical Association are offering pension plans to their members.

Personal Trust Funds. Trust companies and personal trust departments of commercial banks, which take title to property and manage it for the beneficiaries of trusts, are discussed in Chapter 25; but, because most of the assets in these trusts are purchased in the capital market, they are treated here briefly.

Almost two thirds of the assets of personal trusts are invested in stocks and the remainder in state and local government obligations, U.S. government obligations, mortgages, and miscellaneous assets. The investment in stocks of personal trusts are considerably larger than those of investment companies, which are the specialists in holdings of corporate stock.

Generally, there is little public interest in the personal trust departments of commercial banks as the number of persons affected is small compared with the number of bank depositors, holders of life insurance policies, and participants in private pension funds. The range of investments in private trust funds is usually wider than in those of insurance companies and private pension funds, but, in the investments of all three groups, safety of principal, yield, and appreciation are factors more important than liquidity.

INVESTMENT COMPANIES

Investment companies are financial institutions that raise funds in the capital market mainly by the sale of shares (stock or trust certificates) to individual investors and invest the funds thus raised chiefly in marketable corporate securities. They are agencies through which funds of participating investors are combined and invested in diversified securities so as to prevent loss of principal (the law of averages, which assumes that gains on some securities will offset losses on others). Theoretically, the individual investor is protected because he owns a prorata share of all the securities held by his investment company, but, because a fraction of zero is always zero, diversification means nothing unless assets of an investment company have value. In all types of investment companies, the objective is to provide individual investors with safe and profitable employment of funds and to relieve them of the burden of direct responsibility of management of their savings. Their main appeal is to small savers, whose enthusiasm for investment company shares varies with stock market prices.

Most investment companies state their objectives as being safety, growth, or income, or some combination of the three. The achievements of investment companies, even in the same category, vary widely. The past record and prospects for the future of one investment company may fit the needs of the aged who want income, and that of a second company may fit the needs of the young who want appreciation (and so on for the needs or desires of others).

In the Investment Company Act of 1940, Congress classified investment companies as general management, unit investment trust, and face amount certificate companies, of which there are several varieties. The general management type includes the "open" or mutual and the "closed-end" types of companies. The one of major interest is the "mutual" or "open-end" general management company, which has no fixed amount of capital but follows the policy of issuing new shares and retiring old shares according to the demand (see

TABLE 21–3

OPEN-END INVESTMENT COMPANIES
(In Millions of Dollars)

Year or Month	Sales and Redemption of Own Shares			Assets (Market Value at End of Period)		
	Sales*	Redemp- tions	Net Sales	Total†	Cash Position‡	Other
1956.........	1,347	433	914	9,046	492	8,554
1957.........	1,391	406	984	8,714	523	8,191
1958.........	1,620	511	1,109	13,242	634	12,608
1959.........	2,280	786	1,494	15,818	860	14,958
1960.........	2,097	842	1,255	17,026	973	16,053
1961.........	2,951	1,160	1,791	22,789	980	21,809
1962.........	2,699	1,123	1,576	21,271	1,315	19,956
1963.........	2,460	1,504	952	25,214	1,341	23,873
1964.........	3,404	1,875	1,528	29,116	1,329	27,787
1965.........	4,359	1,962	2,395	35,220	1,803	33,417
1966.........	4,671	2,005	2,665	34,829	2,971	31,858
1967.........	4,670	2,745	1,927	44,701	2,566	42,135
1967—May....	357	258	99	39,847	2,608	37,239
June.....	375	225	150	40,795	2,503	38,292
July.....	425	222	203	43,064	2,515	40,549
Aug.....	347	249	98	42,663	2,370	40,293
Sept.....	352	246	106	43,585	2,244	41,341
Oct......	409	270	139	42,652	2,218	40,434
Nov.....	468	231	237	43,262	2,653	40,609
Dec.....	501	242	259	44,701	2,566	42,135
1968—Jan......	556	316	240	42,466	2,679	39,787
Feb......	451	260	191	41,533	3,409	38,124
Mar.....	557	243	314	42,412	3,919	38,493
Apr.....	618	309	309	46,179	3,923	42,256
May....	502	366	136	48,054	3,495	44,559

* Includes contractual and regular single-purchase sales, voluntary and contractual accumulation-plan sales, and reinvestment of investment income dividends; excludes reinvestment of realized capital gains dividends.
† Market value at end of period less current liabilities.
‡ Cash and deposits, receivables, all U.S. government securities, and other short-term debt securities, less current liabilities.
Source: *Federal Reserve Bulletin*, July, 1968, p. A–45.

Table 21–3). Sales and purchases are on the basis of the current value of each share.

The rapid growth of mutual general management companies following World War II was due primarily to two features—continuous offering of shares to the public and redeemability of shares. Usually sales are in excess of redemptions; as a result, there is a net flow of savings into securities. Unless limited by its charter to a specific class or classes of securities, the management of such a company has discretion in the choice of investments. Since these companies are created primarily to permit their investors to participate indirectly in the stock market, 90 percent of their assets are in stocks and the remainder in corporate bonds, U.S. government obligations, cash, and miscellaneous assets.

Mutual funds generally issue but one class of shares and, although there are an increasing number of exceptions, they usually add a "loading" charge to the market price of each share. However, some mutual companies are selling directly to the public without adding a "loading" charge and with or without a small sales charge. The market price is computed daily when new shares are sold. Whether the average performance of a share of mutual company stock is better or worse than the market average depends on management. If it is better, management deserves some credit; if worse, diversification has been the main service of the mutual company. The investor's contract permits him to withdraw his funds at the current value of his shares, minus a service charge made on withdrawals. The earnings on the investments of the mutual funds, after payment of expenses, are paid as dividends to their stockholders. Currently, there are 435 mutual funds, most of whom are members of the Investment Company Institute, which holds over 75 percent of the industry's net assets (see Table 21–4). Mutual funds may offer voluntary savings plans that permit the investor to pay in a fixed sum (which may be as little as $20) each month for a definite number of years (usually 10), and the loading charge for the period is deducted in the first year.

A second type of general management investment company is the closed-end company, whose capital structure is similar to that of other corporations. After the original distribution, generally no new stock is issued, and new investors must buy stock from other stockholders (some of these companies have their shares listed on stock exchanges). Some of the companies of this type also issue notes and bonds, thus giving their stock an element of leverage.

At the other extreme from the general management investment

company is the unit or fixed or semifixed company, in which management has little or no discretion as to investments. They are usually organized for a specified period of time under provisions of a trust indenture or similar legal instrument. The promoters select the securities, and a bank or trust company acts as custodian of the securities, collector of the income, and distributor of the earnings of the trust to certificate holders (the beneficiaries of the property held in trust). Funds are invested in securities at the beginning of the trust, and management is given little or no power of substitution. The arguments for this type of management are that diversification is provided,

TABLE 21–4

INVESTMENT COMPANIES, JUNE 30, 1967

Type	Number of Companies			Estimated Value of Assets (Millions of Dollars)
	Active	Inactive	Total	
Management open end (mutual)	435	24	459	$44,557
Management closed end	161	41	202	7,549
Unit investment trust	141	32	173	4,963
Face amount certificate	6	2	8	1,108
Total	743	99	842	$58,177

* Source: Securities and Exchange Commission, *33rd Annual Report for the Fiscal Year Ended June 30, 1967* (Washington, D.C.: U.S. Government Printing Office, 1968), p. 106.

expenses are kept at a minimum, expert management is furnished by the management of the various corporations whose securities are purchased, and the danger of mismanagement by those in charge of the trust is avoided.

A few investment companies have been organized to offer investment trust certificates to investors on the installment plan. Generally, payments are made to a trustee bank over a 10-year period, and the funds are used to buy certificates of interest in the underlying securities. The holder of certificates is entitled to receive the market value of his certificates, which is based on his pro rata interest in the underlying securities. Loading charges are in addition to the cost of the trust shares or certificates; and, of the amount paid in, a percentage of the early payments is used to cover expenses.

During the fiscal year ended June 30, 1967 promoters introduced a new type of investment company, and nine of them have registered with the Securities and Exchange Commission. They are known as capital leveraged companies because their capital is divided into two parts, with one half contributed by "capital shareholders" and the other half by "income shareholders." The latter are entitled to the income of the fund for a specified period of time, such as 12 to 18 years, and then to a liquidation value. The capital shareholders get the appreciation value of the company's assets minus the liquidation value of income shares. Of the companies organized during fiscal 1967, all except one were closed-end companies. The open-end company sells both types of stock as a unit and redeems them as a unit.[16]

Finally, there are a few so-called "face amount" companies that sell certificates on the installment to investors. The companies contract to pay holders either a stated sum of money on a specified date, commonly 15 or 20 years in the future, or the cash-surrender value of their investments prior to maturity, provided that the holders meet all the terms of their contracts. During the first years, when the investor's equity in the plan is small, lapses on payments tend to be high, and the amount returned on the early payments (cash-surrender value) is small. The chief criticism of the different types of contractual plans is that the "front-end load" charges are too high—up to 50 percent of the first year's payments (and some states do not permit their sale). A bill in Congress would prohibit "front-end load" plans and permit deductions of no more than 20 percent of total investments for sales commissions in any one year and no more than 64 percent of a total commission during the first four years of a person's participation in a plan. However, unless a person is sure of his ability to complete his investment program, contractual plans should be avoided because the penalty for discontinuance is too high.

Some investment companies offer a systematic investment plan that is combined with life insurance. Although this arrangement provides a means of giving one's family added financial protection, the same results may be achieved less expensively by separating the two. Some individuals want an investment fund that permits regular withdrawals for special purposes, and many companies offer reinvestment privileges that permit distributed dividends and capital gains to be retained. Other things being equal, the average investor should select a fund with low operating costs (normally, the larger the fund, the lower the percentage operating cost relative to total net assets) without a "loading" charge and one which is a good performer and fits his needs.

The Investment Company Act of 1940 requires investment com-

---

[16] Securities and Exchange Commission, *33rd Annual Report for the Fiscal Year Ended June 30, 1967*, pp. 107–8.

panies to register with the Securities and Exchange Commission, which is responsible for their supervision, the purpose being to assure the public honest management, cheaper selling costs of new securities, sounder capital structures, and greater publicity as to their affairs. A bill in Congress would permit national banks to establish mutual type funds which were forbidden by a federal court in 1967 in a ruling against the First National City Bank of New York. This bill would also authorize the National Association of Securities Dealers, a trade organization, to establish "reasonable" charges by mutual funds on sales, but if the association failed to act "responsibly" the way would be clear for the Securities and Exchange Commission to fix them. At the present time, these charges are as much as 9 percent of what a person invests, which is regarded as too high. Congress would leave it to the courts to establish "reasonable annual fees" to be paid to a second company for advisory services. Customarily, they are equal to one half of 1 percent of total assets, which may mean an annual payment of millions of dollars for some funds.

SECONDARY MARKETS FOR SECURITIES

The popularity of investments in bonds, stocks, and other long-term securities depends in part upon the liquidity of the capital market. Although millions of individual investors operate through institutions, as noted earlier, these institutions and other individuals invest directly in the capital market, particularly in the secondary markets for securities, which have developed in New York and other financial centers. The middlemen in these markets are securities dealers and brokers who buy and sell for their own accounts or as agents for others.[17] Purchases and sales are made in the over-the-counter market and on organized stock exchanges, which are but associations of brokers and dealers. In the over-the-counter market, trading is of the negotiated type; in the organized exchanges, the auction type of buying and selling exists. Although the two types of markets are unlike in practice and procedures, their functions and purposes are similar (conversion of idle funds into earning assets).[18]

The expression "over-the-counter" market is a loose term ap-

---

[17] The *Commercial Code*, Art. 8–303, defines a broker (broadly enough to include a dealer) as one "engaged for all or part of his time in the business of buying or selling securities, who in the transaction concerned acts for, or buys a security from or sells a security to a customer."

[18] Sometimes large institutional investors, such as charitable foundations, mutual funds, and trust departments of banks, trade directly with one another, thereby avoiding payment of commissions to brokers.

plied to the activities of dealers, brokers, bankers, and others in buying and selling unlisted securities. The Securities Exchange Act of 1934 defined the over-the-counter market as one including all transactions in securities that take place otherwise than upon a national exchange. In essence, it consists of markets characterized by unlimited entry both from the viewpoint of persons trading therein and securities traded. Those who specialize in this type of business may have private-wire systems to other brokers and dealers located in the United States and/or abroad, or they may be one-man firms that trade only in local markets.

The shares of most banks and insurance companies and of many public utility, railroad, and industrial companies are traded in the over-the-counter market. This market is the only medium for marketing securities offered to the public for the first time (later they may be traded on an organized stock exchange). In addition, there is an enormous over-the-counter bond market wherein corporate long-term notes, bonds and debentures and obligations of the federal, state, and local governments are traded.

Brokers and dealers belong to a self-regulating group, the National Association of Securities Dealers, Inc., which is registered with and subject to the supervision of the Securities and Exchange Commission. The association's chief activity has been to raise business standards of all over-the-counter brokers and dealers and to devise a uniform business practice code. It may take, and has taken, disciplinary action against members for violation of the Association's rules. Facts concerning violations by different firms are brought to the attention of the Association by the Securities and Exchange Commission for whatever action the Association may find desirable. An "aggrieved party of disciplinary action" may request a review from the Securities and Exchange Commission, as provided by law.

Brokers and dealers who are members of security exchanges provide the best-known secondary market for securities. In a broad sense, a security exchange is the meeting place for buyers and sellers of securities. A more modern and correct definition is: "A security exchange is an unincorporated association or incorporated company, the members of which trade in securities for others and themselves."

Securities exchanges whose business is predominantly interstate are, since 1934, under the general regulation of the Securities and Exchange Commission and are called "national securities exchanges." At the present time, there are 14 exchanges registered with the Securities and Exchange Commission. The largest, and by far the most important, exchange is the New York Stock Exchange, where stocks and bonds of national and international importance are bought and sold. It is a voluntary organization—an association—and, as such, it is subject to internal regulation. Membership is now at 1,366,[19] and admission is dependent upon getting a member to retire in the applicant's favor, a favorable vote of the committee on admission, and satisfaction of certain other requirements, including payment of an initiation fee. The term "seat" on a stock exchange was first used literally, but now it is a trade term denoting membership, which gives the holder the right to transact purchases and sales of securities on the floor of the exchange.

Individuals or firms having seats on the New York Stock Exchange, the "Big Board," are classified as: inactive members, who rarely go near the exchange but retain their memberships for investments or for social or noneconomic reasons; "wire houses," who execute orders that are received locally and by wire from branch offices and correspondents in American and foreign cities; commission brokers, who buy and sell for their firms' clients; floor brokers (called "two-dollar" brokers), who are not affiliated with stock-exchange firms but execute orders for other members, particularly commission brokers; specialists, who are assigned by the Exchange to one or more stocks and act as floor brokers for other brokers and as traders for themselves; floor traders, who buy and sell for their own accounts; odd-lot dealers and brokers, who buy and sell lots of less than 100 shares to commission brokers and others; and bond dealers and brokers, who deal in bonds for their own accounts and for customers.[20]

The New York Stock Exchange has about 3,650 "allied" members (those who are general partners or voting stockholders in member firms but have no trading privileges as members of the exchange), who are under the rules and discipline of the exchange. Some brokerage firms own more than one seat, and five have 10 or more seats; so

[19] A "seat dividend" of one fourth of one seat was declared in 1929, raising the number of memberships from 1,100 to 1,375, and in 1953 a seat-retirement plan was adopted with the intention of reducing the number to 1,300 by 1963. Originally, under the plan, purchases could be at $45,000 or less, but in 1957 the amount was increased to $60,000 (or less). Because the retirement prices have been low, relative to market prices for seats, only nine seats have been retired to date.

[20] Although some members of the stock exchange offer no general brokerage service to the general public, an increasing number of investment houses have gone into the brokerage business. On the other hand, many brokerage houses, through mergers and otherwise, now do an underwriting and distributing business. Although the former type of business involves already issued securities and the latter, new security offerings, both necessitate an extensive sales organization for wide distribution of securities.

the number of member organizations is only 662, of which 62 are corporations. The member organizations operate about 2,700 main offices in the United States and abroad.

The general public makes purchases or sales on the stock exchange through commission brokers. A prospective buyer or seller merely goes to any broker's office or branch (of which there are several in every city of any size) and places his order to buy or sell. In the case of buying, if he has not already made credit arrangements with the broker, he must deposit cash or acceptable securities. The order will be executed, and the securities will be delivered within a reasonable time. It is, of course, taken for granted that the brokerage house has a member on the floor of the exchange or a correspondent relationship with some member of the exchange on which the order is to be executed.

The New York and other stock exchanges are "continuous auction" markets, wherein the various securities are assigned to different places on the floor of the exchanges (called "posts") where buy and sell orders are taken for execution. At each of the 18 posts, where the shares of about 75 corporations are traded, there is competition between both buyers and sellers. The individual traders who act as both brokers and dealers at each post are registered with the Exchange as "specialists" in one or more stocks. It is their duty to maintain "fair and orderly" markets in the securities in which they deal, buying or selling as dealers when the market is "thin" (that is, insuring that an order will meet a counterpart at a fair price).

In order to prevent fraud, each stock certificate must have the signature of a registrar and a transfer agent. Each corporation whose stock is listed on the New York Stock Exchange is required to have a transfer agent or office in the financial district of New York and a bank to act as registrar. When title to stock changes, a new certificate is issued and the old one destroyed. The duties of the registrar are routine (entailing checking on the number of new shares issued as compared with the old). After signing a new certificate, it is returned to the transfer agent along with the old one. Then the transfer agent destroys the old certificate and gives the new one to the broker.

FEDERAL REGULATION OF SECURITIES MARKETS

The investment banker has a dual role—he is the advisor of issuers regarding securities to be offered investors and he must satisfy investors. Thus, there may be a conflict which may result in neglect of one in favor of the other, as would be indicated by the record of the 1920's and 1930's. In order to reduce the number of fraudulent acts and unfair practices in the sale of securities, the federal and many state governments now regulate the investment banking and brokerage businesses.

The Securities and Exchange Commission was created in 1934 to assume the responsibility for supervision of the Securities Act of 1933 (previously under the administration of the Federal Trade Commission) and the Securities Exchange Act of 1934. Subsequent legislation has made the Commission responsible for the Public Utility Holding Company Act of 1935, the Trust Indenture Act of 1939, the Investment Company Act of 1940, and the Investment Advisors Act of 1940. Under provisions of Chapter X of the National Bankruptcy Act, as amended in 1938, the Commission serves as adviser to the United States district courts in connection with reorganization procedures for debtor corporations (in which there is a substantial public interest).

The Securities and Exchange Commission, which began operations in September, 1934, under the chairmanship of Joseph P. Kennedy, consists of five members and has a supporting staff of experts—accountants, engineers, lawyers, security analysts, and others. The general objective of the laws that it administers is to protect investors and the public against malpractices in financial or securities markets. To this end, use has been made of registration and licensing requirements for security dealers and brokers, registration of specific issues, and civil and criminal prosecution for malpractices.

The laws provide for public disclosure of pertinent facts about new issues and those traded over-the-counter and on national securities exchanges, but they do not insure against the issuance of worthless securities. It provides for civil and criminal penalties for those who fail to make full disclosure of facts and/or misrepresent them. Although dishonesty cannot be prevented, it can be apprehended and those guilty prosecuted. Regulation of trading in securities on exchanges and in the over-the-counter market requires, among other things, that each officer, director, and all others owning 10 percent or more of any class of registered equity securities report monthly on changes in his holdings.[21] In enforcing the laws and the regulations

---

[21] When an "insider" makes a profit from a "sure-thing" transaction in the stock of his own corporation (for example, selling just before a bad earning statement is issued or a cash dividend is omitted or purchasing just before favorable news is released), Sec. 16 of the Securities Exchange Act permits the corporation or any security holder in its behalf to recover these profits (defined as including transactions completed within six months in equities of the corporation with which the person is associated).

under the laws, the Commission has cooperated with securities markets, different associations, and state enforcing agencies. The Commission maintains regional offices, has its own staff of investigators, keeps files on persons connected with illegal or fraudulent securities practices, and may report violations of the law to the attorney-general of the United States for criminal prosecution. Among the various trade and other associations working with the Securities and Exchange Commission are the National Association of Security Dealers, Inc., the Investment Bankers Association of America, national exchanges, the National Association of Investment Companies, the National Better Business Bureau, Inc., and local better business bureaus. Many states now have their own agencies to regulate securities selling, and they have done much to supplement the work of the Securities Exchange Commission, but fraudulent and/or worthless stocks will be sold in the United States as long as there are dishonest persons.

SUMMARY

The capital market, wherein the demands for and supply of long-term funds meet, is dominated on the supply side by institutional investors. The intermediaries in this market are the investment bankers, who underwrite and distribute securities. An original issue of securities may be sold directly to investors (private placement); to the highest bidder (competitive bidding); or through investment bankers, who may purchase the issue outright for resale, guarantee the sale of the issue, or take the issue for sale on a best-effort basis.

By placing issues directly with investors, the issuers avoid the costs entailed in public distribution through the facilities of investment houses and in registration of issues with the Securities and Exchange Commission (required of most publicly offered private issues). When credit risks are small and the securities are of standard quality, requiring little credit investigation, the issue may be sold by competitive bidding (required of some securities such as issues of state and local governments, public utility companies, and certain issues of railroad companies).

Life insurance companies, the most important single group of investors in the capital market, are both customers and competitors of investment bankers in bidding for issues of securities. The competitive position of these companies has been strengthened by the rapid growth of their assets, the increase in competitive bidding, and the provision in the Securities Act of 1933 that has encouraged private placement by exempting such issues from registration. At the present time, life insurance companies are absorbing most of the corporate bond issues and are financing many business needs by making term loans.

Private pension funds are expanding rapidly and, like insurance companies, are heavy buyers of corporate bonds. In addition, they have invested heavily in corporate stocks. The personal trust departments of banks are now the chief investors in corporate stock, holding more than the specialist in this field, the investment company. There are several types of investment companies, but the "mutual" is the most important. Investment companies sell their securities to investors and reinvest these funds in other securities. Their main purpose is to provide small investors with diversification of risks and expert management.

The secondary markets for securities include the over-the-counter market and security exchanges, of which the New York Stock Exchange is the most important. The individuals and firms having "seats" on this stock exchange are divided into seven categories according to their activities, and it is through the commission brokers that the general public makes purchases and sales of securities listed thereon. The various laws and regulations that have been adopted to protect investors and the general public against malpractices in financial and securities markets are administered by the Securities and Exchange Commission, created in 1934. To this objective, use has been made of (1) registration and licensing requirements for security dealers and brokers, (2) registration of specific issues, and (3) civil and criminal prosecution for malpractice. The capital market includes the customer loan market as well as the open market, but the activities of savings and loan associations, mutual savings banks, and other direct lenders are discussed in later chapters.

QUESTIONS AND PROBLEMS

1. Identify: (*a*) capital market, (*b*) investment security, (*c*) issue, (*d*) investment banker, and (*e*) syndicate.
2. Analyze: "An investment banker is a merchant—a merchant of securities." (Boston Better Business Bureau, *Facts You Should Know about Investment Banking* (Boston, 1957), p. 2.)
3. Analyze: "Ever buy a stock or bond fresh from the issuer? If you did, you paid a specific price—the only time a price of a security is ever 'pegged' in a perfectly legal manner." ("Bankers—Wall Street Style," *Financial World*, June 28, 1967, p. 8.)
4. Explain: (*a*) competitive bidding, (*b*) private placement, (*c*) underwriting, and (*d*) distribution of a security issue.
5. Distinguish between (*a*) an investment broker and a dealer, (*b*) auc-

tion and negotiated securities markets, and (*c*) primary and secondary markets for securities.

6. Analyze: "Some new equities have been jumping to fat premiums immediately after being offered, recalling the wild and wooly days of 1961–62 when, as now, science and high technology stocks were all the rage." (*Financial World*, June 28, 1967, p. 9.)

7. Analyze: "The investment flexibility permitted life insurance companies by statute has been gradually increased since 1906, and it is now greater than that available to commercial banks, mutual savings banks, and savings and loan associations although still less than that available to private pension funds." (Report of the Commission on Money and Credit, *Money and Credit, Their Influence on Jobs, Prices and Growth* [Englewood Cliffs, N.J.: Prentice-Hall, Inc., 1961], p. 177.)

8. Analyze the effect of the following on the investment policy of an insurance company: "An insurance company sets promises to pay against promises to pay: thus it is in a hedge position, in which any loss in the value of its assets caused by inflation is offset by a decline in the value of its obligations."

9. Analyze: For Americans 65 years old or over, numbering 19 million, "sociologists have completed a study . . . [that] proves (1) the standard of living among persons 65 and over is declining . . . as their life expectancy increases and . . . (2) those planning to retire can expect to 'go broke.'" (Manufacturers Hanover Trust, *Pension Bulletin*, August, 1967, p. 4.)

10. Discuss: "Investment companies also must file periodic reports . . . and certain 'insiders' of closed-end companies are subject to the insider reporting and 'short swing' trading rules." (Securities and Exchange Commission, *33rd Annual Report for the Fiscal Year Ended June 30, 1967* [Washington, D.C.: U.S. Government Printing Office, 1968], p. 105.)

CHAPTER 22

Urban Mortgage Credit

FOR ITS economic growth, the United States is dependent to a considerable extent on the increase in expenditures not only for goods and services but also for residential and business property, including farms. Being financed with long-term credit, residential construction is sensitive to changes in interest rates. As a result, home building is an important stabilizing factor in the business cycle, increasing during recessions and recovery periods and declining during business booms (see Chart 22–1).

The volume of home building and home improvement is largely dependent upon funds supplied by such intermediaries as mutual savings banks, life insurance companies, savings and loan associations, and savings departments of commercial banks. The flow of savings into residential financing has been encouraged by several government agencies, such as the Federal Home Loan Bank System, the Federal Housing Administration, and the Public Housing Administration in the urban-financing field and into the agricultural mortgage field by the Farm Credit Administration.

MORTGAGES

General Characteristics. The term "mortgage" is one of the oldest legal terms pertaining to security transactions. The forerunner of the modern mortgage was an outright conveyance of title to the mortgaged property by the debtor (mortgagor) to the creditor (mortgagee), subject to the condition that the mortgagor could regain title to the property upon payment of the debt when due. In case of failure to make payment when due, the mortgagee secured an unconditional title to the property, a fact which resulted in many hardships until courts of equity permitted the debtor to recover his property within a specified time after the due date. This right or "equity of redemption" is now a characteristic of the modern mortgage.

Although the concept of a mortgage as being a conveyance of a defeasible legal title to property still exists in some states, it is regarded as a security transaction for the most part. Practically any type of tangible property and interest in property (such as rent, life estates, and vested remainders) may be mortgaged. The mortgagor retains his legal and equitable title, and the mortgagee obtains a lien to secure

CHART 22-1

PRIVATE NONFARM RESIDENTIAL CONSTRUCTION

(Seasonally Adjusted Annual Rates)

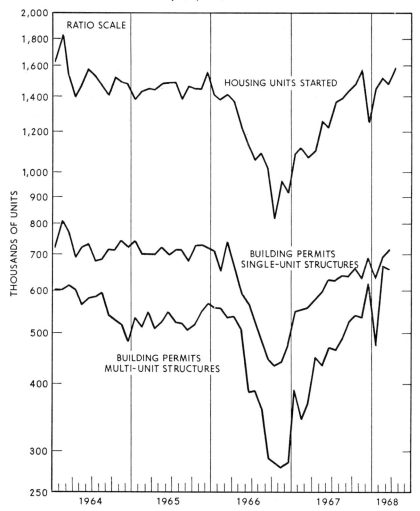

Source: Federal Reserve Bank of New York, *Monthly Review*, June, 1968, p. 109.

payment of the debt. Nevertheless, the mortgage document still retains its form as a conveyance of title accompanied by a detailed description of the property, seal, delivery, and acknowledgment. Since it is merely a security document, the mortgage is accompanied by a promissory note specifically secured by the mortgage.

If the mortgagor fails to meet the terms of his contract, the mortgagee may take court action to protect his interest. Following judicial hearings, the court may render a judgment for the debt and direct sale of the property at public auction ("foreclosure sale"). The lender usually attends the sale and bids for the property, but if the property sells for less than the mortgage claim, he may secure a "deficiency judgment" on the mortgage note for an amount to satisfy the unpaid balance.

Mortgage Debts.   One of the most common ways to classify urban real estate mortgage loans is according to the type of property pledged, that is, commercial, industrial, specialized property (churches, garages, or theaters), apartments, and owner-occupied or rental residential homes. Of the total mortgage debt, over 64 percent is secured by one- to four-family houses, 28 percent by apartments and business property, and the remainder by farm and other types of real property.

Residential mortgages are based on a wide variety of properties which differ as to age, location, quality of construction, and type of building. More than 80 percent of homes are purchased with the use of credit, and such transactions are normally evidenced by contracts called mortgages. Each contract is for a small amount as compared with debt contracts of business firms; however, relative to the income and assets of the average purchaser of real property, the amount of funds needed is substantial. So, when the typical individual buys a home, he usually makes a down payment, pledges the property as security for a loan, and signs a contract to meet interest and principal payments, to pay taxes and special assessments, to insure the property, and to maintain it in good physical condition.

The investment status of one fourth of the nonfarm mortgages outstanding has been enhanced by being insured or guaranteed by the Federal Housing Administration or the Veterans Administration (see Table 22–1). Being underwritten by agencies of the federal government, these mortgages are freely negotiable in the capital market. Trading in nonconventional mortgages has been facilitated by creation of the Federal National Mortgage Association ("Fannie Mae")

TABLE 22-1

MORTGAGE DEBT OUTSTANDING FOR SELECTED YEARS
(In Billions of Dollars)

End of Period	All properties				Nonfarm								
	All Holders	Other Holders†			All Holders	1- to 4-Family Houses			Multifamily and Commercial Properties			Mortgage Type	
		Financial Institutions*	U.S. Agencies	Individuals and Others		Total	Financial Institutions‡	Other Holders	Total	Financial Institutions	Other Holders	FHA-VA-Underwritten	Conventional
1941....	$ 37.6	$ 20.7	$ 4.7	$12.2	$ 31.2	$ 18.4	$ 11.2	$ 7.2	$ 12.9	$ 8.1	$ 4.8	$ 3.0	$ 28.2
1945....	35.5	21.0	2.4	12.1	30.8	18.6	12.2	6.4	12.2	7.4	4.7	4.3	26.5
1962....	248.6	192.5	12.2	44.0	233.4	166.5	140.4	26.0	66.9	46.6	20.4	69.4	164.1
1963....	274.3	217.1	11.2	45.9	257.4	182.2	156.0	26.2	75.3	54.9	20.3	73.4	184.0
1964....	300.3	241.0	11.4	47.8	281.3	197.7	170.5	27.2	83.6	63.5	20.1	77.2	204.1
1965....	326.0	264.6	12.4	49.0	304.8	213.2	184.6	28.6	91.6	72.2	19.4	81.2	223.6
1966....	347.1	280.8	15.7	50.5	323.7	223.7	192.3	31.4	100.0	80.0	20.0	84.0	239.7
1967....	369.5	298.9	18.5	52.1	344.4	236.1	202.0	34.1	108.3	87.9	20.4	88.2	256.2

* Commercial banks (including nondeposit trust companies but not trust departments), mutual savings banks, life insurance companies, and savings and loan associations.

† U.S. agencies are FNMA, FHA, VA, PHA, Farmers Home Administration, and Federal land banks, and in earlier years, RFC, HOLC, and FFMC. Other U.S. agencies (amounts small, or current separate data not readily available) included with "individuals and others."

and the development of mortgage dealers and brokers (see below).[1]
Fannie Mae trades in the secondary market for nonconventional
mortgages in order to improve the "distribution of investment capital
available for home financing."

Mortgage lenders will sell their nonconventional loans to the
Federal National Mortgage Association when they cannot obtain a
better price for them in the private market. The association will make
commitments to buy so many million dollars in nonconventional
home loans, at a specified interest rate. Usually, the demand for
mortgage funds exceeds the supply, and the commitments are sold at
public auction. The interest rate is determined by the extent to which
the price is above or below par (after allowance is made for the one
half of 1 percent service charge).[2]

Mortgage Liens. Most of the real estate mortgages outstanding
are secured by first liens or claims against the property pledged; but,
under certain conditions, second and even third mortgages are used.
The claim of the holder of a second mortgage is junior to that of the
first mortgage holder, and that of the third mortgage holder is junior
to the second mortgage holder as well as the first mortgage holder.
The promissory notes used with second mortgages are usually shorter
term than those used with amortized mortgages.

Second mortgages appear most frequently when residences are
sold by owners to individuals who are unable to finance the seller's
equity in the property. For illustration, an individual may sell his
$15,000 house on which there is a $10,000 mortgage to a buyer having
but $1,000 for a down payment by taking a second mortgage for the
remainder of his equity. When building contractors accept second
mortgages from home buyers, they usually sell them at generous
discounts to individuals who specialize in investing in them. National
and state-chartered banks and most institutional investors are prohibited from investing in second, third, and other junior mortgages.

Amortized Mortgages. Other things being equal, the soundness
of a mortgage note is increased if provisions are made for repayment

[1] In the Housing and Urban Development Act of 1968, the functions of the
Federal National Mortgage Association were divided between two new corporations:
(1) Federal National Mortgage Association, which will be a government-sponsored
agency owned by mortgage companies and other users, and (2) the Government
National Mortgage Association, which will continue to operate the "special assistance," management, and liquidating functions of the old corporation. See Title VII,
Public Law 90–448, August 1, 1968.

[2] For illustration, the accepted prices for Fannie Mae's 90-day commitments to
buy 6.75 percent ceiling-rate nonconventional home mortgage loans—per $100 of
outstanding principal balance—ranged from $90 to $96.25 at one Monday auction. See
Wall Street Journal, August 27, 1968, p. 24.

of the principal and payment of interest and other charges on the installment plan. In the past, the typical mortgage loan was made on a straight-term loan basis for no longer than five years and for but 50 percent of the appraised value of the mortgaged property. The contract called for periodic interest payments (monthly, quarterly, or semiannually) but no installment payments on the principal. It was understood that mortgagors would repay their second mortgages and that first mortgages would be extended at maturity to suit the mortgagors' convenience. This procedure was abandoned during the 1930's when many loans were not renewed and others, which were repayable on demand, were called. The most popular of present-day mortgages call for monthly payments that include payments on principal, interest, insurance, and property taxes. The monthly payments are approximately uniform, with the amount for interest declining and the amount for principal repayment increasing during the life of the mortgage. This type of loan contract, first used by savings and loan associations, received national attention when used by the Home Owners' Loan Corporation during its lending period from 1933 to 1936.[3]

The amortization of mortgages has permitted lenders to make safe loans for longer periods of time and for larger amounts relative to the value of property pledged as security for loans. As a result, smaller original down payments are required, the need for second mortgages has been lessened, and monthly payments have become smaller with the lengthening of maturities. At the same time, lenders are appraising pledged property more carefully and are placing greater reliance on the current and anticipated income of the borrowers. Institutional lenders customarily require borrowers to use the amortized mortgage.[4]

Other Features. The standard mortgage agreement may be modified to meet special situations. For illustration, when the amount of the proposed loan exceeds the value of a single property available as security, the mortgage agreement may be drawn to cover two or

[3] In 1933, Home Owners' Loan Corporation was created to refinance mortgage debtors who were delinquent on home mortgage payments. The Corporation's lending period was limited to three years during which time loans of over $3 billion were made. The maturity dates of refinanced mortgages were extended from 3–5 years to 15–18 years.

[4] In some business transactions, straight mortgages are preferred. In such cases, since the borrower pays only interest during the term of the mortgage with the full amount of the debt coming due at maturity, the principal is usually refunded (a common practice in the public utility industry as in the case of refunding mortgage bonds).

more properties as in the case of a new real estate subdivision, a railroad, or a public utility company (called a blanket mortgage). Under certain conditions, it may be possible and desirable to create one mortgage to replace several existing mortgages and thus to create a consolidated mortgage.

In many cases the practice of including a clause to prevent additional borrowing under the mortgage contract (closed end)[5] has been replaced by a clause that permits additional borrowing for special purposes, such as improvements or additions to property which are covered by the mortgage (open end). Since such improvements are in the interest of the lender as well as the borrower, the open-end mortgage is widely used in both the home mortgage and business-financing markets. Sometimes the seller is given a mortgage as partial payment for property (purchase-money mortgage) which is given special treatment in insolvency action by creditors.

PRINCIPLES AND PROCEDURES

In lending it is assumed that the safety of the transaction depends in part on the relationship between the amount of the loan and the value of the property pledged as security. Therefore it is necessary to appraise the property and to determine the amount of the loan as a percentage of the appraisal figure (for illustration 60 percent or $6,000 on property appraised at $10,000).

Appraisal of Real Property.   There are various elements that enter into the determination of the value of residential property such as location, neighbors, type of construction, architecture, arrangement of rooms, depreciation, obsolescence, etc. Since residential property has a long life expectancy, these factors must be considered in the light not only of present value but also of anticipated future value. The appraiser may compute value by using one of three approaches: (1) the cost approach, in which replacement or reproduction cost new, less depreciation, plus the value of the land, is computed; (2) the market approach, in which sales prices of comparable properties are obtained; and (3) the income approach, in which a relationship between income and value is sought. Customarily a gross multiplier (using gross income) is used in appraising single-family residences, and capitalization of net income (the capitalization method) is used in appraising multiple-family and commercial properties. Whenever feasible all three approaches are used.

[5] The borrower is permitted to issue second, third, and other mortgages but not a mortgage obligation having the same status as those under the closed-end mortgage.

The accuracy of an appraisal depends on the knowledge and experience of the appraiser; but there are so many factors present (particularly, future changes) that results can be little more than "educated guesses." What today may seem to be a reasonable valuation of a business property may be reduced by 50 percent during a depression. So the lender allows for uncertainties by insisting on a margin between appraisal figures and loan values, which may vary with the amount of risk. The amount of risk, even on identical properties, will vary because of differences in the credit standings of borrowers, maturities of loans, and the presence or lack of credit of a third party (as provided by the Federal Housing Administration and the Veterans Administration).

Maturities.   One of the basic principles of real estate lending is that the owner should have sufficient equity in the property so that he will make every effort to meet the terms of his contract in order to protect his investment. The two means for achieving this is to require (1) a large down payment when a loan is made and (2) short-term maturity periods coupled with large monthly amortization payments.[6] Many lending institutions including commercial banks find that both provisions are covered by law. For illustration, Congress has specified that the maximum loan value of a house may be up to (1) 80 percent of the appraised value when the mortgage is for no longer than 25 years and is secured by an amortized mortgage or other instrument under terms that call for installment payments sufficient to amortize the loan on the date of its maturity; and (2) 66.66 percent when the loan is for no longer than 10 years and is secured by an amortized mortgage or other instrument that calls for installment payments that will be sufficient to amortize 40 percent or more of the principal within a period of 10 years. The margin is much larger when the maturity of the loan is shorter and there are larger repayment requirements (being 50 percent for loans of five years).[7]

The two aspects of modern home mortgage lending that have been most criticized are the length of the mortgage loan and the small down payment required relative to the high loan value given to property being financed. In some cases, 100 percent loans are ar-

[6] Amortization is now defined by the Comptroller of the Currency as "a reduction of the debt principal" on the loan during its life; but no mention is made of a regular schedule of payments. "Current Legal and Regulatory Developments," *National Banking Review,* Vol. I, No. 1 (September, 1963), pp. 135–36.

[7] See also Federal Reserve Act, Sec. 24, par. 1–12, USC 371 as amended. The limitations on real estate loans found in this act do not apply to the loans insured or guaranteed by the FHA, VA, Secretary of Agriculture, or state agencies.

ranged, which means that the debtor makes no down payment except the costs incurred in making the loan (about 50 percent of the Veterans Administration loans made during certain years have required no down payments).

Other things being the same, a small down payment means a larger loan and larger monthly payments, but this increase in monthly payments may be avoided by lengthening the loan period (assume from 25 to 30 years). The conditions under which Veterans Administration loans are made are not typical, but the maturities of some mortgage loans have been lengthened from 25 to 30 years, which has resulted in a reduction of almost 10 percent in the monthly repayment charges on such loans. The soundness of small or no down payment mortgage loans depends upon the income of the debtor, and this factor is being stressed to an increasing extent in all types of mortgage lending. Lengthening the maturities of loans and reducing down payments have contributed to the increase in the amount of mortgage debt outstanding.

Credit Analysis. To an extent not true in the past, the borrower's credit position is being appraised carefully in real estate lending. The payment of monthly installments depends on the borrower's income (anticipated-income theory of lending); and, if this is adequate, the lender may give secondary consideration to the value of property pledged as security. Since the loan is liquidated on the amortization plan, both the size and the regularity of the borrower's income are important. Information as to the tenure of employment, occupation, and length of time in residence in one place is the best measure of an applicant's stability of character. Preferred risks are those who worked for one employer for ten or more years, the government (teachers, policemen, firemen, etc.), public utility companies (electric, gas, or telephone), banks and brokerage firms, and those in the professions (accountants, doctors, lawyers, etc.).

The size of a borrower's income must be sufficient to meet not only mortgage payments but also other household and living expenses. Several "rules of thumb" are applied to arrive at a feasible relationship between annual income and the amount invested in a house; for example, a family should not purchase a house in excess of two and one-half times its annual income or two and one-half to three times its annual income after income taxes. These rules are only a starting point, and other aspects of credit worthiness need to be considered. Of these, the most important is the moral character of the applicant for mortgage credit.

A lender should study the record of the potential borrower for evidence of credit worthiness including his use of an experience in handling grants of consumer installment credit, checking and savings accounts, insurance payments, and meeting of other obligations. Although it would be impossible to measure an applicant's determination to meet all obligations and to avoid those which he cannot meet, this factor is a requisite of mortgage credit. Therefore, among the factors that must be considered is the purpose for which money is borrowed —whether to finance a home which is a "good buy" and to sell it later at a profit, to keep up with the Joneses, to live in temporarily rather than to rent, or to acquire a permanent home. A good moral risk will have an appreciation of the seriousness of his pending obligations and recognition as to the amount he should borrow in terms of his ability to repay. The lender should be informed as to the borrower's current debts, his assets, the purpose of the loan, and the amount he can afford to pay.

Technical Requirements. Since property pledged as security for a real estate loan may have to be sold in future years to satisfy the lender for unpaid claims, care must be taken to draw up legal documents that will give the creditor an enforceable lien. The legal document may be a mortgage trust deed or other instrument upon real property, and an enforceable one can be given only by one who has legal title to the property. Attorney's services are customarily used to check on legal titles to property and to disclose all liens on the property that take precedence over mortgage payments (such as mechanics liens and unpaid taxes, and other governmental liens on the property).

National and state laws usually specify that real estate loans made by institutional investors must be secured by first liens on improved properties. They also permit institutional investors to participate in lease financing by making loans on leaseholds provided the lease "does not expire for at least 10 years beyond the maturity date of the loan" and meets the other legal requirements of mortgage lending (security is first lien on the leasehold which must be on improved real estate, amortization is provided, and the same type of legal documents are used).

Institutional Lenders. The chief institutional investors in the mortgage field are savings and loan associations, mutual savings banks, commercial banks' time and savings deposit departments, insurance companies, and pension funds (see Table 22–2).

Mortgage Companies. The work involved in drawing up

documents to meet the requirements for FHA insurance increases the cost of originating and acquiring these mortgages; consequently, many lenders make only conventional home mortgage loans and/or acquire nonconventional mortgages in the open market from mortgage dealers who originate mortgages and service them after they are sold to institutional investors. As the originator of nonconventional mortgage loans, the dealer is responsible for preparing the mortgage instrument and other documents, inspection and appraisal of the mortaged property, and rating the credit of the borrower. The mortgage company assembles the mortgages originated by it and sells them in large blocks to permanent investors. The company invariably retains the right to service such mortgages—collecting and forwarding amor-

TABLE 22-2

INVESTORS IN MORTGAGE DEBT OUTSTANDING
(In Millions of Dollars)

Investors	1945	1966	1967
Savings and loan associations	$ 5,376	$114,447	$121,893
Life insurance companies	6,637	64,609	67,543
Commercial banks	4,772	54,380	59,019
Mutual savings banks	4,208	47,337	50,490
All others	14,507	66,685	70,652
Total	$35,500	$347,100	$369,600

Source of statistics: *Federal Reserve Bulletin*, July, 1968, pp. A-48, A-49.

tization payments and handling other matters pertaining to the pledged properties. The service fee thereon is the company's main source of income.

In some cases, mortgages are originated by the builder or real estate broker and then sold to a mortgage dealer who, in turn, sells them to long-term investors. However, mortgage companies originate more than two thirds of FHA and VA mortgages and handle an even larger percentage of the sales. Some commercial banks have entered the mortgage originating and servicing business directly or through subsidiary mortgage companies. However, most commercial banks, savings and loan associations, and savings banks retain the mortgages they originate, which are usually of the conventional type.

SAVINGS AND LOAN ASSOCIATIONS

Savings and loan associations are financial intermediaries that are chartered by either the federal or state governments. They are the chief link between savers and families who finance their homes with borrowed funds. Among financial institutions, only commercial banks and insurance companies have more assets.

History. In January, 1831, at Frankfort, Pennsylvania—now a part of Philadelphia—the first cooperative home-financing institution in the United States was formed (Oxford Provident Building Association of Philadelphia County). Today, the descendants of this organization are operating throughout the United States under different names, the most popular of which is "savings and loan association." Since their origin, savings and loan associations have added not only nonborrowing members, who are the principal sources of the fund that they use, but also professional staffs to replace the part-time member-workers of the earlier organizations. Despite the addition of "stock" savings and loan associations, the mutual type is dominant.

Recent legislation permits federal savings and loan associations to issue notes, debentures, and long-term certificates of deposit for the first time.[8] The associations may, but are not required to, use the banking terms "deposit" instead of "share" or "savings account" and "interest" instead of "dividends."

Mutual associations are owned by their savings account holders, who manage them through their boards of directors; but this is not true of stock savings and loan associations which operate as banks, accepting savings deposits and paying interest thereon. The stockholders receive dividends on their investments and elect the members of the board of directors.[9]

Incorporation. Savings and loan associations may be incorporated under state or national law and, at the end of 1967, there were 4,059 state associations and 2,056 federal institutions. On the average, the latter are about twice as large as the former. Those incorporated under national law must be of the mutual type and have the word "federal" in their titles. State-chartered institutions may be either mutual or stock companies (the last type being most important in California, Ohio, and Texas). At the end of 1967, there were 5,341 mutual associations and 774 of the stock type (the latter now operate in 21 states). The states with the largest number of associations at the

[8] See Title XVII, Sec. 1719, Public Law 90–448, 90th Cong., S. 3497, August 1, 1968.

[9] About 25 holding companies have been created to acquire ownership and control of stock savings and loan associations. In 1959 Congress, in order to preserve local management, barred existing holding companies from acquiring additional insured savings and loan associations and prohibited the formation of new holding companies.

end of 1967 were Pennsylvania (707), Illinois (575), Ohio (540), New Jersey (376), and Maryland (306). However, the savings and loan associations with the largest amounts of assets were in California ($27,967 million), Illinois ($12,357 million), and Ohio ($11,275 million).[10]

Branching is more widespread than in commercial banking, being practiced in 45 states, the District of Columbia, Puerto Rico, and the Virgin Islands. At the end of 1967, 1,401 associations were operating 3,333 branch offices, with California leading with 516 and Ohio with 344 branches. Although the savings and loan business has expanded rapidly since World War II, the average amount of assets in an association is still small ($23.5 million).

Insurance Status.   At the end of 1967, savings accounts in 73.4 percent of savings and loan associations were insured by the Federal Savings and Loan Insurance Corporation (including all the federal associations which are required to insure savings accounts with the Corporation). In addition, three states have their own insuring corporations: (1) the Cooperative Central Bank of Massachusetts with 160 members; (2) Ohio Deposit Guarantee Fund with 134 members; and (3) the Maryland Savings-Share Insurance Corporation with 164 members.

Supervision.   The Home Loan Bank Board in Washington examines the federal associations and state-chartered institutions insured by the Federal Savings and Loan Insurance Corporation and noninsured state member associations not supervised under state law. The examinations of insured state associations are usually made jointly with state examiners. In 1966, for the first time in their history, savings and loan associations along with other savings institutions were subject to an interest-rate ceiling on savings accounts. The year before, the Board required savings and loan associations to meet account withdrawals out of their own resources in an amount equal to 1 percent of their savings accounts before requesting loans or advances from their federal home loan banks. This forced them to sell government securities in a depressed market in order to obtain cash to meet withdrawals.

Operations.   The savings and loan associations retain part of their earnings as reserves for future losses, and, in case of need, they may borrow from their district federal home loan banks and commercial banks. Because of the highly specialized nature of their business,

[10] Statistics are from United States Savings and Loan League, *Savings and Loan Fact Book, 1968* (Chicago, 1968).

they have been able to maintain a higher "loan-to-value" ratio and grant longer term loans than other lenders in the market (see Table 22–3).

Although both stock and mutual type savings and loan associations may require their account holders to give notice of their intention to withdraw their savings and require a specified waiting period, they rarely do so. In an emergency, shareholders, being owners, may be required to wait until funds are available; depositors being creditors, cannot be required to wait beyond the notification period.

Savings and loan associations developed and popularized the amortization principle of repayment of loans in the home-financing field. Such loans not only increase the liquidity of the lender but also add protection to the loan. About 60 percent of American families are classified as homeowners, and savings and loan associations have had a major role in their financing.

Although the increased demand for home mortgage credit since World War II has been the primary factor in the rapid growth of savings and loan associations, the managers of these associations deserve credit for taking advantage of their opportunities. They advertise extensively, use well-developed promotional schemes, and offer their customers attractive facilities. For some time, over 80 percent of their total assets have been in the form of mortgages, of which about four fifths have been "conventional" loans. Although many are operating in the national mortgage market, the majority are still local institutions catering to local savers and lending their funds to local homeowners.

During the peak years of the four post–World War II business cycles, the growth of savings and loan associations was interrupted temporarily. The most critical of these periods was in 1965 and 1966 when the industry was most vulnerable to the depressing effects of high interest rates because (1) the industry held about one third of all mortgage loans, (2) individual associations were less liquid because of their previous attempts to fill the gap between mortgage demand and savings by borrowing from the federal home loan banks, and (3) the Home Loan Bank Board's policy was to give "due regard to the overall effects of credit extension on economic stability" as well as to the soundness of the borrowing institutions and mortgage and housing markets. When the Board's policy places stability of the general economy ahead of stability of the mortgage and home loan markets, it increases the problems of savings institutions.

Asset Base. If the savings and loan industry is to avoid a repetition of its 1965–66 experiences, it must improve its liquidity position by reducing its dependence on home mortgages and expanding other assets in its portfolios. In the Housing and Urban Development Act of 1968,[11] Congress amended the Home Owners' Loan Act of 1933 to permit savings and loan associations to broaden their portfolios. Now, federal savings and loan associations may: (1) make consumer loans up to $5,000 for no longer than seven years for the purpose of (*a*) equipping, altering, or improving real property and (*b*) purchasing mobile homes; (2) acquire certificates of deposit issued by insured banks; and (3) invest in foreign housing-aid loans guaranteed by the Agency for International Development (see Chapter 29). Many

TABLE 22–3

CONDENSED STATEMENT OF CONDITION OF ALL SAVINGS AND LOAN
ASSOCIATIONS AS OF DECEMBER 31, 1967
(In Millions of Dollars)

ASSETS		LIABILITIES AND RESERVES	
Cash on hand and in banks	$ 3,408	Savings balances	$124,562
U.S. government securities	9,244	Federal Home Loan Bank	
Conventional loans	109,743	advances and other	
Veterans Administration loans	6,356	borrowed money	4,739
FHA loans	5,794	Loans in process	2,281
Federal Home Loan Bank		All other liabilities	2,463
stock	1,395	General and unallocated	
Real estate owned	1,290	reserves	9,557
All other assets	6,372		
Total	$143,602		$143,602

Source: U.S. Savings and Loan League, *Savings and Loan Fact Book, 1968* (Chicago, 1968), p. 93.

states permit their state-chartered savings and loan associations and mutual savings banks to make all types of consumer loan (see Chapter 24) and invest in corporate bonds and a limited amount of common stock and real estate equity ownership in urban renewal projects.

Competition.   Savings and loan associations and mutual savings banks keep most of their cash reserves with commercial banks. Therefore, when a depositor writes a check on his account and deposits it in his savings account in his savings and loan association (or mutual savings bank), the latter may deposit it in its bank account. In this case, the savings institution would have acquired funds and a new obligation, and the commercial bank would have changed the demand deposit from one account to a second. However, if two banks were involved, one would have lost deposits and the other would have gained deposits; but the banking system would have no change in

[11] Public Law 90–448, 90th Cong., S. 3497, August 1, 1968.

total deposits. This line of reasoning ignores the fact that commercial banks operate their savings departments under different rules than savings and loan associations and mutual savings banks.

From 1960 to 1966, there was a flow of funds from savings institutions to commercial banks' savings departments which are not segregated from the commercial departments of these banks. This meant that such funds could be placed in loans bearing high interest rates prevailing in the market. In contrast, savings institutions were holding mortgage loan portfolios containing individual mortgages whose yields were much below the current returns. As a result, the savings institutions felt their earnings did not justify paying the same high rates being paid by commercial banks; and so they faced the hopeless situation of losing deposits if they did not pay the same interest rates and insolvency if they did.

MUTUAL SAVINGS BANKS

Like savings and loan associations, mutual savings banks are highly specialized institutions that accept only savings deposits and make loans primarily in the urban residential mortgage market. They are defined as banks without capital stock transacting a savings bank business, the net earnings of which inure to the benefit of their depositors after payment of obligations or any advances by organizers.

State-Chartered Mutual Savings Banks.   Mutual savings banks are chartered under the state laws of 17 states located primarily in the northeast (New York, Massachusetts, and Pennsylvania are the chief mutual savings bank states). Depositors, who own their mutual savings banks, are paid "dividends" or interest at a fixed rate, and earnings above the amount necessary to pay expenses and dividends are retained for banking purposes and are accounted for in the surplus. As a result of conservative management, most mutual savings banks have large surplus accounts, and some pay extra dividends periodically.

Although mutual savings banks are mutually owned, they are not so managed. Management is in the hands of a board of trustees, self-appointed at the time of organization. The members of the board hold office for life, and the group elects successors when vacancies occur. In carrying out their managerial functions, the trustees emphasize safety, with earnings being a secondary factor. The savings banks movement owes its origin to humanitarians who wanted to help the poor to help themselves.[12] The basic principle on which the mutual savings bank movement was founded is that depositors provide the funds and are the beneficiaries of the operations of mutual savings banks. In case of liquidation, depositors receive all the assets remaining after expenses are paid.

The Federal Deposit Insurance Corporation insures 80 percent of the deposits of mutual savings banks, and the mutual savings banks in Massachusetts have created their own deposit insurance system, which means that 90 percent of the deposits of all mutual savings banks are protected by insurance of some type. Because of the excellent record of mutual savings banks, some believe that deposit insurance is not necessary and would be a needless expense.

The tendency is for these banks to limit their investments to real estate mortgages and to government and public utility bonds; but some states permit investment in certain classes of corporate stock. Real estate mortgages normally make up over 60 percent of mutual savings banks' assets, with the remaining assets consisting of cash; direct and indirect obligations of the federal, state, and local governments; other bonds, notes, debentures, and promissory notes; and corporate stock.

Unlike commercial banks, mutual savings banks have no legal cash reserve requirement, but they keep vault cash and balances with commercial banks for use in their day-to-day operations (2 or 3 percent of their assets). Although these banks have no capital stock, they have surplus and reserve accounts, and their deposit to net worth ratio is approximately 10 to 1. Because of the nature of their business, outlays for salaries are relatively low as compared to those of commercial banks, and their chief expenses are interest and dividend payments to depositors.

State legislatures usually limit the amount of an individual's deposit kept with one mutual savings bank ($15,000 in New York state); but deposits may be kept with more than one bank or divided among different members of a family in order to circumvent the maximum-deposit rule. (In 1960, a savings deposit distributor company was organized that places deposits in different banks for a fee.) The maximum-deposit rule has been attacked on numerous occasions, but the primary reasons for its continuance are that savings banks are

---

[12] Reverend Henry Duncan is given credit for establishing the first mutual savings bank in Ruthwell Village, Dumfrieshire, Scotland, in 1810. In 1816 the Philadelphia Fund Society and the Provident Institution for Savings (Boston) were organized in the United States (both are still flourishing).

for small depositors, the danger of disturbances resulting from withdrawals of a few large deposits are eliminated, and smaller reserves are needed when a given volume of deposits ($1 million) is divided among a large number of depositors than would be the case with a small number (15,000 as compared to 500).

The mutual savings banks of New York have their own central bank, the Savings Bank Trust Company,[13] which is a member of the Federal Reserve System. This bank accepts deposits, makes loans, and provides mutual savings banks with other commercial banking services. The bank has an excellent research division to assist savings banks in planning their loan and investment programs, and it has been instrumental in bringing about changes in the "legal list" of investments for mutual savings banks.

A peculiar modification of the mutual savings bank developed in New Hampshire. Known as "guaranty savings banks," these institutions have special deposits that are virtually capital stock. After the customary interest is paid to general depositors, the surplus goes to the special depositors. The charters of the banks usually require that special deposits equal 10 percent of the total deposits. The special deposits constitute a guaranty fund to protect the earnings and the assets of general depositors. There are only seven of these banks in the state, and they represent an insignificant part of the savings bank resources of the country. The savings banks in New Hampshire, most of which are of the customary mutual type, hold over one half of the total deposits in that state.

Although mutual savings banks still have their original type of organization, their present size and the well-being of most of their depositors have made nominal the charitable and benevolent purposes for which they were organized (as suggested by some of their titles —for instance, the Emigrant Industrial Savings Bank and the Dime Savings Bank). There are more than 500 mutual savings banks which operate over 1,200 banking offices. Their total resources are in excess of $60 billion, hence their average size is larger than the average-size commercial bank. Because they are relatively few in number and are primarily regional in location, they have not shared as fully in the expansion of savings accounts as have savings and loan associations and commercial banks. In addition to carrying on the traditional savings bank business, mutual savings banks are permitted in some states (Connecticut, Massachusetts, and New York) to sell life insur-

---

[13] For an interesting history of this bank see Adolf A. Berle, Jr., *The Bank that Banks Built* (New York: Harper & Bros., 1959).

TABLE 22–4

CONDENSED STATEMENT OF CONDITION OF MUTUAL SAVINGS BANKS, JUNE 30, 1967
(In Millions of Dollars)

ASSETS		LIABILITIES	
Cash and other cash items:		Business and personal deposits:	
Currency and coin...........$	153.3	Demand...................$	464.2
Demand balances with banks..	534.6	Time......................	57,739.4
Other balances with banks....	374.3	Travelers and other checks...	13.7
Cash items in process of		Government deposits:	
collection................	90.1	U.S. government demand.....	7.0
Securities:		U.S. government time........	0.4
U.S. government............	4,303.8	State and subdivisions—	
States and subdivisions.......	242.5	demand..................	3.0
Federal agencies and corps....	1,263.3	State and subdivisions—	
Other securities.............	6,070.1	time.....................	33.1
Loans and discounts:		Interbank—time..............	1.1
Real estate.................	48,893.4	Total deposits...........$58,262.1	
Commercial and foreign		Other liabilities...............	958.6
banks...................	23.7	Total..................$59,220.7	
Other financial institutions....	27.9	Capital accounts:	
Brokers and dealers..........	76.1	Capital notes and debentures.	3.1
Others for carrying securities.	7.4	Surplus...................	3,424.8
Farmers excluding real		Undivided profits and	
estate....................	1.8	reserves.................	1,504.7
Commercial and industrial....	252.4		
Others to individuals........	853.8		
All others..................	29.1		
Other assets..................	1,100.9		
Total Assets*........$64,153.3		Total Liabilities and	
		Capital Accounts*.....$64,153.3	

* Amounts may not total because of rounding.
Source: Federal Deposit Insurance Corporation, *Annual Report, 1967* (Washington, D.C., 1968), pp. 172–73.

ance over the counter, make consumer loans, and offer mutual fund investments to depositors.

Proposed Federal Mutual Savings Banks. In recent years, interest has developed in national chartering of mutual savings banks so as to strengthen the residential mortgage market. The Federal Savings Institution Act, which combined two bills before Congress —the Federal Savings Association Act and the Federal Savings Bank Act—would permit conversion of existing federal- and state-chartered savings and loan associations and state-chartered mutual savings banks into a "federal savings association." The new institutions would be permitted to use the words "bank," "deposits," and "interest." Their depositors would be creditors and would have the right to vote for directors and on major policy issues.

As compared with those of the current thrift institutions, the new institutions would have broader powers, including the right to (1) make consumer and educational loans and some secured loans which are now prohibited; (2) invest in corporate bonds, in a limited amount of common stock, and in real estate equity ownership in urban renewal areas; (3) raise funds by issuing notes, bonds, and/or debentures as well as regular savings certificates and time certificates of deposit (including those of business corporations if maturities are six months or more); and (4) carry on a limited personal trust business. Branching would be permitted but federally chartered institutions would have to conform to state laws, as is now true for commercial banks.

The proposed law reflects changes that have taken place in the economy during the past 20 years, and its passage would permit thrift institutions to operate as "mixed banking" institutions. However, with no change in the law, some stock-type thrift institutions have obtained these advantages by merging with commercial banks. On the other hand, commercial banks could be required to segregate their savings departments from their commercial departments and then be permitted to operate under the same rules as savings institutions.

COMMERCIAL BANKS AND OTHER INVESTORS

Commercial Banks. Commercial banks rank third in importance among the institutional holders of mortgage loans. Following changes in Regulation Q and the development of an open market for negotiable certificates of deposit (CD's), commercial banks' holdings of time and savings deposits increased substantially. Changes in the permissive interest rates by regulatory agencies have allowed banks to compete more successfully for savings and time deposits; but, because they are subject to more stringent regulation than other financial institutions, commercial banks are more conservative in their mortgage investments, preferring nonconventional mortgages. Some banks prefer to make loans on business properties and apartment buildings, and only as an accommodation will they make loans on one- to four-family dwellings. For as long as commercial banks are permitted to mingle funds received by their savings departments with those of their banking departments, the resources of commercial banks may be used to finance industry to the neglect of the mortgage market.

Other Institutions. Although savings and loan associations and mutual savings banks are the specialists in the field of mortgage credit, other financial intermediaries active in the field include life insurance companies, pension funds that make provisions for specific needs, and commercial banks, which offer practically every kind of financial service. Life insurance companies hold about 20 percent of the total mortgage debt of the United States, and their mortgage holdings represent almost 40 percent of their total assets. Although over 50 percent of their mortgages are of the conventional type, they are also large investors in nonconventional (FHA and VA) and farm mortgages.

Life insurance companies' investments in the mortgage market tend to be secondary to their holdings of corporate obligations and government bonds (see Chapter 21), and pension funds prefer common stock as investments. However, life insurance companies are more concerned with safety in investments than in high yields, and the legal conditions under which they make mortgage loans are determined primarily by the laws of the state wherein they are chartered but, in some cases, they are required to meet those of the states in which they operate. Generally, their investments in mortgages are limited to a percentage of their total assets, and the mortgages which they hold must be based on improved property for no more than two thirds of the appraised value and for no longer than 30 years (20 is typical).

FEDERAL AGENCIES

The federal government has aided homeowners and improved housing by (1) strengthening existing home-financing institutions by providing them with central-banking facilities and insurance of their liabilities (deposits and savings accounts), (2) insuring and guaranteeing mortgage loans, and (3) subsidizing public housing projects.

Federal Home Loan Bank System. The Federal Home Loan Bank System is a central mortgage-banking system which stresses the cooperative principle. It was established in 1932 to help institutions operating primarily in the home mortgage field in order to give stability to the home mortgage market. Membership was open to savings and loan associations, mutual savings banks, and insurance companies. The home loan banks were authorized to make loans to member institutions to insure the availability of credit for homeowners. Two types of loans were authorized: (1) short-term, to provide member institutions with liquidity to enable them to meet unusual, seasonal, and cyclical demands for funds and (2) long-term, to supplement member institutions' local sources of funds. Federal home loan banks are permitted to borrow in the capital market by selling consolidated obligations to financial institutions and other investors. Thus, they combined the liquidity services of the Federal Reserve

System with the long-term mortgage loan services of the federal land banks.

The Federal Home Loan Bank System obtains most of its loanable funds in the capital market by the sale of consolidated obligations, the amount of which outstanding may not exceed 12 times the total capital and reserves of the federal home loan banks. Federal home loan bank bonds may now be purchased by the Federal Reserve System. The volume of new issues varies from year to year (having been $7.2 billion in 1966 and $3.3 billion in 1967).

The structural organization of the Federal Home Loan Bank System is similar to that of the Federal Reserve System, consisting of a supervisory board of three members (the Federal Home Loan Bank Board), an advisory council including one member from each bank and six appointed by the Board, and 12 regional banks which are now owned by member institutions.[14] The Board governs the Federal Savings and Loan Insurance Corporation and charters and regulates federal savings and loan associations. The credit policy of the Board is in keeping with national monetary and fiscal policy of the Federal Reserve System and the United States Treasury. The Advisory Council meets regularly with the Board for consultation on economic, regulatory, and other problems that involve the industry. In addition, the Board has the advice of the chief executive officers of the 12 federal home loan banks, individually and as a group (the latter is designated "Conference of FHLB Presidents").

The work of the Federal Home Loan Bank System is carried on by the 12 regional banks, which are wholly owned by their member institutions. They elect a majority of the board of directors (the other four are appointed by the Federal Home Loan Bank Board for four-year terms). The elected directors serve two-year terms and represent the member institutions of their states. Membership in the System is compulsory for federally chartered savings and loan associations and optional for qualified state-chartered associations, mutual savings banks, and life insurance companies. With the exception of 48 mutual savings banks and one life insurance company, most of the membership consists of over 5,000 savings and loan associations. Eighty percent of all savings and loan associations are members, and they hold 98 percent of the total resources of the industry.

[14] In 1946, the Federal Home Loan Bank of Portland, Oregon, was merged with that of Los Angeles and the new institution was moved to San Francisco. In 1964 the Board reestablished the 12th district and established a bank in Spokane, Washington (taking over part of the functions of the San Francisco bank). *Savings and Loan News,* February, 1964, p. 16.

A member institution may keep demand and/or time deposits with its regional home loan bank. Demand deposits are kept to meet day-to-day needs, such as for withdrawals of account holders, security purchases, and current expenses; and time deposits are kept to care for less volatile needs, such as payments of taxes and insurance premiums collected monthly and paid once or twice a year.

Federal Savings and Loan Insurance Corporation. The Federal Savings and Loan Insurance Corporation (FSLIC) was established in 1934 to insure the accounts in savings and loan associations. An individual account holder's maximum protection is $15,000 in any one insured association. If such an association is forced to close, an account holder has the option of receiving cash or a new account in a solvent institution (payment provisions are the same as for FDIC). In case of closure, a second association may absorb the one in default by taking over its assets and by receipt of a loan from the Corporation. In other cases, the Corporation may make a direct contribution or loan to the association in default in an attempt to rehabilitate it. To date, assistance has been given to account holders in 65 associations, as compared to FDIC disbursements to protect depositors in over 460 insured commercial banks.

Insured institutions pay FSLIC a regular premium of one twelfth of 1 percent of their total savings and credit obligations outstanding (the same as participants in FDIC, but there is no rebate as in the case of banks insured by FDIC). Since 1962, insured associations have been required to make an additional payment equal to 2 percent of their annual net increase in savings, less an amount equal to their required purchases of federal home loan bank stock.[15] These payments are credited directly to the Corporation's secondary reserve, which is now in excess of $2.1 billion. FSLIC may borrow up to $750 million from the United States Treasury to meet insurance obligations (as compared to $3 billion for FDIC). In case of need, FSLIC may require member associations to pay a special deposit equal to 1 percent of their savings balances, which would amount to over $1 billion. In addition, the Corporation may make special premium assessments against member institutions, but these assessments may not exceed one eighth of 1 percent of the individual member's savings and credit obligations.

[15] Until January 1, 1962, member institutions were required to hold stock in their federal home loan banks in amounts equal to 2 percent of their total loans (since reduced to 1 percent). Members are not permitted to reduce their investments, but they are not required to purchase additional stock until their total holdings fall below 1 percent.

Federal Housing Administration. During the early 1930's, the role of the Federal Home Loan Bank System was criticized because it helped institutions rather than homeowners; as a result, Congress provided for an emergency corporation, Home Owners Loan Corporation in 1933, to make loans to homeowners for three years. In 1934, the Federal Housing Administration was established to provide insurance of loans made by others. FHA was designed to insure mortgages against losses due to default. Until 1960, the protection was provided only for institutional lenders, which was an important factor in the predominance of institutional lenders in the home-financing field. Now, loans insured by FHA are being used to finance ownership of new and existing one- to four-family dwellings, apartments (rental, cooperative, and condominium), nursing homes, homes for the elderly, relocation and disaster housing, and trailers or mobile homes.[16]

The Federal Housing Administration, following a plan similar to that used by insurance companies, has accumulated reserve funds to meet claims when borrowers default on their payments. The most important of these funds, the Mutual Mortgage Insurance Fund, was created to carry insurance on residences (one- to four-family units). As the title implies, this fund is mutual; therefore, a home purchaser may receive a rebate when his loan is completely amortized. Under the current law, the interest-rate ceiling on new loans insured or guaranteed by FHA or VA is set by the Secretary of Housing and Urban Development; and, at the present time, it is 6.75 percent, with a charge of one half of 1 percent added to FHA loans for insurance (changes in the ceiling rate do not affect the rate on outstanding loans). The power of the Secretary to set ceiling rates, along with other provisions in the National Housing Act, will expire unless renewed on or before October 1, 1969. FHA is now self-supporting, as all of the funds supplied by the federal government have been repaid.

FHA has made major contributions to the housing industry by establishing and enforcing building standards for units financed by FHA mortgages, by encouraging the flow of private funds into the urban mortgage field, and by insisting on scientific appraisals of property and credit ratings of applicants. During its first 33 years, the cumulative volume of FHA insured loans was about $120 billion. FHA has been of assistance to many Americans in becoming home-

---

[16] FHA insurance of loans to improve existing property and to build nonresidential structures (chiefly garages) is considered under consumer loans (see Chapter 24).

owners by making it possible for them to obtain long-term amortized loans from banks and other lenders that otherwise might not have been available to them. FHA has influenced the mortgage loan market by encouraging commercial banks and nonmonetary intermediaries to enter the home mortgage market more fully.

FHA make no loans. However, by insuring lenders against risks, FHA has made it possible for millions to borrow in order to purchase homes and/or to improve them. Should the borrower default on his obligations, the lender forecloses the mortgage loan and transfers title to the property to the Federal Housing Administration. In return, the lender receives either debentures of the mortgage insurance fund which are guaranteed by the federal government or cash in an amount equal to the unpaid balance on the mortgage plus certain expenses.

Generally FHA loans are for a longer period of time and necessitate a smaller down payment than conventional loans.[17] The interest rate is now fixed by the Secretary of the Department of Housing and Urban Development at a level to meet market conditions. In September, 1965, Congress created the Department of Housing and Urban Development and transferred Federal Housing Administration and Federal National Mortgage Association to this department. Of the various agencies in the home financing field, only the Veterans' Administration continues to function as an independent agency.

Veterans' Administration Loans. The Servicemen's Readjustment Act of 1944, as amended, authorized the Veterans' Administration to guarantee institutional loans made to eligible ex-servicemen for such purposes as the purchase of farms and livestock, business property within the United States, and homes. The chief advantage of a VA loan is that it permits a veteran to purchase a home or other property on reasonable terms without the insurance fee that a FHA borrower must pay on his unpaid loan balance. Usually a VA loan is for a longer term (maximum is 30 years) and based on the rule of "reasonable value," which may be as much as the purchase price of the property. However the amount of the loan is limited to $7,500 or 60 percent of the appraised value of the property, whichever is less. Although there is no down payment requirement, the current law requires the veteran to pay a fee (one half of 1 percent of the amount of the loan when it is closed) into a fund that is used to protect the

---

[17] On new houses, the minimum down payment is 3 percent for the first $15,000, 10 percent for the next $5,000, and 20 percent for the remainder. Maximum loan value is $30,000 for a single-family house, $32,500 for a two- or three-family structure, and $37,500 on a four-family building.

borrower in case of default. The law prohibits any one from charging the borrower a mortgage brokerage commission. Unlike FHA, the Veterans Administration is authorized to make direct loans when the applicant is unable to obtain funds from local lenders in the form of conventional or FHA loans. To date only 3.5 percent of the total VA (or so-called GI) loans have been direct loans. Since the veterans' program has been functioning, it has made loans in excess of $68 billion, of which over one half have been repaid. Under the present law, veterans may use their loan privilege up to 10 years from the date of discharge plus an additional year for each three months of war service.

Public Housing Administration. The functions of the Public Housing Administration are (1) to give financial assistance to local public housing authorities in slum clearance and construction of rental housing for low-income families and (2) to assume responsibility for war housing and other public housing projects (many of which were converted into low-rent housing after the wartime need had passed).

The low-rent housing projects constructed under the United States Housing Act program are administered by local housing authorities, organized under state enabling acts as public corporations. They are managed by boards appointed by the chief executive of the cities in which the housing authorities are located, and each board is responsible for the construction and management of the buildings. Members serve without pay, employing experts and others to administer the projects. The management must keep uniform accounting records and must make periodic reports to state and national housing authorities. Financial assistance by the Public Housing Administration is given in the form of capital loans at low interest rates, and annual subsidies. The financial assistance of local governments most commonly takes the form of making the housing projects exempt from local property taxes.

In the Housing and Urban Development Act of 1968, Congress made provisions for construction of new and enlargement of old housing projects in order to obtain the goal of "a decent home and suitable living environment for every American family," which was first stated in the Housing Act of 1949.[18] Under the current law, emphasis is on the use of the resources and know-how of private institutions and the self-help techniques of individuals.

[18] Housing and Urban Development Act of 1968, Public Law 90–448, 90th Cong., S. 3497, August 1, 1968.

One section of the Housing Act of 1968 provides for mortgage subsidies used to obtain funds to finance low-income family ownership of either single or cooperatively owned multifamily structures. At the same time, Congress made provisions to increase the number of and improve the administration of low-rent housing projects. In addition to mortgage subsidies and rent supplements for low-rent housing projects, other sections of the Housing and Urban Development Act of 1968 authorized subsidies for "flood" and "riot" insurance and different urban renewal projects.

SUMMARY

The volume of expenditures for housing and other forms of real property in urban areas is an important factor in determining the well-being of the economy. If these expenditures are too low, a recession or depression may result; if too large, there may be a business boom, inflation, and creation of conditions that may lead to a depression. Funds used to finance urban real estate developments come from lenders of all types, but particularly from institutional investors. The most important of these financial institutions are mutual savings banks, savings and loan associations, life insurance companies, and commercial banks' savings and time deposit departments. Membership in the Federal Home Loan Bank System is compulsory for federal savings and loan associations and optional for qualified state-chartered savings and loan associations, mutual savings banks, and life insurance companies.

The 12 federal home loan banks are the regional central banks of the Federal Home Loan Bank System, which is the central banking system for savings and home financing institutions. The Federal Savings and Loan Insurance Corporation insures the accounts of federal and qualified state-chartered savings and loan associations. The deposits of most of the mutual savings banks are insured either by the Federal Deposit Insurance Corporation or by deposit insurance corporations organized by mutual savings banks in some states.

The U.S. government has assisted in developing the housing industry by creating and operating certain government agencies. Three methods have been used: strengthening private home-financing institutions by creating the Federal Home Loan Bank System, which includes 12 regional federal home loan banks and the Federal Savings and Loan Insurance Corporation; underwriting home mortgages, as by the Federal Housing Administration and the Veterans' Administration, in order to make mortgages more attractive to institutional investors; and subsidizing public housing projects, as by the Public Housing Administration.

The Public Housing Administration has been helpful in providing emergency housing, chiefly for veterans (as on or abutting most college and university campuses), but its more permanent role is to assist local housing authorities in the elimination of slum dwellings and replacing them with low-rent housing projects.

In general, the government has stressed the use of private credit in the financing of homes, and the actual amount of public funds committed has been small relative to the volume of urban mortgages outstanding. Private home-financing institutions have assumed most of the financial responsibility for the different federal banks and agencies (mutualization of the Home Loan Bank System is now complete, and mutualization of the Federal Housing Administration and Federal National Mortgage Association Funds is in progress). The chief beneficiaries of the direct and indirect aid given by the government have been homeowners—which is as it should be.

QUESTIONS AND PROBLEMS

1. Distinguish between (*a*) a first and a second mortgage, and (*b*) conventional and nonconventional mortgages.
2. Summarize present-day standard terms for most home mortgages.
3. To what extent is the income of the borrower, as compared with the appraised value of the property pledged, the determining factor in justifying current mortgage-lending practices?
4. Compare the organization of a savings and loan association with that of a mutual savings bank.
5. Why were savings and loan associations unable to compete successfully with commercial banks for deposits from 1960 to 1965? How can this situation be corrected?
6. Discuss: "The temporary legislation [of 1966] specifically authorized the FDIC to limit the rate of interest paid by insured mutual savings banks, and it authorized the Federal Home Loan Bank Board to limit the rate paid by insured savings and loan associations. The authority was granted to restrain some thrift institutions from trying to match or to better competitive rates available to savers." (Federal Reserve Bank of New York, *Monthly Review*, September, 1967, p. 169.)
7. Compare the organization and responsibilities of (*a*) the Federal Home Loan Bank System with those of the Federal Reserve System; and (*b*) Federal Savings and Loan Insurance Corporation with Federal Deposit Insurance Corporation.

8. "In 1966, experience indicates that the construction industry, and housing in particular, would bear a disproportionate share of the burden" of restrictive monetary policy. (The First National Bank of Chicago, *Business and Economic Review*, June, 1968, p. 2.) Why?

9. "Of course, bankers will be opposed to [the federal chartering of mutual savings institutions bill] . . . no matter when it is brought to a vote." (United States Savings and Loan League, *Savings and Loan News*, March, 1968, p. 6.) Why?

10. Explain: In New Jersey, "the state's usury law has prompted more and more lenders to turn away from conventional loans and deal more extensively in newly authorized 6.75% FHA and VA financing, which is not covered by the 6% ceiling." (United States Savings and Loan League, *Savings and Loan News*, June, 1968, pp. 10–11.)

CHAPTER 23

Agricultural Credit

IN 1966, the Federal Farm Board assisted the United States Treasury and the Board of Governors of the Federal Reserve System in their antiinflationary policies. The Board approved measures that would channel credit extended by the Farm Credit System into loans that maximize production and reduce inflationary pressures.[1] The System's guidelines for loans sought to channel credit into financing production and marketing of farm products and to defer other requests for loans whenever possible (such as those for refinancing long-term debts). The Farm Credit System was able to exert extraordinary pressure on farmer-borrowers because commercial banks and other lenders were reducing their loans to agriculture, thereby leaving the Farm Credit System to fill the credit gap left by other lenders.

The restraints imposed on the nation's economy by monetary policy were reduced somewhat late in 1966 and the first part of 1967, and were then reestablished in late summer of 1968. Credit policies of the Federal Farm Credit System, as well as those of other financial intermediaries, have a major influence on the economy.

BASIC CHANGES IN AGRICULTURE

Farmers have about the same sources of credit as do small business firms; but, in addition, they have their own special farm credit facilities. Traditionally, farming has been a way of life, the farm having been not only a place of business but also a home, and the resulting mixture of business finance and home or personal finance complicated the problem of lending. In case of foreclosure, the farmer lost both his business and his home. Although this situation still exists in many parts of the country, an increasing number of farms are becoming solely a place of business, with those who operate them living in towns and commuting to work as do most other businessmen. Farming has also become more specialized, which means that farms, as family units, have become less self-sustaining.

[1] The Cooperative Farm Credit System, *34th Annual Report 1966–67* (Washington, D.C., 1968), p. 7.

517

Although advancements in the art of farm management together with contributions of science have made it possible for fewer farmers to raise larger crops on less acreage, the demand for farm products is lagging behind the demand for nonfarm products. Consequently, the increase in farm income has not kept pace with the increase in other sectors of the economy; and the normal shift of resources from agriculture to other areas is preceding too slowly to correct this situation (due in part to sentimental opposition and government policies).

Although the average farmer is an individualist, cooperative banks and mutual associations predominate in the federal farm credit system. Unlike home financing, little use has been made of the government-guarantee principle in the field of agricultural credit. Instead, the federal government has inaugurated a program of price support for farm products linked to the cost of farming, which is even more significant than insurance of farm loans would be. However, among its recommendations for agriculture, the Commission on Money and Credit favored insurance programs covering "mortgage loans featuring low down payments, long maturities, and not necessarily complete amortization" and "intermediate-term credit of three to ten years to help farmers finance the acquisition of the capital assets, other than real estate, required for an efficient farm unit."[2] Of course, loan insurance based on farming and other business ventures would be more hazardous, because of uncontrollable natural causes, than loan insurance based on owner-occupied homes and other types of residential property.

There has been an increase in the volume of farm credit due to (1) the use of more expensive equipment and machinery, more fertilizer, and higher grade livestock; and (2) the increase in prices of land and other things that farmers buy. The average value of farms is increasing—12 percent in 1966 and 8 percent in 1965—and is now $164 per acre or $59,800 per farm.[3] Since 1940, the farm population has declined almost two thirds, the number of farms has been reduced almost one half, and the average size farm has more than doubled (see Chart 23–1).[4] The comparative balance sheet for agriculture, with proprietors' equities being over 5 times claims, shows agriculture to be the most solvent of all modern industries (see Table 23–1).

[2] Commission on Money and Credit, *Money and Credit* (Englewood Cliffs, N.J.: Prentice-Hall, Inc., 1961), pp. 194–95.

[3] The Cooperative Farm Credit System, *op. cit.*, p. 5.

[4] *Economic Report of the President Transmitted to Congress February 1968 together with the Annual Report of the Council of Economic Advisers* (Washington, D.C.: U.S. Government Printing Office, 1968), p. 131.

TABLE 23-1

COMPARATIVE BALANCE SHEET OF AGRICULTURE FOR SELECTED YEARS
(Billions of Dollars)

Beginning of Year	Assets Total	Other Physical Assets — Real Estate	Livestock*	Machinery and Motor Vehicles	Crops†	Household Furnishings and Equipment	Financial Assets — Deposits and Currency	U.S. Savings Bonds	Investment in Co-operatives	Claims Total	Real Estate Debt	Other Debt	Proprietors' Equities
1930	$ 68.5	$ 47.9	$ 6.5	$ 3.4	$ 2.5	$4.0	$ 3.6	...	$0.6	$ 68.5	$ 9.6	$ 5.0	$ 53.9
1940	52.9	33.6	5.1	3.1	2.7	4.2	3.2	$ .2	.8	52.9	6.6	3.4	42.9
1950	132.5	75.3	12.9	12.2	7.6	8.6	9.1	4.7	2.1	132.5	5.6	6.8	120.1
1960	203.5	129.9	15.6	22.3	7.8	9.6	9.2	4.7	4.4	203.5	12.1	12.8	178.6
1965	238.5	161.3	14.4	25.5	8.9	8.6	9.6	4.2	6.0	238.5	18.9	18.6	201.0
1966	255.7	172.2	17.5	27.1	9.7	8.6	10.0	4.1	6.5	255.7	21.2	20.4	214.1
1967	269.5	182.0	18.8	28.9	10.0	8.5	10.3	4.0	7.0	269.5	23.3	22.4	223.8
1968	281.2	191.5	{67.7 (Livestock, Machinery, Crops, Household combined)}				{22.0 (Deposits, Savings Bonds, Co-operatives combined)}			281.2	25.0	24.9	231.3

* Beginning with 1961, horses and mules are excluded.
† Includes all crops held on farms and crops held off farms by farmers as security for Commodity Credit Corporation loans. The latter on January 1, 1967, totaled $447 million.

Source: *Economic Report of the President Transmitted to Congress February 1968 together with the Annual Report of the Council of Economic Advisers* (Washington, D.C.; U.S. Government Printing Office, 1968), p. 305.

CHART 23–1

CHANGING FARM STRUCTURE

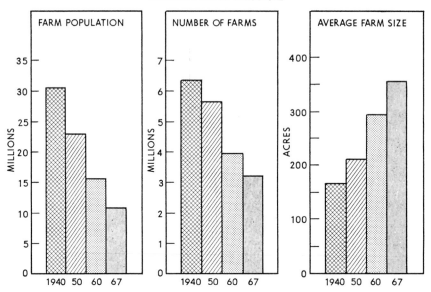

Source: *Economic Report of the President Transmitted to Congress February 1968 together with the Annual Report of the Council of Economic Advisers* (Washington, D.C.: U.S. Government Printing Office, 1968), p. 132.

FARM CREDIT

The dollar amount of loans outstanding to farmers and their cooperative organizations is almost $47 billion, of which 96 percent is in the form of mortgage and nonmortgage loans to farmers and the remainder is loans to farmers' cooperatives (see Table 23–2). In addition to having the same sources of credit as do other business firms of the same size, farmers also obtain funds from one or more cooperative types of institutions in the Cooperative Farm Credit System. About 21 percent of the farm loans outstanding have been made by institutions in this System.

The modern farm is like a small business firm in that it has an inflow of cash as the result of sales, which is offset in part by the outflow of cash to pay for supplies, labor, taxes, debt service, and other items. The surplus of inflow over outflow may be used for farm improvements or to benefit the farmer. Since the day-to-day and month-to-month inflow and outflow rarely coincide, the farmer must borrow to finance interim needs. In addition to his bank and production credit association, a farmer obtains credit from business firms with whom he deals (feed, seed, fertilizer, insecticide, and farm equipment dealers and farm product processors and distributers).

The need for agricultural credit is growing much more rapidly than the ability of commercial banks in rural areas to finance it. The

TABLE 23-2

LOANS OUTSTANDING TO FARMERS AND THEIR COOPERATIVES*

Type of lender	January 1, 1966 Amount (Millions)	Percent of Total	January 1, 1967 Amount (Millions)	Percent of Total
REAL ESTATE FARM MORTGAGE LOANS				
Federal land banks	$ 4,234	20.0	$ 4,908	21.1
Insurance companies	4,813	22.7	5,211	22.4
Commercial banks	2,934	13.8	3,164	13.6
Farmers Home Administration	627	3.0	582	2.5
Individuals and others	8,588	40.5	9,418	40.4
Total	$21,196	100.0	$23,283	100.0
NON–REAL ESTATE FARM LOANS				
Production credit associations	$ 2,580	13.6	$ 3,016	14.2
Federal intermediate credit banks†	140	.7	157	.7
Commercial banks‡	7,664	40.4	8,544	40.2
Farmers Home Administration	715	3.8	735	3.4
Individuals and others	7,878	41.5	8,820	41.5
Total	$18,977	100.0	$21,272	100.0
LOANS TO FARMER COOPERATIVES				
Banks for cooperatives	$ 1,055	60	$ 1,290	60
Members and other individuals	352	20	430	20
Commercial banks	193	11	236	11
Other cooperatives	88	5	108	5
Miscellaneous	70	4	86	4
Total	$ 1,758	100	$ 2,150	100
TOTAL LOANS TO FARMERS AND COOPERATIVES				
Farm Credit System	$ 8,009	19.1	$ 9,371	20.1
Other lenders	33,922	80.9	37,334	79.9
Total loans	$41,931	100.0	$46,705	100.0

* Based on estimates of U.S. Department of Agriculture, 48 states only.
† Loans to and discounts for financing institutions other than production credit associations.
‡ Excludes loans guaranteed by Commodity Credit Corporation.
Source: The Cooperative Farm Credit System, *34th Annual Report 1966–67* (Washington, D.C., 1968), p. 4.

substitution of machinery for labor and other aspects of farm mechanization require intermediate credit in such amounts that rural banks are unable to supply it. Although the Federal Reserve System is empowered to aid banks in meeting short-term and temporary credit needs of their commercial, industrial, agricultural, and other borrowers, the needs of farmers for intermediate credit are not included.

In states permitting branch banking, banks may transfer savings from urban to rural sections through branch offices; in other states, large city banks may participate with rural banks in making farm loans. In addition, a small but increasing number of farmers are reducing their need for credit by leasing rather than buying farm machinery. Most manufacturers of farm machinery have lease arrangements or own subsidiary corporations to lease their products. Fortunately, the Farm Credit System has access to the capital and money markets, which makes it possible for the 12 intermediate credit banks to obtain funds when needed, thus giving a highly flexible element to farmers' short- and intermediate-term borrowing.

In order to change their status from tenant-farmer to owner-farmer or to acquire more acreage, construct buildings, and for other long-term needs, farmers need mortgage credit. The principles of mortgage lending applicable to the urban mortgage field are also applicable to farm mortgages except that in the latter case more emphasis is placed on the pledged property. However, the ability and credit worthiness of the borrower cannot be neglected because repayment is expected from income flowing from the normal operation of the farm.

The modern farm is managed like a small business and many of the same tests of credit-worthiness applied to business borrowers are also applied to farmer borrowers. For illustration, the credit-worthiness of a prospective borrower may be questioned if (1) he has had a large number of small bills outstanding for a considerable time, (2) his record includes composition settlements for debts or bankruptcy proceedings, and (3) he submits inaccurate financial, operational, or other statements when applying for credit.

In addition to moral responsibility, ability to pay is a basic requisite for credit. The results of good farm management will be reflected in the amount of owners' equity and the size of farm income. Capable managers are able to generate adequate income when the size of the farm is in keeping with the farmer's mode of operations and prices for his marketable crops are good. Well-managed farms have (1) high yield per unit of production or low production cost per unit of output, and (2) low overhead cash expenses, includnig living costs.

In farm lending the security pledged may be (1) the item being purchased, such as a tractor or additional land, or (2) the source of liquidation of the loan, such as the cotton crop or livestock that is being fed for the market. The flow of cash resulting from the use of additional equipment or land and the sale of the cotton or livestock should provide the cash needed to retire the debt.

FARM CREDIT ADMINISTRATION

The Farm Credit Administration, established in 1933 to consolidate and supervise all of the existing agricultural credit programs, operated as an independent agency until 1939, when it was placed under the Department of Agriculture. In 1953, the Farm Credit Administration again became an independent agency. Relative to other governmental agencies, the Farm Credit Administration is small, having but 230 employees, of whom less than half are in Washington.

Federal Farm Credit Board. The policy-making and supervisory decisions for the different banks in the farm credit system are made by a part-time Federal Farm Credit Board composed of 13 members, of which one is appointed by the Secretary of Agriculture and the others by the President of the United States from a list of nominees selected by the boards of directors of the different associations that own the 37 banks in the system. (There is one member from each farm credit district).

The policies of the Federal Farm Credit Board and the legal requirements of the law are administered at the national level by the Governor of the Farm Credit Administration and his staff. This staff has a director for each of the three credit service systems—Federal Land Bank System, Federal Intermediate Credit Bank System, and Banks for Cooperatives System. In addition there are divisions which handle examination, accounting and budgeting, personnel, finance and research, and information functions. The staff is responsible for assisting the banks and associations and seeing that they are operated properly. All expenses of the Farm Credit Administration are paid by assessments on the banks and associations in the system.

Supervision. The Federal Farm Credit Board supervises (1) the 12 federal land banks and 695 affiliated land bank associations that make mortgage loans to farmers; (2) the 12 intermediate credit banks and 463 affiliated production credit associations that make short-term and intermediate-term loans to farmers; and (3) the 13 banks for cooperatives that make various types of loans to farmers' marketing, purchasing, and service cooperatives (see Chart 23–2).

The law requires that all banks and production credit associations in the farm credit system be examined at least once a year and that the federal land banks are to be examined whenever the

Governor of the Farm Credit Administration directs (the present policy is at least once every 18 months). During the fiscal year that ended June 30, 1967, the examination division of FCA conducted over 1,070 examinations.[5] As long as there is any government investment in the capital of a bank or association, the United States General Accounting Office may audit its affairs.

CHART 23–2

FARM CREDIT ADMINISTRATION

(Permanent Agencies)

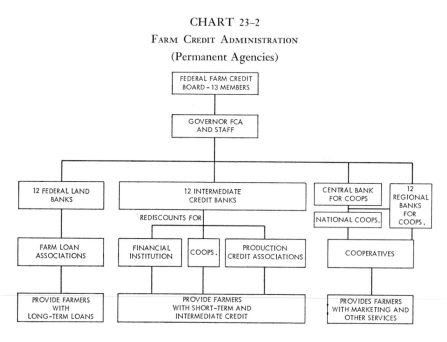

Fiscal Agent. The Federal Farm Credit Administration now employs a fiscal agent having an office in New York City to handle the marketing and other financial matters pertaining to the bonds and debentures of banks and associations sold in the open market to private and other investors (they amounted to $8 billion for fiscal 1967 exclusive of the agent's trading for the investment accounts of the banks and associations). The Federal Reserve banks were authorized by Congress to purchase obligations of federal agencies, including those of the 37 banks in the farm credit system.[6]

The Farm Credit Administration, in cooperation with the

[5] Examinations included federal land bank associations, production credit associations, 37 farm credit banks, the fiscal agent's office, district employee's retirement programs, and other regional activities. *The Cooperative Farm Credit System, op. cit.,* p. 10.

[6] See Public Law 89–597.

United States Agency for International Development (see Chapter 29), is conducting a training program for individuals from undeveloped countries and others from the United States who wish to be foreign technicians. In the training program, the instructor emphasizes the "self-help features of cooperative credit." The participants are taught how U.S. "farmers, with initial help from their Government, have built a dependable viable source of credit."[7]

Twelve Districts. The United States is divided into 12 Farm Credit Districts, and each district has a federal land bank, a federal intermediate credit bank, and a bank for cooperatives. Each district also has a Farm Credit Board that acts as the board of directors for each of the three district banks and supervises their activities. The title of each district bank includes the name of the city in which it is located (such as Federal Land Bank of Springfield, Massachusetts, that serves the First Farm Credit District consisting of the New England States and New York State). Regional headquarters are manned by staffs that perform certain functions for the district banks.

PRINCIPLES

The success of the farm credit system has been due largely to the principles on which the system operates. These principles include (1) cooperative ownership, (2) farmers' control, (3) keeping a private financial institution between the banks and the borrowers, and (4) wide use of investors' money.

Cooperative Ownership. Cooperative ownership is provided by the requirement that any farmer or rancher who borrows from a land bank association or production credit association must purchase capital stock of the association in an amount equal to 5 percent of his loan. The lending institutions, production credit associations, land bank associations, and farmers' cooperatives are required to purchase capital stock of their banks when they borrow from them. Therefore, all of these banks will be owned exclusively by the farmers' associations and cooperatives which, in turn, will be owned by farmers (mutualization is almost complete except for the federal intermediate credit banks).[8]

---

[7] The Cooperative Farm Credit System, *op. cit.*, p. 7.

[8] At the end of fiscal 1967, the federal land bank system was completely owned by farmers but the government owned less than two tenths of 1 percent of the stock of the 463 production credit associations, less than 20 percent of the stock of banks for cooperatives, and 58 percent of the stock and participating certificates of the intermediate credit banks. In eight years the government investments in the system have been reduced from $638 million to $155 million.

The provision for mutual ownership means that each member has a financial stake in the success of his association, and the provision for mutual management means that each director is in a position to protect the interests of the associations as well as those of the farmers he represents. It means also that the credit standing of an applicant for a loan will be reviewed by his neighbors—farmers and ranchers who know his work habits; capacity to farm efficiently; the condition of his land, machinery, and improvements; and his personal, as well as business, spending habits.

Control.   Farmer-borrowers elect the boards of directors responsible for the operation of their local associations, select the officers, and have a voice in appointing members of the most important committees (see Chart 23–3). They also aid in the election of six of the seven members of the district farm credit board which determines district policies for the regional federal land bank, federal intermediate credit bank, and bank for cooperatives (the seventh member is appointed by the Governor of the Federal Farm Credit Administration). Farmers also assist in selecting nominees for membership on the Federal Farm Credit Board.

In addition to supervising the nomination and election of the directors of the 12 district farm credit boards, the Farm Credit Administration also supervises the "nomination polls" for nominees to the Federal Farm Credit Board. For illustration, in 1966 the Governor's Office in Washington held "nomination polls" in the St. Louis and Spokane farm credit districts to pick six nominees (three from each district), from which the President appointed two as members of the Federal Farm Credit Board (one from each district).

Intermediaries.   The third principle on which the farm credit system is organized is the keeping of a private financial institution between the government-owned and financed banks and the borrowing farmers. There are only emergency and temporary exceptions to this standard principle. This type of organization combines local responsibility with government help, lessens the dangers of fraud and political influence, and avoids the type of government administration usually classified as bureaucracy.

Open-Market Financing.   The farm credit banks, like ordinary commercial banks, use other people's money; but, in the case of the farm credit banks, these funds are obtained by the sale of bonds and debentures in the capital and money markets. These credit instruments are secured by the earning assets of the borrowers which are held in trust (collateral trust obligations). In order to strengthen their status in the market, banks in the same system pool their needs for funds by offering consolidated bonds or debentures which are the several and joint responsibility of the banks. Although the banks' equity seems to be more than adequate, Congress placed statutory limits on their debts in terms of equity in order to assure the future

CHART 23-3

FARMER CONTROL OF FARM CREDIT SYSTEM

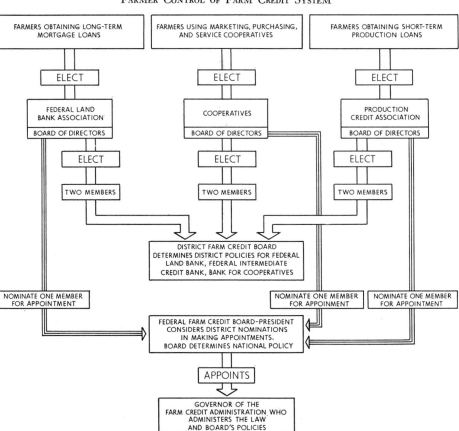

Source: *34th Annual Report of the Farm Credit Administration on the Work of the Cooperative Farm Credit System, 1966–67* (Washington, D.C., 1968), p. IV.

credit status of the banks. For illustration, the federal land banks' debt may be no more than 20 times their capital stock and surplus, and the ratio for federal intermediate credit banks is 15 to 1 (10 to 1 before 1965). Although these banks' securities are not based on government credit, they are similar to those of government-owned corporations insofar as interest rate and credit standing are concerned, and they rank second only to government securities in investment standing.

MORTGAGE CREDIT

The credit needs of farmers correspond to those of industry and business in point of time. In the agricultural field, long-term credit is associated with the purchase of farms, a need which is due in part to state laws requiring equal division of property among children of deceased persons. In many cases, this means either that some member or members of the new generation will mortgage the home place to pay off the other heirs not remaining on the farm, or that the farm will be sold to some outsider who will have to borrow in order to finance the purchase. If the mortgage is amortized during the new owner's life, the mortgage-creating and repaying process will start over again at his death.

During the past 10 years, the value of farms and the cost of equipment to operate them have increased almost threefold in terms of current dollars. This increase in capital requirements has forced farmers in some areas to resort to corporate ownership as a means not only of securing capital but also of providing for business continuity, gaining tax advantages, limiting personal liability, facilitating estate and retirement planning, and avoiding the problem of refinancing with mortgage credit at the death of the owner.[9]

Federal Land Banks. The present cooperative farm credit system had its origin in 1916 when the Federal Farm Credit Act was passed. The original purpose was to help farmers meet their need for "mortgage" or "long-term" credit; and no one seemed to have visualized that within 50 years the farm credit system would be providing farmers with all types of credit, including help for their cooperatives.

During the first part of the present century, although farmers were able to borrow from commercial banks, insurance companies, and others, they looked with envy upon those who were able to borrow in the capital market at lower rates. At times farmers had difficulty in securing adequate amounts of credit at reasonable rates from local sources, and their ability to obtain credit outside their local areas was limited. When provisions were made by Congress for the Federal Reserve System in 1913, the agitation that followed for

[9] G. L. Swackhamer, "The Growth of Corporate Financing," Federal Reserve Bank of Kansas City, *Monthly Review*, May, 1968, pp. 9–19.

creation of a similar central-banking system for agriculture resulted in the passage of the Federal Farm Loan Act in 1916.

Originally, the structural arrangement of the Federal Land Bank System was similar to that of the Federal Reserve System, and it was used as a model in organizing other farm credit systems. Provisions were made for a Farm Loan Board, 12 federal land banks operating within 12 districts, the boundaries of which were drawn to achieve diversified agricultural activities within each district, and ownership by member institutions—the national farm loan associations (now federal land bank associations).

Most of the original capital for the federal land banks was supplied by the federal government, but now all the capital of the banks is owned by the farm loan associations. A borrower from a federal land bank must be a member of his association. Individual membership is contingent on securing approval of an application for a mortgage loan and continues as long as the farmer remains in debt. Loans are repaid on the installment plan, so membership may be for 20 years (or longer, if extensions are authorized).

As few as 10 persons may organize a federal land bank association, and there are no restrictions on the maximum number of members. A farmer-borrower must buy capital stock in his association equal to 5 percent of his loan, and the association, in turn, must buy an equal amount of stock in its district federal land bank. The association endorses and becomes liable for all loans made to its members. Through its loan committee and board of directors, it must approve the application for a loan, and this automatically includes subscription for the association's stock. The land bank's appraiser appraises the land subject to the mortgage lien (the loan committee having made its own appraisal). If the loan application is approved, the transaction will be completed when the association has issued stock to the farmer-member and has endorsed the mortgage note to the federal land bank. This bank will issue its stock to the federal land bank association, which will hold it as security for the loan and will send a bank draft for 95 percent of the mortgage to the farmer through the farm loan association. One of the chief sources of revenue of the associations is the dividends paid on the stock of the federal land banks.

As a result of the policy of credit restriction in force during fiscal 1967, the volume of mortgage financing did not increase for the first time in seven years. During this year, the average-size loan obtained by farmers was $25,438, but 25 percent of the loans was for

$10,000 or less. About 11 percent was for amounts in excess of $50,000, including 1,073 loans for amounts between $100,000 and $200,000, and 373 for more than $200,000.[10] Loans are made for various purposes, such as to refinance debts held by other lenders, improve land and buildings, and buy livestock and machinery.

The influence of federal land banks in the farm mortgage field has been great not only because they have provided farmers with long-term credit but also because of their effect on mortgage-lending practices. When the federal land banks were established, they pioneered in the use of amortized farm mortgages. Largely through their influence, more modern principles of mortgage lending were gradually adopted throughout the farm mortgage credit field—small down payments, higher loan values, careful appraisals, emphasis on farm income, and periodic equal payments that include principal, interest, insurance, and other charges.

Life Insurance Companies. For many years, life insurance companies have been important investors in farm mortgages, and currently their farm mortgage holdings are about equal to those held by the federal land banks. Compared with other lenders in the farm mortgage field, insurance companies operate under fewer legal restrictions, are able to make larger loans in terms of percentage of appraised values, and their funds are more readily available through local agents, branch offices, and mortgage companies. On the average, loans made by insurance companies are larger than those made by other institutional investors.

Commercial and Other Banks. Throughout the history of rural mortgage banking, commercial and other banks have taken an active part in financing farm loans on real estate. Prior to World War I, banks along with individuals and insurance companies provided farmers with most of their credit secured by real estate. The volume of bank lending to farmers declined during the depression of the 1930's until new governmental agencies were created to finance them. However, since World War II there has been a reversal, and now banks are competing actively for farm real estate loans. Surveys of banks' real estate loans indicate that about 60 percent are made to purchase real estate and the remainder to finance farmers' operating needs and purchase of equipment and improvements and to refinance debts.

Among the insured commercial banks, those in small communities with deposits of $25 million or less make about 80 percent of

[10] *Ibid.*, p. 21.

banks' loans on farm land; however, even the largest banks supply agricultural credit. The average-size farm real estate loan made by commercial banks is smaller than that made by federal land banks and insurance companies. Also the size of commercial banks' loans, relative to farm value, is smaller—less than 50 percent as compared to about 60 percent for those of other lenders. Finally, a considerable portion of the over $3.4 billion in farm mortgage loans held by commercial banks represents loans to finance the purchase of small tracts to be added to existing farms.

Farmers Home Administration. During local and regional emergencies, the U.S. government has come to the assistance of those in distress at home as well as abroad. Since 1918, direct government loans have been made to farmers to provide funds to meet emergency seed, feed, and other needs. More than $500 million has been lent, of which more than 80 percent has been repaid. In addition, the Farm Security Administration and its predecessor, the Resettlement Administration, made rehabilitation loans to over a million farmers totaling more than $1 billion.

In an attempt to centralize the emergency lending agencies in the agricultural field, Congress provided for the Farmers Home Administration in 1946, abolishing the Farm Security Administration and the Emergency Crop and Feed Loan Division of the Farm Credit Administration. The Farmers Home Administration makes emergency loans to eligible farmers in flood and drought areas. Such loans average about $3,000 and are for current needs (to replace livestock and equipment and to buy feed, fertilizer, seed, etc.).

The primary function of the Farmers Home Administration is to strengthen family farms and improve rural communities by making and insuring loans made directly to farmers for specified purposes. It also provides advice and assistance pertaining to ownership, operations and development of family farms, repair of housing, soil conservation, and water development. The six classes of loans which this agency is authorized to make are (1) operating, (2) farm ownership, (3) rural housing, (4) emergency, (5) water development and soil conservation, and (6) watershed loans.

Although this agency is financed by appropriations from Congress and with funds from collections, it may enlarge its loan activities by insuring the repayment of funds advanced by private lenders to eligible applicants. Such loans are fully guaranteed by the agency without cost to lenders. The Farmers Home Administration, being within the Department of Agriculture, operates through almost 1,500 county offices, 43 state offices, a central office in Washington, and a finance office in St. Louis. Applications for loans are reviewed by a committee of three, at least two of whom must be farmers, which determines the eligibility of applicants, certifies the value of farms or projects, and reviews the borrowers' progress.

Individuals and Others.   Now, as throughout the history of agricultural lending, individuals hold the largest percentage of real estate loans on farm property. Many of these loans originate when farmers retire and move to the city and also when owners die and title to the land is divided among the heirs, all or most of whom sell their shares rather than operate their inherited land cooperatively. New owners acquire many farms with purchase-money mortgages; but, in some cases, wealthy individuals buy farm mortgages because of their good investment record.

NONMORTGAGE FARM CREDIT

Historically, the chief sources of short-term credit for farmers have been individuals and commercial banks located in rural areas and sales credit provided by merchants and dealers. Among the institutional lenders, commercial banks in farm communities have been most important because they are more numerous, more accessible, and better equipped for lending and providing other financial services on short-term and intermediate-term bases than are other institutions (see Chart 23–4).

Commercial banks make loans to farmers to finance seasonal expenses for livestock and crop production (feed, seed, and fertilizer) and for labor and family outlays (personal and business expenses are usually not separated). In current financing, chattel mortgages are the most common form of security, but unsecured notes are also used. Original maturity of loans is seldom more than one year, but a considerable number are renewed once or twice. Bank loans are made to finance intermediate-term investments for purchases of "feeder" and other livestock, machinery and equipment, land and building improvements, and automobile and other consumer durable goods.

Federal Intermediate Credit Banks.   In 1922, Congress made provisions for 12 banks to rediscount intermediate farm paper, but their activity was not large until after the creation of production credit associations in 1933. The funds of these banks, which are obtained chiefly from the sale of debentures in the open market, are made available to farmers through the farmer-owned and operated production credit associations and over 100 other financing institutions, including commercial banks, corporations affiliated with commercial banks, privately owned business firms, and livestock companies. Farmers now obtain over $5 billion annually indirectly from the federal intermediate credit banks.

CHART 23–4

FARM NON–REAL ESTATE DEBT
HOLDINGS OF SELECTED LENDERS

(Ratio Scale: Billions of Dollars)

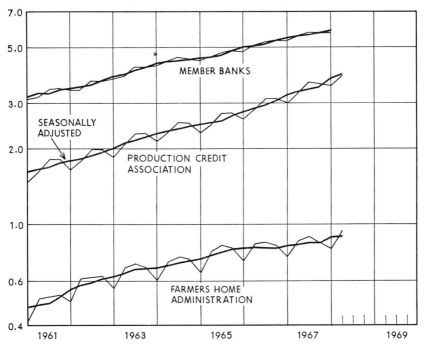

* Change in series.
Source: *Federal Reserve Chart Book*, July, 1968, p. 81.

The original capital of the federal intermediate credit banks was furnished by the federal government; but mutualization was provided for during the Eisenhower administration and eventually all of the stock will be owned by the production credit associations (other borrowers receive participation certificates). New loanable funds are obtained by selling secured consolidated trust debentures, which are the joint and several obligations of the 12 federal intermediate credit banks. They may be issued for as long as five years, but the average maturity is about 9 months between monthly sales of debentures. The individual intermediate credit banks borrow from one another and from federal land banks, banks for cooperatives, and commercial banks. The savings resulting from the lower interest rates at which the banks borrow are passed along to their borrowers.

Interest rates charged by the associations vary because of differences in costs of operation, types and quality of loans, and whether or not secured; but they are usually lower than those of competing commercial banks and other lenders. In addition, the associations' interest charges on loans are based on the actual number of days that each dollar is outstanding, that is, farmers arrange for credit under an annual budget but receive the proceeds of loans only when needed. When funds from the sale of crops, livestock, and other products are available, further savings result when payments are made and loan balances are reduced immediately.

The loans made by the production credit associations include short-term loans, intermediate-term loans, and loans made for capital purposes which may have maturities for as long as 10 years. Unpaid balances for loans made on the annual budget plan may be renewed if credit factors are satisfactory. The short-term loans are used by farmers to purchase feed, seed, fertilizer, and other items, and intermediate-term loans are used to buy livestock, equipment, machinery, and other types of durable producer goods. When farmers apply for loans from production credit associations, they are required to become members by buying stock equal to 5 percent of their loans; after loans are repaid, they may continue membership on a nonvoting basis.

Initially, the production credit associations were financed in part with federal government funds channeled to them through the 12 production credit corporations. When government officials were convinced that ownership could be transferred entirely from the government to farmers without curtailing the associations' operations, the production credit corporations were liquidated. On January 1, 1957, the associations were affiliated with the Federal Intermediate Credit Bank System, and the intermediate credit banks assumed the functions of the former production credit corporations.

Banks for Cooperatives. Farmers are using their cooperatives not only for marketing their products but also as a source of goods which they purchase. The federal government has encouraged the cooperative movement by establishing an Agricultural Marketing Revolving Fund and creating 12 regional banks for cooperatives and a Central Bank for Cooperatives. The revolving fund has total assets of $150 million, of which $112.5 million consists of cash in the United States Treasury, $23.6 million is invested in stock of the Central Bank for Cooperatives, and $13.9 million is invested in the stock of district banks for cooperatives.[11] The regional banks serve the needs of farmers' cooperatives located within their areas and the Central Bank for Cooperatives participates with the district banks in financing larger loans to national marketing and other cooperatives.

Cooperative Associations.   The banks for cooperatives are part of the Cooperative Farm Credit System and are subject to supervision by the Farm Credit Administration (see Chart 23–2). At the regional level, policies are determined by the Farm Credit Board (two of its members are elected by farmers' cooperatives that borrow from the banks for cooperatives). Unlike federal land bank associations and production credit associations, farmers cooperatives are not organized under federal law and there is no legal relationship between them and the banks for cooperatives as is the case with other banks and associations in the farm credit system.

Before borrowing from its bank for cooperatives, a cooperative association must meet the standards set by federal law: (1) The association must be owned by farmers and operated for their mutual benefit. Each member has one vote, and ownership must be so arranged that producers have 90 percent or more of the voting rights. (2) Most of the business of the farmers' cooperative must be (*a*) handling, processing, and/or marketing farm products, (*b*) purchasing, testing, grading, distributing, and/or furnishing farm supplies; and (*c*) providing business and other services. (3) Each association must limit its annual dividends to 8 percent. Like other borrowers from farm credit banks, farmers cooperatives must buy stock in the banks for cooperatives that finance them.

Loans.   Since the banks for cooperatives began operations in 1934, they have made loans totaling $17.9 billion to farmers' cooperatives, and the amount outstanding on June 30, 1967 was about $1.3 billion to over 3,000 borrowers. During the latter part of 1966, the banks for cooperatives, in cooperation with other federal agencies, made a special effort to avoid loans for nonessential purposes in order to lessen inflationary developments.

Loans are either seasonal or term. Short-term loans include commodity loans secured by farm products being marketed (such as dairy products, cotton fiber, wheat, tobacco, livestock, and others) and supplies being purchased (such as feed and fertilizer) and other loans made to supplement the working capital of the associations. The term loans are made to finance the purchase or lease of physical

[11] The Cooperative Farm Credit System, *op. cit.*, p. 42.

property required in handling, storing, processing, and/or merchandising agricultural products, and they are secured by mortgages on the property being financed. Such loans have a maturity of 10 years or less and are repaid on the installment plan.

The Central Bank for Cooperatives was created to finance the regional cooperatives and to make direct loans to some national cooperative organizations. Although some of the latter may have their home offices in an area served by a regional cooperative bank (such as in Chicago or St. Louis), the loan needs of national organizations may be of such proportion as to strain regional resources; hence, the Central Bank was authorized to engage in such loan transactions directly or to assist the regional banks in handling them.

COMMODITY CREDIT CORPORATION

The Commodity Credit Corporation is a federal agency originally incorporated under the laws of Delaware in October, 1933 on a temporary basis to finance the U.S. government price-support program for farm products. In 1948, it was granted a federal charter on a permanent basis. The Corporation's chief function is to handle the farm price-support operations of the United States Department of Agriculture. It is managed by a board of directors under the supervision of the Secretary of Agriculture, who is both a director and the chairman of the board. The Corporation is capitalized for $100 million and may borrow no more than $14.5 billion from banks and other lenders by sale of "participation certificates."

Under different laws, the Commodity Credit Corporation must give mandatory price support to (1) six "basic" farm commodities (corn, cotton, peanuts, rice, tobacco, and wheat), (2) wool and mohair until December 31, 1969, and (3) other commodities and farm products (including barley, oats, rye, honey, grain sorghum, tung nuts, milk and milk products). When either cottonseed or soybean prices are supported, the support price must be at a level set by the Secretary of Agriculture. Price support for other products is discretionary.

Price support may be in the form of nonrecourse loans, purchases, or in other forms (such as incentive loans based on sales of wool and mohair). In making loans, the Commodity Credit Corporation uses the facilities and personnel of the Agricultural Stabilization and Conservation Service. Loans are arranged by producers with their county Agricultural Stabilization Committee at a loan value set in terms of "parity price" at the time the crops are planted. When the crops are harvested, producers may sell them in the market or deliver them to a warehouse or elevator for storage and activate their loan agreements. When loans come due (within 4 to 14 months), the farmer has the option of either paying the note together with storage and other charges and taking title to the products or defaulting on his note, which is in nonrecourse form. In the latter case, title to the commodities passes to the Corporation.

The price-support program is based on the theory that farm prices will be more stable due to more orderly marketing. The companion of the price-support program is limitations placed on all production including acreage allotments, soil-bank programs, and conversion of land into nonfarm channels. Farm products may receive price support by governmental purchase of commodities in order to supply federal agencies, relief and rehabilitation organizations, and foreign governments. The expenditures of the Commodity Credit Corporation, unlike those of the privately owned federal land banks, are included in the federal budget.

Whenever Congress increases the mandatory price-support loans, surpluses pile up in the Corporation's elevators and warehouses and there is not much that can be done by the Corporation except to dump the commodities in foreign markets or to give them away, when so authorized by Congress. Resulting losses would normally force the Commodity Credit Corporation into bankruptcy; but, annually, Congress computes and absorbs the losses (eventually paid for by taxpayers). Attempts to solve the farm-surplus problem by crop control through reducing acreage have failed because farmers, using only their best land and an abundance of fertilizer, produce the same amount on fewer acres. The higher the support price, the more incentive farmers have to intensify their efforts at greater production on fewer acres; and the public pays for surpluses twice—once in the form of taxes and a second time in the form of higher prices.

SUMMARY

The credit requirements of agriculture correspond in time to those of industry and commerce—long term, intermediate term, and short term. The need for long-term credit is associated with the purchase of farms. The farm mortgage debt problem in the United States is linked to our antiprimogeniture laws, which, in most cases, necessitate refinancing of farms each generation. The holders of farm mortgages, ranked in order of their importance, are individuals and miscellaneous lenders, including mortgage companies, life insurance companies, federal land banks, commercial banks, the Farmers Home Administration, and the Federal Farm Mortgage Corporation.

The non–real estate debt of farmers includes intermediate- and short-term debt, and the lenders include both private and federal agencies, as well as miscellaneous lenders, who supply retail and installment credit; and specialists, such as livestock loan companies. The Farm Credit Administration includes 12 federal land banks, 12 federal intermediate credit banks, the Central Bank for Cooperatives, 12 regional banks for cooperatives, and over 1,000 affiliated associations. All of these institutions aid in financing farmers through their member institutions. In creating and administering the institutions within the Farm Credit Administration, emphasis has been on cooperative financing and going to the grass-roots level in determining whether or not loans are to be made.

QUESTIONS AND PROBLEMS

1. In agricultural credit, "personal and business finance are combined." Is this true to the same degree today as it was in the past? Explain.

2. Explain: "The fact that a loan request exceeds a bank's legal lending limit does not mean that the farmer's financial needs cannot be satisfied by that bank." (Robert E. Sweeney, "The Southern Agricultural Bank," Federal Reserve Bank of Atlanta, *Monthly Review*, March, 1967, p. 32.)

3. Distinguish among (*a*) Federal Land Bank System, (*b*) Intermediate Credit Bank System, and (*c*) Cooperative Bank System.

4. Identify: (*a*) Farmers Home Administration, (*b*) Commodity Credit Corporation, and (*c*) Farm Credit Administration.

5. Compare the credit problems of a modern farm with those of a small business firm.

6. Explain: "Total outstanding farm debt . . . has grown by more than five times since the end of World War II, reaching a level of $40 billion at the beginning of 1966." (Federal Reserve Bank of New York, *Monthly Review*, April, 1967, p. 72.)

7. Discuss: "Funds loaned by the Banks [for Cooperatives] come from several sources. In addition to using their own capital, the Banks sell consolidated debentures—short-term securities—to the investing public. To supplement their loan funds between debenture sales the Banks also borrow from commercial banks and other Farm Credit banks. They do not lend government money." (*Banks for Cooperatives and How They Operate*, Circular 40/1–87, [Washington, D.C.: Farm Credit Administration, 1967], p. 6.)

8. Analyze: "Most farm corporations are closely held family corporations. The reasons for incorporating are . . . (1) to facilitate gift transfer of property for estate and retirement planning, (2) to provide

for business continuity, (3) to gain income tax advantages, (4) to limit personal liability, and (5) to improve access to capital." (Federal Reserve Bank of Kansas City, *Monthly Review*, May, 1968, p. 13.)

9. Discuss: "Cooperatives engaged in providing farm supplies are continuing to find one of the best opportunities for saving money for farmers is to move back to mining or manufacturing of raw materials that go into fertilizer, especially the manufacturer of nitrogen. Such operations require relatively large amounts of capital." (The Cooperative Farm Credit System, *34th Annual Report, 1966–67* [Washington, D.C., 1968], p. 41.

10. Analyze: To leave the federal home loan banks and the federal land banks out of the federal budget "seems wrong to me. As the report notes, the Government-sponsored lending agencies to be left out of the budget are widely regarded as Federal agencies, not private ones. They were created by the Federal Government to do a public job, not a private one." (Samuel B. Chase, Jr., "Federal Budget Concepts: A Critique of the Report of the President's Commission," American Bankers Association, *Proceedings of a Symposium on the Federal Budget in a Dynamic Economy* [New York, 1968], p. 38.)

Consumer Credit

᠎ᏗᏗᏗᏗᏗᏗᏗᏗᏗᏗᏗᏗᏗᏗᏗᏗᏗᏗᏗᏗᏗᏗᏗᏗᏗᏗᏗᏗᏗᏗᏗ

CONSUMER CREDIT may be defined as "credit used to finance the purchase of commodities and services for personal consumption or to refinance debts originally incurred for such purposes." Consumer credit includes both sales credit and loan credit. In 1945, consumer credit outstanding amounted to about $5.7 billion, as compared with approximately $100 billion at the present time. Less than 50 years ago, the problem that faced those in need of consumer credit was one of finding a nonusurious lender; today, the problem is to select from the many sources available. Many retailers now advertise credit sales in order to profit from financing them as well as to increase their volume of sales. The cash buyer is no longer the preferred customer. Although the cost burden of the consumer falls heaviest on the poor, those least able to afford it, a college graduate in the $10,000 income bracket may find it easy to "go broke" in this era of easy credit.[1]

COMPOSITION OF CONSUMER CREDIT

Classification. Statistics of consumer credit outstanding are computed by the Board of Governors of the Federal Reserve System and published monthly in the *Federal Reserve Bulletin* (see Table 24–1). Consumer credit is classified as installment and noninstallment credit with each having several subdivisions. Subclasses of installment credit are (1) automobile paper, (2) other consumer-goods paper, (3) repair and modernization loans held by financial institutions, and (4) personal loans.

Installment Credit. The two classes of installment credit are installment sales credit and installment cash credit. The former term applies to credit sales of goods under a contract to pay for them over a period of time in more or less equal amounts, usually each month,

---

[1] "The 191,729 [personal bankruptcies] in the year ended last June 30 were up 9% from the previous year, triple the number 10 years earlier and 18 times as many as were recorded 20 years earlier." *Wall Street Journal*, April 16, 1968, p. 1.

TABLE 24-1
CONSUMER CREDIT FOR SELECTED DATES
(In Millions of Dollars)

End of period	Total	Installment					Noninstallment			
		Total	Automobile Paper	Other Consumer-Goods Paper	Repair and Modernization Loans*	Personal Loans	Total	Single-Payment Loans	Charge Accounts	Service Credit
1939	$ 7,222	$ 4,503	$ 1,497	$ 1,620	$ 298	$ 1,088	$ 2,719	$ 787	$1,414	$ 518
1941	9,172	6,085	2,458	1,929	376	1,322	3,087	845	1,645	597
1945	5,665	2,462	455	816	182	1,009	3,203	746	1,612	845
1960	56,028	42,832	17,688	11,525	3,139	10,480	13,196	4,507	5,329	3,360
1961	57,678	43,527	17,223	11,857	3,191	11,256	14,151	5,136	5,324	3,691
1962	63,164	48,034	19,540	12,605	3,246	12,643	15,130	5,456	5,684	3,990
1963	70,461	54,158	22,433	13,856	3,405	14,464	16,303	6,117	5,871	4,315
1964	78,442	60,548	25,195	15,593	3,532	16,228	17,894	6,954	6,300	4,640
1965	87,884	68,565	28,843	17,693	3,675	18,354	19,319	7,682	6,746	4,891
1966	94,786	74,656	30,961	19,834	3,751	20,110	20,130	7,844	7,144	5,142
1967	99,228	77,946	31,197	21,328	3,731	21,690	21,282	8,267	7,595	5,420
1968, May	100,275	79,270	32,240	20,953	3,699	22,378	21,005	8,508	6,830	5,667

* Holdings of financial institutions; holdings of retail outlets are included in "other consumer-goods paper."

* Note: Consumer credit estimates cover loans to individuals for household, family, and other personal expenditures, except real estate mortgage loans. For back figures and description of the data, see "Consumer Credit," Section 16 (New) of *Supplement to Banking and Monetary Statistics*, 1965, and May 1966 Bulletin.

Source: *Federal Reserve Bulletin*, July, 1968, p. A–52.

CHART 24–1

CONSUMER CREDIT OUTSTANDING
(In Billions of Dollars)

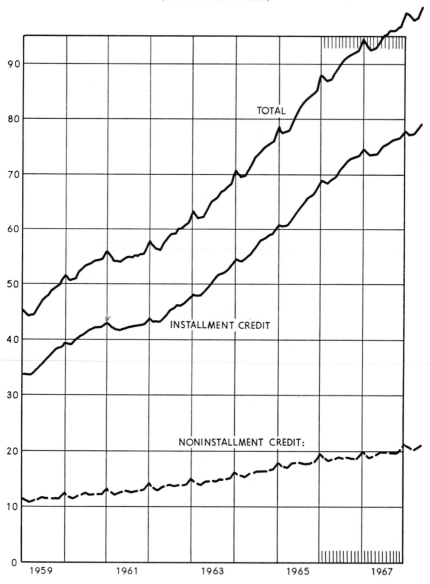

Source: *Federal Reserve Chart Book,* July, 1968, p. 48.

until the entire obligation, including financing charges, is paid. The latter term applies to advances of cash under a contract to repay the debt under terms similar to those specified in installment sales credit contracts. Almost 80 percent of the total amount of consumer credit outstanding is in the form of installment credit (see Chart 24–1), and about 13 percent of the average family's disposable personal income is obligated for such payments. Because only about one half of the families in the United States have installment debts, those having such debts are obligated, on the average, for about one fourth of their disposable personal income for debt payments.

The largest category of installment credit is represented by automobile paper, the volume of which has increased steadily because of the increase in number and price of both new and used cars and the lengthening of the payment period (see Chart 24–2). Installment sales credit is used in financing about 65 percent of new cars and 75 percent of used cars. A second class of installment credit entails installment sales of furniture and household appliances (such as washing machines, dryers, dishwashers, television sets, and refrigerators) and other durable consumer goods (such as boats, mobile homes and trailers, jewelry, and furs). Family size and members' ages have a significant effect on the amount of credit buying, tending to be largest for relatively new households.

The federal government contributed to the growth in the volume of consumer credit in a third category of installment credit by authorizing the Federal Housing Administration to increase the insurance period from three to five years for loans made for alteration, repair, and improvement on existing structures; new buildings for nonresidential purposes; and new structures to be used in whole or part for residential purposes. Under these provisions, FHA has underwritten loans made for new roofs, interior decoration, wiring, and additions of rooms and garages, and has insured sales credit or loans to finance plumbing, heating, air conditioning, and other equipment (but not for items such as barbecue pits, wall-to-wall carpeting, and swimming pools).

Originally, financing institutions were insured against losses on all home improvement loans up to 20 percent of the total (for illustration, if a lender's home improvement loan portfolio contained loans totaling $500,000, all losses up to $100,000 were recovered). In 1954 a change was made in the insurance feature so that FHA insured 90 percent of each individual loan, with the lender assuming 10 percent of the loss on each claim. The home improvement program was intended to operate for 18 months, but it has become a permanent part of the FHA program. The interest rate is subject to change (now 6¾ percent) and the insurance premium of one half of 1 percent is paid on declining balances by the lenders. In order to avoid red tape, insurance fees, and limitations as to maximum interest rates, many lenders are now making noninsured home improvement loans rather than those insured by FHA.

The fourth and last class of installment consumer credit is personal loans repayable at periodic intervals. They include advances of cash to finance purchases of automobiles, home appliances, college

CHART 24–2
CONSUMER INSTALLMENT CREDIT OUTSTANDING
(In Billions of Dollars)

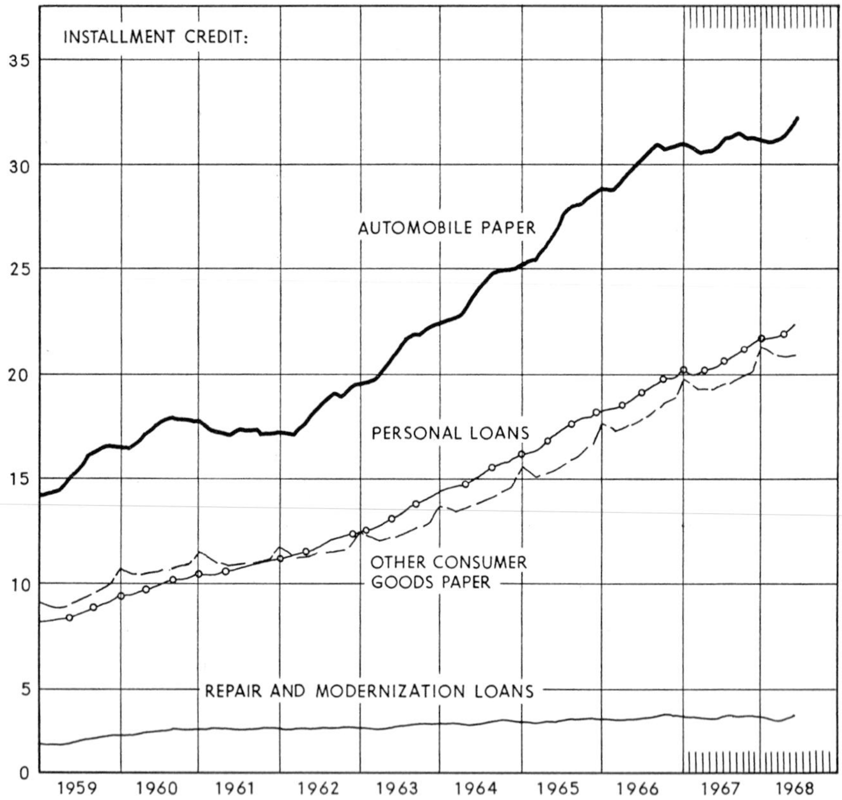

Source: *Federal Reserve Chart Book,* July, 1968, p. 48.

education, insurance premiums, travel, and medical and other services. Under the "check credit" or "ready cash" plan, checks may be written for all types of consumer goods and services up to the maximum stated in the line of credit.

Noninstallment Consumer Credit. The oldest type of consumer credit is noninstallment credit, which makes no provisions other than single payments for consumers' obligations. There are three categories of noninstallment consumer credit: single-payment loans, charge accounts, and service credit (see Chart 24–3).

Single-payment consumer loans are made by commercial banks, savings and loan associations, mutual savings banks, pawnbrokers, and personal finance companies. Charge accounts originate in sales by department stores, other retail outlets, and acceptance of credit cards by service stations and other business units. The charge account method used by retailers and others permits merchandise to be purchased on open-book accounts, as distinguished from cash or installment payments. No credit instrument is used, and no assets are pledged as security. Customarily there is end-of-the-month billing, so

CHART 24–3
CONSUMER NONINSTALLMENT CREDIT OUTSTANDING
(In Billions of Dollars)

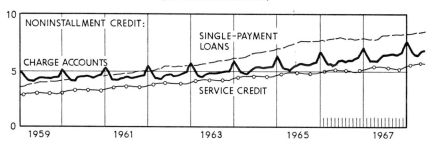

Source: *Federal Reserve Chart Book*, July, 1968, p. 48.

the credit period is short. Traditionally, charge account credit represented noninstallment credit despite the fact that some customers failed to make complete payments at the end of each month. Now, most retail stores offer revolving credit plans whereby a customer pays a fixed amount on his account each month and is permitted to buy up to a specified amount. (This places charge accounts of the revolving credit type in the category of installment consumer credit.) If a customer's purchases exceed the maximum specified, he is billed for one fourth of the excess each month, together with the regular monthly amount and a service charge of 1 to 1.5 percent on the unpaid balance.

Bank credit cards illustrate another variation of traditional charge account credit. Following agreements between a bank and a retail store, the bank will buy a merchant's receivables at a discount ranging from 3 to 6 percent. The store's customers receive credit cards from the bank that they may use to obtain credit from merchants participating in the plan. At the end of the month, the customer receives a bill from his bank covering all of his charge account purchases made from the participating stores (in some plans a fee of 1 percent per month of the amount oustanding is added).

Service credit evidenced by book accounts includes charges made for services such as those of doctors, dentists, public utility companies, and automobile repair firms. Like most other forms of charge accounts, billing is at the end of each month, with payment expected within 10 days. With the increase in charges for services of doctors, dentists, hospitals, and others, plans for shifting the financing from those providing services to financial institutions have been developed, and many are in operation.

SOURCES OF CONSUMER CREDIT

The various sources of consumer credit include credit unions, savings and loan associations, pawnbrokers, industrial banks, sales finance companies, personal or small-loan companies, remedial loan associations, unlicensed lenders, and commercial banks. Although commercial banks were the last to enter the field, they now finance about 40 percent of the total installment credit and over 30 percent of the total noninstallment credit outstanding (see Table 24–2).

TABLE 24–2

SOURCES OF CONSUMER CREDIT FOR SELECTED YEARS
(Amounts in Millions of Dollars)

Institution	1945	1960	1966	1967	1968*
Total Installment Credit	$2,462	$42,832	$74,656	$77,946	$ 79,270
Commercial banks	745	16,672	32,155	33,992	35,450
Sales finance companies	300	11,472	16,936	16,851	16,892
Credit unions	102	3,923	8,549	9,169	9,475
Consumer finance companies†	....	3,670	6,014	6,294	6,361
Other financial	629	1,481	1,911	1,967	2,053
Retail stores	686	5,615	9,091	9,673	9,039
Total Noninstallment Credit	3,203	13,196	20,130	21,282	21,005
Commercial banks	674	3,884	6,714	7,064	7,242
Other financial	72	623	1,130	1,203	1,266
Department stores‡	290	941	n.a.	n.a.	n.a.
Other retail outlets	1,322	3,952	n.a.	n.a.	n.a.
Credit cards§	....	436	874	1,054	1,092
Service credit	845	3,360	5,142	5,420	5,667
Total—All Consumer Credit	$5,665	$56,028	$94,786	$99,228	$100,275

* May, 1968.
† Consumer finance companies included with "other financial" until 1950.
‡ Includes mail order houses.
§ Service station and miscellaneous credit card accounts and home heating oil accounts.
Source of statistics: *Federal Reserve Bulletin*, July, 1968, pp. A–52, A–53.

CASH LENDING INSTITUTIONS

Consumers may borrow in order to (1) pay cash for purchases of durable consumer goods or services (such as education, medical and hospital expenses, and automobile repairs) or (2) obtain general purchasing power for Christmas shopping, travel, vacations, household needs, taxes, and repayment of debts. For illustration, there is usually an increase in consumer loans when property and income taxes are due, during the Christmas shopping season, and when stock market prices decline (suggesting that cash needs are short term). Most consumer loans are small and payable in equal weekly, semi-monthly, or monthly installments. Because of their size and the method of repayment, the cost of administering consumer loans is high. This means that a higher interest rate must be charged to offset the added costs. The borrowers, unlike business firms, are relatively unknown, and their earning capacity may not be increased as a result of the loan. Frequently, a loan is renewed in whole or part, which means that the credit status of the borrower is deteriorating.

In general, three types of loans are made: unsecured loans endorsed by two names (comakers' loans); loan secured by chattel mortgages, wage assignments, insurance policies, and other acceptable collateral; and unsecured loans based upon promises to pay by husband and wife. The chief requisites for consumer credit, even though some loans are secured, are good character and a steady income on the part of the borrower.

With certain exceptions, consumer loans do not increase the ability of the borrower to repay, so payments must be made from his normal income, and this is done most conveniently on the installment plan. A borrower's returning repeatedly for loans means that he is managing his affairs poorly; he is not a good risk, and his application for a loan should be reduced or refused. For this reason, agencies in this field are forced to make special efforts to secure new borrowers by advertising, one of the chief costs of carrying on a small-loan business.

The methods used in analyzing credit risks vary, but as a rule, the basic information is secured from the applicant. He fills out an application blank, which calls for his name, age, marital status, number of dependents, residence (place and length of time), weekly earnings, other income, rent (amount and to whom paid), insurance (amount and beneficiary), real estate (value, title status, encumbrances, and location), and credit references. When the lender requires the signature of comakers, similar but less extensive information is demanded of them. The lending agency usually verifies the data on the information sheet. Special attention is given to answers as to place of employment, length of employment, amount of salary, rent, residence in one place, ownership of real estate and automobiles, and personal habits that have a bearing upon personal finance. General stability of an applicant's record is probably the best barometer of his credit worthiness.

Interest Rates.   Although the legal rates on consumer loans do not lend themselves to comparison because of the different types of loans made and the misleading manner in which lending institutions quote the interest rate, the fact is that many borrowers are paying too much for loans that they secure. The simple monthly rate is normally used by credit unions and small-loan companies operating under an effective small-loan law. When it is quoted as a certain percentage per month on the unpaid balance, the annual rate is 12 times that figure. This annual rate is easily understood, but some lenders and sales-finance companies quote misleading rates using the "add on" method, wherein the customer is told that the rate is $6 or 6 percent per year when the actual rate is nearly double (11.9 percent) that figure, because the borrower is repaying the obligation on the installment plan, which means that he does not have use of the total amount of credit for the entire year.[2] When the discount method is used, the rate is slightly higher because the borrower obtains a loan for the stated amount minus the discount and repays the face amount of the loan in installments (that is, a rate of 11.9 percent per year when quoted at 6 percent). In many cases no interest rate is quoted, and the borrower is merely told the amount of the down payment and monthly payments. In addition, a flat fee may be assessed or included in the payments to cover carrying charges, credit investigation, filing and recording chattel mortgages, and insurance premiums (added to cover the property and the life of the borrower).

The true interest rate on life insurance policy loans is usually lower than the rates charged by other lenders; but this source of consumer credit is available only to holders of policies. Although the true interest rates charged by commercial banks and credit unions are below the average, eligibility for their consumer loans usually de-

[2] The formula for computing the yield on loans discounted in advance and payable in installments is $I = 2PC/(N+1)$ in which I is the annual yield or effective interest rate, P is the number of payment periods in the year, C is the discount rate expressed as a percentage of the net proceeds of the loan and not the quoted rate, and N is the number of equal periodic payments on the note.

pends on the lender being an account holder or possessor of acceptable security. Therefore, factors other than the true interest rate may
determine the source of consumer cash loans. For illustration, a borrower may prefer dealing with a small loan company because of the
privacy of the transaction, or he may choose to deal with a pawnbroker because he needs cash immediately and the assets he has to pledge
are in such form as to be unacceptable to other lenders.

Personal-Finance Companies.   The two pioneers in the development of modern consumer lending were Mrs. Russell Sage, who
endowed the Russell Sage Foundation, and Edward A. Filene, who
financed the studies leading to the development of the credit union
movement. Studies made by the Russell Sage Foundation contributed
to a change in the attitude toward consumer loans—the poor must be
offered loans at fair rates in order to prevent their being exploited by
loan sharks. (The usury laws did not prevent consumers from seeking
loans, but forced them to deal with unscrupulous lenders.) The
federal and state governments, instead of permitting commercial
banks to adjust their interest rates so as to compensate for the greater
risks and higher costs involved in extending certain types of credit,
permitted the organization and operation of credit institutions that are
allowed to lend at higher rates than those applicable to commercial
banks.

In 1911 the Russell Sage Foundation assisted in writing a model
small-loan law that was the basis for the Massachusetts small-loan law.
This law provided for the organization of small-loan companies
whose interest rates, although regulated, were exempt from usury
restrictions. In addition, the lending institutions were carefully regulated as to the maximum amount of individual loans and the basis for
computing interest and other charges.

Personal-finance companies or small-loan companies operate
under provisions of the Uniform Small Loan Law adopted, with
various modifications, by more than 40 states. These companies are
exempt from usury laws applicable to other lenders, but the interest
rates they may charge and the maximum amounts they may lend are
fixed by law. Their lending practices are subject to detailed regulation. For some years, the maximum loan permitted was $300, but in
most states this amount has been increased, generally to $500, in
recognition of the inflation that has taken place during the past 20
years.

The maximum interest rate on unpaid loan balances is fixed at
from 2.5 to 3 percent per month for loans of $500 or less, and usually

a lower rate is applicable to larger loans. The only fee is one to cover actual filing costs. In order to protect borrowers, lenders are required to give a written statement of pertinent information, such as the amount, security, rate of interest, and maturity. Lenders must permit borrowers to repay their loans in whole or in part at any time, and the interest is computed to the exact date of payment. The lender must give a receipt for all payments, and, when the loan is paid, all pledges and paper must be returned.

Small-loan companies make loans based on chattel mortgages, wage assignments, and the unsecured note of husband and wife provided that the borrower is a good credit risk and has been employed at one place for a number of years. The first type—a note secured by a chattel mortage, which usually covers the borrower's automobile or his household furniture—is the most common way in which secured loans are made. The chattel mortage is rarely filed, which may affect its legality, but this policy permits the personal-finance companies to use their most successful advertising slogan—"strictly confidential and private loans."

Normally, the market value of the chattel given as security for personal loans would not cover the loss, and the chief advantage of this type of security is psychological—the borrower prefers to make ever effort rather than go through the humiliating experience of giving up his furniture. The personal-finance companies seldom take such a step; so, in effect, most of their loans are character loans signed by husband and wife. In some states, lenders require borrowers to sign wage or salary assignments as security for their loans.

The cost of credit investigation, collection of delinquent loans, and absorption of losses on bad debts make total operating costs of personal-finance companies higher than those of other types of licensed institutions. The success of companies operating under small-loan laws depends upon careful analysis of applicants and unremitting follow-up until accounts are paid. In comparing interest charges with those of other types of companies, the following facts should be recognized: the rates charged are usually computed on unpaid balances of principal for the actual time the money is borrowed; there are no fees, fines, or other charges,[3] and the interest is computed on a loan basis rather than on a discount basis.

---

[3] Monthly rates are based on the assumption that the regular installment is paid on or before the third day of the month. If the account is delinquent, a greater amount will be charged to interest, which is computed from the last date of payment.

Where small-loan companies have been operated properly, they have made a real contribution by replacing many illegal lenders that had dominated this market for loanable funds. Among cash-lending institutions, the personal-finance or small-loan companies are second in importance only to commercial banks.

There are now over 5,000 personal-finance companies, about one third of which are members of the American Association of Personal Finance Companies, and many of which are members of state associations. Many of the large companies operate separate corporations in different states and branches within states, thus combining the principles of group and branch banking.

Credit Unions. A credit union is a state or federally chartered nonprofit cooperative association "organized for the purpose of promoting thrift among its members and creating a source of credit for provident or productive purposes." There are over 22,200 credit unions in the United States, with total assets in excess of $11 billion. The typical credit union is smaller than the average commercial or mutual savings bank or savings and loan association.

Most credit unions are incorporated and accumulate funds by selling shares to members (17 million in the United States). In some areas, credit unions accept deposit accounts on which they pay a guaranteed rate of interest. From this pool of funds, loans are made to members at an interest rate that may not exceed 1 percent per month on the unpaid balance (a true interest rate of 12 percent which is comparable to the 6 percent discount rate quoted by banks and other lenders). There are no charges incident to making loans, and they are processed in the same way as are loans of banks and other lenders.

Most credit unions provide members with life insurance benefits without charge (premiums being paid by the credit unions). When a member borrows, the insurance is used as loan protection and, in case of death or permanent disability of the borrower, the credit union cancels the loan balance covered by insurance. The amount of insurance depends on the size of the member's savings account, up to a maximum of $1,000 or $2,000, with savings being matched dollar for dollar by insurance if the member is between the ages of six months and 55 years.[4] The responsibility for operating a credit union rests

[4] The amount of insurance carried for those under six months of age and between 55 and 60 years of age is 75 percent of savings, and for those between 60 and 65 years of age, it is 50 percent; but savings deposited before 55 years of age are still matched 100 percent, those made between 55 and 60, by 70 percent, and all after 60 years of age, by 50 percent.

with its directors and officers, who are selected by its members, and their duties depend on the needs of the particular credit union. Policies are determined by members at the annual meetings.

Most of the loans made by credit unions are small, varying from $200 to $750, and, although they are usually evidenced by unsecured promises to pay, some unions require the signatures of two comakers. The most common reason given for borrowing is to pay off old debts, such as those for taxes, medical expenses, funerals, tuition, and so on. However, credit unions also make automobile loans that are secured, and, on the average, these loans are the largest loans made by them. In dollar amount, automobile loans now comprise 30 percent of the loans made by federal credit unions. However, most of the loans made by credit unions must be classified as the remedial type rather than as loans made to finance luxury items.

Credit unions appeal to persons who ordinarily have no bank accounts. Savings in amounts as small as 25 cents per month are encouraged. A member must own at least one share of stock with a par value of $5, which may be purchased on the installment plan. Credit unions are cooperative and are mutually owned and managed. Costs of funds are reasonable, interest rates are limited, and loans are made promptly. The cost of operation is low because there are no large salaries to pay (most of the work is done by members without pay) and the overhead is usually nominal, because rent, heat, and light are donated by the organization around which the credit union is formed.

Most of the credit unions now in operation have been organized since 1930. The passage of the Federal Credit Union Act in 1934 made it possible to organize these thrift and personal-loan cooperatives in all states and in the District of Columbia. The field of membership for each federal credit union is specifically described in its charter, and the chartering laws of most states contain similar specifications. The credit union's board of directors elects prospective new members, who, to be eligible for membership, must be from the field defined in the credit union's charter. Charters are granted to groups having a common bond of association or occupation—factory, store, office, church, club, or trade group.

In 1948 responsibility for the examination and supervision of federal credit unions was transferred from the Federal Deposit Insurance Corporation to the Bureau of Federal Credit Unions (now in Social Security Administration, an agency in the Department of Health, Education, and Welfare). Credit unions are examined periodically by the supervisory agency—once a year by the Bureau of Federal Credit Unions, followed by a written report to the credit union concerned. Wide use is made of standard accounting forms and procedures.

Commercial Banks. Fifty years ago it was difficult to arrange for an emergency personal loan at a commercial bank. Lending in order to finance consumer goods was shunned by banks on the assumption that it was in violation of the thrift principle on which banking was based. The need for borrowing or going into debt to finance consumption was regarded, in general, as a sign of shiftlessness. But, in spite of this attitude, consumers were going into debt to retailers and others for goods and services and were borrowing from pawnbrokers, unlicensed lenders, loan sharks, charitable societies, and friends to finance major and minor household and other personal needs. The right to borrow in order to finance the operation of a business has long been recognized, but the right to borrow to finance the operation of a home is a relatively new concept. At one time commercial banks were primarily institutions that served commerce, but today they are institutions that serve the general public and their communities as well.

Although commercial banks entered the personal-loan field during the 1920's, it was not until the 1930's that they began to make a sizable number of consumer loans. The interest of banks in installment credit was stimulated by their experiences with homeowners who borrowed under Title 1 of the National Housing Act. The personal-loan departments of commercial banks are now foremost among the lenders in the personal-finance field, holding over 40 percent of the total amount of consumer credit and over 50 percent of the total amount of installment credit outstanding. The ability of a consumer to obtain a bank loan depends on a number of factors including ownership of a regular checking account, security, and credit worthiness.

Ownership of a regular checking account (not a special one) wherein an average balance of several hundred dollars is maintained would be favorable to obtaining a bank loan. A passbook is excellent security for a loan and requires little paper work. Terms may be arranged in person or by telephone as soon as the passbook is surrendered and the note is signed. If interest rates are rising, the passbook is even more attractive as security because changes in passbook rates lag behind changes in market rates, and the spread between the two increases. The argument may be advanced that, instead of borrowing, the saver should withdraw funds from his savings account; but, by doing so, he could lose more interest on his savings than he would pay on his loan.

A life insurance policy having a cash surrender value is usually acceptable as security for a bank loan (for as much as 95 percent of the cash surrender value minus the premium for one year). Banks freely make consumer loans secured by stocks and bonds pledged as collateral. Nevertheless, one may need more than acceptable security before a bank will make a loan. Banks want to know their customers, and all unknown applicants for credit are investigated.

In most states the interest rates charged by personal-loan departments of commercial banks are subject to general bank statutes and not to special legislation, as is true of small-loan companies and other "licensed lenders." New York State is an exception—an amendment to the banking code, passed in 1936, permits banks to charge a rate that will yield 1 percent per month (12 percent per year). This law permitted New York banks to broaden the scope of their activities so as to compete more favorably with other agencies in the field. Some consumer loans made by commercial banks are secured by stocks, bonds, savings account passbooks, and/or insurance policies, but co-maker and other loans are made on an unsecured basis.

A new type of lending to consumers is one in which banks extend lines of credit to approved individual loan applicants against which they are permitted to draw checks. The credit lines that may be established vary in size, but most banks specify a minimum and maximum ($120 and $3,000). Interest is charged on the amount of the credit line used and outstanding at a rate of 1 percent per month or some other agreed-on rate; customarily, insurance must be carried to cover the loan, and this adds a few cents to the cost of the loan. Monthly repayments at the rate of one twelfth of the line of credit are required. The banks send monthly statements to the borrowers showing checks drawn, payments made, interest and life insurance charges, the amount of the credit line used, and the amount of credit available. If the borrower makes the monthly payment and the checks paid do not exceed the amount available in the line of credit, the credit becomes available for further use subject to the terms of the agreement. This plan is most popular with professional people and others whose incomes are subject to seasonal fluctuations, and it is used by others to finance unusual expenditures, such as those for taxes, vacations, appliances, tuition, and other items that tend to upset the family budget.

For many years, credit cards have been issued by service companies and retail organizations; but the first bank credit cards were not issued until 1951–52 by the Franklin National Bank of New York, and the plan's major growth started when the Chase-Manhattan Bank introduced a plan in 1958 (followed the next year by the Bank of America).[5] It is estimated that over 1,500 banks now have or are participating in either check credit or credit card plans, and the number is increasing.[6] An important by-product of the use of the credit card system has been a reduction in the number of checks written (many bankers consider expansion in credit card plans to provide a step in the direction of a checkless society).

Other Cash Lenders. The list of miscellaneous lenders also includes industrial banks and loan companies, remedial loan associations, pawnbrokers, mutual savings banks, savings and loan associations, and illegal lenders.

Industrial banks were first organized to receive deposits from and to make loans to workers. There are now two types: those that operate like commercial banks and those that function as personal-financing institutions. The latter raise their loanable funds by the sale of stock and by the sale of "deposit" or "investment" certificates to savers.

Arthur J. Morris, an attorney from Norfolk, Virginia, is given credit for establishing the first industrial bank in the United States and for developing the Morris Plan of banking; there are now several other groups, such as Winsett, White, and Peoples Finance. The first industrial bank, the Fidelity Savings and Trust Company, was established in 1910 in Morris' hometown. The parent company provides Morris Plan banks with copyright forms, literature, and loan plans and gives financial advice and the use of its name. It may provide Morris Plan banks with part of their capital, but most of their stock is locally owned. These industrial banks vary widely in size, corporate structure, and type of business; originally, they specialized in comaker loans repayable on the installment plan. A discount of 6 percent plus a fee of 2 percent is customarily deducted in advance on small loans. Industrial loan companies operate in much the same way as do industrial banks, except that they do not accept deposits.

Remedial loan associations are credit agencies originally established along philanthropic or semicharitable bases, dating from the

[5] Banks had difficulties with their plans and, in 1962, the Chase-Manhattan Bank sold its interest in its credit plan to a new nonbank corporation (Uni-Serv Corporation). The Bank of America solved its problem and now more people use this bank's credit card than that of any other company. In the New York City area, the First National City Bank has more than a million cardholders.

[6] See *Federal Reserve Bulletin*, November, 1967, pp. 1883–92.

first one established in Boston, Massachusetts, in 1869. Although they were among the pioneers in the field of consumer credit, they now number less than 30. In organizing remedial loan associations, capital funds are subscribed by public-minded citizens, and, in order to lessen the profit motive, dividends are limited to 6 to 8 percent by the charters of most of these associations. The Provident Loan Society, located in New York City, is the largest among the remedial loan associations. It has 17 offices spread throughout the city and does a pawnbrokerage business, being one of the city's 130 licensed pawnbrokers. Some of the remedial loan associations are now operating under provisions of the small-loan law.

A pawnbroker is one who lends money on the security of personal property; and, in addition, pawnbrokers customarily buy and sell new and used merchandise and accept valuables for safekeeping. Pawnbrokers are of two types: those who make secured loans, and those who purchase the property offered as security on agreement to resell it to the borrower within a designated time. Pawnshops are patronized by two types of individuals: the traditionally poor, and those who are not poor but are financially embarrassed because of ill health, accident, temporary unemployment, business needs, or requests from relatives. About one fourth of all such loans are made for business purposes, and the remainder for household or personal use. The size of an individual loan depends on the auction value of the article pledged plus the pawnbroker's knowledge of the borrower. The transaction is confidential and requires less red tape than do loans from other institutions in the field. It has been estimated that normally 90 percent of the pledges are redeemed. Greatest profits have been made on large loans and in selling unredeemed pledges.

Almost anything may be pawned, but jewelry is the most acceptable pledge. Most state laws prohibit the taking of goods from minors, intoxicated persons, servants, and apprentices. In order to check on stolen goods, a register must be kept in which the property pledged is described. Some states require a description of the person who pledges the property. The pawn ticket, the pawner's only receipt, shows the length of time allowed for redemption and usually the interest rate. Rates vary from 24 to 120 percent per annum, with 36 percent being considered typical. In New York City, a borrower may obtain a loan for six months and renew it for an additional six months. The interest rate on loans up to $100 is 3 percent per month for the first six months and 2 percent per month for the second six months (for larger loans, the portion in excess of $100 carries an interest rate of 2 percent for the first six months and 1 percent for the second six months).

Mutual savings banks and savings and loan associations and their branch offices are accessible to millions of savers and borrowers throughout the country, and their entrance into the field of consumer financing has been among the most significant developments of recent years. They may soon become second to commercial banks in importance in providing consumer credit to the general public if the national chartering bill is enacted into law.

Until some 50 years ago, illegal lenders dominated the field of consumer credit; and, in spite of hostile public opinion, the amount of business done by unlicensed lenders remains at a high figure, even though it has been reduced in recent years. Although many attempts have been made to eliminate lending at usurious rates, the practice persists. Part of this situation is due to the statutory provisions for maximum legal rates and their interpretation by the courts. Even some legal lending agencies, such as commercial banks, are in doubt as to the legality of contracts at the legal rate of discount plus service fees when loans are repaid over the life of the contract.

The unlicensed lender makes loans on whatever security he can obtain—wage assignments, chattel mortgages on automobiles, or pledged articles left on deposit. In some cases he accepts notes signed by two comakers. In order to avoid charges of usury, the loan may be disguised in some way. When signing the contract, the borrower may agree to pay a larger sum than he borrows. For example, if he makes a pledge to pay $60 of his next month's salary for $50 at the time of the contract, which may have only 15 days to run, the borrower pays $10 for the use of $50 for 15 days, or 480 percent interest on an annual basis. Usual charges made by "salary buyers" are from 20 to 40 percent per month (240 to 480 percent per year).

Salaried men and small wage earners are not the only ones to borrow from unlicensed lenders. Prosecution of usurious lenders in New York revealed that small merchants were frequently paying more than 100 percent per year for their borrowed funds. Most of the illegal loan business is done by individuals operating in single offices, but a number of chain organizations have been formed.

SALES CREDIT

Consumer credit may be linked to the sale of consumer goods, as in the sale of automobiles and household appliances on the installment plan, charge account sales by retail stores, or in rare cases in return for a promissory note. Most qualified creditors use some form of sales credit during a year. The open or ordinary charge account, evidenced by book entries and with end-of-the-month billing, is most commonly used by department stores, specialty houses, and other retailers. A majority of women shoppers use their charge accounts even though they may be able to purchase the same articles at a lower price elsewhere (even worse, the use of charge accounts often leads to overbuying).

Revolving Credit. Consumer buying has been stimulated by the use of revolving credit accounts which permit maintenance of a borrower's credit by installment payment of previously contracted debts while adding to the current debt. Most customers, using these plans, are in the lower or middle income groups. The advantages to the consumer are the ability to make multiple purchases on credit from time to time within agreed-upon limits and to make monthly payments for a fraction of the credit used (assume one sixth). If a customer opens an account under this plan and spends $100 the first month, he will be billed for $100, of which $16.67 is due. He may pay the whole amount or only $16.67. Interest will be charged at the monthly rate of one-half percent on the unpaid balance.

Merchants find using the budget or revolving credit plans advantageous. Experience indicates that it increases their sales and improves their credit ratings with lenders, because a firm with 1,000 customers under contract is more stable than one with 1,000 customers of the "hit and miss" variety. Revolving credit plans have been so profitable that many large chain stores, mail order houses, department stores, and specialty shops, formerly operating on a "cash and carry" basis, have adopted it. Some large retailers now have subsidiaries to finance the consumer credit outstanding (for example, Sears Roebuck and Company and Montgomery Ward).

Credit Cards. Credit cards, many of which are acceptable internationally, have stimulated consumer buying of goods and services. The risk of loss assumed by a credit card holder (which includes 20 million Americans) has been compared to that of the risk of losing a signed blank check. The only protection the owner has in case of loss is prompt notification in writing to the issuer. Promptness is important in order to reduce the time the card may be used fraudulently (that is, between the time of the loss and receipt of the written notification). Unless the owner of the card can prove negligence on the part of the issuer or merchant who honors the card, the owner is liable for unauthorized purchases.

As noted previously, credit obtained from the seller of a service or product that calls for payment over a period of time in approximately equal amounts is called installment sales credit (credit is linked directly, as to amount and security, to the service or goods being financed). The seller or the sales finance company that buys the installment contract protects his interest in the item being financed against theft or sale to an innocent third party by a financing contract. This contract may be a secured agreement, conditional bill of sale, lease, or chattel mortgage signed by the purchaser. Since title to the merchandise remains with the seller until full payment has been received by the latter, a default on any one of the installments means that the remaining payments are due and payable immediately at the option of the holder of the sales contract (acceleration clause).

Sales-Finance Companies.   Sales-finance companies are the specialists in financing the installment sales contracts of automobile dealers and other merchants. As a rule, they do not lend to consumers but buy installment sales contracts from retailers. Some of these companies also finance dealers' inventories and business firms' accounts receivable, thus combining the functions of commercial-sales and sales-finance companies.

Sales-finance companies range in size from local units to those that are national in scope of operations. The latter have branches in key cities throughout the United States, operating a national financing business through these branches. They obtain funds from operations by borrowing in the open market and from bank loans, but dependence on bank loans is decreasing, while borrowing in the commercial-paper market is increasing. Finance companies also use long-term debt obligations. The ratio of total debt to net worth is about eight to one for the larger companies but much smaller for small companies. Thus, large companies are able to trade on equity to a greater extent than smaller ones because of their superior credit standing in the money and capital markets.[7]

In general, sales-finance companies have good credit ratings and are able to borrow at low interest rates. Many of them, being owned or leased, are "captive" companies which, because of their relationship to their parent companies, are handling the financing of their parent companies' credit business. The larger companies act as their own brokers in selling their promissory notes, which may be unse-

[7] Richard T. Selden, "Commercial Paper, Finance Companies, and the Banks," in Deane Carson (ed.), *Banking and Momentary Studies* (Homewood, Ill.: Richard D. Irwin, Inc., 1963), pp. 340–42.

cured or secured by collateral deposited with a trustee (called "collateral trust notes").

Buyers of automobiles and other durable goods customarily apply for the privilege of purchasing goods on the installment plan, support their applications with statements, of their financial positions (income, etc.), and give references as requested. If such an application is accepted (following investigation by the finance company) and a sale is made, the purchaser makes a down payment in cash and/or trades in his used car as a down payment. The buyer agrees to make monthly payments for the remainder of the purchase price according to the terms of the contract (12 to 30 months in most cases). Unless included in the down payment, interest charges, filing fees, and insurance costs are included in the monthly payments. In terms of simple interest, the interest charge is usually 12 percent, on the average, of all unpaid balances. The purchaser's note may be discounted by the finance company or bank at a rate determined by market conditions, maturity, recourse arrangements, and so on.

Protection of Lenders.   In order to reduce its loss in case of repossession of an automobile, the finance company or bank insists on a large down payment and installment payments large enough to offset depreciation. The lender will also insist on the borrower carrying adequate insurance for collision, fire, theft, and so on. In some cases the lender will demand the endorsement of the dealer on the note that is discounted (giving the lender recourse against the dealer). Sometimes a repurchase agreement will be negotiated whereby the finance company (or bank) may require the dealer to buy the repossessed car for the unpaid balance, but the finance company (or bank) loses if the car cannot be repossessed. In order to increase their business, some finance companies assume all the credit risks by waiving endorsements or repurchase contracts (called "nonrecourse companies").

When a product is repossessed by the original seller or the holder of the sales-finance contract, in some states payments made by the buyer are considered to be rent and not recoverable, but in other states part of the amount paid may be refunded. The procedure calls for a public sale at auction and a return to the original buyer of any funds left after the unpaid balance and other charges are cared for. But if the unpaid balance and other charges are not covered by the proceeds from the auction, the creditor may obtain a judgment against the debtor for the remainder.

Prior to World War II, the National Association of Finance

Companies had taken numerous steps to standardize business practices. During the war further standardization resulted from the regulation of consumer credit by the Board of Governors of the Federal Reserve System (Regulation W). The standard terms are based on the following principles: the buyer must have sufficient equity in the property to make him feel that he is a purchaser rather than a renter; the remaining salable value of the property, regarded as a used article, must at all times be greater than the unpaid portion of the price; and the unpaid portion of the price should at all times be small enough to encourage the buyer to complete the payments rather than lose his investment in the property.

The question of how long the payment (repayment) period will be is involved in all types of installment credit. In the case of installment-sales credit, the size of the down payment is also involved. Ordinarily, the longer credit is outstanding, and the smaller the down payment, the greater is the credit risk; for example "going beyond 36 months to 42 months, increases the probability of loss by just about 100%."[8]

Protection of Borrowers. The first rule that should be followed by those who buy on credit is to read the financing contract before signing it. Too often, contracts contain hidden provisions for unwanted services and merchandise, and these may pass unnoticed unless they are itemized. Although buyers normally expect to meet their installments when due, sickness, loss of employment, and/or other emergencies may make payment impossible. The user of installment credit should check for oppressive clauses in his financing contract. These may include: (1) The add-on clause, which covers a series of installment purchases, such as household appliances or furniture, and makes all of the items security for the contract. If the buyer defaults on any one of his payments, he may lose all the goods previously paid for as well as the item being purchased. (2) The "balloon" clause, which provides for low initial installment payments and large ones toward the end of the installment period which the buyer may find difficult or impossible to meet. The result may be signing a refinancing contract on excessive terms or loss of property after having paid most of the obligation. (3) The acceleration clause, which means that all installment payments are due and payable at the request of the creditor when the buyer defaults on one payment. In this case, the

[8] John O. Elmer in *American Bankers,* October 9, 1963, p. 3. Mr. Elmer is Chairman of the American Bankers Association, Installment Credit Committee. Usually, the typical buyer has a minus equity in his car when it is over three years old.

merchandise in question may be repossessed and sold at public auction. As noted previously, the debtor may still be held responsible for any portion of the debt not satisfied by the proceeds of the sale. (4) The wage assignment clause gives the creditor the right to collect the debt by attaching the debtor's wages if an installment payment is not met when due. When wages are garnisheed by a creditor, the employer of the debtor is required by the court to withhold all or part of the debtor's wages until the debt is paid. Because garnishment entails extra work for employers, the latter often discharged the debtor. However, the "Truth in Lending" act (effective July 1, 1969) establishes, for the first time, a national garnishment law restricting wage attachments to 25 percent of a worker's after-tax salary provided it leaves at least $48 of his weekly wage exempt (this amount is subject to change if the minimum-wage law is revised). Furthermore, employers are forbidden to discharge employees the first time their salaries are garnished.

REGULATION OF CONSUMER CREDIT

The oldest objective of regulation of consumer credit is that of preventing exploitation of borrowers by establishing maximum interest rates. Even today, irrespective of general credit conditions, the welfare aspect of consumer credit regulation directed at the prevention of extortion is always present. During the Middle Ages the church banned the taking of interest, and in modern times most governments have enacted so-called "usury laws" that place a limit on the interest rate that may be charged. Compared with businessmen, the applicants for consumer loans are relatively unknown, and the administrative costs and risks assumed in making these loans are relatively high. Too often the low ceiling on interest rates prevented legitimate agencies from making small loans, and, as a result, borrowers were forced to depend on illegal lenders.

State Regulation. Except for those financial institutions that are required to meet standards set by federal law (federal credit unions, federal savings and loan associations, and national banks), the financing standards for institutions financing consumer needs are set by state laws. With a few exceptions, states now have fairly adequate uniform small-loan laws. The principles governing lending under these laws include tailoring repayments to the income of the borrower (usually monthly); permitting prepayment without penalty; stating the charges to cover all obligations as well as normal interest on loans; computing each charge on number of days elapsed between payments, so that the borrower may reduce his total charges in whole or part by prepayment; and providing a written statement showing the schedule of payments, a copy of the statute requiring disclosure, and a copy of the contract. If a wage assignment is used, notice must be provided to both husband and wife.

Where there is adequate regulation, lenders are licensed, are required to post a bond to insure observance of the law, are subject to penalties for violation, and are required to keep adequate records to be inspected by the supervisory officer. Usually, a state official in the banking department is made responsible for enforcement and supervision of the law in the same way as for state banks, savings and loan associations, and credit unions.

Criticisms. Current criticisms of consumer credit practices are directed mainly at the excessive charges made by lenders in states that abound in unlicensed lenders; sales-finance companies that make excessive charges; dealers who expect "kickbacks" from the sales-finance companies, banks, or others who finance their sales; and lenders and dealers who split excessive commissions charged by credit insurance companies. The volume of financing business done by sales-finance companies depends chiefly upon the volume of paper, originated by automobile dealers, stores, and others, that is placed with them. According to the testimony of witnesses before the United States Senate subcommittee, some automobile dealers not only expect kickbacks on finance and insurance commissions or charges but also ask their customers not to finance with credit unions and others who do not follow this practice.[9] Statements of some life insurance companies have indicated that as high as 90 percent of the credit life insurance premiums paid by borrowers have been kicked back as commissions to the dealer through whom the insurance was obtained.[10] The "dealer reserves," "finders' fees," "pack," "kickbacks," and other shady practices are not condoned by the responsible elements in the automobile and other businesses.

Consumer credit is expensive primarily because of the expensive services provided along with the credit, but sales on the installment plan are also criticized because the buyer often pays an excessive price for an inferior article, such as jewelry or a secondhand car, because he thinks in terms of small weekly or monthly payments rather than of

---

[9] *Consumer Credit Labelling Bill,* (Hearings before a subcommittee on Banking and Currency, U.S. Senate, 86th Cong., 2d sess. on S. 2755, March–May, 1960), pp. 539–40.

[10] *Ibid.,* p. 548.

the total cost. Emphasis in installment selling tends to be on the sale of luxury items, thus shifting demand away from more important markets without increasing total demand. Unwittingly, people are encouraged to extend their total debts beyond their ability to pay, causing distress when goods are repossessed or when obligations cannot be met without serious personal sacrifice. Often the chief beneficiary will not be the retailer who sells the goods and services but the lender who finances them.

The fact that licensed agencies have suffered only small losses because of delinquent payments justifies the faith of the sponsors of credit unions, industrial banks, and other small-loan institutions in the honesty and integrity of the workingman, small householder, and professional man of limited income. Nevertheless, one of the most disturbing aspects of the expansion in consumer credit is the rapid increase in the number of personal bankruptcies, which have been at a more rapid rate than the rate of increase in consumer debt. Although the thought of "going through bankruptcy" is distasteful, it may be unavoidable when one's financial affairs are in a hopeless state due to family emergencies, divorce, economic reverses, or just bad management.

Truth-in-Lending Legislation.   In 1968, the "truth-in-lending" bill was approved by Congress, which set the effective date as July 1, 1969. This bill requires full disclosure of the costs of using credit in the acquisition of property and services by creditors to debtors "prior to the consummation of the transaction."[11] The assumption is that many purchases would not be made if buyers were aware of the cost of financing. In his statement supporting the bill, the late President Kennedy wrote:

> The testimony received shows a clear need for protection of consumers against charges of interest rates and fees far higher than apparent without any real knowledge on the part of the borrowers of the true amounts they are being charged. Purchasers of used cars in one study, for example, paid interest charges averaging 25 percent a year, and ranging well above this; yet very few were aware of how much they were actually paying for credit.[12]

The truth-in-lending bill was introduced by Senator Paul Douglas of Illinois in 1961, and it took seven years to clear the United States Congress. Although the bill does not provide for reducing the

[11] Title 1 of the Consumer Credit Protection Act, May 29, 1968 (Public Law 90–321) is called the "Truth in Lending Act." It is published in the *Federal Reserve Bulletin*, June, 1968, pp. 497–504.

[12] See *Truth in Lending Bill* (Hearings before a subcommittee of the Committee on Banking and Currency, U.S. Senate, 87th Cong., 1st. sess., S. 1740), p. 1.

cost of credit on the $100 billion of goods purchased annually on time, it requires retailers and lenders to reveal the cost of credit they offer. Creditors are required to give monthly interest charges on revolving charge accounts as an annual percentage (not 2 percent per month on the unpaid balance); and they may disclose at their option the effective yield on their accounts for a representative period of time.

Congress requires that the "true" annual interest rate be stated on a first mortgage (a practice generally followed by most mortgage bankers), but the requirement for second mortgages is more detailed. The latter transaction must contain a statement that it is a second mortgage and permits the consumer to take three days in which to withdraw from the contract when it covers property already owned. This provision was added to protect homeowners against home repair firms that were tricking credit customers into giving them second mortgages on their homes.

Consumers should be the chief beneficiaries of the truth-in-lending law, but a secondary effect may be to increase consumer loans made by banks, credit unions, small-loan companies, and others operating under an effective small-loan law.

Credit Control. Consumer credit tends to fluctuate cyclically, which suggests the need for using selective devices of credit control (as illustrated by Regulation W) so as to prevent overexpansion of consumer buying during boom periods and the loss of buying power during business recessions. Sales of durable goods, in particular, are subject to wide cyclical swings; so the proposal for economic control of consumer credit is to help smooth our cyclical fluctuations. The volume of consumer credit in use at any one time may be influenced by the use of direct devices of credit control, as illustrated by Regulation W of the Board of Governors of the Federal Reserve System. When consumers are required to increase the amount of down payments and make larger installment payments over a shorter period of time, the effect is to reduce the amount of installment sales credit outstanding. In the case of installment loan credit, the same result may be obtained by requiring larger monthly installment payments and shortening the loan period. The federal government has regulated the volume of consumer credit on three occasions: (1) during World War II, to reduce the volume of credit and use of scarce materials; (2) from September 20, 1948, to June 30, 1949, as an antiinflationary measure; and (3) from September 18, 1951, to May 8, 1952, as a Korean War measure.

The use of Regulation W and similar types of economic regulation is unpopular with automobile dealers and other dealers in durable consumer goods that are customarily sold on the installment plan. While the Board of Governors is not in favor of having its power over consumer credit renewed, many economists feel that the power to regulate consumer credit should be provided by Congress on a standby basis.

The general devices of credit control now favored by the monetary authorities are those which tend to reduce the availability of member-bank reserves and the volume of loanable funds. Not only are commercial banks direct lenders in the consumer credit field, but they are also a source of funds used by other consumer-financing institutions and retailers who finance their own receivables. So a general tightening of credit conditions tends to reduce the amount of consumer credit available, to tighten credit terms, and to bring about a reduction in lending and in sales. The opposite of the foregoing would tend to increase consumer borrowing and credit sales during periods of business recession. Banks are currently required to report loans made to financial institutions under two subdivisions—those to banks and those to others. The latter include particularly those to sales-finance companies, personal-loan companies, and commercial-finance companies.

SUMMARY

Post-Keynesian economic theory recognizes that consumer spending is a dynamic factor in explaining changes in national income; therefore, economists are giving more attention to consumer finance and the sources and uses of consumer credit. When considered from the viewpoint of the economy as a whole, consumer credit enlarges buying power, broadens the market for consumer goods, and permits mass production of goods. One criticism of consumer credit is that it may leave less purchasing power for future buying. However, new buyers, using new consumer credit, may enter the market; therefore, the effect of consumer debt on total spending depends on whether old debt is paid off more or less rapidly than new debt is contracted. From surveys that have been made, one may conclude that, once a person has established a certain standard of living, he will go into debt to maintain it. The continued prosperity of the United States depends, in part, on a steady growth in consumption; for this reason, monetary authorities, economists, businessmen, and others have been giving increased attention to consumer finance.

The growth in consumer debt since the end of World War II is accounted for by several factors in addition to those referred to earlier—the increase in general prices and in disposable personal income—including (1) an increase in the number and variety of consumer goods appearing on the market and in the willingness of consumers to spend, (2) extension of maturities of debt contracts and a decrease in down payments, (3) wider acceptance of the principle of amortization of debts on the installment plan, (4) "catching up" on the acquisition of consumer goods after the war, (5) increased home ownership and its accompanying demand for household furnishings and appliances, and (6) the existence of financial institutions competing actively for consumer loan contracts.

The most important developments in the field of consumer financing have been (1) the rapid increase in the volume of consumer loans and installment contracts owned by commercial banks, (2) the expansion in number and popularity of credit unions, (3) the increased use of credit cards, overdraft credit, and revolving credit plans, and (4) the passage of the "truth in lending" bill. In seeking outlets for loanable funds, banks have captured much of the small-loan and discount business formerly done by personal-loan companies, industrial banks, and discount or finance companies. The aggressiveness of banks, their lower rates, and the prestige of dealing with them have permitted them to secure the "cream" of the small-loan and discount business.

The chief problem of commercial banks is to keep down collection costs so as to show a profit on the smaller margin on which they are forced to operate. The simplest and most equitable solution would be to permit all banks whose deposits are insured by the Federal Deposit Insurance Corporation to charge 1 percent per month on the unpaid balance of all loans made for less than $500.

The loss of some sales-finance business to commercial banks and department stores is forcing some of the sales-finance companies to finance small-loan transactions that were formerly handled by small-loan companies. In addition, some of these companies have gone into the cash-lending business either directly or indirectly through subsidiaries; others are stressing the financing of mercantile credit (trade credit between business firms). The personal-finance and small-loan companies are extending their activities to include the financing of installment purchases in order to compensate for relative losses in volume of loans. For legal and competitive reasons their activities are confined to smaller loans and discounts, but their relative importance is declining.

Credit unions are among the most rapidly growing of the specialized consumer-financing institutions, and they seem to have a secure place in the small-loan business. However, there is little privacy in connection with their lending, and many individuals prefer to borrow elsewhere.

Today, there are two broad classes of consumer credit regulation: the traditional one, which has as its purpose the prevention of extortion of the borrower, and the more modern type of regulation, which has as its purpose the prevention of too much spending and expansion of debts when they would be injurious to the economy.

QUESTIONS AND PROBLEMS

1. Identify: (*a*) consumer credit, (*b*) installment credit, (*c*) consumer credit guaranteed by Federal Housing Administration, (*d*) service credit, and (*e*) sales credit.

2. Distinguish between (*a*) credit card credit and revolving credit, (*b*) credit unions and industrial banks, and (*c*) sales finance companies and personal or small loan companies.

3. What are the most important sources of (*a*) installment consumer credit, and (*b*) noninstallment consumer credit?

4. What is the significance of the following to future consumer lending? "The myriad wants of individuals can be grouped loosely into several basic levels. Recent experience seems to indicate that when income is available to satisfy one level another level appears quickly." (Federal Reserve Bank of Philadelphia, *Business Review*, March, 1964, p. 14.)

5. What roles were played by the Russell Sage Foundation and Edward A. Filene in the development of consumer credit?

6. Discuss: Among lenders "banks and credit unions have continued to increase their share of the market. . . . The major area of slack in consumer borrowing continues to be in home improvement loans." (*Federal Reserve Bulletin*, June, 1968, p. 459.)

7. Discuss: "In fact, the only thing increasing faster than personal debt is personal bankruptcy." (Sally Ryan, *Austin American*, November 28, 1967, p. A–13.)

8. Analyze: "Pawnbrokers offer a service to people who need to borrow cash in a quick and confidential manner. . . . No inquiry is ever made as to a borrower's financial ability, place of employment or purpose of the loan. . . ." (*New York Times*, April 4, 1966, p. 48.)

9. Discuss the effect of the following on the business of savings institutions: "At our current rate of inflation, a man who started work this year and saved a dollar would find when he retired (40 years later) that it would buy only about 21 cents of goods." (P. A. Renfret, "Inflation Hedges," *Institutional Investor*, June, 1968, p. 18.)

10. Discuss: "Sam began by borrowing from friends, but quickly graduated to finance companies. Then he fell . . . into a classic trap: Taking out new loans to pay off old ones. . . . But he could never get ahead enough to begin whittling down the total." (*Wall Street Journal*, April 16, 1968, p. 10.)

CHAPTER 25

Trust Banking

TRUST COMPANIES include specialized institutions and trust departments of commercial banks that perform trust and agency functions for the general public and corporations. They differ from other financial intermediaries in being institutions designed to conserve existing savings. Trust companies take title to property in trust and manager it, most commonly after the death of the creator of the trust and for the benefit of those named in the trust agreement and according to the law. Formerly, trust companies served corporations and wealthy individuals almost exclusively, but now they are managing pension funds in which many small savers participate. Trust departments of banks currently hold in excess of $250 billion in assets.

The desire on the part of individuals to conserve part of their wealth for the benefit of their heirs is as old as humanity and, before the development of corporate fiduciaries in the United States, trust services were performed by individuals (to some extent, individuals still serve as trustees). The old adage, "Three generations from shirt sleeves to shirt sleeves," has been dealt a severe blow by use of the services of trust companies—the spendthrift son or daughter may be prevented from wasting the principal of the estate.

BASIC CONCEPTS

Types of Trust Services. The business of a modern trust company or the trust department of a commercial bank is to settle estates, administer trusts, and perform agency functions for individuals, corporations, associations, governments, and educational, religious, and other public institutions. The trust work of a bank or trust company is usually divided into personal and corporate trust divisions. The personal trust division handles trust work for individuals, including those of executors of estates; administration of trust funds; guardianship; and investment services. The corporate trust division handles the trust and agency business of corporations, including acting as bond registrars, as stock-transfer agents, as coupon-paying agents, and in other fiscal agency capacities (such as performing the escrow functions of the bank).

Trust and Agency Services. Legally, the difference between a trust relationship and an agency relationship is that, in a trust, legal title and control of property is in the hands of one party (trustee) for the benefit of another party (beneficiary), but in an agency arrangement, one party (the principal) authorizes another party (the agent) to act for him in dealing with third parties. Documents providing for the transfer of property from the donor (a living person who creates a voluntary trust) or others under terms of a will (testamentary trust) indicate the duration of the trusteeship, the distribution of income from the principal to the life tenants, and the distribution of the trust property to the remaindermen at the termination of the trust.

Rules against Perpetuities. Perpetuity is an arrangement designed to continue ownership of property indefinitely; but, at an early date, the English courts took the position that it would be harmful for society to hinder the alienation of property because it would tend to undermine commerce, keep property in the hands of the wealthy after they had lost their ability to care for it, and create the basis for the formation of a social caste, with a resulting curtailment of opportunities for individuals. Now the common law, as applied in this country, makes a personal or private trust void if the vesting of the title is for longer than "a life or lives in being and twenty-one years." Furthermore the statutory laws in most states forbid the creation of trusts that extend beyond the period of existing lives and 21 years. Presumably, trusts created for educational institutions, hospitals, and other public institutions that have indeterminate lives may be established in perpetuity; but there is a question as to the legal status of pension plans and welfare trusts wherein individuals are the beneficiaries. Laws have now been passed by more than one half of the states exempting them from the rule against perpetuity.

Trusts and Trustees. When the beneficiary of a trust is an individual (or individuals), it is called a personal trust or private trust. If the beneficiary of a trust is an educational, religious, or similar institution it is called a public trust. When a trust is created as a result of a voluntary agreement between living trustors and a trustee, it is called a voluntary trust. If the terms of the trust agreement become effective during the life of the trustor, it is called a living trust; if the terms do not become effective until after the death of the trustor, and the terms are contained in his will, it is a testamentary trust. Court trusts are those that are arranged by the court having jurisdiction in such cases. A current development is the life insurance trust, which is created during the life of the grantor wherein life insurance policies are made payable to the trust. Although such a trust is a living trust, the only assets may be insurance policies, the proceeds of which become the corpus of the trust at the death of the grantor. Normally, the grantor pays the premiums and reserves all rights under the policy or policies.

Foundations. A trust may be created to provide an income for the maintenance of educational institutions, for equipment and supervision of public parks and playgrounds, or for the support of almost any project. Since property left in trust to finance public and quasi-public institutions (educational, charitable, religious, medical, and the like) is exempt from federal estate taxes and state inheritance taxes, many wealthy men have created trust organizations to which they have given the bulk of their estates (as illustrated by the Cullen, Ford, and Rockefeller foundations). Present federal estate taxes exceed 50 percent of the taxable estate in excess of $2.5 million and 75 percent of the estate over $8 million. Because of these high taxes, it is almost impossible to keep control of an individually owned large business firm more than two generations, except through the device of educational or charitable organizations.[1]

Business corporations have been encouraged to contribute to educational and charitable organizations and to create tax-free foundations by Congress through the federal income tax law, which provides that a corporation may deduct 5 percent of its net taxable income if it is to be used for charitable and other public purposes (more than 5 percent of taxable income in one year if the excess is absorbed in the next five years). While educational institutions have been the chief beneficiaries, some gifts have been for research of particular interest of the donors and some foundations have been created to conduct research for the parent companies.

Tax-free foundations may be organized either as nonprofit corporations or as trusts. Nonprofit corporations are created in the same way as business corporations, except that they have members rather than stockholders. The members, who are often from the founding family or company, elect the directors, and they in turn select the officers. A foundation organized as a trust is formed by the use of an irrevocable trust agreement, and it is managed by a board of trustees selected by the company, individual, or family establishing the trust.

[1] Samuel E. Stewart, "What Is the Trust Market in Our Changing Society?" *American Banker*, October 8, 1963, pp. 32 ff.

Any vacancy on the board is filled by the remaining members of the board of trustees. In addition to strictly charitable institutions, public trusts include those created to finance research, education, and other projects. In recent years, the Ford Foundation has attracted attention because of its size (over $3 billion), the sale of part of its original assets to the general public, and large gifts made to private educational institutions and hospitals.[2] An individual trust may be so large as to require its own officers and the recruitment of its own staff to manage it, or it may be so small (assets less than $50,000) that it may be managed along with hundreds of others of similar size by the trust department of a bank or by a trust company.[3]

Background for Present-Day Trust Activities. For hundreds of years, lawyers and others have acted as trustees and agents for individuals and associations, but the incorporation of trust companies and the grant of trust powers to commercial banks are relatively recent and distinctly American developments. Insurance companies were the first corporations permitted by law to perform trust functions, but until after the Civil War their trust business was a minor activity. The first company to do an exclusive trust business was not organized until 1853. Later, as the trust business developed, many insurance companies reorganized into trust companies, and new trust companies were formed with charters broad enough to permit them to carry on most types of banking.

Since 1900 the trust business has been closely allied with banking, and the modern trust company is one of the best illustrations of the results of the integration movement in banking. Because of the very nature of the trust business, trust companies are responsible for the investment and safety of large sums of money. In addition, they provide many agency services to corporations and others; as a result, they are in daily contact with many business institutions. It was reasonable to expect them to accept commercial and savings deposits from their clients, to make loans, to clear and collect checks, and to perform other banking functions. However, there are many trust companies that perform trust functions exclusively.

With trust companies entering the commercial-banking field, it

[2] Among the better known foundations with assets of more than $250 million are the Carnegie, Duke, Ford, John A. Hartford, Kellogg, Lilly Endowment and Commonwealth Fund, Moody, Richardson, Rockefeller, and Alfred P. Sloan foundations.

[3] Perhaps the first foundation to fit the modern definition is the Peabody Education Fund established in 1867 "to aid the stricken South." *New York Times,* July 11, 1960, p. 35.

was logical for commercial banks to enter the field of trust banking. The Federal Reserve Act of 1913 authorized national banks to carry on a trust business. Until 1962, the trust functions of national banks under the supervision of the Board of Governors of the Federal Reserve System, but in that year Congress transferred all powers over fiduciary activities of national banks to the Comptroller of the Currency.[4] The Comptroller then issued Regulation 9 to replace the Board of Governor's Regulation F, without changes in the latter. After months of study, a new regulation was issued on April 5, 1963.

MANAGEMENT OF PERSONAL TRUSTS

The problems pertaining to the management of personal trusts are those arising from (1) regulation, (2) relationships with beneficiaries, (3) bookkeeping and accounting for assets, and (4) investment of trust funds.

Regulation. Under the regulations of the Comptroller of the Currency, fiduciary permissive powers are no longer divided into categories; now, national banks are permitted to exercise those powers consistent with the ability of the national bank. "On the belief that no bank is only partly competent to exercise fiduciary powers, the Comptroller henceforth deems such National Banks to be possessed of all fiduciary powers which are not in contravention of the laws of the state in which it is located."[5]

All national banks are required by law to separate their trust function from other departments in the bank, keeping the books and records "distinct from other records of the bank." There is no mingling of assets of the trust department with those of the commercial, savings, or other departments of the bank, the only exception being when trust funds are held by a bank as deposits, awaiting investment or distribution. In some states these funds may be used by the bank under authorization of its board of directors, provided that adequate collateral is deposited as security, the deposits being preferred claims on the assets of the bank.

The law specifies that the board of directors is directly responsible for general supervision of the trust department; and Regulation 9

[4] *100th Annual Report of the Comptroller of the Currency* (Washington, D.C.: U.S. Government Printing Office, 1963), p. 14. The transfer of power was authorized in Public Law 87–722, 12 U.S.C., 92a on September 28, 1962. A second law, known as "H.R. 10," authorized on October 10, 1962, offered tax exemption to retirement plans for the self-employed.

[5] Roman J. Gerber, "Current Legal and Regulatory Developments," *National Banking Review*, September, 1963, p. 141. Regulation 9 as revised is published in the *Federal Register*, February 5, 1963, pp. 1111–14.

states that the board may *assign* the performance of its duties to employees, officers, or committees but may not delegate them. The board of directors must approve the acceptance of all fiduciary accounts and the closing-out or relinquishment of all old ones. Furthermore, the law states that all trust funds must be invested by a trust committee composed of three or more members, who must be experienced officers or directors of the bank. This committee must review, at least annually, the assets held in, or for, each fiduciary account. It must "determine their safety and current value and the advisability of retaining or disposing of them; and a report of all such reviews together with the action taken as a result thereof, shall be noted in the minutes of the trust investment committee."

Unless covered by state law, a bank's board of directors determines the policy as to charges for administering trusts which are usually in the form of commissions and fees that may be levied on the value of the assets of the trust or as a percentage of the income from the trust. When a trust is terminated, a final commission based on the principal remaining at that time may be collected. The compensation for a trustee on a will or voluntary trust may be arrived at by negotiation or, in some cases, by law. For New York State, the statutory provisions for compensation for trustees are based on the principal of the trust with levies of 1 percent on the amount paid out; and for that in the trust, it is $5 per $1,000 annually on the first $50,000; $2.50 per $1,000 on the next $450,000; and $2 per $1,000 on all over $500,000. So the annual commission on a $1 million trust would be:

> $250 on the first $50,000 at $5 per $1,000;
> $1,125 on the next $450,000 at $2.50 per $1,000;
> $1,000 on the last $500,000 at $2 per $1,000; or
> $2,375 on the $1,000,000 trust.

The commissions received for accepting and paying out funds as executors, administrators, or guardians are 4 percent on the first $10,000, 2.5 percent on the next $290,000, and 2 percent on all over $300,000. For managing real property, it is 5 percent of gross rent collected.

In only a few states are charges on trust regulated in such detail as in New York, and in many states there are no regulatory laws covering trustees' charges. However, statutory provisions are usually made for executors, administrators, and guardians. Fees and commissions for acting as fiscal agents, such as serving as custodian for securities and supervising investments, are negotiated. Periodic statements of transactions affecting investment and advisory accounts may be required, and supplementary ones may be arranged for by the principal.

Personal Relationships. The executive committee of the Trust Division of the American Bankers Association drew up the following principles to serve as a guide to administration of personal trusts:

Section 1. *Personal Trusts.* In the administration of its personal trust business, a trust institution should strive at all times to render unexceptionable business and financial service, but it should also be careful to render equally good personal service to beneficiaries. The first duty of a trust institution is to carry out the wishes of the creator of a trust as expressed in the trust instrument. Sympathetic, tactful, personal relationships with immediate beneficiaries are essential to the performance of this duty, keeping in mind also the interests of ultimate beneficiaries. It should be the policy of trust institutions that all personal trusts should be under the direct supervision of and that beneficiaries should be brought into direct contact with the administrative or senior officers of the trust department.

Section 2. *Confidential Relationships.* Personal trust service is of a confidential nature and the confidences reposed in a trust department by a customer should never be revealed except when required by law.

Section 3. *Fundamental Duties of Trustees.* It is the duty of a trustee to administer a trust solely in the interest of the beneficiaries without permitting the intrusion of interests of the trustee or third parties that may in any way conflict with the interests of the trust; to keep and render accurate accounts with respect to the administration of the trust; to acquaint the beneficiaries with all material facts in connection with the trust; and, in administering the trust, to exercise the care a prudent man familiar with such matters would exercise as trustee of the property of others, adhering to the rule that the trustee is primarily a conserver.[6]

Trusts vary in size from a few hundred dollars to millions of dollars, and in most cases, the income therefrom is used for the benefit of women and children. Trust funds may also be used for the support of homes, education, care of parents, and the like. In the aggregate, trust institutions are managing more property than at any time in history, reflecting the increase in money incomes and fundamental changes in American life. Furthermore, the increase in life expectancy has led to the creation of many living trusts to give financial security to the beneficiaries during old age.

[6] "A Statement of Principles of Trust Institutions," *Trust Principles and Policies*, a compilation of seven statements of principles and policies of trust institutions that have been adopted by the Trust Division, American Bankers Association, from April 10, 1933 to February 8, 1950 (New York: Trust Division, American Bankers Association, n.d.), p. 3.

While high income taxes have made the accumulation of estates more difficult, increased estate and inheritance taxes have made the preservation of estates virtually impossible for many individuals. Today, many of those who have accumulated modest estates have had previous experience with financial reverses and are desirous of guarding against repetitions; therefore, they are turning to trust companies and trust departments of banks for assistance. The average personal trust is between $200,000 and $500,000, depending primarily on the location of the bank. Currently, trust companies are managing many small individual trusts which can be handled profitably because of the use of electronic data processing equipment and the mingling of funds for investment purposes.

The policy of most banks is to assign individual accounts to the bank's trust officers (the number of accounts assigned to an individual officer varying according to the amount of work involved in each one), so that each officer has the same accounts year after year and develops a satisfactory personal relationship with the beneficiaries. The Trust Division of the American Bankers Association emphasizes the need for trust officers to know the financial circumstances of his clients in order to be able to handle requests intelligently (when a mother asks for money to build a new room or finance a trip to Europe, or junior wants funds for a new car or to start a business). Since most trust agreements allow the trustee some discretion in the disbursement of funds (income and principal), special requests tend to be numerous.

Under the statement of principles cited above, it was stated that steps must be taken to insure the administration of each fund in accordance with the wishes of the creator (trustor) and/or the law as interpreted by the court. Administration becomes more difficult when the trustee is given discretionary powers as to the distribution of principal and/or income of a trust. For example, when the trust agreement states that "each daughter is to have a good car" and the "sons are to have a good education," the trustee must decide what is "good." In cases wherein the beneficiaries of income from a trust are not to inherit the principal when the trust is liquidated, there is conflict of interests between the two groups of beneficiaries that may result in legal action against the trustee if some of the principal is disbursed and the residuary beneficiaries feel the trustee abused his discretion. Conversely, income beneficiaries may sue if the discretionary income is not distributed and they feel that it should be.

Accounting and Bookkeeping.   The regulations pertaining to banks' trust business require that all books and accounts of member banks must be kept in a form approved by supervisory authorities. Each account must be examined annually by a special trust committee of the bank's board of directors and also by supervisory agencies' examiners who give special attention to the auditing, examining, and investing functions of the trustees. In addition to following intelligent investment policies, trustees are expected to provide physical safeguards such as vaults and safe storage places for all assets, and fire, burglary, fidelity, and other types of insurance as may be deemed necessary. Under the leadership of the Trust Division of the American Bankers Association, standard rules and practices are being adopted by most banks.

Accounting has been called "the heart of the trust department" because of the need to give "good information to the board of directors, customers, and other interested parties."[7] Lack of a good accounting system may make it impossible to answer questions of customers and examiners, and this could result in a loss of goodwill and possibly legal action. Courts hold that trustees are responsible for losses when due to their failure to act as the prudent man (and failure to adopt and keep a good accounting system is not the way that a prudent man would operate). The accounting system should provide information "in a form readily available to the trust officer, so that he may know what he must do, when he must do it, and how it shall be done."[8] Although electronic data processing equipment has made accounting and bookkeeping less time-consuming, details must be collected and filed, and forms developed for current operations, and annual accounts reviewed and analyzed.[9] Since each individual account must be segregated from others being handled by a trust department, an institution having a thousand trusts will have to keep a thousand investment, earnings, disbursement, and other bookkeeping records.

Profitability of Handling Trusts. The future of trust institutions and trust departments of banks depends, to a considerable extent, upon their success in keeping down expenses and keeping up income from trust estates. Cost analysis may show that a bank's trust

[7] Noel L. Mills, "A Guide to Setting Up and Operating a Small Trust Department," *Opening and Operating a Trust Department*, reprint from the *Trust Bulletin*, September, 1959 (New York: Trust Division, American Bankers Association, n.d.), p. 2.

[8] Noel L. Mills, "Machines and Systems Needed," reprint from the *Trust Bulletin*, March, 1960, *op. cit.*, p. 21.

[9] *Ibid.*, pp. 22–25.

department is unprofitable, but often the bank derives indirect benefits, such as the use of earnings from trust funds held as deposits pending investment or distribution. The indirect benefits may make the difference between profitability and unprofitability. While it is desirable for a trustee to secure a high rate of return on investment of trust funds, safety of principal must be the major consideration. In order to avoid any suspicion of self-dealing, which is prohibited, banks usually separate the organization for the investment of trust funds from the investment or bond departments of the bank.

Investment of Trust Funds. Although the creator of a trust may give definite instructions as to the character of investments, such as specifying that 50 percent must be in U.S. government securities, 25 percent in municipal or corporate bonds, and 25 percent in gilt-edge common stock, normally he leaves investment policy entirely to the discretion of the trustee. Unless otherwise specified in the trust agreement, the trustee may be limited to investments of trust funds to the so-called "legal" list of securities which usually includes first mortages on real property, government bonds, and the high-grade bonds of public utilities, railroads, and a few industrial corporations. Since 1933 the fear of inflation has led many trustees to seek permission to buy high-grade common and preferred stocks, and some states have made statutory provisions for such investments. However, a more popular arrangement with trust officers is that of leaving the selection of securities to the discretion of trustees. While the laws of a majority of the states have adopted the "prudent man" principle, a creator or grantor of a trust may specify that trust funds be invested in certain types of common stock or other securities.

In cases wherein control of assets in personal trust accounts is shared with other persons (co-trustees), they are usually members of the family. Although such co-trustees may have no previous experience in handling trusts, they may be helpful to beneficiaries who may be inexperienced in business affairs and dislike dealing with "strangers." While a trust company or trustee may be held liable for losses suffered through failure to comply with statutory regulations or instructions contained in trust agreements, they will usually not be held liable if the loss is due to an error in judgment (assuming action was in keeping with the prudent-man theory).

Prior to the authorization of common trust funds, each trust had to be invested separately; and, as a consequence, small trusts lacked diversity and liquidity compared to larger trusts. In an effort to correct this situation, the federal and state governments authorized banks to invest small trust accounts collectively and to issue participation certificates to each trust account. This development of common trust funds originated in 1936 when Congress gave common trusts special tax status in the Revenue Act of 1936, and now most states have passed enabling acts.

Since the trust instrument may specify that funds be invested in certain types of securities—such as mortgages, corporate bonds, or common stock—such trust funds may not be invested collectively unless the latter is limited to similar securities.[10] An increasing number of banks are establishing more than one common trust fund. These may include a fixed-income fund, a common-stock or equity fund, two funds for pension and profit sharing (one income and one equity), a municipal bond fund, and more recently separate funds for self-employed individuals. Along with the increased number of trust funds, there has been a greater increase in the volume of assets in trust funds due partly to the progressive increase in the dollar limit on individual participation, from $25,000 to $100,000, and finally the elimination of the dollar limit. However the rules state that no more than 10 percent of a common trust fund may be acquired by one participant and that no more than 10 percent of the assets in a common trust fund may be invested in the securities of one issuer.[11]

To an increasing extent, banks are being requested to administer employee-benefit funds of various types, including pension, thrift, welfare, profit sharing, and bonus plans set up for the exclusive benefit of employees or their beneficiaries. The problem of investing funds paid in periodically is similar to that inherent in the investment of small trusts; therefore, collective investment of such funds is allowed provided it is authorized by the instruments creating the trusts.[12] The most significant postwar change in the investment of personal trust funds has been the emphasis on common stocks and the decline in fixed-income securities. Many economists and trust experts feel that, in the long run, equities are a better investment than bonds, notes, or mortgages because of the effect of inflation (see Table 25–1).

[10] "Uniform Common Trust Act," *Trust Estate and Legislation* (New York: Trust Division, American Bankers Association, 1961, p. 10. This act has been adopted by all states except Alaska and Iowa, with minor and major modifications by 22 states and with changes by 28 states.

[11] Roman J. Gerber, "Current Legal and Regulatory Developments," *National Banking Review*, September, 1963, p. 140.

[12] In 1961, 36 states had passed laws providing for exemption of pension and profit-sharing trusts from the rule against perpetuities.

TABLE 25–1

TRUST ASSETS OF BANKS, APRIL 1, 1968
(In Billions of Dollars)

Type of Asset	Amount	Percent
Stock........................	$161.7	64.4
Bonds..........................	66.8	27.4
Real estate and mortgages...........	12.5	5.0
Cash and miscellaneous.............	8.1	3.2
Total.....................	$251.1*	100.0

* Since $2.2 billion was not broken down by type of assets, it was not included in the total.

Source: Staff Report for the Subcommittee on Domestic Finance, Committee on Banking and Currency, *Commercial Banks and Their Trust Activities: Emerging Influence on the American Economy* (H.R., 90th Cong., 2d sess., July 8, 1968), Vol. 1, p. 47.

PERSONAL TRUST AND AGENCY SERVICES

The chief types of personal trust and agency functions that trustees are asked to assume are to serve as executors or administrators of estates, trustees under wills of deceased persons or under agreements or deeds of trust, guardians of property of minors and incompetent persons, and fiscal agencies, attorneys in fact, and depositories in various capacities.

Settling Estates. Individuals or trust companies may be appointed to take charge of the settlement of estates under wills (called "executors") or by orders of the court having probate jurisdiction (called "administrators"). In both cases the duties of a trust company or individual trustee are practically the same. They include the receipt of property, payments of all claims against the estate, and division of the remainder among the heirs according to the law or the terms of the will. The authority of the executor is derived from the will, and the authority of the administrator is derived from the intestacy law. However, the administrators or executors cannot take possession of the property until authorized to do so by the court having probate jurisdiction. (Probate means officially proving a will. Under probate the will is certified by the court to be the deceased's last will and testament, and the executor is empowered to act under the terms of the will and the laws of the state controlling the duties and functions of executors.) In the past, the maker of a will usually named an individual as executor, but, at the present time, there is a growing tendency to name a trust company or a trust department of a bank as executor. Because of the nature of the trust activities involved, the duties of executors and administrators are temporary, but the one who serves as executor or administrator may also be asked to act as trustee.

Personal Trusts.   The principal types of personal trusts are testamentary trusts, living trusts, and guardianship accounts. A testamentary trust is one created by the terms of a decedent's will and is composed of those assets transferred to it in accordance with the terms of the will by the executor after the debts, taxes, and other obligations have been paid. The trust will be administered in accordance with the terms of the will which created it.

A trust created by the truster during his life is a living trust. His purpose may be to assure his family of certain income in the case of business losses, or the trust may be created as a gift for the life of an individual or for a limited period of time. A trust is often used as a vehicle for making gifts to minor children which will not be paid to the children until they reach 21 years of age. Although the beneficiaries of trusts are usually persons other than the trustor, he may make himself the beneficiary until his death and by the terms of the instrument provide where the benefits should go at his death either by the terms of the agreement or by payment of the remaining assets to the executors of his estate. In any of these circumstances, the trust agreement may also provide the trustee with discretion to distribute not only the income but also the principal of the trust to or for the benefit of the beneficiaries named.

A guardianship account is an account which is created for one under a legal disability and would include minors, habitual drunkards, idiots, and insane persons. In the case of the death of parents (natural guardians), the protection of minor children and their property is assumed by the state. A guardian for the children may be appointed by will, by deed, or by the probate court. A trust company may serve as guardian of a minor's property and in some cases of his person. The guardianship ends when the ward reaches the legal age or in some cases when he marries. The principal duties of the guardian of the estate of a minor are to accept the property of the ward; to make investments in accordance with the law; to keep accurate records of receipts and expenditures; to render annual accountings to the court; to render a final accounting; and upon the decree of the court to deliver the property to the beneficiary. Habitual drunkards, idiots, and insane persons may be declared incompetent by the state and, therefore, become wards of the state. The courts, upon proper application, appoint guardians of their persons and property. Duties of the guardian, sometimes called conservator or a committee, are similar to those of a guardian of the estate of a minor. The length of time a guardianship is in existence varies according to the needs in the individual case.

Personal Agency Services. Trust companies act as fiscal agents for individuals when they take complete charge of assets of the individual and manage them as if they were trustees except that they do not take title. Formerly such activities were limited to the management of real property, but now this is usually an investment type of account including only stocks, bonds, and other types of personal property. In general a trust company may serve an individual in the same physical capacities in which one individual may serve a second (as a custodian, a managing agent, an investment counselor, a saleman, etc.). Often an individual planning to be absent from his home or business for an extended period of time will employ a trust company to manage his personal affairs. Doctors, dentists, and other professional people also find this type of service helpful in freeing themselves of investment burdens.

One of the more complicated agency services offered by trust companies is the escrow depository. Under this arrangement, property is accepted on deposit and is to be delivered to another individual upon specific conditions. It is a useful device in business transactions where parties are separated by long distances, in real estate transfers where property is in dispute, in connection with alimony payments, and whenever the first party of a contract does not fully trust the second party or vice versa. As an escrow depository, a trust company accepts checks, notes, bonds, and other types of property and holds it until the grantee has fulfilled certain specific conditions. While in escrow, the grantor loses all control over the property.

At the present time, many trust companies are holding investment management accounts wherein they manage investments for individuals. This service is sought by many amateur investors, often after having suffered stock market reverses or having been confused by too much free advice from others. Finally, trust companies act as custodians of property—jewelry, paintings, etc., but most often, securities.

The business of the corporate trustee will increase because of the enactment of the Self-Employed Individuals Tax Retirement Act passed by Congress in 1962, along with the amendments passed in 1966. By this legislation a self-employed individual, as defined by the statute, may deduct from his income 10 percent of his annual income as defined by the act up to a $2,500 contribution to a qualified retirement plan. Unless the plan is restricted to the purchase of insurance or a special United States savings bond, a bank must be named trustee. During the period that the trust is in existence, the self-employed individual pays no income tax on the income earned on the trust or on capital gains realized. The grantor may designate the amount to be placed in insurance, if any, and the amount to be invested in common stock and other securities. Most banks use one or more common trust funds as the investment media for these accounts.

Advantages of Using Corporate Trustees. Although most trust functions may be performed by individuals, trust companies may be better equipped to perform certain specific services. The advantages of the trust companies over individual trustees may be summarized as follows:

1. Trust companies offer continuous administration, which the individual cannot do. Whereas the life of an individual is short, trust companies have perpetual charters. If an individual trustee dies or resigns, a successor must be appointed. This is usually costly, for it involves a complete accounting on the part of the former trustee or his estate, the cost of which is charged against the trust fund.

2. Trust companies offer continuous service at their place of business, but an individual trustee is not always at his home or office; moreover, his residence may be changed many times during the life of the trust. Many annoyances to beneficiaries and losses because of delay may result from these conditions.

3. Trust companies are more responsible than are individual trustees, having had more experience with investments and being more impartial than individuals. Banks are subject to periodic examinations by the government, and their capital resources are large. Trust companies are not, however, responsible for losses of trust funds unless fraud or negligence can be proved.

4. Trust companies have available expert services in the investment, accounting, taxation, and legal fields and have more experience in handling estates—circumstances that make the cost of administration less than is usually the case under management of an individual trustee.

Objections to Corporate Trustees. The chief criticism of corporate trustees is that they are impersonal in their treatment of beneficiaries and trust funds. Many contend that the primary concern of corporate trustees is to keep within the law and to avoid future claims against them for illegal operations, which means that their activities are too passive and too routine in nature. Even when given broad discretionary powers, banks sometimes hesitate to take necessary action, seemingly preferring the safer legal policy of doing nothing. The chief critics of the trust work of banks are their chief competitors, lawyers. However, these criticisms have become less valid because trust officers of banks have done a great deal to create a "father image." Now trust companies are giving more attention to public relations and are building up more friendly relations with lawyers, accountants, and the general public.

TRUST AND AGENCY SERVICES FOR CORPORATIONS

Although trust companies perform agency services for individuals as well as corporations, the need for corporate trust and agency services is confined largely to large centers of population. For this reason, many small banks limit their trust business to agency and fiduciary services to individuals.[13] In administering corporate trusts and agency services, banks are expected to follow the same administrative principles that have been considered under personal trusteeship. "Promptness, accuracy, and protection are fundamental requirements of efficient corporate trust service. The terms of the trust instrument should be carried out with scrupulous care and with particular attention to the duties imposed therein upon the trustee for the protection of the security-holders."[14]

Corporate trust business includes all fiduciary services performed for corporations, educational institutions, fraternal organizations, hospitals, and religious institutions, under relationships created either by expressed or implied contracts or by law in which the principal delegates the transaction of some lawful business to a trust company. The latter managers the affairs and gives an accounting to the principal. The most important corporate fiduciary services rendered by commercial banks are acting as trustee under a corporate mortgage or under reorganization plans, receiverships, etc.; serving as transfer agent, registrar, or paying agent; serving as fiscal agent, attorney in fact, and depository in various capacities; and helping societies and institutions in various ways, including the management of pension and profit-sharing plans.

Trustee under Instruments of Indebtedness. When corporations borrow for long periods, the amounts needed may be too large to be provided by one lender. In some cases of this type, the borrower may make a contract with a broker to serve as trustee of a bond issue.

---

[13] See 100th Annual Report of the Comptroller of the Currency, 1962 (Washington, D.C.: U.S. Government Printing Office, 1963), p. 245.

[14] "A Statement of Principles of Trust Institutions," p. 3.

Through this medium, bonds may be sold to investors in convenient denominations (usually $500 or $1,000). A single mortgage or indenture agreement is usually drawn up and made payable to a bank or a trust company.[15] This mortgage or indenture agreement contains provisions to protect the bondholders. The corporation conveys to the trustee, under certain conditions, title to all or part of its property. This mortgage or indenture agreement is held in trust by the trustee for the benefit of the holders of the bonds which the corporation has issued thereunder.

Prior to 1939 trust companies were not bond trustees in the true sense of the word but merely agents of the bondholders.[16] They rarely took action on their own initiative, being guided by the traditional attitude, which was opposed to taking positive action. Even when trustees were given discretion to act, they rarely did so. As a result, bondholders did not have the protection that the word "trustee" denotes. However, trust companies were faithful in performing their routine functions in connection with their trust under corporate mortgages.[17]

One purpose of the Trust Indenture Act of 1939 was "to bring all indenture trustees up to a high level of diligence and loyalty and to place them in a better position to protect security holders. The means adopted is a requirement that bonds, notes, debentures, and similar debt securities exceeding $1,000,000, in principal amount may not be offered for sale to the public unless they are issued under a trust indenture which conforms to specific statutory standards and has been duly qualified with the [Securities and Exchange] Commission."[18] The trustee is now expected to take action to protect bondholders in the event of default on payment of interest, principal, or some other part of the indenture agreement.

Agent or Trustee in Corporate Reorganizations. The work of

[15] An indenture trustee "shall mean a trustee under a mortgage, deed of trust, or indenture, pursuant to which there are securities outstanding, other than voting-trust certificates, constituting claims against a debtor or claims secured by a lien upon any of his property." (Art. II, sec. 106, chap. X, of the National Bankruptcy Act.)

[16] See Securities and Exchange Commission, *Report on the Study and Investigation of the Work, Activities, and Functions of Protective and Reorganization Committee* (Washington, D.C.: U.S. Government Printing Office, 1937), Part I: "Strategy and Techniques of Protective and Reorganization Committee."

[17] See Trust Indenture Act of 1939 (76th Cong., 1st sess.; Public Law 253). This act gave the Securities and Exchange Commission the power to approve or disapprove of trust indentures under which securities are issued.

[18] *Tenth Annual Report of the Securities and Exchange Commission* (Fiscal Year Ended June 30, 1944) (Washington, D.C.: U.S. Government Printing Office, 1945), p. 5.

trust institutions in the financial reorganizations of corporations is usually passive. They accept the securities deposited with them by one or more of the reorganization committees. After the committees and the courts have worked out an acceptable plan for reorganization, the depository issues the reorganization certificates authorized by them.[19]

Transfer Agent.   The stockholders of a corporation are the owners of its capital stock, and their names and the number of shares held by each are shown on the books of the corporation. If title is transferred to a second party, transfer of the certificate is not sufficient; the title must be passed on in the books of the corporation. This transfer of title may be made by the corporation or by some trust institution appointed as the transfer agent. If a stock is actively traded in on a stock exchange, trust institutions commonly serve as transfer agents, since they are able to transfer titles to stock rapidly and skillfully; but some of the larger corporations, such as the American Telephone and Telegraph Company, have their own transfer offices in New York City.

Registrar.   In order to prevent fraud in the form of illegal issues of stock, the New York Stock Exchange now requires, as a prerequisite for listing stocks, the appointment of a transfer agent and a registrar, both to be located in the borough of Manhattan, city of New York. In addition, the listed company may have several other transfer agents and registrars in different sections of the country. In all cases, the registrar must be a trust institution. The registrar checks upon the transfer work of the transfer agent and receives both the canceled certificate of stock, or a registered bond, and the new stock certificate or bond issued in its place. The canceled certificate is examined to see that it is genuine and that the new certificate is drawn to represent the proper number of shares. Proper entries are made in the registration records, and the registrar's certificate is signed and then returned to the transfer agent. Bonds may be registered in the same way as stock certificates, and the same procedures for transfer of title are followed. Usually, no new bond is issued when ownership changes, but the name of the new owner is placed on the bond and in the books of the transfer agent.

Paying Agent.   Trust companies also serve as payment agents for private corporations, state and local governments, and other debtors. If a trust institution serves as paying agent, the debtor deposits

---

[19] Note new provisions for corporate reorganization in Chapter X of the National Bankruptcy Act (75th Cong., 2d sess.; Public Law 696).

funds with it prior to the interest, dividend, or maturity dates of the obligations. Trust institutions also serve corporations in many of the special-agency capacities in which they serve individuals.

Other Capacities. A trust institution may take complete charge of the assets of a corporation and manage them as a trustee, except that there would be no transfer of title to such assets. A trust company may serve a business firm in the same capacities as one individual may serve a second (as managing agent, custodian, investment counselor, escrow depository, and even liquidating agent in case owners decide to liquidate their business).

TABLE 25–2

TRUST ASSETS BY TYPE OF ACCOUNT, 1967

Type of Account	Amount	Percent
	(Billions of Dollars)	
Employee benefit accounts	$ 72.9	28.8
Private trust accounts	126.2	49.8
Agency accounts	54.2	21.4
Total	$253.3	100.0

Source: Staff Report of the Subcommittee on Domestic Finance, Committee on Banking and Currency, *Commercial Banks and Their Trust Activities: Emerging Influence on the American Economy* (H.R., 90th Cong., 2d sess., July 8, 1968), Vol. 1, p. 34.

One reason for the rapid increase in bank trust business is the growth of pension and other types of employee benefit plans. In 1968, the volume of assets in these funds was estimated to be in excess of $100 billion, of which $72.9 billion was in funds managed by banks (see Table 25–2). The volume of assets in pension funds is increasing because of the expansion of old funds and creation of new ones. By 1980, they are expected to have assets in excess of $285 billion, with banks managing $200 billion.

Community Trust. Trust companies serve as trustees and agents for many types of foundations, educational institutions, hospitals, religious and charitable organizations, and other institutions. The community trust is a fairly recent development in this field, the first having been created in 1914 in Cleveland, Ohio. Under a community trust, gifts and bequests are received by one or more trust companies, which, with the help of an advisory board of citizens, expend the funds for public purposes. The community trust in New York is the largest in this country.

OTHER ASPECTS OF TRUST BUSINESS

Concentration. Of the 13,500 banks in the United States, less than 28 percent have been authorized to do a trust business, and of the 2,890 banks having trust powers, 124 are not using them. The 10 largest banks, ranked according to the volume of their trust assets, hold only 36.8 percent of the total trust assets; but the 10 largest banks, ranked according to the amount of deposits, hold only 23.8 percent of the total deposits of all commercial banks.[20] Furthermore most of the trust business is concentrated in the older and wealthier states (see Table 25–3).

TABLE 25–3

BANK DEPOSITS AND TRUST ASSETS BY STATES

State	Deposits (Millions of Dollars)	Percent	Trust Assets (Millions of Dollars)	Percent	Number of Banks	Number of Trust Depts.
New York	$ 76,724.6	19.42	$ 86,329.9	34.51	303	129
Pennsylvania	23,651.1	5.98	23,861.5	9.54	512	223
Illinois	29,398.9	7.44	22,407.9	8.96	1,062	242
California	41,254.1	10.44	14,287.2	5.11	172	36
Massachusetts	9,015.8	2.28	12,469.2	4.99	154	80
Ohio	18,618.0	4.71	12,360.1	4.94	530	83
Delaware	1,056.7	0.26	6,907.8	2.75	19	10
Connecticut	4,257.7	1.07	5,898.8	2.36	64	33
Texas	20,828.2	5.27	5,035.6	2.01	1,139	163
New Jersey	11,856.2	3.00	4,542.4	1.81	225	121
All others	158,309.6	40.13	56,070.0	23.02	9,336	1,770
Total	$394,970.9	100.00	$250,170.2	100.00	13,516	2,890

Source: Staff Report for the Subcommittee on Domestic Finance, Committee on Banking and Currency *Commercial Banks and Their Trust Activities: Emerging Influence on the American Economy* (H.R., 90th Cong., 2d sess., July 8, 1968, Vol. 1, pp. 62–63.

Conflict of Interest. Among the principles of trust banking, the one that may be violated most frequently is, "It is the duty of a trustee to administer a trust solely in the interest of the beneficiaries without permitting the intrusion of interests of the trustee or third parties that may in any way conflict with the interests of the trust." Conflict of interest could result from a trust holding of large blocks of stock of corporations that are at the same time customers of the bank. In such a case, will the vote of the stock of the corporations be

[20] Staff Report for the Subcommittee on Domestic Finance, Committee on Banking and Currency, *Commercial Banks and Their Trust Activities: Emerging Influence on the American Economy* (H.R., 90th Cong., 2d sess., July 8, 1968), Vol. I, p. 77.

cast in the interest of existing management of the corporation or the beneficiaries of the trust?[21] Many bank directors are, at the same time, directors and/or officers of corporations whose stock is held by banks' trust departments, and this raises the same question of possible conflict of interest.[22] Under modern conditions, there is always the danger that a third party's interest will be given priority over the interests of the beneficiary. Such breaches of trust are punishable under the law, but few beneficiaries are aware of any irregularities in the activities of their trustees; and, if they are, how many are in a position to assume the responsibility for legal action against the trustees? Furthermore, supervisory agencies responsible for regulation of trust business are limited to "ascertaining whether the bank conducts its operations in accordance with the governing trust instruments, statutes, regulations, and sound principles of trust administration. The responsibilities of bank supervisory authorities do not include any control of investments or other important discretionary action."[23]

Proposals for Reform. In registration of securities, Congress has made wide use of the disclosure principle, and in the Staff Report of the House Subcommittee on Domestic Finance the members recommended the application of this principle to the trust business as follows: (1) annual disclosure by each trustee of his aggregate holdings, in all capacities, of corporate stock registered with the Securities and Exchange Commission; (2) disclosure of the contents of the portfolios of all pension funds; and (3) disclosure of proxy voting by trustees of all registered stock.

Most of the danger of conflict of interest stems from the fact that trustees hold voting rights to stocks in their trust portfolios. While most states do not permit banks acting as trustees to vote shares of their own banks, only five have similar laws pertaining to shares of other corporations. Among the proposals to remedy this situation are (1) prohibit bank trustees from investing in more than 10 percent of any stock that must be registered with SEC, (2) prohibit all insured banks from holding or voting their own stock, and (3) prohibit an officer or director of a commercial bank, mutual savings bank, savings and loan association, or insurance company from being a director of any other commercial bank, mutual savings bank, savings and loan association, or insurance company, or any other corporation that has created an employee benefit plan which is managed by the bank.

[21] *Ibid.*, pp. 23 ff.
[22] *Ibid.*, pp. 775–85.
[23] *Ibid.*, p. 8.

When the stock of the founder of the pension plan is not voted, the amount should be subtracted from the total outstanding in determining a majority vote on any question.

SUMMARY

Trust institutions have as their primary functions the protection of private property against waste and loss and the supervision of the transfer of income or title to property (such as from trustor to the beneficiary or of securities bought and sold in the open market). In the capacity of trustee, the trust company takes title to and manages property left in trust by the creator of the trust, as provided for by a trust agreement, a will, and/or the law. Trust companies also perform many agency services for individuals, corporations, governments, societies, and institutions.

Individuals as well as corporations may act as trustees, and in the administration of estates provisions are often made for co-trustees—an individual and a corporation—thereby combining the advantages of havng both kinds of trustees. In investing funds left in trust and distributing the income therefrom, the trustee is required to give primary attention to the wishes of the trustor. Assuming that the trust agreement does not specify the types of investments, in some states the trust must be invested in securities classified as legal investments for trust funds by the state governments. In an increasing number of states, however, the trustees are permitted to invest in securities in which a prudent man would invest under like circumstances.

Services performed for business corporations include acting as trustee under a corporate mortgage, trustee under reorganization plans, transfer agent, registrar, and paying agent. Trust companies also administer funds contributed to educational institutions, research foundations, hospitals, community trusts, and pension and similar plans. Trust companies may be held liable for losses resulting from failure to adhere to instructions in the trust agreement, requirements in the state law, or actions of an imprudent nature. The chief reason why individuals and business firms select trust companies to manage their property is the ability of such institutions to do a better job than individuals can.

QUESTIONS AND PROBLEMS

1. (*a*) What is trust banking? (*b*) Explain the legal difference between a trust and an agency relationship. (*c*) Identify: the "rule against perpetuity."

2. How does the receipt of title to property by a trustee differ from a bank's receipt of the title when a time or demand deposit is made?

3. Assume that a college graduate wants to endow a "Chair of Finance" in memory of his parents. How may this be done through the facilities offered by a trust company?

4. What is the significance of the following quotation from an editorial in a metropolitan newspaper? "The dead hand of obsolescence can never smother or destroy memorial funds left with the New York Community Trust, because the seventeen financial institutions serving as trustees of this great association are empowered to redirect the application of such funds if the purposes for which they were established become out-moded."

5. Distinguish among (*a*) transfer agent, (*b*) registrar, and (*c*) paying agent. What other trust and agency services do banks provide?

6. Discuss: In general, state laws "require that a trustee keep accurate accounts of the assets, which must be segregated; . . . comply with the wishes of the grantor in carrying out the terms of the Trust; . . . not take advantage of his position, and that he confine investments to those permitted by law for trusts, if he is responsible for making investment decisions." (*New York Times*, May, 1966, p. 67.)

7. Analyze: "The profitability of trust operations varied greatly among banks in the District. Of the 58 banks which participated in the survey, only 32 or 55 percent reported that their trust departments were profitable." (Federal Reserve Bank of Dallas, *Business Review*, June, 1968, p. 13.)

8. Analyze: "The fastest growing bank, Republic National of Dallas, is only 42nd in size. No New York City bank . . . falls among the fifteen most rapidly growing trust departments. . . . California banks appear to represent the second most rapidly growing region. . . ." (A. L. Pakkala, "Trust Department Income," *Financial Analysts Journal*, July–August, 1968, pp. 142–43.)

9. Explain: "No area of banking is so fraught with the possibility of disastrous and humiliating losses . . . as the trust field. An incorrect distribution to a beneficiary, . . . incorrect tax analysis . . . are only a few of the multitude of pitfalls which make trust officers old before their time." (Charles H. Mullen, "Food for Thought in Pros and Cons on Small Bank Trust Departments," *American Banker*, September 24, 1967, p. 52.)

10. Discuss: "Commercial banks are acquiring a dangerous 'snow-balling economic power' over big sections of U.S. industry. . . . The confidential nature of trust arrangements . . . means that 'much information on the many relationships between bank trust departments and others have been hidden from the public'. . . ." (*Austin American*, July 15, 1968, p. 14.)

CHAPTER 26

Foreign Exchange

FOREIGN EXCHANGE is foreign money or credit instruments payable in foreign money, and the foreign-exchange market is the market wherein currencies of the world are traded. In the United States, the chief institutions in this market are the large New York banks through which foreign exchange is bought and sold. The demand for foreign exchange originates in the purchase of foreign goods, services, and assets by United States businessmen, travelers, and investors; the supply originates in the sale of goods, services, and assets of foreigners.

FOREIGN-EXCHANGE INSTRUMENTS

Foreign-exchange instruments are the means used to remit money abroad and to extend short-term credit to those engaged in some form of foreign trade or other financial transactions.

Remitting Money Abroad. An individual in need of money abroad may have it remitted by purchasing either a bank check (draft) or a cable or mail transfer. The most commonly used method of sending money abroad is by means of a bank draft drawn in terms of American dollars or the equivalent in foreign money computed at the current conversion rate for the day plus fees. The use of bank drafts in making foreign payments has the same accounting and other advantages as the use of checks in domestic trade. The buyer of a sight draft may arrange for its purchase far enough in advance for it to reach his creditor before the obligation is due. A draft may be sent by mail to any address designated by the creditor, who customarily deposits it with his bank for collection. Personal checks are sometimes used in making payment in foreign countries for items such as gifts, books, subscriptions for newspapers and magazines, and mail order items; but bank drafts, traveler's checks, and bank transfers are usually preferred.

A cable transfer is an order to pay a specified sum of money to the party named in the order (beneficiary) transmitted by cable, telephone or radio by one party (usually a bank) to another party abroad (usually a bank located near the recipient of the funds). When the name of the beneficiary bank is known to the sending bank, the latter may send a cable instructing the bank to credit the recipient's account for the amount. In other cases, the sending bank may instruct the receiving bank to advise the recipient by telephone or mail to identify himself and to receive the funds.

Except in the case of emergencies, businessmen prefer mail transfers because the cost of the cable adds to the price paid for goods.[1] Cable transfers are most commonly sent by one banker to another as principal, with the cable-transfer company as agent; but the cable company may also act as principal in such transactions (as Western Union does in domestic transactions). Cable transfers are sent in code, and, to avoid fraud, key words are used for identification at the receiving end.

When transfers are made in terms of the U.S. dollar, as they sometimes are because of the strong position of the dollar in international exchange, instructions may be given to the paying bank or agent to make payment to the beneficiary for the equivalent in local currency at the "rate of the day" or to hold and wait for conversion instructions from the beneficiary. If payment is to be made in local currency, the equivalent would be found by dividing the number of dollars by the rate of exchange used in conversion (assume $2.40, if in English pounds). Although the time needed to transfer an order by cable is a matter of minutes, such transfers from the United States to Europe are usually completed the following day because of the difference in time.

A mail transfer is similar to a cable transfer in all respects, except that the instructions are sent by mail rather than by cable, wire, or radio. The purpose of using a mail transfer rather than a cable transfer is to avoid the cost of the cablegram, which is paid by the buyer of the foreign exchange. Both cable and mail transfers are essentially cash transactions, and, since an airmail letter can be delivered within one day, mail transfers are almost as fast as wire or cable transfers. The buyer of a cable, wire, or mail transfer receives no credit instrument but merely a confirmation of the transaction.

In addition to the kinds of foreign exchange most commonly

[1] The cost of sending a cable order is the price of the foreign money, as quoted at the cable rate of exchange, plus the cost of the cablegram. For example, the cost of transferring 10 to London would be $27.60, assuming the cost of the cable to be $3.60 and the cable rate of exchange to be $2.40 for the English pound ($3.60 + $24.00).

provided by commercial banks, other kinds are provided by other institutions in the foreign-exchange market. These include the United States Post Office and the American Express Company, which provide postal and express money orders. Postal money orders may be expressed in terms of dollars or in terms of certain foreign monetary units. In most cases the orders are expressed in terms of the American dollar, which means that the sender is not sure of the amount of foreign money that is being sent because the order in dollars involves a conversion rate that is unknown until the order is cashed. In making transfers to Great Britain, France, and certain other countries, "foreign currency orders" may be purchased at the conversion price for these countries. In a few cases the buyer sends the order directly to the payee, but in most cases the funds are transmitted between postal authorities. The sender receives a receipt, and the local post office sends the order to one of the money-order exchange offices. The latter sends an advice (containing a list of all such orders, with complete information as to payers, payees, and addresses of payees) to the foreign post office. Then the foreign post office notifies the payees where to call for their money. The United States usually has an adverse balance on postal money orders, which is settled each week through banking channels.

In 1882 the American Express Company introduced a satisfactory method of making small payments at home and in foreign countries in the form of an express money order. Express money orders are issued through the offices of the company, banks, and other agents of the company. Orders may be cashed at banks and hotels as well as at the offices of the American Express Company. The company maintains offices in principal cities in this country and in certain foreign countries and has representatives or correspondents in other cities. Many metropolitan banks are now selling their own money orders, which are cheaper to service than bank drafts (cost-analysis figures indicate that the cost of such bank money orders is about one half that of bank drafts).

Bills of Exchange. The oldest and most important among the credit instruments used in financing foreign trade is the bill of exchange. In financial circles, a bill of exchange, or simply "bill," is an order to pay drawn by one person (the seller or the one who is to receive payment) against a second person (the buyer or the payer). A bank draft, or simply a "draft," is an order to pay drawn by one bank (the payee) on a second bank (the payer). The bill of exchange customarily states the number of days or months before due and the amount, for example "30 days after January 15, 1969 pay to John Smith $2,500 for value received." Because bills of exchange are drawn by the creditor (drawer) on the debtor (drawee), the instrument is not valid until it has been "accepted" by the debter. "Acceptance is the drawee's signed engagement to honor the draft as presented. It must be written on the draft, and may consist of his signature alone."[2] Bills of exchange may be domestic or foreign, depending on whether the drawee or acceptor is domiciled in the United States or abroad.

Originally, bills of exchange were drawn only on merchants, but now they are most commonly drawn on banks. If a bill of exchange is drawn on a bank and accepted by a bank, it is called a "bankers' acceptance" if it is drawn on and accepted by a name other than a bank, it is called a "trade acceptance." By using a bill of exchange, the purchaser of goods may sell the goods before paying for them; and, at the same time, the seller of the goods has received an instrument that he may sell (discount) in the money market at a low interest rate.

The use of the bill of exchange permits trading on credit terms that otherwise would be impossible. When an American exporter sells goods to a foreign buyer he rarely sells on terms commonly used in the United States (such as 2 percent 10 days, net 30 days) because of distances between parties, differences in legal systems and language, lack of information as to the buyer's creditworthiness, and factors that may delay collection. By using a bill of exchange, the seller has written evidence of his claim in the form of a negotiable credit instrument that has been signed (accepted) by the foreign buyer or his bank.

During the early history of international trade, buyers customarily authorized sellers to draw bills of exchange on them; but, after a period of time, sellers realized that bills carrying the name of a large and financially strong merchant as acceptor had better credit standing than those drawn on smaller and less well-known merchants. As a result, sellers arranged with buyers to have their bills accepted by better known houses. The fact that such bills were more negotiable and salable at higher prices led to the practice of acceptors charging a fee or commission for their services. When the volume of their acceptance business justified doing so, some of these firms relinquished their mercantile activities to concentrate on financing foreign trade. These firms are now known as merchant bankers or accepting houses.

Prior to passage of the Federal Reserve Act, national banks were

[2] *Uniform Commercial Code*, sec. 340(1).

not authorized to accept bills of exchange and were prohibited from opening foreign branches; hence, most of the foreign trade of the United States was financed by London banks in terms of sterling exchange. (A few state-chartered banks accepted bills and operated foreign branches before World War I.) Fundamental changes in the international trade and financial position resulted from World War I; and, in a very short time, American banks were financing the foreign trade of many foreign countries as well as that of the United States.

In connection with the use of bills of exchange, two things should be kept in mind: (1) banks and acceptors expect their customers to pay them an amount equal to the bills accepted by them either at or prior to maturity; and (2) accepting bills are sold in the money market which means that, during the interim between the date of acceptance and maturity of the bill, the trade transaction is financed by the owner of the bill (institutional investor, business firm, bank, or other investor), who earns the discount during the time he holds the bill. Most economical financing exists when there is a well-developed acceptance or commercial bill market as well as strong accepting institutions (thereby assuring the existence of prime bills and competition for them).

FOREIGN EXCHANGE RATE

The exchange rate is the price of foreign money stated in terms of domestic money (see Table 26–1). In the United States, the direct-price method of quoting foreign-exchange rates is usually used (for illustration, the Mexican peso = 8 cents); but where the second unit is the same as the U.S. dollar (such as the Canadian dollar), the

TABLE 26–1

FOREIGN-EXCHANGE RATES FOR SELECTED COUNTRIES
(In Cents per Unit of Foreign Currency)

Currency unit	1963	1964	1965	1966	1967	1968*
Argentina (peso).	0.72447	0.71786	0.59517	0.48690	0.30545	0.28470
Canada (dollar)..	92.699	92.689	92.743	92.811	92.689	92.846
West Germany (mark).......	25.084	25.157	25.036	25.007	25.084	23.032
India (rupee)†...	20.966	20.923	20.938	16.596	13.255	13.228
Japan (yen).....	0.27663	0.27625	0.27666	0.27598	0.27613	0.27636
United Kingdom (pound)‡.....	280.00	279.21	279.59	279.30	275.04	238.46

* June, 1968
† The Indian rupee was devalued from 4.76 to 7.5 rupees per dollar, effective June 6, 1966.
‡ The pound sterling was devalued on November 18, 1967.
Source: *Federal Reserve Bulletin*, July, 1968, p. A–90.

foreign unit may be quoted as being at a premium or discount. In London the indirect-price method is used, which means that one unit of English money will be given for the quoted number of U.S. dollars (for example £1 = $2.40).

In New York, a foreign monetary unit is sold under different terms, and so the buying rates for the English pound sterling may be quoted by one bank as $2.397 for a cable transfer, $2.394 for a sight draft, and $2.385 for a 30-day sight draft, with lower prices for longer maturities. (Selling prices may be slightly higher.) Even the quoted prices may be "shaded" in favor of customers for various reasons such as the size of the transaction, quality of the credit instrument, and the relationship between the seller and the buyer. Similar differences will be applicable to other banks because the market is closely knit by telephone lines.

Cable exchange usually has the highest rate or price because the buyer obtains funds immediately and the seller releases them immediately. Airmail permits rapid movement of demand and sight drafts; therefore, mail transfer prices are not much lower than cable because cable is often paid the next day in Europe, due to the difference in time.

The spread between the price of cable and time drafts is determined by the loss in interest in the market for the time period between origination and payment. Thus, the higher the interest rate and the longer the time period, the greater is the spread between cable and time drafts; and conversely, the lower the interest rate and the shorter the time period, the smaller is the spread between cable and time drafts. At times, there are national and international forces at work in the foreign exchange market that cause all rates to move up and down together.

Forward or future exchange embodies a contract for delivery and payment of foreign exchange at some time in the future, with the rate of exchange being fixed at the time the contract is negotiated. A brief statement indicates the rights of the buyer and the obligations of the seller. No money changes hands because delivery and payment are in the future, hence the name "future" or "forward" exchange.

A forward-exchange transaction usually provides for the delivery or purchase of forward exchange on a fixed date (such as one month up to six months), but it may provide for purchase or sale of foreign exchange over a period of time at the customer's option. In the latter case, the option may never be used, so the date merely indicates when the option terminates. Banks and dealers customarily offset their purchases and sales of foreign exchange wherever possible. For illustration, a bank may contract to deliver a "cable" transfer of 12.4 million Mexican pesos to a second party in 60 days at a rate of exchange of 8.0645 cents. At the end of the 60 days, the spot rate for the peso may be 8 cents, but this would have no effect on the contractual rate of exchange. Usually, the forward exchange rate is quoted at a discount or premium in terms of the spot rate.

The behavior of the exchange rate depends in part on the type of foreign exchange system. For nations that accept and adhere to the principles adopted by the International Monetary Fund (see Chapter 27), the price or the sight rate of exchange would fluctuate above and below the par of exchange within limits established by the Fund. When countries are not adhering to the principles of the Fund, the rate of exchange is determined by the demand for and supply of foreign exchange or foreign money in the market. It may fluctuate freely with no upper or lower limits, but may be subject to exchange control and other interventions by the central bank and/or government (see Chapter 27).

FOREIGN-EXCHANGE MARKETS

A bank, dealing with its customers, buys and sells different foreign currencies in both the spot and forward markets. Usually purchases are offset by sales, and any difference at the end of the trading day is settled by exchanges with other banks.

Interbank Market. Although foreign exchange is bought and sold in every community in the United States, the principal foreign-exchange market is in New York, where large commercial banks, foreign-exchange dealers and brokers, subsidiaries and agents of foreign banks, some investment houses, commodity and securities brokerage firms, and the Federal Reserve Bank of New York, as agent for the Federal Reserve System and the United States Treasury, buy and sell foreign exchange to one another at wholesale prices. The inventories of these wholesalers consist of balances with foreign banks, which are replenished by purchases of foreign exchange.

In New York, commercial banks find it convenient to use the services of one or more of the seven exchange brokers, most of whom specialize in handling all of the leading currencies, such as the Canadian dollar, the pound sterling, or the Swiss franc. By matching up a bank's bid to buy or its offer to sell foreign exchange with others in the market, the broker makes it possible for the banker to concentrate on his banking business. If there is an imbalance between orders to buy and orders to sell in the market, the foreign-exchange rate will change—rising when orders to buy are large relative to orders to sell. Changes in exchange rates may attract additional banks as buyers or as sellers and also speculators.

Gold is no longer permitted to assume its historical role as the regulator of the exchange rate and of the international balance of payments; and so, the monetary authorities have greater responsibility for stabilization of foreign exchange rates. If the supply of foreign exchange in the market exceeds the demand, the rate tends to fall; and so the Federal Reserve Bank of New York buys the foreign currency. Conversely, when the demand for foreign currency exceeds the supply, the rate tends to rise; and so, the Federal Reserve Bank of New York sells foreign currency. The Federal Reserve Bank of New York uses resources provided by the Federal Reserve System and the United States Treasury in ways consistent with the policies of the Open Market Committee and the Treasury.

The foreign-exchange market, as organized today, has changed little through the years. The principal change has been the entrance of the Federal Reserve System; however, commercial banks, now as always, play the major role as dealers in the market. The commercial banks which act as dealers operate directly or through a few intermediaries (foreign-exchange brokers and dealers). When a broker or dealer receives an order from a bank's foreign exchange department, he will call the other banks in sequence until he finds one on the "other side of the market" and negotiates with it for the desired amount of foreign exchange. If the amount required is large, the order may be divided among several brokers and/or dealers and filled after negotiating with several banks. The banks which act as dealers have direct lines to their dealers and brokers and a small number of foreign corporations, and most of their foreign business is handled by teletype machines. Only about 15 New York banks are active in the foreign exchange business and these include the First National City Bank, Chase Manhattan, Morgan Guaranty, and Chemical Bank and Trust. In addition, there are banks in Boston, Chicago, Dallas, and San Francisco that trade in foreign exchange and also about 30 private banks and agencies of foreign banks, most of whom are located in New York.

Foreign-Exchange Department. The internal organization of a bank's foreign-exchange department will vary from bank to bank, but there will be sections or divisions to serve commercial customers, who finance with letters of credit; and foreign correspondents and other customers, who buy and sell securities for their own accounts. There will also be sections or staff personnel responsible for the bank's trading in exchange and making of futures contracts; collecting foreign credit instruments; paying when ordered by cable, mail, or over the counter (called "foreign tellers"); receiving and sending cables, telegrams, and radiograms; and keeping records of the balances of foreign correspondents and other customers, of the bank's deposits in foreign currencies abroad, and of the general assets and liabilities of the department. The commercial-bill brokers are the specialists who buy and sell bills of exchange that originate in exports of merchandise. They usually represent business firms that prefer to send their bills of exchange directly to New York instead of selling them to local banks. The commercial-bill brokers may also buy and sell foreign exchange, arrange for foreign-exchange contracts, and sometimes maintain foreign accounts. Most of their business is done with banks in New York and in foreign countries.

"FUTURES" OR "FORWARD" MARKET

In foreign trade, there are hazards other than those associated with the credit standing of the purchasers of goods—misunderstandings caused by differences in languages, units of weights and measures, laws and trade practices, and currencies. A major hazard, not present in domestic trade, is the "risk of exchange."

Risk of Exchange. If a cotton dealer in Houston sells cotton to an English manufacturer when the exchange rate is $2.40, he expects to receive $2,400,000 in return for a £1,000,000 sale if the exchange rate is the same when he is paid. But, if the exchange rate is $2.395, he will lose $5,000 on the transaction; if the exchange rate is $2.405, he will have a $5,000 profit on the transaction. Since he does not choose to speculate, he arranges with his bank to sell it a forward contract for £1,000,000 with the terms drawn so as to coincide with the due date for his spot draft for £1,000,000. Irrespective of the rate of exchange when the sale terminates and the cotton is paid for, the cotton broker knows how much he will receive (the amount in the forward or futures contract).

The advantage of forward-exchange transactions is that it enables merchants, banks, and traders—once they are committed to make or receive payments in foreign currency—to eliminate the risks arising from fluctuations in foreign-exchange rates. If an exporter of goods is selling abroad, he may want forward exchange as protection against loss if there is a decline in that rate of exchange. Then, despite a decline in the rate of exchange, the exporter has a contract that permits him to deliver that amount of domestic money to the seller of the futures contract. Since the rate of exchange may move up as well as down, a buyer of foreign goods may protect himself by a forward or futures contract, which calls for the future delivery of a cable or demand draft for a certain number of monetary units at the current exchange rate plus the premium being quoted on such futures contracts.

Commercial Banks. One method of hedging, as practiced by banks, consists of offsetting a sale or purchase at "spot" prices by a purchase or sale for future delivery, thus practically eliminating the loss or gain resulting from price fluctuations. As a matter of policy, commercial banks rarely speculate on the future of foreign-exchange rates. They prefer to forgo the potential profits in order to avoid potential losses on uncovered foreign-exchange transactions.

If one assumes an increase in a bank's spot obligations to its customers, the bank is normally protected by offsetting sales or purchases of spot exchange in the interbank market. This so-called "marrying-up" may not be complete. In case a bank has committed itself to sell more foreign exchange than it has arranged to buy, the bank may purchase or "swap" for more exchange in the interbank market in order to have each day's total purchases and total sales equal. Banks would make greater use of the forward market to adjust their positions if such a market existed in all currencies. However, even where there is a futures market in a currency, a bank may still prefer to use the spot market, because it may be easier and cheaper to match forward commitments in this market. Banks and dealers are reluctant about making forward commitments because any delay in their execution could be expensive.

Other Participants. Participants in the foreign-exchange market other than commercial banks may be willing to take a speculative position. When they expect a foreign currency to appreciate in value, they buy it in the spot market in the hope of selling it later at a profit. However, this transaction entails the use of cash, which can be avoided by using the futures market. (A certain thinness exists in all forward or futures markets except for the English pound sterling, the Canadian dollar, the German mark, and the Dutch guilder.)[3]

Interest-Rate Arbitrage. In order to protect themselves against the risk involved in international lending, commercial bankers, corpo-

[3] Allan R. Holmes and Francis H. Scott, *New York Foreign Exchange Market* (rev. ed.; New York; Federal Reserve Bank of New York, 1965), pp. 44-46.

rate treasurers, investment bankers, securities brokers, and individuals hedge in the forward market when they make short-term international loans. These hedge transactions pertain most frequently to government Treasury bills, but they also include investments in commercial paper notes and bills of exchange. When possible, lenders take advantage of any interest rate differential existing in the foreign-exchange market as compared to the domestic interest rate without assuming the risk due to changes in the foreign-exchange rate by hedging.

When the interest rate on Treasury bills is 6 percent in London and 4 percent in New York, a profit may be made by shifting funds to London if prices for exchange in the spot and forward markets permit. A bank in the United States may lend in the London market by purchasing a mail transfer and forwarding instructions that the funds are to be lent in London for 60 days (or a specified number of days) at the highest rate prevailing in that market. In order to bring home the funds in 60 days, the bank also arranges to sell the same amount of money plus the accrued interest in the forward-exchange market. To make the transaction profitable, the difference in interest rates in the two markets must be enough to offset the costs, including the discount on forward exchange (see Table 26–2). For illustration, it would not be profitable to invest in London when the interest rate is 2 percent higher than in New York if the rate for pound sterling cable or mail transfer is $2.41 and the 2-month forward exchange price is $2.39, because the discount in the futures market would more than offset any interest-rate differential.[4]

Arbitrage. Arbitrage in foreign exchange is the operation wherein foreign exchange is bought and sold in the same or different markets simultaneously in order to make a profit from discrepancies in prices. In order to operate successfully between two or more markets, an arbitrager must be well informed as to current prices in these markets and must be able to communicate orders to buy and sell for immediate execution. Arbitraging is usually done by large banks having foreign-exchange departments and by foreign-exchange dealers. Sometimes large investment houses and brokerage firms have divisions that arbitrage in foreign exchange and commodities as well as in securities.

[4] A $100,000 cable would cost $241,000 and the futures contract would provide $241,390 ($239,000 plus $2,390 interest), a net return of $390; but the same $241,000 invested at home would yield $1,606.67 for the same period.

Although the margin of profit in arbitraging is small, the amounts dealt in are large. The financial success of such operations depends upon the speed with which they are performed, because purchases and sales tend to eliminate maladjustments in prices. The economic effect of arbitrage is to keep the major foreign-exchange markets in alignment with each other.

In arbitraging in the exchange markets, there may be two, three, or more exchange markets involved. Assuming no restrictions exist, a hypothetical illustration of two-point arbitrage is as follows: At a

TABLE 26–2

ARBITRAGE ON TREASURY BILLS
(Percent per Annum)

	United States and United Kingdom				
	Treasury Bill Rates				
Date	United Kingdom (Adjusted to U.S. Quotation Basis)	United States	Spread (Favor of London)	Premium (+) or Discount (−) on Forward Pound	Net Incentive (Favor of London)
1968					
February 2....	7.38%	4.81%	2.57%	−2.59%	−.02%
9....	7.32	5.01	2.31	−2.60	−.29
16....	7.21	4.93	2.28	−2.68	−.40
23....	7.29	4.96	2.33	−2.86	−.53
March 1....	7.24	5.00	2.24	−3.09	−.85
8....	7.15	5.06	2.09	−7.01	−4.92
14....	7.15	5.33	1.82	−8.75	−6.93
22....	7.00	5.21	1.79	−4.78	−2.99
29....	6.95	5.14	1.81	−7.33	−5.52
April 5....	6.90	5.23	1.67	−4.83	−3.16
11....	6.97	5.37	1.60	−4.33	−2.73
19....	6.97	5.50	1.47	−3.83	−2.36
26....	6.90	5.49	1.41	−4.53	−3.12
May 3....	6.94	5.44	1.50	−4.06	−2.56
10....	6.92	5.52	1.40	−4.95	−3.55
17....	6.94	5.75	1.19	−5.28	−4.09
24....	7.03	5.70	1.33	−6.10	−4.77
31....	7.06	5.65	1.41	−6.79	−5.38
June 7....	7.03	5.62	1.41	−6.10	−4.69
14....	7.00	5.64	1.36	−4.45	−3.09
21....	7.03	5.32	1.71	−4.29	−2.58
28....	7.03	5.26	1.77	−5.23	−3.46
July 5....	7.03	5.35	1.68	−5.56	−3.88

Source: *Federal Reserve Bulletin*, July, 1968, p. A-89.

particular moment, if the sterling cable rate on New York is $2.40½, and the dollar rate in London is $2.40¼, there is a possibility of a one-fourth point arbitrage profit. The New York operator may sell a £100,000 cable for $240,500, and, to meet this obligation, he instructs his agent or partner in London to obtain £100,000 by selling a cable on him for $240,250. The arbitrager has a gross profit of $250. This process may be repeated as long as there is any discrepancy in rates in different markets, but the fact that sterling exchange is being sold in New York will tend to lower its price, and the fact that dollar exchange is being bought in London will tend to raise its price. So the difference of one-fourth point will be of short duration. Thus, it is obvious that the activities of arbitragers tend to have a stabilizing effect on the foreign-exchange market.

Arbitraging differs from speculation in that arbitraging involves the making of a profit from differences in prices at a particular time, while speculation involves the attempt to profit from changes in prices over a period of time. If the calculations of the arbitragers are correct and the orders to buy and sell go through as scheduled, no risks are involved, but in speculation risks are always assumed by the speculators.

Speculation.   Speculation in foreign exchange is the buying or selling of foreign exchange with the expectation or hope of making a profit from a change in the rate of exchange. Most speculation in foreign exchange is done by individuals and private bankers (brokerage houses and foreign-exchange dealers) rather than by commercial bankers. If speculators expect a rise in exchange rates, they may take a long position in the market, purchasing or agreeing to purchase sight or cable exchange in the present with the expectation of selling it in the future at a higher price. Most speculators prefer to operate in the forward or futures market because it is cheaper.

If speculators expect a decrease in the foreign-exchange value of a currency, they may contract to deliver the currency at a future date at a given price, expecting to cover in the spot market for demand or cable at a lower price. For illustration, a speculator may agree to deliver £100,000 in 30 days at the current cable rate of $2.40½, and, if the rate goes below $2.40½, he may make a speculator's profit. The bank will have covered its 30-day "forward" commitment by buying a 30-day time draft in the "spot" market. During periods of international disturbances, there are opportunities for tremendous profits; in fact, they were so great during the early 1930's that international speculators and bankers were charged with creating conditions that made it impossible for certain countries to remain on the gold standard. At present, the opportunities for making profits from speculation in foreign exchange are limited, and the risks are great because so much depends on what governments may or may not do. For the most part, speculation in exchange is done by the experts, and the amounts involved now are small compared with those involved prior to 1930.

FOREIGN FACILITIES

Prior to the enactment of the Federal Reserve Act, the foreign banking needs of businessmen and others in the United States were cared for mainly by English banks. The first major step taken by Congress to change this situation was that of authorizing national banks having paid-in capital and surplus of $1 million to establish and operate foreign branches under regulations of the Federal Reserve Board. At the same time, national banks were permitted to accept bills of exchange, the most widely used credit instruments in foreign-trade financing.

Currently, American banks may operate in foreign countries (including U.S. overseas areas and trust territories) under any or all of the following methods: (1) establishing and operating foreign branches, (2) creating subsidiary corporations under state or federal laws, (3) purchasing ownership interest in foreign banks, and (4) establishing correspondent relationships with foreign commercial banks. The procedure used in a particular case will depend on the size of the bank, the type of operation, and the laws and conditions in the country where business is to be conducted.

Branches. By the end of 1967, 15 member banks were operating 295 branches in 54 foreign countries and overseas areas of the United States (Puerto Rico, 16; Virgin Islands 10; Canal Zone, 2; Guam, 2; and Turk Islands, 1). Of the foreign branches, 280 are operated by eight national banks, with those of the First National City Bank of New York being the most numerous. There are 133 branches of American banks in Latin America and 63 in the Far East (12 in Japan and 10 in Hong Kong).[5]

Foreign branches of American banks are helpful to foreign branches and subsidiaries of American business corporations and to Americans traveling extensively abroad. The largest number of

[5] *Fifty-Fourth Annual Report of the Board of Governors of the Federal Reserve System Covering Operations for the Year 1967* ((Washington, D.C., 1968), pp. 323–24.

branches of American banks is in Argentina (25), where banking facilities are not as fully developed as in the United States. The second largest number is in England, where banking facilities per capita are more fully developed than in the United States.

The foreign branches of American banks are supervised and examined by the Board of Governors, which has the power to increase, decrease, or modify the number and operation of foreign branches. During 1967, the Board approved 62 applications for permission to open new foreign branches. The general policy is to permit a national bank to establish a new branch bank in any country where it already has a branch after giving 30 days' notice to the Board.

National banks' foreign branches have been permitted to engage in operations that the parent banks are prohibited from entering on the plea that they needed such authorizations in order to compete with indigenous banks and branches. These operations include: (1) underwriting and distributing obligations of the government of the country where the branch is located; (2) acquiring and holding securities of the central bank, clearing houses, development banks, and governmental entities of the foreign country; (3) guaranteeing customer loans; (4) making loans secured by second liens on unimproved real estate without regard to limitations as to amount or amortization requirements; (5) extending credit to banks' executive officers up to $50,000 for the purchase of foreign residences provided the transaction is reported promptly to the home office; and (6) paying higher interest rates on deposits of officers and employees of the banks than on other deposit accounts.[6]

The accounts of each foreign branch must be segregated from those of other branches and the home office; and, at the end of a bank's fiscal year, the profit or loss accrued at each branch must be transferred to the general ledger as a separate item. Although the Board of Governors is responsible for supervising and regulating foreign branches of American banks, the Comptroller of the Currency may demand that national banks operating foreign branches furnish his office information as to these branches. As stated above, a national bank which meets the necessary qualifications may invest directly or indirectly in foreign banks; however, the total amount invested in banks and their subsidiaries in order to finance international transactions may not exceed 25 percent of the bank's capital

---

[6] Board of Governors of the Federal Reserve System, *Foreign Activities of National Banks*, as revised effective March 15, 1967 (Washington, D.C., 1967), pp. 1–3.

and surplus.[7] In addition, the Board of Governors must be kept informed as to the status of the foreign banks in which national banks have investments.[8]

"Agreement Corporations." The requirement that a national bank must have $1 million in capital and surplus excluded small banks from participating in foreign branching. In 1916, Congress authorized national banks to buy stock and participate in corporations created to do a foreign branch-banking business. Two corporations of this type were already in operation under state laws; so Congress permitted national banks to participate in similar organizations if the latter "agreed" to submit to regulation by the Federal Reserve Board (hence the name "agreement corporation"). In 1919, Congress did what it had failed to do earlier, that is, made provisions for chartering foreign banking corporations under federal law. Bankers find federal chartering preferable to state chartering (it avoids double supervision and regulation); and at the end of 1967, there were five agreement corporations and 46 federal banking corporations.

"Edge Corporations." "Edge corporations," named for their sponsor Senator Edge of New Jersey, are federally incorporated subsidiaries of American banks that have been created to operate a "foreign banking and financing" business. An Edge corporation must have a minimum capital of $2 million, and a majority of the stock must be owned and held by American citizens or by corporations or firms which are controlled through ownership by citizens of the United States.

Under the law and Regulation K of the Board of Governors,[9] Edge corporations have the power to (1) receive deposits within and outside of the United States (except savings deposits) if they are related to transactions with foreign countries, (2) issue and accept bills of exchange drawn upon them, and (3) issue letters of credit and perform other functions related to foreign trade. The powers of these corporations are broader than those of the foreign-exchange depart-

[7] The 25 percent limitation does not include ownership of stock acquired to prevent a loss on loans, but such stock must be disposed of in 12 months. *Ibid.,* pp. 4–5.

[8] As long as the United States remains "Number 1" among the nations of the world, it should anticipate anti-American demonstrations. So, the Board of Governors permits foreign branches to suspend operations during "disturbed conditions." However, during such periods of suspension, the staff must strive to serve depositors and other customers. The manager must make a full report to the main office and to the Board of Governors through the bank's Federal Reserve bank.

[9] Board of Governors of the Federal Reserve System, *Corporations Doing Foreign Banking or Other Foreign Financing under the Federal Reserve Act,* amended March 15, 1967 (Washington, D.C., 1967), pp. 3–9.

ments of banks. For illustration, they are authorized to acquire and own shares of foreign corporations when the acquisition (1) is incidental to the extension of credit to a corporation, (2) consists of shares in a foreign bank, or (3) is otherwise likely to further the development of trade of the United States. Without the prior consent of the Board of Governors, the total investment in stock of a foreign corporation may not exceed $200,000 or 25 percent of the corporation's shares. Although Edge corporations' investments in foreign financial institutions have been their most publicized activities, their banking operations are more important.

Some Edge corporations carry on banking operations similar to those of foreign departments of large commercial banks. In fact, many interior banks that are prohibited from opening branches in seaboard cities organize and operate Edge corporations in New York City.[10] These subsidiaries make loans to finance foreign trade and foreign investment, enter into acceptance and letter-of-credit agreements with customers, and handle various transactions for both Americans and foreigners.

At one time, many inland banks found it difficult to offer their customers trade-related banking services such as handling documentary evidence; but now their subsidiaries are able to give the same services as New York banks. Inland banks prefer opening banking and subsidiary offices in New York over other cities because of the volume of trade that moves through that center. Furthermore, the New York office permits them to participate in the foreign-exchange, international lending, and other markets located in New York.

Some Edge corporations carry on foreign financing operations through ownership of foreign commercial banks (most of them do not limit their operations to short-term financing). They may, directly or through subsidiaries, act as holding companies, owning stock of foreign nonbank corporations.[11] Their ownership of stock includes issues of factors, brokerage and underwriting firms, development banks, trust affiliates, and commercial and industrial firms such as electrical appliance, public utility, transportation, shipbuilding, steel production, and other companies. Many of the undertakings of the Edge corporations are in cooperation with local interests (joint ventures) because the laws of many countries require that 50 percent or more of a firm's shares be owned by its own nationals.

[10] David L. Martin, "Edge Act Corporations Performing the Roles of Foreign Departments," *American Banker*, September 25, 1967, pp. 20 ff.

[11] Federal Reserve Bank of Richmond, "Edge Act Corporations and International Banking," *Monthly Review*, June, 1966, pp. 2–5.

Correspondents. Despite the increase in number of foreign branches and subsidiaries of American banks, the greater part of the foreign-exchange business of American banks is still conducted through correspondent banks. Like their domestic counterparts, foreign correspondent banks provide a wide variety of services for their customer banks who keep deposit with them. With the increase in the importance of the U.S. dollar, more American banks have acted as correspondents of foreign banks. The modern practice is for American banks to keep relatively small balances abroad and for foreign banks to keep relatively larger balances with American banks. Among the currencies commonly traded in the "free" world, the United States ranks either first or second, which reflects the wide use of the dollar in settling international debts. Many foreign banks keep most of their interbank balances in the United States, and the foreign-trade invoices of some countries are in American dollars rather than in their domestic currency units.[12]

FINANCING FOREIGN TRADE

When the terms of sale stipulate that financing is to be with a bill of exchange with a maturity of 30 days after being presented for payment, the documentary set (usually including the bill of lading, insurance policy, commercial invoice, and consular invoice) is retained by the exporter or his agent until the bill of exchange is accepted. This arrangement provides the seller with security until the bill is accepted, after which he must rely on the acceptor's credit standing. If the seller is uncertain as to the integrity of the buyer, he should insist on acceptance by an American or an indigenous bank. If the foreign buyer prefers to use the services of a local bank rather than an American bank, he will arrange for "acceptance credit" with the former in favor of the American seller. The document which contains the terms of the acceptance credit, known as a letter of credit, is used by the accepting bank to notify the seller of the arrangement.

After receipt of the letter of credit, the seller will meet the terms of sale and ship the goods as directed. Then, with the help of his local bank, he will draw a bill of exchange for the total cost of the goods being shipped and present it for acceptance through banking chan-

[12] Note: "Most of our external trade is invoiced in U.S. dollars or sterling and not in Canadian dollars, with the result that the exchange conversion problem is usually left to the Canadian firm rather than its foreign customer or supplier." *1964 Report of the Royal Commission on Banking and Finance* (Ottawa: Queen's Printer and Controller of Stationery, 1964), p. 295.

nels. After acceptance, he may keep the draft until maturity and then present it for payment, or he may obtain cash immediately by (1) selling the bill of exchange to his banker or in the acceptance market, (2) pledging the bill of exchange as security for a bank loan, (3) arranging for insurance of a second bill of exchange in the acceptance market. The third procedure is usually followed when the bill of exchange is drawn on a name other than a bank and takes months to collect (see Chart 26–1).

Before an accepted draft matures, the buyer will usually have sold the goods and will remit cash to the bank that issued the letter of credit so that it may pay the bill of exchange at maturity. The cost of financing will equal the discount on the bill when sold by the original owner, plus the accepting fee and any service charge made by the buyer's own bank (which may not be the same bank that accepted the draft). To further clarify the use of letters of credit and bankers' acceptances, let us assume that a store in New York is buying cloth from a manufacturer in London, England. The letter of credit is issued by a New York bank, and it contains the following terms: the time of the draft to be drawn is 30 days; the expiration date of the terms is June 10, 1968, the amount is to be approximately $10,000; and the documents to be provided by the seller of the goods must include a commercial invoice, an ocean bill of lading, an insurance certificate, and a consular invoice.

A copy of the letter of credit will be mailed to the seller in London; or, under certain circumstances, the terms may be cabled by the bank to its correspondent in London, and this correspondent will notify the seller in writing.[13] On receipt, the letter of credit is examined by the seller, and, if he finds the terms in agreement with the sales contract, he proceeds to prepare the goods for shipment. He makes out a commercial invoice, secures a consular invoice from the American consul in London, insures the shipment with a marine insurance company, and obtains a bill of lading from the steamship company when he delivers the merchandise.[14] These and any other minor documents that may be necessary are then taken to the seller's

---

[13] One copy of the letter of credit is retained in the files of the issuing bank, and a nonnegotiable copy is furnished the customer for his own record. In addition to the regular letter of credit, there is a revolving form—a circular letter of credit. For example, under a circular letter of credit, drafts may be drawn in amounts up to $x per month for a period of y months. It may be cumulative or noncumulative—that is, drafts not drawn for the full $x in one month; they may or may not be drawn in excess of the amount at a later period.

[14] Other documents that may be required are a certificate or statement of origin, a certificate of quality, and a weight certificate.

CHART 26–1

FINANCING AN EXPORT TRANSACTION BY BANKERS' ACCEPTANCES

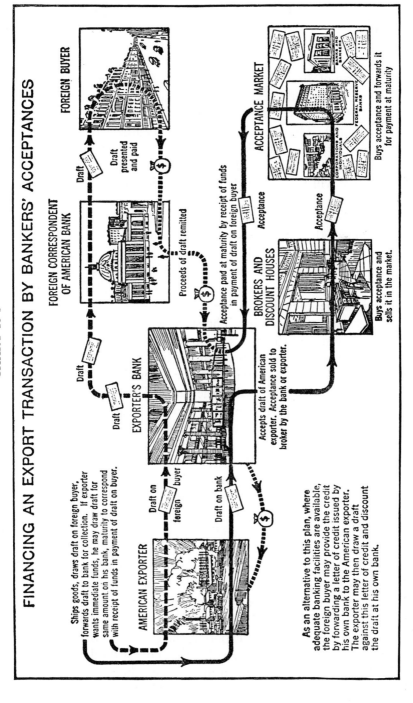

AMERICAN EXPORTER

Ships goods, draws draft on foreign buyer, forwards draft to bank for collection. If exporter wants immediate funds, he may draw draft for same amount on his bank, maturity to correspond with receipt of funds in payment of draft on buyer.

Draft on foreign buyer

Draft on bank

EXPORTER'S BANK

Accepts draft of American exporter. Acceptance sold to broker by the bank or exporter.

Draft

Draft

Proceeds of draft remitted

FOREIGN CORRESPONDENT OF AMERICAN BANK

Draft

Draft presented and paid

FOREIGN BUYER

Acceptance paid at maturity by receipt of funds in payment of draft on foreign buyer

Acceptance

Acceptance

BROKERS AND DISCOUNT HOUSES

Buys acceptance and sells it in the market.

ACCEPTANCE MARKET

Buys acceptance and forwards it for payment at maturity

As an alternative to this plan, where adequate banking facilities are available, the foreign buyer may provide the credit by forwarding a letter of credit issued by his own bank to the American exporter. The exporter may then draw a draft against this letter of credit and discount the draft at his own bank.

bank, where a draft equal to the selling price of the goods is drawn, say, $10,000.

The dollar credit is usually sold to the seller's bank, so the draft will be drawn in favor of the exporter's bank. Since the draft will have a term of 30 days after acceptance, and it may take the draft a week to be received in New York by mail, the amount paid the seller may be $9,975 (assuming a one fourth of 1 percent discount on the face amount). The draft, with documents attached, will be sent by mail to a New York bank acting as correspondent for the London bank. When the draft and accompanying documents reach New York, they will be sent to the bank that issued the original letter of credit.

The bank issuing the letter of credit will check the documents to ascertain whether the terms have been complied with. If the documents are correct, the bank will stamp the draft "accepted," and then date and sign it. (In case of a sight draft, the bank will pay it and immediately debit the account of the customer.) The accepting bank will retain the documentary set and then give it to the New York store against a trust receipt. The store will use the bill of lading to obtain possession of the goods as soon as they arrive.

On or before the maturity of the bankers' acceptance, the store will pay the bank, which will remit or otherwise settle for the bankers' acceptance. The disposal of the bankers' acceptance in the interim between acceptance and payment depends upon instructions. Thus, the use of a letter of credit not only involves the guaranty of the bank but also permits the creation of a credit instrument that can be sold at a small discount in the "bill" market.

In effect, a bankers' acceptance is a predated certified check that permits the exporter to receive payment without waiting weeks or months for the goods to reach the importer and for remittance by the latter by mail or cable (depending on the terms for payment). The checklike quality is given a bankers' acceptance when the accepting bank places its credit behind this credit instrument by endorsing it on its face (acceptance), which makes the bank primarily responsible for it. The accepting bank charges the importer for this service at a rate that is most commonly 1.5 percent on an annual basis.

After acceptance, the exporter, the exporter's bank, or whoever has purchased the acceptance will either hold it until maturity or sell it in the acceptance market. In many cases, the accepting bank may act as the selling agent, selling the bankers' acceptance either directly to another bank or through an acceptance broker or dealer. The proceeds from the sale of the acceptance will be paid to the exporter or to the one who has acquired the time draft from him. When the acceptance comes due, the holder turns it over to the accepting bank for payment. As previously noted, by this time the importer will have received the goods and presumably sold them and will have funds with the accepting bank to meet payment of the obligation.

OTHER USES OF ACCEPTANCE CREDIT

Domestic Trade.　American banks may be requested to finance domestic shipments of goods with the use of acceptance credit. Financing procedure involves the same general steps already noted. The bill of exchange is drawn by the seller under terms started in the letter of credit, is secured by shipping and other documents, and then is sent to the accepting bank for its acceptance. The drawer of the accepted draft obtains funds immediately and economically by selling the accepted draft through a broker, or a bank, in the acceptance market. When the draft matures, the accepting bank pays the draft with funds provided by the purchaser of the goods.

Shipments between Foreign Countries.　An American accepting bank may receive a request to finance a shipment of goods between a European seller and a South American buyer. The former is willing to sell goods to the latter, provided that he arranges through his bank for the issuance of a letter of credit by a New York bank. If this is done, the financing proceeds as follows: The European exporter ships the goods to the buyer, draws a draft on the New York bank, and discounts it with his bank. The European bank forwards the draft to its New York correspondent bank to be presented to the American bank for acceptance. At maturity the American bank meets the draft with funds provided, through banking channels, by the importer located in South America.

Storage of Goods.　In order to promote orderly marketing of goods, particularly agricultural staples, it is necessary to hold them from season to season. Owners may secure financial help from local banks under ordinary lines of credit or from the Commodity Credit Corporation, but it may be preferable to borrow in the acceptance market. The owners may arrange for a line of acceptance credit, permitting them to draw drafts on the accepting banks. After acceptance, the drafts are sold in the bill market, and the beneficiaries will have funds with which to purchase more staples or to finance other needs. The acceptance credit is secured by warehouse receipts, and these receipts are exchanged for trust receipts when the goods are removed from the warehouse. The bills of exchange are liquidated with funds received when the goods are sold.

Risks caused by market fluctuations may be removed by requiring owners of the staples to sell futures contracts in the commodity market when the acceptance credit is given. If the price of the commodity falls, the loss is offset by the profit on the futures contract. When transactions are protected by this commodity-hedging operation, many banks will give acceptance credit to finance storage of staples for as much as 90 percent of their market value. Similar problems arise in financing the storage of goods that may not be of American origin and that may be stored in a foreign country. Accepting banks usually ask for satisfactory evidence of storage (warehouse receipts) and for letters of guarantee from actual takers of the credit.

Creating "Dollar Exchange."   One important special use of acceptance credit is to make dollar exchange available to those buyers of American goods who are in poorly developed financial centers. By "dollar exchange" is meant New York drafts or other drafts drawn on banks in the United States. This type of financing gives rise to finance bills, a device for borrowing among banks that has been used widely abroad. Conditions under which member banks may finance with finance bills are limited by law and regulations of the Board of Governors of the Federal Reserve System. The purpose of using finance bills is to make credit of American banks available to banks in underdeveloped areas so that they may finance the purchase of American goods.

Normally, buyers of goods in most foreign financial centers are able to secure adequate dollar exchange from their local banks. But assume that steamships stop but once a month at some Central American port, that the one bank in the community keeps a balance of only $25,000 with its New York correspondent bank, and that there are no exchange dealers in the community. During the seasonal buying period, the steamship unloads $100,000 worth of goods sold by exporters in New York to the local merchants. There is an immediate need for $100,000 in New York drafts, which the local banker is unable to provide with his $25,000 balance in New York.

Assume that the Central American banker had previously opened a line of dollar-acceptance credit with a New York bank. Under this credit agreement, he draws a 30-day time draft for $80,000, which he sends to New York to be accepted and then sold in the acceptance market. The proceeds from the sale will be credited to his deposit account in New York. In the meantime, the Central

American banker will have sold New York drafts to his customers for $100,000. He knows that the time draft will have been sold and that funds are available in New York to take up his sight drafts when presented. During the next 30 days he can build up his deposit in New York so as to take up the time bill at maturity.

Financing Foreign Travel. One function of banks and exchange dealers is to provide travelers abroad with acceptable means of payment for services, hotel accommodations, and goods. Three credit instruments have been created to finance travelers: traveler's checks, traveler's letters of credit, and internationally recognized credit cards. Traveler's checks are printed blanks that may be purchased from banks, express companies, leading hotels, and other agencies, both here and abroad. The purchaser signs his name in the upper left-hand corner of each blank. The checks may be in denominations varying from $10 to $1,000. When issued, the agent collects the full value of the checks and usually a commission of 1 percent (during periods of high interest rates the commission may be waived).

When a traveler's check is cashed at a bank, hotel, store, or some other place, the traveler signs his name in the lower left-hand corner in order to make it negotiable. (In some foreign places, merchants give discounts of up to 25 percent on goods paid for with American traveler's checks.) The checks may be secured in terms of dollars, sterling, francs, or other currencies. If they are in terms of dollars, they will be paid in foreign countries at the prevailing rate of exchange for sight drafts on New York. To avoid this risk of exchange, traveler's checks may be made up in terms of the currencies of the countries in which traveling is planned.

Three out of every four American travelers use traveler's checks amounting to more than $3 billion per year; but, when staying abroad for a long period of time or planning expensive purchases, traveler's checks may be inconvenient to carry in bulk (checks for more than $50 are less acceptable than smaller denomination checks). To overcome this difficulty, travelers may arrange with their banks either to forward additional funds when requested or to issue them traveler's letters of credit. The latter are issued in two parts: the introduction or instruction part and the identification part, which contains the owner's signature. (To prevent misuse in case of loss or theft, the two documents should be carried separately.)

The principles involved in the use of traveler's letters of credit are the same as in the use of commercial letters of credit. The issuer (bank) makes it possible for the beneficiary (traveler) to purchase goods and services in foreign countries. The letter of credit is a printed form of letter addressed by a bank to its correspondents in foreign countries. It authorizes the beneficiary named in the letter to draw drafts on the issuer, which the correspondent banks are requested to honor. Since this letter of credit establishes the credit of the holder, it is similar to a commercial letter of credit. Because it is addressed to more than one bank, it is sometimes called a "circular letter of credit." The charge for issuing a letter of credit is usually one half of 1 percent of the face amount. After proper identification, a draft is drawn in the presence of the foreign correspondent who is to cash it (the correspondent bank's name is selected from the list in the letter of credit). The draft is sent for payment through banking channels to the bank on which it is drawn. The drafts are unsecured (clean bills), and extra care is taken to see that fraud is not committed.

In order to clarify the use of the traveler's letter of credit, let us assume that Mr. White is planning to travel throughout western Europe, and, in addition to a small quantity of cash and traveler's checks, he wants to use a traveler's letter of credit. He goes to his local bank and arranges for one for $2,000 by depositing and/or assigning his account for $2,000, or depositing and assigning $2,000 worth of marketable securities, or simply signing a paper guaranteeing to pay the drafts as presented. In addition to the letter of credit, the bank gives him a special form of letter of introduction on which he writes his signature. This is known as a "letter of identification" and is used in connection with the letter of credit. This, as well as the letter of credit, will be officially signed by his bank. Since all correspondents have received copies of the official signature, they will be able to determine whether or not the documents are authentic.

On arriving in London and desiring pounds sterling for shopping and other needs, Mr. White checks the list of correspondents and notes the name of the Chase-Manhattan Bank. He checks the address and then goes to the West End Branch of the bank, which is located at 51 Berkeley Square. In order to obtain a draft for £100, he presents his letter of identification and letter of credit. On a blank provided by the bank, he draws a dollar draft for the equivalent of £100 ($240). The bank checks the documents to make certain that the time has not expired, that the letter has not been exhausted by previous withdrawals, and that the signatures are correct. If no further identification is necessary, the bank cashes the draft, provided that it shows the number given in the letter of credit and that the signature of Mr. White is authentic. Before returning the letter of credit to Mr. White, the London bank indicates in the space provided on the reverse side the amount of the draft, date of negotiation, and its own name. The bank charges a small fee for its services. The amount of each withdrawal is listed by the banks providing the cash and when the amount is exhausted, the letter of credit is returned to the issuing bank (any unused portion may be presented to the issuing bank for redemption).

Credit cards are being used to an increasing extent to meet travel needs. Extra care must be taken to see that foreign currency charges are correctly stated and that the amount of credit card bills is accurately converted into dollars before payment (all receipts for purchases should be kept until final settlement). The use of credit cards reduces the risk of being short of cash and permits traveling on credit ("see the world and pay later"). Usually there is no difficulty in exchanging paper money when traveling from country to country, but coins may not be exchangeable; however, conversion of surplus currency is expensive and should be avoided if possible. For those planning to remain in a foreign country for a considerable length of time, it may be advantageous to open a checking account with a local bank or a branch of an American bank.

SUMMARY

Foreign exchange consists primarily of balances on deposit in foreign banks which are used to meet foreign obligations of American businessmen, travelers, investors, and others. Title to these balances is transferred with the use of foreign-exchange instruments, which are classified as cable and mail transfers, and sight and time drafts.

The foreign-exchange rate is the price of a unit of foreign money in terms of the dollar. Since there are many different rates, the rate of exchange for accounting purposes is usually the cable rate (but sometimes economists think of the *rate* as the price of sight bills of exchange). The prices paid for foreign money vary, with "cable" being the most expensive, and the longest time drafts being the cheapest. The prices of a foreign currency will rise or fall together, but the spread among the different time drafts will depend upon maturity and the discount rate prevailing in the market where they are paid.

Bankers extend acceptance credit to their customers by permitting them to draw drafts on their banks, which they accept. This makes the drafts a primary obligation of the accepting banks and readily negotiable in the bill or acceptance market. Member banks may accept drafts to finance exports, imports, domestic shipment of goods, storage of goods, and the creation of dollar exchange. Banks also sell traveler's checks and traveler's letters of credit. But much of the foreign export trade of the United States is financed with the use of trade drafts, which are orders (time or demand) that are drawn on buyers by the sellers of goods.

Foreign-exchange markets have transfer, credit, and hedging functions. How well the foreign-exchange markets perform their functions depends, in part, on the activities of speculators and arbitragers in the market. Speculators buy and/or sell foreign exchange with the expectation of making a profit out of changes in prices over a period of time, while arbitragers buy and sell foreign exchange in order to make a profit from price discrepancies in the same or different markets at the same time. Most of the foreign-exchange business is in the hands of large commercial banks and certain specialists in New York, although foreign exchange is bought and sold in every community in the United States. In recent years, subsidiaries and branches of American banks have increased in importance, doing business not only with branches and subsidiaries of American corporations but also with native businessmen and governments.

QUESTIONS AND PROBLEMS

1. What is meant by (*a*) foreign exchange, (*b*) cable transfers, (*c*) mail transfers, (*d*) foreign bank drafts, and (*e*) time drafts?

2. Distinguish between (*a*) the "spot" and "forward" exchange markets, (*b*) "sight" and "time" exchange, (*c*) speculation and arbitrage in foreign exchange, and (*d*) a bank loan and a grant of acceptance credit.

3. Describe the foreign facilities that American banks may use to finance foreign exchange and other needs of their customers.

4. What provisions has Congress made for the supervision and regulation of American banks' activities in foreign countries?

5. "Many Inland Banks are considering the establishment of Edge corporations in New York City and other ports." (*American Banker*, September 9, 1967, p. 22.) Why?

6. Outline the steps involved in financing an import of goods with the use of acceptance credit granted by an American bank.

7. How may acceptance credit be used other than for financing foreign trade and foreign travel? Explain.

8. Discuss: "Exchange rates are prices for currencies expressed in terms of other currencies. It is a basic fact . . . . that exchange rate fluctuations for most currencies in trading for immediate delivery . . . are

limited to narrow margins around a single fixed price. . . ." (Alan R. Holmes and Francis H. Scott, *New York Foreign Exchange Market*, [rev. ed.; New York, Federal Reserve Bank of New York, 1965], p. 27.)

9. Explain: A "bank operating in North Carolina would not be able to establish a branch in New York City for the purpose of conducting foreign operations, but it could acquire such an office through the formation of an Edge Act subsidiary. Many banks have used this device for precisely this purpose." (Federal Reserve Bank of Richmond, *Monthly Review*, June, 1967, p. 5.)

10. Analyze: "Whether or not it is profitable to move short-term funds from one center to another depends, not only on the additional interest that might be gained by so doing, but also on the relation of the two currencies in the spot and forward exchange markets." (Alan R. Holmes and Francis H. Scott, *op. cit.*, p. 52.)

CHAPTER 27

International Transactions
৯৯৯৯৯৯৯৯৯৯৯৯৯৯৯৯৯৯৯৯৯৯৯৯৯৯৯৯৯৯

IN THE United States domestic factors have greater influence on monetary policies than in most other countries. This is due to this country's productive capacity, large international reserves, and output which is chiefly for the domestic market. More attention is currently being given to international problems because of the balance-of-payments deficits, the loss of gold reserves, and the shift from an international gold standard to an international exchange standard. A number of domestic programs have been created and others have been proposed to improve the U.S. balance-of-payments position. In order to reduce dependence on gold as international money, new sources of reserves have been created and old ones have been strengthened.

NATURE OF THE BALANCE OF PAYMENTS
Credits and Debits. The balance-of-international-payments or international-transactions statement of the United States is a record, presented in balance sheet form, of the money value of economic transactions between residents, business firms, governments, and other institutions in the United States and the rest of the world for a period of time (see Table 27–1). Within the balance-of-payments statement, there are two broad classes of items; credits, those giving rise to immediate claims by the United States on the rest of the world; and debits, those giving rise to immediate claims on the United States by the rest of the world. The debit items for the United States are its expenditures abroad, including those for goods and services imported, remittances and pensions sent abroad, United States economic and military aid, grants, and government and private investments. The credit items for the United States are the foreign expenditures in the United States, including those for goods and services exported, remittances, pensions, and investments in the United States.
Double-Entry Payment Ledger. The transactions that include transfers of financial assets and resources between residents of the

TABLE 27–1

U.S. INTERNATIONAL TRANSACTIONS, 1967
(In Millions of Dollars)

Item	Credit	Debit	Net Credit	Net Debit
Goods and services:				
Merchandise adjusted, excluding military...	$30,463	$26,980	($ 3,483)	
Military transfers and expenditures........	2,174	4,319		($ 2,145)
Transportation..	2,701	2,965		(254)
Travel.............................	1,641	3,170		(1,429)
Other services (fees, royalties, U.S. government and others)...............	3,831	1,183	(2,648)	
Income on foreign investments...........	6,783	2,277	(4,506)	
Total........................	$46,593	$40,894	$ 5,699	
Unilateral transfers to foreigners:				
Private remittances (net)...............				(835)
Military grants of goods and services......				(90)
Other U.S. grants.....................				(1,765)
U.S. pensions and other transfers........				(448)
Total (net).....................				$ 3,949
Transactions in U.S. private assets:				
Direct investments...................		$ 3,026		
Foreign securities newly issued in U.S.....		1,597		
Redemption........................	$ 469			
Other transactions in foreign securities.....		123		
Claims reported by U.S. banks...........		455		
Claims reported by U.S. residents, other than banks........................		712		
Total (net).....................				$ 5,445
Transactions in U.S. government assets, except reserves:				
Loans and other long-term assets.........		3,583		
Foreign currencies and other short-term assets..............................	219			
Repayment on credit...................	1,003			
Total..........................				$ 2,362
Transactions in U.S. official reserves:				
Gold..............................	1,170			
Convertible currencies.................		1,024		
Gold tranche position in IMF............		94		
Total..........................			$ 52	
Transactions in foreign assets in the U.S.:				
Direct investments.....................	153			
U.S. securities other than Treasury issues..	994			
Long-term liabilities reported by U.S. banks.............................	965			
Other liabilities reported by nonbank residents...........................	513			
Liabilities of U.S. government except marketable or convertibles.............	451			
U.S. government marketable or convertible bonds and notes.....................	411			
Deposits and money-market paper held in U.S.............................	3,111			
Total..........................			$ 6,599	
Errors and omissions (net)..................				$ 595
Total..........................			$12,351	$12,351

Note: Totals may not equal because of rounding.
Source of statistics: *Survey of Current Business*, March, 1968, p. 23.

United States and foreign countries are based on the double-entry bookkeeping principle kept by the Department of Commerce. If "goods are exported and payment received in the form of a check drawn against an account of a foreign resident in a U.S. bank, the credit entry would be a merchandise export, and the debit entry the corresponding decline in U.S. liabilities to foreigners . . ." (a foreign resident's checking account in a United States bank is a liability). While the system used by the International Monetary Fund is different, in both cases the principle is that each item that crosses international boundaries has some item offsetting it on the other side of the balance-of-payments statement. The total of all credits or receipts is

CHART 27-1
U.S. BALANCE OF PAYMENTS, 1967
(In Millions of Dollars)

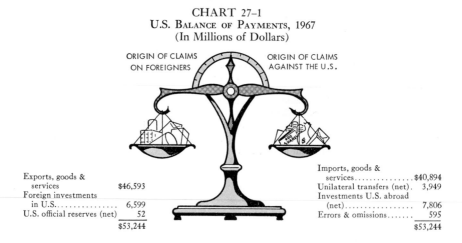

ORIGIN OF CLAIMS
ON FOREIGNERS

ORIGIN OF CLAIMS
AGAINST THE U.S.

Exports, goods & services	$46,593	Imports, goods & services	$40,894
Foreign investments in U.S.	6,599	Unilateral transfers (net)	3,949
U.S. official reserves (net)	52	Investments U.S. abroad (net)	7,806
		Errors & omissions	595
	$53,244		$53,244

supposed to equal all debits or expenditures; but, since they never do, it is necessary to include the item "errors and omissions" in the balance-of-international-payments statement or balance sheet.

Similarity to Balance Scale. The balance-of-payments statement may be thought of as a balance scale (see Chart 27–1) on which "credits" or claims on foreigners are placed on one side and "debits" or claims against the United States are placed on the other, with gold and short-term credits added to the "light" side to bring about equilibrium. Over a period of time, the scale could be brought into balance by adding to the light side or subtracting from the heavy side as needed.

As Checking-Account Accounting. Another way of regarding the international balance-of-payments accounting system is to compare it to the procedure followed in keeping a personal checking account. One has a surplus when the amount in one's checking account shows an increase over the last accounting period and a deficit if the amount has decreased. However, some asset may have been acquired on credit; hence, to complete the analysis, one would have to add these liquid obligations to the net change in the checking account to arrive at a true picture of the deficit or surplus for the accounting period. If there are too many outstanding obligations to be met, one's checking account may be replenished by selling long-term securities or borrowing long term. While this procedure would provide immediate cash, it would not be a long-run solution.

The international balance of payments is in equilibrium when, at the existing exchange rate, there is no continued flow of monetary gold and/or short-term capital in one direction. A deficit exists when there is a continued outflow of monetary gold and short-term capital; a surplus exists when there is a continued inflow of these items. (However, one qualification is necessary: for a gold-producing country an outflow of gold must be treated, in whole or part, as a merchandise export rather than as an indication of a deficit.)

The existence of a balance-of-payments deficit or surplus is considered to be an indicator of a country's international well-being and its ability to retain international reserves in amounts sufficient to support the standard monetary unit. A temporary deficit or surplus is normal, but a chronic one indicates that a country may be in serious disequilibrium with other countries with whom it trades. The ideal situation would be one wherein there would be no deficit or surplus but this could only be achieved when all countries operated on exchange control systems or on a system of flexible exchange rates.

COMPONENTS OF THE BALANCE OF PAYMENTS

The balance-of-payments items may be classified in many ways, but the one used here is to divide the items as credits and debits with each divided into (1) goods and services, (2) unilateral transactions, (3) capital transfers, (4) errors and omissions (a residual item), and (5) changes in reserves and liquid asset holdings of the United States.

Goods and Services. The first item in the balance-of-payments statement, "goods and services," is an estimate of the dollar value of goods and services exported from and imported into the United States. In 1967 exports of goods and services, excluding military, amounted to $46.6 billion, or $5.7 billion more than imports of these items (see Table 27–1). The most important item among the goods and services account is merchandise, which is sometimes referred to as the "visible" items of international trade. When a country has an excess of exports over imports, it is said to have a "favorable balance of trade" (which has characterized the position of the United States during the past 100 years).

In recognition of the effect of the large amount of merchandise financed by American grants and loans on our balance of payments, Congress now requires that "aid" grants and loans be spent in the United States rather than in foreign countries so as to ease the burden of maintaining a balance between credits and debits. Tying aid to domestic payments permits export trade to expand without calling upon the foreign-exchange market to finance them (the American taxpayer will pay the bill). Other steps taken to increase exports of the United States include: keeping American goods competitive by resisting proposed increases in prices, labor and other costs, modernizing plants, lowering taxes, encouraging new product design, entering into trade agreements with foreign countries, and lowering tariffs.

Other important items in the current-account section of the balance-of-payments statement include service items (payments for travel, transportation, and miscellaneous services) and income from investments. These are often referred to as "invisible" items of foreign trade to distinguish them from movements of goods and specie or the "visible" items of foreign trade. American tourists spent $3.2 billion abroad, but about one half of this unfavorable balance-of-trade item was offset by expenditures of foreigners ($1.6 billion) in the United States. The administration discouraged Americans from traveling abroad and foreign spending by reducing the duty-free limit on goods brought home from $500 to $100. Furthermore, consideration is being given to levying a tax on Americans traveling in foreign countries that will vary with per-day expenditures above a certain amount.

On the other hand, the Department of Commerce has established the United States Travel Service (most countries have had such services for many years) to attract and help travelers from abroad. About one half of the foreign tourists in the United States are from Canada and Mexico. When Americans and tourists from foreign countries travel on American-owned planes and ships, they prevent a further increase in the overall balance-of-payments deficit.

Currently, Americans are receiving interest, dividends, royalties, and other payments on their investments abroad which amount to $6.7 billion, as compared with similar payments to foreigners of $2.3 billion. In addition, the United States is receiving $2.8 billion for other services, such as insurance fees and royalties on motion pictures and television shows, and is making similar payments to foreigners of $1.3 billion (see Table 27–1). However, the surplus on "goods and services" items has been declining and it is one of the most discouraging aspects of the attempts to reduce the U.S. balance-of-payments deficit.

Unilateral Transfers. The term "unilateral transfers" refers to movements of goods, services, money, and capital items from one country to another without payment in any form. They include gifts in kind (goods and services) and gifts or grants of money and other capital items. At one time, they consisted chiefly of personal remittances by immigrants to relatives in foreign countries, pension checks sent abroad, and gifts to churches, educational institutions, and charitable and other organizations. Today, unilateral transfers consist of private remittances, military grants of goods and services, other U.S. grants, U.S. pensions and other transfers (see Table 27–1). Gifts and grants received from foreign countries are credit entries, but, for convenience in presentation, only the difference between the two appears on the balance-of-payments statement.

The basic purpose of U.S. foreign aid, now less than $3 billion annually, is to aid developing and newly emerged nations and others in creating their own defense programs. The critics of U.S. policy claim that the United States could overcome its balance-of-payments deficit by eliminating foreign-aid programs. This would be true if other things remained the same. However, most foreign-aid dollars are spent in the United States, and the elimination of foreign aid would be reflected in statistics showing exports of goods and services.

Investments. The capital-account sector of the balance-of-payments statement records the estimates of changes in capital movements between the United States and the rest of the world. A U.S. purchase of a foreign financial asset is a debit item because such a transaction causes immediate foreign claims against the United States to increase; conversely, the sale of U.S. securities to foreigners is a credit item because it increases the immediate claims of the United States against the rest of the world. (It may be helpful to identify American foreign investments as *debit* items by thinking in terms of imports of stock certificates, bonds, and other credit instruments; conversely, to identify foreign investments in the United States as *credit* items in terms of exports of stock certificates, bonds, and other credit instruments.) American investments abroad are sometimes institutional in nature, such as the direct investment of an American corporation in one of its subsidiaries abroad. Included among the foreign investments are capital contributions to international organizations (see Chapters 28 and 29).

Although the private flow of U.S. capital to foreign countries is currently far in excess of the offsetting flow of foreign capital to the United States, the largest part of U.S. foreign investments is direct, being made by American corporations in their own subsidiaries and branch organizations in foreign countries.

Interest rates are usually lower in the United States than in foreign countries, so foreign governments and business corporations prefer to borrow in the U.S. capital markets. Each issue of foreign securities sold in the United States adds to the balance-of-payments deficit; and so the U.S. government is applying a so-called "interest-e-qualization" tax to foreign loans made and securities sold in the United States. This tax does not cover direct investments and loans made through foreign branches and subsidiaries of banks, so a second part of the program was to appeal to businessmen, bankers, and others to cooperate in voluntarily limiting their foreign investments. Under this Voluntary Cooperation Program, the Federal Reserve System established guidelines for banks and other financial institutions[1] and the Department of Commerce formulated guidelines for American corporations to limit their foreign investment with American funds. (The interest equalization tax and voluntary restrictions do not apply to Canada and developing countries.)

Restrictions on capital movements offer only temporary relief because the long-run effects are undesirable. Trade follows dollar investments, hence restrictions lower the foreign demand for American goods; reduce the future flow-back of dividends, interest, royalty, fees, and other payments; and diminish the growth and efficiency of the economies of foreign countries. Fortunately, the U.S. government's purpose is to moderate rather than stop the outflow of capital. Currently, American corporations are financing more of the capital needs of their foreign branches and subsidiaries by using foreign earnings or borrowing in foreign capital markets.

Errors and Omissions.   Although "errors and omissions" is not always an important item in the balance-of-payments statement, it is included to cover errors due to difficulties in pricing and because of legal and illegal shifts of assets which have not been recorded (omissions). The latter is usually largest during periods of international financial disturbances when funds are moved in a search for safety

[1] See *Federal Reserve Bulletin*, November, 1967, pp. 1869–76.

(due to fears of devaluation and other factors). In recent years, this item has been unfavorable to the United States which may indicate a movement of funds from this country because of lack of confidence in the dollar.

Gold and Liquid Assets.   Currently, gold is sharing more fully its traditional role as an international means of payment and as reserve money along with the American dollar, the English pound sterling, and other "key currencies." Reserves are kept to insure the debtor's ability to meet current or near-future claims against him. The extent to which reserves are adequate to meet liquidity or reserve needs depends on the amount of short-term claims. As long as reserve assets grow faster than claims, their adequacy increases; when claims grow faster than reserve assets, their adequacy decreases. So, a particular volume of reserves has little significance because the concept of adequacy is a relative one. Furthermore, the liquidity of assets and the nature of liabilities may be affected by any number of changes that may take place. Gold is still the most attractive form of international reserves because its value is not subject to change; however, gold is noninterest bearing and its handling and storage presents minor problems.

Among the new sources of international reserves are "credits" with the International Monetary Fund in the form of "ordinary" or "special" drawing rights (see Chapter 28). The change in the U.S. "tranche" position noted in the balance-of-payments statement refers to the United States "quota" minus the Fund's holdings of the dollar. Other measures taken to strengthen the liquidity position of the United States are currency agreements that entail "swaps" of currency, enlargement of IFM quotas, and establishment of borrowing facilities by so-called Group-of-Ten countries (see Chapter 28).

MEASURING THE DEFICIT OR SURPLUS

The purpose for which the international transactions statement is to be used will affect the manner in which it is presented in summarized form. A common use of the statement is to measure the amount of a country's deficit or surplus in its balance of payments for a period of time. In the United States, interest in the deficit (or surplus) is due to the fact that it is considered to be an important indicator of the economic strength of the dollar in international markets. Due to the continuing balance-of-payments deficits of the United States over the past 10 years, there has been a loss of confidence in some centers in the ability of the government to maintain the current value of the dollar in terms of gold. Despite the fact that all the Presidents of the United States during this period have assured the world that the dollar would not be devalued, many expect the official price of gold to be increased, eventually.

The balance-of-payments statement does not show a deficit or surplus (see Table 27–1) but one does exist which appears in accounts that make up the totals. Therefore, the problem is to separate the transaction items into two groups: one showing transactions that cause the deficit or surplus and a second showing transactions used to finance the deficit or surplus. The accounts in the first group are called "above the line" items and the others are called "below the line" items. The latter measure the balance-of-payments deficit (see Table 27–2).

Official Reserves.   At the present time, the free countries of the world are operating on an international foreign-exchange standard, and gold is only one of the official reserve items. In 1967, U.S. gold stock declined by $1,170 million, but there was an increase of $1,024 million in the holdings of foreign currencies plus an increase of $94 million in the gold tranche position of the United States (see Chapter 28). Although there was a relatively small increase in total reserves, the decline in gold stock meant a decline in the quality of reserves.

The U.S. dollar is now being used by foreign governments, foreign central banks, and international financial organizations as part of their official reserves. Hence, the net change in the reserve position of the United States is found by adding to the change in its official reserve position any decrease in the liquid and certain nonliquid liabilities of the United States to foreign agencies. Normally, one does not include nonliquid assets among reserves, but most of those used in this case are nonmarketable medium-term convertible government bonds that may be exchanged for cash at any time (see Table 27–3).

Balance-of-Payments Deficit.   In 1967, while the "official reserves" of the United States were decreasing, its liquid liabilities to foreign official agencies were increasing by $3,353 million ($2,062 million plus $1,291 million). Finally, one adds the net change in the "official reserves" of the United States ($52 million) to the increase in liabilities that count as foreign official reserves in order to obtain the deficit of the United States, $3,405 million (see Table 27–3).

The emphasis on changes in official reserves as an indicator of the deficit or surplus in the international balance of payments is due to the monetary authorities' responsibility for maintaining stable ex-

TABLE 27-2

U.S. BALANCE OF PAYMENTS, 1965–67 *
(In Millions of Dollars)

Item	1965	1966	1967
Exports of goods and services—Total*	$39,147	$43,039	$45,693
Merchandise	26,244	29,168	30,463
Military sales	844	847	1,272
Transportation	2,390	2,589	2,701
Travel	1,380	1,573	1,641
Investment income receipts, private	5,376	5,650	6,163
Investment income receipts, government	512	595	622
Other services	2,401	2,617	2,831
Imports of goods and services—Total	−32,203	−37,937	−40,893
Merchandise	−21,472	−25,510	−26,980
Military expenditures	−2,921	−3,694	−4,319
Transportation	−2,674	−2,914	−2,965
Travel	−2,438	−2,657	−3,170
Investment income payments	−1,729	−2,074	−2,277
Other services	−969	−1,088	−1,182
Balance on goods and services*	6,944	5,102	4,800
Remittances and pensions	−1,024	−1,010	−1,284
1. Balance on goods, services, remittances and pensions	5,920	4,092	3,516
2. U.S. government grants and capital flow, net	−3,375	−3,446	−4,127
Grants,† loans, and net change in foreign currency holdings, and short-term claims	−4,277	−4,680	−5,128
Scheduled repayments on U.S. government loans	681	806	996
Nonscheduled repayments and selloffs	221	428	5
3. U.S. private capital flow, net	−3,743	−4,213	−5,446
Direct investments	−3,418	−3,543	−3,027
Foreign securities	−758	−482	−1,252
Other long-term claims:			
Reported by banks	−232	337	284
Reported by others	−88	−112	−301
Short-term claims:			
Reported by banks	325	−84	−739
Reported by others	428	−329	−411
4. Foreign capital flow, net, excluding change in liquid assets in U.S.	278	2,512	3,077
Long-term investments	−68	2,176	2,235
Short-term claims	149	269	390
Nonliquid claims on U.S. government associated with—			
Military contracts	314	341	68
U.S. government grants and capital	−85	−213	−85
Other specific transactions	−25	−12	−1
Other nonconvertible, nonmarketable, medium-term U.S. government securities	−7	−49	470
5. Errors and unrecorded transactions	−415	−302	−595
A. Balance on liquidity basis: BALANCES			
Seasonally adjusted (=1 + 2 + 3 + 4 + 5)	−1,335	−1,357	−3,575
B. Balance on basis of official reserve transactions:			
Balance A, seasonally adjusted	−1,335	−1,357	−3,575
Plus: Seasonally adjusted change in liquid assets in the U.S. of:			
Commercial banks abroad	116	2,697	1,265
Other private residents of foreign countries	306	212	394
International and regional organizations other than IMF	−291	−525	−208
Less: Change in certain nonliquid liabilities to foreign central banks and govts.	100	802	1,274
Balance B, seasonally adjusted	−1,304	225	−3,398

* Exports of goods and services excludes Department of Defense shipments of grant aid and military equipment and supplies under mutual security programs. Transactions other than changes in foreign liquid assets in the United States and in U.S. monetary reserve assets—seasonally adjusted.

† General imports including those for immediate consumption plus entries into bonded warehouses.

Source: *Federal Reserve Bulletin*, June, 1968, p. A–70.

TABLE 27–3

<small>Balance-of-Payments Settlement Transactions</small>
(In Millions of Dollars)

	1960	1962	1964	1966	1967
Balance on official reserve basis:......	−3,403	−2,702	−1,564	266	−3,405
Official reserves (− is an increase)...	2,145	1,533	171	568	52
Gold.........................	1,703	890	125	571	1,170
Convertible currencies.........	...	17	−220	−540	−1,024
IMF gold tranche position.......	442	626	266	537	−94
Liquid liabilities to official agencies...	1,258	919	1,075	−1,595	2,062
Certain nonliquid liabilities to official agencies*.................	...	250	318	761	1,291
Reported by U.S. private residents.......................	...	...	149	793	839
Reported U.S. government......	...	250	169	−32	452
Balance on liquidity basis:.............	−3,901	−2,204	−2,800	−1,357	−3,571
Official reserves (− is an increase)...	2,145	1,533	171	568	52
Gold.........................	1,703	890	125	571	1,170
Convertible currencies†........	...	17	−220	−540	−1,024
IMF gold tranche position......	442	626	266	537	−94
Liquid liabilities to all foreigners.....	1,756	671	2,679	789	3,519
Official agencies.............	1,448	457	1,075	−1,595	2,062
Commercial banks‡...........	140	−138	1,454	2,697	1,262
Other foreign residents and unallocated§.................	−167	140	343	212	413
International and regional organizations................	335	212	−243	−525	−218

† The United States first used foreign convertible currency as a reserve in 1961.
‡ Includes deposits of foreign branches of U.S. banks and foreign commercial banks associated with their U.S.-dollar-denominated liabilities to foreign fiscal agencies.
§ May include U.S. government bonds and notes held by foreign commercial banks.
* Beginning in 1962, the United States Treasury issued nonmarketable medium-term convertible bonds to foreign central banks in return for deposit credit. The Treasury regards them as medium-term obligations, but foreign central banks treat them as liquid assets.
Source: *Survey of Current Business*, June, 1968, pp. 34–35.

change rates. The larger a nation's reserves relative to its international liabilities, the more time it has to bring its international transactions position into equilibrium. The chief criticism of the official reserve transaction measure of a deficit or surplus is that it excludes private dollar claims which are sometimes closely related to central-bank policies. This would be true in France, where the most important banks are owned by the government, and in South America, where exchange control is in effect.

There are many reasons for not treating private claims against the United States in the same way as official claims. (1) Many foreigners hold the U.S. dollar because of its acceptability and status as international reserve currency, and they will continue to hold dollars as long as the United States is a "world banker" (see below). (2) Many American banks lend to foreigners on the same terms as to

Americans, including requiring compensatory balances not subject to withdrawal. (3) Americans sometimes place funds on deposit in foreign banks which the latter invest in liquid assets of the United States. Because foreign bankers are mindful of their foreign obligations, it is unlikely that these liquid assets will be converted into foreign currency.

It may be misleading to assume that no part of the private assets of the United States would be available in case of international need because these assets are convertible into foreign currency. They may be and, at times, have been purchased by monetary authorities in the foreign-exchange markets. The term "liquidity" is a relative one, subject to sudden change. For illustration, with no change in the amount of international reserves, when there is a general confidence in the dollar, the liquidity position of the United States seems to be much better than at other times when there is a lessening of confidence.

The Office of Business Economics in the United States Department of Commerce computes the balance-of-payments position of the United States not only in terms of change in official reserve transac-

CHART 27–2
OFFICIAL RESERVE-TRANSACTION AND LIQUIDITY BASES
(Billions of Dollars)

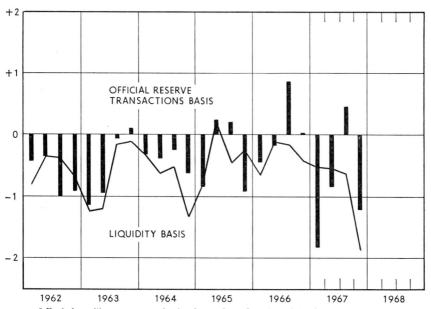

* Excludes military grants and related transfers of goods and services.
Source: Board of Governors of the Federal Reserve System, *Federal Reserve Chart Book,* June, 1968, p. 82.

tions plus increases or decreases in liquid and certain nonliquid liabilities to foreign official agencies but also in terms of official reserve
transactions plus liquid liabilities to all foreigners (see Chart 27–2).
The resulting computed deficit may be larger because of the inclusion
of liquid liabilities to foreign commercial banks, foreign residents, and
others not included above. On the other hand, it may be smaller
because it does not include among liabilities the nonliquid obligations
to foreign agencies (see Chart 27–3).

CHART 27–3
Foreign Liquid Assets in the United States
by Holder, 1957–67

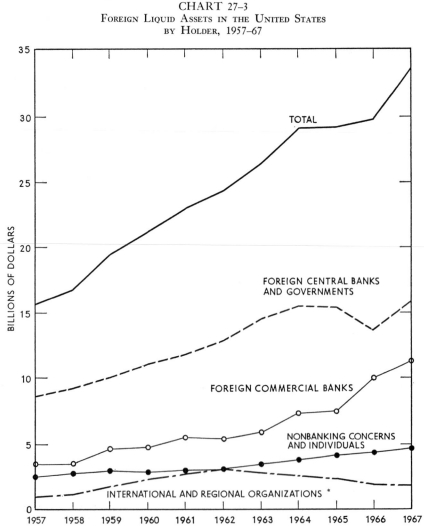

* Excluding IMF dollar holdings arising from U.S. currency subscriptions to the Fund and
from IMF transactions in dollars with the United States and other members.
Source: Federal Reserve Bank of New York, *Monthly Review,* June, 1968, p. 117.

The central bank may influence the size of the dollar holdings of all private investors in foreign exchange by operating in the forward exchange market. By selling foreign exchange in the forward market, the Federal Reserve Bank of New York assures private investors that they may take their assets home later at a more favorable rate of exchange. Although such procedures tend to blur the distinction between "official" and "private" dollar exchange, such changes are short run and do not interfere seriously with the long-run forces affecting the U.S. balance of payments.

The use of the liquidity balance as a guide to policy is criticized because it treats short-term private claims of foreigners below the line but does not place similar claims of U.S. residents on foreigners in a similar position as liquid assets. This means that private liquid assets may not be used to offset private liquid claims, so the balance-of-payments deficit is reported to be much larger than it would be if reporting were consistent.

The justification for the unequal treatment is that U.S. liabilities held by private foreigners are a potential threat to U.S. international reserves because foreign governments may (and do) order them to be surrendered to their monetary authorities in case of need (see below); while the United States has never followed such a policy. The fact that the dollar serves as an international currency reserve places a special responsibility on this country's monetary authorities to balance its holdings of official reserve assets against both official and private liabilities (see Table 27–3).

WORLD BANKER

Since 1950 the gold stock of the United States has been reduced by about 50 percent from the abnormal highs that characterized much of the period following devaluation of the gold dollar in 1934. At the same time, the United States increased its short-term debt by more than $24 billion. Rather than cash their balance-of-payments claims against the United States, most foreigners prefer to invest them in short-term promises to pay.

Currently, total foreign assets of the United States are $122.3 billion as compared with total liabilities of $69.6 billion. Over 85 percent of the foreign assets of the United States consists of direct investments and other long-term claims against foreigners. About 46 percent of the remaining assets consist of United States holdings of foreign currency and other short-term assets, and the remainder includes commercial and banking claims against foreigners. The latter represent short-term claims, but there is some question as to their liquidity because a large percentage is against countries in the least industrialized sections of the world (Africa, Asia, and South America). The overall balance of payments situation of the United States would be more comfortable if the foreign assets held by the United States were in a more readily available or more liquid form. The United States has assumed the role of a modern commercial bank—borrowing short and lending long.

At the end of 1967, foreigners owned $69.6 billion of assets of the United States of which $33.5 billion were in the form of marketable or short-term United States Treasury securities, demand and time deposits, and money-market instruments such as bankers' acceptances, commercial paper, and negotiable time certificates of deposit. Although holders of these assets buy and hold them for numerous reasons, all reflect the use of the U.S. dollar as a means of international payments and as a store of value.[2]

Monetary Authorities. Foreign central banks and governments have accumulated large holdings of U.S. assets including marketable U.S. government issues, special issues of the United States Treasury, demand and time deposits, bankers' acceptances, negotiable time certificates of deposit, and other prime short-term money-market assets. Of the $15.5 billion held by them at the end of 1967, monetary authorities in western Europe held about 65 percent; in Asia, 20 percent; in Latin America, 6.5 percent, and the remainder was held in Canada and the rest of the world. In addition, free-world monetary authorities also held $1.5 billion of U.S. notes and bonds including marketable issues and special issues that are not marketable but are convertible into cash or short-term United States Treasury notes.

The International Monetary Fund (see Chapter 28), the World Bank (International Bank for Reconstruction and Development), and a few development banks (see Chapter 29) are important investors in U.S. liquid dollar assets which amounted to $1.5 billion at the end of 1967. The holdings of IMF were due largely to reversible gold sales and to mitigate against the effects on the U.S. balance of payments of gold purchases by countries that needed the gold to pay for their 1965 IMF quota increases (see Chapter 28). The World Bank and the regional development banks often accumulate funds that they invest

[2] Federal Reserve Bank of New York, *Monthly Review*, June, 1968, pp. 117–24.

temporarily in the United States, pending the completion of lending arrangements with borrowers.

Foreign Commercial Banks.   Liquid assets in the form of U.S. dollars are popular not only with national and international bankers and other monetary authorities but also with foreign commercial banks, business firms, and individuals. However commercial banks hold a higher percentage of such assets in the form of demand deposits, including those in foreign branches of U.S. banks and foreign central banks. The remaining liquid assets are usually used to acquire earning assets, such as bankers' acceptances, time deposits, and time certificates of deposit because the earnings on these assets are not subject to the federal income tax when held by foreign corporations.

Ownership of U.S. liquid assets by foreigners has been stimulated by the establishment of foreign branches and agencies by U.S. banks. At the same time, American banks, through their branches, subsidiaries, and agents, have been able to borrow funds in the Euromarket that they have transferred to their home offices. In the balance-of-payments accounting, the foreign branches and agencies of U.S. banks are treated as foreigners, and for each dollar borrowed in Europe they receive a deposit or some other type of liquid asset, thereby adding to the total (reaching a peak of $4 billion in mid-December 1966). By offering attractive interest rates on behalf of their head offices in Canada, agencies and affiliates of Canadian banks in New York have been able to obtain large deposits from U.S. corporations. Canadian banks customarily protect themselves from loss on American dollar deposits by acquiring dollar assets. They place matching funds in their offices in New York to be used to finance operations in the money market and short-term loan market (such as loans to securities brokers and dealers).

Foreign Nonbank Corporations and Individuals.   Monetary authorities and foreign commercial banks are the chief owners of foreign-held liquid assets of the United States; but holdings by foreign private nonbank firms and individuals have increased steadily and amounted to over $4.5 billion at the end of 1967. The chief reason for holding these assets is to care for their liquidity needs; but many Latin Americans hold United States short-term time and savings deposits and money-market instruments as an escape from domestic inflation and currency uncertainties. Among European nonbank holders are foreign-owned life insurance companies operating in the

United States, which hold not only short-term deposits and money-market instruments but also United States Treasury bonds and notes.

FOREIGN EXCHANGE SYSTEMS

Throughout the history of international trade, nations have been confronted with imbalances in their international transactions statements. The adjustment process was simply one of reducing the supply of money in the deficit country. This decrease in the amount of money tended to lower general prices, decrease national income, and reduce spending. Foreigners found the market less attractive, so imports declined; domestic businessmen sought markets for their products abroad, so exports increased. The decrease in the money supply tended to increase interest rates, so the export of capital declined and the import of capital increased, thereby aiding in bringing the balance of payments into equilibrium.

Gold Standard.   When a country is on the gold standard, the export of gold will cause a decline in general prices because of tie between the amount of money and gold. Presumably, an outflow of gold results from a deficit in the country's international transactions balance. In order for the central bank to check the loss of gold, deflationary monetary policies must be adopted. Hence, the Federal Reserve Banks would raise their discount rates and the System would reduce its investments in the open market by selling or buying fewer government securities. Bank reserves, the quantity of money, costs, and prices would all decline. Lower costs would stimulate output, and lower prices in the domestic market would encourage exports. Because prices in the home market would be lower than abroad, buying at home would increase, and imports would decline. Eventually, these changes would correct the imbalance in the international transactions of the United States. In case of an inflow of gold and a surplus in a country's balance of payments, the opposite steps would be taken by the monetary authorities.

When countries operate under the gold standard, parity between their currencies is fixed in terms of the gold content of their monetary units, interchangeability of currencies is permitted, and the sight rate of foreign exchange fluctuates around the par of exchange and within the "gold points." The latter is found by adding the cost of exporting gold to the par of exchange to get the "export" point and by subtracting the cost of importing gold from the par of exchange to get the "import" point. The cost of moving gold includes the cost of preparing for shipment, insuring, mint charges, and loss of interest on the sum while in transit. In practice, gold shipments are usually initiated only in large amounts by banks, bullion dealers, and other specialists because the use of gold in payment would not be economical for individuals. Higher exchange rates discourage foreign buying by increasing costs and thereby lessening the demand for foreign exchange and reducing its price. Conversely, lower exchange rates increase the demand for foreign exchange and increase its price. As in the case of foreign investment and foreign travel, fluctuations in exchange rates affect balance-of-payments equilibrium.

The effects of gold imports and exports on a domestic economy are not automatic but depend on the aggregate of individuals who control the country's power of investing and spending. Their behavior may modify the effects of imports or exports of gold; conversely, their behavior may intensify these effects. One danger of an excessive outflow of gold is that it may result in recession or depression, discouraging investments. Furthermore, the automatic correctives of the gold standard are incompatible with the current goals of economic policy—to achieve full employment, economic growth, and stable prices. Hence central banks and governments intervene to offset the loss of gold by increasing the volume of reserve credit and to neutralize the effects of gold imports by decreasing the volume of reserve credit. Thus, when a country has a large supply of gold, it may insulate itself against many of the depressing effects that normally accompany the loss of gold, operating, in effect, upon a managed currency system. Conversely, many of the inflationary effects of gold imports may be offset by central-bank and government absorption of reserves so that they do not affect the domestic economy.

In a modern economy, even without central-bank interference, there is no certainty that adjustments would be along the lines anticipated when gold flows out of a country. Money wages and other costs of production tend to be fairly rigid, making it difficult to lower prices in response to the influence of loss of reserve money and higher interest rates. Instead of lower prices, the result may be a decline in employment, production, and exports. Automatic operation is a desirable characteristic of the international gold standard, but, for proper functioning of this standard, flexibility of domestic prices and noninterference by central banks and governments is required. Present-day economists no longer visualize the international gold standard as an automatic gold standard, but the principles under which it operated do have an important place in the International Monetary Fund

Agreement and the type of international monetary system anticipated therein (see Chart 27.4).

Flexible Exchange-Rate System.   When countries are operating on the gold standard, there is no wide fluctuation in exchange rates caused by changes in supply and demand. Fluctuations are confined to the limits set by the gold points, and the norm around which the sight rate of exchange fluctuates is the par of exchange. When operating under a fluctuating exchange-rate system, exchange transactions continue to entail the purchase and sale of credit instru-

CHART 27–4
FOREIGN-EXCHANGE RATE
(Weekly Averages of Daily Figures) *

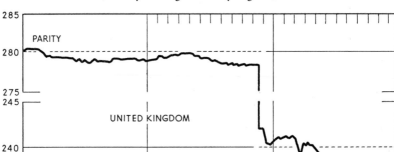

* Foreign-exchange rates are certified to the United States Treasury by the Federal Reserve Bank of New York for customs purposes.
† The United Kingdom devalued the pound sterling on November 18, 1967 from 280 cents to 240 cents in terms of the United States dollar.
Source: *Federal Reserve Chart Book,* July, 1968, p. 93.

ments, but gold movements are not used to keep the sight rate of exchange within the gold points. International bankers can no longer obtain gold at fixed prices, so gold is not permitted to perform its traditional function, that of stablizing exchange rates. In addition, international reserves would no longer be needed, and the burden on domestic economies from unrestricted gold movements would be eliminated. Equilibrium in the balance of payments would result from fluctuations in the exchange rate.

Assuming that two countries are operating on a freely fluctuating exchange system or on the so-called "paper standard," there is still a norm around which the exchange rates fluctuate—the purchasing-power par of exchange. The purchasing-power par theory of exchange is that a rate of exchange will be established that equates the domestic purchasing power of the two currencies. The formula for determining it is as follows:

$$\frac{\text{Index number — Country A}}{\text{Index number — Country B}} \times \text{old par of exchange} = \text{Purchasing-power par}$$

For example, if the United States and Great Britain have paper standards and the index number of prices in the United States is 150 and that of Great Britain is 200, the purchasing-power par is computed as follows:

$$\frac{150}{200} = \times\$0.240 = \$1.80$$

If the purchasing-power par is $1.80 and the market rate of exchange is $1.50, it is obviously to the advantage of Americans to purchase goods in England, where the equivalent of $1.50 spent for a bill of exchange will buy $1.80 worth of goods. An increase in purchases abroad would tend to bring the actual exchange rate and the purchasing-power par together. The adjustment would be a three-way process: Buying abroad would make it necessary for merchants to go into the exchange market to purchase exchange, and the rate of exchange would tend to increase. Buying goods abroad would tend to increase prices in that market. A decrease in purchase of goods in the United States would tend to lower the prices of goods in the domestic market. The first movement would tend to increase the exchange rate, and the last two movements would tend to lower the purchasing-power par. For example, if prices should go up 10 points in England and down 10 points in the United States, the new purchasing-power par would be:

$$\frac{140}{210} \times \$2.40 = \$1.60$$

Assume also that in the meantime, the market exchange rate had increased 10 cents (from $1.50 to $1.60). The exchange rate and the purchasing-power par would thus be brought together.

If the exchange rate is above the purchasing-power par, just the opposite of these movements would tend to take place. That is, goods would tend to be purchased more freely in the United States and less freely abroad, the rate of dollar exchange would tend to rise, domestic prices would tend to increase, and foreign prices would tend to decrease. In computing the purchasing-power par, the most satisfactory results are secured when only prices of goods bought and sold in international markets are considered. When sheltered goods are considered, differences in purchasing power of money in two markets may be great. Further deviations of the exchange rate away from the purchasing-power par norm may result from capital movements, domestic price control, and other restrictions placed on the markets; herein lies the chief weakness of the purchasing-power parity doctrine. In practice, exchange rates may undergo changes, although there may be stability in the commodity price levels of the countries being compared.

While the foregoing discussion has emphasized the relationship between the purchasing-power parity of exchange and the market rate, the mechanism whereby exchange-rate fluctuations tend to keep the balance-of-payments statement in equilibrium is of primary interest. If foreign goods and services are being imported excessively by Americans, exchange rates will tend to increase, and this will mean that higher prices (when converted into dollars) will have to be paid for foreign goods, thereby checking imports. Foreign-exchange rates are high in New York, which means that American goods may be purchased more cheaply (in terms of foreign currencies), and this will stimulate American exports. Thus, by discouraging imports and encouraging exports, fluctuations in foreign-exchange rates will tend to curtail American imports and to stimulate American exports, bringing into equilibrium the relationship between exports and imports.

Conversely, if American goods and services were being exported excessively, the fluctuations in exchange rates would tend to correct this situation. The price of American dollars in foreign markets would be high, and the price of foreign currencies in New York would be low. The first would discourage foreign purchases of American goods, and the second would encourage the purchase of foreign goods by Americans. This would tend to bring into balance the relationship between exports and imports by reducing the former and by increasing the latter, and there would be no balance-of-payments deficit.

If there are free foreign-exchange markets, fluctuations in exchange rates become a major factor in bringing about equilibrium in the balance of payments. A fall in the rate of exchange or price of the U.S. dollar of 25 percent would tend to increase sharply the export or credit items and to decrease sharply the import or debit items. The foreign purchasing power of U.S. residents would be reduced and that of foreigners would be increased. If only commodities are included, an equilibrium rate of exchange would be established without involving gold movements, and, as already noted, this rate would tend to correspond to the purchasing-power parity of the two monetary units involved.

The freely fluctuating exchange system has not been adopted internationally, but has been forced on or adopted by individual countries. Although favored by some economists, it is opposed by most bankers and businessmen, who contend that it would subject them to a capricious exchange market. The proponents point out that bankers and businessmen could protect themselves from exchange risks by operating in the futures or forward-exchange market. However this market is not available in all currencies at the present time, but this situation would be rectified if all countries adopted a freely fluctuating exchange system. Under such a system, the international liquidity or reserve problem would cease to exist because there would be continuous adjustment in the rate of exchange, reflecting the demand and supply situation. Under such circumstances, monetary authorities could devote themselves exclusively to domestic problems of unemployment, economic growth, and stable prices. In effect, a domestic policy would be substituted for the international one.

Although the flexible exchange system contains the mechanism for correcting any disequilibrium in balance-of-payments statements, it discourages international transactions and contains no effective check on inflation. National governments may follow independent monetary policies in regard to domestic affairs, but they cannot ignore the effect of these policies on their external affairs. Inflation between the two World Wars discredited the flexible exchange system and after World War II the world returned to the gold-exchange system (see Chapter 28).

CONTROLLED EXCHANGE SYSTEM

In practice, few countries permit exchange rates to bring about equilibrium between the inflow and outflow of goods and services, because fluctuating exchange rates tend to create as well as to correct situations that are in disequilibrium. If the price of the U.S. dollar is falling, speculators are encouraged to sell bills of exchange in New York, bankers will find it profitable to shift funds away from New York, foreign buyers of American goods and services will tend to wait for lower prices, and American importers will tend to enlarge their purchases from abroad in order to avoid higher prices (in terms of the dollar). All of these capital and goods movements will tend to accelerate the fall in the price of the dollar.

Orderly exchange markets are desirable, so most countries have used or are using some type of foreign-exchange control—fixed prices of foreign exchange and regulation of the demand for and supply of foreign exchange. In adopting foreign-exchange control measures, countries may have objectives other than elimination of the disturbing effects of fluctuating exchange rates. For example, if nations are buying heavily abroad, it is desirable to keep their exchange rate above the purchasing-power par norm in order to get the most goods and services from what they have to spend. But, in order to sell, they may want to keep their exchange rates below the purchasing-power par norm—in fact, they may try to do both at the same time by introducing a multiple exchange system, with one rate for one purpose and a second rate for a second purpose.

Foreign-exchange control means the detailed control by governments over the exchange markets and complete, or almost complete, suppression of free dealings in exchange. This form of control was initiated in Germany in 1931. It was adopted by most warring countries at the outbreak of World War II and has been continued to date in many countries. Usually, it is introduced in order to support a foreign-exchange value of a currency at a level above its international purchasing power. In addition to a government nomopoly of the exchange market, direct exchange control usually includes a licensing system for the import and export of goods, control of foreign assets of nationals, regulation of foreign investments, and specifications of the amount of funds that individuals may take out of the economy.

Having a monopoly of the supply of foreign exchange, the control authority must decide on its apportionment for commodity imports, debt service, tourist expenditures, and other items. The next type of decision involves the distribution of the funds among different countries. This power permits all types of international favoritism, often in violation of most-favored-nation clauses in existing treaties. For example, applicants for exchange who want to buy American goods may be refused, while applicants who want to buy French goods may be sold exchange.

Further complications arise because of the question of the distribution of available exchange among different commodities. These decisions make it possible to favor certain industries at the expense of others, to favor industry at the expense of agriculture, and to bring about a redistribution of national income among the domestic classes. For instance, manufacturers of chemicals may be permitted to buy abroad, while manufacturers of cloth may be forced into bankruptcy because they cannot secure raw materials from abroad. Finally, the exchange authority must allot exchange among competing business firms, a source of one of the most vicious types of abuse in exchange regulation. For example, Firm A is permitted to buy exchange and therefore raw materials abroad, but Firm B is denied foreign exchange and is forced to get along with inferior domestic substitutes, to change the nature of its business, or to liquidate. Thus, arbitrary administrative decisions are substituted for the old system of free exchange, in which price serves as the mechanism of allotment.

In a system of free exchange, if the total demand for foreign exchange for all purposes is greater than the total supply, its price rises until supply and demand are balanced. There is therefore no problem of discriminating among buyers in different fields and among individuals in the same field. "The less urgent needs are excluded by price, and there is no direct interference in the process of production and trade. Vested interests do not grow up which are dependent on the continuance of an artificial system of control and allocation and which accordingly resist any attempt to change that system.[3]

The control agency controls not only the use of foreign exchange but also the supply. Exports are the most important source of exchange, and the owners of the resulting bills of exchange are required to sell all or part of them to the exchange authorities at a price fixed by the control agency. Exchange is then available to finance government payments abroad and to sell to importers and to others. If the plan in operation permits the exporter to retain a part of his foreign exchange, he may use it to buy goods abroad or he may sell it to an importer at a negotiated price, which is usually above the official buying price.

In addition to the seizure of bills of exchange resulting from exports, the exchange authorities may increase their holdings of foreign exchange by requiring all persons to report and to surrender title to all bank balances abroad, all foreign securities, and all other foreign assets, including real estate. Imports of foreign currency may be tolerated, but, since some currencies (such as the American dollar) are widely hoarded, the exchange-control authorities may prefer to

[3] League of Nations (committee composed of members of the Economic and Financial Committee), *Report on Exchange Control* (Geneva: League of Nations, 1938), p. 39.

have it exchanged for domestic money at the port of entry. Domestic currency may be taken out of the country by tourists, but limits are placed on the amount that may be imported.

As short-term capital movements are the most dynamic among the items in the balance of payments, exchange control was first introduced in many countries in order to prevent these short-term debt transfers from causing exchange disturbances. Governments commonly decreed that nationals must pay their interest and principal charges into a fund at the central bank. These payments were made in domestic currency calculated at the debtor country's official exchange rate. The coupons of foreign bondholders were then presented to the central bank for payment. In some cases arrangements have been made for payment of principal, but the conditions under which these funds can be utilized vary greatly. Usually, these "blocked balances" or bank accounts may be used to purchase goods within the country where they are held and may be sold to tourists for expenditures within the boundaries of the country.

Ordinarily, no international banker will place funds in an exchange-control country where he knows restrictions will be placed on their withdrawal. So in order to have normal capital movements, confidence in the future of exchange-control countries must be reestablished. Experience suggests that this may not be expected so long as these countries follow any policy of exchange control which prevents the creditor from receiving, in free exchange, interest, dividends, and installment or other payments on principal. Therefore, exchange control tends to restrict international lending and to shrink the total volume of transactions involved in the balance-of-international-payments statement (unless offset by government lending).

Parallel to restrictions on exchange markets are restrictions placed on foreign trade by countries whose governments limit the purchase of goods by import quotas, licensing systems, and protective tariffs. In addition, governments have made discriminatory bilateral agreements that have practically closed certain markets to other countries. Among these agreements were the prewar "barter" and "clearing" agreements that Germany made with her satellite countries and the postwar agreements between Russia and the nations in her sphere of influence—the Molotov Plan for eastern Europe. Another agreement, less sweeping in nature, was the Anglo-Russian exchange of grain and other Soviet products for English manufactured goods. Under agreements of that type, individuals as well as governments may participate. Buyers in each country pay for the goods purchased by remitting to their central bank or some other government agency. From the funds received, each control agency pays exporters in their own country for the goods shipped to the other country. Thus goods are purchased and sold without the use of foreign exchange, settlement being made by domestic drafts. Final settlement of any balance between the two countries is made by the exchange authorities of the countries according to prior arrangements.

A major problem inherent in clearing agreements is that of arriving at the correct exchange rate to be used. In the past, trade was often carried on at artificially high prices, and this tying together of the economies of two countries at an artificially high price level tended to deprive these countries of freedom of action in dealing with other countries operating at the international price level. Since trade with the larger country was relatively more important to the smaller country, the economy of the smaller country was more seriously affected, and the shock to it was greater when other markets had to be found.

SUMMARY

The statement of international transactions or balance of payments of a country is the record of the money value of economic transactions between the residents, business firms, governments, and other institutions of that country and the rest of the world for a period of time. The balance-of-payments statement may be thought of as a balance scale, with each addition on one side necessitating an addition on the other side to keep it in equilibrium. Now, any change in a country's deficit or surplus is measured in terms of changes in its official international reserves or in terms of changes in its liquidity balance. Changes in the United States liquidity balance are generally recognized as being most significant because of the status of the dollar as an international reserve unit. Nevertheless government economists have been criticized for treating changes in the U.S. liquid obligations to private foreigners as "below the line" items but treating changes in private U.S. claims on foreigners as "above the line" items. This means that any increase in short-term private capital claims against the United States tend to weaken its liquidity position, but a similar outward flow does not strengthen it. The justification given for this difference in treatment is that private liabilities on the United States are readily transferable to foreign official holders of reserves to whom the United States is committed to sell gold; but U.S. private claims on foreigners are not readily available to the American authorities for use in protecting the U.S. dollar in foreign-exchange markets.

When operating on the gold standard, gold movements involve more than balancing international transactions because they affect interest rates, price levels, and international movements of goods and services. When countries keep the value of their currencies tied to gold, the norm around which exchange rates tend to fluctuate is the par of exchange; when countries are on paper standards, the norm is the "purchasing-power par."

Most countries are committed to a fixed rate of exchange which may be under either a direct control system or an international gold-exchange standard system. Restrictions on exchange markets are usually paralleled by restrictions on foreign trade. Hence, foreign trade, investment, and travel are placed in a straitjacket by devious devices in countries where direct control is practiced. The United States has been the leader in the movement to eliminate these restrictive practices, which were deeply embedded in many countries because of prewar, war, and postwar emphasis on economic nationalism. One of the reasons for creating the International Monetary Fund was to have an international agency to assist in the establishment of a multilateral system of payments in respect to current transactions and in the elimination of foreign-exchange restrictions which interfere with the growth of world trade. Perhaps no aspect of the international payments system is more widely accepted among officials than adherence to a fixed rate of exchange and avoidance of direct exchange control.

The United States is pledged to the policies of maintaining peace and eliminating poverty which can be achieved only in an expanding worldwide economy. The hope for solution of the U.S. balance-of-payments deficit problem lies in increasing the export-import surplus sufficiently to permit continuance of the United States as an international banker, while keeping its economic and military commitments abroad without resorting to direct foreign-exchange control. But one should not conclude that the deficit is "all bad," because the increase in dollar liabilities has given the United States additional funds to invest and an opportunity to replace nonearning gold assets with earning assets.

QUESTIONS AND PROBLEMS

1. Identify: (*a*) balance-of-international-payments statement, (*b*) favorable balance of trade, (*c*) balance-of-payments deficit, (*d*) "below the line" items, and (*e*) "above the line" items.

2. Explain: "In the fourth quarter [1967] . . . the composition of U.S. reserve assets underwent a major change. Gold holdings declined $1,012 million, while holdings of convertible currencies increased $1,145 million and the U.S. gold tranche position in the IMF improved $48 million." (*Survey of Current Business*, March, 1968, p. 15.)

3. Explain: "In recognition of opposing views . . . the United States recently adopted two measures of its international payments position —the 'liquidity' balance and the balance on 'official reserve transactions.' " (Federal Reserve Bank of Kansas City, *Monthly Review*, September–October, 1966, p. 14.)

4. Discuss: The "deficits in the balance of payments may be largely associated with large capital outflows . . . [Now] the United States assets abroad at $111.8 billion far exceed liabilities $60.4, leaving a net asset position of $51.5 billion." (First National Bank of Chicago, *Business and Economic Review*, November, 1967, p. 6.)

5. What are the major components of the balance-of-payments statement? Which ones tend to be favorable items? Unfavorable items?

6. What steps has the U.S. government taken to improve the trade balance and to make the balance on foreign travel less unfavorable?

7. Discuss: "The United States . . . now acts in the world as a 'financial intermediary,' lending long and borrowing short. The resulting rise in foreign dollar holdings counts as a deficit as the balance of payments is now defined [and] it will persist as long as capital movement is free." (*New York Times*, February 8, 1966, p. 49.)

8. Explain: The U.S. dollar and English pound sterling are international currencies without any act of Congress or the British Parliament because they met the various needs of foreign individuals, foreign commercial banks and foreign official institutions more efficiently then other financial assets could. (B. S. Karlstroem, "How Did They Become Reserve Currencies," *Finance and Development*, September, 1967, pp. 209–17.)

9. Explain: "The market rate of exchange tends to fluctuate around the purchasing-power par of exchange when a country is operating on an inconvertible paper-money standard and has a free exchange market."

10. Analyze: "The attainment of equilibrium in the balance of payments is likely to require, in addition to restraint of demand at home, a vigorous economic expansion in other industrial countries, together with a greater willingness on the part of those countries to let competitive U.S. goods enter their markets." (*Federal Reserve Bulletin*, April, 1968, p. 361.)

CHAPTER 28

International Monetary System

FOLLOWING THE CLOSE of World War II, financial and political leaders were searching for a type of international monetary system that would be less restrictive than the gold standard of the 1920's and that would offer greater stability than the paper standard of the 1930's. Through international cooperation, the solution arrived at was centered around the International Monetary Fund. Although many alternate suggestions have been made during the interim since that time, most financial leaders believe that the international system currently in effect should be kept and improved.

BACKGROUND FOR INTERNATIONAL MONETARY ORGANIZATIONS

Gold, as the basis for the international monetary system, dates from the 1870's when the United States, France, Germany, and other nations used it to replace other monetary standards including paper money, silver, and bimetallism. The governments of many countries selected gold as their monetary standard because Great Britain had been on the gold standard since 1821, and they wanted to share in the expansion of commerce and industry of which Great Britain was the leader. The international gold standard worked successfully as long as the participating countries abided by the terms of this standard.

Nations operating under the gold standard defined their currency units in terms of gold, which meant that all currency units had a common base and a fixed value relationship with each other. Gold coins issued by participating countries could be exchanged at rates based on the relative amount of gold therein; and currencies convertible into gold had the same acceptability in international transactions as gold coins. This gave the world stable exchange rates and an integrated price system, thereby encouraging international trade and investment.

International Trade. International payments are due primarily to trade transactions, but those resulting from international investment, travel, and other service transactions are becoming increasingly important. The growth of international trade and production was fostered by the international price system that permitted countries to base output in accordance with the principle of comparative costs. At one time, countries operated on the assumption that they should only buy things abroad that they could not produce at home; the current theory is that the world's total production will be maximized when each country specializes in producing those things over which it has the greatest comparative advantage over other countries.

During the gold-standard era, industrial production increased, world trade flourished, per-unit costs declined, and the advantages resulting from greater specialization spread throughout the world. Although the principles of international trade and the international gold standard did not replace nationalism, the gold-standard system had provided a monetary basis for an impressive increase in production and in the standard of living. Therefore, it was not surprising that nations returned to this system after the devastation of World War I and their postwar inflationary experiences with fiat paper money issued to finance the war and the reconstruction that followed.

Modification of the Gold Standard. The increase in the use of silver coins, paper money, and deposit currency at a faster rate than the increase in gold money led to a *de facto* debasement of the gold standard which made it necessary for central banks to depend more fully on monetary management and less on the automatic workings of the gold standard. During the 1920's steps were taken to economize on the use of gold by discontinuing gold coinage and using foreign exchange to supplement gold as reserves. These economy measures could scarcely be avoided because gold production was lagging behind the demand for gold for monetary and nonmonetary purposes.

By 1928, a gold-exchange standard had been established and the world was experiencing record industrial production; then, one country after another was caught in a credit crisis which was followed by suspension of gold payments. The main weakness of the gold-exchange standard was an inability to cope with financial stress and crises.

Competition in Depreciation. During the Great Depression, many countries adopted the policy of depreciating their currency units in order to increase their exports and to increase employment (a policy referred to as exporting unemployment). The main disadvantage of this policy is that it encourages similar action by other countries. Once started, competition in depreciation seems to follow and to continue until all countries have devalued their monetary units. At any time, a new wave of depreciation may be started if one major country reduces the international value of its currency.

Any advantage gained from depreciation is usually temporary because prices in the depreciator's market tend to rise if for no other reason than the increase in international demand for its goods. The reduction in purchasing power of the depreciator's currency in foreign markets where raw materials and other goods are purchased will also contribute to higher domestic costs and prices. If this country is a debtor country, it will mean that the burden of its international debts will be increased; if it is a creditor country, depreciation will cancel a portion of its foreign credits in terms of real income.

Retaliation by other nations against depreciator nations may take forms other than competitive depreciation. These measures include raising tariffs to offset any trade advantage gained by the depreciator country, establishing quotas to limit imports in order to assure domestic producers a certain percentage of the domestic market, licensing imports, entering into bilateral barter agreements whereby goods are exchanged for goods rather than money; and making trade agreements with other countries that block out the depreciator's goods from their markets.

When goods are purchased abroad, they are usually paid for in foreign money, and, by allocating available foreign exchange, a country may direct or control its imports. Gradually, the control of foreign exchange was linked to import control by requiring would-be importers to obtain import licenses before applying for foreign exchange.

In order to have foreign exchange to sell, governments required exporters and others to sell their foreign exchange in whole or part to their governments at the latter's official price. The policy may also require nationals to surrender title to foreign stocks and bonds and other liquid assets in order to increase the foreign exchange reserves of the central bank.

Once the foregoing methods of international economic warfare are perfected, as they were during the 1930's, they may be applied against nations other than those who have depreciated their currencies (such as enemy countries during war or a strong competitor, such as the United States since World War II). When limits are placed on the use of foreign deposits and other international reserves, they may or may not be applied uniformly. There may be differentiation with respect to the ownership of deposits (as between residents and nonresidents and/or between foreign central banks and other nonresidents), to the purposes for which the deposits are to be used (as current transactions and capital transfers, travel, and other purposes), and to origin of the deposits (between old and new and/or between prewar and postwar).

Equalization Funds. Not all the international financial developments during the 1930's were of the type that handicapped and suppressed international trade, travel, and investments. Some countries created stabilization funds, which sought to minimize government interference in the exchange markets and to maintain free foreign-exchange markets. For illustration, when the United Kingdom abandoned the gold standard in 1931, it created an Exchange Equalization Account to stabilize the value of the pound sterling. Unlike the English Equalization Account, the American Stabilization Fund, provided for in the Gold Reserve Act of 1934, was used very little because of the strong international position of the dollar, the stress on domestic recovery, the link to gold, and the greater degree of economic and political stability in the United States as compared with some foreign countries.

Tripartite Agreement. Between 1930 and 1944, the most important international movement to cooperate on policies and procedures designed to stabilize exchange was the Tripartite Agreement of 1936. The participants (the United States, Great Britain, France, Belgium, the Netherlands, Switzerland, and later the Bank for International Settlements) contracted to sell gold to one another at fixed prices which were to be unchanged unless 24-hours' prior notice was given. In effect, it consisted of little more than the participants acting as agents for each other in support operations in foreign-exchange markets. When World War II started in 1939, the Tripartite Agreement became of secondary importance when economic controls replaced free markets in order to enhance the war effort.

Trade Needs. In approaching the postwar monetary problems, it was apparent that stable exchange rates and free-exchange markets were requisites if international trade, investments, and travel were to be financed with the minimum of risks. Attainment of these requisites would relieve merchants, bankers, and others from the fear that their receipts might be reduced by depreciation of foreign-currency units and that their funds might be "blocked" and would have to be spent according to the dictates of a foreign government. By their nature, these problems are international in their effects and require international cooperation for their solution. Emphasis was on creation of an international monetary system wherein gold was used as standard money with escape clauses and safeguards that would permit it to function while recognizing both national and international interests. In addition, it was apparent that large sums would be needed for reconstruction and development.

Experiences of the 1930's indicate that it would be impossible for any country acting alone to improve its balance-of-payments position by devaluation and placement of restrictions on trade and capital movements unless other countries were willing to accept the adverse effects on their balance-of-payments positions. The monetary and trade problems of the interwar period provided the background for the establishment of the International Monetary Fund and the International Bank for Reconstruction and Development.

Bretton Woods.   Representatives of 44 nations met in July, 1944, at Bretton Woods, New Hampshire,[1] and approved the Articles of Agreement for the International Monetary Fund and the Articles of Agreement for the International Bank for Reconstruction and Development (World Bank). The actions of these representatives were not binding on their governments, and the governments of several of the original 44 nations have taken no action on the Agreements.[2] However, in addition to those at Bretton Woods, others have approved, and by July, 1968, there were 107 members. Both the Fund and the World Bank are cooperative ventures, being owned, controlled, and operated by and in the interest of members.

INTERNATIONAL MONETARY FUND

Organization.   The Board of Governors of the International Monetary Fund and the International Bank for Reconstruction and Development is the policy-making group for both organizations. Each member country selects one Governor and his alternate as representatives at annual meetings of both organizations. The general policy is for the appointment to be filled by the Finance Minister, Secretary of the Treasury (as for the United States), or a similar

---

[1] Department of State, *Proceedings and Documents of the United States Monetary and Financial Conference, Bretton Woods, New Hampshire, July 1–22, 1944* (Washington, D.C.: U.S. Government Printing Office, 1948), Vols. I and II.

[2] The United States was the first country to take action on the agreements. The Bretton Woods Agreements Act was approved by the President on July 31, 1945 (59 stat. 512). The Bretton Woods Conference provided that, when the governments representing 65 percent of the total subscriptions accepted and signed the Articles of Agreement, they would be effective. Action was required before the end of 1945, and on December 27, 1945, all but seven of the original 44 nations had signed the Articles of Agreement, and, subsequently, three of the seven have been admitted. The only important nonacceptor was Russia.

high-ranking government official who is in a position to speak for his country in international affairs. The Board of Governors meets once a year in the capital of a member country, and the speeches and activities at these meetings are published in the *Summary Proceedings of the Board of Governors*.[3] The work of the Fund is assigned to a group of executive directors and a staff of over 600 from over 50 countries.

Board of Executive Directors. Of the 16 executive directors and their alternates, 5 are appointed by their governments and 11 are elected to represent countries grouped together for this purpose.[4] The number of votes each executive director has varies according to the member country's subscription or that of the group of countries an executive director represents. For illustration, the U.S. director casts 51,850 votes or 22.22 percent of the total, and the director for Japan, Burma, Ceylon, Nepal, and Thailand, as a group, casts 10,630 votes or 4.55 percent of the total.[5] The executive directors are full-time employees of the International Monetary Fund. They have two-year terms, but there are no restrictions on the number of terms they may serve.

Purposes. The purposes of the International Monetary Fund are (1) to promote international monetary cooperation through a permanent institution that provides the machinery for consultation and collaboration on international monetary problems, (2) to facilitate the expansion and balanced growth of international trade, thereby contributing to high levels of employment and real income, (3) to promote exchange stability and to avoid competitive exchange depreciation, (4) to assist in the establishment of a multilateral system of payments in respect to current transactions, thereby eliminating foreign-exchange restrictions that hamper the growth of trade, (5) to provide members with resources with which to correct temporary maladjustments in their balances of payments, and (6) to shorten the duration and lessen the disequilibrium in the international balance of payments.

Consultation and Collaboration. The International Monetary Fund is a semipolitical type of organization whose accomplishments

[3] The 22nd annual meeting of the International Monetary Fund was held in Rio de Janeiro, Brazil, in September, 1967 under the chairmanship of the Honorable Erik Brofoss, Governor from Norway.

[4] The five countries having appointed directors are the United States, United Kingdom, Germany, France, and India. These countries hold almost 46 percent of the total votes.

[5] For the names of executive directors and the number of votes each controls, see International Monetary Fund, *1967 Annual Report* (Washington, D.C., 1967), pp. 162–63.

cannot be measured in terms of dollars and cents. Officially, it began operations on March 1, 1947; but, prior to that date, there were consultations with member countries on international and national monetary and trade policies and such consultations have continued to be among its most important functions. With the emergence of new financially inexperienced countries, it is fortunate that permanent international machinery exists to provide advice and services.

Technical Assistance. One of the major responsibilities of the Fund is that of sponsoring the expansion and balanced growth of international trade, thereby contributing to a higher level of income and employment. So often contributions of capital funds through economic aid and loans by the United States and international development banks have failed to accomplish what was expected because many of the recipient countries lacked personnel trained in business administration and engineering. The Washington headquarters of the Fund operates an Institute offering 20-week courses in English to residents of member countries and seminars to special groups for shorter time periods. The main purpose is to provide training in national and international monetary policy, fiscal policy, and financial analysis for representatives selected from central banks and government employees.

Exchange Stability. In order to achieve greater economic stability and growth, member nations agreed to establish stable exchange rates and to eliminate competitive exchange depreciation. Furthermore, it is the duty of the Fund to assist in the establishment of a multilateral system of payments in respect to current transactions and to eliminate exchange restrictions that hamper the growth of trade.

Each member government agreed to limit fluctuations in its spot exchange within 1 percent and to refrain from changing its par of exchange except when necessary to correct a fundamental disequilibrium in its balance of payments (but by no more than 10 percent without concurrence of the Fund). It was understood that at times, after returning to free-exchange markets and stable rates, there may be temporary deficits in countries' balances of payments which will result in losses of international currency reserves and gold. To maintain the par of exchange and to avoid exchange restrictions, the Fund provides temporary resources to the deficit countries from contributions of members (normally, 25 percent in gold and 75 percent in each country's own currency). The Fund is authorized to lend only to correct temporary imbalances, because long-term commitments must be avoided if its assets are to be used as a revolving fund.

Quotas. The International Monetary Fund is financed by contributions or quotas of member countries, the amount of which depends on the member's ability to pay as indicated by national income and the importance of its international trade. Since voting and borrowing privileges are in proportion to the amount of members' contributions, some member countries have requested and obtained enlargements of their quotas.[6]

"Borrowing." As a prerequisite to borrowing from the Fund, a member must have met its subscription (quota) and established the par value of its currency in terms of gold or the U.S. gold dollar (that is, agreed to an accounting rate of exchange). When a member "borrows" from the Fund, it exchanges its own currency for the currency it borrows. To insure equitable treatment of members and to maintain liquidity of the Fund's resources, limits are placed on the amount that any one country may withdraw in one year and have outstanding at one time. The Fund insists on repayment within a reasonable period of time (repayment is the reverse of the borrowing transaction). The ability of the IMF to help individual members was increased when larger quotas were authorized in 1959 and 1965 and subsequently paid. Although the Fund does not increase the world's supply of international reserve money in its "ordinary operations," it helps to maintain the stability of exchange rates by making more reserve money available to nations in need of them.

The Fund's policy is to make borrowing by members automatic for amounts equal to their gold contribution (25 percent of their quotas). If a country's quota is $100 million, it may borrow $25 million; but if it has already withdrawn the equivalent of $15 million, its so-called gold tranche position is $10 million. Since member countries may use their gold tranche drawings freely, they customarily include them in estimating their liquidity positions or ability to meet their current foreign claims (see Table 28–3).[7] The amount of a country's gold tranche decreases as the amount of its currency in the

[6] During fiscal 1967, Peru, Korea, and Vietnam requested and obtained larger quotas. *International Monetary Fund Summary Proceedings of the Twenty-Second Annual Meeting of the Board of Governors* (Washington, D.C., 1967), pp. 262–64.

[7] Member countries normally pay 25 percent of their quotas in gold and the rest in their own currencies. So, a country's gold tranche would be $100 - 75 = 25$ percent of its quota, before there are any transactions in its currency. The gold tranche declines as a country draws from the Fund by giving its currency in payment. When it draws 25 percent of its quota, the Fund's holding of its currency is 100 percent and its gold tranche is zero. Conversely, when a country's currency held by the Fund decreases because "loans" have been repaid or other members have drawn on its currency, the country's gold tranche increases, and when none of its currency is left, its gold tranche will be 100 percent of its quota.

Fund increases. A member country may borrow in excess of its gold tranche if it meets certain conditions; but, before borrowing in excess of 100 percent of its quota, it must obtain a special waiver from the Fund. (Borrowing arrangements may be made on a standby basis.)

Earnings and Expenses. Part of the gold in the International Monetary Fund was used to buy U.S. government securities to obtain additional income with which to operate. The ordinary earnings of the Fund are derived from charges made for the use of the Fund's resources. At the time of a drawing, a service charge of one half of 1 percent is made. If a member arranges for a standby agreement, the fee charged is .0025 of the amount minus the member's gold tranche. If the Fund holds more of a member's currency than its quota, no charge is made for the first three months, but thereafter a charge is made depending on the amount of the excess and the time period.[8] It is these charges which constitute the International Monetary Fund's chief source of revenue. All charges are paid in gold, and the amounts paid are applied to the member's most recent drawings (the first in-last out principle). When the Fund's holdings of a member's currency have been reduced to an amount equal to its quota for at least one year, the progressive charges cease and revert back to the lowest applicable rate.

Expenditures of the Fund seem small for such a large organization. They include expenditures for the staff for salaries, travel, and other compensation, which make up over two thirds of the total. Soon after the Fund was organized, investments in U.S. government securities were authorized to provide income during the period when the Fund was not active as a "lender." Today, income from these investments and net income from operations are being used to build up the Fund's reserves.

ELIMINATION OF FLOATING RATES AND EXCHANGE CONTROL

The representatives of the nations attending the Bretton Woods Conference realized that international growth and prosperity were dependent in part on an increase in trade among nations and that this

[8] The charges now in effect are (1) after three months, 2 percent per annum for the first 15 months for holdings of less than 50 percent above the country's quota; (2) 2 percent per annum for 9 months for holdings in excess of 50 percent but less than 100 percent above the quota; and (3) 2 percent per annum for 3 months and rising by one half of 1 percent each 6 months for holdings in excess of 100 percent of the quota. When the rate reaches 4 percent per annum, the member and the Fund consult on means of reducing the obligation. After an agreement to repurchase one's currency, the rate is not permitted to exceed 5 percent; but if no agreement is reached, it may increase to 6 percent.

could be achieved with greater surety under a system of fixed exchange rates and stable currencies, unhampered by direct exchange control.

Par Value of Exchange Units. An early activity of the Fund was to establish a foreign-exchange policy which all member countries pledged to observe. This consisted of agreements to establish par values and to maintain the sight rate of exchange within 1 percent above or below this par value without placing any restrictions on current international payments (except for "scarce" currencies). A fixed rate of exchange not only removes the uncertainty of costs or prices involved in international trade, travel, and investments but also tends to contribute to the more efficient distribution of international resources among the nations of the free world with beneficial effects on the general economic welfare. It also subjects countries to the "discipline of gold and currency losses" when there is a deficit in their balance of payments due to inflation, international shifts in the use of capital and other resources, changes in competitive position, foreign government expenditures, and expenditures of tourists abroad. This discipline is beneficial provided it does not lead to curtailment in production and other reactions that could cause a recession and adversely affect general welfare. A good international money system will provide enough liquidity to correct imbalances in payments in time to avoid resorting to devaluation or abandonment of the fixed exchange-rate system. A country may devalue its currency 10 percent but any change in excess requires the approval of the International Monetary Fund. However, the Fund favors realistic rates and permits changes in par values to correct fundamental disequilibriums.

In 1946, the par values for 32 countries and a number of nonmetropolitan areas were announced, but, by September, 1949, it was evident that the par values of many countries were too high. With permission of the Fund, a wholesale revision of rates in Europe and elsewhere of about 30 percent was made over a period of several months. Since that time, only a few changes have been made, of which the most unusual were the increase in the rate for West Germany from 23.8 cents to 25 cents and for The Netherlands from 26.3 cents to 27.6 cents.[9] In 1967, with the approval of the Fund, Great Britain devalued its currency by 14 percent (which was accompanied or followed by Ireland, Denmark, and other countries whose international reserves are in the form of sterling exchange).

Removal of Direct Exchange Control. The second part of

[9] The change in par value for West Germany became effective on March 6, 1961 and that for The Netherlands, the next day.

the Fund's exchange policy pertains to the elimination of direct exchange control on all current accounts (except in cases where the Fund may have exhausted its supply of a particular currency and declared it to be scarce). Under the Articles of Agreement, nations are permitted to control exchange fluctuations due to capital movements. Some member countries felt that they needed exchange control to protect their limited international reserves, hence some did not remove their exchange control devices and others removed them only in part. Although the Fund tolerated this situation, in 1950 it began the publication of existing exchange control restrictions in its new *Annual Report on Exchange Restrictions.* Two years later, the Fund began consultations with members on their exchange restrictions, seeking methods whereby they could be removed. The greatest step forward was that taken in 1958–59 when western European countries removed most of their restrictions on current transactions. Complete removal of direct exchange control by underdeveloped countries seems remote; and no permanent solution may be expected until the export surplus of these nations becomes sufficient for them to keep a larger part of their resources as reserves and still achieve the goals of economic growth and higher per capita income. Nevertheless, they are committed to a policy of avoiding exchange restrictions, discriminatory currency practices, and multiple exchange-rate systems. Although convertibility of currency into other currencies was still a national responsibility, it was one that was to be achieved in cooperation with other countries through membership in the International Monetary Fund.

INTERNATIONAL MONETARY RESERVES

Currently, international monetary reserves consist of gold, official holdings of foreign currencies, and drawing rights on the Fund. Because gold, unlike credit instruments, is not subject to quality changes, it is still the preferred form of international monetary reserve. However, one disadvantage of gold is that it is not interest bearing and another minor one is that it presents problems in handling. Like the size of an individual's bank account and holdings of other liquid assets, the size of a nation's gold reserves and the amount of its officially held foreign balances and short-term foreign credit instruments reflect its liquid position among the countries of the world. Gold is still the only completely acceptable kind of money; and, although the percentage of nongold reserves in use is increasing, gold still makes up the bulk of international reserves (see Table 28–1).

Prior to the organization of the International Monetary Fund, it was assumed that any nation had the right to change its monetary unit at will, even though such action had worldwide effects upon the economies of other nations with which it carried on trade and had financial transactions. By accepting the International Monetary Fund Articles of Agreement, nations adopted a code of behavior that,

TABLE 28–1

GOLD RESERVES OF CENTRAL BANKS AND GOVERNMENTS
(In Millions of Dollars)

Year	World*	United States	International Monetary Fund	All Others
1957	38,765	22,857	1,180	14,730
1958	39,445	20,582	1,332	17,530
1959	40,195	19,507	2,407	18,280
1960	40,505	17,804	2,439	20,260
1961	41,100	16,947	2,077	22,080
1962	41,475	16,057	2,194	23,190
1963	42,305	15,596	2,312	24,380
1964	43,015	15,471	2,179	26,365
1965	43,230	13,806	1,869	21,285
1966	43,185	13,235	2,652	27,300
1967†	41,600	12,065	2,682	26,855

* Excludes the U.S.S.R., other eastern European countries, China mainland.
† Preliminary.
Source: *Federal Reserve Bulletin*, June, 1964, p. 786; and June, 1968, p. A–86.

among other things, involved the surrender of a part of the freedom to modify their monetary units.

If defining a country's monetary unit in terms of gold is to have significance, some provisions must be made whereby those who have rights to this currency may convert their rights into gold or gold equivalent on demand; so the second rule of the international gold standard is that international convertibility in gold or gold exchange must be provided. The smooth functioning of a domestic monetary system depends on the free interchange of all kinds of money at par throughout the areas served, and, although the problems are more complicated, an international monetary system must have this same interchangeability of currencies at or near par. A fixed rate of exchange increases the interdependence of free-world countries and tends to draw them closer together on all world ventures (political and military as well as economic).

Although gold is the most important form of international reserves, its percentage of the total has declined from about 75 percent in 1949 to 53 percent at the end of 1967. Until the end of 1964, the monetary gold stock increased at an annual rate of 1.4 percent of the total gold reserves, but it has declined since that time (see Table 28–2). This decline in the world's monetary gold stock has been due to an increase in the demand for gold for nonmonetary purposes, particularly hoarding.

The expansion in the monetary reserves of the free world have been largely in the form of dollars and sterling balances. Due to the balance-of-payments deficits of the United States and Great Britain,

TABLE 28–2

GOLD PRODUCTION, 1956–67
(In Millions of Dollars at $35 per Fine Ounce)

Year	World*	South Africa	Canada	United States	Australia	Others
1956	975.0	556.2	153.4	65.3	36.1	164.0
1957	1,015.0	596.2	155.2	63.0	37.9	162.7
1958	1,050.0	618.0	158.8	61.6	38.6	173.0
1959	1,125.0	702.2	156.9	57.2	38.1	170.6
1960	1,175.0	784.4	161.1	58.8	38.0	132.7
1961	1,215.0	803.1	156.6	54.8	37.7	163.0
1962	1,290.0	892.7	145.5	54.5	37.4	159.9
1963	1,355.0	960.1	139.0	51.4	35.8	168.7
1964	1,405.0	1,018.9	133.0	51.4	33.7	168.0
1965	1,440.0	1,069.4	125.6	58.6	30.7	155.7
1966	1,445.0	1,080.8	114.6	63.1	32.0	154.5
1967	1,410.0	1,068.7	103.7	53.4	28.4	155.8

* Estimated: excludes U.S.S.R. and other eastern European countries, China mainland, and North Korea.
Source: *Federal Reserve Bulletin*, June, 1963, p. 787, July, 1968, p. A–87, and October, 1968, p. A–87.

these currency reserves reached a level that caused concern among International Monetary Fund members, government officials, private bankers, other financial interests, and even the general public. Doubts regarding the ability of the United States and British governments to keep the value of their currency units equivalent to gold at $35 per fine ounce caused many to hoard gold bars, coins, and other forms of gold. Speculators expected the price of gold to rise and that there could be no potential loss, aside from the loss of interest, involved in hoarding gold. Hence, it is not surprising that most of the gold produced during the 1960's plus some placed on the market by the Soviet Union went into hoards and other nonmonetary channels. By 1967–68, the chief suppliers were withholding gold from the market in the expectation of an increase in the official price (see Chart 28–1).

In mid-March, 1968, the central bankers of seven commercial and industrial nations agreed to (1) suspend the London gold pool,

CHART 28–1

<small>Gold: Estimated New Supplies and Absorptions, 1951–68</small>
(In Millions of U.S. Dollars)

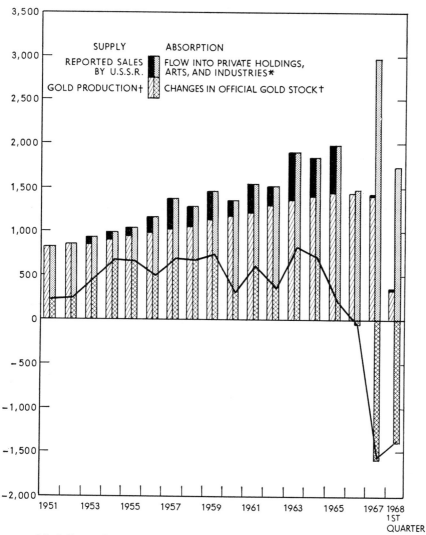

* Including purchases by mainland China amounting to the equivalent of $150 million in 1965, $75 million in 1966, and $20 million in 1967.
† Excluding CMEA countries, mainland China, etc.
Source: International Monetary Fund, *Annual Report of the Executive Directors for the Fiscal Year Ended April 30, 1968* (Washington, D.C., 1968), p. 86.

(2) stop buying from and selling gold to the general public, (3) permit the market price of gold to seek and maintain its own level, and (4) sell gold to one another and cooperating central banks at the official price of $35 per ounce. If new reserves are not to be obtained in the gold market, the future needs for international liquidity must be met by an increase in the supply of credit money. At the end of 1967, the international reserves of the United States were $17.83 billion (see Table 28–3).

TABLE 28-3

UNITED STATES INTERNATIONAL RESERVES, 1961–67
(In Millions of Dollars)

End of Year	Total Reserve Assets	Gold Stock		Convertible Foreign Currency	Reserve Position in IMF
		Total	In Treasury		
1961..........	18,753	16,947	16,899	116	1,690
1962..........	17,220	16,057	15,978	99	1,064
1963..........	16,843	15,596	15,513	212	1,035
1964..........	16,672	15,471	15,388	432	769
1965..........	15,450	13,806	13,733	781	863
1966..........	14,882	13,235	13,159	1,321	326
1967..........	17,830	12,065	11,982	2,345	420

Source: *Federal Reserve Bulletin*, June, 1968, p. A–73.

ADEQUACY OF INTERNATIONAL RESERVES

The question of the adequacy of international reserves has received considerable attention in recent years. Unfortunately, inflation tends to absorb any surplus a country possesses; hence, preventing a scarcity of reserves depends upon attaining a high degree of general price stability. The two aspects of the problem of international reserves are the total amount and the distribution of reserves among nations.

The term *liquidity*, as used in credit analysis, has the same connotation in international and domestic finance. It means the ability of a debtor to meet current and other short-term claims against him at any time. This ability depends on the amount of the debtor's current assets relative to his current obligations. Because of the number of variables, it is difficult to estimate any country's liquidity position accurately. Certain countries have resources that permit them to acquire new reserves which are classified as supplements to reserves (such as conditional credit facilities available in the International Monetary Fund and credits resulting from "swap" arrangements).

Swap Arrangements.   In order to combat disturbances in the foreign-exchange market that followed revaluation of the German mark and Dutch guilder, the Federal Reserve Bank of New York (as agent for the Federal Reserve System and in cooperation with foreign central banks) started trading in foreign exchange markets. In order to have sufficient funds with which to operate, the Federal Reserve Bank of New York built up a network of reciprocal credit or "swap"

TABLE 28–4

FEDERAL RESERVE RECIPROCAL CURRENCY ARRANGEMENTS

	Amount of Facility (In Millions of Dollars Equivalent)	
Other Party to Arrangement	December 31, 1966	December 31, 1967
Austrian National Bank	100	100
National Bank of Belgium	150	225
Bank of Canada	500	750
National Bank of Denmark	...	100
Bank of England	1,350	1,500
Bank of France	100	100
German Federal Bank	400	750
Bank of Italy	600	750
Bank of Japan	450	750
Bank of Mexico	...	130
Netherlands Bank	150	225
Bank of Norway	...	100
Bank of Sweden	100	200
Swiss National Bank	200	400
Bank for International Settlements:		
Dollars/Swiss francs	200	400
Dollars/authorized European currencies other than		
Swiss francs	200	600
Total	4,500	7,080

Source: *Fifty-Fourth Annual Report of the Board of Governors of the Federal Reserve System Covering Operations for the Year 1967* (Washington, D.C., 1967), p. 278.

arrangements with the central banks of Western Europe, Canada, Mexico, Japan, and the Bank for International Settlements (see Table 28–4).

Euro-Dollar Market.   World liquidity has been increased by the growth of the Euro-dollar market, which developed from practically nothing in 1958 to over $25 billion at the present time. This market for lending and borrowing the dollar and other important convertible world currencies is located primarily in Europe. The chief intermediaries in the market are large commercial and private banks, merchants, and a few investment houses. Funds flow into the market from commercial and central banks all over the world, from official monetary institutions and other government agencies, commercial and industrial enterprises, and individuals.

The commercial banks in London and other European cities make the Euro-dollar market in the sense that they are willing (1) to accept Euro-dollars in the form of time deposits in large amounts, such as $1 million or more (using negotiable certificates of deposits in some cases), and (2) to make short-term loans primarily to European borrowers and to a lesser extent to American and Japanese borrowers. The unique characteristic of this market is that each transaction takes place outside the country where the currency originates, that is, the Euro-dollar market is outside the United States, and the Euro-sterling market is outside the United Kingdom. Funds are lent for periods from as short as one day to as long as 18 months.

The market affects not only the interest rates in different countries but also the "spot" and "forward" rates in the exchange markets because interest arbitrage is a common practice. Funds, which are obtained by the market in the form of deposits, are lent to business enterprises to finance industrial or commercial transactions or retained by a bank to improve its reserve or liquidity position. Of the $25 billion held outside the United States, $14 billion is owned by foreign central banks and other foreign governmental agencies, $7 billion by commercial banks outside the United States, and the remainder by other foreign holders.[10] Often the Euro-dollar market and the Bank for International Settlements are ahead of the Fund in providing liquidity.

Ratios.   In addition to international reserves having been increased, supplementary credit arrangements have increased their effectiveness. A number of ratios have been formulated to measure the adequacy of reserves. The most important of these is the ratio between a country's official reserves and its foreign trade. A variation of this ratio is one that relates a country's official reserves and existing credit arrangements to the amount of imports of merchandise on the assumption that a larger supply of reserves is needed when the import trade of a country increases. However, most international transactions are financed privately and therefore the relationship between mer-

---

[10] See Oscar L. Altman, "Euro-Dollars," *Finance and Development*, Vol. IV, No. 1 (March, 1967), p. 13.

chandise imports and official reserves is remote. It should be remembered that the functions of official reserves are to settle imbalances in a country's international transactions and to be used to prevent excessive fluctuations in its exchange rate.

Today, an important question is: Are the world's reserves sufficient to permit the free trade of nations and to maintain fixed exchange rates without direct exchange control and still have sufficient reserves to finance the economic growth of individual nations? In the aggregate, the supply of reserves may be adequate for all three purposes as measured by tests such as the relationship among reserves, money supply, domestic growth, and the price level; or the relationship of reserves and the claims that may be brought against them due to balance of payments deficits.

However, regardless of the adequacy of reserves in the aggregate, the fact that they are poorly distributed throughout the world means that more international reserves are needed. Currently, the major industrial and high-income countries have sufficient reserves while the underdeveloped countries are in chronic need of them. Another variable in the question of worldwide adequacy of reserves stems from their composition and the vulnerability of key currencies that make up an increasing percentage of the total.

Special Drawing Rights. After four years of study and discussion, the countries of the "free" world reached an agreement on a plan to supplement existing international monetary reserves by means of "special drawing rights" on the International Monetary Fund. In submitting the outline for the plan to the Board of Governors at its annual meeting in Rio de Janeiro, Brazil, in September, 1967, the managing director stated that the plan was based on the principle "that the international community should be able to control reserves instead of the reserves controlling the community."[11] This plan will provide the means to create additional reserves in amounts deemed necessary, eliminating the risk that the world will suffer from a lack of liquidity if and when needed.[12] Some bankers, economists, and others regard the plan as the most significant step taken in the international monetary field since the establishment of the International Monetary Fund in 1944.

The report to the Fund recommending procedures, within the framework of the Fund, for obtaining supplementary international

[11] International Monetary Fund, *Summary Proceedings of the Twenty-Second Annual Meeting of the Board of Governors* (Washington, D.C.; 1968), p. 22.

[12] *Ibid.*, pp. 271–79.

reserves was the result of discussions and negotiations among committee members representing the Fund and the "Group of Ten" (the countries that participated in the Fund's general arrangement to borrow). The group rejected the suggestion to create a new type of money and accepted the principle of creating new reserves by borrowing under conditions established by the Fund.

Since the beginning of its operations, the International Monetary Fund had made its resources available to member countries which had contributed them in accordance with their quotas under the condition that such borrowing must be repaid in from three to no more than five years. The creation of the special drawing rights will not reduce or impair the existing ability of member countries to draw currencies of other countries from the Fund.

Special drawing rights (SDR's) are to be created and allocated on the books of the Fund as credit to participating members in proportion to their quotas. The SDR units are to have the same value as the gold dollar defined as 0.888671 grams of gold. The Fund will determine the initial number of SDR's to be created and allocated among participants. If a member country does choose to participate in the plan, it must accept SDR's when offered in amounts that will not cause its SDR holdings to exceed three times its quota, and it may use them to make "official" settlements with other countries (but not to private institutions or individuals). There may be some delay in putting the special drawing-rights plan into operation because 85 percent of the voting power of the participating members is required on determination of the base period, the timing of this period, and the allocation of the special drawing rights.

When the special drawing-rights system begins to function, each participating member will be assigned a specified number of SDR's that it may draw during the first basic period (assume five years). The amount of each participating member country's special drawing rights will depend on its quota in the Fund. If the executive directors of the Fund start by authorizing $1 billion SDR's, the United States share would be about $246 million; the United Kingdom's, $117 million; West Germany's, $47 million; and so on for each country. Presumably, governments would count their SDR's as part of their international reserves. Each participating country must keep an average of 30 percent of its special drawing rights on deposit with the Fund over the base period; and, if it uses more than 70 percent of its allotment, it must reconstitute enough of them to reestablish its 30 percent balance.

The special drawing rights have been referred to as "paper gold" and, if one accepts the concept of "inviolability of international obligations," they may be as safe as gold. Nevertheless, gold may be preferable as a reserve because there is no reconstruction requirement attached to its use; and, in addition, it would be safer in case of a major war. Interest is to be paid to the holders of SDR's, and this advantage may be sufficient to cause many countries to use them freely for reserve purposes. Originally, special drawing rights were considered to be a supplement to gold but, if current gold policies are continued, they may become the most important form of international reserves.

BANK FOR INTERNATIONAL SETTLEMENTS

The Bank for International Settlements, established in 1930 in Basel, Switzerland, was originally expected to become a world bank; but, due largely to the reluctance of the United States, it has developed into a central bank for European central banks. According to the original plan, the Bank's seven central-bank sponsors (Belgium, France, Germany, Italy, Japan, United Kingdom, and the United States) were to be represented permanently on the Bank's board of directors by their presidents or governors and a second appointed director. Other participating central banks were to be represented as a group, with the number of directors limited to 25.

Each of the seven sponsoring countries was allotted an equal amount of the Bank's stock, which the central banks could purchase or sell to others. The capital was guaranteed by the original subscribers—the five European central banks and two private banking groups acting in the place of the central banks in Japan and the United States (J. P. Morgan and Company, the First National Bank of New York, and the First National Bank of Chicago). Other central banks were given the privilege of subscribing, but few did so because of the chaotic international conditions during the early 1930's. The charter of BIS was revised in 1950, and all European central banks, except the Bank of Spain and the State Bank of the U.S.S.R., have subsequently purchased stock. The shares held by the Japanese banking group were repurchased by the central banks that were founder members, most of whom retained their stock. All the American-held stock was sold in the United States market, and most of it has been resold to Europeans (but there are still a number of scattered private shareholders). The rights to representation and to vote are not linked to ownership, so the status of BIS as a central bank for central banks is assured (about three fourths of the outstanding stock is owned by central banks).

Compared to the World Bank and the Fund, the authorized

capital of the Bank for International Settlements is small, 500 million
Swiss gold francs, of which about one fourth has been paid in (equal
to 41 million current United States gold dollars). About 40 percent of
the total assets of about $2.6 billion is in gold. As indicative of U.S.
policy at that time, the Federal Reserve Bank of New York was not
permitted to participate officially in the plan for international cooperation, and the United States has never taken its seat on the board of
directors. However, the Federal Reserve Bank of New York now acts
as the correspondent bank for BIS in the United States. The Bank for
International Settlements is managed by a board of directors composed of the presidents or governors of the five founding European
central banks, a second director appointed by each, and three elected
directors from among the presidents or governors of other central
banks (at present, the Netherlands, Sweden, Switzerland, and their
nominees).

The powers of the Bank for International Settlements are less
restrictive than are those of the Fund or the World Bank. They
include the rights to (1) buy and sell gold and gold bullion, bills of
exchange, Treasury bills, and other securities for its own account or
for the account of central banks; (2) make secured advances to or
borrow from central banks; (3) act as depository and correspondent
for central banks and arrange for the latter to act in similar capacities
for it; (4) carry on credit operations for banks and others, in any
market, provided that the central bank in the country where the
money market is located does not object; and (5) enter into special
agreements with central banks to facilitate the settlement of international transactions among them. However, the Bank for International
Settlements may not (1) issue notes payable at sight to bearer, (2)
"accept" bills of exchange, or (3) make advances to government. The
Bank's principal dealings are with central banks but it also participates
in "swaps" and other international cooperative ventures. The Bank's
income is derived from its loans and investments and commissions
collected for acting as agent for the European Monetary Agreement
nations, the European Coal and Steel Community, central banks,
governments, international financial organization, and others.

The Bank for International Settlements acted as trustee and
reparation agent in the collection of German reparations until these
payments were ended by the Hoover International Debt Moratorium
(June 20, 1931). During the spring and summer of 1931 the Bank
made loans and organized lending syndicates to meet the international
crisis of that period, but, when England left the gold standard in

September, 1931, the Bank ceased making international loans to keep currencies tied to gold. During the trying months of the international economic crisis, the Bank was a rallying place for the officials of the central banks of the world and served as "a common center of contact, counsel, and collaboration." During World War II the Bank's activities were almost suspended and its place in the postwar world was in doubt (in its final declaration, the Bretton Woods Conference recommended that BIS be liquidated). After World War II, BIS worked on troublesome postwar problems and soon found a place for itself, chiefly as a central bank for European central banks. The Bank has continued to work for stable exchanges and for better international monetary, credit, and trade conditions. Its annual report has come to be one of the most important documents of its kind, eagerly awaited by government officials, bankers, economists, and others.

SUMMARY

The countries of the free world suffered from a breakdown in the international payments system in the 1930's which was accompanied by a decrease in production, employment, and general prices, as well as political extremism that led to World War II. In planning the rebuilding of the international monetary and economic system that cumulated in the Bretton Woods Conference in 1944, representatives of the Allied world proposed the creation of an international monetary fund and international development bank. By the end of 1945, the necessary number of members (based on quotas) had accepted the Fund Agreement and World Bank plan.

The allover objective of the International Monetary Fund is to increase prosperity among all member countries. The Fund possesses sufficient flexibility so that there has been an increase in membership each year, from 30 in 1945 to 107 in 1968. Each member subscribes for a share of the capital (called "quota") in an amount being determined by the country's financial ability. Quotas are reviewed every five years and increased according to the need for international reserves (50 percent in 1959 and an additional 25 percent in 1964–65). The Fund has also arranged to supplement its resources in case of need by borrowing arrangements with the 10 largest members of the Fund. The most important change in the international monetary field was the establishment of the two gold price system in mid-March 1968 and the creation of special drawing rights, which is now in process. The use of SDR's is expected to provide a permanent supply of international reserve money, because the credits which will be advanced to participating members need not be repaid.

Member countries are committed to a fixed rate of exchange and to unrestricted exchange on current accounts in international transactions. In case of temporary disequilibrium in their balance-of-payment situations, they may draw on the Fund. Ordinary drawing privileges and repayment requirements are designed to keep the Fund's assets in a liquid condition.

The soundest international monetary system cannot guarantee achievement of national objectives of any given country. Although the existence of a supplementary source of reserves does not solve the problem of balance-of-payments deficits, it gives deficit countries (such as the United States) more time and freedom to adjust their economic affairs. The future of the international monetary system depends on how wisely the United States and other major countries manage their national affairs, including keeping labor costs below the increase in productivity, preventing inflation, maintaining sustainable growth, solving the balance-of-payments deficit problems, and preventing the waste due to wars.

QUESTIONS AND PROBLEMS

1. Identify: (*a*) gold standard, (*b*) competition in depreciation, (*c*) principle of comparative cost, (*d*) Bretton Woods Agreements, and (*e*) "borrowing" from the International Monetary Fund.
2. Distinguish between: (*a*) Board of Governors and Board of Directors of the International Monetary Fund, (*b*) ordinary and "special" drawing rights from the Fund, and (*c*) fixed and floating rate of exchange.
3. What problems faced the world at the end of World War II? Was the creation of the International Monetary Fund a step in the right direction? What are the purposes of the International Monetary Fund?
4. Analyze: In 1946 "the International Monetary Fund was thought of as a vehicle for reestablishing a form of international gold standard, or more accurately a form of gold-exchange standard. Such a conception, however, did less than justice to the revolutionary character of the accomplishment." (Ralph A. Young, "Making Peace with Gold," *The Morgan Guaranty Survey* [New York, Morgan Guaranty Bank, June, 1968], p. 7.)
5. Analyze: "Judged by the sustained increase in world trade and output of the last twenty years, the gold exchange standard has served its purpose well." (Pierre-Paul Schweitzer, "World Payments Problems," *International Financial News* [Washington, D.C.: International Monetary Fund, June 14, 1968], p. 201.)

6. Criticize: As "the existing stock of monetary gold is sufficient in view of the prospective establishment of the facility for Special Drawing Rights, they no longer feel it necessary to buy gold from the market. Finally, they agreed that henceforth they will not sell to monetary authorities to replace gold sold in private markets." ("Meeting of Governors of Central Banks Contributing to the Gold Pool: Communique," *Federal Reserve Bulletin*, March, 1968, p. 254.)

7. Explain: A "large part of the additions to reserves in the last 8 years were in the form of dollar holdings of foreign governments and these increases resulted largely from the U.S. balance of payments deficit. . . . If new gold output goes to private uses and the United States deficit is eliminated, how are the nations of the world to add to their reserves?" (Federal Reserve Bank of Richmond, *Monthly Review*, June, 1968, p. 4.)

8. Explain: The "Fund's transactions during 1967 were conducted mainly with developing countries. There were no drawings by the United States or the United Kingdom, and the total net of both members was reduced during the year. Those of the United Kingdom declined from $2,410 million to $1,509 million, and those of the United States from $905 million to $792 million." (International Monetary Fund and the International Bank for Reconstruction and Development, *Finance and Development*, March, 1968, p. 53.)

9. Analyze: "First, SDR's will be more readily available than the credit that the IMF now provides through drawing in the credit tranches." (Federal Reserve Bank of New York, *Monthly Review*, January, 1968, p. 10.)

10. Discuss: An increase in the price of gold "is neither necessary nor desirable as a solution to the problem of international payments imbalance or to the problem of assuring adequate growth in international reserves. It would be highly disruptive and highly inequitable." (William McC. Martin, Jr., "The Price of Gold Is Not the Problem," *Federal Reserve Bulletin*, February, 1968, p. 120.)

CHAPTER 29

Development Banks

MUCH OF the planning for political and economic development during and following World War II was on an international basis with the creation of the United Nations in the political area, the international Monetary Fund in the field of money and short-term credit, the International Bank for Reconstruction and Development in the area of investment banking, and the rejected International Trade Organization in the field of international trade. Soon thereafter a number of regional development banks were created to help rebuild the economies of former belligerent nations and to promote the growth of developing countries.

The large international and regional institutions were organized to channel funds from the more highly industrialized countries to the less developed ones. Multinational agencies are now making over $5 billion available annually to emerging countries, and new banks are being organized to serve certain sections of the free world exclusively. The idea has permeated to lower levels, with development banks being formed on national and local bases. The purpose is to achieve a faster rate of economic growth—expanding the ability of nations to produce more goods and services that their people need and want.

Among the development banks operating on an international scale, the most important are the International Bank for Reconstruction and Development, popularly known as the "World Bank," the International Development Association, and the International Finance Corporation. Regional banks that serve particular sections of the world include the European Investment Bank, Inter-American Development Bank, and the Asian Development Bank. Numerous other development banks operate on national or local levels.

BACKGROUND

Economists have been interested in economic growth since the beginning of economic theory. Their interest has gradually shifted from the high regard for money and the enrichment of the state by an increase in treasuries, to the present-day stress on expansion in national and per capita real income.

Accelerating Growth. The concept of normal growth contains allowances for increases in productivity and in population. The increase in productivity is an index of the efficiency with which the nation's resources are used to produce goods and services measured in terms of output per machine, per unit of capital, or a combination of both. The most comprehensive measure of productivity available is output per unit of labor and capital because it is an indicator of the productive efficiency of all resources.

During the past 100 years, the increased efficiency of capital and labor and the growth in population have contributed about equally to the expansion in output. Since World War II, the strongest stimulus to economic growth has been research and development. The public and private laboratories have contributed new products, technologies, production methods, managerial procedures, and industries. In addition, the amount of new information available for current and future use has been doubling every 10 years. One of the major functions of foreign aid is to share this new information with developing countries.

Reconstruction Period. During the early stages of the reconstruction period following World War II, most of the U.S. aid came directly from the United States Treasury. Foreign assistance was provided through lend-lease, United Nations Relief and Rehabilitation Administration (UNRRA), and under the Marshall Plan and its successors. In his speech of June 5, 1946, General Marshall stated: "Europe's requirements for the next three or four years of foreign food and other essential products . . . are so much greater than her present ability to pay. . . . It is logical that the United States should do whatever it is able to do to assist in the return of normal economic health in the world, without which there would be no political stability and no assured peace." After a number of meetings the Organization for European Economic Cooperation (April 16, 1948) was created, and its membership eventually included 17 European nations and Japan. When the broad objectives of the European relief program had been achieved, the United States government aid program was directed at economic development in underdeveloped countries through the World Bank and its two subsidiaries as well as regional development banks.

The United States government has continued its program of economic aid through the Agency for International Development (AID); Public Law 480, which authorized the Agricultural Trade

Development and Assistance Program; and the Export-Import Bank of Washington, which was organized to make loans and guarantees to facilitate the export and import trade of the United States.

Each year, it has become more difficult for the sponsors of our various aid programs to obtain the needed legislation and appropriations from Congress; but the ultimate end of these programs and the day when the job of economic development can be turned over to international, regional, and private agencies does not seem to be in sight. Since United States public funds are involved in the functioning of several of these international organizations, the National Advisory Council on International Monetary and Financial Problems was created in order to coordinate the policies of the representatives of the United States in the Fund and the World Bank with the agencies of the U.S. government in lending and other matters. It must be remembered that borrowed dollars are usually spent in the United States, which means that the demand for American products is increased.

Aiding Developing Countries. Most of the nonindustrialized countries have natural resources but lack the capital and trained personnel to use them effectively. Some of the grants and loans made to such countries have been "frittered away" on useless or wasteful projects which demonstrated the need for more effective planning and supervision and better trained personnel. Although the United States has reduced its foreign aid below the level of the decade followingWorld War II, it is still giving economic aid along with other countries such as France, West Germany, the United Kingdom, Japan, and others that have been recipients of U.S. aid.

The 17 members of the Organization for Economic Cooperation and Development contributed $11.4 billion in 1967 in private and public capital funds to less developed countries. The United States accounts for the largest actual flow of capital, having supplied almost one half of the total. Of the 1967 foreign investment in underdeveloped countries, almost 40 percent was private funds which took the form of direct investment and purchases of securities. In March, 1968, the United Nations Conference on Trade and Development at its meeting in New Delhi, India, set the goal for each industrialized nation's investment in underdeveloped countries at 1 percent of its gross national product.

The key to further betterment in living standards at home and abroad is a continuing rise in productivity through the use of more efficient plants and equipment, improvements in workers' skills, and a reduction in the birth rate. It is assumed that, as developing nations become more industrialized, the population explosion will come to an end, and any increase in population will be due primarily to a reduction in the death rate. The United Nations labeled the 1960's as the "Decade of Development," and this description seems justified in view of the improvements wrought by the development banks and other agencies in the economies of the developing nations which contain half of the world's population. Their steel production has increased threefold, their industrial production has doubled, and transportation systems have been improved and expanded. The gross national product of some countries is expected to double during the 1960's (including Greece, Taiwan, Israel, Nicaragua, Korea, Panama, Spain, and Thailand).

Although the growth in industrial production has been impressive, many of the changes are not reflected in the size of the gross national product because the time lag between investment and benefits flowing therefrom may be years. For illustration, money being spent on education of children in underdeveloped countries may not benefit the economy for 12 or more years. Furthermore, investments in electric power, roads, water systems, and other public utilities are made, in part, in anticipation of future needs.

Industrial investments are usually made to meet demand, but manufacturing projects may be delayed by lack of trained personnel. Improvements in agricultural methods seem to be the most logical objective for investment in underdeveloped countries, but use of new machinery and equipment means displacement of existing farm laborers and an increase in unemployment. Unfortunately, the increase in production of agricultural products has not been sufficient to feed the increased population in developing countries. Now, the World Bank and the International Finance Corporation are giving more attention to production and use of fertilizers.

WORLD BANK GROUP

The World Bank group is composed of the International Bank for Reconstruction and Development, generally known as the "World Bank," and its two affiliates, the International Finance Corporation (IFC) and the International Development Association (IDA). These organizations are associated with the United Nations and have the status of special agencies. They share both a common administration and a common objective—to improve the standard of living in member countries by providing financial and technical assistance through governments, governmental agencies, and other organizations in member countries. The two affiliates were created to make investments of the type which the World Bank was prohibited from making. The lending and other activities of the international development banks are supplemented by other organizations that are not classified as banks. In a free society, economic growth is the result of activities of individuals, business concerns, and governments; but, in the beginning of a new development program, more rapid results may be achieved by making loans to governmental agencies that are made responsible for special projects (such as those based on natural resources).

International Bank for Reconstruction and Development. The second of the so-called Bretton Woods "Twins" is the International Bank for Reconstruction and Development (World Bank). As stated in the Articles of Agreement, the main purpose of the Bank is "to assist in the reconstruction and development of member countries by facilitating the investment of capital for productive purposes, including the restoration of economies destroyed or disrupted by war, the reconversion of productive facilities to peacetime needs and the encouragement of the development of productive facilities and resources in less developed countries."

The World Bank is supervised by a board of governors (identical with that of the Fund) that meets once a year, 20 full-time executive directors and their alternates, a president, vice president, and staff members. (The Bank now has over 600 employees.) The Board of Governors is composed of one representative from each member country appointed by his national government. The representatives chosen are usually individuals who hold cabinet positions, such as finance minister or secretary of the treasury, and who are able to present the views of their governments on international financial questions.

Of the executive directors, five are appointed by the five largest shareholders of the Bank—United States, France, West Germany, United Kingdom, and India—and the remaining 15 are appointed to represent the other member countries. The Board of Governors, by a four fifths majority of the total voting power,[1] may increase the number of executive directors (it has increased the number from 12

[1] Each member country has voting power equal to 250 votes plus one additional vote for each share of capital stock held. This means that the United States has 22.22 percent of the total voting power (51,850 votes); United Kingdom, 10.56 percent (24,650 votes); West Germany, 5.25 percent (12,250 votes); France, 4.33 percent (10,100 votes); and India, 3.32 percent (7,750 votes). See International Monetary Fund, *1967 Annual Report* (Washington, D.C., 1967), p. 162.

to 20). The executive directors, who appoint their own alternates, are responsible for the general operations of the Bank and such other functions delegated to them by the Board of Governors. As in the case of the Fund, member countries deal with the Bank only through their Treasuries, central banks, stabilization funds, and similar fiscal agents.

The Articles of Agreement of the World Bank require each member country to subscribe for capital stock in an amount determined by the formula used to fix the quotas of countries for the International Monetary Fund. At the end of 20 years of operation, 107 members had subscribed to $22.9 billion of the Bank's capital stock (the total is increased when new members join and decreased when members withdraw). Of the subscribed capital, only $2 billion has been paid in and the unpaid portion is subject to call at any time. The Bank finances with borrowed funds, but the existence of its capital stock (actual and potential) is a factor in the high credit rating of the Bank's bonds and debentures, because investors know that the unpaid portion of the U.S. subscription is in excess of all the Bank's debts.

Almost from the beginning, the World Bank has been both a lender and a borrower, obtaining most of its loanable funds by borrowing from private investors in the United States, Canada, and the countries of western Europe. Although Switzerland is not a member of the Bank, it has opened its capital markets to it. When bonds and notes are sold in member countries, they are denominated in the currencies of these countries, but it does not follow that all the bonds or notes are purchased and held by private investors in these countries. Although interest rates are low, the bonds are popular with investors, and their investment rating is about the same as that of government issues.

In Article III of its Articles of Agreement, the World Bank is authorized to make or participate in making loans in amounts equal to its unimpaired paid-up capital and surplus, and out of funds raised in the market of a member, or "otherwise borrowed by the Bank." In addition, it may guarantee in whole or part loans "made by private investors through investment channels." The Bank's loans may be to governments and governmental agencies and to private enterprises if domiciled in a member-country's territory, provided the loan is guaranteed by the member-country's government or a governmental agency (government credit must be behind loans).

In order to increase its credit assistance to borrowers, the World

Bank may (1) sell its loan paper to commercial banks and other financial institutions to free funds for further lending, (2) participate with other banks in making loans so that its available funds may be stretched over more loans, and (3) guarantee loans made by other lenders. The Bank determines the terms and conditions of loans (amount, interest, maturity, amortization, and dates of payments) commissions charged in connection with them. The loan contract specifies the currency or currencies in which a loan is to be repaid.

Interest rates on loans obtained through the World Bank are 1 percent above the Bank's cost of borrowing funds, and they now reflect the high interest rates prevailing in the United States and other countries throughout the free world. To an increasing extent, bond issues of the World Bank are being sold in Canada, West Germany, Switzerland, and other foreign countries. About one third of the loans are made to finance electric power plants and their facilities, one third for transportation facilities such as railroads, ports, and transport equipment; and the remainder for miscellaneous projects, including the establishment of development banks.

In its lending operations, the World Bank follows certain techniques that necessitate answers to: (1) will the borrower repay the loan (creditworthiness); (2) are the proposed projects the best for the member country (selection of projects); (3) are appraisals of the projects satisfactory in terms of economic, technical, managerial, organizational, commercial, and finance aspects; and (4) are there provisions for general supervision of projects. India, the largest member country, is also the largest debtor. Other large debtors include Japan, Mexico, Pakistan, Colombia, and Brazil.

Funds borrowed through the World Bank affect the balance of international payments of the national governments involved. Therefore the U.S. director must approve the loan before dollars are lent. By 1950, the Bank recognized that the ability to use capital productively ("know-how") was lacking in many areas and that the need for trained personnel to administer economic programs was imperative. However, it was not until January, 1956 that the Economic Development Institute of the World Bank was opened; and since that time, the institute has broadened its training by offering "a modest technical assistance program."[2]

The Articles of Agreement permit the Bank to make loans only for specific purposes and require it to give due attention to economy

---

[2] John H. Adler, *The Economic Development Institute of the World Bank*, reprint from *The International Development Review*, Vol. V, No. 1 (March, 1963).

and efficiency and see that the proceeds of the loans are used only for those purposes for which they are granted. In addition, proceeds of a loan are to be made available only to meet expenses of a project when they are actually incurred. In order to carry out these conditions, the World Bank not only controls the disbursement of funds but also supervises the physical development of the projects financed.[3]

In their operations, the World Bank and its subsidiary, the International Development Association, are more "headquarters-centered" than most other international organizations. Although there are two regional offices in Africa and one in Europe and "resident representatives" in developing countries, about 95 percent of the permanent staff members are in Washington.[4] The Bank and IDA carry out their tasks by means of periodic visits by staff members for a few days or longer to developing countries and by sending missions to survey economic conditions, to review and appraise old and new projects, and to make recommendations. The latter cover not only the proposed projects but also how they are to be financed. The World Bank is not only an international financial institution but also a development agency that provides a wide range of technical assistance to its members.

International Development Association.   The high credit standards set in the Articles of Agreement for loans granted by the World Bank prevent the Bank from financing many worthwhile governmental development projects. Consequently, in 1960, the owners of the Bank established the International Development Association (IDA) to make substandard loans. Its resources are used to finance a variety of development projects in underdeveloped countries. As an affiliate of the World Bank, IDA has the same management but fewer member countries (98 as compared with 107 at the present time, but the memberships change annually), and subscribed capital of $1 billion.

IDA has two classes of members: Part I member countries provide most of the funds used for projects, and Part II countries are recipients of loans. (In recent years, some of the Part II countries have become suppliers of development aid as well as being recipients.) The International Development Association makes loans and/or extends credit to private or public institutions to finance specific projects which may or may not be revenue-producing (such as sanitation

[3] Norman G. Jones, "Disbursing World Bank Loans," *Finance and Development, The Fund and Bank Review*, March, 1967, pp. 51–56.

[4] David Gordan, "The World Bank's Mission in Eastern Africa," *Finance and Development*, March, 1968, p. 37.

projects, water facilities, and highways). Loans made by IDA are repayable in foreign exchange and those made to date are subject to a service charge of three fourths of 1 percent. Repayment on such loans begins after 10 years at an annual rate of 1 percent for the next 10 years and thereafter 3 percent for the last 30 years.

The International Development Association may use its own discretion in seeking the appropriate member country's guarantee prior to making a private loan, but to date, all loans have been made on government credit. From the viewpoint of the borrower, one advantageous feature of the repayment terms is IDA's willingness to accept the debtor's own currency. Although IDA advances hard currency, it may be repaid in soft currency for which there may be little or no international demand. IDA is using the same policies as those used by the World Bank in the disbursement of funds and supervision of projects being financed (with surprisingly good results).

The United States has about the same percentage of shares (32.06 percent) of IDA's capital as in the other international organizations and is among the Part I nations that paid their subscriptions in gold or freely convertible currency over a five-year period. The Part II nations pay only 10 percent of their shares in gold and convertible currency and the remainder in their own currencies, which can neither be converted into other currencies or used to finance exports from the borrower country without its consent. This means that Part II members make only a token contribution to the International Development Association.

The board of governors, executive directors, president, and staff members of the World Bank serve ex officio in the same capacity in IDA; so, at least for some time, there will not be separate officers and staffs. IDA, which has been called the "lady of easy virtue," was expected to be used by "neutralist nations" and others who may wish to avoid other lending agencies for political reasons; but the list of projects and their location in its annual reports seems to indicate that IDA is popular among the same countries that also use the World Bank. Doubtless, some loans made by IDA could have been made by the World Bank but were shifted to IDA because of the easier terms and conditions. Much of the credit granted by IDA, now in excess of $1.7 billion, has been used to finance improvements in transportation systems in developing countries. IDA obtains loanable funds from subscriptions of members, earnings, loans from the World Bank, and contributions from governments.

The credit position of some member countries is due not only to the size of their total debts but also to the nature of their maturity structures. Some loans have maturities of only three to five years, when maturities of 10 to 15 years would have been more appropriate. In some cases, the structure of the debt is so unfavorable that half the outstanding amount must be repaid in five years. Furthermore, the problem of financing this foreign debt has been made more difficult by the decline in world prices of their principal export products.

IDA loans are made because of balance-of-payments difficulties, and there is no intention on the part of the sponsors to subsidize foreign projects at only three fourths of 1 percent service charge on loans of 50 years; hence IDA lends only to governments which lend funds to public or private revenue-producing enterprises on terms that reflect the local capital market rates. The "second round" of lending that IDA is preparing for includes assistance to the 30 new nations that have become members. They will need not only re-sources but also technical assistance in preparing projects to be financed. In addition to the type of loans that IDA has been making, it anticipates granting others for agricultural and educational purposes. The latter seems to be one of the new frontiers that IDA is con-sidering.

The pressure on developing countries to provide the type of education needed for the various skills in an industrial country is so great that outside help may be needed. The existence of surplus labor has prevented the mechanization of agriculture because of the number of families dependent on subsistence farming. In many countries, land reform has consisted of breaking up large estates into small subsistence farms with a decline in productivity.

International Finance Corporation.   Soon after the World Bank began operations in 1946, it became apparent that there was need for private capital which the Bank was not authorized to supply; consequently, the staff of the Bank suggested the creation of a new corporation that would be permitted to lend directly to private busi-ness without a government guarantee of loans. In response, the Inter-national Finance Corporation (IFC) was created in 1955 and began operations the next year. This corporation now has 85 members and total subscribed capital of $100,150,000. In 1965, IFC was authorized to borrow directly from the World Bank in an amount up to four times its capital and surplus. IFC has a separate staff from that of the World Bank and IDA and it follows different operating procedures because the problem is one of selecting projects to be financed with venture capital rather than projects requiring debt capital.

The International Finance Corporation has financed relatively small corporations by granting loans of from $2 to $3 million. It may finance as much as 50 percent of an enterprise but assumes no responsibility for management of the firms financed. It avoids financing projects where private capital may be obtained on reasonable terms. The original IFC loan contracts provided for participation in profits, for conversion of its interest into share capital in whole or part, and/or interest of a nonfixed type (being in many respects an equity-type transaction similar to those involved in small-business investment company financing in the United States). In 1960, after four years of experience with this type of arrangement, the president of IFC recommended that the charter be changed so as to permit direct investment in equities; and, it was approved by the required number of member countries the following year.

IFC takes minority equity participation in manufacturing, development and other companies in underdeveloped countries.[5] Customarily, the Corporation combines equity purchases with long-term loans; but straight equity financing is increasing. Now, there is very little financing by purchases of convertible debentures and practically none without equity features. However, there is no plan for IFC to hold equities of companies permanently, and the Corporation has sold some shares to private investors. A number of IFC investment ventures are shared by Edge corporations, which are affiliates of American commercial banks, but it never provides all of the capital of foreign ventures. The IFC realizes that a large reservoir of private capital exists in many underdeveloped countries and that this needs to be tapped if continued economic expansion is to become a reality in such countries. The Corporation takes an active role in establishing national and local development companies (being an important source of equity funds for 17 development companies in 15 countries). The Corporation also assists in developing foreign capital markets by underwriting securities, thereby broadening ownership of many family-held or closely held companies.

REGIONAL DEVELOPMENT BANKS

The problems of international lending have been approached from a regional as well as a worldwide point of view; and, while there are obvious advantages in the regional approach, there is danger that the world's economy will be divided into blocs, with the loss of some multilateral trade, growth, and worldwide economic stability. On the

---

[5] David Grenier, "IFC: An Expanded Role for Venture Capital" *Finance and Development*, June, 1967, pp. 133–42.

other hand, there are certain problems that may be handled more efficiently on a regional than on an international basis; as a result, a number of regional financial institutions have been created, and a few of these are considered here.

European Investment Bank. The European Investment Bank was established in 1958 by the European Economic Community or Common Market countries.[6] It was financed by members' subscriptions to authorize capital and with funds raised from the sale of bonds in capital markets (primarily in Europe). The main purpose of the Bank is to finance projects in less developed sections of the European Economic Community and associated areas. Most of the funds have been invested in the southern part of Italy (Sicily, Sardinia, and the southern part of the peninsula). In addition, Greece and Turkey, the two associates of the European Economic Community, have received a small amount of financial aid from the Bank.

The headquarters of the European Investment Bank is located in Brussels, an area well served with funds; hence, the Bank has developed into an important investment bank for the Mediterranean area. Most of its funds have been used to finance industrial enterprises such as chemical, iron, and steel companies, transport and power projects, and a few agricultural ventures. The financing needs of specific projects may be met only in part by loans obtained from the Bank.

Loans are made in the six common-market countries for public and private enterprises; but any member country may veto proposed loans in order to protect itself from those politically inspired. The lending capacity of EIB is $2.5 billion, and it may raise additional funds by selling bonds and notes in the capital market (one fifth have been sold in the U.S. market). The Bank's interest rate is the same as that charged by commercial banks and other lenders.

In 1963, EIB established a Special Section, which is separately managed and financed to provide long-term loans on special terms when projects being financed seem to justify doing so. To date, Turkey has been the only country that has obtained funds from the Special Section. The European Economic Community has also made provisions for the European Development Fund, which is not a Bank. The Fund makes grants to help finance welfare and other projects in the colonies and dependent territories of members and also in the independent associates of the European Economic Community that were formerly colonies of members. The chief beneficiaries of these

[6] See "Some Development Banks Considered—International, Regional, and National," *Midland Bank Review*, February, 1967, pp. 12–24.

funds have been former colonies of Belgium and France located in North Africa.

Inter-American Development Bank. The Inter-American Development Bank, which began operations in Washington in October, 1960, exports capital to Latin-American countries (except Cuba) to facilitate economic growth. The United States is the chief subscriber to the Bank's capital, which is divided between the Bank's two independent parts, one for "ordinary" transactions and the other for "special operations." In addition to its paid-in capital, the Bank also borrows in the capital markets of the world but chiefly in the United States.

Ordinary loans made to private enterprises and public bodies are repayable in the currency in which the loans were made (usually U.S. dollars). These loans usually provide only one half of the capital needs of specific enterprises and their maturities are usually for 12 years or less when made to finance private ventures, but they may be up to 20 years when made to finance public projects. Most of these "ordinary" loans have been made to finance industrial, mining, agricultural, electric power, transportation, and water supply projects.

The "Fund for Special Operations" of the Inter-American Development Bank is separate from the rest of the bank's operations. The loans of the department are made on terms that seem appropriate for handling "special circumstances" in specific countries. These loans are made on easier terms and for ventures that cannot meet the standards set by other lenders. Although some of the loans are made in the same areas as those made by the ordinary department of the Bank, those made by the Special Operations division tend to emphasize financing research projects, preinvestment studies, project preparation, urban and rural community development, river basin surveys, and research pertaining to natural resources.

When possible, the Bank channels its funds through national development banks. It strives to maintain high operating standards by controlling and supervising projects and budgeting the funds used for different undertakings. The Bank has been instrumental in establishing the Central American common market (El Salvador, Guatemala, Costa Rica, Nicaragua, and Honduras) and the common-market central bank, the Central Bank for Economic Integration.[7] The Inter-American Development Bank also administers financial aid provided by other countries to Latin American countries and the Social Prog-

[7] J. W. Crow, "Economic Integration in Central America," *Finance and Development* (March, 1966), pp. 58–66.

ress Trust Fund created by the United States to provide technical and financial assistance to social development projects. The Bank's policies are decided by a Court of Governors composed of one representative from each member country. The day-to-day operations are the responsibility of a board of seven directors.

African Development Bank. The African Development Bank has been in existence since 1964, and its membership is open to all independent African nations, except South Africa. The members have subscribed to all of the $250 million capital stock, only part of which has been called. Although equity interest in the Bank is limited to African nations, the Bank expects to use its borrowing power to obtain funds in the European and other capital markets. In addition, each member may be required to lend to the Bank in proportion to its subscribed capital to finance its exports of goods and services that are required for specific projects to other member countries.

Asian Development Bank. The purpose of the Asian Development Bank, organized in 1966, is to encourage economic growth and cooperation among the countries of Asia and the Far East. Membership is open to both the developing nations of the area and developed nations which are members of the United Nations or any of its specified agencies (at the present time, there are 18 of the former and 12 of the latter, including the United States).[8] The authorized capital of the Bank ($1 billion) is divided equally into "paid-in" and "callable" shares, of which no less than 60 percent must be owned by regional members. The stock, initially subscribed for, is payable in five equal installments, 50 percent of which must be in gold or convertible currency. Like most development banks, the Asian Development Bank is to provide financing for specific projects, including those forming a part of regional, subregional, or national programs. The financial assistance may be in the form of direct loans, participation in loans, guarantee of loans, or investment in equity capital.

The Asian Development Bank is required to avoid using a disproportionate amount of its resources for the benefit of any one member. It may set aside 10 percent of its paid-in capital to establish one or more special funds to finance "soft" currency loans or specific projects (which must be administered separately from the ordinary operations of the Bank). Provisions for management of the Bank, whose head office is in Manila, are similar to those of the World Bank

[8] *Japan's Growing Role in Development Assistance* (Washington, D.C.: United States—Japan Trade Council, 1967), pp. 4 *ff*.

with a Board of Governors, Board of Directors, President (who must be from a regional member country), and one or more vice presidents. Members' voting strength varies with the number of capital shares held.

Other Development Banks. Currently, the United Nations, World Bank and its subsidiaries, the United States, and other nations are sponsoring the formation of additional development banks throughout the world on national and/or local bases. The most common reason for establishing development banks is to provide credit on reasonable terms for private or public projects. In developed countries, governmental authorities often take the initiative in making provisions for financing development projects and creating financial machinery to fill the "gap" in existing financing structures.

During past wars and depressions, the United Kingdom, United States, Italy, and other industrial nations have created financial institutions to meet special needs. Some of these have been temporary and others have become permanent additions to their countries' financial structure. The United States provided for small investment companies in the Small Business Investment Companies Act of 1958, to finance small companies in need of venture capital. In addition, many states and cities have organizations designed to attract or build new businesses. Perhaps the most successful forerunner of modern development organizations is the Tennessee Valley Authority, created by an act of Congress in May, 1933.

In addition to the development banks previously considered, many more having similar functions have been created to operate on a smaller scale. These include local, national, and some so-called regional development organizations (such as the Fund for Arab Economic Development established by the government of Kuwait in 1962 and the privately owned Adela Investment Company of Luxembourg, which operates in Latin America). Among the oldest national development banks are the National Financiera of Mexico (1933), Industrial Development Bank of Turkey (1950), Banco National do Desenvolvimento Econômico of Brazil (1952), Industrial Credit and Investment Corporation of India (1954), Yugoslav Investment Bank (1956), Industrial Development Bank of Israel (1957), Pakistan Industrial Credit and Investment Corporation (1957), Banque Nationale pour le Développement Economique of Morocco (1959), and Industrial and Mining Development Bank of Iran (1959).[9] An even

[9] *Midland Bank Review*, February, 1967, pp. 12–23.

larger number of national development banks has been formed since the end of 1959.

As soon as the International Finance Corporation was permitted to purchase and own stock in private companies, it exchanged its investment in debentures issued by two private development banks in Colombia for their stock; and, since that time, it has invested in development banks in various underdeveloped countries. The development banks have been of use to the World Bank and the International Finance Corporation because they prefer to make loans and capital investments through development companies and banks. Unfortunately, many of the public development corporations have not been administered wisely and are being reorganized and others have ceased to operate; but two industrial corporations that have excellent records are the development banks of Puerto Rico and Japan.

The development bank in Puerto Rico was established in 1942 with capital of $2.5 million and currently it is about 5.5 times that amount; but more important than its financial success has been the new industries and increased employment that have followed. It has served as a model for many countries, particularly those in Latin America.[10]

Since 1951, the investment development company established in Japan has had a spectacular record. It has been engaged in helping to finance private business by providing long-term funds which are used to rehabilitate and expand the Japanese economy. Its success and size (assets of over $2.2 billion) permit it to raise funds in the New York capital market. In the future, with IFC taking an important part, there is expectation of greater development of privately owned or "mixed" development banks which are to be partly financed by the government under private management. The retiring president of the International Finance Corporation summed up his views as follows:

My forty years of financial and business experience make me an advocate of prudent financial structures. I, therefore, see great importance in IFC's right to provide and stimulate the flow of equity capital. . . . By underwriting or providing stand-up commitments it can provide facilities . . . for the growth of capital markets. The ability to draw capital from large numbers of people is a necessary element for sustained growth of modern business. It is the basis of capitalism.[11]

[10] John H. Mudie, "The Role of the Government Development Bank in Puerto Rico's Economic Program," unpublished doctor's dissertation (Austin, Texas: University of Texas, 1960).

[11] Robert L. Garner, *An Address at the 1961 Annual Meeting of the Board of Governors* (Vienna, Austria, September 21, 1961) p. 3.

AMERICAN FOREIGN AID

In view of the various international financing institutions that have been created, one would expect that the money and capital needs of the underdeveloped countries had been carded for adequately; but, although the economic progress made since World War II has been greater than during any other period in history, the underdeveloped nations are desirous of pushing their national incomes to new records. At first it was assumed that, after the original capital investment, the growth in the economy would permit the developing countries to finance future growth without outside capital, but now it is evident that outside capital will be needed for a long time.

Agency for International Development. The Agency for International Development (AID), which is administering most of the loans and grants of the U.S. government, was organized in 1961 by combining the Development Loan Fund, the International Coopera- tion Administration, and other smaller governmental units. Its pur- pose is to serve as an additional source of funds for financing eco- nomic development in the free world and to reduce or eliminate barriers to international trade and the flow of private capital. Specific grants are made to finance technical training and development proj- ects in underdeveloped countries. The assistance grants are com- monly used to help finance cash imports.

Under current policy, all loan funds must be spent in the United States, which may not always be the best market in which to buy; and grant funds may be spent anywhere except in the 19 industrial coun- tries (chiefly those of western Europe and Austria, Canada, New Zealand, and Africa). If commodities are purchased, none may be obtained in the United States if it has a net import of that commodity. While restrictions on spending AID funds may be helpful to U.S. business, it is often harmful to the recipient of the funds. By follow- ing a worldwide procurement policy, buyers may often cut the cost of industrial and other equipment by 50 percent. Although develop- ment loans have a maturity of 40 years at low interest rates and are repayable in dollars, it is often cheaper to pay a higher interest rate and borrow from the World Bank or some private agency.

From the beginning, AID faced urgent requests for substantial funds from Latin American governments; but the administrator an- nounced the policy of the Agency in these words: it is the "first duty to help those of the less-developed friendly countries that make efforts to help themselves. . . ."[12] Later, after teams of experts visited different Latin American countries, they recommended the formation of more development banks or institutions in that area.

Agricultural Trade Development and Assistance Program. Agricultural surpluses owned by the U.S. government as a result of its price-support program have been used in part in the aid program of the United States since the beginning of World War II under lend-lease, United Relief and Rehabilitation Administration, the Marshall Plan, and all of the programs which have followed. However, aid given in the form of agricultural products was not treated under a separate program until Congress passed the Agricultural Trade Development and Assistance Act in 1954 (Public Law 480). Agricultural surpluses include both those owned by the government and those privately owned and declared surplus by the Secretary of Agriculture. Title IV of the Act, added in 1959 and first used in 1961, provides for the sale of surplus farm products on a long-term credit basis (maximum 20 years) at low interest rates.

Export-Import Bank of Washington. The Export-Import Bank of Washington was organized in 1934 primarily to stimulate U.S. exports by insuring individual shipments against credit loss and making loans to foreign governments. The Bank is authorized to conduct a general business and to make loans of any type for the purpose of "financing and facilitating" the foreign trade of the United States. It makes intermediate-term and long-term loans to finance the purchase of equipment, materials, and/or services for economic or self-supporting development projects. The Bank finances or guarantees medium-term export credit and provides short-term and intermediate-term export credit insurance. In its operations, the Export-import Bank is closely allied to commercial banks and the Foreign Credit Insurance Association of New York (made up of about 70 insurance companies). Usually, the Bank assumes one half of the credit risk and all of the "political" risk.

As directed by Congress, the Bank's function is to supplement and encourage private capital (not compete with it) and to make loans for specific purposes that offer reasonable assurance of repayment. The Bank is financed by the United States Treasury, which made $6 billion available to finance the export trade of the United States.

[12] *New York Times,* October 4, 1961, p. 23.

The Export-Import Bank is prepared to aid in financing both imports and exports of products and the purchase of engineering and other technical services in the United States. Most of its experience has been with the financing of exports for which it offers credits for the benefit of individual exporters in the United States and a line of credit to a foreign government, foreign bank, or foreign firm to facilitate the purchase of specific goods (material and equipment) and services in the United States.

The Export-Import Bank is managed by a board of directors, of which the Secretary of State, or someone appointed by him, is the chairman. The National Advisory Council on International Monetary and Financial Problems acts as an advisory council for the Export-Import Bank. This council (NAC) coordinates all foreign lending by the U.S. government and is a sort of international monetary- and credit-control council, consisting of the Secretary of State, the Secretary of the Treasury, and the Secretary of Commerce, the chairman of the Board of Governors of the Federal Reserve System, the American director of the International Monetary Fund, and the president of the Export-Import Bank (or a substitute that may be designated by any of the foregoing).

FINANCING THROUGH PRIVATE AGENCIES

In spite of the emphasis on government assistance to foreign countries since the end of World War II, private investments in foreign countries by American corporations, individuals, and banks in developing countries have been substantial. The commercial banks help in the capital flow to these countries and to mobilize local capital and to channel it into desirable projects. Investment subsidiaries of commercial banks formed under the Edge Act are investing directly in foreign private companies, and commercial banks are assisting private development banks with funds and in other ways.

Much of the flow of private investment has been in the form of direct investment rather than the purchase of securities. The greatest flow of private capital has been to Canada and Europe, but substantial amounts have gone to Latin America, the Middle East, Asia, and Africa. Along with this flow of capital has gone the know-how or technical assistance, of which there has been a shortage in underdeveloped countries. The danger in the expansion in large-scale government lending is that it may discourage private lending and cause the liquidation of some of the loans outstanding. However, the private-capital market has been expanding throughout the free world, and the general effect of the lending by different international and regional agencies seems to have been supplementary rather than competitive.

The establishment of successful private capital markets in foreign countries has been facilitated by U.S. aid, development corporations, and other institutions. Industrial countries that have retained exchange control and other restrictions on capital movements have handicapped the development of their own capital markets and have also shifted much of the burden of supplying capital to the world to the United States. Most foreign countries need investment dealers, brokerage firms, and stock exchanges to encourage the purchase of stocks and bonds. As noted in earlier chapters, American commercial banks have followed their customers abroad through branch offices, subsidiaries, or correspondent relationships with foreign commercial banks; and an increasing number have organized Edge and Agreement corporations. The export of capital by the private sector of the U.S. economy is more likely to increase than to decrease. The most promising areas for a greater flow of U.S. capital are the countries in Latin America, Africa, and the Middle East.

SUMMARY

At the Bretton Woods conference in the summer of 1944, plans were made for the International Bank for Reconstruction and Development and the World Bank, whose main function was to grant or guarantee long-term foreign currency loans to member nations for specific approved productive purposes. The Bank organized subsidiary institutions in 1956 and in 1960. The first, the International Finance Corporation, was created to assist in financing private projects on an equity or convertible loan basis. The second, the International Development Association, was established to make development loans to member countries that may have had difficulty in borrowing on conventional terms because of their balance-of-payments positions. In addition, numerous regional and national development banks have been created.

In 1945, there was an urgent and immediate need for rebuilding shattered economies of Europe, Asia, and North Africa; but the present need is to aid the developing countries of the free world. The problems involves not only developing natural physical resources of these emerging nations but also their human resources, which means that foreign aid will be required for a long period of time.

QUESTIONS AND PROBLEMS

1. Compare the International Monetary Fund and the World Bank as to organization and management.
2. How do the functions of the World Bank differ from those of the International Finance Corporation? Why was the International Finance Corporation added? The International Development Association? The Inter-American Development Bank?
3. Explain the justification for the provision that necessitates the prior approval of a country's representative on the Board of Governors, whose currency is being borrowed from the International Monetary Fund. From the World Bank. What United States group advises the American representative when dollars are requested?
4. What are the functions of the Export-Import Bank? Does it duplicate the work of the World Bank? Explain. How do the activities of the Export-Import Bank compare with the amounts of loans and grants made to foreign governments directly by the United States Treasury?
5. Analyze: "Besides the loan portfolio and special reserve, the [World] Bank's obligations have behind them the Bank's unqualified right to call upon all member governments for the uncalled . . . portion of their capital subscriptions. . . . The United States obligation alone is $7.41 billion. . . . ." (International Bank for Reconstruction and Development, *The World Bank Policies and Operations* [Washington, D.C., 1957], p. 28.)
6. What justification was there for expecting a small increase in investment (expanding the machinery of production) to be sufficient to stimulate growth in a developing country without additional foreign investments? Explain.
7. Analyze: "The World Bank has approved a loan equivalent to $50 million to Yugoslavia to help complete the construction of the last major link in its railway network. . . . The loan is for 25 years with interest at 6¼ per cent. It will be made to the Yugoslavia Investment Bank, the main channel in Yugoslavia for foreign development loans, and it is guaranteed by the Government of Yugoslavia." (International Monetary Fund, *International Financial News*, April 5, 1968, p. 109.)
8. Discuss: "The total outstanding obligations of the [World] Bank amount to about $3.4 billion, of which about $2.6 billion is denominated in U.S. dollars . . . more than 55 percent of the Bank's total outstanding debt and some 41 percent of its U.S. debt is held by investors outside the United States." (International Monetary Fund, *International Financial News Survey*, May 10, 1968, p. 145.)
9. Explain: In addition to underwriting public offerings of shares International Finance Corporation has helped to develop capital markets "through support for private development finance companies." (International Finance Corporation, *Annual Report 1965–66*, Washington, D.C. 1966, p. 11.)

10. Analyze: "There has been a growing recognition . . . that domestic efforts constitute the central element in economic progress and that assistance . . . can only reinforce the essential of domestic efforts." (Organization for Economic Co-operation and Development, *1966 Review* [Paris, France, 1966], p. 66.

CHAPTER 30

Foreign Banking Systems

THE BANKING systems of Canada, England, and France have influenced and have been influenced by banking practices in the United States; however, there has been considerably more concentration in commercial banking abroad than in the United States because of their wider acceptance of branch banking. Foreign banks customarily receive their charters from one source, the national government; hence, the banking structures abroad show greater uniformity than in the United States. However, banking practices tend to be the same throughout the free world, so there is a great deal of similarity among operations of the banks in the United States, Canada, England, and France.

CANADIAN BANKING SYSTEM

The Bank of Canada. The central bank of Canada, the Bank of Canada, is owned by the Dominion government and serves as its fiscal agent, acting as depository and taking charge of public-debt operations. The Bank has a monopoly of note issue, holds reserve deposits of the chartered banks, acts generally as a bankers' bank, carries on all customary central-banking activities, and owns and operates a subsidiary corporation, the Industrial Development Bank, which is a source of capital funds for private business firms when such funds cannot be obtained elsewhere.[1] The Bank of Canada began operations on March 11, 1935, and rapidly assumed an important place in Canadian banking. The head office is in Ottawa, and, subject to governmental approval, the Bank may establish branches at home or abroad (none has been established, but the Bank does operate nine agencies in different sections of Canada).

The board of directors of the Bank of Canada is appointed by the government, and, with the approval of the government, the board selects the chief executive officers—governor, deputy governor, and

---

[1] *The Industrial Development Act* (Ottawa, Canada: Printed by Edmond Cloutier, Law Printer to the King's Most Excellent Majesty, 1949), pp. 3–16.

assistant deputy governor. The executive committee, which consists of the governor, deputy governor, and a director selected by the board, meets weekly and exercises the powers of the board of directors but submits all decisions to the board for review. The Canadian Minister of Finance and the Governor of the Bank of Canada consult regularly on monetary policy and how it is related to general policy. In case of unresolved differences, the issues are settled by the government.

Although modified somewhat during wars, the objectives of the Bank of Canada are basically the same as those provided in the preamble of the Bank of Canada Act of 1934, which is as follows: To "regulate credit and currency in the best interests of the economic life of the nation, to control and protect the external value of the national monetary unit and to mitigate by its influence fluctuations in the general level of production, trade, prices, and employment, so far as may be possible within the scope of monetary action, and generally to promote the economic and financial welfare of the Dominion. . . ."[2]

Unlike the United States Employment Act of 1946 and other legislation pertaining to the monetary and credit policies of the Federal Reserve System, the Canadian law specifically recognizes the necessity for stabilizing general prices and the external value of the Canadian dollar as monetary objectives. The Royal Commission on Banking and Finance (sometimes called the Porter Commission for its chairman, the Honorable Dana H. Porter, Chief Justice of Ontario) suggested that the preamble be broadened to direct the "Bank to use its powers to promote the general economic and financial welfare of the nation and to contribute to the achievement of such goals as rising productivity, a high and stable level of employment, the protection of the national monetary unit, and the development of an efficient and flexible Canadian financial system, and the maintenance of a sound external financial position."[3]

Among the instruments of credit control, the Bank of Canada depends for the most part on open-market operations—buying and selling government securities to influence the reserve positions of chartered banks. In addition to percentage reserve requirements for deposits, the Bank of Canada has the authority to specify secondary reserve requirements that may consist of notes and deposits of the

[2] *Bank of Canada Act* (Ottawa, Canada: King's Printer and Controller of Stationery, 1949), p. 3.

[3] *1964—Report of the Royal Commission on Banking and Finance* (Ottawa, Canada: Queen's Printer and Controller of Stationery, 1964), p. 539.

Bank of Canada, Treasury bills maturing in one year or less, and day loans made to investment bankers. Moral suasion, without the use of formal instruments of credit control, has been used effectively because of the fact that there are only 10 chartered banks in Canada.

The chartered banks adjust their reserve positions either by changing their day-to-day call loans to authorized investment dealers or by changing their investments in treasury bills; and, only rarely do they use their rediscount privileges at the Bank of Canada. The Canadian investment dealer, unlike his American counterpart, has access to the discount window of the Bank of Canada. Most of the earning assets of the Bank of Canada are in the form of Dominion and provincial government short-term and other securities. In order to permit Canada to take part in international cooperative ventures, Parliament permits the Bank of Canada to accept interest-bearing deposits from foreign central banks and international financial organizations.

Like central banks the world over, the lending power of the Bank of Canada is due primarily to its right of note issue. The Bank is authorized to pay cumulative dividends of 4.5 percent per annum and, after setting aside reserves for bad debts, depreciation of assets, pension funds, and other items "properly provided for by banks," the "rest fund" (surplus) kept equal to paid up capital, the remainder of earnings, after dividends are paid and other adjustments are made, are paid to the government.

Currency.   Following the formation of the Confederation in 1867, the Dominion government took control over currency and repealed all provincial currency acts that were in conflict with federal control. Changes continued to be made in authorized currency circulation, but the most significant ones occurred in 1934 when the central bank took over control of paper money issues from the chartered banks, retired these issues over a 15-year period, and replaced those issued by the Dominion government.

The Canadian coinage system is similar to that of the United States and had the same standard unit until 1962. Canada has abandoned convertibility of its currency into gold and now keeps the value of its foreign exchange in terms of the United States dollar at 92.5 cents (plus or minus 1 percent). On April 30, 1940, the gold reserves of the Bank of Canada were transferred to the Foreign Exchange Control Board, and the requirement that the Bank keep a reserve of gold equal to no less than 25 percent of its note and deposit liabilities has been abolished.

Commercial Banks.   A Canadian commercial bank is best described as a "bank of branches." Generally, head offices of commercial banks neither lend money nor accept deposits, but they operate branches that do their banking business.[4] The 10 chartered commercial banks operate more than 5,400 domestic branches and about 150 foreign branches. In a sense, the Canadian banking system dates from the formation of the confederation in 1867 when the Dominion Government was given control of banking and currency. Currently, the federal parliament has exclusive power to charter commercial banks and pass laws governing their operations; but trust and loan companies and other financial institutions are organized under provincial laws.

Commercial banks, originally local institutions, became regional and then national institutions with the growth of the country and improvements in transportation and communications. Although the charters of the early banks did not specifically authorize them to establish branches, they did not prohibit them from doing so. Consequently, branch banking soon spread from the larger cities to smaller communities.

Early Canadian bank charters were similar to that of the first Bank of the United States, containing in some cases the same clauses and phraseology. The Dominion Bank Act of 1871 reflected this influence, and so it is "generally agreed that the Canadian banking system is a direct descendant of the first Bank of the United States. . . ."[5] The Bank Act of 1871 gave the commercial banks charters for but 10 years, and ever since the unique policy of giving decennial charters and renewals has been followed when practical. This policy forces the legislature to appraise its banking system periodically and has brought about many improvements. These revisions led to the provision for a central bank, the Bank of Canada, and, 10 years later, to the organization of the Industrial Development Bank, a subsidiary of the Bank of Canada. In addition, there are 10 commercial and 2 savings banks that operate under federal laws. Some of the Canadian banks are among the largest in the world and 5 of them have nationwide branch banking systems as well as foreign branches. Commercial banks, operating under provisions of the Dominion Bank Act, are called "chartered banks."[6]

The head office of a Canadian bank, being the administrative

---

[4] For a description of the work of a head office, see "The Head Office of a Bank," Bank of Nova Scotia, Toronto, *Monthly Review*, April, 1949.

[5] *Report of the Royal Commission on Banking and Currency in Canada* (Ottawa: J. O. Paternaude, Printer to the King's Most Excellent Majesty, 1933), p. 15.

[6] *1964—Report of the Royal Commission on Banking and Finance*, pp. 113–46.

center, receives daily reports of the positions of branches, maintains the primary and secondary reserve positions of the banks, keeps surplus funds invested or lent "on call" to investment dealers, examines the branch offices, makes required reports to the government, and formulates loan, personnel, and other policies of the bank.

The chartered banks are managed by boards of directors of at least five members, 75 percent of whom must be Canadian citizens who are "ordinarily" residents of Canada. In addition, each director must be a stockholder and meet the requirements that no one may serve after 75 years of age. Each board of directors, the great majority of whose members are businessmen, elects the bank's president and vice president from among their own members. However, after July 1, 1971, members of the board may not comprise more than 20 percent of the board of directors of any corporation. Furthermore, a director of a chartered bank may not be a director of (1) a trust or loan company, (2) a Quebec savings bank, (3) a company holding more than 10 percent of the voting shares of a trust or loan company or a Quebec savings bank, or (4) a director of another chartered bank.[7]

The minimum subscribed capital for chartered banks is $1 million, half of which must be paid in before business may commence. Actually, each Canadian chartered bank's capital is many times this minimum, and most of the banks have surplus (called "rest") accounts equal to or in excess of their paid-in capital. Under current rules, banks find it easy to sell new shares because the par value may be as low as $1 and may not exceed $10. Since 1954, banks may refuse to offer shares to residents of countries wherein more information is required in public disclosure laws (such as in the United States).

Canada no longer approves of foreign ownership of its banks. In 1965, the Finance Minister proposed that when more than 25 percent of a bank's issued shares are held by one owner, resident or nonresident, the bank's liabilities may not exceed more than 20 times the issued shares. A bank could request authorization for a capital increase from the Treasury Board with little or no hope for approval. This proposal was aimed at the smallest of the Canadian banks, the Mercantile, which is owned by the First National City Bank of New York.[8] Later, two new Canadian banks (the 9th and 10th) were created, including the Bank of Western Canada, which was 50 percent

[7] H. H. Binhammer, "Canada's Revised Banking Legislation," *The National Banking Review*, June, 1967, pp. 497 ff.

[8] *New York Times*, May 31, 1965, p. 20.

owned by two British companies. Under provisions of the present law, the First National City Bank of New York has until 1972 to reduce its ownership interest in the Mercantile Bank to no more than 25 percent.

As in the United States, restrictions have been placed on the ownership of voting stock of other corporations by the chartered banks. For illustration, a chartered bank may not acquire more than 10 percent of the voting stock of a loan or trust company or any other corporation if the cost of the voting stock is more than $5 million, and if less the total acquisition may not be equal to more than 50 percent of the company's voting stock. (This rule does not apply to corporations owning bank premises and certain service corporations.) However, this ruling will stop the establishment of subsidiary corporations created to provide mortgage credit to business firms (chartered banks may make these advances directly).

Canada's chartered banks are permitted to engage in "such business generally as appertains to the business of banking," but they are not permitted to issue bank notes intended for circulation in Canada. They receive personal checking accounts, current accounts, and personal and corporate savings accounts. Although the latter may be subject to notice prior to withdrawal, notice is seldom required; and, in practice, many individuals use their personal savings accounts as a means of payments as well as an instrument for saving.

In 1954, the Bank of Canada was authorized to vary minimum cash reserve requirements of chartered banks from 8 to 12 percent, but this power was not used. In 1967, this provision was eliminated and the American system of requiring a specified percentage reserve ratio for demand deposits (12 percent) and another for time deposits (4 percent) was adopted. In addition, the central bank may require chartered banks to keep secondary reserves against deposits in the form of notes and deposits of the Bank of Canada, short-term Treasury bills and day loans to investment dealers. After a month's notice, the central bank may impose a secondary reserve requirement of 6 percent, and may increase it by 1 percent per month until a maximum of 12 percent is reached (vault cash other than Bank of Canada notes does not count as part of the required legal reserves).

Personal accounts are checking accounts of individuals, and "current accounts" are those of business firms. Collection and other fees are regulated by law, and in this as in many other instances, Canadian banks are subject to stricter regulation than are banks in the United States. Checks are cleared and collected rapidly and efficiently through 52 clearinghouses operated for the chartered banks by the Canadian Bankers' Association. The results of these daily clearings are reported to the Bank of Canada and are settled each day by crediting and debiting clearing balances kept there for this purpose by the chartered banks.

Branch-bank managers may make individual loans up to a maximum set for them by the head offices. Requests for loans above this maximum are passed upon by a district supervisor or the head office. Loan policies are similar to those in the United States, large loans being made under lines of credit. Business firms customarily use but one bank, and customer-bank relations are usually of long standing; as a result, there is little or no delay in obtaining credit when requested. Restrictions have been placed on the amount of credit that may be extended to an officer of a bank and on the circumstances under which a loan may be made to a director of a bank or to any firm or corporation in which he is interested (which goes farther than the restriction on borrowing by officers in the United States). The volume of these loans to "insiders" appears as a separate item on monthly bank statements as published by the Minister of Finance.

In order to facilitate lending to business firms, the banks merely receive an assignment of merchandise or grain pledged as security for loans. The legal result is that the banks become preferred general creditors. Periodically, the scope of lending by Canadian banks has been broadened (as in 1954, when "livestock" was defined to include poultry, and "fisherman" to include partnerships and corporations). In 1954, banks were permitted to make consumer loans secured by chattel mortgages (automobiles, household goods, and other forms of movable personal property) but it was not until 1965 that banks were authorized to accept such mortgages as security for business loans up to 75 percent of the value of the property pledged as security. Consumer loans are made on a discount basis with an effective interest rate of 11.78 percent. In Canada, as in the United States, banks have found consumer lending to be very profitable.

In general, the types of loans made by Canadian banks are similar to those made by banks in the United States, including commercial, personal, home improvement, farm improvement, and loans for other purposes. The maximum rate was 6 percent except on small personal loans, but after a short transitional period, Parliament abolished the interest-rate ceiling on bank loans (effective January 1, 1968). In 1954, banks were permitted to make insured home mortgage loans; but, by 1959, they had withdrawn from this market because of the 6 percent ceiling on them.

In the new Bank Act, National Housing Act mortgage loans may be made at the current market rate; and, for the first time, conventional home mortgage loans may be made provided the amount of the loan does not exceed 75 percent of the value of the property securing the loans. Under the new law, the total amount of residential loans was limited to 3 percent of a bank's total deposits plus its outstanding debentures the first fiscal year, and thereafter a bank is permitted to increase such loans at the rate of 1 percent per year until the total reaches a maximum of 10 percent (1973). For the first time, commercial banks in Canada were permitted to sell subordinate debentures provided: (1) they have maturities of at least five years, (2) they are not callable until after five years, and (3) the principal amount of those outstanding after 1970 is not in excess of 50 percent of the bank's paid-up capital and surplus.

Like commercial banks in the United States, the chartered banks of Canada offer numerous financial services in addition to the basic ones of accepting deposits and making loans. They are active in financing foreign trade and buying and selling foreign exchange. Their investments consist chiefly of obligations of the Dominion, provincial, and municipal governments.

The Canadian Bankers' Association, organized in 1890 as a voluntary association, was incorporated by an act of Parliament in 1900 "to effect greater cooperation among the banks in the issue of notes, in credit and control and in various aspects of bank activities." All banks to which the Dominion Bank Act is applicable must be members. The Canadian Bankers' Association performs may cooperative services for banks,[9] and it sponsors the important education program conducted by Canadian banks. This program is similar to that of the American Institute of Banking. However, most of the success in training the well-managed staffs, for which Canadian banks are famous, is due to the existence of the branch-banking system and the opportunity it offers management to shift personnel from position to position according to individual administrative records. The personnel of a branch may be small or large—may number two or three or several hundred.

Canada Deposit Insurance Corporation. In 1967, Parliament made provisions for deposit insurance in Canada by incorporating the Canada Deposit Insurance Corporation (CDIC). This corporation is

[9] The Porter Commission recommended that the clauses in the Canadian Bankers' Association Act "which give the Association the right of operating the clearing system" be repealed and an association of all clearing institutions, including the Bank of Canada, be formed. *1964 Report of the Royal Commission*, pp. 393–94.

owned by the government (authorized capital is $10 million) and managed by a Board of Directors consisting of a chairman appointed by the government and four officials of the federal government.[10]

Federally chartered banks and loans and trust companies must be members of the deposit insurance system, and the provincially chartered loan and trust companies that accept deposits may be members. Individual deposits are insured up to a maximum of $20,000, but the Corporation may prevent liquidation of financially distressed institutions by purchasing their assets and making advances (in effect guaranteeing deposits 100 percent). As in the United States, the deposit insurance corporation may inspect member institutions and suggest means whereby they may achieve higher banking standards.

The insurance premium is levied annually on banks' insured deposits (not total deposits as in the United States) and it is equal to one thirtieth of 1 percent of insured deposits or $500, whichever is the larger. When the insurance fund is adequate, the Corporation may reduce the premiums.[11] As in the United States, deposit insurance was adopted over the protests of Canadian bankers, who felt that it was not needed. However, the contention of Parliament was that deposit insurance would increase public confidence in deposit institutions and enhance banks' competitive position among other financial institutions, because many of the local credit unions and other competing organizations already had mutual insurance plans.

Quebec Savings Banks. The two Quebec savings banks which operate branches in Montreal and Quebec were organized under provisions of the Federal Savings Bank Act. Most of the savings functions which federally chartered savings banks were expected to perform are being handled by chartered banks, trust and loan companies, and credit unions. The original restrictions on savings banks' investments have been modified to permit these banks to make secured and unsecured personal loans and conventional and nonconventional mortgage loans on residential property.[12] Currently, unsecured personal loans may not be more than 5 percent of deposits and in an amount not to exceed $5,000; nonconventional home mortgage loans may equal 60 percent of a bank's deposits; and a conventional mort-

---

[10] The four officials are the Governor of the Bank of Canada, Deputy Minister of Finance, Superintendent of Insurance, and Inspector General of Banks.

[11] The authority of CDIC to reduce premiums is written so that a member that has paid premiums for five years may not be required to pay additional premiums except one sixth of 1 percent on new insured deposits. The Corporation may sell bonds and debentures to the general public and may borrow from the government in an amount not to exceed $500 million at one time. See H. H. Binhammer, *op. cit.,* p. 500.

[12] *1964—Report of the Royal Commission on Banking and Finance,* pp. 147–54.

gage loan may be for 60 percent of the value of the property pledged as security or up to $100,000, whichever is the smaller. The banks may invest in federal provincial, municipal, and other securities in an amount up to 50 percent of their paid-up capital and surplus (rest account).

The Quebec savings banks are required to hold a cash reserve equal to 5 percent of their deposits in the form of Bank of Canada bank notes or deposits or as deposits in chartered banks. In addition, they must hold a secondary reserve of 15 percent of deposits in cash and/or federal or provincial securities. The deposit accounts are similar to commercial banks' personal savings accounts and are used in the same way—as both checking and savings accounts.

Credit Unions. The credit union movement began in 1900 when Alphonse Desjardins started the first peoples bank (Caisse populaire) in Lévis, Quebec.[13] As in the United States, their growth in number (in excess of 4,600) and membership (21.2 percent of the population as compared with 8.5 percent in the United States) has been rapid.[14] The activities of the credit unions in Canada are similar to those in the United States, and many Canadians have found these cooperative societies better able to meet their financial needs than other financial institutions.

Mortgage Loan and Trust Companies. The modern mortgage loan companies originated as "terminating" building societies (similar to the origin of savings and loan associations in the United States).[15] These companies obtain their funds from depositors and by sale of debentures and their investments are chiefly in residential mortgages. The 25 mortgage loan companies of Canada deal with the general public through their main and branch offices.

Part of the business of trust companies is similar to that of mortgage loan companies except that they place more emphasis on security investment. However they differ from other financial institutions in that they are permitted to act as trustees and to conduct other fiduciary activities. The 35 trust companies deal with the general public through their main and branch offices, offer both check and savings deposit accounts, and sell guaranteed investment certificates to attract corporate accounts. They are closely related to commercial banks through stock holdings, contracts, and in other ways.

Consumer Finance Companies. Sales finance and consumer

[13] *Ibid.,* pp. 155-71.
[14] *International Credit Union Yearbook 1966* (Madison, Wis.: Cuna International Inc., 1967), pp. 10 ff.
[15] *1964—Report of the Royal Commission on Banking and Finance,* pp. 173-99.

loan companies are among the specialists providing consumer credit.[16] Although finance companies are the only major financial institutions not subject to special regulation, loans for less than $1,500 are regulated by the government. About 80 percent of the sales finance business is done by 10 companies operating through over 1,100 branch offices; and a like number of companies have close to 90 percent of the small loan business. Frequently sales finance companies make no direct loans to consumers but concentrate on purchase of installment sales contracts written by automobile and other dealers in durable consumer goods. In addition to functioning as consumer finance companies, they act as commercial finance companies in extending credit to dealers.

Other Financial Institutions. In areas such as agricultural and small-business financing, Canada has created specialized institutions to provide credit needs not cared for by commercial banks and other institutions. In addition, the government has used the insurance or guarantee device to direct loans into special areas.

Canadians keep most of their savings deposits with commercial banks, but the postal savings system and specialized savings institutions are also important. Some of the specialized savings institutions are owned by the provincial governments, and the two in Quebec offer both time or savings accounts and checking-account services.

There are more than 100 investment houses that act both as brokers and as dealers. They have formed the Investment Bankers' Association of Canada. In the Dominion, there are seven different stock exchanges, the two oldest and most important being the Montreal Stock Exchange and the Toronto Stock Exchange.

The Canadian Royal Commission recommended that the definition of the word "banking" be broadened to include financial institutions other than chartered banks and that the Dominion Banking Code be extended to include them.[17] If Parliament were to approve of these proposals, the effects on competition and other aspects of commercial banking would be far reaching. The Bank of Canada would gain new customers if the reserve requirement were made applicable to financial institutions other than the chartered banks. Unlike nonmonetary financial institutions in the United States, many of those in Canada accept checking accounts.

---

[16] *Ibid.*, pp. 201–22.

[17] The Commission would include all private financial institutions issuing banking liabilities. This would include transferable and nontransferable demand claims and time or term obligations maturing or redeemable within 100 days of the time at which notice of withdrawal is given by the customer or within 100 days of the time of the original issue. *Ibid.*, p. 378.

BRITISH BANKING SYSTEM

The British banking system that serves not only Great Britain but also many areas throughout the world consists of (1) a central bank, the Bank of England, (2) commercial banks called "joint-stock" or "clearing" banks, (3) merchant banks, also known as accepting houses, and (4) savings banks. In addition, agencies, offices, and branches of foreign and overseas banks are located in Great Britain. Other domestic financial institutions include discount houses and bill brokers, hire-purchase finance companies, insurance companies, securities markets, investment companies, and a number of specialized institutions that have been created to provide intermediate- and long-term credit to industry.

Bank of England. The Bank of England was established in 1694 as a commercial bank for the specific purpose of lending money to the king (William III). Although all of its capital was invested in government loans, the bank was permitted to use this debt as security for an equal amount of bank notes. The Bank was a joint-stock company (the only one in England engaged in banking until 1826) with limited liability which was not extended to other banks in 1858. During its early history, the Bank of England occupied a unique position among private bankers of the period, but it did not practice central banking until the middle of the 19th century.

The Bank of England performs normal central-banking functions, including (1) acting as banker, agent and adviser to the national government, (2) being the only source of paper currency, and (3) functioning as the banker for other banks. As fiscal agent, the Bank manages government deposits, pays interest on the national debt, floats new government loans, and acts as custodian for gold used by the Treasury for international settlements.

In 1844, the Bank of England was divided into two departments, the note-issue and the banking departments, on the assumption that the Bank could carry on an ordinary banking business as well as functioning as a central bank. The functions of the note-issue department are routine, issuing Bank of England notes up to a fixed amount (the fiduciary issue) and issuing additional notes in exchange for equal amounts of gold or gold bullion. Although the Bank's balance sheet is still divided into the issue and banking departments, the division is nominal because the Bank is now organized into a number of departments, the most important of which are: (1) Cashier's Department, which is concerned with note issue, banking operations, affairs of the eight branches, and the Exchange Equalization Account;

(2) Accountant's Department; (3) Overseas Department; and (4) Economic Intelligence Department.

Although the "fiduciary issue" is fixed by law, the Treasury may, without statutory approval by parliament, increase or decrease the amount in case of need for a period not to exceed two years (giving flexibility to the note-issue system). In 1939, practically all of the Bank's gold supply was transferred to the Exchange Equalization Account; and the Bank's notes are now covered by government securities, with the exception of a small amount backed by gold and coins. The latter are struck by the Royal Mint, sold at par value to the Bank of England, and then used to meet requests of commercial banks.

The Bank of England is not required to keep a reserve against its demand-deposit liabilities; and, since 1931, it has not been required to convert its obligations into gold coin or gold bullion. The banking department counts the Bank of England bank notes as an asset and uses them to meet its obligations. These notes are also used by commercial and other banks for the same purpose. In practice, all kinds of English money are interchangeable for Bank of England notes, which are not freely convertible into gold coin or gold bullion. At the present time, the government is maintaining convertibility of its foreign exchange arising from currency transactions in gold and gold exchange and is keeping the value of its currency equivalent to $2.40 per pound sterling.

Customarily, the commercial or joint-stock banks do not borrow from the Bank of England; instead, they adjust their reserve positions through the bill market by calling loans to bill brokers or by selling bills in the market. If more of the resources of the Bank of England were to be used, the increase would result from the Bank's open-market purchases of bills or the Bank's advances to bill brokers. This means that about 12 specialists, chiefly discount companies and private firms, are the "buffers" between the Bank of England and the joint-stock banks. Most of the trading in the bill market today is in treasury bills rather than bankers' and trade acceptances.

While the Bank of England uses open-market operations and changes in rediscount rates as devices of credit control, it also uses moral suasion effectively and a system of "special deposits." The last is a new instrument of monetary control, first used in April, 1960, and requires the commercial banks to keep a percentage of their gross deposits in the Bank of England. This percentage may be increased to discourage expansion of credit or decreased to encourage it.

In addition to being the central bank for the English Banking System, the Bank of England has some ordinary commercial-bank characteristics that date back to the time when central banks were also ordinary commercial banks. When it was recognized that deposits and bank notes differed only in form, the Bank began to withdraw from the commercial-banking business. The Bank of England was the first bank to become aware of and accept the responsibilities of a central bank. Gradually it assumed its role as the bank of issue, custodian of bank reserves, "lender of the last resort," regulator of the money supply, and bank for the settlement of clearing balances. The Bank is highly skilled in transactions in foreign exchange and in the money market, and has special relations with foreign central banks and international financial organizations.

Prior to World War I, the Bank of England was solely responsible for the country's monetary policy, but since that time it has consulted with the Treasury before acting on important policy matters. In 1946, the law which shifted ownership of the Bank from private hands to the government also made the government responsible for monetary policy. The Bank now acts as the agent of the government in carrying out monetary policy rather than as an independent central bank.

Management of the Bank of England is in the hands of a Court (board of directors) composed of a governor, deputy governor, and 16 directors appointed by the Queen. The governor and deputy governor are appointed for five-year terms, and the directors for four-year terms. As many as four of these directors may be designated as "executive" directors to serve on a full-time basis, and the remainder are part-time directors selected from the fields of banking, business, shipping, and organized labor.

Commercial Banks. The commercial banks of England are organized under the Companies Act as joint-stock companies. One of the main features of the British banking system is the small number of domestic banks (22) and the large number of branches (over 14,000). The British Bankers Association has 55 members, including three from North Ireland, five from Scotland, and twelve from other parts of the British Islands. Although the banks of Scotland and North Ireland keep deposits with the Bank of England, their relationship to the Bank of England is not as close as that of the "clearing" banks. The checking system is widely developed in England, with checks being cleared for the most part through the clearinghouse in London (the branches send them to their main office). Settlement of unfavorable balances is made with checks drawn on the Bank of England.

Commercial banks hold three classes of deposits—"current accounts" or demand deposits, savings accounts for small savers, and "deposit accounts," subject to seven days' notice of withdrawal. Interest is paid on savings and deposit accounts but rarely on current accounts. (The interest rate is usually 2 percent below the discount rate of the Bank of England.) In 1960, a checkless system of payments was introduced whereby the payer instructs his bank to credit the accounts of his payees (such as department stores, telephone and utility companies, etc.). The payer then sends one check to his bank in payment. The "credit advice" contains the names of all creditors, names of their banks and branches, and the amount owed each. Clearing is done through a "credit clearing" meeting of the London Clearing House.

English banks customarily keep a cash reserve of 8 percent of deposits with the Bank of England to be used to meet seasonal demands for cash and to settle clearing balances. Each bank reports its reserve position each week on the same banking day. Commercial banks keep a second liquidity ratio—holding cash, bills discounted, and call loans in an amount of 28 percent or more of their total deposits. There is a seasonal movement in this liquid assets—deposit ratio (from 28 to 31 or 32 percent). During November-December the London clearing banks keep a ratio of 31 or 32 percent in order to permit the normal decrease in liquid assets that occurs during the first quarter of the year without infringing on the 28 percent minimum liquid assets ratio. Because banks report their positions for the middle of the week, the normal weekend outflow of cash and first-of-the-week inflow does not affect reported cash and liquid assets ratios.

English banks are large buyers of trade, Treasury, and other bills of exchange. (The trade bill is important as a foreign trade document, but it is used infrequently in domestic trade.) In Great Britain, as in the United States, the most important type of bill of exchange is that used as a means of borrowing, best illustrated by the Treasury bill. Although banks buy other government securities, they usually limit their purchases to those maturing in five years or less.

The most important assets of commercial banks are loans and advances to their customers. These may be in the form of "overdraft" credit made under previously arranged-for overdraft lines of credit for a definite time and for a specified maximum amount. Overdraft credit is customarily used to finance seasonal working capital needs of business. During this lending period, the borrower writes checks to pay expenses, and when checks are written in excess of his deposit account, he pays interest on the amount of the excess (overdraft). Banks also make personal and other loans for fixed amounts and definite periods of time, with emphasis on short-term and intermediate credit. The clearing banks have subsidiary corporations that make hire-purchase (installment) advances to individuals to purchase automobiles and other goods on the installment plan, and other subsidiaries that are used to finance overseas transactions, exports, and investments. Furthermore, English banks are now equipped to give their customers various types of other services including trust, investment, safekeeping, credit cards, foreign travel, and preparation of income tax statements.

Merchant Bankers. The merchant bankers, also known as accepting houses, are located in the City of London. The original function of the merchant banker was to finance foreign trade by accepting bills of exchange. By adding his name to the obligations of smaller mercantile firms, the quality and liquidity of the "accepted" paper was improved. As their business increased, some of the merchant bankers gave up their mercantile business and specialized in accepting bills of exchange for others. In addition, merchant bankers make loans of acceptance credit to manufacturers and other firms so they can finance their needs for short-term funds by drawing term bills and selling them in the money market. Accepting houses assist foreign trade and international finance by confirming the credit of buyers, accepting and lending Euro-dollars and other foreign money, acting as managers of investment trusts, writing marine and other types of insurance, operating travel agencies, providing and managing ships, serving as agents in the export and import of goods, and providing numerous other services.[18]

Issuing Houses. The merchant bankers, as well as other financial institutions, function as investment bankers for their customers by acting as underwriters or sponsors for securities that are sold to the general public. They also use their own funds to sponsor small companies which for various reasons are not financed publicly; they assist in reorganizations, mergers, and purchases of other business firms; and they act as advisors on financial and other problems. The issuing houses have formed their own association, called the "Issuing Houses Association," having between 50 and 60 members (including the 17 members of the "Accepting House Committee").

[18] See *Jardines Today* (London, England; Jardine, Matheson Group Companies, n.d.).

Foreign and Overseas Banks. Because London has been a leading financial center for several hundred years, most of the large commercial banks of the world maintain offices, branches, or subsidiary corporations in London. In addition, there are 28 British and Commonwealth banks with offices in London that carry on most of their business overseas. These British Overseas and foreign banks—numbering over 100—are primarily engaged in financing trade between Great Britain and the countries wherein they operate. They deal in foreign exchange, thereby providing the means for shifting money from one international center to another. At times when their assets are not fully employed in financing international trade, their unencumbered funds and reserves are invested in the London money market.

Savings Banks. In addition to the savings accounts kept in commercial banks, English depositors keep large sums in the postal savings banks and the 79 trustee (savings) banks which operate 1,375 banking offices. Trustee banks were created to help small savers having no business accounts. Now, they not only accept savings accounts but also permit their customers to open checking accounts. In the United Kingdom, as in the United States, there has been a growth in the sale of savings bonds and in participation in employee pension plans, with an increasing percentage of employees being subject to "contractual savings."

The Post Office Savings Bank, established in 1861, now has over 23 million deposit accounts that range in size from 10 shillings ($1.20) to £5,000 ($12,000), plus accumulated interest and payments from other accounts. Although management and records are centralized in London, deposits may be made in any of the 21,000 post offices of Great Britain. The statutory interest rate on deposits is 2.5 percent. In June 1966, Parliament provided for investment accounts that permit payment of a higher interest rate to depositors with minimum balances of £50 in their ordinary accounts (the maximum is £5,000). Withdrawals are subject to one month's notice; but, unlike the first £15 of interest on deposits in the Post Office Savings Bank, the interest on investment accounts is subject to the income tax. The funds received by the Post Office Savings Bank are invested by National Debt Commissioners.

Trustee savings banks, which are similar to the mutual savings banks in the United States, have two departments: the Ordinary Department, which operates under the same conditions as the Post Office Savings Bank, and the Special Investment Department, which operates under the same conditions as the investment account division of the Post Office Savings Bank. The funds of the trustee savings banks are invested primarily in guaranteed government securities and local government obligations (such as bonds and mortgages), under the general supervision of the National Debt Commissioners.

Building Societies. The activities of the building societies, which number over 600, are similar to those of savings and loan associations in the United States. In addition to selling "shares" to savers, these societies accept deposits bearing an agreed-upon rate of interest, usually one fourth of 1 percent lower than the dividend rate on shares. Both are subject to notice of withdrawal, the time period being one month for deposits and from one to six months for shares, depending on the rules of the individual society. The required income tax is paid by the societies. The main function of building societies is to make mortgage loans on owner-occupied dwellings and occasionally on farms, industrial buildings, shops, rental houses, and blocks of flats. Loans are usually repaid monthly (the amount includes interest and principal payment) over a period of years ranging up to 30 years. The organization and activities of the societies are subject to supervision and regulation by a government agency, the Registry of Friendly Societies, which administers the Building Societies Act 1962.[19]

Registered Provident Societies. The Registered Provident Societies of Great Britain include a number of small mutual companies such as friendly societies, industrial and provident societies, trade unions, certified loan companies, and railway savings banks. These societies have been defined as "voluntary associations formed for the purpose of raising by the subscriptions of the members, funds out of which advances may be made for the mutual relief and maintenance of members, their wives or children, in sickness, infancy, old age or infirmity, or for kindred purposes."[20]

Hire-Purchase Finance Companies. In Great Britain, as in the United States, there has been an increase in sales of consumer goods on the installment plan, called "hire-purchase" contracts. More than a century ago, railway wagons or cars were financed on the installment plan by finance companies, but the rapid growth of these companies has been due to financing automobiles. Since the close of World War II, the growth of finance houses was further accelerated when they began to finance the needs of industry for equipment,

[19] *British Financial Institutions*, prepared by Reference Division, Central Office of Information (London, England: Her Majesty's Stationery Office, 1966), pp. 48–50.
[20] *Ibid.*, p. 51.

machinery, and plants. Although approximately 1,500 firms are engaged in financing hire-purchase transactions, most of this business
is done by the 39 members of the Finance House Association.[21]

Most of the assets of the finance houses are in the form of
installment paper, of which two thirds is based on consumer and
commercial purchases of automobiles and the remainder on industrial
and building equipment, household appliances, and other goods.
Other earning assets of the finance houses consist of advances and
loans. Most of the funds used by the large finance houses are obtained
at home and abroad in the form of large deposits (the minimum being
£500) which bear a higher interest rates than other short-term paper.
The smaller finance houses secure their funds from the general public.

Special Finance Corporations.   Several specialized finance
corporations have been formed to finance the intermediate- and
long-term capital needs of companies unable to obtain funds from
traditional sources. These corporations include the following: (1)
Finance Corporation for Industry, Ltd., whose capital is owned by
insurance companies, investment trust companies, and the Bank of
England. (2) Industrial and Commercial Finance Corporation, Ltd.,
which is financed by the sale of stock to the London clearing banks
and Scottish banks. (3) Commonwealth Development Finance Company, Ltd., which is a private company established in 1953 to assist in
financing commerce with the Commonwealth countries. (4) Technical Development Capital, Ltd., which was formed in 1962 to finance
technical development and innovations. (5) Ship Mortgage Finance
Co. Ltd., which was established in 1951 to aid shipbuilding. (6) Commonwealth Development Corporation, which was formed by the
government in 1948 (name changed in 1963) as the Colonial Development Corporation, to finance development projects such as public
utilities, housing, transportation, agriculture, commerce, and industry
in the Commonwealth countries. (7) Agricultural Mortgage Corporation, Ltd., was formed in 1928 to make long-term loans (up to 50
years) secured by mortgages on farm land and buildings in England
and Wales. (8) Scottish Agricultural Securities Corporation, Ltd.,
which provides long-term mortgage credit to farmers in Scotland. In
addition, there are over 400 life insurance companies that operate a
"life" or general insurance business and manage pension plans and
300 investment trusts whose activities are similar to their counterpart
in the United States.

[21] *Ibid.,* p. 39.

FRENCH BANKING SYSTEM

In 1945, in a sweeping reform law, the French government provided for reorganization of the French Banking System. First, the government purchased the stock of the Bank of France and of four large commercial banks. These banks were then placed under the management of directors selected, for the most part, by the government. As a second step, remaining banks were required to register as banks of deposit, as business banks (*banques d'affaires*), or as long-term or intermediate credit banks. After self-classification, each bank was given one year in which to adjust its business to standards as provided for its class. All banks were then to be subject to regulation as provided for in other sections of the law. The standards set for deposit banks limited their underwriting and other investment banking activities, and the standards set for business banks limited their deposit banking business. The other classes of banks were specialized institutions that, for the most part, had been operating under special statutes (savings, agricultural, mortgage, people's banks, etc.).

There are now three separate authorities responsible for the regulation of the banking system. (1) In 1945 a National Credit Council was created to advise the government and to take general responsibility for credit policy (a sort of national monetary- and credit-control council such as has been recommended in the United States). The Minister of Finance is the president of the Council, the Governor of the Bank of France is the vice president, and all the economic departments of the government are represented. There are 38 members, and their function is to make general studies and recommendations. (2) In 1941 the law provided for a Banking Control Commission of five members. This is a supervisory agency, authorized to impose penalties if its requirements are not met. (3) The Bank of France, in its capacity as a central bank, is largely responsible for carrying out the policies of the National Credit Council.

Bank of France. One of the chief objectives in forming the Bank of France in 1800 was to make credit both cheap and available. Like the Bank of England at that time, the Bank of France made funds available to individuals, commercial borrowers, banks, and the government.[22] It was this dual role of the Bank of France, functioning as a central bank as well as an ordinary commercial bank, that justified

---

[22] Karl R. Bopp, *Bank of France Policy: Brief Survey of Instruments, 1800–1914*, reprint from the *American Journal of Economics and Sociology*, Vol. II, No. 3, pp. 229–44.

the operation of over 650 branches and agencies through which the Bank brought its services directly to the general public. For years, the Bank of France competed with other banks for ordinary deposits, transfer (*giro*) accounts, and loans; but, since World War II, it has become mainly a central bank.

The Bank of France (Banque de France) has a monopoly of note issue (acquired completely in 1848), which is more important in France, wherein checks are used less than they are in English-speaking countries. The Bank of France was established (by Napoleon in 1800) without a charter, but in 1803 its organization and powers were laid down by law. Throughout most of its history the Bank was owned privately and managed conservatively, having suspended specie payments only twice prior to 1914 (1849–50 and 1870–77).

During World War I the heavy commitments of the Bank of France to war financing caused inflation in general prices. Between the two World Wars, France continued to have currency and other financial problems, and the French franc decreased to less than one tenth of its prewar value. World War II increased France's financial burdens by increasing its outlays for war, occupation costs of the German army, and postwar reconstruction.

On December 2, 1945, the government nationalized the Bank of France, acquiring title to all stock in exchange for bonds. The chief administrative officers have been appointed by the nominal head of the government (the Emperor or the President of France) throughout the history of the Bank. Now, as before nationalization, the President of France appoints the governor and two deputy-governors. The three officials plus two *censors* and twelve *conseillers* (directors) make up the membership of the General Council. Seven of the directors are appointed by the Minister of Finance on nomination by cabinet members to represent various groups, one is elected by the staff of the Bank, and four are ex officio members representing certain public credit institutions.

In carrying out its credit policies the Bank of France has used open-market operations and changes in the rediscount rate, but major dependence has been on various selective or direct-control devices. These consist of requirements that commercial banks hold a certain amount of their resources in short-term government paper and refer requests for large loans to the Bank of France for approval. In addition, limits (ceilings) were placed on the amount of rediscounting with the Bank of France, except for certain types of paper. At times, use has been made of a secondary ceiling to cover supplementary borrowing, but at a penalty rate, at the Bank of France. For a long period of time the commercial banks did not need to borrow from the Bank of France, and this handicapped its functioning as a central bank.

The inflationary pressures to which France was subject led to the de Gaulle government and a reform program, which was started in December, 1958. Reform measures had as their objectives keeping down budgetary deficits; eliminating escalator clauses in labor contracts (except for minimum wages), debt or bond contracts, cost-of-living subsidies on food and fuel and public utilities; liberalizing both foreign and domestic trade; and providing for a new monetary unit, the "new franc," worth 100 old francs (introduced in 1960). With the change to more conservative financing, France has enjoyed unprecedented prosperity, favorable balances of trade, large gold imports, and unusual political stability.

Deposit Banks (*Établissements de Crédit*). About the middle of the last century a number of chartered banks appeared, including three of the most important deposit banks in France—Crédit Industriel et Commercial, 1853; Credit Lyonnais, 1853, and Société Générale, 1864. There are now six large incorporated deposit banks that are national in scope of operation, having about 300 branch offices in Paris and more than 4,000 in the provinces. The four large banks that have been nationalized to do about two thirds of the commercial-banking business in France.[23] One of the two large banks that have not been nationalized is technically a Paris bank (Crédit Industriel et Commercial), but it holds an investment interest in groups of regional banks; and the other (Crédit Commercial de France) has a less complete coverage of branches than the other large banks. The 22 regional banks include 12 that are associated with the Crédit Industriel et Commercial.

In addition to the national and regional branch-banking systems, there are local provincial banks, some of which have branch offices. There are also many small banks in Paris that operate as unit banks, but their interests are not confined to Paris even though they have no branches. In the provinces, as in Paris, there is a tendency for the smaller banks to be absorbed by larger banks or to die out with the

---

[23] The four banks are Crédit Lyonnais, Société Générale, Comptoir National d'Escompte, and Banque Nationale pour le Commerce et l'Industrie. The other two members of the Big Six were exempt because their business was not national in scope. The Crédit Industriel et Commercial does have national coverage through its affiliates in the provinces (12 regional banks and their branches). The deposit business of the Crédit Commercial de France is more regional in nature.

passage of time because their survival depends upon personal relations, which may be discontinued after the death of certain individuals. Nevertheless, there is a demand for personal services that family concerns provide most satisfactorily.

As one of the important money markets of the world, Paris is the locale of a number of subsidiaries, branches, and offices of colonial and Franco-foreign banks and of foreign banks. Among the foreign banks there are 15 that are incorporated outside of France (such as branches of the Chase-Manhattan Bank of New York, Midland Bank, Ltd., and the Morgan-Guaranty Trust Company of New York), and 11 others are French companies under foreign control (such as Morgan et Cie and the First National Bank of New York, France).

Prior to 1946, deposit banks were subject to no general banking regulations and were free to develop banking along various lines, except note issue, which was a monopoly of the Bank of France. There were no legal ties (as in the United States) or formal ties (as in Great Britain) between the Bank of France and the deposit banks. At the end of World War II the earning assets of the commercial banks were largely in the form of government securities, and now treasury bills and other short-term securities comprise only 15 percent of total assets, with over two thirds of total assets being in commercial discounts, loans, and overdrafts.

Other Financial Institutions.   Other financial institutions of France include (1) business banks (*banques d'affaires*), (2) savings institutions, (3) agricultural banks, (4) mortgage banks, and (5) miscellaneous institutions.

1. *Banques d'affaires* are similar to investment houses in the United States, their chief function being to help finance the capital needs of new and old business firms. Some of the early investment bankers were of Swiss Protestant antecedents, such as Hottinguer, Mallet, Mirabaud, and Vernes; others were of Jewish origin, such as Oppenheim and Rothschild. These *hautes banques* (higher banking houses) carried on investment banking, foreign exchange, arbitrage, and deposit banking. Their scope of activities was even broader than that of American private banks, such as the old J. P. Morgan and Company and Kuhn, Loeb and Company. These French banking houses owned most of the stock of the Bank of France before 1936, and, because of directorship, investments, and close family connections, they controlled most of the French economy, as well as having "interests" throughout the world.

In addition to the *hautes banques*, the "aristocracy of French banking," there were smaller and less influential private banks in Paris (bringing the number of such banks to more than 50, of which 6 were incorporated). Today, these banks are classified as *banques d'affaires* (business banks). They accept deposits but differ from other banks in their extensive participation in promotion of new industrial enterprises and underwriting of existing corporations, often holding blocks of shares and maintaining a close relationship with the corporations concerned. These banks have no branches and use the large deposit banks to market securities; therefore, they often have a large ownership interest in the deposit banks (*établissements de crédit*) so as to be sure of their cooperation in merchandising securities.

Under provisions of the banking act of 1945 the *banques d'affaires* were required to register as either investment or business banks, but they were permitted to accept deposits under limited circumstances, which are linked more or less directly to their function of providing investment funds.

2. Saving institutions include ordinary savings banks (*Caisses d'Epargne Ordinaires*) and the postal savings system (*Caisse Nationale d'Epargne*). The ordinary savings banks include those operated by municipalities, whose directors are appointed by the government, and mutual savings banks, operated by self-perpetuating boards of directors (as is the case with mutual savings banks in the United States). The ordinary savings banks which number 550 operate over 2,200 branch offices and they have been regulated by the national government since 1835. Except for the legal provision for audits, interest, investment of funds, and reserves, each savings bank is managed by its own board of directors.

The postal savings system, established in 1881, was modeled after that of Great Britain. Each post office is authorized to accept deposits and to transfer accounts from one post office to a second. In addition, they accept accounts on which checks may be drawn but more frequently, are used to make transfers on written instructions. Deposits of savings banks are invested by the *Caisse des Dépôts et Consignations*, a government agency created to manage insurance, trust, savings, and pension funds.

3. Agricultural banks include numerous cooperative institutions which have been promoted by the state. There are local and regional cooperatives as *Caisse Nationale de Crédit Agricole* (a government institution) and independent cooperative associations. Loans are usually for short terms, and funds are obtained by the sale of stock to members, from depositors, and by borrowing from the appropriate

regional office (which in turn borrows from the national office). The agricultural credit system resembles a pyramid, with more than 6,000 local associations, affiliated with 98 regional associations that, in turn, are assisted by the national association—a state institution with broad powers over the system.

4. Mortgage banks are both rural and urban credit institutions. Since most of the French farmers have owned their land for generations, there is little need for farm mortgage credit. (French families are small, estate settlements cause little demand for additional credit, and larger properties seldom change hands.) Although residential mortgage loans are more frequent, the demands for new credit are small because of the stationary population. However, the agricultural cooperative banks grant some long-term mortgage credit to farmers. War-damaged buildings have been rebuilt with assistance from the government (through municipal and departmental institutions), but mortgage banking is less widely developed in France than in most other countries.

One of the oldest credit institutions in the field of mortgage banking, *Crédit Foncier de France*, established in 1852, has been a model for new mortgage banks in other countries. This institution uses its own capital, reserves or surplus, deposits, and especially bond issues which are sold to the general public. The Bank's funds are traditionally invested in mortgages on residential property, but in recent years lending to local governments has been emphasized. The amount of bonds that this bank may have outstanding at one time is limited to 50 times its capital (as compared with 20 for federal land banks and home loan banks in the United States). The bank's operations are national in scope, and all its activities are under the supervision of the government, which appoints the governor and two deputy governors. Affiliated with *Crédit Foncier de France* is the *Sous Comptoir des Entrepreneurs*, which finances the building trade.

5. Miscellaneous financial institutions include foreign banks' representatives such as branches or subsidiaries—Morgan et Cie, Morgan-Guaranty branches, National City Bank of New York (France, Chase-Manhattan branches, Barclays Bank (France), and many others. In Paris, there are security houses or brokerage firms and various types of specialists, including two bullion brokers, discount houses that operate in the money market as either brokers or dealers (the most important is the *Compagnie Parisienne de Réescompte*, which is the official broker for the bank of France), and banks that make intermediate- and long-term loans. In addition, there are peo-

ple's banks which have special charters similar to those of cooperative societies.

The *banques populaires* (people's banks), or credit unions, were created to provide credit for small businesses either by loans or by guarantees of loans made by others. Since they tend to lend to those who cannot get credit accommodations from other lenders, their record reflects the emphasis on social policy rather than a lack of sound bank management.

In France, the pawnbrokerage business has been a state monopoly since the French Revolution. It is operated under the name of *Crédit Municipal* and has a chain of 22 establishments. A loan may be for as little as $2, and anything of value may be used as security. The annual interest rate charged on loans is 10 percent.

SUMMARY

The banking system of the United States has influenced and has been influenced by the banking systems of other countries. At the central-banking level, the United States has 12 central banks, while most other countries have but one, but, because of the concentration of policy decisions in the hands of the Board of Governors of the Federal Reserve System and the Federal Open Market Committee, this difference is chiefly technical. Most of the central banks established prior to the creation of the Federal Reserve System originated as ordinary commercial banks with ordinary commercial-banking functions as well as central-banking functions, but the newer central banks have been patterned after those of the United States, that is, they have been created as banks of issue, bankers' banks, and bankers for their governments. In recent years the older central banks have been emphasizing their central-banking functions to an increasing extent and have been curtailing their commercial-banking functions; as a result, the activities of central banks the world over are not very different from those of the Federal Reserve banks in the United States. Unlike the situation in the United States, most foreign central banks are owned by their governments.

The greatest difference between the organization of commercial banks in the United States and of those in foreign countries is the operation of large numbers of branch offices. In many foreign countries, most of the commercial banking is done by fewer than 10 banks, with their hundreds or thousands of branches. When computed on a per capita basis, the people in most foreign countries are served better, in terms of the number of banking offices, than are the people of the

United States. Abroad, as in the United States, banking is generally subject to detail regulation (the most important exception being the United Kingdom, where tradition is a determining factor). Credit-control policies are determined by central banks and governments, with perhaps the latter being more important abroad than in the United States.

With the possible exception of France, no foreign country has achieved a degree of complexity and completeness in the noncommercial-banking field as great as that found in the United States. In most foreign countries there is a tendency to expand existing sources of credit available to homeowners, farmers, and consumers rather than to create new credit-granting institutions. The more complex noncommercial-banking systems in the United States are due, in part, to legal restrictions on commercial banking, the local nature of most commercial banks, and the complexity of American laws resulting from the existence of 51 legislative bodies. In the United States local or state groups are continually experimenting with some new type of bank or association arising out of some special need (some of these have been adopted later by the national government).

The commercial banks in the United States hold over one half of the commercial-banking resources of the world, and the noncommercial-banking institutions hold an even larger percentage of the world's investment-banking resources. In a comparison of the banking facilities of the United States with those of foreign countries, the dominant position of the United States must be kept in mind. For example, the New York City banks alone hold more assets than do all the banks in England, and the two largest banks in the United States have more assets than do all the commercial banks in Canada.

QUESTIONS AND PROBLEMS

1. Justify this statement: "The Canadian banking system is a direct descendant of the first Bank of the United States. . . ." Explain why the American system did not develop along similar lines.

2. Explain and give the advantages of the decennial chartering and renewal policy in Canada.

3. Compare the functions of (*a*) the Bank of Canada with those of the Federal Reserve banks in the United States and (*b*) the "chartered" banks in Canada with those of the commercial banks in the United States.

4. Explain: "In the United States a system of local 'unit' banks was deliberately fostered, but in Canada the first Dominion legislation explicitly allowed branch openings and thereby encouraged a sys-

tem of national banks to develop." *1964—Report of the Royal Commission on Banking and Finance* (Ottawa: Queen's Printer and Controller of Stationery, 1964), p. 113.

5. Is commercial banking in Great Britain more, or less, concentrated than in the United States? In Canada? In France?

6. Explain: In the United Kingdom "regulation of banks is in the main effected by 'suasion' rather than statute, and particularly is this so in matters of monetary regulation." (*Midland Bank Review*, November, 1967, p. 18.)

7. Describe the "overdraft" system of lending. Compare with the type of bank lending common in the United States. What are the advantages of the first to the borrower? Are banks justified when they charge a higher rate for overdraft loans than for other types, assuming that other things are the same? Explain.

8. "The Bank of France is the greatest and in many respects the strongest of the banks of the world, and its development exhibits many of the most interesting phases of banking history outside of Great Britain." (C. A. Conant, *A History of Modern Banks of Issue* [5th ed.; New York: G. P. Putnam's Sons, 1915], p. 38.) Is the first part of this statement, first made in 1902, still true?

9. Identify the French "deposit" banks and "business" banks. How do their activities compare with those of commercial banks and investment houses in the United States?

10. Explain: "Direct borrowing [at the bank of England] is not available to the commercial banks, and the borrowing done by discount houses tends to be limited by the penalty effect of the discount rate, which remains consistently above most money market rates." (Peter G. Fousek, *Foreign Central Banking: The Instruments of Monetary Policy* [New York: Federal Reserve Bank of New York, 1957], p. 34.)

Index

Commercial letter of credit, 92, 609–17
Commercial loan theory, 243, 361–62, 362 n
Commercial paper, 34–35, 113–16
Commodity Credit Corporation, 367, 407, 536–37
Common stock, 98–100, 213
Common trust funds, 578–79
Community trust, 587
Compensatory balances, 118–19, 277–78
Compensatory budgetary principle, 400–402
Compensatory spending principle, 367–68
Competition in banking, 206–7, 242
Competitive bidding, 111–12, 464–65
Comptroller of the Currency, 139, 193, 200, 203–5, 295, 345–46, 573
Condition statement of banks and the monetary system, 43–44
Conditional sales contract, 94
Conflict of interest in trust banking, 588–90
Consumer credit, 540–68
  analysis of, 547–48
  composition of, 540–46
  criticism of practices, 563–64
  interest rates, 548–49, 559–65
  regulation of, 369, 561–66
  sources of, 546–60
  in Canada, 703–4
Consumer prices, 434, 435
Consumer spending, 415–16
Consumption and money, 3–4
Controlled exchange system, 641–45
Conservation cycle of loans, 272
Cooperative associations, 535
Cooperative Farm Credit System, 525–26, 532–36
Corporate stock, bank ownership of, 248–50, 308
Corporate trustee, 583–84
Corporations, trust and agency services for, 584–87
Correspondent banking, 140–41, 176–78, 243, 254–55, 609
Correspondent banks' services, 294, 609
Cost factor, 80, 440–43
Cost-of-living index, 61–62, 437, 447
Cost-price and cost-push inflation; *see* Inflation
Cost theory, 440–42
Costs and prices, 75, 440–43
Council of Economic Advisers, 443–44
Countercyclical debt management, 423–30
Countercyclical spending, 419–23
Creation of deposits, 55–57

Credit, 84–85; *see also* Consumer credit; Farm credit; Loans; *and other specific topics*
  elastic system of, 150–51
  instruments, 83–91
  lines, 277–78
  mobility of, 150
  revolving, 272, 545
  transactions, 84–85
  urban mortgage, 488–514
Credit analysis, 268
  in real estate lending, 496–97
Credit cards, 188–89, 285, 545–46, 554–55, 558–59, 617
Credit control; *see also* Board of Governors of the Federal Reserve System
  consumer financing and, 565–66
  discount policy and, 379–98, 362–63
  instruments of, 379–98
    coordination of, 396–98
  moral suasion and, 395–96
  open-market policy and, 364–65, 370–72
Credit department, 267–69
Credit instruments, 83–91
  dishonor of, 89–90
Credit policy; *see* Monetary policy
Credit risk, 292–93, 308, 547–48
Credit system, 83–87
Credit unions, 551–53
  in Canada, 703
  in France, 719
Creeping inflation, 446–50
Currency, 10–14, 20–23, 34–35, 47–55; *see also* Money; Paper money; *and other specific topics*
  banks' need for, 250–56
  "blocked," 651–52
  Canadian, 696
  devaluation of, 36–37, 649–51, 657
  "scarce," 657
Customer loans, 259–60

D

Dealers and brokers, 103–4, 120–21, 271–72, 480–83
Debentures, 96, 224, 532–34
Debt, 7, 15–16, 85–87; *see also* Consumer credit; Credit; Mortgages; *and other specific topics*
  services relative to the public, 327–28
Debt burden argument, 424
Debt financing, 224–25
Debt management, 400–430
Defalcation risk; *see* Fraud
Deferred availability, 180
Deferred payments, standard of, 7
Defense spending, 419
Deficit financing, 367–68

Loans; *see also* Credit; Credit instruments; *and other specific topics*
accommodation, 270
agricultural, 282–88; *see also* Farm credit *and other specific topics*
bank, 144–45, 267–88
  to examiners, 287
  to officers, 286–87
  classes of, 282–86
comaker, 547
customer, 259–60
demand for, and money position, 255–56
discounts and, 315–21
endorsement, 270
expansion in, 391
to farmers, 520–23
  by cooperatives, 535–36
of Federal Reserve banks, 314, 315–21, 379–83
installment, 243, 285
interest rates on, 276–77
  regulation of, 286–88
investments and, 259–61
maturity of, 271–73
mortgage; *see* Mortgage credit; Mortgages; *and other specific topics*
negotiating terms of, 269–70
policies and practices as to, 272–82
real estate, 284–85, 287–88; *see also* Mortgage credit *and* Mortgages
screening, 375
secondary reserves and, 258
security for, 270–71
self-liquidating, 243
single-payment, 545
syndicated, 278–79
term, 272–73, 278–80
working capital, 272–73
Loans and investments, 259–61
as cause of bank failure, 247
secondary reserves and, 258
Locked-in theory of banks' investments, 375–76, 427

M

Magnetic Ink Character Recognition System, 10, 171, 181
Mail transfers, 593–94
Management of bank funds, 241–65
Management of bank portfolio, 297
Margin requirements, 392–94
Market for federal funds, 106–10
Market for the national debt, 426–27
Market; *see* Capital markets *and other specific topics*
Matched sale-purchase, 389–90
Maturity arrangement of investments, 257, 293

Medium of exchange, 4–6
  qualities of a good, 9–14
Member bank reserves; *see* Reserves
Member banks, 163–64, 195–96; *see also* Banks; Commercial banks; *and other specific topics*
foreign branches of, 605–7
discounts and loans from Federal Reserve banks, 315–21
reserve requirements, 107, 226, 252–56
reserves; *see* Reserves
  vault cash as, 16
state, 162–63
tradition against borrowing by, 381–82
Merchant bankers, 136–38
  English, 709
Mint ratio, 23–26
Monetary authorities, 599, 634–35
Monetary gold; *see* Gold
Monetary history of the United States, 20–40
Monetary management, 7–8
Monetary policy, 357–76
coordination of fiscal and, 453–57
evolution of, 357–76
inflation and, 372–74
instruments of, 379–98
legal reserve requirements and, 254
wars and, 362–66, 369–74
Monetary standards; *see* Gold standard; Paper standard; *and other specific topics*
Monetary system
banks and, 43–44
international, 648–69
of the United States, 20–40, 43–58
Monetary theory and the business cycle, 359–61
Monetary unit, 6, 39–40
Money; *see also* Currency; Paper money; *and other specific topics*
characteristics of, 9–17
coins and paper, 10–11
commercial banks as source of, 169–90
concept of, 43
consumption and, 3–4
creation and destruction of, 55–58
demand and supply of, 70
denominations of, 12–13
distribution and, 2–3
full-bodied, 20, 26, 43
functions of, 4–9
gold; *see* Gold *and other specific topics*
illusion, 434
instruments, 91–95, 103
legal qualities of, 15–17
nature of, 1–18
"near," 44
policy and liquidity needs, 251

*This book has been set in 11 point Janson,
leaded 2 points, and 10 point Janson, leaded
1 point. Chapter numbers and chapter titles
are in 14 and 18 point Memphis Medium.
The size of the type page is 27 by 46½ picas.*